PRAISE FOR ANDREW CARROLL'S
WAR LETTERS

"Andrew Carroll has given America a priceless treasure. These letters are intimate, deeply personal portraits of the courage, sacrifice, and sense of duty that made this country."

—Tom Brokaw

"These war letters are more deeply moving, more revelatory, and more powerful than any dispatch from the front. It's the truly *felt* history of what war is all about."

—Studs Terkel

"In the sweep of history, the experience of the lone soldier is often lost, but in this breathtaking collection the individual voices of the men and women who have served this nation come to life with a power and an eloquence that is both gripping and unforgettable. I can think of no better way to understand the horrors of war than to read the words of those who have been caught in its grasp, and these extraordinary letters offer some of the most dramatic eyewitness accounts of war imaginable."

—Stephen E. Ambrose

"Andrew Carroll has assembled a collection of previously unpublished letters that run the gamut of wartime emotion. . . . An excellent compilation that I enjoyed reading very much—and believe you will, too."

—John Glenn

"It was a letter that moved me to write *Flags of Our Fathers*. A letter my dad wrote four days after he helped raise the flag on Iwo Jima. My father honored his country. And Andrew Carroll honors us all with his gift to the nation of the superb *War Letters*."

—James Bradley, son of flag-raiser Doc Bradley

"[T]he power of these voices from various fronts . . . is undeniable, and the sentiments and observations they record have a compelling immediacy."

—*Publishers Weekly*

"This wonderful collection of war correspondence is . . . a treasure. . . . For scholars, a wealth of primary-source material is provided here. General readers will find it an informative and deeply moving reading experience."

—*Booklist*

WAR LETTERS

Extraordinary Correspondence
from American Wars

EDITED BY
ANDREW CARROLL

FOREWORD BY
DOUGLAS BRINKLEY

WASHINGTON SQUARE PRESS
New York London Toronto Sydney Singapore

All of the author's earnings, minus limited expenses incurred in the preparation and support of the book, will be donated to nonprofit organizations, memorials, and institutions, particularly those working to honor and remember the men and women who have served this nation in wartime.

Owing to space limitations, the permissions can be found on page 499.

Copyright © 2001 by Andrew Carroll

Originally published in hardcover in 2001 by Scribner

ISBN: 0-7434-1006-8

First Washington Square Press trade paperback printing May 2002

10 9 8

WASHINGTON SQUARE PRESS and colophon are
registered trademarks of Simon & Schuster Inc.

For information regarding special discounts for bulk purchases,
please contact Simon & Schuster Special Sales at 1-800-456-6798 or
business@simonandschuster.com

Cover design by John Fulbrook; cover photos by Joseph Scherschel/Timepix,
Adrienne McGrath/Skouras Design

Printed in the U.S.A.

In memory of
my uncle FRANK W. HARTMANN (1920–1999)
and
my godfather JONATHAN H. "JACK" LASLEY (1910–2001),
two of the most honorable veterans I have ever known.

CONTENTS

World War I

WORLD WAR II

THE KOREAN WAR & THE COLD WAR

———————— *Extended Correspondence* ————————

——————— ~ ———————

The Vietnam War, the Persian Gulf War, Somalia, & Bosnia

——————— *Extended Correspondence* ———————

FOREWORD

There is many a boy here today who looks on war as all
glory, but, boys, it is all hell. You can bear this warning
voice to generations yet to come. I look upon war with
horror.

> —General William Tecumseh Sherman,
> in a speech to the Grand Army
> of the Republic Convention,
> August 11, 1880

Like most great old soldiers, General Sherman knew whereof he spoke in
his gut hatred for war: Sixteen years before he made his starkly poignant
appeal to future generations, he had been supreme commander of the
Union army in the West, and it was he who had slashed and burned a
fiery swath across Georgia, sacked Atlanta, and marched on to the sea with
an indomitable brutality that sealed the triumph of the North in the
U.S. Civil War.

But how it must have pained him to know what he had done, to have
seen the blood spilled and the devastation wrought at his own orders;
how he must have ached, as he revealed to those boys a decade and a half
later, that posterity should grasp, and heed, his heart-felt horror of war.

Indeed, Sherman stands in a long line of military leaders whose battle
scars would yield a profound understanding of human belligerence and
all its attendant atrocities. And the most important thing experience
teaches these thinking warriors—from fifth century B.C. Greek naval
commander-turned-historian Thucydides on down the millennia—is
the ancient truth philosopher George Santayana articulated so well at the
beginning of the twentieth century: "Those who cannot remember the
past are condemned to repeat it."

War Letters helps us all remember and learn from the wars of the past,
seen firsthand and described here in the words of a broad cross section of
American men and women. Covering the Civil War, World Wars I and II,

21

Korea, the Cold War, Vietnam, the Persian Gulf War, and the interventions in Somalia and Bosnia, each of the letters in this remarkable volume is published here in its entirety for the first time. Inclusions were carefully culled from the more than fifty thousand pieces of American wartime correspondence editor Andrew Carroll amassed over the last few years in his search for what he calls "this nation's great undiscovered literature."

The objects of his quest were not politicians' grandiloquent exhortations unto the breach or jingoistic calls to arms, but personal letters affording authentic, unfiltered glimpses of the realities of war. What Carroll wanted to get across is the notion Confederate cavalry hero John Singleton Mosby—echoing General Sherman—expressed in his 1887 memoir of the Civil War, that "War loses a great deal of romance after a soldier has seen his first battle."

Fans of Rambo-esque exploits will have to look elsewhere for chest-thumping: *War Letters* instead presents a series of moving testimonials from both ordinary and celebrated men and women—impassioned evocations of love and sacrifice, duty and honor, fear and confusion, courage and perseverance, rage and the intimations of mortality that spark it. A number of these letters were written not from the battlefield or barracks, but the homefront; others offer the unique perspective of the combat journalist or the nurse in the trenches. Taken together, these messages make for a powerful look at the eternal mystery of man's impulse to reach for arms rather than the wisdom of the Golden Rule.

The earliest letters date from the start of the Civil War, when a moment of truth was upon the nation as never before or since. Enraged by the 1860 election of Republican Abraham Lincoln, who had vowed not to permit any territory that allowed slavery to join the United States, seven southern states seceded from the Union, formed the Confederacy, and elected their own president—former senator from Mississippi Jefferson Davis—all before Lincoln even took the oath of office on March 4, 1861. A month into his administration, Lincoln faced a fateful decision: The federal garrison at Fort Sumter in Charleston, South Carolina's harbor—then under the authority of one Major Robert Anderson—was running so short on supplies the post had to be either restocked or abandoned at once.

The Union army's then commanding general, Winfield Scott, favored withdrawal, a move the nation's new president considered acceptable, provided it would inspire the loyalty of the border states. But anti-Confederate sentiment was building in the North, where pulling out might have been taken as a sign of weakness, so Lincoln boldly decided to reinforce Fort Sumter instead, leaving Anderson—surrounded by hostile

Confederate forces, but undaunted—to hunker down and protect the American flag and all it represented.

Overnight, Anderson became a symbol for the fight to preserve the Union. Letters poured into the stronghold at Charleston, thanking the garrison leader for his grit and grace under the tremendous pressure to surrender. Particularly encouraging words came in a moving missive from the former governor of Massachusetts, Marcus Morton, written just days before Confederate General Pierre G. T. de Beauregard began pounding Fort Sumter with some four thousand shells. "At a moment when the hearts of all true friends of the Union were heavy with apprehension," Morton wrote, "when distrust in the efficiency of Republican Institutions seemed about to settle upon the land; and men began to doubt whether the coming day would dawn on a people enjoying the blessings of Constitutional Liberty or a people drifting into disorder and anarchy, the intelligence of your self-reliant, wise and patriotic conduct in the harbor of Charleston, as it flashed from point to point, reanimated their wavering hopes, restored their waning confidence, and gave reassurance that they still possess a national Government." Morton continued, in the letter included here, that "[t]his is not the time nor the occasion to enter upon any discussion of the merits of the unhappy controversy which menaces the Republic; nor to enquire upon whom rests the responsibility for the perils which environs us. Your heroic action admonishes us that our first thoughts and efforts should be devoted to the maintenance of the Union as it was founded by our wise and patriotic Fathers and bequeathed to us, that we, in our time, may transmit it, in all its integrity and glory, to our successors."

The Civil War, which began when Anderson reluctantly surrendered Fort Sumter after two days of relentless Confederate bombardment, exacted the most staggering loss of human life in our nation's history: More than 370,000 Union and 260,000 Confederate soldiers were killed, while another 275,000 of the former and 100,000 of the latter went home maimed. The appalling bloodshed on both sides left many wounds, some of which still have not healed. Yet as Governor Morton noted so eloquently in the letter presented here, with our freedom comes the obligation to preserve and protect the principles of the Declaration of Independence and the United States Constitution for future generations—no matter the cost, or how deep the lasting scars. For all its terrible consequences, it is important to remember that Anderson's steadfastness at Fort Sumter was in two of history's noblest causes: the preservation of the Union and the abolition of slavery in America. "Sometimes gunpowder smells good," as Ralph Waldo Emerson averred. "Now we have a country again."

The very loftiness of those ideals that sustained the United States through its direst crisis also informs perhaps the most telling theme in this collected correspondence. In general, the letters from the Civil War and the two world wars have an upbeat and optimistic ring, and are more often than not brash with good-natured confidence. By contrast, the GIs of the Cold War era, from Korea to Vietnam and beyond, sent home accounts fraught with doubt and confusion and openly questioning whether risking death in a Chosin Reservoir crater or on a Mekong Delta rice paddy made any sense, or did any good, for Old Glory or anything else.

Although most of the letters collected here bear the obscure signatures of regular folk, quite a few were penned by figures of note. Editor Andrew Carroll's celebrity selections include such luminaries as Civil War nurse Clara Barton putting her thoughts down by campfire light on the cold still December night before the bloody Battle of Fredericksburg, legendary cavalry officer George Armstrong Custer recounting to his sister a hair-raising reconnaissance mission against rebel troops in Virginia, and a prepacifist General William T. Sherman gloating to friends about the burning of Atlanta. *War Letters* also turns up written proof that during World War I General John "Black Jack" Pershing vigorously advocated equal treatment and rights for African-American servicemen, and reveals how Benjamin O. Davis Sr., our nation's first African-American general, found inspiration in the eloquent words of Abraham Lincoln during World War II.

Social worker Jane Addams is represented in a letter she wrote to President Woodrow Wilson on October 29, 1915, in her capacity chairing the Women's Peace Party, criticizing his administration for starting a military buildup aimed at preparing America for war. In one startling letter General Douglas MacArthur lashes out at whoever might be behind the "campaign of vituperation" he insisted was mounted against him after the People's Republic of China entered the Korean War. There are even a few personal missives sent by then Joint Chiefs of Staff Chairman Colin Powell and General H. Norman Schwarzkopf after the 1990–91 Persian Gulf War, and a surprisingly powerful denunciation of McCarthyism from none other than public TV's festive "French Chef," Julia Child. Before becoming a gourmet icon, the then Julia McWilliams had worked in both clerical and low-level policy positions at the U.S. Central Intelligence Agency's precursor, the Office of Strategic Services. *War Letters* portrays a side of Child her cooking shows never did. In a gallant March 12, 1950, letter she wrote to a fellow Smith College alumna to protest McCarthyite red-baiting witch hunts of liberal-leaning professors at her alma mater. "In this very dangerous period of our history, where, through fear and confusion, we are assailed continually by conflicting opinions and strong appeals to the emotions, it is imperative that our young people learn to sift truth from half-truth; demagoguery from democracy; totalitarianism in any form, from liberty," the future French Chef declared. "The duty of Smith College is, as I see it, to give her daughters the kind of education which will ensure that they will use their minds clearly and wisely, so that they will be able to conduct themselves as courageous and informed citizens of the United States."

The most affecting of *War Letters*'s big-name epistles is the heartbreaking note former President Theodore Roosevelt wrote to a family friend shortly after his son, Quentin Roosevelt, was killed during World War I. Thanking Mrs. Harvey L. Freeland for her condolences, Roosevelt admitted: "It is hard to open the letters from those you love who are dead; but Quentin's last letters, written during his three weeks at the front, when of his squadron on an average a man was killed every day, are written with real joy in the 'great adventure.'" The grieving father continued: "He was engaged to a very beautiful girl, of very fine and high character; it is heartbreaking for her, as well as for his mother; but they both said that they would rather [he] never come back than never have gone. He had his crowded hour, he died at the crest of life, in the glory of the dawn."

The letters that follow also detail a few wartime incidents—or reactions to them—that place readers in the front row of history. One such tale unfolds in a letter Army Cpl. Robert S. Easterbrook penned to his parents from the bedside of Japan's ex-premier, Hideki Tojo, after the enemy leader made a failed attempt at suicide. Written in grisly diary form, Easterbrook chronicled to the exact minute, every detail of Tojo's blood transfusions, apparently for posterity. "In my next letter I'll send a piece of his shirt," the corporal promised his mother. "It has blood on it—but <u>don't</u> wash it. Just put it away in my room."

This peculiar note turned up in a bundle of old photographs, postcards, and news clippings that Debra Beyerlein bought for a dollar at a yard sale in June 1982. Sixteen years later, after reading a "Dear Abby" column about Andrew Carroll's Legacy Project, Beyerlein mailed him the bundle. Now, thanks to *War Letters,* precisely what happened to Tojo after he tried to kill himself is part of recorded history.

It makes for a delightful subtext to this volume, not just that Carroll discovered these letters at all, but that "Dear Abby" helped him do it. Consider, for example, that until Abigail Van Buren's syndicated column on Carroll's search appeared in his newspaper, Horace Evers had given but scant thought to the historical value of an old letter he kept in a trunk in his mobile home in Florida. When Carroll received it, any doubt about the keepsake's value disappeared, and not just because then Army Staff Sergeant Evers had written it on a sheet of Hitler's personal stationery he had procured firsthand from the Führer's Munich apartment on May 2, 1945, only days after the Nazi leader killed himself in his Berlin bunker. Indeed, it is what Evers reported back home on this stationery that makes it so remarkable—his account of what he had seen at the Nazi concentration camp at Dachau. "In two years of combat you can imagine I have seen a lot of death, furious deaths mostly. But nothing has ever stirred me as much as this," Evers recounted. "The first box car I came to had about 30 what were once humans in it. — All were just bone with a layer of skin over them. . . . Bodies on top of each other — no telling how many — Filthy barracks suitable for about 200 persons held 1500. 160,000 persons were originally in the camp and 32,000 were alive (or almost alive) when we arrived. — There is a gas chamber and furnace room in one barracks. — Two rooms were full of bodies waiting to be cremated. . . . How can people do things like that? I never believed they could until now."

War Letters is full of searing first-person accounts that leave it clear just how much some principles are worth fighting for. What makes this book so poignant, however, is its constant echo of a melancholy note, previously published, that Supreme Allied Commander Dwight D. Eisenhower wrote home one night in April 1944, just weeks before the D-Day invasion. "How I wish this cruel business of war could be completed quickly," he confided in it to his wife, Mamie. "Entirely aside from the longing to return to you (and stay there) it is a terribly sad business to total up the casualties every day—even in an air war—and realize how many youngsters are gone forever. A man must develop a veneer of callousness that lets him consider such things dispassionately, but he can never escape a recognition of the fact that back home the news brings anguish and suffering to families all over the country. . . . War demands real toughness of fiber—not only in the soldiers [who] must endure, but in the homes that sacrifice their best."

Though hewn of pretty tough fiber himself, Eisenhower would remark that the hardest part of his job during World War II came on Sundays, which he set aside for the mournful chore of signing the thousands of condolence letters that had to be sent to the families of GIs killed in the European theater. To soothe the pain of putting his name to these starkly bureaucratic letters—government casualty certificates, really—Ike looked to the classics of war poetry, from Homer's *Iliad* to World War I–era Siegfried Sassoon.

For Eisenhower understood that however gripping the battle stories, nothing can capture the rending agonies of war as good poetry can, especially when it's written in a foxhole as artillery fire screams overhead. It was one thing, Ike's long experience had proved, to read in a textbook that more than 116,000 American soldiers died in World War I—and quite another to take on the question British war poet Wilfred Owen raised in his posthumously published "Anthem for Doomed Youth": "What passing-bells for those who die as cattle? / Only the monstrous anger of the guns. / Only the stuttering rifles' rapid rattle / Can patter out their hasty orisons."

Sadly Owen never got to learn that he had penned some of the most celebrated verses to come out of World War I: He was killed in action on the Western Front a week before the armistice. A similar fate had claimed another Ike favorite, Alan Seeger, an American who had joined the French Foreign Legion when the Great War broke out. Seeger was killed in 1916 fighting the Germans in France, shortly after writing his great poem "I Have a Rendezvous with Death," the chorus of which begins, "I have a rendezvous with Death / At some disputed barricade," and ends, "And I to my pledged word am true, / I shall not fail that rendezvous." It was Seeger's poem that inspired Franklin D. Roosevelt's famous line, "This generation of Americans has a rendezvous with destiny," and was later adapted by President John F. Kennedy for his demand that the United States put a man on the moon within a decade.

The personal papers collected in *War Letters* conjure the same emotions as the likes of Owen and Seeger in a plainer poetry of their own. Whether the author is Union surgeon William Child writing home after the ferocious Battle of Antietam to ask rhetorically who permits such bloodshed or Staff Sergeant Daniel Welch describing the surreal scene of carnage he saw along the coast road as he passed Kuwait City up in flames, the letters here haunt the soul the way good war poems do, perhaps out of the same awareness of knowing what the authors did not: that, in Owen's memorable line, so many of their eyes would soon "shine the holy glimmers of good-byes."

It seems appropriate that so much of this volume draws from "last letters" written by servicemen before being killed in action—and that they were, so many of them, just teenagers suddenly tossing not baseballs but hand grenades at other, equally innocent kids—recalling Herman Melville's observation in his 1866 book *Battle Pieces* that "[a]ll wars are boyish and are fought by boys."

That's what makes it so hard, and so worthwhile, to read the sweet letter Richard Cowan wrote to his mother on his twenty-second birthday, before going off to fight in the Battle of the Bulge. By and large Cowan's is a fairly sophisticated meditation on mortality, but his youthful exuberance can't help but burst through in the end. "Pretty convinced I'm grown up, ain't I, Mom?" he teased. "Well, I still count on you tucking me into bed when I get home."

Another point *War Letters* underlines is the incredible range in human relationships, as seen in the contrast between Cowan's note home and the one Kate Gordon sent her son, stationed overseas during World War I, urging him to "live," unless God willed otherwise, in which case he should "die with courage." And then there is the powerful last letter of Dean Allen of Delmar, New York, who was drafted into the Army, put through Officer Candidate School, and sent to Vietnam in 1969. Writing home to his schoolteacher wife, Allen confessed his fear of losing any of the men in his platoon. "Being a good platoon leader is a lonely job," he explained. "I don't want to really get to know anybody over here because it would be bad enough to lose a man—I damn sure don't want to lose a friend." Four days later Allen was killed after stepping on a land mine.

Yet for all the horror in these pages, it would do their authors a disservice to dwell on the lamentations rather than on their playful good cheer, even under the most harrowing circumstances. After all, most were responses written in the glow of youthful vigor boosted by the latest news from home affirming that life was still normal there—that Dad was still boasting about the tomatoes bursting ripe in his backyard garden, that Little Brother had smacked his first stand-up double, or that Sis had been accepted at the local university. Indeed, there is comfort to be found in the mundane details of everyday life back in the United States—the score of a Friday night football game, the cut on a smart linen dress that was such a steal at the Salvation Army store—these simple bits of news have always been the rare joys of soldiers far from home. In truth, for every Dear John letter giving notice to a GI that he had just been dumped by his best girl, a thousand others served as warm reminders of Mom's cooking up a storm for the holiday picnic under the oak tree down by the pond—and it is in the same home-and-hearth spirit that the Yanks, Johnny Rebs, doughboys, GIs, and grunts who fought our wars always wrote back, and still do.

Indeed—one of the purest, gentlest, and most old-fashioned evocations of mom-and-apple-pie patriotism in this book appears in one of its last entries. Written from Bosnia in September 1996, Major Tom O'Sullivan's birthday letter to his little boy concludes thus:

> There aren't any stores here in Bosnia, so I couldn't buy you any toys
> or souvenirs for your birthday. What I am sending you is something

very special though. It is a flag. This flag represents America and makes me proud each time I see it. When the people here in Bosnia see it on our uniforms, on our vehicles, or flying above our camps, they know that it represents freedom, and, for them, peace after many years of war.

This flag was flown on the flagpole over the headquarters of Task Force 4–67 Armor, Camp Colt, in the Posavina Corridor of northern Bosnia-Herzegovina, on 16 September 1996. It was flown in honor of you on your seventh birthday. Keep it and honor it always.

Love,

Dad.

In the end, it is the sort of warmth that radiates from Major O'Sullivan's note to his son that makes *War Letters* so extraordinary. For much of the correspondence collected here is the simple exchange of assurances of caring and support, mother to son, brother to sister, husband to wife, friend to friend. And it is in this communication among loved ones that those lofty ideals of liberty that make America great are passed on. As shown here, every American generation from that of the Civil War to the Bosnian intervention has wanted its progeny to know that war is cruel and to be avoided at any cost—except, that is, when conflict is the only way to preserve the integrity of our constitutional values and democratic principles. As the inscription on a statue of William Tecumseh Sherman in Washington, D.C., notes, quoting a speech he delivered in St. Louis shortly after General Robert E. Lee's glorious surrender, "The legitimate object of war is a more perfect peace."

—Douglas Brinkley
Director, Eisenhower Center
of American Studies and Professor of History
at the University of New Orleans
January 1, 2001

INTRODUCTION

Behind the Lines

Nothing I had ever seen, or read, or been told about war, prepared me for the letters I was about to receive. I had braced myself for graphic descriptions of bloodshed and stories of brutality and suffering, and I suspected there would be intimate letters to wives and girlfriends written by forlorn soldiers who, in so many cases, later died in battle.

What caught me off guard were the personal messages enclosed with every war letter.

Three days after Abigail Van Buren announced in her November 11, 1998, column that a new initiative, the Legacy Project, had been created to honor American veterans by seeking out and preserving their wartime correspondence, our tiny mailbox in a neighborhood post office was flooded with the first of fifty-thousand letters. I was thrilled by the deluge and hoped that, within these bins of mail, I would discover gripping, previously unpublished accounts of Gettysburg, Meuse-Argonne, Pearl Harbor, D-Day, Khe Sanh, and Desert Storm—all written at the time these dramatic events were unfolding.

But after tearing into the envelopes, I was stunned to find deeply moving letters addressed to me. Many described the bittersweet experience of rereading these wartime correspondences, especially those by family members who were killed in action—or, if they did survive, had come home permanently changed. Attached to a handful of correspondences from Vietnam, for example, was this note: "Dear Sir, Please accept these letters that my brother had written to my mother. My brother is missing (not a POW). He was never right after he returned home and one day he was just gone. I hope to make his life worth something. I miss him very much."

Fastened to a bundle of yellowed World War II memorabilia was a brief letter, penned in barely legible handwriting; "I am a widow 85 years old and my husband and only son have passed. My husband served in Patton's Third Army. There is no one I can give these my husbands letters to so you may have them. Please remember him." There was no return address. A similar package was sent in by a woman whose husband was still alive but afflicted with Alzheimer's. She feared that when she and her husband died, all of his correspondences would be thrown away. Along with his letters were photographs of the two of them, strikingly beautiful, taken when they were probably no more than eighteen or nineteen years old. Almost sixty years had passed, and the handsome young private who mailed passionate letters to his fiancée was now an elderly man incapable of recognizing his wife at all.

"[My grandfather] passed away in the late '70s when I was a child and was such a curmudgeon when I knew him," noted Karren Reish, who contributed several letters by her maternal grandfather, Walter Schuette. "I found these letters as a teenager and they made me cry." Indeed, Schuette's wartime letters are poignant expressions of love addressed to his wife and their infant daughter, Anna Mary (Karren's mother). "You will never know the joy I knew when I received word that you had arrived," Schuette wrote to his baby girl from England a week after she was born. "Should God decree that you never know your father I want you to have this sample of my handwriting. . . . I place you now in the hands of God. May He care for you and love you. May He see fit that we shall see one another very soon and keep us together into eternity." Schuette returned home alive and was able to read his letter to Anna Mary personally. But the tender, homesick correspondent was not the man Karren Reish knew. Like others who saw combat, he did not talk about the war with anyone—not his friends, not his children, not even his wife. While a self-imposed humility prevents many veterans from recounting their war days, there is another reason for their reticence: What they saw, what they lost, and what they endured was horrific beyond words. A tempest of painful memories rages behind many gruff exteriors, and the only way for them to bear this anguish is not to discuss it. I began to understand this silence once I started focusing on the war letters themselves.

"All along the beach, men were dying of wounds. Maybe you will think this is cruel, but I want you to know what it was like," Pfc. Richard King wrote to his parents in 1945 about the fighting he experienced on Saipan and Okinawa. "Mortar shells dropping in on heads, and ripping bodies. Faces blown apart by flying lead and coral. . . . Shells would hit, and bury you, or blow you out of your foxhole. The Catholic Chaplain was killed as he was blessing each foxhole. An artillery shell cut him in half at the waist."

France, 1918. Writing to his wife from a hospital bed after the St. Mihiel Offensive, 1st Lt. Ed Lukert listed the close friends he had lost in the war: "Lt. Gamble, killed. Lt. Airy killed by a shell. Lt. Horton, who used to live at the Dyer House in Chickamauga Park, killed by shell fire.

His clothing was blown off his body, and his body was minus all limbs, but right arm. Lt. Jones, B Company (the funny fellow you liked to hear talk) shot thru the head by a machine gun. Lt. Boatwright, same."

Sgt. John Wheeler, fighting in Korea, told his father about the day he was shot: "I found out that I got hit twice that day. The first was a bullet that went through part of my right temple, through the right ear and out the back of my head never going all the way into my head, but grazing it leaving quite a scar and a hole in the ear. Good thing it didn't go all of the way in, or I would have come home sooner than anticipated, in a pine box."

I was three years old when U.S. troops pulled out of Vietnam in 1973, and no one in my immediate family has ever served in the armed forces. War had always been a remote, almost abstract concept to me. Even the fighting in the Persian Gulf, which I vividly recall watching live on television, seemed distant and unreal. When it was over, far from sobering me to the realities of warfare, Desert Storm only convinced me—at the time—that wars were won quickly, easily, bloodlessly.

Over a year earlier, just before Christmas 1989, a fire swept through my family's home in Washington, D.C. Thankfully, no one was hurt (even Claude, our cat, bounded out safely), but almost all of our possessions were destroyed. As I walked cautiously through the burnt-out shell of our house several days later, it suddenly occurred to me that all my letters were gone. The clothes, the furniture, the books, just about everything else could be replaced, but not the letters. Admittedly I had nothing historically significant, only correspondences with high school friends traveling abroad and, alas, more "Dear John" letters than most overseas army divisions receive collectively. But it was crushing to realize that all of these personal letters were gone forever, curled up into ash and washed away. I was unaware of it then, but the experience of losing everything in the fire inspired in me a lifelong passion for letters and, ultimately, the Legacy Project, itself. For that alone, the fire was something of a godsend.

Ed Stoch heard about the Legacy Project in November 1998 and sent in a remarkable letter he wrote after he was wounded in the Battle of the Bulge. From his hospital bed in England, Stoch mailed a three-page letter to his parents back in Cleveland, Ohio, to let them know he was still alive. At the bottom of the third page, a handwritten postscript asked: "Say, how about that fruitcake you promised me, huh?" What is notable about the seemingly innocent appeal is that Ed Stoch did not write it. The censors did. Rather ingeniously, the mail handlers were soliciting care packages from the homefront and then pocketing the goodies on their way back. The soldiers didn't know the requests were being made, and the parents didn't know the food was being intercepted. It was the perfect crime. Stoch sent me a photocopy of the fifty-six-year-old letter and, still miffed, added above the forged handwriting: "The Rats!" As trivial as it may appear, this small spark of mischief in a tiny corner of the world brought war to life and humanized it in a way that was more personal and more powerful to me than any recitation of battle-related statistics or casualty counts.

Some of the most affecting letters are those by servicemen and women trying to downplay the horrors of combat. Writing to an old friend back in Dallas on May 13, 1944, S. Sgt. Bob Brown, a B-24 turret gunner stationed in England, described a recent dash through German antiaircraft fire: "That flak is really rough on your nerves—especially when you can hear it burst. Once I bent over to pick up my flak suit & a piece of flak knocked a hole 4 in. round in the exact spot that my head had just vacated—also a hunk of flak hit my ball turret while I was in it & bounced off—Gee, I was really scared. These Germans are really serious about this whole thing & if they aren't careful they are liable to hurt someone."

Lance Corporal Thomas P. Noonan articulated the madness of the Vietnam War in a brief, whimsical letter to his sister in New York: "Please disregard any small note of flippancy that might reveal itself in this letter," Noonan wrote on October 17, 1968. "I try to avoid it, but when one is having such a good time it is hard not to be cheerful. I've thrown off the shackles of silly society. I've cast out my razor, divorced my soap, buried my manners, signed my socks to a two-year contract, and proved that you don't have to come in out of the rain. I scale the mountains, swim the rivers, soar through the skies in magic carpet helicopters. My advent is attended by Death and I've got chewing gum stuck in my mustache." These lighthearted bursts of spontaneity and levity become heartbreaking, however, when one recognizes the real dangers they were facing. S. Sgt. Bob Brown, twenty-two years old, was shot out of the sky only six days after he wrote to his friend in Dallas, and Lance Corporal Noonan was killed five months after writing to his sister. He was twenty-five.

Every effort has been made to transcribe the letters featured in this book exactly as they were written, mistakes and all. The intent is not to embarrass the correspondents but merely to capture their distinct personalities and nuanced writing styles. Certain errors also suggest the conditions under which these letters were written. Many correspondents wrote by moonlight in filthy trenches and flooded foxholes. One Civil War soldier resorted to using blackberry juice for ink. Punctuation and spelling errors abound because letters were written in haste, and certain words are indecipherable because rain or melted snow caused them to blur. Some of the servicemen, including George S. Patton, were dyslexic, and it is further evidence of how vital letters were to them that they would struggle for hours to write what would, in the end, amount to only a few pages. To clean up these letters or disrupt their natural pacing with one "[sic]" or bracketed notation after another, I believe, only diminishes what makes each letter so unique in the first place.

In the one hundred and forty years of warfare covered in this book, billions of letters, postcards, telegrams, V(ictory)-mails, and, more recently, e-mails, have traveled over continents and oceans to sustain the bonds of family and friendship. Although there are very few V-mails included here, they are referred to throughout the World War II chapter and represent the bulk of American correspondence during the 1940s. Created to handle the onslaught of letters overwhelming the U.S. postal service, V-mails were free and quick, but provided correspondents with only one short, preprinted page to express themselves. That page was sent through a machine to be photographed, and then negatives from thousands of V-mails were placed on a single roll of film and flown to a processing center, where they were developed and then forwarded to their recipients. At one point during the war, so many wives and girlfriends were kissing their V-mails before sending them off that the lipstick was building up and jamming the machines. It was known as the "scarlet scourge."

Few themes run more conspicuously through every generation of wartime correspondence than the yearning for mail. Letters were one of the few, tangible connections to loved ones, and servicemen and women pleaded and pined for even a word from home. "Say you old slab of lopsided tin-eared Jackass," one World War I soldier wrote to his friend, Elmer Sutters, in the States, "what's wrong with you anyhow. Got writer's cramp or what? Pick up a pen for the Love of Pete and write to your old buddie in France." Union private Columbus Huddle begged his father back in Ohio to write to him more frequently. "I have sent two letters to America and received no answer yet," Huddle reminded his father on April 10, 1862, "it is such a pleasure to get a letter here in this foreign land." (Huddle was in Tennessee.) Some soldiers were even more demanding. "You really giped me in your last letter," a young private groused to his friend Tessie Greenberg back in Brooklyn.

> A soldier looks forward to a letter as a means of relaxation and some consolation to a certain extent and to what is going on back home and last but not least, a friendly man to man talk. He doesn't expect a quiz program, and he'd rather not hear about the troubles or sickness that the sender of the letter is having at the time. And before I stop bringing you down any further, how about writing so I can understand what the hell you are writing without having to put my eyes

within an inch of the writing so I can make it out. Okay, I'm through.
Boy, I'll never hear the end of this.

Regrettably, Tessie's response has not survived.

And herein lies the sense of urgency that fuels the Legacy Project.
Throughout our country, old war letters are regularly being destroyed,
misplaced, lost to fire and water damage, or thrown away. These letters are
the first, unfiltered drafts of history. They are eyewitness accounts that
record not only the minute details of war but the personal insight and perspective no photograph or film reel can replicate. And each one represents
another page in our national autobiography. Millions of these letters—
maybe more—remain tucked away in attics, basements, and closets in
every community in America. It is exhilarating to think of what is yet to be
uncovered. But it is equally as discouraging to consider, if these letters are
neglected, what may be lost forever.

During a trip to London in the fall of 1999 to research American war letters at the Imperial War Museum, I encountered an elderly English gentleman who related to me how he and his countrymen prepared for war in
the summer of 1939. Fearing massive bombings and a full-scale German
invasion, English citizens in numerous towns and villages meticulously
dismantled the stained glass windows of their churches and distributed the
individual fragments throughout the community. The townspeople then
hid the small pieces of colored glass in biscuit tins and bowls of sugar. After
the war, the glass was collected and reassembled.

What struck me about the story was how analogous it seemed to this
book. Individually, the war letters collected here are distinct, finely cut
works of art, some more polished, some rougher around the edges, but
each one exquisite in its own right. Together, they create a larger narrative:
the story of Americans at war against themselves and other nations. It is a
story of immeasurable suffering and astonishing violence. But it is also a
story that encompasses tales of heroism, perseverance, integrity, honor, and
reconciliation. The individual letters infuse the story with its humanity,
while the collection as a whole demonstrates the story's breathtaking
size and scope.

There is another story these letters tell, but it is more obscure and
harder to discern. Occasionally it reveals itself when a soldiers assures his
mom or his wife that "everything's fine" and not to fret. It is most evident in the relatively few letters that have survived by these mothers and
wives imploring their loved ones to let them know all is well. This particular story is not about the men who fight. It is about the women on the
homefront.

Theirs is a story largely unrecorded because the servicemen hundreds or thousands of miles away could not, for the most part, save their letters from home. They wanted to, and they tried, but ultimately it was impractical; there was no place to stash so much mail, and, even if there were, the letters were unlikely to outlast the jungles of Vietnam, the frozen mountains of Korea, the muddy battlefields of Europe, or the sweltering islands of the Pacific. Most letters from the homefront that have survived are correspondences marked "return to sender" because the recipient was dead. (The delay in wartime mail delivery also meant that letters by the deceased kept coming home days and even weeks after he had been killed in action.)

"I am just about frantic for fear you were in danger yesterday," Alice House wrote on December 8, 1941, to her eighteen-year-old son, Paul, stationed at Pearl Harbor. "I walk around doing my work, ironing, doing the dishes, and everything else, saying my prayers. . . . I would be terribly grateful if I could get just one word from you, SAFE." (Petty Officer House was onboard the USS *West Virginia* when it was struck, but he leapt into the flaming waters and was rescued.) In every war women like Alice House waited and worried, never knowing when to expect a visit from a military chaplain or a telegram beginning with that pulse-stopping first line: "The Secretary of War desires me to express his deep regret that . . ." And if that notification did come, their lives were instantly shattered. "There are no words to describe how I felt. I was so empty," Theresa O. Davis wrote thirty years after her son, Richard, was killed in Vietnam. "I pretended to be brave. But inside, the empty space just grew bigger."

I have learned, through what letters of theirs have been preserved, of the private pain these women have carried with them over the years. There are, of course, millions of men who quietly grieve for lost brothers and sons and fathers and best friends, but I emphasize the women only because they are so often overlooked. The resilience and compassion of these women is extraordinary to me, and they have taught me and so many others the human cost of war and the internal scars it leaves behind. They are also the ones, I have discovered, most responsible for organizing, deciphering, transcribing, and saving America's war letters. This book would not have been possible without the letters these women have held on to and safeguarded for future generations. They have kept these voices alive and ensured that the men and women who have served this nation will always be remembered. For their generosity, their sacrifice, and all that they have endured, this book is dedicated to them.

—Andrew Carroll
Washington, D.C.
January 28, 2001

THE CIVIL WAR

All the firing had ceased, everything was calm and still after the awful storm save the awful shrieks of the dying and wounded which were great came from every quarter in every direction. Cries for help, for water, brother calling for brother, comrade for companions. In ten feet of where I lay was a Pennsylvania Yankee with his bowels shot out. He was lying in the branch. He begged for water, for a blanket and said that he was freezing. Some of the boys lifted him out of the branch and wrapped a blanket around him. We left before daylight. I don't know what became of him.

—Undated letter by Capt. William Harris Hardy,
with the Confederate Army, to his wife, Sallie

Truly we know not the horrors of war till peace has fled.
—*Pvt. Elijah Beeman, with the Union Army,*
to his sister Ann, April 26, 1862;
Beeman was killed five months later

Abolitionist Aaron Stevens, Writing to His Brother in 1858, Warns That Slavery Will Only Be Done Away with "By the Sword"
&
Stevens Bids Farewell to His Brother from Jail Before Being Hanged for Participating in John Brown's Raid at Harpers Ferry

Fierce debates over the issue of slavery had imperiled the creation of the American colonies from their earliest days. Delegates to the Second Continental Congress refused to sign the Declaration of Independence until severe, antislavery language written by Thomas Jefferson—ironically, a slaveowner himself—was expunged. Forty-four years later Jefferson articulated his own ambivalence on slavery in a letter to John Holmes, a member of the Massachusetts Senate: "We have the wolf by the ears," Jefferson wrote on April 22, 1820, "and we can neither hold him, nor safely let him go. Justice is in one scale, and self-preservation in the other." Tensions mounted as violent encounters flared throughout the nation. In 1831 a slave named Nat Turner led a two-day insurrection in Virginia that left an estimated fifty-seven white men, women, and children dead. In 1837 a white newspaper editor, Rev. Elijah P. Lovejoy, was shot to death in Illinois by a mob infuriated by his abolitionist views. Beginning in the early 1840s fugitive slave Frederick Douglass traveled throughout the North describing to audiences the brutality he had experienced under his master's whip. Harriet Beecher Stowe further exposed the horrors of slavery in her 1852 best-seller Uncle Tom's Cabin. *An explosive clash, like the one erupting in Kansas in the 1850s between pro- and antislavery factions, seemed increasingly likely on a national scale, and some—like Aaron Dwight Stevens— were literally praying for its arrival. A veteran of the Mexican War, Stevens was a skilled soldier who wanted to use his military expertise to hasten slavery's demise. As expressed in the following letter to his brother in Minnesota, he believed its end would come only through bloodshed.*

Spring Dale Cedar Co. Iowa
Aug: 2nd 1858.

My Dear Brother,

It seames a long time since I had a letter from you. I have been traveling about so much that I'v not been able to write offtiner.

I think I told you before that I was in the cause of <u>human Freedom,</u> but I did not give you the particklures. We left Kansas to strike Slavory at the heart, and we had things all arrianged to do it, and would of done so, but for a trator. one of the party had a falling out with the head one and for gold turned trator to himself his country and his god; you may think it not best to do it by the sword, but I tell you it never will be done away except by the sword, and every year it is getting worse, and then think of the thousands who are murdered yearly, you are aware of how they do things down south. I suppose you know

I suppose that they work there Slaves on those big plantations hard enouf to kill them in seven years, they can make the most of them in thatt way, so you see there is thousands of them murdered yearly, and would you not think it best to do away with Slavory in a year or two by loosing a few thousands in war than to have thousands of them murdered yearly for god knows how many years, and to think how many of them have been murdered before this.

I am aganst war, except in self defense, and then I am like Pattrick Henry, when he sayd "<u>give me Liberty or give me death.</u>" I do not think we shall be able to go on with it this year, but I think the time is acoming when it will be done. it leaves us in rather bad circumstances for we had sackraficed all we had to the cause, but we are willing to give up life it self for the good of humanity.

how is the times in Minisoti I suppose they are about the same as else where. I have not heard from Father for a long time nor eny of the rest of our folkes. I had a letter from Lemuel about four months ago. he was well then I would like to see him very much, and o. how I wish we could all meet once more.

give my love to your wife, and tell her I should like to see her very much. you must excuse me for writing this short lettor.

I will send you my likeness. it is not a very good one, but then you can see how I look somewhat. I wish you would send me yours and you will gratley oblige your

Loving Brother
A. D. Stevens

(Please write as soon as you get this.)

Over a year after writing this letter, Stevens joined forces with John Brown, a man who was equally as impassioned about eradicating slavery through violence. On October 16, 1859, Brown, Stevens, and seventeen other men, including five blacks and twelve whites, seized the federal armory in Harpers Ferry, Virginia (now West Virginia) in an attempt to rally the local slaves in a rebellion that, Brown antici-

pated, would spread throughout the South. The raid was a disaster. Not a single slave heeded Brown's summons, and Brown and his men found themselves surrounded in the fire engine house, first by armed townspeople, and then by United States Marines under the command of U.S. Army Lt. Col. Robert E. Lee. Ten of Brown's men, including two of his sons, were killed. Aaron Stevens was shot several times but lived. Captured and tried, the surviving men all received a sentence of death, and Brown was hanged on December 2. (Standing in the crowd of 1,500 to watch the execution was a young actor named John Wilkes Booth, who conceded that Brown was "a brave old man.") Aaron Stevens's hanging did not take place until over three months later. On March 13, 1860, Stevens, unrepentant and ready to die, wrote a final letter to his brother from the Charles Town Jail.

My ever dear Brother.

    I sit down for the last time, without doubt, to communicate a few thoughts to thee. I am in excellent health and very happy. Sister Lydia is with me, and she is as brave as ever I was very glad to see her, it is now over nine years since I last saw her. it does not seem so long. how fast the time flies. I should like to see you my Dear Brother very much, but shall have to wait untill we meet in the Spirit-world. What joy it will give me to meet you and all other kind friends there.

    I hope Dear Brother you will investigate the spiritual theory for it is such pleasure to <u>know</u> that we shall all meet sooner or later in the Spirit-land, than mere <u>belief</u>. It has been very <u>consoling</u> to me during these trying times. I hope you will be one of those lovers of <u>truth</u> and <u>right,</u> and help redeem the world from sin and oppression of all kinds, and as you love yourself as you love man, as you love woman, as you love God, work with your head, heart, and hands, for the happiness of yourself and <u>all</u> the <u>world.</u> be careful and not think too much of self. this is one great thing we should all conquer.

        Give my love to your wife, and little one and say Farewell.

        Farewell my Dear Brother we meet again beyond the tomb,

            god bless you and yours

        A. D. Stevens

The deaths of Brown and his men galvanized both sides of the debate over slavery. Southerners were outraged that Brown, a "traitorous, cold-blooded killer" whose sanity was questioned even by his supporters, had become a martyr. But to the abolitionists, the raid on Harpers Ferry heralded the possible end of one of the foulest of all human creations. "This day will be a great day in our history," wrote the poet Henry Wadsworth Longfellow on Brown's execution, "the date of a new Revolution—quite as much needed as the old one."

~~∾~~

Marcus Morton Sends Fort Sumter's Maj. Robert Anderson a Message of Support in His "Hour of Imminent Peril"

South Carolina was the first to go. Mississippi was next. And then Florida, Alabama, Georgia, Louisiana, and Texas. Enraged by the 1860 election of Abraham Lincoln, who vowed he would not allow slavery in new territories joining the United States, the seven Southern states seceded from the Union and elected their own president, the former U.S. secretary of war and senator from Mississippi Jefferson Davis, before Lincoln even took the oath of office. "I have no purpose, directly or indirectly, to interfere with the institution of slavery in the states where it exists," the president stated in his March 4, 1861, inaugural address. But Lincoln also declared he would use the "power confided in [him] to hold, occupy, and possess the property and places belonging to the government." This included Fort Sumter in the harbor of Charleston, South Carolina, which, surrounded by thousands of Confederate militiamen and artillery batteries, was rapidly running out of provisions. For weeks Maj. Robert Anderson and his modest garrison received no supplies or reinforcements, but they remained in the fort despite mounting pressures and threats to evacuate. As word of Anderson's plight spread through the Union, heartfelt letters of admiration poured into the fort, including one from Marcus Morton, the former governor of Massachusetts.

> Taunton Mass April 8 1861
> Major Robert Anderson USA
> Commanding Fort Sumter
> Charleston S. C.

Sir,

At a moment when the hearts of all true friends of the Union were heavy with apprehension; when distrust in the efficiency of Republican Institutions seemed about to settle upon the land; and men began to doubt, whether the coming day would dawn on a people enjoying the blessings of Constitutional Liberty or a people drifting into disorder and anarchy, the intelligence of your self-reliant, wise and patriotic conduct in the harbor of Charleston, as it flashed from point to point, reanimated their wavering hopes, restored their waning confidence, and gave assurance that they still possess a national Government.

This is not the time nor the occasion to enter upon any discussion of the merits of the unhappy controversy which menaces the Republic; nor to enquire upon whom rests the responsibility for the perils which environ us. Your heroic action admonishes us that our first thoughts and efforts should be devoted to the maintenance of the Union as it was founded by our wise and patriotic Fathers and bequeathed to us, that we, in our time, may transmit it, in all its integrity and glory, to our successors. We trust that this may be accomplished by an exercise of the same disinterested spirit by which they were animated, and by the same rational means which they employed.

We trust that reason and reflection may carry to the minds of our Fellow Countrymen, in every section of our widely extended and diversified territory, the conviction that there can be no grievance, which may not be better and more certainly redressed, in the Union, than out of it; and that the sum of all existing evils, real or supposed, is but the dust of the balance when weighed against a single one of the dreadful consequences, which must inevitably follow in the track of dissolution.

We trust that God, in infinite Goodness, may avert the horrors of fraternal strife; and that under His providence, the Flag, which, heretofore, has floated in glory over land and sea, the hope of the world, may never be stained by fraternal blood. But come what may come, we but utter, what we believe to be the honest sentiment of the Country, when we repeat and adopt, the memorable words, which, in a similar crisis, gave hope and confidence to the nation.

"Our federal Union—It must be preserved."

Entertaining these sentiments, and recognizing in you a man and a soldier, who in the hour of imminent peril, had the forethought to conceive, and the patriotism and courage to perform an Act necessary to the preservation of the authority and entirety of the Union, even at the risk of self-sacrifice, the citizens of the Ancient Town of Taunton, desire to present to you an expression of their admiration and gratitude, and as a testimonial of their appreciation of your character and of the eminent services rendered the Republic, the undersigned, by their authority and in their name and behalf, begs your acceptance of the accompanying <u>Sword,</u> confident, that, by your hand, it never will be drawn without just cause, or returned, dishonored, to its scabbard.

> In behalf of the inhabitants of Taunton,
> With high personal considerations
> I am Your Obedient Servant,
> Marcus Morton

Just after 3:00 A.M. on April 12 Major Anderson received a polite but unwelcome message from two Confederate officers: "By authority of Brig General Beauregard Commanding the Provisional Forces of the Confederate States we have the honor to notify you that he will open the fire of his Batteries on Fort Sumter in an hour from this time. We have the honor to be Very Respectfully Yr. Obt Svts." Anderson refused the ultimatum, and at 4:30 A.M., the Confederate forces began their assault. Anderson and his sixty-eight soldiers were bombarded by an estimated 4,000 shells for a day and a half before they finally surrendered. (Miraculously, no one was killed in the onslaught.) Cheers erupted throughout the Confederacy as the "American" flag above Fort Sumter came down. "We have humbled the proud flag of the Stars and Stripes," boasted the governor of South Carolina, "that never before was lowered to any nation on earth." Pierre G. T. Beauregard, who directed the attack, had learned his artillery skills over twenty years earlier while a cadet at West Point. His instructor was Robert Anderson.

~

P. Burns in Tennessee, Observing the "Spirit of War" Overtaking the Country, Laments to a Friend the Misery to Come

Immediately after the Confederate victory at Fort Sumter, President Lincoln ordered the remaining states and territories to dispatch militiamen to fight for the Union. Virginia, Tennessee, Arkansas, and North Carolina refused, siding with the Confederates. President Lincoln appealed to Robert E. Lee, a hero of the Mexican War, to lead the entire federal army. Although Lee considered slavery "a moral and political evil," he declined. "I cannot raise my hand against my birthplace," he wrote to a friend. (In June 1862 Lee would be given command of the Confederate's single largest military force—the Army of Northern Virginia.) Accusations of betrayal and treason would tear friendships and families apart as soldiers and officers made their alliances. Both sides expressed enthusiasm for the contest to come, which many presumed would be settled quickly. But not everyone was sanguine about the impending clash, as evidenced in a prescient letter from P. Burns in Tennessee to his friend Ann Maceubbin in Missouri.

Nashville, June 10, 1861

Miss Ann:

Thinking it would not be amiss to drop you a few lines to let you know what was going on in the confederate states and also when I was going to return. I take the present opportunity after the noise & bustle of the election is over.

After leaving your quiet & beautiful town, I arrived the same evening in St. Louis. Procured your music with the exception of a few pieces which I could not get in the City. They cost me more than I expected but I suppose not more than common. I went to the free state of Illinois found all my folks and stade over a week. Started then for this city, as the boats quit running down the river had to come by railroad all the way rather tiresome business.

Found people in Illinois fixing for war, came through Indiana they were fixing — crossed Kentucky they were preparing. Arrived in my old State of Tennessee and never saw the like. Men women & children are imbued with the spirit of war. There are over 80 thousand under arms in this State & men swair that they will not submit if it costs the last man in the state. I can hear the fife & drum from morning until night & see men in rank & file all day & every car that comes into town crowded with soldiers. I see some of my cousins that was but little boys when I left here seven years ago drilling every day. There are thousands of soldiers passing through this State every day from the South on their way to Virginia. Some here think that Maryland will become a great battlefield some of these days, if so I will feel for Susan. An invaded country is no place for ladies.

I found quite a change in this city & my relations since I left seven years ago. My relations have grown in numbers size & wealth. They received me with a great deal of hospitality. Some of my Aunts ran & kist me as they would one of their sons. They insist that I must stay untill fall but I have to refuse their kindness. I have long sympathised with the people of the South and I now sympathise more than ever they are a generous & noble people. The election that was held on the first went off very quiet in this city nearly all for separation & dispatches from other parts say nearly all are for separation every man was let vote the way he saw propper. Some had feared the result and thought there would be bloody times at the election.

Ann it makes my heart sick to think of the State of our once happy and yet beloved country for there is no history that tells of any country that was ever happyer than ours — and now to see two brave and warlike armys armed with all the deadly instruments that art and wealth could procure marching over our once peaceable country and to think when they meet in the bloody battle fields what destruction they can and what misery they can produce. But Ann what is most horrid of all in this contest is that brother will meet brother and father will meet son in the strife for there are but few families in the north but have members of that family in the South and the people of the South are in the same way—as for myself no matter what side I might take might bring me in contact with a brother or a cousin or unkle & god forbid that I should ever be found in the arms against either.

The people of the north by blockading the ports think they can starve the people of the South but they will fail for I never saw a better prospect in my life for an abundant crop.

Ann if no providential hinderance I will be in your town by the 27 inst but should I not be prompt to the day do not dispair for a day or two for these are squally times and a person might be frustrated in their calculation. You may hear that people are prevented from leaving this State but believe it not. The mails will be stopt here in a day or two. If you see propper you can drop me a few lines to Moro, Illi as I will call there as I return.

No more at present but remain with cincerity
Your friend
P Burns

P.S. Excuse haste

～つ

Lt. Ai Thompson Writes to His Father After the U.S. Army's "Disgraceful" Loss at Manassas (Bull Run)

The first major confrontation of the Civil War occurred just twenty-five miles from the White House. Hundreds of spectators, some carrying picnic baskets and champagne, rode out from Washington to watch over 35,000 Union soldiers as they marched into Virginia. Under the direction of Gen. Irvin McDowell, the Union army planned to capture the new Confederate capital at Richmond and strike a swift and fatal blow to the secessionists. Waiting to intercept them at Bull Run, a meandering creek near the Manassas railroad junction, was Gen. P. G. T. Beauregard, hero of the victory over Fort Sumter. When the two armies clashed on July 21, Beauregard's outnumbered forces were driven into near retreat. "The day is ours," exclaimed McDowell. But standing firm—like a "stone wall"—in the middle of the Confederate line was Gen. Thomas J. Jackson. Emboldened by Jackson's resolve and the arrival of reinforcements, the Confederates launched a fierce counterattack, and the Union forces withdrew. In a letter to his father in New Hampshire, twenty-eight-year-old Union Lt. Ai Thompson related the confusion and, in his view, cowardice that led to the federal army's first major defeat of the war. (The Zouaves, alluded to in the letter, were soldiers who wore bright scarlet and blue uniforms with trimmed jackets and either a turban or a fez, all styled after elite French troops. At Manassas, they suffered some of the heaviest casualties.)

Camp Sullivan
Washington D.C.
July 24 1861

Dear Father,

A great battle, as you have heard, has been fought. The Federal forces were badly cut up and retreated in the most disgraceful disorder, and all on account of unskillful generalship. But, thank God, Gen. McDowell has been withdrawn and Gen. McClellan is coming to take his place on this department.

On Sunday morning last at 2 o'clock Col. Burnside's Brigade left their place of temporary encampment, which is between Fairfax C.H. and Centerville and about 2 miles this side of the latter place, with their blankets on their shoulders, their haversacks full of hard bread, their canteens of water, with heavy muskets and cartridge boxes full of ammunition, but with hearts as light as were their falling footsteps, which latter were almost as noiseless as the shining of the full faced moon which lighted them on over turnpike, thro' forest and thro' field to disastrous defeat and to death. It seemed to me as I watched the movement of those four thousand men as we were marching onward in the solemn stillness of the early Sabbath morn, that a phantom army was issuing forth from the mists of the night; armed with brightly burnished weapons of silver and gold. But you don't want poetry nor sentiment now.

We marched on, as I have said, over miserable turnpikes, thro' magnificent forests of oaks from two till nine AM. It was about nine, or as near as I can tell, when their pickets first fired on ours and in a very few moments the battle began in earnest. We were in the woods when the firing began and the balls whistled thro' the trees past our heads in double quick. We had marched at least 15 miles and with all our burdens we were somewhat jaded and ill prepared for immediate action. But, we were upon the enemy unexpectedly and must fight. The men threw away their blankets, rushed thro' the woods into the open field in the direction of the enemies' fire. We soon saw that they had every advantage of us. They were under cover of woods, we could not see them, only a few of their pickets. Their batteries were all around us, except in our rear and command almost every position we could possibly take to do them any injury. Sherman's Battery and the R.I. Battery did us much service and them great injury but we had to fire uphill and they down and they could see us but we could not see them. The battle lasted from five to six hours and during the whole time the Federal forces were without a competent head to direct their movements. I don't think with a more skillful General and the same number of men we could have dislodged the enemy from their stronghold, but we might have thrown them out perhaps and had a fair fight of it.

Regiment after regiment of our troops advanced up the hill in solid column towards the enemies batteries and discharged volley after volley into the rebel ranks but every one retreated in disorder and confusion leaving many dead and dying on the field. With painful anxiety I watched the successively retreating columns. Till I saw the bloody Zouaves advancing up the hill in the face of the enemy's fire, the blood of the murdered Ellsworth crying to them from the ground to be avenged and then I thought of victory. But the Goddess of victory perched not on their banner; they too retreated in great disorder, leaving three hundred of their brave fellows dead or dying on the field. It was now evident that unless some other plan of attack should be adopted, it would be impossible to drive out the enemy. But how could our forces be rallied, scattered as they were in every direction and many of their officers dead or wounded, and the General commanding clearly deficient in military skill and nowhere to be seen. A great and fearful retribution awaits those incompetent men who take upon themselves the responsibility of a division of the Army, a brigade or a regiment, or a company even, and I hope that the people of New Hampshire will bear this important fact in mind when they organise other regiments.

But you want to know where the N.H. 2nd was and what they did during the battle. They were nowhere and did nothing. This latter is a sweeping statement and needs to be qualified a little. When we first entered the field from the woods we were ordered, by whom I don't know, to take a position about 1/2 of a mile on a terrace from where we then stood in line. Our position before the order was in rear of Ricket's Battery, as I supposed to support it in case it should be charged upon by the enemy. But we obeyed orders of course, went to the terrace, drew up in line awaiting orders, all the while cannon balls and shells flying and bursting about our ears. But no orders came and no enemy was in sight, excepting forty or fifty who were secreted under a fence within musket reach. No sooner did our men see them than they drew up and blazed away without orders from Col. or Capt. The rebels under the fence couldn't stand the fire and ran for the woods. One poor fellow near by where I stood was shot thro' the body and he fell almost lifeless to the ground. He belonged to Company H. I suppose he was hit by a ball from one of the fellows under the fence.

We could not have been placed in a more favorable position for the enemy to cut us in pieces and there was not a rebel to be seen after those few retreated to the woods. Our men began to grow unsteady under the enemy's fire, our commanding officers didn't seem to know what to do. Marsten is plucky and rash but he was not born to command. Lt. Col. Fiske attempted to rally the men but in spite of his tardy efforts they retreated beyond the reach of the rebels fire, and it was a most disorderly and disgraceful retreat.

We fell back perhaps fifty or a hundred rods out of reach of the rebel cannon and after great efforts on the part of some of the company officers

the men were got in line and drawn off to their first position to the rear of
the battery. Here we remained for some time without discharging a musket, but constantly exposed to the enemy's fire and our men being
wounded at almost every shot. Here Col. Marsten was wounded in the
arm. A rifle ball struck him in the right arm near the shoulder, penetrated
to the bone where it changed direction, followed the bone to the shoulder
blade, turned again and went down and lodged in the right breast where
it remained till he got to Washington.

From this position we were ordered to advance in front of the battery,
out of range of course and nearer the enemy's infantry which was under
cover of woods. Here we remained a long time with orders to fire when
we could see a mark, which was not often. It seemed to me that the sun
was scalding hot and no tea to drink. Again we were ordered to move and
take a position nearer the enemy which we did, but before doing so Col.
M. had returned to the field with his arm in a sling, made us a brief speech
which was full of pluck, said he was with us again and would be with us so
long as he could.

But to speak the plain truth, he was useless as a commander when
unwounded and we knew it, and what could we expect of him in his present condition, notwithstanding his plucky speech made while his face was
distorted with intensest pain. But he went with us about half way to the
place we were ordered to occupy, where we halted for a while and the last
I saw of him on the field he was squatted on his haunches in a ditch packed
full of men who had jumped in there to escape the rebel fire, which was
thick and hot upon us. But they exposed themselves to greater danger as
I thot and told them at the time, by lying down, for in our then position,
nothing could hit us but falling balls and shells, and in a reclining position
they exposed more surface than when standing. My philosophy they
couldn't comprehend and urged me with tears in their eyes to abandon
such dangerously false ideas and fall in with them. But I was incorrigible
and stood upright and they lay still.

After having several men terribly wounded here by bursting shells we
took our position halfway up the hill towards the enemy, where we were
ordered to lie down on our faces, which most of the officers and men
obeyed. They lay there in that disgraceful, because unnecessary, position
without firing a musket or seeing an enemy, and the next order was to get
up and retreat. And we did get up and we did retreat and we scarcely
stopped till we got to Washington.

Thus did the Gallant New Hampshire 2nd Regiment acquit itself on
Sundy the 21st day of July Anno Domini 1861. Every order was a blunder
and every movement a failure. Had the men been left to themselves with

their muskets and ammunition they could and would have done the enemy serious injury, but as it was I don't believe they killed a single rebel except what the rifles may have picked off. I am sorry, yes, I cannot but weep to tell this sickening tale of the Gallant 2nd Regiment from N.H. of which so much was expected. There was no fault in the men thank God: they are brave fellows as ever heard the music of whistling bullets, and it was too bad to expose them to be cut down and mangled, when they could not return the enemy's fire. But so it was and may it be a wholesome lesson to those men in New Hampshire who are anxious to put themselves at the head of the other regiments which are to be raised.

I think we shall have trouble in reorganizing our regiment. Col. M. will not be able to take command for some time yet, but if he should be, I don't think the men would go to battle under him with any heart. As for the other field officers, they are not reliable and have not the confidence of the men. Our adjutant had business in Washington on the day of the battle and was not with us. How we shall be officered and by whom I cannot say. Many of the company officers have said they never would march under the same officers again. I cannot foretell the result. Perhaps we may conclude to try it once more.

Our loss is small, not over 10 men were killed on the field, but many, I don't know the number, came off badly wounded. Most of the wounded are alive and accounted for but two or three it is supposed fell into the hands of the enemy and were murdered.

Eight or ten of our company were wounded, some badly, some slightly. All but one poor fellow who had his leg torn badly with a cannon ball are accounted for.

I cannot write any more now.

Your son,
Ai B. Thompson

By the end of the battle, more than 4,500 Union and Confederate soldiers were either dead, wounded, or taken prisoner. Shaken by the defeat and fearful that more states (such as Kentucky, Missouri, and Maryland) might join the Confederacy, President Lincoln called for the enlistment of 100,000 new troops and placed the Union army under the command of Gen. George B. McClellan, who had successfully driven Rebel forces out of West Virginia. Arrogant but admired, the thirty-four-year-old McClellan transformed the dispirited, untrained Army of the Potomac into a skilled, invigorated fighting force. There was, however, one small problem—he did nothing with it. The overly cautious McClellan blamed conflicting reports, inadequate supplies, incompetent staff, the weather—essentially, everyone and everything—for refusing to engage the Rebels. "If General McClellan does not want to use the army," the president fumed after months of inaction, "I would like to borrow it for a time." Animosity between Lincoln and McClellan—who referred to the president as "nothing more than a well meaning baboon"—would, as the war continued, only grow.

~

Imprisoned Confederate Spy Rose O'Neal Greenhow Excoriates U.S. Secretary of State William Seward for the "Military Dictatorship" He and President Lincoln Have Established

Just as they had done in the young nation's previous conflicts, women—both in the North and the South—made invaluable contributions to the war effort. They organized food drives, tended family farms, labored in factories, served as nurses in hospitals, and raised funds for relief efforts. An estimated 400 women even disguised themselves as men and enlisted as soldiers. Many women assumed a less visible though no less dramatic role by working as spies. One of the most famous was Rose O'Neal Greenhow, a Washington socialite whose connections provided her with extraordinary access to political and military leaders. In early July Greenhow sent a coded message to Gen. P. G. T. Beauregard, alerting him that Union troops would soon be heading through Manassas. ("But for you," Jefferson Davis later praised Greenhow, "there would have been no battle of Bull Run.") On August 23 Greenhow was arrested, and after three months in jail, she sent a scathing letter to Secretary of State William H. Seward.

Washington, Nov. 17th, 1861,
398 Sixteenth Street.

To the Hon. Wm. H. Seward,
Secretary of State:

Sir—For nearly three months I have been confined, a close prisoner, shut out from air and exercise, and denied all communication with family and friends.

"Patience is said to be a great virture," and I have practised it to my utmost capacity of endurance.

I am told, sir, that upon your ipse dixit, the fate of citizens depends, and that the signature of the ministers of Louis the Fourteenth and Fifteenth was not more potential in their day, than that of the Secretary of State in 1861.

I therefore most respectfully submit, that on Friday, August 23d, without warrant or other show of authority, I was arrested by the Detective Police, and my house taken in charge by them; that all my private letters, and my papers of a life time, were read and examined by them; that every law of decency was violated in the search of my house and person, and the surveilance over me.

We read in history, that the poor Marie Antoinette had a paper torn from her bosom by lawless hands, and that even a change of linen had to be effected in sight of her brutal captors. It is my sad experience to record even more revolting outrages than that, for during the first days of my imprisonment, whatever necessity forced me to seek my chamber, a detective stood sentinel at the open door. And thus for a period of seven days, I, with my little child, was placed absolutely at the mercy of men without character or responsibility; that during the first evening, a portion of these men became brutally drunk, and boasted in my hearing of the "nice times" they expected to have with the female prisoners; and that rude violence was used towards a colored servant girl during that evening, the extent of which I have not been able to learn. For any show of decorum afterwards was practiced toward me, I was indebted to the detective called Capt. Dennis.

In the careful analysis of my papers I deny the existence of a line I had not a perfect right to have written, or to have received. Freedom of speech and of opinion is the birthright of Americans, guaranteed to us by our Charter of Liberty, the Constitution of the United States. I have exercised my perogative, and have openly avowed my sentiments. During the political struggle, I opposed your Republican party with every instinct of self-preservation. I believed your success a virtual nullification of the Constitution, and that it would entail upon us the direful consequences which have ensued. These sentiments have doubtless been found recorded among my papers, and I hold them as rather a proud record of my sagacity.

I must be permitted to quote from a letter of yours, in regard to Russell of the London Times, which you conclude with these admirable words: "Individual errors of opinion may be tolerated, as long as good sense is left to combat them." By way of illustrating theory and practice, here am I, a prisoner in sight of the Executive Mansion, in sight of the Capitol where the proud statesmen of our land have sung their paeans to the blessings of our free institutions. Comment is idle. Freedom of thought, every right pertaining to the citizen has been suspended by what, I suppose, the President calls a "military necessity." A blow has been struck, by this total disregard of all civil rights, against the present system of Government, far greater in its effects than the severance of the Southern States.

Our people have been taught to contemn the supremacy of the law, to which all have hitherto bowed, and to look to the military power for protection against its decrees. A military spirit has been developed, which will only be subordinate to a Military Dictatorship. Read history, and you will find, that the causes which bring about a revolution rarely predominate at its close, and no people have ever returned to the point from which they started. Even should the Southern State be subdued and forced back into the Union (which I regard as impossible, with a full knowledge of their resources), a different form of Government will be found needful to meet the new developments of national character. There is no class of society, no branch of industry, which this change has not reached, and the dull, plodding, methodical habits of the poor can never be resumed.

You have held me, sir, to man's accountability, and I therefore claim the right to speak on subjects usually considered beyond a woman's ken, and which you may class as "errors of opinion." I offer no excuse for this long digression, as a three months' imprisonment , without formula of law, gives me authority for occupying even the precious moments of a Secretary of State.

My object is to call your attention to the fact: that during this long imprisonment, I am yet ignorant of the causes of my arrest; that my house has been seized and converted into a prison by the Government; that the valuable furniture it contained has been abused and destroyed; that during some periods of my imprisonment I have suffered greatly for want of proper and sufficient food. Also, I have to complain that, more recently, a woman of bad character, recognized as having been seen on the streets of Chicago as such, by several of the guard, calling herself Mrs. Onderdonk, was placed here in my house, in a room adjoining mine.

In making this exposition, I have no object of appeal to your sympathies, if the justice of my complaint, and a decent regard for the world's opinion, do not move you, I should but waste your time to claim your attention on any other score.

I may, however, recall to your mind, that but a little while since you were quite as much proscribed by public sentiment here, for the opinions and principles you held, as I am now for mine.

I could easily have escaped arrest, having had timely warning. I thought it impossible that your statesmanship might present such a proclamation of weakness to the world, as even the fragment of a once great Government turning its arms against the breasts of women and children. You have the power, sir, and may still further abuse it. You may prostrate the physical strength, by confinement in close rooms and insufficient food—you may subject me to harsher, ruder treatment than I have already received, but you cannot imprison the soul. Every cause worthy of success has had its martyrs. The words of the heroine Corday are applicable here: "C'est la crime qui fait la honte, et non pas l'echafaud." My sufferings will afford a significant lesson to the women of the South, that sex or condition is no bulwark against the surging billows of the "irrepressible conflict."

The "iron heel of power" may keep down, but it cannot crush out, the spirit of resistance in a people armed for the defence of their rights; and I tell you now, sir, that you are standing over a crater, whose smothered fires in a moment may burst forth.

It is your boast, that thirty-three bristling fortifications now surround Washington. The fortifications of Paris did not protect Louis Phillippe when his hour had come.

In conclusion, I respectfully ask your attention to this protest, and have the honor to be, &c.,

Rose O. N. Greenhow

Greenhow's accusations were not without merit, and throughout the war President Lincoln was criticized even by his supporters for acts that were deemed unconstitutional. Most egregiously, in the minds of many, Lincoln suspended the writ of habeas corpus—a citizen's most basic protection against imprisonment without due course of law. It is believed that during the war over 13,000 Americans were temporarily jailed without a formal charge, hearing, or trial. After being incarcerated for almost a year, Rose O'Neal Greenhow was released in 1862 and banished from the Union. She left for Europe in 1863 to generate support for the Confederate cause and promote her autobiography. While returning home on a blockade-runner in the fall of 1864, a federal gunboat was sighted near Cape Fear, North Carolina, and Greenhow, fearing for her safety, asked to escape to shore in a rowboat. The small craft capsized, and Greenhow, purportedly weighed down by gold sovereigns earned from the sale of her book, was drowned.

~∿

Lt. James Trathen of the MS *Bark* Describes to a Friend a Burial at Sea and Several Encounters with the Confederates

Mocked by critics as the "Anaconda Plan," Gen. Winfield Scott's April 1861 proposal to suffocate the South economically through naval blockades won the attention of President Lincoln, who shared Scott's belief in the need for long-term strategies. Northerners initially derided the plan as unnecessary (the war, after all, would be over shortly), and Southerners scoffed at the idea that the Union could cut off their 3,500 miles of coastline. Both sides, however, came to recognize the necessity of having warships to patrol coasts and rivers, control commercial routes, and fire upon enemy troops on land. The Union navy ultimately outnumbered the Confederate navy three to one, but Southern mechanics were skilled at transforming steam frigates into ironclad warships that could wreak havoc against the Union navy's wooden vessels. (Confederate engineers even created the Hunley, *the first submarine in history to sink a ship in battle—although it sank itself in the process.) In a letter to a friend in New York, James Trathen of the MS* Bark, *writes about skirmishes with Confederate forces trying to overrun Fort Pickens, which, though situated in Florida and guarding Pensacola Harbor, was still in Union hands.*

Gulf Squadron
Midnight off Fort Pickens Nov 29th 1861

Dear Sir,

It is with much pleasure I avail myself of this opportunity to send you a few lines altho as yet nothing of much interest has occur'd. I left New York on the 5th inst after a detention of several days off the Battery. The ship was in good turn well arm'd and mann'd, and a fine set of officers. We had not proceeded far before a very fierce storm broke upon us, and soon brought our Gallant little ship under small sails.

On the third day from New York we entered the Gulf Stream with the Lightning and Thunder raging horribly around us, and the fierce Gale and high sea threatning destruction to us every minute. In the midst of this one of our best Seamen fell from the mast head very near the place where my first officer and my self were standing, which instantly killed him and cast a gloom over the whole ship.

There is nothing that can happen on board ships that will affect a sailor more than the Death of a shipmate in this way. Ten men killed in a Battle produces less despondency. It was two days after the sad incident occured before we could Bury him which was the most impressive scene I ever beheld. The Gale was still fierce and the sea running very high making it impossible to stand on Deck without having a firm hold of the Rigging or other support. The corps lay on the Deck secur'd up in a Hammock. The whole crew grouped around in front of me bareheaded with their hair streaming in the wind, looking both wild and sad with now & then the Sea washing over us.

All the officers were gather'd around me near the Cabin Door, heads uncovered when I commenced and read part of the Funeral Service of our Church as much as circumstances would permit. The Body was Launched into the Sea. The gloom seemed immediately to pass away from the faces of all and things resumed their usual routine. And after a tedious voyage of fifteen days we arrived at Key West on the 19th inst, replenished our stock of water and sailed for this place the next day and arrived here on the 27th inst just too late to share in a small fight between our Fleet, Fort Pickens and the Rebel Batteries which resulted in nothing but the loss of a few men on both sides. Yesterday the Rebel Fort McCrea opened fire again and we all thought we were going to have a good time, but after the Enemy had fired a few shots all became still again and here we are laying frowning at each other in silence.

I have just received orders from Commodore McKean to proceed to Texas and Blockade the Coast from Galveston to the Rio Grande where the Rebels have full and uninterrupted Trade. The frigate Santee being the only ship there & she is too large to be effective to do this Service perfectly. We want many more Naval vessels. I regret very much I am not attached to Commodore Dupont's Squadron. I should like to have stepped on the Traitorous Dominions of South Carolina.

The magnitude of the work before us becomes more and more apparent as I get into it. Our Country seems sad and Bleeding at every pore. I cannot think the People of the North are in earnest as yet, nor will they be until we suffer more. Surely the time has already arrived to take hold of the work before us with energy & determination. The way we are working now it seems to me will only bring universal ruin & exhaustion to both parties.

You will please excuse this short & incoherent Epistle, for while I am writing I am momentarily expecting a Signal from the Flag officer to repair onboard the Niagra which is grandly laying on the Bay within Five Hundred yards of my Ship. This place Pensacola cannot be taken without a land force of Ten Thousand men. The Government must be the Judge whether it is worth that cost or not.

Your Friend & Obedt Servant
James Trathen
Lieutenant Commanding

Over four months later, in March 1862, one of the most celebrated naval battles of the Civil War took place at Hampton Roads, Virginia, where a blockading Union fleet was hammered by the CSS Virginia *(originally named the USS* Merrimack)— *a massive, iron-plated warship that was virtually unsinkable. On March 8 the* Virginia *handily sank the USS* Cumberland, *set the USS* Congress *ablaze, and ran the USS* Minnesota *aground. By nightfall there were 250 Union casualties, and the* Virginia *was positioned to return and destroy the USS* Minnesota *and the rest of the fleet. But early on the morning of March 9, an even more indestructible vessel— the Union navy's USS* Monitor, *built entirely out of iron—slipped into the harbor and confronted the* Virginia *head-on. The two ships unleashed a torrent of shot and shell on one another for hours. Unable to sink or even seriously damage the* Monitor, *the* Virginia *withdrew. Naval warfare would never be the same.*

~⌒

Patience Black Sends Her Husband, James, News from the Home-front and a Reminder of How Much He Is Missed
&
Sgt. Maj. James Black, Writing from "Lone Some Camp," Vows to Patience That His Love for Her Will "Burn Forever"
&
Union Soldier William Mayberry Scolds His Wife After Hearing Rumors That She Has Been Unfaithful

"I would rather write to you than to eat when hungry," expressed a Confederate ser-geant major from Texas named James Black to his wife, Patience. Letters were one of the few, tangible connections soldiers and their loved ones could look forward to and cherish during their separation. (Recognizing it was unnecessarily cruel for families of soldiers to receive death notices and other devastating news at postal service windows, the U.S. Government inaugurated free home mail delivery in about fifty Northern cities in 1863.) Letters also offered soldiers—who endured long periods of boredom interrupted by moments of sheer terror—a quiet time to reflect on their lives before the war. Few luxuries bolstered a soldier's morale more than a personal missive from a sweetheart or family member back home, even if there was little to report. Patience Black wrote the following letter to her husband on February 22, 1862, reassuring him with an understated poignancy that, although away, he was not forgotten.

My Dear Husband

This is a Saturday evening and every one is as merry as they well can be, all but me and my heart is aching with sadness I have been in the deepest blues all day. I did not expect a letter this evening as Mr. Riley wrote you had a bad rising on your hand which excused you not writing. I have nothing to write to you, my darling, but judging you by myself I will write something if it is not much.

We had an egg nog this evening all the children are slightly intoxi-cated. Ida is the funniest thing alive. Mat is in the same situation. Uncle Jasper is here he and Hatt will leave for Henderson next Tuesday morn-ing. Hatt is in ecstacies. Aunt Mary has moved to the Brazos. We will be all alone soon. I wish you would come up some evening and spend the night with us. I for one will appreciate your presence very highly. I have been expecting a letter from Sister Mollie but have received none. I will write to her again before long, perhaps she did not get my last letter. Pap brought his sheep home again. Good many of them died while Mr. McDaniel had them. They are doing tolerably well now.

I see so many things to remind me of you every day. I walk the same road that I have walked with you though by myself. I thought for some time past my health was improving but this week I have been able to do nothing but nurse my knitting and look at others work. I have knit you two pair of cotton socks. Mother is spinning thread for pants. My tonsils are sore and I will have to burn them again.

Jess Ellison has returned on furlough of forty days, he looks rather worsted I suppose his health is far from being good. He is gone to see his Mother now; he left all the Boys in fine health. Two of Widow Anderson's sons Jim and Anges were captured while in a scouting party in Kansas and shot for refusing to be loyal to Northern power also one Murphy who once lived with McFall's wife here on Bosque.

Dunk McLennan was here last Sunday he has no idea of going to war. Mr. Alexander and Mrs. Taylor called to see us this morning. Bell looks very much like herself though some what older. I sympathize with her exceedingly for Mr. Taylor has enlisted for the war. Mrs. Carter has a Miss Jessie Beauregard in her family. Will Dutch is dead. I do not know with what disease he died unless it was Strychnia. She left seven little ones to mourn her loss though we have distributed them among kind friends who doubtless will do their duty by them.

I do wish you would come to see us. I find my subject to be uninteresting and inexhaustable so I will leave it as it is getting late. Do not let anyone see this letter. Hatt wishes you to write to her. Pap and Mother send their love to you all. Present my love to Jim and Will. Take care of yourself Jimmie. Now I shall soon meet you in the land of dreams so Good Bye Bless you

Yours
Patience

Write soon   tell me how you are pleased

James reminisced in his correspondences as well, and in the following letter, he also gently teased Patience about her suspicions he was being unfaithful while away.

Lone Some Camp

Dearest Patience:

I received your welcome letter of the 15th inst two days ago, and I was indeed glad to hear from you, for I was afraid you were sick when you only have a scratched ankle.

I have nothing interesting to write you. Everything here is the same yesterday, today, and tomorrow.

Patience what shall I write you? Shall it be more word of friendship? Oh no, my heart prompts my pen to the most wedded love. If I had never known you that flame would have been unkindled in this bosom but once set burning it will burn forever. You are associated with every thought and every action of my existence.

Last night while lying on the parapit (for I slept there) viewing the starry heavens, I almost lived over the last two years. They were associated with many happy recollections. There was but one solitary cloud to mar my future happiness (this bloody war) and I hope very soon it will be dissolved. I will then be the happiest of the happy.

Patie, I sometime think of our Government affairs and the way they are carried on until I am half crazy; and the present moment is the time of times I write and hardly know what I have written. I do so much wish I were at home with you and little Joel. I know he looks mighty funny in his little trousers. I can imagine I see him tottering around.

You will hear if I make love to the girls, ha. I would like to know how you would hear it. There is not one hear that would dare tell it, for they are guilty of the same crime, if it be a crime to love a pretty woman. We have not been visited by the Ladies for the last few days.

I have heard not talk for the last few days of our regiment leaving here though we are subject to be ordered away at any hour. There are no leaves of absence given to any, but those that get sick furloughs.

It is very warm here. There is no shade except the tents, and they are so low that I had almost as soon be in the sun.

The men are still deserting from here occassionaly. There were seven Yankee negroes deserted two nights ago. I hav'n't heard whether they went to the Yankee Fleet or no. There is a great deal of dissatisfaction among the troops here. Many of them are whipped

I don't know whether you can read this letter or not. I have to write on my knees and it is very badly written.

You say you are sorry I can find nothing more interesting than your letters. You know you are telling a story for you wouldn't have me think otherwise than my interests were in you and your letters.

Although there is no indication that James Black, who returned home alive and well after the war, was ever unfaithful, infidelity was a problem confronted by many couples. Upon hearing through word of mouth that his wife had been seen with another man, Union soldier William Mayberry dashed off the following terse rebuke. (It is not clear to whom or what the phrase "Smack Rits" refers.)

Culpeper Court House Va
August 7th 1862

My Dear Wife

I was glad to hear from you and that you were pretty well but I suppose that beau of yours that you picked up on the picnic fanned you so much that you caught cold,

He better look out   I know how to shoot or I'll box your ears when I come home   you never said whose picnic it was, or who you knowd that I knowd or anything about it I heard of it last Saturday night

I hope you are better and Willie and Mary are ditto. Glad to hear you got the money.

Smack Rits—for me I dream of being home nearly every night but when the drum beats in the morning I wake up and find I ain't there

Your loving husband
WWM

~~~

Twenty-Two-Year-Old 2nd Lt. George A. Custer Tells His Sister Ann of a Memorable Scouting Mission Near Rebel Troops

"If it is to be my lot to fall in the service of my country and my country's rights," George Armstrong Custer wrote to his sister Ann before he left West Point at the age of twenty-one, "I will have no regrets." Within a year the ambitious and spirited Custer, who graduated at the bottom of his class, would be cited for bravery in his first battle (Manassas) and appointed as an aide to Gen. George McClellan. On March 11, 1862, Custer wrote again to Ann to describe a reconnaissance mission near the Warwick Courthouse in Virginia that proved more eventful than planned. (Near the end of the letter, which appears to concern the well-being of friends and family, the text is difficult to read due to comments Custer wrote directly over these lines, though from a different angle. Many correspondents did this to save paper.)

My dear Sister

I hope you will forgive me for writing to you before you have answered my last letter. I have a few minutes of leisure just now and presumed you would like to hear from me. We are here facing the rebels   our army numbers about one hundred thousand more or less, the number of the rebels is unknown but it is supposed to be about equal to ours. we have been camped in sight of them for four days

The only reason why we have had no general battle is that the roads have been so muddy as to prevent our heavy siege guns from coming up as fast as we wish, but they have commenced arriving and the weather has become good so that a great battle will certainly come off in a day or two. They have been firing at us and we at them ever since we came here but few are killed on either side, perhaps about fifteen a day on our side.

I was sent out two days ago with a larger party to find where the enemy had their batteries we rode as far as safety would permit us to take our horses and then left them concealed in the woods. we then had to crawl on our hands & knees to keep the rebels from seeing us. The party then was halted while another officer and myself went forward (on our hands & knees) with our spyglasses to examine a rebel battery which our negro guide had told us was just over the brow of the hill, up which we were then crawling.

on top of the hill stood two chimneys of a house which the rebels had burnt down that morning. we crawled up behind these two chimneys which concealed us very well and from behind which we examined the rebel battery which was only about five hundred yards from us. after we had acquired all the information possible we started to return to our party but just as we did so the rebels discovered us and fired a shell at us we saw the discharge and fell flat on our faces in order to avoid it the shell passed over us and exploded over our party beyond one of the fragments struck one of our men tearing off his arm. we allowed no grass to grow under our feet after that.

Yesterday one of our Generals was sitting down to his dinner when the rebels fired a cannon ball which struck so close to him as to spatter the dirt all over him and his dinner There is scarcely an interval of ten minutes during the day that our men and the rebels do not fire at each other. both parties keep hidden as well as possible but as soon as either party shows themselves they are fired at, and at night when it is too dark for either party to see the other so as to shoot or be shot at they will both come out from their hiding places and holler at each other calling all sorts of names and bragging what they intend to do and then as soon as daylight begins to appear the party which sees the other first fires at him and that puts a stop to the conversation until night comes again when the same thing occurs again but we will soon decide the question with them. The great battle will probably come off before this reaches you. Gen McClellan is here to lead us so we are certain of victory. . . .

Tell <u>all</u> my friends my address and write soon. Give my love to Riley, Emma, and Aut.

Your affectionate Brother
Armstrong

Custer would go on to serve with distinction in numerous battles, including at Gettysburg and Appomattax, and he finished the war at the age of twenty-five as a brevet major general. Custer's fame soared from the mere heroic to the legendary after the war when, as an "Indian fighter" leading the Seventh Cavalry, he and over 200 of his men confronted Lakota Sioux and Cheyenne warriors on June 25, 1876, at the Battle of Little Bighorn. Custer, as has been frequently noted, lost.

~~

Union Soldier Columbus Huddle Writes to His Father After Nearly Being Killed at the Battle of Shiloh

As Gen. George McClellan stalled in the East, an obscure general named Ulysses S. Grant was on the move in the West, capturing Fort Henry and Fort Donelson, two vital strongholds on the Tennessee and Cumberland rivers. One month later, in April 1862, Grant was encamped with over 40,000 of his men at Pittsburg Landing, Tennessee, waiting to join forces with Gen. Don Carlos Buell's Army of the Ohio. On Sunday morning April 6, Gen. William Tecumseh Sherman, put in charge of the Union camp by Grant, was surveying the area through field glasses when he suddenly saw Rebel soldiers come crashing through the woods. "We are attacked!" Sherman yelled. A bullet slammed into an orderly by his side, killing him instantly. Sherman galloped off to alert his men that a small Confederate force was fast approaching. In fact, the Rebel soldiers were the first wave of 50,000 troops under the command of Gen. Albert Sidney Johnston. (Pierre G. T. Beauregard was his second in command.) By Sunday night, the Confederate forces were on the verge of triumph. The Rebels' elation was tempered, however, by the news that General Johnston had bled to death after an errant bullet severed an artery in his leg. But any hopes that Beauregard, now in charge, had of adding to his victories at Fort Sumter and Manassas were shattered when Buell's men arrived Monday morning to reinforce Grant. Grant immediately went on the offensive, and by late afternoon Beauregard had no choice but to withdraw. Columbus Huddle, who barely survived the battle, wrote to his father in Ohio to grieve the loss of one soldier in particular. (George, alluded to in the letter, was Columbus's step-brother.)

April 10/62

Dear Father

with sadness I sit down to write you a few lines to let you know that I am still liveing and well but with sorrow I will have to tell you that poor George was layed low by a rebbel ball last sunday morning

the rebbels attacked us on picket guard and drove us in by firing on us with a six pounder shells and then we fell back on the regiment and was attacked in the woods and George was killed the first fire by a musket ball passing through his left hip him and me was right together he in the front rank and me just behind him in the rear rank we was lying down when he was shot I did not think when he first fell that he was killed I thought that he was just shot through the leg but we had to retreat back a little distance and when I went back to see how bad he was hurt he was laying on his face <u>dead</u>

I had to just leave him lay as our regiment had to retreat back and I did not get to see him any more till the battle was over then I went to him and layed him out strait as well as I could and I had to leave him till the next day when we brought him in and burried him as decent as we could which was pretty well only he had no coffin but he was put in a sepperate grave by himself all that was killed in our regiment was put in seperate graves our regiment suffered severly

I suppose there was two hundred or over killed and wounded in our regiment there was three killed as far as we have found out and eight wounded in our company Henry Miles that little corporal in our mess was one among the killed I came off pretty safe I did not get a wound but I had three bullet holes put through my blouse one through the sleave one through the pocket and one through the shoulder but as good providence ordained none of them wounded me

I was in the fight from Sunday Morning about sunup till Monday in the afternoon when the secesh run like turkeys then I passed over the battel field tongue cant describe the sight that I seen dead secesh and Union men all lying together some tore to pieces by cannon balls and shells but most of the secesh was shot in the head by our rifles as we could not fire without good aim

sunday about noon I was standing behind a tree the cannon balls and shells flying thick around and the secesh was about fifty yards from me when I looked out and saw a man holding the secesh Flag I took deliberate aime at his brest and fired the flag droped and the man too but the flag was not to the ground befor another one picked it up and befor I had time to load and fire they was so near onto me that I had to retreat back so I did not get a shot at him I did not fire a lot the whole two days with out good aim and I think I brought one every time for I was generly behind trees and had a good rest

April the 11th   as I did not get time to finish my letter yesterday I thought I would try and write a few more lines and close I was detailed on police to day for to finish burying the dead as we are not quite done yet it is awfull to see the battle ground to day and very disagreeable as the dead horses are not buried yet and a good many men lay out in the field to be buried yet

I cant tell you the number that was killed   I suppose you will heare about as soon as me for the papers will tell you before you get this but I saw one grave that had one hundred and forty two dead secesh in and that is only a mere shaddow to what was killed in the battle   well I will have to stop writing about the battle for I suppose you will here sooner about it than you will get this letter only I think you will hear that it was one of the hardest fights that has ever been fought in America.

Enclosed you will find some of the trimming of a secesh officers coat sleave that I took off Monday evening after the battle   he was killed by a shell that nearly cut him entirely in two near the spot that I stood on Sunday when I shot the flag officer   I could not get any thing else that I could sen to you so I thought I would send you this   all so you will find a secesh bill that calls for 50cts enclosed   I would like for you to keep those things for I got the money from a nice Tennessee lady about 18 years old that I got acquainted with while on picket and the tape please save to remember me and the battle   that is if I should happen to never get home but I think there is no danger as secesh is about played out   I think you may look for me home in a few months for we have about wound them up

I do wish you would write   I have written two letters and got no answers   if you direct just like I tell you the letter will be sure to come for it cant help it   I will soon have to close to go on inspection as our armes has to be inspected this evenings   please tell the boys to writ to me   that is my friends Geof Flynn and Webb for it is such a pleasure to get a letter here in this foreign land   I got a letter from america last evening that came in a letter that was sent to George Manuel by Mollie Reynolds   I have sent two letters to America and received no answer yet

tell all the folks that I said I have been in one of the hardes battles that ever was fought in the new world but I never want to get in another one for it is not what it is cracked up to be to get in such a fight as that was although I will not run if I get in one for more gets shot in the back runing than those that stands up to the mark like men   that is my motto   anyhow poor George died like a soldier with his face to the foe   poor George let his ashes sleep in the land of Tennessee for he is decently buried only he had no coffin but he was buried deepe so that he will never be disturbed   it is impossible to send him home for all the officers that was killed was buried here   they cant be sent home   the burying ground that the killed was buried in out of our regiment is layed out regular   each man put in a separate grave about four feet deep and three feet apart

Well Father I will have to close now   please writ me a letter as you have not written to me since I have been in Tennessee   so Good bye or from your son

C. Huddle

Of the 100,000 Rebel and Union soldiers at Shiloh, which was named after a nearby Methodist meetinghouse, a full quarter of them were either killed, wounded, or taken prisoner—more casualties than in the American Revolution, the War of 1812, and the Mexican War combined. Northerners and Southerners were stunned by the enormity of the carnage. For the first time, Beauregard, the illustrious Confederate hero, saw his reputation tarnished, and Grant was blamed for not anticipating Johnston's attack and was temporarily demoted. Although it would have been inconceivable at the time that any single battle could produce more staggering losses in a mere two days, indeed, the worst was yet to come.

~~

A Union Soldier Unleashes a Fury of Insults on the Officers, Doctors, and "Rebbles" Making His Life Unbearable
&
Francis Christiance Assures His Wife That, Despite a Newspaper Story to the Contrary, He Is Certain He Has Not Been Shot for Desertion
&
Charles E. Bingham Describes to His Wife the Execution of a Deserter

"I had a dim notion about the 'romance' of a soldier's life," a young man wrote after a particularly ferocious battle in 1861. "I have bravely got over it since." Similar sentiments were being voiced in letters home as the hardships of war became increasingly intolerable. Aside from the persistent and numbing fear of being killed, soldiers endured seemingly endless marches in suffocating heat, incessant fatigue, ubiquitous lice, chronic illness, and rations that were sometimes no more than a few pieces of stale hardtack (essentially, flat dried biscuits) and gritty, watered-down coffee. Soldiers often toned down their complaints so as not to worry already anxious loved ones back home. But one Iowa soldier, writing after the Union victory over Gen. Sterling Price's Rebel troops at Iuka, Mississippi, felt no such impulse and ranted emphatically about his maladies, his contempt for his officers and doctors, and, most heinous of all, an apparent shortage of alcohol. (Barely legible, the letter has no salutation or closing with the soldier's or the recipient's name, but these may have been on other pages lost over time.)

Octobr the 25 1862
camp Near Corrinth Miss
2nd Iowa cavalry co F Rosecrans Armie

wel I am flat off my ass this eavning once more A Driveing Away at the olde trade again I have thought of every thing that I can think and come to the conclusion that this soldiering is A Durnd Dry bisnes

A fealow can get A cussing any time he is A minde to stick his head out of his tent and if he attemps to stay in it they will come in and kick him out & if A fealow does not feal very well and goes on the sick report the Dr will mark him for fight duty and then he has more to do than he had Befor he reported sick   they will make him tend to all the olde sick horses that thare is and thare is jenerly about a Dosen of them   where a fealow is well, they cant ask him to tend to nun but his own so when A fealow gets started down hill here it is the liberty of every one to give him A kick that fels that way Disposed

A sick man in the armie is like A poore boy A shucking   he has No rite to say anything   if you object to do anythin and say you are not Able they will say god dam you go to the hospital then and if he goes to the hospital by him self the Dr will ask him what in hell he wants thare   if he is able to walk or stand up he will tell him that he guesses he is trying to play off and will go to work and tell about how many thousand thare is in the hospitals now an expence to the government just a doing what you are he will say then   then he will up and cuss you again so if you feel able to walk or any way to get back to your quarters you will think it is better any place than here so you will turn and go back to your company again and stay till you cant turnover then perhaps the company officers will go to the Dr and tell him that thare is A poor Devil over there in the company that seams to be prity damd sick and if he can any way conveinienttly send the ambulance over and get him   so then you will get off to the hospital the soldiers heaven one would think to see A newspaper account of it but sure

I dout one bit but what the goverment does provid every thing that is necessary to make A soldier comfortable but the men that is imployt to take care of it is what plays the dickens with everything thare they will set in those fine tents drink thare Regular two quarts of uncle sams good whisky every day that hes furnished expressley for medical purposes

Just so long as A soldier is well and can go ahead and do every thing he is A good fealow but let him get sick and ask to be excused from duty then you will here him get it from all sides <u>the damd lazzy sonofabich he is Afraid to go to the Drs for fear he will ketch hell from him they will say get</u>

<u>out of this if you cant get on the sick report you cant get any favors from me</u> so if A fealow can walk he has got to toddle or else be tied to a tree

the newspapers will tel you what great care our medical aids take of the wounded but I have seen A little of that too while I was suposed to be A damd privet and did not no anything. I seen them here at Corrinth when they was A taking care of the wounds of our men thare sufering for the want of care while they was dressing the wounds of the Rebbles, <u>it mad me curse the day I was bornd,</u> I thought it was time to take care of them after ours was all mad comforttable   I dont wonder at the Rebbles A going ahead with such great confidence   they have nothing to fear if they fall in to our hand   wounded or prisners they no that they will live and have the Best of care

I am not Discouraged at all but I cant see any end to the war as when we are A going to conker the Rebbles the way the north is A caring on the war   it is true this Regment has made some very Pointed Demonstrations towards distroying Baretts men and property   I will venture to say that us and the 4th Cansas has distroyed more Rebble property and freed more neegrows than any other two or all the rest of the Regments in the servis

Stealing horses and Burning Bildings and killing cattel and sheep is A thing we are A geting noted for   whare ever we finde A horse we take him if we have any use for him at al if he is better than the one we use an turn him out and change   it is very true we get halled up for it once and A while and get the Bracelets on our legs for it   but we dont have to ware them A weeke or so and then all is over about that matter

thay may talk about the generalship that was used at Iuka by general Hamilton   but thare is A few that is left that can tell how the matter was arangd   I saw the account of it in the papers and I expect you seen the same and I say what I seen was A Damd unmitigated lye and not a word of it true about general Hamiltons being on the ground all the time. he just marched his men towarze Iuka till the enimy met them and then as we just went to firing in confusion, hamilton did not no where his men was nor him self either   I passed his head quarters the next day and I should think he from the looks of the wine bottles that lay in the Rear of his tent was haveing A glorious olde Drink

I expect thare was more of our men killed by our own men thare than the Rebbles kill for us because thare was hardly a Regment but was fired in to by our own men   and some more than once   because they was scatered all over the woods and could not tell who each other was

and when they found Price was A Retreeting they sent co F and B of this Regm and too compainies of the 4th Cans to cut of his retreete (A force of 40,000 men) and we run on to them about sun up and they fired in to us and we had A little skirmish and they turnd A Battry on us and was obliged to fall back and get Reinforcements we dismounted and sent an ordeley to general hamilton telling him what was wanting the ordeley found him A slepe with his Bodygard around him with orders not to allow him to be dis turbed till he wake up, so we kept falling back till we found they was not A folowing us up and then we advanc again and that time we found about 50000 cavalry rite under A hill just A wating for us so we scud back again

we dun that four times and all the time sending for reinforcement they was thar redy to come all they wanted was the order from Hamilton, and we never got them till about 4 oclock and then Price had got clear A part. when he came up the 2nd Iowa stood thar and he found that Price was gon he ordered that cavalry, ses he, folow him up and give his Reargard <u>hell</u> of course the order had to be obeyed it went A head And found A Reargard of about 50000 cavalry and A Battery of six guns well suported by infantry thare was A wicked little fight took place and the Rebbles Run our loss was light

thou the pursuit of Price was ended about 5 miles south of Iuka and over that five miles is whare our troops Dun thare hard marching they was put over that five miles in about 9 hours

Hamilton tells that he folowed Price till his men was compleetley give out, sor footed and all this but I dont think thare was any sorefooted ones unless they stumped thare toes on some thing that way

But we all supose our generals noes thar Bizz I will quitt I dont supose you will bleave half of this any way

I supose you would not like to write to A frind so I shant ask you to all I ask of you is to reed this

Griping about insufferable conditions was not uncommon, but a number of soldiers took a more drastic step: they deserted. During the Civil War an estimated 280,000 Union and 104,000 Confederate soldiers were classified as deserters—to date, the highest rates recorded in American wartime history. (At the height of the Vietnam War the numbers peaked at 7.4 percent, compared with an average of about 11 percent in the Civil War.) Punishments for desertion varied from receiving a mere reprimand to being flogged, imprisoned, branded on the face with a "D," or, in the most serious cases, shot. The latter was rare; executions could have a counterproductive effect on troops, and the vastly outnumbered Confederacy could hardly spare the men. Newspapers were quick to report when executions were carried out, serving as cautionary reminders to those tempted to flee. But these reports were not always accurate, as a mortified young Union private named Francis Christiance discovered one day while reading the paper.

Alexandra Heights, Oct. 7, 1861.

Dear Wife,

I this day received an issue of the Star and Times containing the following paragraphs which no doubt overwhelmed me as much as it certainly must have done you. "To be shot: Francis Christiance deserter from the ranks of Capt. Truax'es Company, one which we have known for a long time was sentenced to be shot and perhaps met his faith at noon to-day. We have not given this fact publicity before, we did hope for and do not yet despair of a reprieve for the misguided soldier though the fact that this terrible punishment is meted for a second offense seems to abide it:—"

I simply deny in to each and every specification contained in the above.

1st. I am not shot.

2nd. I am not sentenced to be shot.

3rd. There has not been here the slightest supposition among the men or myself that I was to be shot.

4th. I never deserted from Capt. Truax'es Company nor have I ever been tried for any charge for desertion. From whence these false assertions could have originated I cannot surmise. But if he has feeling for a kind and loving wife, a houschold of children, not to say of the grief that fills your heart at this report, he certainly would not be humanity to contradict it.

This afternoon Col. Jackson has received a letter requesting the transmission of my dead body to my wife, my feeling may better be imagined than described. The editor of the Star certainly should bare a great deal of the blame for publishing a rumor leaving a whole family on the foundation of what must have been a mere rumor, but this is not the first nor I suppose the last kindness we will receive from those we left behind.

Truly your loving and yet living husband,
Francis Christiance.

Another Union soldier, Charles Bingham, wrote to his wife, Sarah, to describe in chilling detail the execution of a deserter, whose death he witnessed firsthand.

August 9 1863
Same old camp 6 miles from Rebbys

My dear wife

i seat myself again to pen a few lines to you again as it is Sunday and did not think that i could let the day pas without a little conversation with you and it may be that you are engaged at the same business at this moment i would like to know if you are out but i supose that the day will be spent in visiting with happy friends and neighbors and i would not wonder if you had a quite a good time at it i hope that you will

i tell you what it is it is so hot here that it aint comfortable a setting in the shade and do nothing i had a letter from mother two or three days ago she was well at the time she is to work out there for ten shillings per week and she says that this fall she is a coming out to see you if she lives

the day before yesterday the execution of a man took place out in front of our camp it seems as though he had enlisted some three times getting a big bounty each time and then desert again i stood and watched the execution of him the division that he belonged to was marched out the band playing a lively tune all the while untill they formed a hollow square then came the officer on horse back then came the pallbearers four in number carrying his coffin the one that i spoke of in one of my other letters close to them was the chaplain and the criminal keeping the step as firm as if he was going out on parade

next came the band playing his death march in fine stile but it did not seem to affect him in the least and following them was 12 with loaded guns and i think there was four others with loaded guns in reserve so if the first did not make the work of death complete the others could finish it at once

they marched in and sat the coffin down and took their position behind the man the chaplain then stood by him and made a prayer and shook hands with him bade him good bye and steped back

the officer approached him and he steped forward took off his cap and blouse laid them down alowd himself to be blindfolded and then took a seat on his coffin the officer shook hands with him and bade him good by and steped back to the twelve exicutioners the criminal then raised his hand three times holding it out straight the last time but he did not hold it long before the death messengers hit him he fell from of his coffin and lay there kicking

the officer steped up and called the others they stood there they came puting their guns quite close to him and let drive and that was what all called butchering and then my company right ahead guide right march pass in review pass and the whole division passing by where he lay and so back to their quarters and so ended the life of a Deserter

So i have give you as good an idea of the matter as I can but believe me that i dont want to see any more such proceedings The first shots i did not mind so much but when the others came up and almost put their guns against his breast and head it all most made me sick and as many as was seen at gettysburg laying dead it did not cast as mutch solemnyty over the troops as that one mans death did and what will his wife think when the news reaches her for i have heard that he left a wife and two children

well i must drop this and wind up i am well and doing well and god grant that this bad mess of scribling may find you in good health the weather has been exceedingly hot for all i thought that it was getting colder please write as often as i remain your kind and affectionate husband and shall till death give all the love that you can spare to them that kneeds it only keepe what you want.

Charles E. Bingham, Sarah J. Bingham
so good by for this time

~⌐

In the Aftermath of the Bloodshed at Antietam, an Anguished Maj. William Child Asks His Wife, "Who Permits It?"

With the exception of a few critical victories—such as Admiral David G. Farragut's capture of New Orleans, the South's largest and most active port—the late spring and summer of 1862 did not augur well for the Union. Despite having a superior number of troops, Gen. George B. McClellan was outwitted and outmaneuvered throughout Virginia's Peninsula by Gen. John Magruder and Gen. Joseph E. Johnston in April and May. In early July just five miles outside of Richmond, McClellan was forced into retreat during the Seven Days' battle by Robert E. Lee, newly appointed to lead the Army of Northern Virginia. An exasperated President Lincoln ordered the Union troops to evacuate the peninsula and head north, where the majority of them would serve under Gen. John Pope. Pope fared even worse; at the second battle of Manassas (Bull Run) in late August he lost five times as many men against the Rebels as had been lost there over a year earlier. Desperate for a decisive triumph and anxiously watching Robert E. Lee and his army march into Maryland, President Lincoln reluctantly placed the Army of the Potomac under the control, once again, of George McClellan. And once again McClellan, with almost twice as many troops, thought he was outmanned and proceeded tentatively, allowing Lee the time to concentrate his forces at Sharpsburg, Maryland. The two armies descended on one another along Antietam Creek on September 17, 1862 with unprecedented fury. With more than 23,000 casualties, Antietam remains the bloodiest one-day battle in American history. Major William Child, a surgeon with the Fifth Regiment New Hampshire Volunteers, cared for many of the soldiers wounded in the fighting. Overcome by the sheer immensity of the suffering and incredulous that a civilized society allowed it to continue, Child appealed to his wife and family back home for emotional comfort and support.

> U.S. General Hospital
> at Smokestown
> near Sharpsburg Md.

My Dear Wife:

It is now evening. I am very much better than I have been, but am yet as yellow as an orange. There is nothing of interest here to write unless I give you some of our hospital operations. How many patients we have I do not know—probably four hundred and fifty certain. The wounds in all parts you can think, but seven tenths of all have suffered amputation. Many die each day. Some are doing well. No one can begin to estimate the amount of agony after a great battle. We win a great victory. It goes through the country. The masses rejoice, but if all could see the thousands of poor suffering dieing men their rejoicing would turn to weeping. For days our wounded after the last great battle lay in and about old barns and in the yards on straw. It was impossible to take care of them all for three or four days—and were not all removed from the barns for three weeks. Now many will recover to live a poor maimed old soldier—while others are fast going to the grave.

When I think of the battle of Antietam it seems so strange. Who permits it? To see or feel that a power is in existence that can and will hurl masses of men against each other in deadly conflict—slaying each other by the thousands—mangling and deforming their fellow men is almost impossible. But it is so and why we can not know.

But I must go to bed. I think of you every day and dream of you every night.

Tell Clinton to be a good boy—be kind to his ma-ma and his sister. You must let him go up to his grandfather and his grandmother—and Uncle Hazens. Keep him well clothed this fall and winter—and Kate—kiss her for me. Tell her pa-pa has not forgotten his "daughter." O what I would not give to see you all. Well we will patiently wait. Time will soon pass away and we shall meet again and I hope to be able to live in our own happy home. I only hope to be able to obtain enough to live comfortable and improve our house and farm. For several days I have been in my own mind making plans of what I would do when I do get home if I am able. But we will live in remembrance of our full duty to ourselves our children and our Maker. I too often forget it I know.

Good night. Kiss the babes for me.

Write soon and often and tell others to do so.

Tell me all the news you can about everybody that you think I would like to know. It seems a year since I left Bath and two years since I heard from there, but again good night—good night—God preserve us all.

As ever, Wm

Major Child eventually made it home to his family after the war. The immediate consequences of Lee's narrow defeat at Antietam were enormous and far-reaching. George McClellan was relieved of his command—permanently—and replaced by Ambrose Burnside. (President Lincoln was irate that McClellan had ignored his direct order to continue after the badly weakened Army of Northern Virginia, which gave Lee the time to regroup and rebuild.) Most significantly, Lincoln now had the opportunity to announce the Emancipation Proclamation, which declared all slaves in the "rebellion" states to be "forever free" after January 1, 1863. Critics were quick to point out that these were precisely the states over which the Union had no control and that the proclamation did not free the slaves in the border states (which Lincoln still feared might ally themselves with the Confederacy). But despite its limitations, the document was a potent symbolic statement that infused great moral force into the war. "I hail it as the doom of Slavery in all the States," thundered former slave and revered abolitionist Frederick Douglass during a speech in New York. "We are all liberated by this proclamation."

~

Nurse Clara Barton Portrays to Her Cousin Vira a Hushed, Moonlit Camp, "Still as Death," on the Eve of the Battle of Fredericksburg

Of the 3,000 women who served as nurses in the Civil War, one earned particular distinction and even international acclaim for her compassion, heroism, and fearlessness. Known as the "angel of the battlefield," Clara Barton stood under five feet tall and was forty years old when the war began. Barton first assisted troops stationed in Washington, mending their clothes, helping with letters home, and distributing stationery, delicacies, tobacco, and brandy. But after learning of the primitive conditions sick and wounded soldiers endured due to lack of medical supplies and the inattention of overburdened doctors, Barton vowed to aid the men directly. Often working without sleep and at considerable personal risk—a bullet passed through her sleeve as she tended to a young soldier at Antietam—Barton affixed bandages, dug shrapnel out of men's flesh with her penknife, applied compresses and slings, cooked meals, and offered solace to frightened, homesick boys. Barton was also a prolific and poetic letter writer. On the eve of the assault on Fredericksburg, Virginia, she described to her cousin Vira the dark, almost haunted calm of camp before the storm of battle.

Head Quarters 2nd Div.
9th Army Corps—Army of Potomac

Camp near Falmouth, Va.
Dec. 12th, 1862–2 o'clock A.M.

My dear Cousin Vira,

Five minutes time with you; and God only knows what those five minutes might be worth to the maybe-doomed thousands sleeping around me.

It is the night before a battle. The enemy, Fredericksburg, and its mighty entrenchments lie before us, the river between—at tomorrow's dawn our troops will essay to cross, and the guns of the enemy will sweep those frail bridges at every breath.

The moon is shining through the soft haze with brightness almost prophetic. For the last half hour I have stood alone in the awful stillness of its glimmering light gazing upon the strange sad scene around me striving to say, "Thy will Oh God be done."

The camp fires blaze with unwanted brightness, the sentry's tread is still but quick—the acres of little shelter tents are dark and still as death, no wonder for as I gazed sorrowfully upon them, I thought I could almost hear the slow flap of the grim messenger's wings, as one by one he sought and selected his victims for the morning sacrifice. Sleep weary one, Sleep and rest for tomorrows toil. Oh! Sleep and visit in dreams once more the loved ones nestling at home. They may yet live to dream of you, cold lifeless and bloody, but this dream soldier is thy last, paint it brightly, dream well. Oh northern mothers wives and sisters, all unconscious of the hour, would to Heaven that I could bear for you the concentrated woe which is so soon to follow, would that Christ would teach my soul a prayer that would plead to the Father for grace sufficient for you, God pity and strengthen you every one.

Mine are not the only waking hours, the light yet burns brightly in our kind hearted General's tent where he pens what may be a last farewell to his wife and children and thinks sadly of his fated men.

Already the roll of the moving artillery is sounding in my ears. The battle draws near and I must catch one hour's sleep for tomorrow's labor.

Good night dear cousin and Heaven grant you strength for your more peaceful and less terrible, but not weary days than mine.

Yours in love,
Clara

Well aware of President Lincoln's frustrations with McClellan, the normally timid and self-effacing Gen. Ambrose Burnside was determined to act boldly against Lee's army at Fredericksburg. Incredibly, both to Union and Confederate officers,

Burnside ordered his men to advance against the Rebels' main position behind the stone walls of Marye's Heights. "Murder, not warfare," is how one of Burnside's own generals characterized such an attack. But Burnside was insistent, and the first wave of soldiers rushed headlong into what would later be described as a "sheet of flame." As predicted, the men were butchered. A second wave was ordered, and a third and a fourth. One by one they were cut down. Fourteen assaults in all were sent before Burnside recognized the futility of the attack and, openly sobbing, withdrew his troops. Even Robert E. Lee, although victorious, was sickened by what he saw: "It is well that war is so terrible. We should grow too fond of it."

~

Dr. Calvin Fisher Reports to His Brother Alfred the "Awful Scene" at Chancellorsville and the Fate of Several Civilians Caught in the Crossfire

"May God have mercy on General Lee, for I will have none," boasted Joseph "Fighting Joe" Hooker in April 1863, the new commander of the Army of the Potomac. With twice as many soldiers as Lee, Hooker was not unjustified in his confidence. Hooker drafted a plan that entailed splitting his 130,000 troops and overwhelming Lee's 60,000 men, entrenched at Fredericksburg, from both the front and the rear. But Lee was devising his own plan. Leaving behind a small force at Fredericksburg, Lee rushed the majority of his troops to a densely wooded area called "the Wilderness" to intercept Hooker. After a fierce surprise attack on May 1 the Union forces scurried in retreat. Early on May 2 Lee divided his army again, sending an estimated 30,000 soldiers under the command of Thomas "Stonewall" Jackson. Just after 5:00 P.M. Jackson struck, and once again Hooker's forces were caught off guard and routed by the Confederates. Hooker set up his headquarters at a roadside inn, known as both Chancellor House and Chancellorsville, and ordered fortifications around the perimeter in the event of a renewed offensive. It came the next morning; the Rebels battered the Union troops and shelled the inn relentlessly. Hooker himself was nearly killed after a pillar he was leaning against was smashed to pieces by an artillery round. Against the advice of his officers, Hooker ordered a retreat. Calvin Fisher, a Pennsylvania doctor who had been in Chancellor House during the siege, described the assault to his brother Alfred.

Camp Hancock, Va. May 19th 1863

My Dear Brother:

I long have been awaiting a letter from you but as yet have received none. I suppose that you are aware that since I last saw you I have been north on sick leave on account of partial loss of the sight of my right eye. I was much afraid of Amanrasis as there was dilation of pupil and discolored sight. My trip did not appear to benefit me much but since my return the sight has somewhat improved but is yet far from well.

I am sorry I did not call in to see you as I was to Boalsburg about ten days. I do not know whether I shall continue in the service much longer as probably if it does not get better I shall ask to be transferred to some Hospital North where I can better take care of myself. Frank is well is now chief of the Signal Corps of this army, expects promotion to a major—and will in all probability be sent first to the Carolinas then to New Orleans where he expects to spend the summer. This will be a fine position for him and enables him to travel.

Well Alfred I have seen my first battles was under fire for four successive days. On the time of the great flight on Sunday I was ordered by Genl Hancock to take charge of the wounded and remove them to the brick house known as the Chanceller House. On arriving there I was immediately detailed by the Medical Director of the Army to remain in the building, and in case of the retreat of our Army to voluntarily remain as a prisoner in order to take charge of our wounded.

Soon after our lines were forced back beyond the house. When this building being the central point of attack was perfectly enfiladed with shot and shell. Every moment it was struck   at one time whilst dressing a wounded leg a shell struck the chimney, when the whole thing came in with a tremendous crash nearly falling in on me. The shot flew then in all directions. Some wounded officers who were in the building at the time remarked that never in the history of the war was there such terrible fire, so concentrated at that one point.

After a while the building took fire by the explosion of a shell when commenced an awful scene. The wounded had to be carried out in the midst of this terrible storm of iron hail coming from both Armies to a place of safety. I had them removed to a place of safety as fast as possible. Many were killed in the transit, but to crown all there were about a dozen or more women in the cellar of the building. When told that the building was on fire and that they must run the gauntlett between those fires then commenced a scene I pray God I may never again witness another such. Their screams were heartrending. One had her leg shot away, another the side of her face. Another was killed and of the others I know not.

After I was told that all were out of the house I thought that I would run through the lower part of the building to see whether all were out. It was well I did so   in one room I found four poor fellows unable to move. I had them carried off, then went and put on my Haversack, threw my overcoat over my arm, went to examine the scene. It was anything but a pleasant one. The house was on the point of falling in. The Rebs about 100 yds off coming on a charge bayonet. I thought I had performed my duty and would if possible try and regain our own lines. I started on the run but it was so warm that I stopped and took it in a walk. Oh how the bullets whizzed by me. One struck my sash at my waist, but thanks to a merciful Providence I received no injury and reached our lines in safety.

Our regiment fought like tigers. We had killed or wounded 177 men about 30 killed. Col Beaver was severely wounded in the abdomen. Daul Kelber received a severe wound in the shoulder. George Ishler was killed. Lieuts Bible and Ferguson were killed. If you can get a copy of the Bellefonte Central Press of this week which will publish all. William Weaver son of John Weaver of Pine Grove was killed. Capt. Andrew Mosser died since of Fever contracted on the march. I never was nearer worn out in my life than after that battle.

Al, I am afraid that Genrl. Hooker did not manage the battle rightly. As the enemy were retreating at the same time we were I for my part cannot understand the necessity of our recrossing the river. Please write soon. If possible see the Surgeon General of Harrisburg and find out whether on account of the condition of my eyes I could not be transferred to some Hospital in Penna as I do not wish to resign yet am fearful I must if I remain in the field.

> Closing with my Love from your affec Brother
> address 148th Pa   C S W Fisher
> Hancocks Division 2 corps
> Army of the Potomac

After learning of the Union withdrawal, President Lincoln was incredulous: "My God! My God!" he exclaimed, "What will the country say?" On June 28, Lincoln replaced Hooker with George Gordon Meade. Lee had masterminded his greatest triumph of the war, but it was a Pyrrhic victory; he lost over 12,000 out of his 60,000 men, more than one fifth of his army. (The Union forces suffered 17,000 casualties out of 130,000—more men, but a smaller percentage.) Lee was devastated by one death in particular. As Stonewall Jackson and his staff were returning from a reconnaissance mission, nervous Rebel soldiers, seeing silhouettes approaching in the darkness, opened fire, killing two of Jackson's aides outright and hitting Jackson in the right hand and left arm. Doctors sawed off Jackson's arm below the shoulder, but, despite early hopes of a recovery, he died in bed on May 10. The Army of the Potomac and the Army of Northern Virginia, tired but tenacious, both headed north. In less than two months they would clash again in a small Pennsylvania town called Gettysburg.

~⌒

Samuel Cabble, an African-American Private in the Union Army, Promises His Wife That Slavery, the "Curse of This Land," Will Be Crushed
&
Capt. Francisco Rice Assures His Wife That "Although the Day May Be Dark as Ever," Their "Sacrifices Have Not Been Made in Vain"

In the beginning of the Civil War African Americans pleaded with and even peti-tioned the government for the opportunity to fight. But it was to no avail. Political and military leaders feared it would only stimulate recruitment efforts in the South, and many held the racist view that blacks were cowardly, lazy, and untrainable. But as Union casualties escalated and the military command recognized the need for increased manpower, small regiments of black troops were formed starting in the sum-mer of 1862. After issuing the Emancipation Proclamation, President Lincoln launched an aggressive campaign to recruit black soldiers. On July 18, 1863, the Massachusetts Fifty-fourth, the first all-black regiment organized in the North, demonstrated extraordinary courage against impossible odds during an attack on Fort Wagner in South Carolina. Other regiments would also shatter every stereotype hurled at them. Despite being underpaid, assigned menial tasks, and given inferior medical attention, young black men continued to volunteer in droves. An estimated 180,000 African-American soldiers served in the war, representing nearly one-tenth of the Union army, and over 37,000 of them died. Twenty-one-year-old Samuel Cabble (possibly Cabel), an escaped slave, enlisted with the Massachusetts Fifty-fifth Volunteer Infantry in June 1863. Soon after, Cabble sent the following letter to his wife back in Missouri. (Correspondences by slaves are exceedingly rare; slaves still in captivity were punished severely—even put to death—if they were caught writing or reading any materials, particularly letters.)

Dear wife i have enlisted in the army i am now in the state of Mass-achusetts but before this letter reaches you i will be in north carolina and though great is the present national difficulties yet i look forward to a brighter day when i shall have the opertunity of seeing you in the full enjoyment of freedom

i would like to no if you are still in slavery if you are it will not be long before we shall have crushed the system that now opreses you for in the course of three months you shall be at liberty. great is the outpouring of the colored people that is now rallying with the hearts of lions against that very curse that has separated you and me yet we shall meet again and oh what happy time that will be when this ungodly rebellion shall be put down and the curse of our land is trampled under our feet

i am a soldier endeavry to strike at the rebellion that so long has kept us in chains. write to me just as soon as you get this letter   tell me if you are in the same cabin where you use to live. tell eliza i send her my best respects and love ike and sully likewise

i would send you some money but i no it is impossible for you to get it   i would like to see little Jenkins now but i no it is impossible at present so no more   but remain your own afectionate husband until death

Samuel Cabble

At close to the same time that Samuel Cabble (who survived the war) sent his letter, thirty-one-year-old Francisco Rice was writing to his wife, Adelia, to articulate the cause for which he was fighting.

> *Our prospects of triumphant success in this great effort to maintain inviolate the blessings of government achieved by our fathers in the american revolution are brighter now than they ever have been . . . [But w]hen I think of your sufferings I cannot restrain my tears. Yes, the ragged and bronzed soldier has shed many, many a bitter tear when thinking of and listening to the recital of the wrongs inflicted upon my people—my wife, my children.—Our enemies are a vile and barberous race. Hystory does not give account of so wanton and wicked a war waged with so much atrocity and inhumanity, as that now waged against us by the infernal Yankee nation.*

Rice was a Confederate captain from Alabama under General Nathan Bedford Forrest. A doctor by profession, Rice served as a state senator before the war and maintained a small family farm. While he was away fighting, Union troops plundered his farm and drove off his livestock. In late May 1863 Rice expounded on his hatred of the Yankees and his allegiance to the ideals he believed were at issue in "the war of Northern aggression." (The last page of the letter is missing.)

Spring Hill Tenn May 25/63

My own dear Wife

We are again at this place Picketting in front of Franklin after an absence of one brief month. The seenes through which we have passed, and the part we have enacted in this great <u>Tragidy</u> will be properly recorded in the hystory of this revolution. I will not detain you with a detail of our march from this place to Courtland Ala.—the fight at Town Creek or the expedition from there to Rome Ga. and the capture of Col. Strait and his Brigade of Independent Rovers, within 20 miles of that place.

Dark and angry clouds are now hanging over us in the Southwest, which almost dims the light that has arisen in the north east. Our constitutional rights having been denied us,- the Chart of our liberties ignored, our country and homes desecrated, our women insulted and robbed of their substance, we are driven to the necessity of staking our all upon the final result of this bloody contest. We take the position assigned us and are determined to risk our chances for the future amid the general wreck, although the day may be as dark as ever lowered upon patriots struggling for freedom.

I hope the end is coming, the fury with which this war is now being prosecuted cannot continue long. The dark clouds will soon give way to the sunshine of peace, and liberty and free government be more firmly established than ever before.

"All this is familiar as household words." Within this brief period, the enimy has measured armes with us upon more than one well fought battlefield. Our powers of indurance have been tested and the patriotism of our citizens of every age and sex sorely tried.

Dark and angry clouds are now hanging over us in the Southwest, which almost dims the light that has arisen in the the north east. Our constitutional rights having been denied us.—The Chart of our liberties ignored, our country and homes desecrated, our women insulted and robbed of their substance, we are driven to the necessity of stakeing our all upon the final result of this bloody contest. We take the position assigned us and ar determined to risk our chances for the future amid the general wreck, although the day may be as dark as ever lowered upon patriots strugling for freedom.

I hope the end is comeing. The fury with which this war is now being prosicuted cannot continue long. The dark clouds will soon give way to the sunshine of peace, and liberty and free government be more firmly established than ever before.

During this time many a noble Son of the South has fallen in defense of that liberty to which we are entitled by the laws of nature and of nature's God. These sacrifices have not been made in vain. A just God will award us our proper place among the nations of earth. Those now clad in mourning will again be made to rejoice and our land to bloom and blossom as the rose. The names of our departed comrades will be kept as precious jewils and transmitted to generations yet unborn, as the bright luminaries of the 19th century. But though hystory should never repeat their names or honest men report their fame, the justice of our cause demands that these offerings should be made. Our Redeemer for our sake suffered upon a Roman Cross, and why should not we a degenerate race suffer by the hands of wicked men.

I know that you and my children have a just claim on my time, my talents and my life, the two former at present though painful to you, for the time being is surrendered, the latter I know you can never be willing to give up. And I firmly believe that you will not be called upon to make the sacrifice. I am impressed with the belief that I will survive this struggle and return at the close of the war in safety to your fond imbrace, there to remain while we both are permitted to live.

But enough of this. My health is good. There is no sickness among the members of my company who are here. Wife you alone can imagine the pleasure it gave me to see you and be with you.

I exceedingly regret that I could not be with you longer. I feel that I have not been treated with due courticy by my superior officers.

Rice survived the war and returned to Alabama, where he and Adelia raised five children.

～

Capt. William T. House Writes Under the "Whistling Bullet" to His Fiancée, Linda Brigham, During the Siege of Vicksburg
&
Captain House Expresses to Linda How Thrilled He Is by the "Grand Sight" of the Defeated Rebels

Situated on high bluffs over the Mississippi River and heavily defended by Rebel troops with formidable artillery, the town of Vicksburg was virtually unassailable. And it was, in the words of Confederate President Jefferson Davis, "the nailhead that held the South's two halves together." If Vicksburg should fall, the Confederacy would be divided by the Mississippi, and the transport of weapons, troops, provisions, and other necessities between the east and the west would be critically hindered. Gen. Ulysses S. Grant gambled that the only way to conquer the city was to march down the west side of the Mississippi thirty miles past Vicksburg, cross the river, march back up through Jackson, and attack from the rear. Even his chief lieutenant William T. Sherman argued against the plan. But Grant gave the order, and on May 19—after trekking for 200 miles and vanquishing Rebel forces at Port Gibson, Raymond, Jackson, Champion Hill, and Big Black River Bridge—the Union troops finally arrived at Vicksburg. Grant's men hurled themselves at the city but were forced into retreat after Gen. John Pemberton's 31,000 soldiers and 100 cannons ripped them to pieces. With tens of thousands of reinforcements on the way, Grant decided simply to surround, shell, and starve the city until it capitulated. Twenty-six-year-old Capt. William T. House, with the Thirty-second Missouri Infantry, wrote to his fiancée, Linda, throughout the siege. The following was sent three weeks after Grant's first major assault. (The letter ends abruptly and without a signature. House also censored himself when repeating certain profanities—such as "damned," "hell," and "devil"—used by other men.)

Camp near Vicksburg Miss
June 6th 1863

Dearly loved Lind

From the precincts of my sometimes sanctorum which by the way is a small tent o'er which the whistling bullet often flies that carries death to so many, I sit down to write to you my dear friend with the same feelings of security that I would were I comfortably situated in Old Stephenson of Ills. However let me say were I there with you present I should be happy, happy indeed in the realization of the bright hopes of which I so often think namely (to be with her I love).

O how often I think of you even in the hour of battle when I see my fellow soldiers and officers falling around me pierced by the rebels bullet or torn and mangled by their bursting shells, but of this I must not write, and I turn from such soul sickening sights to thoughts of her I love or to the bright and happy hours passed at my pleasant home and those who are yet in the enjoyment of its peace and quiet. To say I am in the least disturbed by the din of battle, the roar of cannon or the bursting of infernal shells I can not, for they have become such familiar sounds that I doubt whether I shall enjoy the first peaceful quiet silence which must soon reign supreme after the fall of Vicksburg.

Sometimes both armies will cease firing for fifteen minutes or a half hour at a time. Soon the camp rumors will begin their flight and inquiries will arise without number as to what can have happened to cause the change. However soon again is herd the booming of cannon where at once all conclude that matters are all right and that the cessation was only to afford variety or to see how odd it would seem and go quietly to their places apparently content. One would suppose they enjoyed their position as well as any they had seen since their enlistment into the Army, or rather would were it not for the almost unendurable heat from which God and the suffering soldier who lies night and day in those hot and sultry rifle pits and shoots at rebels only knows how we suffer from its effects.

Besides this they are nearly all seemingly at home and amid a storm of bullets are as jocular and frolicsome as at a sociable or tea party. They often talk backward and forwards with the Rebel who occupy pts just a little in from ours. I was quite amused the other evening when posting pickets at the conversation which passes between one of my boys who we had sent to reconoirter the position of Rebel Pickets who were a fiew steps in our advance & who we could faintly see in the dark. A Rebel Hailed him when the following colloquey passed between the pickets.

Yank (for such they name us & they hate Yankees) what are you doing?
Yank Reply, Posting Pickets.
Reb, what for?
Yank to keep you Rebs from coming over to our lines.
Reb. O! Ha! Ha! You needn't do that for Old Pemberton has out a bigger guard than you dare have for the same purpose.
On annother occasion Reb says wouldn't you like to come over & get some corn cakes.

Yank, No thank you plenty to eat over here. Our northern gals furnish us with plenty of Nick Nacks and fine things.

Reb, come 'cross & get something to drink.

Yank, Never mind we've plenty of rum and whiskey which we took at Jackson.

Reb, when are you over to camp in city.

Yank, in about a week when we think you hungry cusses have eaten all the state Victuals on hand.

Reb, What are you fighting for.

Yank, to whip you d——d Rebels. Yank (jumping up in full view shouts) Hurrah for Abe Lincoln!

Reb, Go to h—l!

Sometimes one of the boys will holler at them while another watches to shoot him the moment he shows his head & often send one of them to the other side of Jordan. At times they will stop for a while and black-guard and then shout out, take care of your D——d old head or I'll shoot it or get out of the way for I'm going to shoot and after firing they'l exclaim how do you like that or Does that suit you.

Occasionally they blackguard on the nigre question invariable winding up with swearing a Blue streak by both parties.

For over a month and a half the townspeople—mostly women, children, and slaves—of Vicksburg withstood a rain of fire as Grant's 200 cannons shelled them from the land, and Rear Adm. David Dixon Porter's gunboats pummeled them from the Mississippi. "It is such folly for them to waste their ammunition like that," scoffed one citizen. "We'll just burrow into these hills and let them batter away as hard as they please." But hunger proved more threatening than artillery rounds. After a few weeks civilians and soldiers alike resorted to eating mules, and then cats, dogs, and even rats— the flavor of which one individual declared reassuringly was "fully equal to that of squirrels." As disease, exhaustion (mental and physical), and a shortage of drinking water taxed the limits of human endurance, the townspeople and the army finally relented. Vicksburg surrendered on July 4, 1863. Captain House, writing again to Linda, could barely contain his excitement at being present at this momentous event, which he considered more historic than Cornwallis's surrender to George Washington at Yorktown in 1781.

Fourth July in the Afternoon of 1863

Lind

I have just returned from a view of the rebel works in & about Vicksburg and tired and much fatigued & almost smothered by the burning and oppressive heat of to day yet I must add some to the wild exatic note

I wrote this morning. I as soon as permission was granted to us to cross, I in company with a fiew other officers went over on the top of their works & witnessed the grand spectacle on this glorious day—of the Rebels Marching out & laying down their arms & equipments thus acknowledging themselves fairly beaten by our victorious army. It was a grand sight one which I witness with feelings of the greatest delight of the victorious soldier who is delighted with the success of his labor. Slowly they marched out of their works in front of our lines & between both armies & Regt lay down their arms colors & equipments & with a slow & measured tread they returned within their own lines betraying a deep sence of mortification at being obliged to capatulate.

Some cried like children when they lay down their arms   others cursed and swore while a fiew seemed Gay and happy and much pleased with the prospect of being relieved from the duties of a soldier's life & the deadly fire which we were constantly pouring on upon them. We as an army silently witnessed their acts which were so varied as to make the scene truly interesting & much the Strangest one I ever thought to witness.

I have often looked upon the picture of the Surrender of Lord Cornwallace & wished I could have witnessed the scene but this day I have beheld one greater than that & one I shall never forget.

I have often to day wished Mr. Crary was here to enjoy the scene with us   he would be fairly beside himself with excitement.

Rebeldom is gone out now where we them whiped in this part of the South & the war will end soon & we return to home sweet home.

Please give to Mr. Crary & enclosed order & if he gets it I will have him pay the same to you. I have between five & six hundred I wish to send to you but at present it is not safe to do so. Communication is often interrupted. Want to send all I can to pay for that Missouri Ranch.

Yours
Will

Many Vicksburg residents would not celebrate the Fourth of July again until World War II.

~

Pvt. John H. Burrill Sends His Fiancée, Ell, a Brief but Graphic Description of the Battlefield at Gettysburg

In late June of 1863 Robert E. Lee was on the offensive, invading the North through Maryland and Pennsylvania. It was an enormous risk—if his army were destroyed the repercussions would be catastrophic. But with less manpower and fewer resources than the Union, Lee believed the South's only hope for maintaining its independence was to thrash the Union army so severely it would demoralize the North and lead to peace negotiations. On the morning of July 1, Lee's infantry collided with Yankee cavalry just northwest of Gettysburg, Pennsylvania. By evening the Rebels had pushed the Union forces east and south to Culp's Hill, Cemetery Hill, and Cemetery Ridge. Both sides urgently sent for reinforcements and within hours approximately 75,000 Rebel and 90,000 Union troops were converging on Gettysburg for what would become the largest battle ever fought in North America. After fierce—and ultimately failed—attacks on the Union's right and left flanks, Lee ordered an assault down the middle at Cemetery Ridge. On July 3 an estimated 12,000 Rebels launched one of the most fateful charges of the war straight into the waiting Union guns. It was a bloodbath. "Arms, heads, blankets, guns, and knapsacks were tossed into the clear air," recalled one Northern officer. Some Rebels rushed so close to the Union line that soldiers were firing directly into each other's faces. Within hours it was over, and thousands of corpses littered the once tranquil fields of Gettysburg. Pvt. John Burrill, of the Second New Hampshire Volunteers, wrote a short message to his fiancée of the horrendous cost of victory and one especially shocking casualty.

Gettysburg, Pa. July 6th 1863

Dear Ell,

This is the third letter I have written you since receiving any from you but such is the peculiarity of them. My last was from Emmetsburg before our fight here. I just wrote a line home this morning.

It rained then and we were expecting to leave and did, but came back soon from where we started. We have packed up once more since, but did not go.

You will want me to tell you of the battle. It was awful. Language will not convey an idea.

We were not under fire till 2 or 3 o'clock in the afternoon. We then got under a fierce artillery fire, but with no damage. We then moved to another position near a peach orchard. Then under another heavy fire that made the earth tremble and the air shook and was so full of smoke you could not see. A good many of our Regt. were shot here.

We were supporting a battery. We were soon ordered to move forward which we did. We drove them, but what is that? They have turned back and are on our right flank. We have to fall back. They pour an awful fire into us. Men dropped fast. They could not stand it. We were forced to yield our ground. Other troops soon came—the 6th Corps. Our regiment went into the fight with 338 men. All we can muster now is not far from 175. Our company has 3 killed and 15 wounded—some of the latter are slight. A loss of 17 officers out of 30. The loss of our Corps is 4600, or about, one-half.

I went over the battlefield before the men were buried and they lay awful thick, I can assure you. I have been over other fields but never one like this. In one place I counted 16 in a spot no larger than your kitchen. It was a hard sight. They had turned black and swollen to twice their natural size.

Yesterday was the day I went over it. In going over, I saw one man who did not look like the rest. He was not black nor swollen. He was alive. He could move one of his hands a little. I went up to him and saw the top of his head was blown off. I gave him a little water—got some help—put him on a blanket and carried him to an old barn where he would get attention. He was about as hard a looking man as I ever saw and I have seen many. I have seen men torn in pieces in almost every shape and mind nothing about it, but not so with this one.

The Fitzwilliam boys are all well but J.B. Fiske. He is wounded and I don't know where he is. Will write some more next time. Write soon and oblige,

yours truly,
Johnny

There were over 51,000 casualties in all at Gettysburg—28,000 Confederate, 23,000 Union. Watching his soldiers getting slaughtered, Lee was overheard to say, "All this has been my fault." (Lee offered his resignation, but Confederate President Jefferson Davis would not accept it.) As the Rebel army limped back to Virginia, they learned that Vicksburg had fallen on July 4 as well. President Lincoln was relieved by the Union triumph, but infuriated that Meade did not pursue the Army of Northern Virginia aggressively enough and destroy it while he had the chance. Meade countered that his men were too weary to do so. Over four and a half months later, on November 19, President Lincoln traveled to the battlefield to dedicate the Gettysburg National Cemetery. The president's speech would be criticized by reporters and even friends as "dull," "commonplace," and a "flat failure." But over time, Lincoln's Gettysburg address would be hailed as one of the most profound and influential orations delivered in the course of American—if not world—history.

⤳

Capt. David Embree, a Veteran of Numerous Battles, Reflects in a Letter to His Sister, Rose, on the Horror—and Exhilaration— of Combat

On September 9, 1863, General William "Old Rosy" Rosecrans, head of the Union Army of the Cumberland, captured Chattanooga, Tennessee, without a single loss of life. Imbued with confidence, Rosecrans ordered his troops to pursue Gen. Braxton

Bragg and his Army of Tennessee into Georgia. The Rebel and Union forces—125,000 soldiers in all—descended on one another near Chickamauga Creek on September 19 and 20. Bragg lost more men, but "won" by driving Rosecrans back to Chattanooga. Combined, the two sides suffered more than 35,000 casualties in less than forty-eight hours. Capt. David Embree, a young attorney from Indiana who fought at Chickamauga, had received a letter beforehand from his fourteen-year-old sister Rose asking what it was like to be in a battle. Embree replied with the following. ("Bleucher," alluded to in the letter, was Prussia's Gebhard von Blücher, whose timely arrival helped the British defeat Napoleon at Waterloo. Louisa is Embree's other sister.)

Dear Sister

Yours of the 16th ultimo came to hand after about two weeks traveling. It with one from Perry at the same time is the only letters I have got from home since the Battle here. I have not seen Jim since Pa was here, at that time spent one day in the 38th. He was in our camp about a week ago, but at the time I was out on a foraging expedition. We are camped north west of town and their camp is rather east of town. We are perhaps nearly three miles apart. I intend to visit their camp in a day or two when it is not too cold as it is now.

You ask me something about how one feels when in the hottest of a battle.

Well I believe I can tell you. There is no man, however brave he may be, who does not when the storm begins to rage fiercest around him;

when he sees a friend on the right and another on the left, stricken down and quivering in the agonies of death;

when he sees the serried ranks of his foe coming upon him undaunted and pouring their deadly fire out toward him, making the air quiver and hiss with the rapid movement of all manner of projectiles, from the keen sound of the little bullet that sings on its errand of destruction like the buzzing of a fly, to the bomb shell that goes by you like a thunder bolt, overcoming all obstacles;

I say there is no man who when the first wave of such battle as this surges upon him, does not involuntarily and mentally appeal to God for protection.

But after the man soon begins to fire at his foe, this animates him. He will soon in the earnestness of his purpose seem to forget that there is danger. His heart throbs wildly, the life blood hurries like a race horse through his veins, and every nerve is fully excited. The arm of the weak man becomes endued with almost a giant's strength. His brain is all alive; thought is quick, and active, and he is ten times more full of life than before.

Although his reason may assent to the simple statement that he might be killed in an instant, yet his <u>feelings</u> seem to give the lie to it. He seems so full of life that it is hard for him to realize that death is so near. And then again as the waves of battle roll on and as he finds that perhaps the foe are gaining on him a feeling of despondency comes over him and he asks himself if the terrible waste of life he sees shall indeed prove fruitless.

He watches the time to see what he can hope for. If the foe are driving back his lines he longs for night to close the combat. Like a great warrior he exclaims "Would to God, that night or Bleucher, one would come!"

It is terrible to hear the singing of a bullet and follow its course as it flies on its way and then to hear that keen whistle of the little piece of lead suddenly terminate in a dull crush, as the ball leaps through the brain of some friend beside you. I noticed one case particularly like this. The ball came obliquely from the left and front and passed several feet in front of me. It seemed that I could hear it singing almost from the time it left its bed in the rebel's gun, and as it swiftly came I knew where it was going, by the sound.

Suddenly I heard the same ball go crash! against something and I knew by the sound that it had burst a human skull. I barely had time to look around a few minutes to my right and then I saw Sergt. Chauncy Goldsmith quivering and dying. This happened when we were not very hotly engaged and when our men were not firing else I could not have heard the singing of the bullet. We were all kneeling in among some bush, and every one of us could not refrain from casting a glance at the dying man who lay there trembling in every limb and the blood spirting from his nostrils and the wound in his forehead. In the heat of action such scenes do not much affect one but at a time like this it is awful indeed.

On the night of the 31 as I passed over a part of the field to visit the 38th I could see by moonlight the poor dead men with their faces upturned and cold eyes gleaming in the moonlight. Then one could think of Sir John Moore's burial, especially where the words come in "and we bitterly thought of the morrow," for "on the morrow" I expected to see a much more terrible battle fought.

I have come to the conclusion that Shakespeare is right when he says "There's a destiny that shapes our ends rough hew them how we may." And that Destiny is Deity that shields and protects, or permits to be stricken down, as his wisdom chooses.

Tell Louisa I will write to her shortly. Give my love to all

Your Brother
D. F. Embree

After Rosecrans's men were pressed back to and besieged at Chattanooga, President Lincoln sent Ulysses S. Grant to the rescue and replaced Rosecrans with George Thomas, who had saved Union forces from a total rout at Chickamauga. On November 24, the reinvigorated troops wasted little time trouncing the left flank of Bragg's Rebels at Lookout Mountain, just outside of Chattanooga. Yelling "Chickamauga! Chickamauga!" the Union soldiers charged into Bragg's main line at Missionary Ridge and sent them scurrying. President Lincoln was elated; he had finally found the general with the talent, steel will, and daring required to lead the entire Union army. Rumors of Grant's drinking were immaterial to the president: "Can you tell me where he gets his whiskey?" Lincoln is reported to have said, "I should like to send a barrel of the same brand to every general in the field."

~

Martha Liggan Tells the Mother
of a Confederate Soldier of Her Son's Last Moments
and Denounces the "Vile" Yankees
Who Let Him Die

"On to Richmond!" had been the rallying cry of the Federal army from its inception. But one by one each of its commanding generals was unsuccessful. None of them, in the opinion of President Lincoln, had the decisiveness, grit, and competence to be victorious—except Ulysses S. Grant. On March 9, 1864, Grant was given supreme control over all armies of the Union, and he was determined, no matter the cost, to hunt down and destroy the Army of Northern Virginia once and for all. Lee, outnumbered, was equally as resolved to inflict on Grant such enormous casualties that the North would lose its will to continue the war. Grant's 118,000 soldiers set out for Richmond on May 4, and waiting for them, near Chancellorsville in an area known as "the Wilderness," was Lee with only 60,000 men. Lee had faced an even larger number of troops against "Fighting Joe" Hooker a year earlier at the same place—and won. Indeed, history would repeat itself; after two days of fighting, Grant sustained 17,000 casualties, Lee only 8,000. But unlike his predecessors, Grant pressed on. He could spare the men. Lee could not. Grant headed for Spotsylvania, and, again, Lee was ahead of him. Attack followed counterattack, leading to savage hand-to-hand combat. Grant lost more troops, but Lee failed to repel the Union army, which marched deeper into Virginia. In late May, just days before the historic Battle of Cold Harbor, Rebel and Union cavalry skirmished at Matadequin Creek. Gravely wounded in the fight, Confederate soldier O. H. Middleton was cared for by a local woman named Martha Liggan. Liggan wrote to Middleton's mother to describe her son's fate. (Several letters and words, such as "t" and "the," are missing in places.)

Long Meadow Hanover
County Va
Mrs Middleton

Dear Madam

I now seat myself to reply to your letter for the purpose of giving you the particulars concerning the death of your noble son, who was mortaly wounded here on 30th of May.

The ball sruck the left arm between the shoulder and the elbow, entering the body little below the arm pit passing through the lungs, came out under the left shoulder blade bone. Our Cavelry was repulsed here, about seven O'clock P. M. Your son was brought to the house about sun down, by my father and one of the Yankeys. They found him a very little distance from the house. It is supposed he had been lying there some time, for he was very near speechless, when they got him here. I bathed his wound, washed his face and hands. That revived him very much. He would raise his head from the pillow and speak very distinctly. I asked him his name. He told me O. H. Middleton. I asked him his father's name and address. He told me the same name he was named after his father. The reason we asked him those questions, we could see that he would die, and we thought if he died we could let his relatives know where he died. I think he suspicioned why we asked him those questions, for he asked us please to write and let his father know that he was wounded.

He was conscious until two hours before he died. He died about three O'clock in the morning. Just a little while before he became delerious, he said, Oh! my dear mother if I only could see you once more before I die! While delerious, he would call some names I suppose of his companions, such as Tom, Charlie, and Jerry. The last I heard him say was Mr Blake please send for the surgeon. He suffered very much, But he bore it very patiently, like the rest of our noble Sons.

Sometimes he was resless, because we couldn't move him on the bed to ease him, his wound was so painful. I do assure you your son resieved the very best attention we possible could give him, being in the enemy's lines. We hardly knew ourselves having the enemy all around us, and enoying us with there numerous questions.

Although your son was a stranger to me, I have shed many a tear over his corpse and now over his grave. He is buried in our family burying ground, But not coffined as we wish him to be. He was wraped in a blanket. My father is now in the reserve class militia, he says if he can come home, him and another one of our neighbors are going to take him up before he decays and put him in a coffin, so that his remains can be removed more conveniently.

He didn't receive any surgical attention at all. We tried to get him a surgeon and beged the yankeys to send him one, But it was impossible to get one. He would ask us please to try to get him a surgeon. He thought something could be done for him. Oh, he did crave a surgeon. We asked the Yankeys to let us send for our family physician, they told us no they could not do that. Oh, vile and unfeeling wretches, I hope they may receive thier reward.

M. E. L.

It had been almost a month since the Union army had begun its southward march, and despite tremendous gains, Grant had lost a staggering 50,000 soldiers. (Many generals were killed in the campaign as well, including John Sedgwick, who uttered perhaps the war's most memorable last words. After being warned by his men he was too close to Rebel lines at Spotsylvania, Sedgwick retorted, "They couldn't hit an elephant at this dist—" just as a sniper's bullet struck him down.) The slaughter at Cold Harbor in early June, however, would severely jeopardize Grant's support among Northerners and even his own troops. Lee, with less equipment and fewer men to move, had raced ahead of Grant to Cold Harbor, a mere six miles from Richmond. On June 3 Grant ordered a head-on assault. Thousands of Union soldiers who rushed the entrenchments were slain in the first ten minutes of the blitz. In all, Grant had 12,000 casualties. Lee had 1,500. Newspapers and even Mary Lincoln referred to Grant as a "butcher" unfit to lead. But there was only one man Grant had to appease, and his confidence was unwavering: "I begin to see it," read a dispatch Grant kept in his pocket as he maneuvered south of Richmond to Petersburg, "You will succeed. A. Lincoln."

～◡

Sgt. Thomas Bowen Provides His Mother with an Eyewitness Account of the Disastrous Battle of the Crater at Petersburg
&
Lt. Col. William Pegram, with the Confederate Army, Describes for His Wife the Same Battle, and Justifies the Massacre of Surrendering Black Troops

In theory, the plan was rather ingenious. Hoping to end a bloody stalemate between Union and Confederate forces at Petersburg (a vital railroad junction south of Richmond), a regiment of Pennsylvania coal miners spent a backbreaking month tunneling underground to the Confederate lines 500 feet away and packing 8,000 pounds of gunpowder beneath the unsuspecting Rebels. Ideally, after blowing the front line to pieces, the Union troops would advance swiftly toward the remaining—and almost certainly shaken—Confederate defenses and capture Petersburg. Before dawn on July 30 the fuse was lit, and the explosion, which could be heard for miles, sent Rebel soldiers and debris over a hundred feet into the air. All that remained was a smoldering crater 250 feet across and more than three stories deep. Cheers erupted on the Union side as they began their assault. And then everything went wrong. Instead of running around *the crater,* Union troops charged directly into it. *Without ladders, they found it impossible to scale the thirty-foot dirt walls. Confederate soldiers, who had retreated after the terrifying blast, realized their tactical advantage, rushed to the crater's edge, and rained a steel blizzard of bullets down on the cornered men. Union sergeant Bowen wrote to his mother two days after the disaster to relate what he had witnessed.*

Camp near Petersburg Va. Aug. 1st/64

Dear Mother,

Please excuse all mistakes & the poor writing for I'm not in very good spirits today & don't feel much like writing. We have had another row in which although we were not actually engaged yet we were formed so near the scene of conflict that shell & shot payed their respects to us rather too devotedly to suit me. We had two men killed & seven wounded. The account of the affair will probably be found in the papers before this reaches you, but still I can give a feeble description of some of the things which probably the paper will not mention.

In the first place the day before yesterday at 1 o'clock in the morning we were aroused & ordered to fall in. We packed up & at 2 o'clock marched out to the Norfolk R.R. down which we marched toward Gen. Burnside's front line. Reaching a deep cut in the road we halted & were ordered to sit down in our places & make no noise. This excited my <u>hump of curiosity</u> to such a degree that I disobeyed orders enough to climb the steep bank where I had a good view of the rebel & union lines, which are at this point not farther apart than from your house to James Fosters. Nothing unusual seemed to be going on as I could see.

I sat down wondering what was up untill, a little after daylight, just 5 A.M. to the minute, when all at once I heard a loud rumbling noise—felt the earth tremble & in a second after saw a large rebel fort nearest our line flying in all directions. It seemed to be lifted bodily from its foundations & hurled to pieces. Men, cannon, wheels & logs and all were sent flying into the air at the same moment both rebel & union guns opened fire in one simultaneous roar all along the line, & the air was in a moment alive with rushing iron, shreaking & whistling around in all directions.

Under cover of the dense canopy of smoke that settled like a shroud of death over the doomed fort, our forces charged & drove the rebels, who still lived, out of that line of works, & out of a line further back. Musketry added its sharp rattle to the din of battle, & at this time it was a scene of terror indeed. The rebels rushed fresh troops forward & our forces did the same thus the fight continued without an interval of rest untill 7 o'clock when our forces had driven the enemy back at every point & remained victors.

As soon however as the rebels fell back, whipped, their artillery on the right, left & front of the portion of the works which we captured turned a murderous cross fire on our forces, & we were forced to fall back to our own line.

Nearly all the troops engaged on our side were the colored troops of Burnside & they would have continued the charge into the city itself if the command had been given. They are regular black devils on a charge, & don't know when to stop. From the rebel Brig. Gen. that we captured we learned that there were about four hundred men blown up in the fort. What our loss is I don't know yet but it must be heavy from the grape & canister poured into the flanks of the charging party. The rebels worked all night digging out the men from the ruins. The rebel dead & wounded as well as our own on the field could not be got off by either party untill this morning.

Think of what the poor fellows suffered lying two nights & nearly two days under the burning sun, on the hot sand, without even a drink of water. I went out on a hill yesterday several times & with a pocket glass I could see hundreds of poor fellows squirming & rolling around on that open field. Some who could, of course, crawled in during the night, but a great many could not.

I saw one poor black, who had both legs broke above the knee, who, by lying on his back & using his elbows managed to reach our line. He was all night getting over about twenty rods. I don't think the operation paid, for I believe we lost nearly as many men as the rebs & our lines have not advanced any.

Well I'm not supposed to judge, so I'll not.

Don't fear for me. If I live to get my discharge I will promise to come direct home by the shortest rout & not stop by the way. If I make all connections by rail & boat & am not delayed in Washington getting a settlement of accounts you may expect to see me, if ever, on the 18th of this month. I intended to stop in York a day or two but as you are all so anxious I should not, why I'll obey orders & slide through.

I have your letter & Grandma's of the 28 July but don't feel like writing enough to answer today.

My respects to Mrs. Helman, Mrs. Dun &
Fagan & all other friends.
Ever your Aff't. Son
C.T.B

Of the more than 4,000 Union troops killed or seriously wounded in and around the crater, hundreds were African Americans. And one of the worst fates imaginable for a black soldier was to fall into Rebel hands; unlike whites, who were taken prisoner, blacks were often executed on the spot. Lt. Col. William Pegram, a battalion commander in the Confederate's Third Army Corps, wrote to his wife, Jenny, on August 1 about the Battle of the Crater and the murder of black soldiers who tried to surrender. It was a punishment Pegram heartily sanctioned. (The letter's salutation and signature could not be located. The bombproofs Pegram alludes to were shallow trenches.)

I suppose you all have gotten, before this, a correct account of the affairs on Saturday. It was an exceedingly brilliant one for us.

The enemy avoided our mine & ran theirs under Cousin Dick's Batty. They blew it up about daylight, & taking advantage of the temporary confusion & demoralization of our troops at that point, rushed a large body of whites & blacks into the breach. This turned out much worse for them in the end. The ever ready Mahone was carried down to retake the line with his fine troops, which he did, with comparatively small loss to himself, & great loss to the enemy. I never saw such a sight as I saw on that portion of the line for a good distance in the trenches, the yankees, white & black, principally the latter, were piled two or three or four deep.

A few of our men were wounded by the negroes, which exasperated them very much. There was hardly less than six hundred dead—four hundred of whom were negroes. As soon as we got upon them, they threw down ther arms to surrender, but were not allowed to do so. Every bombproof I saw had one or two dead negroes in them, who had skulked out of the fight, & been found & killed by our men. This was perfectly right, as a matter of policy. I think over two hundred negroes got into our lines, by surrendering & running in, along with the whites, while the fighting was going on. I don't believe that much over half of these ever reached the rear. You could see them lying dead all along the route to the rear, while there was a temporary lull in the fighting, after we had recaptured the first portion of the line, & before we recaptured the second, I was down there, & saw a fight between a negro & one of our men on the trench. I suppose that the Confederate told the negro he was going to kill him, after he had surrendered. This made the negro desperate, & he grabbed up a musket & they fought quite desperately for a little while with bayonets until a bystander shot the negro dead.

It seems cruel to murder them in cold blood, but I think the men did it had very good cause for doing so. Gen Mahone told me of one man who had a bayonet run through his cheek, which instead of making him throw down his musket & run to the rear, as men usually do when they are wounded, exasperated him so much that he killed the negro, although in that condition. I have always said that I wished the enemy would bring some negroes against this army. I am convinced, since Saturday's fight, that it has a splendid effect on our men.

After the Battle of the Crater, the showdown between Grant and Lee deadlocked at Petersburg with no end in sight, and the two sides fortified themselves behind a maze of trenches. (The foul, vermin-infested living conditions were a grim foreshadowing of what American soldiers would endure during World War I.) Abraham Lincoln was convinced he was going to lose the 1864 presidential election and looked to William Tecumseh Sherman, marching with ruthless determination toward Atlanta, for a desperately needed Union victory. Sherman had no intention of disappointing the president.

Extended Correspondence

Gen. William Tecumseh Sherman Defends Himself Against Those in the South Who Call Him a "Barbarian," Denounces Unsupportive Northerners, and, After Conquering Atlanta, Asserts That the "People of Georgia [Now] See We Are in Earnest"

War, to Gen. William Tecumseh Sherman, was neither romantic nor glorious. It was destructive beyond comprehension and relentlessly cruel. But few commanders waged war with more ferocity than Sherman himself. "War is the remedy our enemies have chosen," he contended, "and I say let us give them all they want; not a word of argument, not a sign of let-up, no cave in till we are whipped—or they are." Striking out from Chattanooga in early May 1864 with 100,000 men, Sherman was under orders from Grant to shatter Joseph E. Johnston's combined Confederate armies and seize Atlanta. Sherman vowed to "make Georgia howl," inflicting so much damage and suffering on the South the very spirit of the rebellion would be crushed entirely. "We can make war so terrible," Sherman declared, "and make them so sick of war that generations [will] pass away before they again appeal to it." Sherman emphasized often in his letters that he bore no personal animosity toward the South; indeed, having spent most of his adult life there, many of his oldest friends were Southerners. One of them, Annie Gilman Bowen—the only pro-Union member of a secessionist family—maintained a friendly correspondence with Sherman during the war. In the following letter to Bowen, Sherman laments how he is perceived by her rela-

tives, but, in his characteristically impassioned style, declares that the South is solely to blame for whatever terror is to come.

Head-Quarters, Military Division of the Mississippi,
In the field, near Marietta Geo. June 30 1864.

Mrs. Annie Gilman Bowen,

Baltimore Md.

Dear Madam,

Your welcome letter of June 18 came to me here amid the Sound of Battle, and as you say, little did I dream when I knew you playing as a school girl on Sullivan's Island beach, that I should control a vast army pointing like the swarm of Alaric towards the Plains of the South.

Why oh why is this? If I know my own heart it beats as warmly as ever towards those kind & generous families that greeted us with such warm hospitality in days long past but still present in memory, and to day were Frank and Mrs. Porcher, or Eliza Gilman, or Mary Lamb or Margaret Blake, the Barksdales, the Quashes, the Poyas, indeed any and all of our cherished circle—their children, or even their children's children to come to me as of old, the stern feelings of duty & conviction would melt as snow before the genial sun, and I believe I would strip my own children that they might be sheltered.

And yet they call me barbarian, vandal, a monster, and all the epithets that language can invent that are significant of malignity and hate. All I pretend to say on Earth as in Heaven, man must submit to some arbiter. He must not throw off his allegiance to his Govt. or his God without just reason & Cause. The South had no Cause, not even a pretext. Indeed by her unjustifiable course she has thrown away the proud history of the Past, and laid open her fair country to the tread of devastating war. She bantered & bullied us to the Conflict. Had we declined Battle, America would have sunk back coward & craven meriting the Contempt of all mankind. As a Nation we were forced to accept Battle, and that once begun it has gone on till the war has assumed proportions at which even we in the hurly burly sometimes stand aghast. I would not subjugate the South in the sense so offensively assumed, but I would make every citizen of the land obey the Common Law, submit to the Same that we do—no worse no better—our Equals & not our Superiors.

I know and you know that there were young men in our day, men no longer young but who control their fellows, who assumed to the Gentlemen of the South a Superiority of Courage & Manhood, and boastingly defied us of northern birth to arms. God knows how reluctantly we accepted the issue, but once the issue joined like in other ages, the Northern Races though slow to anger, once aroused are more terrible than the more inflammable of the South—Even yet my heart bleeds when I see the carnage of Battle, the desolations of homes, the bitter anguish of families, but the very moment the men of the South say that instead of appealing to War, they should have appealed to Reason to our Congress, to Our Courts, to Religion and to the Experiences of History then will I say Peace— Peace— Go back to your point of Error & resume your places as American Citizens with all their proud heritages.

Whether I shall live to see this period is problematical, but you may, and may tell your mother & sisters that I never forgot one kind look or greeting, or ever wished to efface its remembrance, but in putting on the armor of war, I did it that our Common country should not perish in infamy & dishonor.

I am married—have a wife and six children living in Lancaster Ohio. My career has been an eventful one, but I hope when the clouds of anger & passion are dispersed and Truth emerges bright & clear, you and all who knew me in early years will not blush that we were once close friends. Tell Eliza for me that I hope she may live to realize that the Doctrine of "Secession" is as monstrous in our Civil code, as Disobedience was in the Divine Law. And should the Fortunes of War ever bring your mother, or sisters, or any of our old clique under the Shelter of my authority I do not believe they will have cause to regret it.

> Give my love to your Children,
> & the assurances of my respect to your
> honored husband. Truly,
> W. T. Sherman Maj. Genl.

Convinced that Joe Johnston's inability to halt Sherman's steady march toward Atlanta was a weakness of will, Jefferson Davis replaced Johnston with thirty-three-year-old John Bell Hood as commander of the Confederate army. Hood, who was crippled in the arm at Gettysburg and had lost a leg at Chickamauga, took the offensive and attacked the Union forces repeatedly outside of Atlanta in late July. After several failed assaults, costing 20,000 men, Hood withdrew his army behind the city's ramparts. Sherman had no desire to repeat previous Union disasters by storming entrenched positions only to have his soldiers wiped out in waves. So he cut off supply routes to Atlanta and began a constant bombardment that would last a month. During the siege, Sherman received a letter from a friend named Silas Miller, who occasionally sent gifts and kept Sherman informed on political and social matters in Northern cities like New York, where riots had flared the previous year after a draft was announced. (Immigrants, unlike wealthier citizens, did not have the means to pay "commutation fees" of several hundred dollars or hire replacements to avoid enlistment, and they lashed out most vehemently against blacks, whom they blamed for the war. Mobs set fire to their homes, churches, and even an orphanage, and at least two black men were lynched.) As the presidential campaign reached its final months in August 1864, tensions in the North between "traitorous" Copperheads—the antiwar wing of the Democratic party—backing George McClellan and "negro-hugging worshippers" of Abraham Lincoln were at a fever pitch. Sherman, though displeased, was not surprised.

> Headquarters, Military Division of the Mississippi
> In the Field, Near Atlanta Geo.
> 1864 Aug. 13

Dear Miller,

I have your last letter from the Galt House, also the box of cigars (five boxes well put up in a larger one) sent by you through Col. Sawyer. I fear, my Dear Friend, I am taxing your kindness & generosity beyond the bounds of propriety. Mrs. Sherman has repeatedly asked me if I had paid you for certain blankets washed and other matters almost out of my memory, and unless you limit your acts of benevolence to the poor & distressed soldier from down in the Land of Dixie I must begin to look about to square accounts.

But I assure you I am far from unmindful of these repeated favors & only hope I may have it in my power to reciprocate them. Besides laboring with an earnest & I believe patriotic desire to build up & fortify a Govt. worthy of the land we have inherited I am not aware that I have merited at your hands such bounteous Gifts.

I have read your observations concerning matters & things North, and though what you say is painful to contemplate still to me not alarming. Anarchy is one of the steps through which we are doomed to pass before men become tamed to a degree to deserve civilized Govt. In a country where the People Rule, the local prejudice of each spot has its representation. If you have a tooth ache you little heed the pains of the poor fellow in the next room with a broken leg.

So the People of New York, feeling high taxes and the little vexations caused by this war, little heed the dangers & trials through which we pass, and go on with their own notions. Little dreaming that this whole Land is so united in interest that a disease pervading one part will reach & poison the whole unless it be eradicated & cured. The Copperheads at the North are a voting people, who, simpletons as they are, think that upon their votes enemies will lay down their arms. Why these fellows in Atlanta have a more supreme contempt for the sneaks in Indiana & New

York who claim to be the Friends of Peace, than they do for this Army that is pounding away for their destruction.

The time is not yet for reaching these fellows, but when the Army begins to make itself felt at the North, and tell these sneaks who are trying to control the Policy of the Country in the absence of the Army, that there is no such thing as property without Govt. and that if they don't behave themselves they shall have no vote, they will change their tune, for their money & property will go and they be left mere sojourners in a land they would not fight for in its hour of danger.

I believe the draft will be made & enforced—that our armies then having an unfailing supply of recruits to take the places of the dead, wounded & sick, we can go on making swathes through the South that cannot be patched up. I can easily pass round Atlanta now & go on but for the Present prefer not to do it, but when the time comes I will. I want to see the Virginia Army in motion again. Also one from Mobile. It is no use besieging Mobile. An Army can make a circuit round it, cutting all its communications.

Fort Morgan too can be watched by a single ship & cannot be supplied. Its days are numbered. If our armies were promptly reinforced, we are now in position to strike home.

I am sorry to see Bullitt & others in trouble. This is no time for them to breed trouble. They should defer the discussion of abstractions till we have Peace. If you see Bullitt tell him as much for me, that he is intelligent enough to know that at a time like this we should sink our opinions on minor matters and deem the Great End Union—then if any wrongs have been done, any false policy pursued, we can sit down & reason together and Truth will prevail—when a ship is on fire is no time to question the authority or discretion of the Captain. I am determined to move from Kentucky to Foreign parts all disturbing elements. Let the blows fall where they may. Longer forbearance would be criminal.

W. T. Sherman
Maj. Genl.

On August 31, just over two weeks after writing this letter, Sherman launched a final, massive assault against Hood's army, driving the overwhelmed Rebels out of the city. On September 2, 1864, Georgia's most dreaded nightmare was now reality—William Tecumseh Sherman had captured Atlanta. The mayor and councilmembers implored Sherman, who had ordered all citizens (regardless of age or health) to evacuate the city, to be merciful. Sherman was unmoved. "You cannot qualify war in harsher terms than I will," he scolded in a now-famous letter dated September 12;

Now that war comes to you, you feel very different. You deprecate its horrors, but did not feel them when you sent car-loads of soldiers and ammunition . . . into Kentucky & Tennessee, to desolate the homes of hundreds & thousands of good People who only asked to live in Peace . . .

Now you must go, and take with you the old and feeble, feed and nurse them, and build for them, in more quiet places, proper habitations to shield them against the weather until the mad passions of men cool down, and allow the Union and peace once more to settle over your old homes in Atlanta.

Sherman added a conciliatory note: "But, my dear sirs, when peace does come, you may call on me for any thing. Then will I share with you the last cracker, and watch with you to shield your homes and families against danger from every quarter." (Sherman's sentiments were not disingenuous; at war's end he recommended such mild terms of peace that he was accused of treason by many in the North.) Writing to Silas Miller again, Sherman relates some lighthearted observations about Duke, his finicky but eventually accommodating horse, as the two rode victoriously into Atlanta.

Headquarters, Military Divison of the Misssissippi
Atlanta Sept. 22, 1864

Silas Miller, Esq.
Dear Friend,

You have seen enough in all conscience and heard enough also to satisfy you that I made the riffle and got into this Forbidden City, and as I promised you I rode Duke in, that is the horse you gave me. I did so on purpose changing my saddle to him about 3 miles out.

Duke at first did not like this outdoor life & rough living—was particular about his meals, and city like would not drink water out of the creek or mud holes. The truth was he was a City Gent and looked on this out door life with contempt and was gradually showing the effect. But I have a most excellent fellow who humored him & gave him water in a bucket etc., & kept him along till the horse began to see that he was duly enlisted for the war and in for it when he began to mend. He is in fair order now and in perfect health and seems to like getting into town again, though he must observe that this is not Louisville.

Telegraph gives good news from Sheridan.—Next will be Grant, and then we must maul the wedge another bit and the log will split in due time. So thinks Old Abe the Rail Splitter.—I've got my wedge pretty deep and must look out that I don't get my fingers pinched.

Audenried goes up with my dispatches and can tell you every thing. I have the place pretty well cleaned out, & regulated. And the People of Georgia see we are in earnest and won't let trifles stop us.—I have forbidden all citizens to come, but as you may have an "irrepressible" desire to come I send you a Pass, and you may explain the exception on the grounds of belonging to the Christian Commission.

Yr Friend,
W.T. Sherman
Maj Gen

The news of Sherman's conquest injected a shot of energy into Abraham Lincoln's foundering presidential campaign. Ulysses S. Grant, still entrenched at Petersburg against Robert E. Lee, fired a one-hundred-gun salute in Sherman's honor (in the direction of Lee's army, of course). Grant also approved Sherman's proposed "march to the sea," a 300-mile campaign of destruction across Georgia. After burning almost a third of Atlanta to the ground, Sherman headed east in the beginning of November with over 60,000 troops, who tore down, ripped up, ransacked, looted, hacked, smashed, and threatened almost everything in their path. On December 22 Sherman sent a telegram to a grateful (and, with considerable debt to Sherman, reelected) president: "His Excellency Prest. Lincoln—I beg to present you as a Christmas gift the City of Savannah." South Carolina was next. "Here is where treason began," one of Sherman's men stated with rising fury, "and, by God, here is where it shall end!"

James Paxton Relates to His Friend Val Giles the Torments He Endured While a Prisoner in a Union POW Camp

Despite the infamy of William T. Sherman's brutal rampage across the South, both sides engaged in savage, often unprovoked acts of violence throughout the war. Confederate general Nathan Bedford Forrest, most notoriously, had hundreds of disarmed and surrendering black soldiers killed at Fort Pillow, Tennessee, in April 1864. Few atrocities, however, equaled the widespread, vicious treatment of both Confederate and Union prisoners of war. Men were starved, indiscriminately shot, and denied the most rudimentary medical care and sanitation, causing tens of thousands to suffer horribly and eventually die of disease and exposure. In many camps, like the infamous Andersonville in Georgia, the main source of water was also the sewer. (On November 10, 1865, Andersonville's ruthless commandant Henry Wirz was hanged for "war crimes." He was the only Confederate officer to be executed. Clara Barton, who would go on to establish the American Red Cross, made it her mission to try to identify and honor the 13,000 unknown soldiers who perished at Andersonville.) James Paxton, writing to his friend Val Giles years after the war, recounted his experiences at Camp Morton in Indiana, where over 1,700 Rebels died. Morton was considered one of the "best" camps—Union or Confederate. ("Sutlers," mentioned throughout the letter, were private merchants who followed armies and sold goods to the soldiers. The first page of this letter is missing.)

In the fall of 1863 General Joe Shelby made a raid into Missouri from Arkansas. I went along, intending to help Colonel D. C. Hunter recruit men who wanted to come to Dixie, but was betrayed by a fellow soldier—a Judas—before I had gone far into the state. We were a short time at Springfield, then a few weeks at St. Louis, and finally reached Camp Morton early in November, 1863.

For the first time in my life my clothing was fully searched and everything of mine, even my pencil and penknife, were taken from me. What money I possessed being Confederate, was of no value, and therefore no loss. At first we thought our confinement would be temporary and expected an early exchange, but weeks grew into months and then came the news of no exchange.

Immediately after this our rations were reduced to the point of starvation. One-half a loaf of broad, called "duffers" by the prisoners, and about six ounces of poor beef constituted a day's rations. Coffee and vegetables were cut off entirely and the sutler was forbidden to sell us anything of a substantial nature. It was claimed by the Federals that this was in retaliation for the starved condition of their soldiers in southern prisons. We prisoners sympathized with the northern prisoners, as we knew the south could not furnish regular rations to her own soldiers, as it was the policy of the northern troops to devastate the south as a means of putting down the rebellion. That it was successful, though a fearful policy, was shown by Sherman's march to the sea, torch in hand. When someone remonstrated with him for this he is said to have replied, "War is hell anyway." The effect of reduced rations on strong, healthy men was to render them frantic with hunger, while it did not harm others so much.

Camp Morton was named In honor of Oliver P. Morton, war governor of Indiana. It was located a mile or two north of Indianapolis, on a plat of ground. The old stock sheds were used for barracks, and the grounds were fenced with a box wall of fourteen-foot planks, stoutly nailed. On the outside was a platform about four feet from the top of the wall, on which guards were stationed. This enabled them to protect over half their bodies, and yet they could see all over the prison.

The land inside the prison lay nearly level with the exception of a drain running through it from the south to the north. This creek was called by the prisoners the Potomac. The barracks were built along the north and west walls of the prison, at a distance of about thirty feet from the walls. Some native trees were enclosed, which gave good shade in summer. Under these trees the prisoners would gather for rounds of pastime. Some would meet for worship, some for Masonic exercises, and still others for gambling purposes. The money used in gambling was sutler's tickets, furnished in lieu of money to those who were fortunate enough to have friends inside the Federal lines. Gambling seemed to be the means of distributing the tickets among the prisoners. These tickets could be used at the sutler's and sometimes the prisoners could get things from the outside through the friendly guards. All were scantily clothed, and very few had sufficient bedding.

The winter of 1863–64 was an unusually hard one. New Year's Day, 1864, was the coldest day I ever saw. Several were frozen to death; others were so injured that they fell sick, and the "old gray horse" was kept busy hauling out the dead. The prisoners, having lost all hope of exchange, began to devise means of escape. Sam Metcalf of Kentucky organized a squad to break over the wall. They charged the wall at dusk, but only Metcalf succeeded in getting over and escaping. The others were caught and tied up by the thumbs to a rack, and then, stretched up on tip-toes, were left standing as long as they could bear it. This was called "riding Morgan's mule" by the prisoners.

After this they tried mining under the walls. A tunnel was started under a bunk and in the direction of the wall, the loose dirt being carried in our haversacks and emptied into the Potomac or scattered about where it would not be noticed. But most of the tunnels were detected before completion. Finally a few men dug a tunnel in the east end of the barracks, and by keeping it secret from their nearest friends, managed to get it beyond the prison walls and succeeded in escaping just before day. They were never caught, but disaster came to some of their friends whom they had told of the tunnel. They told their friends whom they had left behind that they would cover the mouth of the tunnel with planks.

The Federals discovered the tunnel but they kept quiet. At a late hour, when all was quiet in and out of the prison, a party led by a prisoner named James Barnhart occupied the tunnel head to foot in an endeavor to escape. As Barnhart raised the plank he was filled with bullets from the guns of the waiting guards. Such a scramble as ensued from the prisoners in the tunnel you never saw. All that could regained their barracks, and those who were not so fortunate had to ride "Morgan's mule." The federals had the prisoners dig a ditch inside the wall to prevent a further tunneling. A party headed by James Bowers and A. C. Norwood, both Texans, attacked the guards with sticks and stones, and by means of ladders which they had made secretly, succeeded in scaling the wall and escaping. Bowers was recaptured, and the Federals, admiring his bravery, did not punish him, but only required him to promise not to try to escape again. There were other escapes, which I do not recall or have not time to give the details.

Among the 400 prisoners in Camp Morton there were many of a high order of talent, who, though dressed in the ordinary prison garb, had been men of high order of culture at home. One of the most unassuming of these was Lieutenant James A. Corry of the southern engineer corps. He was a native of Georgia. Plain, modest and unassuming he preferred to pass as a common private but little by little his comrades became aware of his talents, and his Christian fortitude and upright conduct won the respect and warmest friendship of all his comrades. I have often wondered if his relatives knew of his death (by pneumonia) in this far-off prison home.

We had preachers among us, and under the shade trees of Camp Morton many sinners came to a knowledge of their Saviour.

The guards were often unscrupulous and tyrannical men, and kept the prisoners in a constant state of fear by their threats. One lieutenant would strike them with brass knucks, and one sergeant shot three prisoners to death with scarcely a shadow of excuse. Yet many of the guards were gentlemen and did many kindly acts for the prisoners, as their opportunity offered. Col. A. A. Stephens, the commandant, was pleasant and courteous to the prisoners.

The prisoners were so pressed by hunger that when citizens allowed their dogs to follow them into the prison the dogs were often entrapped, killed and eaten. This constant hunger often drove some men to steal each other's rations. To stop this Col. Stephens allowed us to organize a court to try the offenders and inflict punishment for theft. The usual punishment was forty lashes, save one, on their bare backs, the prisoner being bent over a barrel. The culprit had the advantage of witnesses and a fair trial by jury. The sentence was placed for execution several days ahead. A powerful South Carolinian stole a "duffer," and many of the prisoners thought he would never submit to the punishment without force, but after studying over the matter he said the punishment was just, and submitted. When hunger pinched many would commit petty acts of theft who would have been honest under other conditions.

Governor Morton and the legislature visited us in February, 1865. As they drove by in carriages and viewed the long line of prisoners called out for inspection the governor was heard to say: "What a fine looking body of men." We hardly knew whether he was in jest or earnest.

I had now been in prison about eighteen months, and the meager fare and privations were making serious inroads on my health. I wrote to an uncle—Green Paxton—in Louisville that I did not think I could live much longer in prison. Through his friends he succeeded in getting a release for me from President Lincoln. I should tell you that there was another man whose name I have forgotten, was released at the same time. He was from Louisiana, but his father lived in Indiana. We walked down to the city, and this man, having a few dimes, we enjoyed our first meal for many months. Through my friend's father we met a member of the Indiana legislature, who provided us with tickets to Louisville, which we reached next morning. This member was very kind to us, asking us many questions about our prison life and expressing sympathy for us. I am sorry to have forgotten his name.

Arriving at Louisville my companion took the train for his home out in Indiana and I hunted up my uncle. My uncle received me cordially, took me to a barber shop, where I enjoyed a good bath and shave, also gave me the nicest suit of clothes I ever had and took me to his home to rest and recuperate from my eighteen months' imprisonment. All this time I was in a state of bewilderment and could scarcely realize what was passing. I had suffered from confinement, hunger, and was poorly clad in prison and could scarcely realize that I was free to go at will, and was respectably clothed and had plenty of wholesome food. Passing into the parlor of my uncle's house I caught the reflection of myself in a mirror and though there was something familiar about the image, I actually did not know myself, but thought it was an older brother, but by degrees the idea dawned upon me that it was myself.

As I came to realize the great change in my life and thoughts of mother, home, and loved ones came into my mind, I dropped into a chair and shed tears. My aunt, observing that I often stopped before a mirror, asked me if I thought myself pretty. I told her no, that I was trying to renew acquaintance with myself.

Some few weeks after my release General Lee surrendered and the war came to a close. A little while before this I met you for the last time in front of the Louisville hotel. You recognized me and told me some of your plans about surrendering, but I never saw you afterwards. I came to Texas in 1866, married and settled in Fannin county; remained there until 1871, when I removed to my present location in Jones county, near Anson, which is my post office.

James Paxton

Union Soldier Charles George Sends His Wife, Ellen, a Letter from Appomattox, Announcing That "General Lee Has Surrendered!!!!"
&
Mary Custis Lee, Wife of Robert E., Tells Her Cousin That the North "Achieved by Starvation What They Could Never Win by Their Valor"
&
Maj. William Child Exclaims in a Letter to His Wife: "I Have Seen the Murder of the President of the United States"

March 1865. The Confederacy was in ruins. Cities and towns throughout the South had been decimated. Food was scarce. Mass desertions plagued the Rebel army. On the political front, Abraham Lincoln had been sworn in for his second term on March 4—five weeks after the U.S. Congress passed the Thirteenth Amendment to the Constitution, abolishing slavery in America forever. (The amendment was ratified later that year on December 6.) And after nine months of sporadic attacking and counterattacking, Robert E. Lee's exhausted and diminishing Army of Northern Virginia remained entrenched at Petersburg, facing an army several times its size commanded by Ulysses S. Grant. On April 2, Union troops finally broke through the Petersburg line, forcing Lee to retreat, and Richmond, the Confederate capital, was evacuated. Pursued by Grant, the Rebel troops struggled west toward Amelia, Virginia, where Lee expected to find rations waiting for his famished men. But when they arrived, nothing was there. After a ferocious confrontation on April 6 at Sayler's Creek, Lee lost another third of his army. Grant sent Lee a message the next day urging him to spare "further effusion of blood" and surrender. Lee refused, attempting one last dash to Appomattox Court House, where, again, he hoped to find provisions. General Philip Sheridan's cavalry raced ahead of the Rebels and seized the food and supplies. By April 9, Palm Sunday, Lee recognized the inevitable. Attired in an immaculate gray uniform, Lee met with Grant—fifteen years younger and dressed in rumpled, mud-splattered clothing—to discuss a formal surrender. Throughout the war Charles George had sent hundreds of letters, many of them written in blackberry juice, to his wife, Ellen, back in Vermont. After three years of service, George was able to report from Appomattox the news that he, and literally tens of millions of others, so urgently wanted to hear.

<u>Monday Morning—April 10, 1865</u>

<u>HURRAH!!!!</u>   <u>HURRAH!!!!</u>   <u>HURRAH!!!!</u>
<u>GENERAL LEE HAS SURRENDERED!!!!</u>

Peace is near at hand!! — Oh! My dear Ellie!! I cannot express to you the emotions of my heart. Yesterday was the most eventful day of the war. A day that will never be forgotten!!! Never were such demonstrations of joy exhibited as there was from five to eight o'clock. I will explain to you first the situation of the armies and try to tell you something about the enthusiasm of the 6th Corps.

Friday operations proved to be a severe blow to Lee. Sheridan had got him in a tight place — captured several thousand prisoners and obliged him to burn his wagon trains. We left Farmville about 9:00 A.M. Saturday — after traveling a few miles we came upon the burned train — the roads were strewn with the debris of camp equipage — kettles, secretary desks, papers, books, and everything belonging to Headquarter wagons were scattered over the road for miles. About 600 wagons were burned. After marching about 4 miles we began to hear cheering ahead. Pretty soon it came to us — General Lee had sent in proposals for a surrender and made terms of peace. Grant sent back that he had no authority to make peace. He would accept nothing but an <u>unconditional surrender</u>. That day the 2nd and 5th Corps got another haul of prisoners and wagons. Sunday morning we heard firing at the front and were hurried on.

The first news we heard was that Lee had sent a flag of truce again — wishing to have an interview with Grant. Grant sent word again that he would accept nothing but an unconditional surrender! — Lee sent word again that he would not surrender then. General Thomas had taken Lynchburg with only the 4th Corps and a division of cavalry attacking in the rear and in the battle captured about 45,000 prisoners. Everything was then in readiness to attack on all sides — we had him surrounded and his army was so reduced that he could not whip either side. The 2nd Corps were in readiness for a charge. — Our Corps was massed about two miles in their rear — Grant then sent word to Lee that he would give him till 5:00 P.M. to surrender. The story is soon told — Lee came to terms and Grant renewed his previous title of

<u>"Unconditional Surrender Grant"</u>

And Ellie, when the news reached our Corps, such a scene of excitement I never have witnessed. About half an hour later it was confirmed by Grant, Meade and Staff riding by. Cannons were immediately whirled into position and commenced firing — such a hollering I never heard. Cheer after cheer went up — hats thrown high into the air — men throwing their arms up and swinging their caps and every other type of demonstrations of joy were going on. I began to think the Band ought to play a part too — I found Herbert playing with only five members! Hail Columbia — the rest soon joined. As we played I looked at our division in front of us — there everything was in motion — the air was full of caps and hats — officers from General Seymore down to Lieuts. were on their horses "riding every which way!" Flags were waving — cheer after cheer from thousands of soldiers rent the air and it seemed as if there would be no end to the noise. Just try to imagine, if you can, seeing all this and hearing the yelling of the men batteries firing blanks and bands playing (other bands took up the strains). It is almost impossible to describe the joy these men were showing. For an attempt to describe it think of <u>bees</u> when they are swarming and imagine every one to be a man and you will get a faint idea.

What a week's work! In one week we have eaten up Lee's whole army — taking large mouthfuls every day. He had about 80,000 men, and now all that armed force is powerless. It is now proof positive of the great wisdom of General Grant, by the help of God, that this is the time we have been so anxiously waiting for, for so <u>long</u>. There will be no more war! The forces will speedily surrender I think. The question now is, how long will we be kept here — I think we shall be home in a month from today, at the fartherest. They will settle the business as speedily as possible and discharge us to save expense. There will be negroes and veterans enough left to garrison the Ports.

The story is that Lee surrendered to the 2nd and 6th Corps because they were the only ones who ever broke his lines! There is no other news this morning. We are wondering what we shall do next, and where we shall go. We are now within 25 miles of Lynchburg and not far from 100 miles of the city of Petersburg. I wouldn't wonder but that we will go to Harper's Ferry.

Did I tell you that when we passed through Petersburg on April 3rd we saw President Lincoln? (I don't remember) — he was on horseback and was surrounded by a crowd of colored people shouting, "God bless Massa Lincoln". Everyone was cheering and at the same time asking for something to eat — "give me some hard-tack"

Today is rainy and cold — the mail goes out at 6:00 p.m. and it is now 5:00 — I expect mail tonight. My dearest love to you always.

—Your Charlie

Sensitive to the humiliation felt by Lee and his defeated soldiers, Grant, upon hearing his men explode into cheers and fire their guns in celebration, ordered them to stop. "The war is over," he declared, "The Rebels are our countrymen again." (The war, in fact, was not entirely over; small isolated actions continued in the South and West for months. The last Confederate troops laid down their weapons in June 1865.) Grant also offered Lee rations for his starving army. "This will be very gratifying," Lee replied, "and do much toward conciliating our people." Lee then told his mostly speechless, broken-down soldiers to "go home now" and become "good citizens" to their country, soon to be reunited again. But thoughts of reconciliation came harder to Robert E. Lee's wife, Mary Custis. (Mrs. Lee was unable to leave Richmond during the invasion due to the pain from severe arthritis, and a Union cavalryman who happened to be black was posted at her house to ensure her safety. She demanded he be replaced with a white man. He was.) Writing a short letter to her cousin Mary after the official surrender, Mrs. Lee justified her husband's actions and reflected on what he, their sons Fitzhugh and Robert—who both served in the war— and the South itself had endured. (There is no salutation to the letter, and the reference to "our President" is to Jefferson Davis, who had fled Richmond by train.)

I have just heard my dear cousin Mary of an opportunity to write to tell you that we are all well as usual and thru' the mercy of God all spared thru' the terrible ordeal thru' which we have passed — I feel that I could have blessed God if those who were prepared had filled a soldiers grave. I blessed Him that they are spared I trust for a future usefulness to their poor unhappy country. My little Rob has not yet come in but we have reason to think he is safe.

Tho' it has not pleased Almighty God to crown our exertions with success in the way & manner we expected yet we must still trust & pray not that our will but His may be done in Heaven & in earth. I could not believe I'd tell you of the startling events that have been crowded into the last few weeks, but I want you all to know that when Gen'l Lee surrendered that the enemy by their own account had nearly 80 thousand men well provisioned & equipped while ours had been out 7 days with only 2 days rations that they were fighting by day & marching all night without even time to parch their corn their only food for several days, that even in this exhausted state they drove back the hosts of the enemy but could not follow up their advantage that had Grant demanded an unconditional surrender they had determined to sell their lives as dearly as possible & cut their way thru' his encircling hosts, but the conditions he offered were so honorable that Gen'l Lee decided it was wrong to sacrifice the lives of those brave men when no object could be gained by it.

For my part it will always be a source of pride & consolation to me to know that all mine have risked their lives fortune & even fame for so holy a cause — We can hear nothing certain from our President — may God bless & protect them — we can only pray for them — our plans are all unsettled. Gen'l Lee is very busy getting up his army matters & then we shall probably go to some of those empty places in the vicinity of the White

House. Fitzhugh has gone down there to see what he can do but that place is an utter scene of desolation — so is our whole country & the cruel policy of the enemy has accomplished its work too well. They have achieved by starvation what they could never win by their valor & nor have they taken a single town in the South except Vicksburg that we have not evacuated. Dear Cousin write me about you all & how you manage to exist would that I were able to help you. I do not think we shall be here very long therefore unless you can write at once you had better wait till you hear from me again.

The girls & the General write in love. He is wonderfully well considering all he has endured. Nanny South's wife is fine & several of her boys who have come in — Love to all friends.

Ever affectionately yours,
M C Lee

After the fall of Richmond, and before Lee's surrender, President Lincoln wanted to visit the old Confederate capital firsthand. "Thank God I have lived to see this," he remarked, walking through the demolished city on April 3, "It seems to me that I have been dreaming a horrid nightmare for four years, and now the nightmare is over." On April 14—exactly four years to the day the American flag was lowered in defeat at Fort Sumter—a cheerful, visibly relieved President Lincoln went to Ford's Theatre with his wife and two guests to see a comedy, Our American Cousin. *Soon after the president's sole bodyguard stepped away, John Wilkes Booth walked quietly behind the president and fired a single shot into his head. Major William Child, a surgeon from New Hampshire who had treated wounded soldiers throughout the war, was in Ford's Theatre across from the president when it happened. Still reeling from the historic event, he dashed off the following letter to his wife.*

Washington, D.C.
Apr. 14. 1865

My Dear Wife
    Wild dreams and real facts are but brothers. This night I have seen the murder of the President of the United States.
    Early in the evening I went to Fords Theater. After a little time the President entered—was greeted with cheers. The play went on for about an hour. Just at the close of an interesting scene a sharp quick report of a pistol was heard and instantly a man jumped from the box in which was the President, to the stage—and rushing across the stage made his escape. This I saw and heard. I was in the theatre—and sat opposite the Presidents box. The murderer assassin exclaimed as he leaped "Sic Sempur Tyrannis"—"Thus always to tyrants."

I never saw such a wild scene as followed. I have no words to describe it.

Sect. Seward was also wounded by a knife about the same minute. The city is now wild with excitement. The affair occured only an hour since.

Are we living in the days of the French Revolution? Will peace ever come again to our dear land? Are we to rush on to wild ruin?

It seems all a dream—a wild dream. I cannot realize it though I know I saw it only an hour since.

W.C.

Abraham Lincoln died the next day at 7:22 A.M. It was the first time in American history a president had been murdered, and it marked the beginning of a period rife with social and political animosity. Enraged Northerners accused Southern leaders of conspiring to have Lincoln killed. Southerners fumed about the arrest and imprisonment of their former president, Jefferson Davis. The United States Congress imposed draconian laws on the South, inciting subversive, white supremacist organizations like the Ku Klux Klan. But the majority of the country was sick of war and sick of fighting. Spoken just five weeks before his death, the words of Lincoln's second inaugural address—"with malice toward none, with charity for all"—resonated deeply. The United States of America was a nation again, and four million men, women, and children—approximately one in every eight Americans—were freed from bondage. "Strange, (is it not?)," the poet and war nurse Walt Whitman mused, "that battles, martyrs, blood, even assassination should so condense—perhaps only really, lastingly condense—a Nationality."

∼

In the Bitter Aftermath of the Civil War, Union Soldier William Byron Tries to Win the Heart of Caroline Tally, an Attractive Young Confederate Woman

It is not entirely certain how William Byron, a Union soldier from Lafayette, Indiana, first made the acquaintance of Caroline Tally from North Carolina. But once he did, he was smitten. Serving in Charlotte as part of a postwar occupying force, Byron tried to court Tally through a series of almost ostentatiously romantic letters. Tally's brother John had been killed at Cold Harbor—"he was shot through [the] forrade wright above the eye[, and] his brains were all shot out," a relative wrote of his death—and Yankees were not held in high regard by the the Tally family. Caroline Tally, herself, seemed to indicate she did not believe Union soldiers had the most impeccable reputations, and Byron entreated her to change her mind. (The fact that he repeatedly spelled her last name incorrectly was not, one can safely assume, helping his prospects.)

Headqurs
June the 10 1865

Miss Caroline Tully,

You may perhaps feel disposed to censure the writer of this note as a presumptuous fool to place so much reliance upon the generosity of one who is an entire stranger as to pay his addresses upon paper, yet whatever my excuses for this method may be, accept my assurance in the absence of more substantial evidence, Lady, that I am actuated by motives both honerable and Beneficial.

Having from the first of our slight acquaintence conceived an intense admiration for your apparent resignation to the misfortune of past events and your evident regards for Christianity—combined with a quick sense of distinguishing right from wrong—and a desire to do good I can not but desire a more intimate acquaintence.

Considering these qualities one may well risk something in the way of personal pride to Cultivate an acquaintence with the posessor of such Valuable accomplishments more especially when the posessor is a fair Lady whose society are always sought after by Soldiers of either Army.

Perhaps your opinion of the Federal Soldiers Based upon petty acts of abuse and insult which you may have sustained at the hands of Unreasonable and rowdy Soldiers extends to include all who wear the Blue yet permit me to assure you again that in seeking your valuable and interesting Society I am influenced by none but purely Beneficial motives as to the result of our acquaintence I desire not from impudent curiosity, but future benefits to accquaint myself perfectly with the Society of the South which has undoubtedly—to a certain extent been misrepresented. The hospitality, generosity, and confiding liberality of that Class of citizens whom circumstances have brought me in contact with demonstrates their excellence

And as our Brigade expect to remain in the vicinity of Charlotte some time yet to come I trust you will lay aside the prejudices of an inheritance and cultivate Sentiments beneficial to the accquantence of one who is not disposed to intrude upon your Alonelyness (one might say) unless insured of a welcome.

Should an acquaintence prove objectionable in your estimation although much I should regret your objections I would not risk the honor of a soldier by pressing my entreaties. I am allready ashamed of my previous frequent calls without apparent purpose let this explain the past and the future.

Your Obt Servant
O S Byron

Despite his assurances to the contrary, Byron was unyielding.

Gen'l Grungers Head Qurs
New Greensboro NC

Miss Caroline Tully
Charlotte NC

Perhaps you will be eaqually surprised and annoyed at my persistent indeavors to Cultivate an accquaintince which circumstances seem to oppose Yet it seems that I can never forget one whose aimiable qualities have made such a deep impression upon my mind and heart & which I am afraid in this case are entirely to susceptible & yet anxiety in behalf of one whom I reverence with that adoration which is in fervor eaqual to that Spirit or Sentiment which lights the christeon on his Path to heaven, that, same instinct, bids me hope for the happy day when this bondage which controls my hearts desire, May cease, and I be Permitted to return to Charlotte on the Banks of the little Brooklet which winds its way through the Meadow close by Mrs Tullys and leaning confidingly upon My arm was Miss C—or rather Mrs C for in My innocent dream of Happiness there was no Barrier to that joy which in Reality would transport me to the sweetest Realms of Bliss would that I could meet your sweet Countnance in day, as well as Night dreams.

If I am spared my life untill my return from the North Whither I start to morrow morning—I shall seek consolation in your decision in regard to the termination of our acquaintenship the first dilicate Business which I undertake upon my return & In the meantime sweet Carrie How pleasent it woulde be to Recieve a few lines from you which might bid me hope for the consumation of that blessed Event which ~~might~~ would afford to us, a life of Happiness.

How Pleasant it would be to have a Nice Beautiful Residence in the sunny South, and More Plasant yet to enjoy the treasure, which in My innocent imaginations should share my Connubial Happiness. Please Miss Caroline do Not allow the Predjudices of others to influence you in your decision But write to me the Pure Sentiments of a Mind free from Criticisms of Intended Friends; or restraints of a Natural Modesty.

With anxiety I shall await your answer for upon it depends my whole Future course of life one word will either bring to me a life of Happiness or of Misery so Remember in your hands I place the issue of my future God grant that yours may Prove a wise decision

I am Very Respectfully
Your Obt Servt and Ardent Admirer
William Byron

It is believed that Tally and Byron did meet, but her parents—still grieving over the loss of their son Charles during the war—prohibited Caroline from ever seeing her Northern suitor again.

~~~

Joshua Chamberlain Returns to the Field Where He Was Shot and Recalls, in a Letter to His Sister, the "Horrible Carnage" That Took Place That Day

In a war of innumerable heroes, he was among the most revered. On July 2, 1863, Col. Joshua Lawrence Chamberlain led a spectacular bayonet charge at Gettysburg against approaching Rebels after he and his men ran out of ammunition. (Chamberlain, a college professor before the war, was awarded the Congressional Medal of Honor for his courage and leadership in saving a strategically important stronghold at Gettysburg.) Almost a year later, at Petersburg, a bullet slammed into Chamberlain's right hip and tore through his midsection, severing arteries and fracturing his pelvis before exiting from his left hip. He barely survived. After the war he was elected governor of Maine four times, and then became president of the prestigious Bowdoin College. In January 1882 Chamberlain, fifty-three, was riding back on a train from Florida, where he had been looking for new business opportunities. (He also thought the climate might benefit his ailing wife, Fanny.) In the following letter to his sister Sarah, Chamberlain described his visit to the nation's capital, which he found populated by too many self-promoting politicians, and his journeys through the South, including a nostalgic return to Petersburg. Seventeen years after the war, the battle-scarred field—like the nation and the old soldier, himself—were all, quite literally, still in the process of healing.

<div align="right">Washington Jan 29 1882</div>

My dear Sister:

I am so far on my way home & write a word to let you know where my movements are leading. I made quite a visit to Florida, & saw much there to invite energetic and resolute young men. There are great opportunities to get health & wealth, & also to do good, & to help other people.

I was most warmly received by all sorts of people, & had many invitations to take positions of responsibility—which naturally suits my temperament & aspirations. I always wanted to be at the head of some enterprise to transform the wilderness into a garden—both materially & spiritually—to be a missionary of civilization & of christianity at once. Here is a great chance to do it, & in my own Country, which is peculiarly dear to me. It would be a delight to me now to give my energies to bringing forward the true results of all our struggle & sacrifice for the Country, & to secure the blessings of so great a victory for the right.

As yet I have made no plans, for I owe a duty yet to the College, and must see that all fulfilled before I think of new fields.

Health surely could be found & kept in that wonderful clime where the sea sands & corals have made a land of strange contrasts of soil, & the days & nights are glorious above, & the airs sweeping from the atlantic & the Gulf keep a constant & delicious evenness of temperature.

I mean to take Fanny there next winter, & think it would cure her of all her ills.

It may be I shall have more to say & do about Florida by & by.

Friday I visited the battle fields of Petersburg & spent 4 hours in trying to identify the spot where I fell on the 18 of June 64 in leading a charge upon the Rebel works.

All is changed there now. What was a solid piece of woods through which I led my troops is now all cleared field, & the hill side so smooth then is now grown up with little clumps of trees—marking some spots made more rich perhaps by the bloody struggles enacted on them.

At last, guided by the railroad cut & the well remembered direction of the church spires of the city, I found the spot—or a space of 20 or 30 feet within which I must have fallen. It is now a plowed field—too rich, I suppose, since that 18 of June to be left barren by the owner—& there are in it the remnants of a last years cornfield.

Standing & musing there remembering how I thought of mother in that calm ebbing away of life amidst the horrible carnage, I looked down & saw a bullet, & while stooping to pick it up, another & another appeared in sight & I took up six within as many feet of each other and of the spot where I fell. You may imagine what the havoc must have been that day and for 17 years relic hunters have been carrying away lead & iron from that field—amounting, I was told, to cart-loads. I could easily no doubt have found many more had I searched, or kicked away the earth a little. But these I have, & that other that made so straight a way through me, will do.

You can not imagine, I believe, what thoughts came over me, as I thought of all those who stood there on that day—for & against—& what it was all for, & what would come of it—& of those who on the one side & the other thought there was something at stake worthy of dearest sacrifice.

Such thoughts never would end, had one time to ponder & it is well perhaps that the common cares & the inexorable duties of life call us away from too long thoughts.

Another study is this capitol. Here are gathered the representatives of all sections & parties & creeds & countries, within little space. It is like a spectacle—a scene in an amphitheater. Here is the little world around which the whole great country moves.

Self-seeking marks too many faces, & all the strifes of peaceful times less noble often than those of war,—are seen here in their little play, or great one, as the case may be.

All is not evil here, however, I went to a church thronging with earnest people this morning, & heard words of deep impressiveness, & witnessed a wonderful scene of infant baptism which also set me to thinking long of how we are responsible for each other.

I shall hasten home now, & shall hope to see you before long. Trusting you are all well & happy under God protecting love & care

> I am
> Your affectionate brother
> Lawrence.

WORLD WAR I

Sitting on head of cot, map case on knee and head ducked beneath canvas leanto against side of company officer's wagon. The war news continues to be the best ever. We're licking the tar out of the Germans and I'm a live part of it. The spirit of the boys is great and they are brimming over with confidence. These are stirring times and regardless of my personal outcome I'm glad to be a part of it.

—*Lt. Robert F. Mitchell to Winifred Bostwick,*
October 6, 1918;
Mitchell was killed nine days later.

Social Activist Jane Addams Warns President Woodrow Wilson of the Consequences of Preparing for War Instead of Advocating for Peace
&
Mrs. M. Denkert Implores Jane Addams to Continue Her Antiwar Efforts on Behalf of "Poor Stricken" Mothers Everywhere

Shot by a teenaged Bosnian Serb named Gavrilo Princip on June 28, 1914, while visiting Sarajevo, Archduke Franz Ferdinand—heir to the Austro-Hungarian throne—assured those who rushed to his aid, "It is nothing." But Ferdinand died only moments later, igniting a diplomatic firestorm that swiftly consumed all of Europe. Austria-Hungary swore retaliation against Serbia for the assassination. Russia vowed it would protect Serbia. Germany, allied with Austria-Hungary, declared war on Russia. When German forces marched through Belgium in early August to invade France, a Russian ally, Great Britain declared war on Germany. The long-standing powder keg of suspicion and animosity between the Central Powers (primarily Germany, Austria-Hungary, Bulgaria, Turkey) and the Allies (including Russia, France, Belgium, Great Britain) had finally exploded. The United States wanted no part of it. The war, asserted President Woodrow Wilson, was one "with which we have nothing to do, whose causes cannot touch us." The vast majority of the country agreed. But when a German submarine torpedoed the British liner Lusitania *on May 7, 1915, killing 128 vacationing Americans, the nation was jolted, if only temporarily, from its apathy. Antiwar activists feared the attack would dash any hopes for a negotiated peace. Jane Addams, the famed social reformer and chairwoman of the Woman's Peace Party, was particularly concerned by Wilson's call to increase the production of armaments and double the size of the army to ensure the country's preparedness for war. Addams sternly reminded the president of the potential repercussions of his actions both to the world and his own legacy.*

October 29, 1915
To the President of the United States,
Washington, D. C.

Dear Mr. President:

Feeling sure that you wish to get from all sources the sense of the American people in regard to great national questions, officers of the Women's Peace Party venture to call to your attention certain views which they have reason to believe are widespread, although finding no adequate expression in the press.

We believe in real defense against real dangers, but not in a preposterous "preparedness" against hypothetic dangers.

If an exhausted Europe could be an increased menace to our rich, resourceful republic, protected by two oceans, it must be a still greater menace to every other nation.

Whatever increase of war preparations we may make would compel poorer nations to imitate us. These preparations would create rivalry, suspicion and taxation in every country.

At this crisis of the world, to establish a "citizen soldiery" and enormously to increase our fighting equipment would inevitably make all other nations fear instead of trust us.

It has been the proud hope of American citizens who love their kind, a hope nobly expressed in several of your own messages, that to the United States might be granted the unique privilege not only of helping the war-worn world to a lasting peace, but of aiding toward a gradual and proportional lessening of that vast burden of armament which has crushed to poverty the peoples of the old world.

Most important of all, it is obvious that increased war preparations in the United States would tend to disqualify our National Executive from rendering the epochal service which this world crisis offers for the establishment of permanent peace.

Jane Addams

President Wilson assured both Addams, who later received the Nobel Peace Prize, and the rest of the country that he had no intention of seeing the United States mired in the fighting abroad. "He Kept Us Out of War" became his 1916 campaign slogan, and it proved successful; Wilson was reelected. Americans continued to be shocked by news wires reporting the sheer enormity of the carnage overseas. An estimated 19,000 British soldiers were killed on the first day of combat along the Somme River in France. Over 700,000 French and German soldiers were lost at Verdun. The Russians suffered nearly one million casualties during the Brusilov Offensive on the eastern front. And this was all in 1916 alone. The U.S., although firmly behind the Allies in spirit, was by no means unanimous in its support; Irish Americans loathed the British, Russian-American Jews had fled their homeland because of anti-Semitism, and many German Americans still had emotional and often direct family ties to Germany. One German American, Mrs. M. Dunkert, wrote to Jane Addams and begged her not to yield to those who were pressing for war

and denigrating Addams's crusade for peace as antipatriotic and futile. Dunkert's
sentiments were shared by many American parents, regardless of nationality, terrified
of sending their boys to fight in what was increasingly being seen as a never-ending
bloodbath. (Sir Edward Grey, alluded to below, was the British foreign secretary.)

Johnstown, NY

Dear Madam:

Will you have enough patience to listen for a few minutes to the words of the obscure writer of this? I trust you will, since it is nothing that I want for myself.

As an introduction I wish to say I am a German-American woman, who came here to this country as a young girl 27 years ago. I am happily married now for over 20 years, my husband having been born and brought up in Moscow, Russia, the latter loving his native country as much as I love mine.

We are, through God's grace, the parents of two big, healthy boys, and it is, when with motherly pride I look at them, that my heart is wrung at the thought of all those mothers not alone in Germany, but in all the warring countries, who have to send forth these treasured tokens of God, either never to see them again or else to get them back crippled or blind or demented. The thought of this is making my own joy in my boys appear almost like a crime to me!

Oh, dear Miss Adams, is there no way out of this fearful nightmare? Must nations go on, killing each other by the thousands, though their own feelings are revolting, in doing it? Is there nobody and nothing that will stop this terrible slaughter and save our poor stricken sisters what yet may be saved for the one or the other?

Ever since I read in the paper of the answer you, dear Madam, received from Sir Edward Grey, when you appealed to him for peace, that "the proposals for peace must come from the neutral nations," and that "if for instance 6 proposals were submitted, there might be one among them which would eventually be acceptable to all the parties concerned."—ever since that time I have prayed and hoped you would take these words as a hint, as it seems to me they were meant, and that you would use your great influence here in Washington with the representatives of the neutral nations there, to push on the noble task you and your sister workers had set for themselves, when starting on your trip abroad.

Pray, dear Madam, let me beg and implore you for the sake of all our sorrowing sisters, do not throw over this work because a few shallow fools ridicule it in the papers! What do they care about all those breaking hearts three thousand miles away! Such people will be among the loudest to applaud you, should you push on this work successfully! And you will have success! But believe it, the warring governments themselves are sick of what they have got themselves into and would gladly stop if they could save their pride in doing so.

Once more, dear Madam, keep up your brave fight and emperors and kings and ministers and mankind will bless you for it for all times!

Yours devotedly,
Mrs. M. Denkert

*There was no single event that triggered President Wilson's declaration of war. Certainly the repeated and fatal attacks on American merchant ships by German submarines (*unterseebooten *or U-boats) were a decisive factor. As was the public release in March 1917 of the Zimmerman Telegram, a coded message from Germany's foreign secretary Arthur Zimmerman to the German minister in Mexico, proposing an alliance between the two countries and promising Mexico the return of Texas, Arizona, and New Mexico after their presumed victory over the United States. (Zimmerman had once menacingly reminded James Gerard, the American ambassador in Berlin, that there were 500,000 German-born reservists in the States who would "rise up against the government" in the event of war. Gerard shot back that, if so, the U.S. had "501,000 lampposts from which to hang them.") With these and other provocations in mind, President Wilson stood before the Congress on April 2, 1917, and delivered one of the most impassioned speeches of his presidency. "The world must be made safe for democracy," he urged. "[T]he day has come when America is privileged to spend her blood and her might for the principles that gave her birth and happiness and the peace which she has treasured. God helping her, she can do no other."*

~

Pvt. Lester Hensler, Heading Overseas, Assures His Parents He Is Excited to Be Off to War—"a Man's Game"

*With less than 130,000 soldiers (and 80,000 national guardsmen), the United States was far from a world military power. Six weeks after the official declaration of war on April 6, 1917, Congress passed the Selective Service Act, drafting more than 2 million men into service. Another 2 million volunteered. Of the 4 million troops, nearly one in five was an immigrant. (During the war, mail censors had to scrutinize letters penned by soldiers in dozens of different languages.) President Wilson and his administration propagated a sweeping campaign to unify the country behind a single, "noble crusade" for democracy. Draftees were given parades. Movie stars pitched Liberty Bonds. Inflammatory films—*To Hell with the Kaiser—*were produced. (Anti-German hysteria, not unexpectedly, blazed nationwide. German Americans were harassed and beaten, and at least one was lynched.) The campaign*

had its desired effect: American soldiers, imbued with patriotism, were now fully per-
suaded they were embarking on a daring adventure to save the world from tyranny.
Lester Hensler, a twenty-six-year-old private from Cincinnati, expressed this gung-
ho spirit in a letter home moments before heading out with the American Expedi-
tionary Forces. (German soldiers were often referred to as "Huns" or "Boche," a
derogatory French word for Germans.)

Camp Meade, Md.

Dear Mother and Father

Well Mother, this is the proudest day of my life. We leave for "over there" tonight, and I am thankful that I can take a place among men who will bring freedom to the world. I do not want you to worry about me at all, for I am coming back and will be 100 percent better for having gone, for in the army one gains a knowledge of life, that is impossible to gain elsewhere.

All I want of you all is to "Keep the home fires burning" and it will not be long until we will come marching home our mission accomplished, and happy to have suffered the hardships of war.

When you speak of me in France, do not do so with a heavy heart, do it in a proud way, for it is indeed, a thing any parent should be proud of.

I feel this way about it I would rather die in war, than to have stayed out and lived a "Coward" and a "Slacker" and Mother there are many of those and think just how their parents must feel when ask about their son or sons.

This is a man's game, and let me tell you Mother when Bat. "E" 312 F.A. (which is recognized to be the best of Bat. Of Field Artillery in the U.S. army) starts in there is going to be a long line of Huns in line at roll call in hell for breakfast. I would like to have my picture made in my overseas outfit but I will not have a chance. One of the boys, my buddie, had a camera, and we will take some pictures over there and I will send you some. Well I will say good bye to all and "<u>don't worry</u>."

Love and best wishes
Your loving son Lester

P.S. Put this number down someplace and don't lose it. In case anything happens you will need it to get my insurance. "2.695.642"

Lester Hensler would return home after the war, almost to his disappointment, without even a scratch.

～

Kate Gordon Sends a Letter to One of Her Three Sons on His Way to Europe, Telling Him to "Live—or, if God's Will, Die with Courage"

Even parents, once so reluctant to see their boys go off to battle, shared in the patriotic fervor after the official declaration of war. Kate Gordon watched as three of her sons—Luke, John, and Jimmy—left their home in New York for Europe. Gordon addressed a short letter to one of her boys (it cannot, however, be confirmed precisely which one), admonishing him to maintain his pride and dignity throughout his experience, regardless of what should happen.

My dear boy,

Your father says to tell you that he will give his son to his country, but that he will be _____ (never mind what!) if he will give all his new suspenders. He says you pinched three pairs from the top drawer of his dresser—he adds that he "is on to your curves."

Nora says you were very wise to take them, and she would give you all of hers, if she had any! Betty says to tell you that she hears Jack Ellis sails next week;—I know just how his mother will feel for those ten days while he is crossing. But she wouldn't have had him stay at home, any more than I would have had you! All the same, she won't have a good night's sleep until she hears he has landed. I keep thinking what a different world it will be to mothers; when you all come marching home again!

And when you do come marching home old fellow bring me back the same boy I gave my country,—true, and clean, and gentle, and brave. You must do this for your father and me and Betty and Nora;—and most of all, for the daughter you will give me one of these days! Dear, I don't know whether you have even met her yet,—but never mind that! Live for her or if God wills, die for her;—but do either with courage,—"with honour and clean mirth!" But I know you will come back to me—

Mother

Jimmy, age eighteen and the youngest of the three boys, would be killed in the war. John and Luke would return home to the States in 1919, but Luke would die three years later from medical complications resulting from a mustard gas attack in October 1918.

Ship's Cook 3/C Hugh Alexander Leslie Writes Home
After Surviving the Sinking of the USS *President Lincoln* from
a Submarine Attack

The first vanguard of American troops were rushed to France in late June 1917, though it would be months before they saw combat. The threat of being killed, however, confronted servicemen even before they made it to the front lines; the large, lumbering troop ships on which they sailed traversed thousands of miles of mined and submarine-infested ocean before reaching Europe. (In the three years before the war, German U-boats attacked twenty-eight U.S. ships, killing over 200 Americans.) The voyage was especially perilous for the ships' crews, who traveled between the States and France time and time again. Hugh Alexander Leslie, a cook aboard the USS President Lincoln, *described to his family back in Kenedy, Texas, the sense of panic and desperation aboard the ship—especially of those who couldn't swim—after being torpedoed less than 500 miles from France. (The "gun cotton" Leslie refers to was used to make explosive powder.)*

My Dearest and beloved parents and brothers & sisters:

I received your most kind and appreciated letters sinse I hit the old U.S.A. Again, I suppose you read about us losing our good ship Lincoln by two torpedos from an enemy sub. Also the lives of 24 of our shipmates and 3 of our officers, our pay masters/Dr and a Lieutenant taken prisoner by the Germans.

I sent you a telegram as soon as I arrove in New York. I suppose you recived it in a fiew hours after it was sent. I just written old N. S. a 26 page letter when I got in for he wanted to know all about the sinking of our home the Pres. Lincoln.

There is no need of me writting you all about the details of the brave crew of the Lincoln. Captain Foote complemented us again and again on our coolness, bravery and obedience to orders, officers and men of the crew.

We was 480 miles off the coast of Brest France at 9 o'clock a: m: while we were stirring the bryan to the tune of about 12 knots an hour. She sank in 37 minutes after the two torpedos hit forward and aft parts of the ship. The explosions of the gun cotton was so violent, it stuned a number of the crew and tore enormous large holes in her hull on the port side. I and the other ships cooks were on watch in the galley when the first one hit forward and just as I stept out the galley the second one hit, right under the aft galley where we had just had dinner all set. it knocked me flat on the deck and a shower of salt water & wreckage of hatch covers came falling all round me. it tore the galley upside down and wounded some of the fellows in there.

The ship began listing to the port very rappidly. we all fell in our B deck as usual, as no more than an abandoned ship drill, as we had them ever sinse we were on the ship. the general alarm bell was ringing, and the cyreene was blowing keen blasts as a signal of danger. also the coarse whistle used in a fog was also blowing as for help. She looked like a large animal or a cow or a horse that was shot on the left side, and groaning for help as they go down side way, the same with our ship, looked as if she knew she was sinking.

There wasnt a man left the ship until the order was given to abandon ship by the captain. Our pay master and asso. p. m. were so excited they lost their heads. the pay master is all ways in charge of the comesary branch, the chief comesary stewards, cooks & bakers, me. The cooks & bakers of the 9th division were busy throwing off life rafts until the waves were almost washing over the deck. all the pay master would do was to run up and down the deck rubbing his hands. I told him to jump off and grab a line to a life boat or raft, if he couldn't swim. I told him she was sinking rappidly. He said, "No Leslie, jump and save yourself." He took off his gun and dropped it on deck, and a Negro grabbed it and blew his own head off with it as the ship was sinking. The last I saw, him and others was going as high as he could on the ship.

I jumped and swam to a raft. it taken some good swimming to swim to one of those rafts in a choppy sea as that. some of the rafts were lashed to the ship and with the ship, some of our best friends lost their lives, when she went down. I was within 15 foot of it when she disappeared. We were in the water 15 hours before the destroyer picked us up that night. We went back to Brest and come abord the Great Northern, to steam back to the states. she is a fast ship, a 23 knotter an hour. we made this trip in seven days. you can take it for me I was glad to be back here.

The government gave us a full bag of clothes, as we lost everything we had. I hit the water with a pair of white pants, an undershirt, an apron & white hat. We are a crew with out a ship, or a dog with a home. We are on the Antigne, one of the ships that was with us when we got hit. We are just staying here waiting for orders to go to the Navy yard or barracks.

I will knock off at present   as ever   H. A.

Although initially in good health after his rescue, the fifteen hours Hugh Alexander Leslie spent in the ocean weakened his lungs, and he died of pneumonia months after returning to the States. He was twenty-one years old.

~⌒

Ambulance Corps Driver George Ruckle Describes to His Family a Failed German Offensive and the Skills American Soldiers Brought to the Fight

&

Maj. Edward B. Cole Provides His Two Young Sons with a Lighthearted Account of His Experiences in France

By the fall of 1917 the Allies were in a state of alarm. A meager 86,000 U.S. troops were on the battlefields of France (three times that many British soldiers were lost in the third battle of Passchendaele alone), and it would be months before the vast majority of American forces were primed for combat. Vladimir Lenin's Communist revolution, which had appealed especially to war-weary peasants, led to an armistice between Russia and Germany, releasing over one million German soldiers from the eastern front. The reinvigorated German army launched a massive assault in March 1918, and U.S. troops, although still relatively inexperienced, were thrust into battle to stave off an invasion of Paris. In late May and early June the Americans fought with distinction at Cantigny and Chateâu-Thierry on the Marne River, just fifty-six miles—well within range of Germany's heavy artillery—east of the French capital. (An estimated one million Parisians fled the city during the spring.) George Ruckle, serving with the ambulance corps, reported back to his family in Dumont, New Jersey, on how American troops helped French and British forces blunt the German juggernaut.

Dear Father, Mother & brothers,

This is the first chance I have had to write to you in over a week. We have just come back from the front where our division took part in holding back the Germans in one of their biggest drives of the war. This is the first German offensive which failed to make any gains and our boys not only held them back but counter attacked in several places.

The offensive was started by the Germans with a terrific barrage which began at 12.05 Monday morning and the French say it was the most intense since the beginning of the war. It was a creeping barrage and in some places the ground looked as if it had been plowed up, it was so full of shell holes and then all roads for a distance of 15 miles back were continually shelled.

When the barrage started there were 2 lieutenants and 5 of us men with three ambulances stationed in an abandoned village right behind the second line of defense and when the first shells began to come over we retired to a cellar that was about four feet high and crouched there waiting for a call. The first call came at 2 o'clock and Lauber and I started out for the ambulance which was parked in the yard back of the cellar in which we were. Just as we stepped out a shell whistled by and we ducked back in the cellar.

We tried a second time and got out allright and the sight that met our eyes was awe inspiring. The whole sky was a bright red and in three or four places where ammunitions dumps were burning, the flames were leaping into the air while here and there in the village houses were burning. The din was terrible, thousands of big guns were going off so rapidly that it made one continual roar punctured now and then by one mightier than the rest when an ammunition dump went up.

The road we rode along was lit up as bright as day and we reached the first aid station safely, being the first ambulance to reach that section. The wounded had just begun to arrive so we filled up our ambulance and started back for the hospital.

The bombardment kept up all that day and the next night and we ran continually for 48 hours with practically nothing to eat, but then everyone was so busy and our nerves were at such a high tension that we weren't hungry.

I'll never forget some of the sights I saw and how bravely our men and the French bore their wounds. Men with arms and legs torn off would never utter a groan during the whole trip to the hospital. At one place some new batteries came up and their horses were picketed in a clump of trees. I saw a shell land in the middle of them and the next minute there was a pile of 50 or 60 dead horses. The roads too were littered with dead horses and mules and overturned kitchens and supply wagons.

But as heavy as the German barrage was our boys held firm and our artillery sent back two for every one that came over. German prisoners said our artillery did horrible execution among their line troops and we know they were piled high in "no man's land."

One of our batteries that uses the French 75's, a three inch shell, was sending them over so fast that a captured German asked to see our 3 inch machine gun.

The French say they never saw such wonderful work as done by our boys and the whole division got a citation from the French General in command of this section.

The Germans call us barbarians, they don't like the way we fight. When the boys go over the top or make raids they generally throw away their rifles and go to it with trench knives, sawed off shot guns, bare fists and hand grenades, and the Bosch doesn't like that kind of fighting. The boys from Alabama are particularly expert with knives and they usually go over hollering like fiends—so I don't blame the Germans for being afraid of them.

At hand to hand fighting the Bosch is no match for our boys and any American soldier will tell you he can lick any two Dutchmen. Where the Germans shine is with their artillery and air service.

We captured a large number of prisoners, I don't know just how many but it must have been a large number. Whole squads would come over and give themselves up and at one place a squad of machine gunners were captured and offered to turn their guns on their own men, but the American Lieutenant in command of the Americans who captured them wouldn't allow it.

We carried a number of German wounded and everywhere they got the same treatment as the French or our own men. At one dugout they had an unwounded prisoner, a young boy about 17, and he helped us load the wounded in the ambulance and tried in every way to help do something. He was a nice looking young fellow and I couldn't help liking him.

All of the prisoners were well equipped and each man had a map of the territory they were supposed to have taken in the drive. Most of them said they were glad they were captured and that Germany would soon have to give in, but a few were defiant and one of them said it didn't make any difference how many Americans were over here, Germany would whip them all. One wounded German kept crying out in the ambulance that was taking him to the hospital saying, "Mein Goot, Mein Kaiser."

Well, I guess I've written enough about the fight so will talk about something else.

I found a bunch of letters waiting for me when I got back last night and haven't had time to read them all yet. I read the latest one from home to see if everything was OK and was relieved to find it was.

So Jamesie was expected to sail July 6th. If he did he is over here by now and I might get a chance to see him soon. All the boys you know including Elliot and Lauber came through safe and are well.

I will close now hoping this finds you all well,

With love to all,

George

Almost immediately after the U.S. army's triumph at Chateâu-Thierry, a brigade of marines with the Second Division attacked fortified German positions on June 6 just west of the town in Belleau Wood. Outnumbered, gassed, and raked by machine-gun fire, the marines were nearly overwhelmed. When retreating French troops advised the Americans to do the same, Capt. Lloyd Williams barked,

"Retreat? Hell, we just got here." Resorting to hand-to-hand combat, they tena-ciously fought back and prevailed over the Germans on June 26. But their losses were staggering; the marines suffered approximately 5,200 casualties, almost half of their strength. One of those wounded was Edward B. Cole, a Marine Corps major who left behind his wife, Mary, and two young sons, Charlie (age ten) and Teddy (age eight) to serve in France. Cole frequently wrote to his family back in Brookline, Massachusetts, to give them updates on his well-being and general whereabouts, and, six weeks before the attack at Belleau Wood, Cole sent his boys the following letter. ("Prince" is Cole's horse.)

April 22nd, 1918

Dear Charlie and Teddy:

I have received several very nice letters from you both. What a time you did have with the measles, did you not? Well the time to have them is when you are young so you will not catch them when you get older. Prince is quite well and sends his love to you both, he says that when we get back to the United States that he will be very happy to let you ride him provided that you feed him regularly with sugar. He and I went to the front line trenches the other day at least Prince went part way, but just now we are back in our headquarters.

A short time ago Capt. Curtis and I were in our mess room eating breakfast when 'Blooie' went a big shell just outside the window. I got a piece of toast mixed with a swallow of coffee in the wrong channel of my throat and Capt. Curtis, well the last I saw of him he was easily outrunning a 9.2 shell in the direction of the dugout. Somehow I caught up with him at the entrance and we passed in neck and neck for a dead heat. It ain't no disgrace to run when you are skeered. These 9.2 shells are almost as tall as Teddy. How would you like to shoot one in your air gun. Where I am writing this letter is behind the lines and the Bosche have only shelled us once but a dugout entrance leads into my office so you can see I resemble a prairie dog sitting in front of its burrow ready to duck in if danger comes its way.

We see lots of airplanes here   it reminds one of Pensacola except that when it is a German plane our anti aircraft guns fire at them. They do not hit many, but they keep them high and away. The Germans have lots of balloons in the air like the one you boys and mother went up in while we were at Pensacola. The French have a lot of them also. Where I sleep is a little three room cabin or hut that you would like to own for it would be just the thing for boy scouts. At night we have to darken all the windows so the lights will not show— that is to prevent the German airplanes from interrupting our sleep with bombs. I do not think you would like that part of the hut life quite so well, do you?

Yesterday I saw a mule that had been killed by shrapnel fire. The French had skinned him and were cutting him up to eat. The meat looked rather tough to me but I do not see any reason why it should not be wholesome so some day when I get a chance I shall try a mule sirloin. I wonder if it will be as good as that pole cat stew. Good gravy! My men got a few helmuts the other day but had to turn them in so I can't send you one. Anyway they were not the right kind as they had no spikes on top. Now I know you boys have no yellow streak because you are doing better in school and I am always so proud of you when you do well and when mother writes me that you are not doing well in your studies it makes me very unhappy so if you want to help your old dad away over here—away from you and who is fighting for you just study hard and do your best in school.

The woods here are full of wild flowers, violets and many other pretty varieties. One could pick a boquet for the table in a very few minutes but the only boquet that we have picked for the table is one of dandelions and those we cooked and ate. Yum! Yum! some boquet. Are both you boys going to be promoted this year but then of course you are. I have not seen Uncle Charlie for two months but he is not far from here and is doing well for which we should all fel feel very proud.

How do you like the picture of your dad, dug out and the little accelerator behind him. One thing over here the more rank one has the better dug out, sometimes that makes me wish I were president.

Now I must close but I want you both to do something for me. Go to mother, put both your arms around her neck and give her a kiss for dad and tell her that although dad scolds her sometimes in his letters and is pretty much of an old grouch, he loves her with all his heart and the poetry she sent him about the ship sailing over the sea is very beautiful and she was a darling to send it. Now boys be good and take care of the only girl in our family.

Dad

On June 13, one week after the marines launched their attack at Belleau Wood, Mary Cole received a letter from her brother-in-law, Brig. Gen. Charles H. Cole, stating that her husband had been wounded in both arms, both legs, and on his face after a grenade exploded directly in front of him. "Luckily for him," Gen. Charles Cole wrote after visiting his brother in the hospital, "his eyes were not hit, (something miraculous). Today the doctor told us that, unless something unforeseen happens, he ought

and many other pretty varieties
One could pick a boquet
for the table in a very few
minutes but the only boquet
that we have picked for the
table is one of dandelions and
those we cooked and ate.
Yum! Yum, some boquet.
Are both you boys going
to be promoted this year
but then of course you are.
I have not seen Uncle Charlie
for two months but he is
not far from here and
is doing well for which we
should all ~~fee~~ feel very proud.

9.2

Dad.

Dugout

to survive. Tell Charlie and Teddy there is no braver man in the American Army than their daddy." Something unforeseen happened two days later; severe blood poisoning spread rapidly throughout Cole's system and, despite two amputations to stem the advance of the infection, Maj. Edward B. Cole died on June 18. In October 1918 the United States Navy christened destroyer no. 155 the USS Cole *in his memory.*

In a Cable to Gen. Peyton March, Gen. John "Black Jack" Pershing Praises the "Colored Soldiers" Serving with the AEF

He was "Nigger Jack" to those who loathed him, and there were many. A gruff, obstinate, and highly disciplined graduate of West Point, John ("Black Jack," as he was more commonly known) Pershing distinguished himself in the Spanish-American War, the Philippines, and Mexico, where he pursued Pancho Villa after the rebel leader murdered American citizens. Impressed by Pershing's strong will and indomitable character, President Wilson appointed him, over five other senior generals, commander of the Allied Expeditionary Forces when war was declared against Germany. During the Spanish-American War, Pershing had led the all-black Tenth Cavalry (hence the derogatory nickname) in Cuba. While many opposed drafting African Americans, Pershing lauded black troops as being, from his own experiences, as "reliable and courageous" as whites and encouraged their enlistment. More than 380,000 served in World War I, 10 percent of whom were in combat. Pershing was discouraged to hear from Washington reports of incendiary rumors circulating about black soldiers, and on June 19, 1918, he sent the following to Gen. Peyton March:

Confidential

Adjutant General
Washington

Reference to your cablegram 1523, the stories probably invented by German agents that have been widely circulated among colored people in the United States to the effect that colored soldiers in France are always placed in most dangerous positions and sacraficed to save white soldiers; that when wounded they are left on ground to die without medical attention etc. are absolutely false.

The following are the losses as reported up to June 18th in the 4 colored combat regiments now in France: 369th Infantry, died of wounds 3; died of disease 8; severely wounded 2; 370th Infantry, died of wounds 0; died of disease 3; severely wounded 0; 371st Infantry, died of wounds 0; died of disease 8; severely wounded 0; 372nd Infantry, died of wounds 0; died of disease 3; severely wounded 0. These figures show conclusively that negro troops have not thus far occupied positions as dangerous as those occupied by white troops and that their physical condition is excellent.

A tour of inspection just completed among American negro troops by officers of the Training Section, these headquarters, shows a comparatively high degree of training and efficiency among these troops. Their training is identical with that of other American troops serving with the French Army, the effort being to lead all American troops gradually to heavy combat duty by preliminary service in trenches in quiet sectors. Colored troops in trenches have been particularly fortunate, as one regiment had been there a month before any losses were suffered. This almost unheard of on western front.

Exploit of colored infantrymen some weeks ago repelling much larger German patrol killing and wounding several Germans and winning Croix de Guerre by their gallantry has roused fine spirit of emulation throughout colored troops all of whom are looking forward to more active service. Only regret expressed by colored troops is that they are not given more dangerous work to do. They are especially amused at the stories being circulated that the American colored troops are placed in the most dangerous positions and all are desirous of having more active service than has been permitted them thus far. I cannot commend too highly the spirit shown among the colored combat troops who exhibit fine capacity for quick training and eagerness for the most dangerous work.

Pershing.

Despite their oft-expressed desire to fight, African-American troops were segregated in the U.S. Army and relegated to mostly non-combat duties. The French, however, welcomed them into their own forces with open arms, and awarded one of the most famed black regiments—New York's 369th Infantry, the "Harlem Hell Fighters"—with over 150 croix de guerre medals for their valor. Only the soldiers of the 369th Infantry received a hero's reception upon their return home; many black veterans were specifically targeted for abuse and harassment after the war, and some were even lynched.

~

Writing to His Nine-Year-Old Son, Warren, Gen. John Pershing Explains Why He and His Troops Are Fighting in France

On the morning of August 27, 1915, a year-and-a-half before America went to war, a newspaper reporter named Norman Walker called the office of Gen. John Pershing in Fort Bliss, Texas to confirm a tragic story coming over the wires about Persh-

ing's wife and children. Certain the voice at the other end was a military aide, Walker inquired about the deaths at Gen. Pershing's residence in San Francisco. "What has happened!?" demanded the voice. It was Pershing, himself. Norman stumbled through the report as the general listened: Mrs. Pershing, only thirty-five, and their three daughters—ages eight, seven, and three—were all killed when a fire swept through their house at the Presidio. Only six-year-old Warren was pulled out alive. Less than a year later, Pershing was sent to Mexico in the Punitive Expedition against Pancho Villa and in June 1917 he was off to Europe to lead American forces in the war. Notoriously stern and reserved before the fire, Pershing became even more withdrawn in its aftermath. Pershing demonstrated great warmth and tenderness, however, in his letters to Warren, who was living with his Aunt May in Lincoln, Nebraska. The general wrote the following to his son on October 10, 1918.

My dear Kiddie:

I have your letter of Sunday (no date) written on letter paper with the Stars and Stripes on one edge. It makes very pretty writing paper. The letter was No. 8 so I suppose you can tell the date but I cannot.

I have often promised in my various letters that you should come to France while I am still here, and I am going to keep this promise and you may count upon it. I do not know just when it will be nor how I shall arrange it, but we can work that out a little bit later.

I want you to come so that you yourself can see something of the army and see something of France. I want you to know while you are still a boy something of the fine patriotism that inspires the American soldiers who are fighting over here for the cause of liberty. They are fighting as you know against Germany and her Allies to prevent the rulers of Germany from seizing territory that does not belong to them and from extending their rule over the people of other governments who do not wish to be ruled by Germany. I might add that in order to do this the German army, under orders from the Ruler of Germany, has committed most serious crimes, and for that also we are fighting in order to punish them.

I want you to see some of the battlefields of France with me, over which the American soldiers have fought in carrying out the great purpose of our people. It will enable you to realize later in life just what sacrifice means and just what degree of sacrifice our army is called upon to make and which they have made and are making bravely and courageously.

I think that you should talk this over with your Auntie and I want you to regard it, of course, as confidential, and let me have any suggestion that you and she wish to make regarding it. In the meantime, work as hard as you ought to work giving yourself plenty of time for play and exercise in the open air, to the end that you may prepare yourself as well as the average boy prepares himself, or better, for whatever calling you may follow in life. And might I add, as I have already said to you, that it is my hope that you will always be what I believe you to be—a very manly, upright, honest, industrious, wholesome, wide-awake boy. I look forward to your companionship with a great deal of pleasure, and after the war is over we can have many good times together.

Give my love to your Aunties, and believe me, as always,
Yours affectionately,
Papa

General Pershing kept his promise to Warren, and in March 1919 the general and his son were reunited in France. Outfitted in a miniature officer's uniform, Warren toured the country with his celebrated father.

~⌐

John E. Bott Tells His Son Harry, in France with the AEF, Joyful News of a Recent "Arrival" to the Family—Followed by a Devastating Loss

A nineteen-year-old private named Reynold Thomas, writing to his mother, confessed what happened when he pulled her photo out of his pocket and mused on his life back home: "[All] of a sudden I was conscious of your picture becoming blurred, and finally I could not see it at all. The tears were coming, and I burst out crying loudly and souly. I was homesick, homesick for the first time in my life." Thomas's sentiments were not uncommon. Never before had so many young American men been sent to serve in a foreign land for so long. And that loneliness and sense of distance became all the more excruciating when soldiers received word from loved ones in the States that something truly terrible—or, absolutely wonderful—had occurred in the family. Few, however, were hit with both at once. Serving in France, Harry Bott received a letter from his father relating two dramatic events from their home in Provo, Utah—news that would be overwhelming under any circumstances, but especially so to a young soldier separated from his family by thousands of miles of ocean. (Connie was Bott's sister-in-law, Olive was his wife, and Louise, alluded to but not mentioned by name, was Bott's stepmother. His own mother had died when he was a boy.)

Dear Son

be strong and have faith in the future and rest assured that all has been done that could be done   you have a fine little Baby Girl   she is 5 days old to day and is doing well and she will be waiting for you when you return but your dear wife has passed to the other side to day.

Dear Boy it is sad news — but remember God's Will not ours to be done   she did not die from the effects of childbirth but the flu was the cause   now Dear Boy be brave and remember the Baby will want your care and attention when you come back again   Uncle Herman also lost his wife 2 weeks ago from the same cause she was only 16 hours —

oh my dear Boy   can hardly write you this sad news — I saw Bishop Buttle and told him   he said he would take me out in his car   he will no doubt be at the funeral — it has not been arranged for as yet my wife has got a severe cold she can not go there   Connie can not go either on account of her Baby   there has been and is now lots of People taken away from the same cause   we would have sent you a cable but we had no assurance that it would reach you

Well Harry   rest assured everything will be looked after in the best possible manner it can be done   we all sympathize with you   and all yours and Olive's Friends condole with you in this sad hour   may God bless you and keep you strong and well and all will be well

I must close   I will write more again in a few days   The Girls and wife send you their Love and Sympathy in which I do too   may God give you strength to bear your burden is my prayer for you

from your Father

Bott's wife had died from the "Spanish Flu," as it was known, an influenza pandemic of epic proportions; in 1918 and 1919 it claimed the lives of over 500,000 Americans in the States and tens of millions of people around the world. Although 43,000 U.S. soldiers overseas died from the flu, Bott, himself, was spared. But he would not see his baby daughter or be able to visit his wife's grave until he returned home from the war in 1919.

~

Pvt. Walter Bromwich, Writing to His Pastor, Begins to Question the Role of God in War

The intoxicating exuberance with which so many soldiers had left the States was soon tempered by their introduction to a new, technologically "advanced" form of warfare. Machine guns, flamethrowers, tanks, airplanes, and poison gas made it possible for armies to wipe out tens of thousands of men in a single battle. The trenches in which the soldiers lived were disease- and rat-infested, mud-soaked burrows, made all the more unbearable by the stench of human waste and rotting corpses. The new century's promise of a peaceful, civilized world where machines would serve—not annihilate—humanity seemed rapidly to be deteriorating into barbarism. Some soldiers began to reexamine their idealism, their purpose, and their faith. In a brief but thoughtful letter to his pastor in Pennsylvania, Pvt. Walter Bromwich emphasized that, although still a believer, he was questioning the notion of a benevolent God in a spectacle so incomprehensibly horrible as war.

Dear Reverent:

Here I sit in my little home on the side of the hill thinking of the little church back home, wondering how you are getting along. Don't think I am down-hearted because I am writing you, but it's a queer thing I can't explain, that ever since I volunteered I've felt like a cog in a huge wheel. The cog may get smashed up, but the machine goes on, and I know I share in the progress of that machine whether I live or die, and that seems to make everything all right. Except, perhaps, when I lose a pal, it's generally one of the best but yet it may be one of the worst. And I can't feel God is in it.

How can there be fairness in one man being maimed for life, suffering agonies, another killed instantaneously, while I get out of it safe? Does God really love us individually or does He love His purpose more? Or is it better to believe he makes the innocent suffer for the guilty and that things will be squared up some day when those who have escaped suffering here will suffer, and those who have suffered here will escape suffering. Sounds rather calculating, doesn't it, and not a bit like the love of a Father.

What I would like to believe is that God is in this war, not as a spectator, but backing up everything that is good in us. He won't work any miracles for us because that would be helping us to do the work He's given us to do on our own. I don't know whether God goes forth with armies but I do know that He is in lots of our men or they would not do what they do.

Do write me and let me know how the church is getting along.

Remember me to all—especially The Altar Guild, and tell them to "carry on" the war work. My motto is "carry on." So here's good-luck to all.

Yours sincerely,
Pvt. Walter T. Bromwich
Company A   6th U.S.—Engineers
American Expeditionary Forces

Four months after writing this letter, Bromwich was shot in the back and head during combat. After extensive hospitalization, he recovered fully from his wounds.

Theodore Roosevelt Sends a Letter of Deep Gratitude
to Mrs. H. L. Freeland, Who Consoled Him
After a Heartbreaking Loss

Fifty-nine years old, almost blind in one eye, overweight, and suffering from a host of illnesses, former president Theodore Roosevelt was denied his request to lead a division of men into battle during World War I. (There is speculation that Roosevelt's ridicule of President Woodrow Wilson as "yellow" and a "molly-coddle pacifist" before the war did not help his appeal.) He was, however, able to send overseas what amounted to a small army of Roosevelts—his four sons, Quentin, Archie, Kermit, and Theodore ("Ted") Jr.; Ted's wife, Eleanor, who went to work in France with the YMCA; and his son-in-law, Dr. Richard Derby. Twenty-year-old Quentin, the youngest and most jovial of the four boys, was especially eager to serve and, despite poor eyesight, became a fighter pilot (he memorized the military eye chart to pass his physical). Fearless almost to the point of being cocky, Quentin was thoroughly exhilarated by aerial combat. "You get so excited," he wrote home after his first dogfight, "that you forget everything except getting the other fellow." On July 11 he described his first kill:

> *I was out on high patrol with the rest of my squadron when we got broken up, due to a mistake in formation. I dropped into a turn of a vrille [a dive]—these planes have so little surface that at five thousand you can't do much with them. When I got straightened out I couldn't spot my crowd any where, so, as I had only been up an hour, I decided to fool around a little before going home, as I was just over the lines. I turned and circled for five minutes or so, and then suddenly,—the way planes do come into focus in the air, I saw three planes in formation. At first I thought they were Boche, but as they paid no attention to me I finally decided to chase them, thinking they were part of my crowd, so I started after them full speed. I thought at the time it was a little strange, with the wind blowing the way it was, that they should be going almost straight into Germany, but I had plenty of gas so I kept on.*
>
> *They had been going absolutely straight and I was nearly in formation when the leader did a turn, and I saw to my horror that they had white tails with black crosses on them. Still I was so near by them that I thought I might pull up a little and take a crack at them. I had altitude on them, and what was more they hadn't seen me, so I pulled up, put my sights on the end man, and let go. I saw my tracers going all around him, but for some reason he never even turned, until all of a sudden his tail came up and he went down in a vrille. I wanted to follow him but the other two had started around after me, so I had to cut and run. However, I could half watch him looking back, and he was still spinning when he hit the clouds three thousand meters below. . . .*

Three days later Quentin was shot down behind enemy lines. After word of Quentin's death was reported by the media, thousands of condolence letters poured into the Roosevelts's home in Oyster Bay, New York, and the former president responded to each one with at least a brief note of appreciation. But there was something about a letter from a Mrs. Harvey L. Freeland that particularly struck Roosevelt, and he sent the following handwritten reply.

Sagamore Hill
Aug 14, 1918

Dear Mrs. Freeland,

Last evening, as we were sitting together in the North Room, Mrs. Roosevelt handed me your two letters, saying that they were such dear letters and that I must see them. As yet it is hard for her to answer even the letters she cares for most; but yours have so singular a quality that I do not mind writing you of the intimate things which one can not speak of to strangers.

Quentin was her baby, the last child left in the home nest; on the night before he sailed, a year ago, she did as she always had done and went upstairs to tuck him in bed — the huge, laughing, gentle-hearted boy. He was always thoughtful and considerate of those with whom he came in contact; a week ago a letter from him, written two days before he was killed, came to a devoted member of our family, Mary Sweeny, the chambermaid, who loved Quentin as if she had been his nurse; a gay, merry letter.

It is hard to open the letters coming from those you love who are dead; but Quentin's last letters, written during his three weeks at the front, when of his squadron on an average a man was killed every day, are written with real joy in the "great adventure." He was engaged to a very beautiful girl, of very fine and high character; it is heartbreaking for her, as well as for his mother; but they both said that they would rather have him never come back than never have gone. He had his crowded hour, he died at the crest of life, in the glory of the dawn.

My other three boys are just as daring; and if the war lasts they will all be killed unless they are so crippled as to be sent home. Archie apparently has been crippled by his two shell wounds, but has been struggling against being sent home. Ted has been gassed, and is now with his gallant little wife in Paris, with two bullet wounds; he will be back at the front in a few weeks. Kermit won the British Military cross in Mesopotamia, but is now under Pershing. My son in law, Dick Derby, a major in the Medical Corps, has been knocked down by a shell, but after a week in hospital is back at the front. A good record, isn't it?

All four left their wives, and their children, born and unborn. And in view of your liking the chapter of my autobiography for which I care most,

I venture to say that the five boys, who as fighters have won distinction against the greatest modern military nations—I wish I could tell you some of their feats!—are so gentle, and are just as clean and good as girls. And I am just as proud of my daughters and daughters in law as of the boys. And we have such darling little grandchildren, and they are such comforts.

Yes, the two anniversaries I always remember are our engagement day and our wedding day; but I have succeeded in hopelessly befogging myself as to whether my wife's birthday is on the 8th or 6th of August (it's really the latter) and every year have to be enlightened on the subject by slightly impatient offspring.

Is your husband in the army? Give him my warm regards; and your mother and father and sister. I wish to see any of you or all of you out here at my house, if you ever come to New York. Will you promise to let me know?

Faithfully yours
Theodore Roosevelt

Incredibly, the Roosevelt family retrieved the mangled axle from Quentin's plane and displayed it prominently in their home at Oyster Bay. In 1941, when World War II was declared, Archie, Kermit, and Ted Jr. all served again. Only Archie, who was hit by shrapnel and severely wounded in 1944 in the South Pacific, would come home alive; Ted died of a heart attack over a month after leading troops on D-Day, and Kermit, who had fought depression and alcoholism his entire life, committed suicide on June 4, 1943, while on active duty in Alaska.

～

On the Eve of the First Major U.S. Offensive at Saint-Mihiel, Lt. David Ker Tells His Mother What He Wants Her to Remember in the Event of His Death
&
Col. George S. Patton Writes to His Father After Saint-Mihiel, Which Was "Not Half So Exciting" as He Had Hoped

By the late summer and early fall of 1918, the German army, which had once dismissed the American forces as "mongrels," were on the defensive. Just before dawn on September 12, an estimated half a million U.S. troops tore into the stronghold at Saint-Mihiel in the east of France, which the Germans had held since the beginning of the war. The night before the attack, Lt. David Ker, a Columbia University student who had left college to enlist, wrote to his mother back in New York City in the event that she, his sister, Elizabeth, and his fiancée, Mary, should never hear from him again.

September 11, 1918

Dear Mother,

Tomorrow the first totally American drive commences, and it gives me inexpressible joy and pride to know that I shall be present to do my share. The plan of attack has been carefully worked out, and every precaution taken to ensure the success of the big undertaking. I have just returned from a visit to some of the troops, who are to make the attack, and I am so proud to be a member of an army such as ours, that I am at a loss to express what I feel.

The rugged and heavily wooded character of the country makes the task which we face extremely difficult, and the losses are almost certain to be considerable. Success, however, will mean so much that almost any price would be cheap to pay for it. Should I go under, therefore, I want you to know that I went without any terror of death, and that my chief worry is the grief my death will bring to those so dear to me. Since having found myself and Mary, there has been much to make life sweet and glorious, but death, while distasteful, is in no way terrible.

I feel wonderfully strong to do my share well, and, for my sake, you must try to drown your sorrow in the pride and satisfaction, the knowledge that I died well in so clean a cause, as is ours, should bring you. Remember how proud I have always been of your superb pluck, keep Elizabeth's future in mind, and don't permit my death to bow your head.

My personal belongings will all be sent to you. Your good taste will tell you which to send to Mary.

May God bless and keep you, dear heart, and be kind to little Elizabeth, and those others I love so well.

David.

The end.

Although triumphant, the Americans sustained 7,000 casualties in the thirty-six-hour offensive. Lt. David Ker was among the dead. Another young officer wrote a similar "last" letter to his wife, Beatrice, in the event he was killed: "I have not the least premonition that I am going to be hurt and feel foolish writing you this letter but perhaps if the thing happened you would like it. . . . The only regret I have in our marriage is that it was not sooner and that I was mean to you at first. . . . It is futile to tell you how much I love you. Words are as inadequate as is love for a person like you. . . . Beat I love you infinitely." The officer was thirty-two-year-old Col. George S. Patton, who had served with John "Black Jack" Pershing during the Pancho Villa Punitive Expedition in Mexico and then went to France in 1917 as Pershing's aide. Patton was eventually put in command of the light tank brigade at Saint-Mihiel, marking the first time the U.S. Army had employed tanks in battle. Patton, of course, survived the battle, and he chronicled his experiences—including a brief encounter with a brigadier general named Douglas MacArthur in a typed letter to his father. (The erratic punctuation and occasional spelling mistakes in the letter were a result of Patton's dyslexia.)

September 20 1918

Dear Papa

We have all been in one fine fight and it was not half so exciting as I had hoped, not as exciting as affairs in Mexico, because there was so much company. When the shelling first started I had some doubts about the advisability of sticking my head over the parapet, but it is just like taking a cold bath, once you get in, it is all right. And I soon got out and sat on the parapet. At seven o clock I moved forward and passed some dead and wounded. I saw one fellow in a shell hole holding his rifle and sitting down I thought he was hiding and went to cuss him out, he had a bullet over his right eye and was dead.

As my telephone wire ran out at this point I left the adjutant there and went forward with a lieutenant and four runners to find the tanks, the whole country was alive with them crawling over trenches and into the woods. I t was fine but I could not see my right battalion so went to look for it, in doing so we passed through several town under shell fire but none did more than throw dust on us. I admit that I wanted to duck and probably did at first but soon saw the futility of dodging fate, besides I was the only officer around who had left on his shoulder straps and I had to live up to them. It was much easier than you would think and the feeling, foolish probably, of being admired by the men lying down is a great stimulus

I walked right along the firing line of one brigade they were all in shell holes except the general (Douglas Mcarthur) who was stan ding on a little hill, I joined him and the creeping barrage came along toward us, but it was very thin and not dangerous. I think each one wanted to leave but each hated to say so, so we let it come over us. The infantry were held up at a town so I happened to find some tanks and sent them through it I walked behind and some boshe surrendered to me. At the next town all but one tank was out of sight and as the infantry would not go in I got on top of the tank to hearten the driver and we went in, that was most exciting as there were plenty of boshe we took thirty.

On leaving the town I was still sitting sidewise on top of the tank with my legs hanging down on the left side when all at once I noticed all the paint start to chip off the other side and at the same time I noticed machine guns, I dismounted in haste and got in a shell hole, which was none too large every time I started to get out the boshe shot at me. I was on the point of getting scared as I was about a hundred yards ahaed of the infantey and all alone in the field. If I went back the infantry would think I was running and there was no reason to go forward alone. All the time the infernal tank was going on alone as the men had not noticed my hurried departure. At last the bright thought occurred to me that I could move across the front in an oblique direction and not appear to run yet at the same time get back. This I did listening for the machine guns with all my ears, and laying down in a great hurry when I heard them, in this manner I hoped to beat the bullets to me. Sometime I will figure the speed of sounds and bullets and see if I was right. It is the only use I know of that math has ever been to me.

I found the Major of the infantry and asked him if he would come on after the tank. He would not as the next battalion on his left had not come up (he was killed ten minutes later) Then I drew a long breath and went after the tank on foot as I could not let it be going against a whole town alone. It is strange but quite true that at this time I was not the least scared, as I had the idea of getting the tank fixed in my head. I did not even fear the bullets though I could see the guns spitting at me, I did however run like H - - - On reaching the tank about four hundred yards out in the field I tapped on the back door with my stick, and thank God it was a long one. The sergeant looked out and saluted and said what do you want now Colonel , I told him to turn and come back he was much depressed. I walked just ahead of him on the return trip and was quite safe. We now got five tanks and decided to attack the town but on of the tanks started shooting at our machine guns and I had to go out again and stop it. A third time I went out as the tanks were keeping too far to the right but the last time was not bad as the machine gunner were mostly dead or chased away by the tanks. We took the town, 4 field gun and 16 machine guns.

Then I walked along the battle front to see how the left battalion had gotten on. It was a very long way and I had had no sleep for four nights and no food all the day as I lost my sack chasing a boshe, I got some crackers off a dead one (he had not blood on them as in Polks story) they were very good but I would have given a lot for a drink of the brandy I had had in my sack. The Major of the left battalion was crying because he had no more gas   He was very tired and had a bullet through his nose, I comforted him and started home alone to get some gas. It was most interesting over the battle field like the books but much less dramatic. The dead were about mostly hit in the head. There were a lot of our men stripping off buttons and other things but they always covered the face of the dead in a nice way.

I saw one very amusing thing which I would have liked to have pho-tographed right in the middle of a large field whwere there had never been a trench was a shell hole from a 9.7 gun the hole was at least 8 feet deep and 15 across on the edge of it was a dead rat, not a large healthy rat but a small field rat not over twice the size of a mouse. No wonder the war costs so much.

On the thieteenth we did nothing but on the fourteenth the left battalion personally conducted by me went to hunt for the enemy. We found the only place on the entire front where for the space of half a mile there were no troops we went through and were attacked by the boshe we drove them six miles, took a town, Joinville, on the Hindenburg line, battery of field guns 12 machine guns but no prisoners, then finding that we were eight miles ahead of our own line, and that all the canon in that part of Germany were shooting at us we withdrew with only four men hit. I was in at the start of this very fine feat of arms, but not at the finish as I was ordered back just after thetanks started and before we knew the boshe were there. We withdrew that night total loses 4 men killed 4 officers and 4 men wounded.

I am writing this in what was once a house but what is now a sort of quay. The boshe shell us at seven thirty each night it is now that time so I will stop and put this in an envelope . This is a very egotistical letter but intersting as it shows that vanity is stronger than fear and that in war as now waged there is little of the element of fear, it is too well organized and too stupendous. Iam very well much love to all

Your devoted son

The war would soon become significantly more "exciting" several days later when a German machine-gunner opened up on Patton and a small band of infantry. "It is time for another Patton to die," he remembered thinking moments before a bullet ripped through his left thigh. (Patton's grandfather, fighting for the Confederacy, was killed in the Civil War.) Patton was evacuated to a hospital and recovered in full. Over twenty years later he would become one of the most formidable—and controversial—generals of World War II.

⁓

In an Impassioned Letter to His Wife, Gertrude, 2nd Lt. Francis M. Tracy Declares That Their Separation Has Only Intensified His Love for Her

"Snookie Darling," 2nd Lt. Francis M. Tracy wrote to his wife, Gertrude, on September 1, 1918, "This is Sunday night, and just outside my billet, some of the dear boys of my platoon are singing love songs about honest to God women, back in the 'land o' dreams.' Small wonder then, that I should think of you. . . ." An orphan

raised by the Catholic Church in upstate New York, Tracy was a law student at the prestigious Georgetown University when he first met Gertrude Colman, who was still a teenager attending "finishing school" in Washington, D.C. When Colman went on an unchaperoned date with Tracy, she was abruptly expelled from school. Colman and Tracy soon fell in love, and they married when she was only eighteen. They were together for almost eleven years before Tracy was shipped off to France, and he frequently wrote to his "sweet, willful, fighting, loving, and beloved angel" while he was serving wih the Ninety-first Division. Recognizing that he had not exactly been a model husband back in the States, Tracy emphasized in his letters home how dearly he missed her and that his love for her had only grown. Tracy sent the following on September 20, 1918:

Dearest Woman,

Finished your letter last evening, but had to cut it short, as we moved into a new area last night. Have a few moments to spare, so am going to resume my chat with you, the beginning and the end of my temporal ambitions. Perhaps you will consider it an extravagant statement, but it's true, just as true as the fact that during this period of separation, there has come a new strong, more spiritual love into my heart for the dear precious woman who has suffered so much, as I am only now beginning to thoroughly understand, at my hands.

For a person who really desires to see the triumphs of his or her better self, and I confess to such desires, on occasions, war is a wonderful aid. You know there is an old saying, which runs like this, "When the devil was sick, the devil a monk would be. But when the devil was well, the devil a monk was he," and I believe that mortals are more or less that way, that fear of what may be awaiting them across the "great divide" makes virtuous men and women, but it isn't fear that I am speaking about now, my girl, but the coming to understand in the midst of almost inconceivable desolation and suffering caused by nothing else but bestial passion, what a mad, devilish thing, uncontrolled passion is, and the indulgence of small whims, is a sad, sad thing as I know now, to my sorrow and everlasting regret. My one prayer is that I may be privileged to have one more opportunity to try to make you happy. I trust it will be granted me.

You and your Daddy, would have had a good laugh, not so sure of you but I am certain that your father would have enjoyed it, the other night, when a wild boar, ran amuk thru our camp. We were peacefully sleeping in our "pup" tents, when Mr. Boar, came into our little tented burg and started down the main street, looking for trouble. He must have been a Hun boar, for he suddenly took it into his head to see how many tents he could tear up before he got plugged, and he surely did cut a swath while he lasted. Fortunately no one was hurt and it is a wonder too, for he had a pair of tusks in his nether jaw, that could have plowed up a ten acre lawn. However the boys soon trimmed his tusks for him, just as they are trimming the fangs of the rest of the Boche.

This is several days later my dear, the uncertainties and the unlooked for, in war, having compelled me to leave off writing you, at a time, when I would have to preferred to keep on. But—"C'est la Guerre." "It is war" as our French brothers put it, and if you were here just now, you would conclude that war is no place for a woman. Have had a number of exciting experiences, of late. The Boche dropped a few shells along our line of march and then an airplane came along and tried to cut a few frills with his machine gun. The delightful feature of the whole proceeding was the fact that not one of the boys was even scratched. Oh we are enjoying our European "vacation" immensely.

Received a letter from you yesterday, enclosing a number of pictures which were taken in Tacoma, and one delightfully sweet one of yourself taken at Salem. You look like a sweet spirit just stepping forth from the dim and distant fifties, or the era of hoops and pantalets. My girl, my girl, how I do miss you. I didn't think it possible for one to be possessed of the longing I have for you. At night I lay awake and think and think of you, the roar of the big guns, giving way before the press of mental pictures of you. I go back and retravel again the entire road that we have known together. Back to the old sweetheart days, over ten years ago, the little girl as I first knew her, comes to me again just as wistfully sweet and ingenuous as she was then, all arrayed in white, or pink or lavendar, from her little pumps to the hat on her dear shock of gold. Do you remember the frocks? I used to wonder then, if the general color scheme prevailed all the way from the outer garments, thru mysteries of lingerie and laces, to the dearest most ravishingly attractive body that ever set a man's blood on fire.

If I had to go over the same road with you again, I am quite sure the way would be easier for you. The mistakes I have made, the heart aches I have caused you stand out like the shell holes that deface much of this country, that once, was so beautiful. I am learning my lesson, honey, and this experience, this absence from you is burning its brand into my soul, as nothing has ever done before. But God knows I deserve all the punishment I am getting, and I accept it as most penance. I know full well, that it is doing me a world of good. May it continue, until I am safe to be turned loose among civilized peoples. Must break off again. Will continue tomorrow. Good night and God bless and preserve you.

—Write—write. Your devoted Hubby

Although the official notification would not arrive until November 6, 2nd Lt. Francis Tracy was killed on September 27, 1918. A colonel in Tracy's regiment reported to Gertrude, who had asked for details about her husband's death, that Tracy had been "struck by a piece of high explosive shell which went over his head, landed about 100 yards past him, exploded, & threw the piece backward—one of those strokes of fate so unaccountable for. He was unconscious and never felt pain or knew what hit him."

Goldie Marcellus Mails Her Husband, Edward, a Love Letter— Which He Promptly Returns with Commentary

It cannot be determined precisely why, when, or how Goldie Marcellus and her husband, Edward, settled on their unique epistolary system. Possibly it was to save paper. Or Edward may simply have been a man of few words. But whatever the reason, after receiving her handwritten expressions of affection from the homefront, Edward, a clerk stationed in German camps overtaken by the Allies, would type succinct, sometimes teasing remarks directly on her letters and then return them to her. The following is just one example. (His words are in bold.)

Dear Husband,

This is a Sat. afternoon and I have the work all done and washing on the line. **Smart girl** I do not know what they would do without me I must say. I am sure very tired. You see Mamma is sick at Proctor Hospital & Dad away and Gladys is not real strong & Hila will not work too hard **No** for fear she might spoil her ~~buty~~ beauty. **Yes, Booty is right.**

Mother is getting along just fine now. **That's good.**

Excuse this writing for my arm is so tired. When I was home I did not know what work was. **I didn't think so.** I received a letter from Pearl. **Why don't she write to me?** She is not well at all poor girl. I think she will never get strong now. She says that her husband comes home at night and does up all of her housework. **Very nice of him.** It is hard on him, but it sure is nice that he is so willing to do it. Your mother goes over and does the washing & ironing and the baking. **and talking** So you see that she must be a very weak woman. **Yes, you are right** One should be so happy if they have good health.

I took your picture to church with me. (You see I just must have you with me that is all.) **That is a catastrophe**

Everyone thought you sure was a fine **fat** looking young man. Our preacher's wife, a most lovely lady, said "your husband sure is nice looking" and the preacher said "not only he, but he is the posseser of a nice looking young wife." I will look more pretty when you get home, **dots gut for I will be more happy.** I want to keep myself looking well for you and you alone. We both must keep our health at any cost, for health and looks go well together. I hope and pray you can come home soon.

Your picture stands right in front of me this very moment. **Why don't you send me some of yours? I have worn yours out already.** I can hardly believe it is you. The only part that looks natural is your eyes. **And what about them?** I just have to kiss that sweet fat face every time I look at your picture. Well I must stop a bragging on you for you might run away with some pretty girl over there. Ha. Ha. **There isn't any.**

It is a setting in for a rainy evening.

Mother is getting along just fine and I think we will bring her from the hospital by next Sunday. I think she is strong now. It seems so lonesome with just women about the home. Just think we have three of the best men on this earth and every one of them is miles from home.

Ed I get all of your letters now, but they all come in bunches about every two weeks. **Glad you get them anyway.**

There is an article in the High School paper about Me. It is on my efficiency in Type. They have sent it to Hazel & Stella or I would clip it out for you. **Can you afford to buy another?**

So some of the men in your Co. go with girls. **No, not girls, fraulines.** Well dear Ed, I expect there is much more of "not being loyal" by the girls over here. **Yes, I know all about them.** I just read in the paper where a returned soldier came back only to find the one he had been true to in love with another man, so he killed her. **Yes, you'll find the members of the A. E. F. are not afraid to kill.** I do not believe in killing but she really got what she deserved I must say. I guess one side is as bad as the other.

Do not even let Herb know this, but I prayed for Gladys C. not to give him up & marry some other man too sickly to fight for his own country. Several weeks ago she came to me on her way home from work, her eyes filled with tears and said "Goldie, oh help me out, you are a married girl and one of my dearest friends." **I really am not surprised at this but do not tell her I said so.** I won her on the point that she did not know men at all, if she would turn untrue to Herb he being such a strong man, would just go all to pieces **Yes, I believe he would** and just throw his life away. Well she went home and thought it over and now "all is well" and Herb is alone shining in Gladys' sky. **Good, you're a missionary too.** Oh, I have read some of Herb's letters and Ed his future entirely rests with that girl. I sure am happy over the outcome.

Oh See it is mail time and I do want to get this in the box by 4:30. So I will have to close. (I could write to you by the hrs.)

Take good care of yourself and I will do the same. So By By my dear hubby, I enclose all love for you

From your loving wife,
Goldie
Ed

Ed Marcellus survived the war and returned home alive and well.

─────────── *Extended Correspondence* ───────────

1st Lt. Edward Lukert Promises His Wife, Mabel, He Has No Interest in Dying for His Country, Shares His Thoughts After Watching Men Get Killed, and, After Being Wounded Himself at Saint-Mihiel, Assures His Wife There Are Young Soldiers in More "Terrible Shape" Than He

"About the war, let me say that it is quite different from the description one reads in the <u>Saturday Evening Post,</u>" explained twenty-five-year-old 1st Lt. Ed Lukert to his wife, Mabel, back in Philadelphia. "In print it reads: 'A shell burst close at hand. A patrol met resistance. A raid was repulsed . . .' etc., etc., Oui, Oui Madame! But what a different story I shall someday tell if called upon." In fact, Lukert was able to tell much of his story to his wife through his correspondence,

which, unlike the letters of the enlisted men who served under him, were more forth-
coming about the graphic details of war. Lukert, as an officer in the Fifth Division
of the Allied Expeditionary Forces, was responsible for censoring the mail, and it
was therefore easier for him to send home observations others could not. On June
18, 1918, Lukert wrote to his wife after having been gassed—but only mildly, and
in training. (Dan Boone, mentioned in several of the letters, was a friend who
served with Lukert in France.)

June 18, 1918

Dearest Girlie:

Do you smell gas also? We were all subjected to several different kinds of it today, with and without masks, and as usual, I cannot rid my clothes of the odor. It is sure awful stuff, honey. Deadly and usually insures a slow horrible death. There is one kind which kills quickly, Chlorine, but I do not prefer any kind or brand myself. I'll use the gas mask if possible, with all its discomforts and smell.

I had to have a photo taken today for another "Officer's Identification Book" which every officer must carry. It provides for a small size bust, without head-gear, so when I receive same, I will send you copies. I believe they take the book when your body is found and send the photo to the War Dept to be placed on the Honor Roll. Won't you be proud to have your Hubby's picture on a nice magazine page, all fringed with black? Ha! There's no danger tho. You'll have me back soon. The war cannot last for-ever, you know, and even if it does, I will return to you safe and sound eventually.

Unlike the majority of other boys, I am not over here to "die" for my country. I came over to live for it, and after I have helped make it possible for others to live in peace and happiness, I'll be back to continue living for you. Then we'll be happier than we would have been had you not sent me over. You know it too! Just like Dan Boone said today, "It's a great privi-lege, gentlemen, truly a great privilege to be able to assist in making the world safe for Democrats!" Hurrah for Bryan, yes, and all the party.

That fellow Boone is a funny duck, you know that tho without my saying so.

Heaps of love for you wifie dear—
Ed

"My health? Great! It never was better and never could be," Lukert once again tried
to assure his wife. "There really isn't any more danger here than at home. There are
no big buildings to fall down on us, neither are there any trolley cars to grind us to
dust. There are lots of shells, true, but really they are harmless. All you do is duck

when one comes anywhere near." Mrs. Lukert didn't believe a word of it; nor, for that matter, did her husband. Only a few days earlier during a routine training exercise, Lukert witnessed an accident that jarred even him.

July 1, 1918

Dearest Girlie:

Our "Big Show" yesterday was quite a success tactically, but had a very bad ending.

At the very beginning of the Artillery Preparation, the Red Boys had a short burst of shrapnel wounding one man a mile back of the lines and killing three horses. The man's wound was not serious, so everyone began boasting that this had been the most successful show yet. Especially so did they boast when our contact Aeroplane seemed to get hit, and in falling, shoot "everything OK" rocket.

The Pilot claimed engine trouble and later told me that he had a strenuous time keeping from falling in the enemy trenches which were at that time under heavy fire from our big guns. Anyway, he pulled out of it, and managed to land in a nearby wheat field. When the attack was finally over, Boone and I walked over to see him make repairs. It was then he told us about the apparent engine trouble and his brave attempt to keep from falling—not that he minded, but "Mac there (observer) wasn't used to it."

The pilot was a fine looking chap, and since I knew "Mac," I lingered quite awhile, and was even invited over for a party at 8 o'clock. It was 3:30, so we turned for home. Near the bridge, we met Watkins, who stood watching the attempt to get the aeroplane to rise. He wagered that "Mac" was sure scared by this time, and we all laughed. An instant later, the machine took the air and went sailing away real low. About a hundred yards further on, the plane seemed to stop suddenly. The tail went up, and the next second it crashed to earth. It no sooner hit the ground before we saw flames shoot up and envelope the entire frame.

Ten minutes later we got a message saying that the only human remains were several blackened bones, including one skull. Think of it! Isn't that dreadful! Since I have been over here I have seen several dead men, but never before have I been so impressed with the uncertainty of life's length here, and the necessity of keeping the lamp filled with oil, at all times.

I suppose I was impressed the more because I was in conversation such a few minutes before with the men themselves. Even to this minute I can see the Pilot's advice as to air service, burning bright in my mind. I mentioned the fact that his must be a great life, so full of exciting incidents. He laughed and said "You too? They all get that way when they see us tearing around overhead, but it's not so wonderful after all—after you're in it." Here he laughed again and continued. "I've been in it some time now, and

of course, since I'm in I've got to see it thru." And he did, poor chap. He
saw it thru some ten minutes later.

> With love in heaps
> From your hubby,
> Ed
> X X X X

*Lukert often became philosophical in his letters, and touched occasionally on matters
of faith and justice. On July 18 he wrote with extraordinary impartiality: "The
War must end soon, so pray real hard, dearest, for a speedy and just peace, irrespec-
tive of which side it is. Do not pray that we win the war, neither pray that my life be
spared. Our enemy prays likewise, you see, and likewise his wife prays that his life
be spared. . . . Some of us say we know God is with us, but who knows? The Germans claim the same thing. Pray God to have mercy upon us and grant us peace."
Several weeks later Lukert watched a battle being fought in a distant valley, which
prompted the following:*

> August 19, 1918

Dearest Wife:

Last night there was a terrible bombardment downstairs, which might
have been a raid or a small attack. I could see the flash of German guns all
along the line from here, but I could only hear our own. It surely was
a pretty sight. What impressed me most, as I looked down upon them, was
the insignificance of man and all his terrible weapons of war. They looked
like toys, down there, and I am no where near as high as Heaven. Wonder
what we poor creatures and our murderous guns look like from up there?

We are a poor people, know it? It makes me feel sorry for everybody,
but "we two," that they must settle differences by going to war. Why in
the dickens should we have to kill each other to settle a matter of opinion
or a matter of liberty or rights? We should have these things, and when
they are denied, it should only be necessary to call attention to the matter
of injustice to have it rectified. Don't you think so?

Sometime ago I told you about capturing a Hun. Remember? Well, I'm
mailing you his cap today, after having had it washed and cleaned up a bit.

> Heaps of love xxxxx
> Your Hubby,
> Ed

*On Friday September 13, 1918—"the most luckless of unlucky days"—a twisted
shard of metal slammed deep into Lukert's right thigh after a shell exploded during
the offensive at Saint-Mihiel. "This morning," he wrote from the hospital, "I woke
up to the fact that I occupy bed 13 in Ward 13, and am attended by a Safety Valve of*

a nurse who wears the number 13 on her tunic. Can you beat it?" In fact, Lukert considered himself extremely lucky. Many around him—some of them close friends—were killed. Those who survived Saint-Mihiel were still fighting, and Lukert, racked with guilt, felt he should be with his men.

October 13, 1918

Dearheart:

Here I am, still lounging around at the Hospital when I should be with the boys at Verdun. I'm beginning to feel as if I were "beating" something, especially so, since my wound has entirely healed up and I am once more able to walk without a rheumatic limp. Of course, it is still a bit tender, but I cannot see why I should stay here longer, unless it's because I complained the other day of sharp pains near my knee. Now I suppose, they'll attribute this to the tiny piece of metal left in me which they did not get during my last operation. They'll probably want to take another X-ray—hope not. It hasn't bothered me very much since tho, and I'm going to insist that it will be all right if left alone. That's what the Chief Surgeon told me after the last attempt.

You know, dear, some of the boys here are in terrible shape. I feel awfully sorry for them. Yesterday I went thru several wards to see if there was anyone there I knew. Several boys I saw had lost both legs, others had all sorts of compound fractures which caused them to be strapped down, while others had shrapnel wounds as big as a dinner plate. Fragments of shell do make horrid wounds. Bullets are not bad, clean and small, but chunks of iron from high explosives are dreadful. I am very, very fortunate to have escaped so lightly from such a hole as I found myself in that Friday night. At one time, I gave up all prospects of coming back. But I made the mistake of figuring them as courageous fighters as my own men.

All afternoon we had been subjected to heavy artillery fire, while in the open digging trenches, and the knowledge of my tremendous losses in killed and wounded had the effect of shattering my nerves a bit. Then the wounded—they worried me too. I had them carried into a shelter where a first aid dressing could be applied. Some were bleeding to death, others were in terrible pain and groaning pitifully. At intervals, I would go in to cheer them up, and lie to keep their spirits up. I told them we would soon get reinforcements and then I could send them back. We had litters enough I suppose, for we captured quite a few in a German Ambulance, the day before, but I couldn't spare the men. I had orders to hold that woods, and we held, while my strength was reduced from about a hundred and fifty to thirty in less than twenty-four hours.

All these things—wide-eyed dead men gazing at you with a cold stare, wounded men trying to suppress groans, the smell of sulfur and the sickening stench of blood in the shelter almost made me wish they would close on us and capture what few remained after the rush. But the men did act wonderfully. They never gave a single thought to retire, even when they knew the Huns outnumbered us frightfully, and had us penned in on three sides. I just gave one order when they offered a reasonably good target: "Fire at will—retire to edge of woods when they reach that abandoned field piece!" And we did give them H___. But the Huns were afraid to rush us. They dropped to the ground on the open side behind a small hill and from there opened up with their machine guns, waiting for the other Huns to get behind us in the woods. At that time I had no idea we'd ever get away, but later I picked up more hope, when I saw how afraid they really were.

"C" Company on my right, I hadn't heard from, but I supposed they were almost wiped out. Early in the day I had sent them a reinforcing platoon of 30 men too!

But well, we got out, as you know when we got the order. But I hated to obey it. "Abandon dead and wounded. Withdraw to right rear and fight your way back. Support covers you in rear on crest of four-five." Well, we picked out the wounded I thought might live, and we carried them back, or rather dragged them. Those I thought would die anyhow, we left where they were, and the others we piled in a shelter and closed the sand bag door.

Most of them survived and were sent for at dawn the next morning in the wake of our relief's attack.

Other outfits had just as hard a time. I saw men who had been only slightly wounded dead after two days' exposure to the cold and mud. They were further to the rear too, where the stretcher bearers could reach them; but in such odd corners they were never found in time. Just think of their suffering. Isn't it dreadful? Considering all these things I suppose the boys here are lucky at that, but still I feel sorry at their suffering.

War is terrible, but with all we're glad we're here trying to stop it. After all, it is really the wives and mothers etc. of those boys with the glassy eyes who do the real suffering. They are thru suffering. They are laid away in countless graves but a telegram is dispatched to the "nearest kin," who lives to remember and mourn and grieve.—It is not we who pay the price.

And then, the mourners. I could write pages on my own ideas in the matter, and I dare say I know of others who agree with me, but, well . . . .

With heaps of love & xxx
Your loving Hubby
Ed

It was the grimmest of roll calls. Writing again to his wife from his hospital bed, Luk-ert began to reflect on the friends and fellow officers he had lost in the war. (Lukert him-

self would recover and return home in 1919.) "These men I saw myself and know were casualties. Lt. Gamble, killed. Lt. Airy killed by a shell. Lt. Horton, who used to live at the Dyer House in Chickamauga Park, killed by shell fire. His clothing was blown off his body, and his body was minus all limbs, but right arm. Lt. Jones, B Company (the funny fellow you liked to hear talk) shot thru the head by a machine gun. Lt. Boatwright, same. Lt. Adams killed by a bayonet thru the neck." Later, Luk-ert thought back on the evening before the men left the States. "What gets me," he noted gravely, "is to think of that last night at Camp Merritt, and the hopes of everyone pres-ent to return. Remember the party? Reeves, Newphur, Harting and their better selves? Mrs. Newphur and Harting are widows now. Pretty sad I should say. But that's war I guess."

A Soldier Sends a Dramatic "Yarn" to His Friend Elmer J. Sutters About the Meuse-Argonne Battle—the Final, Major Clash of the First World War

Almost one-third of the Americans killed in the war lost their lives during the Meuse (River)-Argonne (Forest) campaign, which was in fact three successive strikes begin-ning on September 26, 1918, against entrenched German troops. The densely wooded, rolling terrain of northeastern France favored the Germans, who had been fortifying their lines since they captured the region four years earlier. Virtually none of the U.S. soldiers involved in the first wave of the attack had ever been in battle before. But with support from the French, the troops made slow but steady progress against fierce resistance. As the second phase commenced in early October, two battalions of Americans were pinned down in a ravine for five hellish days. When the Germans suggested they surrender, the Americans yelled back certain expletives that, even untranslated, could be easily understood to mean "NO." Reinforcements were rushed in, and the troops were saved. The third assault, which began on November 1, bat-tered the Germans into a full surrender a week and a half later. The Meuse-Argonne offensive lasted forty-seven days and involved 1.2 million Americans. One of these soldiers vividly described, in a quirky and almost whimsical style, the decisive cam-paign to Elmer J. Sutters, an old friend back in the States. (The soldier, whose full name cannot be determined, sent the letter after the war, when censorship was lifted.)

Cote D'Or France

Dear Old Bunkie,

Now don't go into epileptic fits or something like that when you read this letter, that is because I sent one to you as I know I haven't written you a letter for some time. Too busy with Uncle Sam's affairs just now and am working to beat hell.

I guess you would like to know of a few of my experiences over here while the scrimmage was on so I'll give you a few little yarns.

We were in the line up at Thiacourt (St. Michel Sector) at first and although we did no actual fighting as we were in reserve at first and then in support, we got a lot of strafing from Jerry in the nature of Artillery fire and Air raids.

But in the Argonne Forest was where we got in it in earnest and even if I do say it myself, the good old Lightning (78th) Division will go down in history as second to none for the work they did there.

It was here, old man, that I got my first Hun with the bayonet. That was on the day prior to taking Grandpre and we had just broke through the enemy first line defenses when this happened.

We were pressing through a thicket when this big plug-ugly Hun suddenly loomed up in front of me and made a one-armed stab at me with his bayonet. You can make a hell of a long reach this way, but it's a rather awkward thrust as the bayonet makes the rifle heavy at the muzzle when you've got hold of your rifle at the small of the stock like this guy had. A homelier guy I never saw before in all my life and he'd make two in size compared to Dad and you know what a big man my old Dad is.

Well you can imagine that this bud did not catch me unawares.

I was ready for him. I thought I was going to have a pretty stiff one-sided fight on my hands, with the odds in his favor, but he was a cinch. Before I even realized it myself I parried off his blow and had him through his throat. It was my first hand to hand fight.

It was all over in a second, that is it for Jerry. He never even made a shriek. He went down like a log.

It was hand to hand all the way through that section of the woods as it was considered a vulnerable point, but we finally cleared them out and opened up the way for an attack on Grandpre itself.

The 311th Infantry supported by the 310th stormed the neighboring heights to the north of Grandpre making the town intenable and enabled the 312th and the 309th Infantry regiments to make a dash for the citadel.

We took it, but at heavy cost. I lost a buddie in that last charge. If short five or ten yard dashes can be called a charge and I certainly didn't have much love for the Boches after he went west. We can't mention any names of boys who were killed in our letters so I'll have to postpone it until I get home but he came from New Hampshire and a whiter fellow never lived. He was the only child too, old chap and his parents certainly have my sympathy.

Although I don't know his people I wrote a letter to them trying to make it as soft as I could. Well, he gave his all to the cause and you can't expect a fellow to do more. If a fellow goes down, its up to the next one to carry on and make them pay dearly for every life taken. You know what I mean.

I know that the first thing you would ask me when you see me again for the first if I was afraid. Now I am not going to stick my chest out and exclaim "Like hell I was" or anything of the sort. I sure was afraid, and you and any other chap would be too, but what I was afraid of most was that I would be yellow.

If a fellow gets a yellow streak and backs down the other boys won't have anything to do with him and that was what I was afraid of the most, of getting a yellow streak.

But I didn't. I was as plucky as any other doughboy and carried on all the way through and although I didn't get as much as a scratch I had many a close call. Enough of them to make a fellow's hair turn white. I crouched for three hours one night up to my waist in water in a shell hole waiting for our barrage to lift.

The water was like ice and there four or five dead Huns floating around in it too. Not very pleasant, eh?

While sneaking about the ruins of Grandpre "Mopping Up" we came across a Prussian Chap in a ruined building with a rifle. He was a sniper, alive and the reason he was still there was because he could not get out although the opening was big enough for him to crawl through. During the bombardment the roof of the building had fell through in such a way as to pin him there by the feet and although he was practically uninjured he could not get himself free. I'll explain better when I see you, as I can tell it better than I can write it. He begged us to help him and although we had been cautioned against treatury one of the fellows who was with me put down his rifle and started to crawl through to free him. The moment he got his head and shoulders through the hole which had been smashed by a shell, by the way, this Hun hauls off and lets him have a charge right square in the face.

Poor Dan never knew what happened. His face was unrecognizable. We didn't do a thing but riddle that hole, we were that furious, and we didn't stop shooting until our magazines were empty.

That Hun was the dirtiest skunk that ever lived, but even now I've got an idea that he thought Dan was going to do for him. Dan was some husky boy and boasted of being a foot-ball player somewhere out in Tennessee where he came from. I've mentioned his name as Dan but that is not his name at all. I've just got it down here so I can write my story out better.

Up near Brickemay we ran into another pretty stiff proposition. We had to fight through the woods that seemed to be full of machine gun nests. We had just cleared out one of them with hand grenades and while we were sneaking up a rather steep hill, thickly wooded, we saw these Huns suddenly appear and run about a dozen paces and disappear down into a clearly camouflaged dug-out.

The Yanks were pressing the Huns hard, they were some of the Famous Prussian Guard too, and after these three birds had gone down into their hole we sneaked right up. There were three of us together, all Buck Privates. I took a hand grenade out of my bag, pulled out the retaining pin and heaved it down into the dug-out. That's the only and safest way of getting a Hun out of a dug-out. There was a helluva an explosion in about six seconds. I threw two more down to join the first and keep it company. Well after the big noise had stopped down there we crept down to investigate.

There was only one room down there, a big concrete affair and only one entrance, the one we came down, and that room was a mess. There were fifteen dead Huns down there and the walls, floor and ceiling were splashed with red, so you can see what damage a hand grenade can do. I don't know whether my grenades killed them all, we didn't have time to accertain, as we had to hurry right out again, but I know I got the three we saw beating it down there.

I was also with a detachment of men who took a dozen prisoners out of a dug-out and the worst of the whole thing was that they were only mere kids.

Just think of it old man. Mere kids, that is the most of them and they all expected to be killed immediately.

They were all scared stiff. We bagged the lot and sent them to the man under guard.

Well I was there to the finish old man and we had just mashed Fritz's last resistance up near Sedan when we were relieved by a French Division who captured Sedan next day.

We had opened the way for the French to take Sedan and although we did not actually take the city, we can claim credit for making it a quick sure thing.

We were near Brickemay again on our way back out of the lines when I and another chap, Louis Becker, were ordered to proceed by the narrow-gage railroad to Grandpre and report to the Division Casual Detachment. When we got there I was attached to the Quatermasters' office as orderly and Becker was installed in the Q.M. Warehouse at the railroad.

Fritz pulled off a peach of an air raid that night, and although there was danger for everyone it certainly looked funny to see these S.O.S. chaps step about while the music was in progress.

It was about 7:30 pm and quiet, yes very dark outside when the thing started and he came back again and again at regular intervals of ten minutes and bombed hell out of everything in sight, but what he really wanted to get and that was our Supply and Ammunition Depots. Anyhow we were all sitting in the office and I was telling them of some of my experiences when the thing started.

Fritz dropped one of this famous "Benzine Cans" somewhere in the vicinity with the usual salvo.

Emediately there was a wild stampede in the office to get out. They all piled out into the road and beat it hellbent for election up the road. Now there is only one sane thing to do and I did it. Nothing heroic about it old man, just common sense and it wasn't the first time I did it either, even though my heart was trying to pound a hole through my ribs at the time. I went outside and walked out on the railroad and lay down flat in a shallow trench I had stumbled upon between to sleepers along the tracks and I stayed there all night too. It was an organized raid, or rather a general raid and I saw the flashes from the exploding bomb all around me all night.

These crazy stiffs in the Q.M. office did nothing but run up and down the road and railroad all night trying to find a dug-out to crawl into when you couldn't even see your hand if you held it six inches away from your nose, it was so dark. I couldn't see the boobs, but I could hear them all night, they made such a racket shouting to one another and running about like hens with their heads chopped. It wasn't their fault that none of them got hit that night as he came mighty close at times. He did get some up in the town, six killed and twenty-two including a major wounded out of the 6th Division.

He came so close that one bomb struck right near a small wooden shack where the Engineers use to store tools and blew that thing to hallaballoo.

That shed stood only about 100 or 150 yards from where I was laying, a safe place but rather uncomfortable as I was laying on a lot of broken stone, and a big piece of that shed came down ker-smak only six feet from where I was.

Oh boy! I felt like getting up then and scooting for another place but I didn't. That thing couldn't do anymore damage after landing once so I stayed where I was and it was a good thing I did.

The next instant another landed right on the railroad and exploded with terrific force.

You see it landed right on the railroad, a good hard resisting substance, and that was what made it so loud.

This one burst about 500 yards away from me, but those things can kill at 1,000 yards and the concussion lifted me up out of this trench between the rails, about a foot or so in the air and I came down again ker-flump. It wasn't a pleasant sensation, but nothing hit me and that was better than anything. I got a good thump though. The concussion of the bomb hitting and exploding on a concrete like road bed was what lifted me off the ground.

At 500 yards too. You can imagine the awful kick to one of these "benzine cans" that Jerry sprinkles around on Supply and Ammunition Dumps and Depots.

Well I guess this will be all for just now so with best regards and good wishes to you, Elmer, Mother Sutters, Pop, Mutt, and all the kyoodles. I close.

Your Old Friend and Comrade in Mischief
Dickwitch

P.S. Say you old slab of a lop-sided tin-eared Jackass, what's wrong with you anyhow. Got writer's cramp or what? Pick up a pen for the Love of Pete and write to your old buddie in France.   Dick

~⌒⌒

After Peace Is Declared, Lt. Lewis Plush Reflects in a Letter to His Parents on the Haunting Images of War He Will Never Forget

At 11:00 A.M. on November 11, 1918, "the war to end all wars" was finally over. Elation surged like an electric current through the Allied armies and nations. "No doubt the people in the States went wild over the signing of the armistice," Ira Schubert wrote from France to his sweetheart back in Chicago, "But you can't imagine the feelings of the boys who went through the hardships one encounters in a war-swept country. The only way they could celebrate the victory was to pat each other on the back and thank Almighty God that they survived the greatest ordeal man ever went through." The "ordeal," in fact, was beyond comprehension. Tens of millions of men, women, and children had been killed, and famine and disease were rampant. (American deaths in the war numbered approximately 116,000—53,000 from combat, 63,000 from illness and injury.) For twenty-six-year-old Lt. Lewis Plush, like so many millions of others, the nightmare of what had been endured and witnessed would be forever seared in memory. Writing home to his parents in Pomona, Cali-

fornia, Plush—a recipient of the Distinguished Service Cross for his heroism as a combat pilot—shared his somber postwar sentiments.

Aboard the S.S. <u>Regina</u>

Dear Father and Mother,

Now that it is all over, what is there to look back upon? The fifteen months in France have been like a book with strange chapters, a book that one reads and casts aside as impossible, but a book that leaves a lasting grip on the imagination.

I used to watch the small planes as they manoeuvered in the air and felt that I presumed too much when I hoped to fly one myself. Flying became a reality when I learned to fly a clumsy and safe Caudron. After that came the Nieuport school with its three types of training planes, the 23-meter double control, the 18-meter solo, and finally the 16-meter scout plane. And then the work in acrobatics, formation flying, combat practice, and a month's course in aerial gunnery.

"Training completed and ready for active duty at the front" sounded like a voice in a dream. A few days later I was at the front.

I fly again my first flight over the lines when everything was new, mysterious, and awful. The imprint of that picture will never fade, and I will always see a picture, not of war and destruction but of beauty and peace. There below, far below, is picture after picture slowly passing by, set in thick frames of clouds, colors, and shadows, and white dazzling light. There on my right is Metz, and off to the left lays Nancy, like a jewel set in dark green. One is a German city, the other French. Can it be that the men who inhabit each are bitter enemies and fight to kill?

I was soon to discover that this peace was only the calm before the storm. And when the storm did break in sudden fury on the morning of Sept. 12 , I saw my picture of peace shattered and torn.

I live again that eventful day. It is before dawn and the guns pound and hammer the enemy. The whole skyline of the north is luminated by continuous flashes. Now it is dawn and we leave the ground to play our small part in a mighty struggle. Low clouds and a light rain forces low flying, so from our altitude we see a great army in action.

I see again great tanks waddling and lumbering their way toward Montsec with khaki-clad troops hanging thick on their backs and following in the rear. The roads are jammed with troops, pursuer and pursued. Scattered troops run into woods and out as the whole region is spotted with bursting shells. A tank is on its side here, a shattered truck there, horses running madly in their blind flight. The enemy are in absolute confusion by the rapid advance of our own troops. The fury of the storm did not last long but the story of the St. Mihiel offensive will never be erased.

I see and live again the long weeks of struggle in the Argonne region, where dodging "archies" became a routine duty, bombing raids a daily occurrence, and strafing enemy troops a dangerous but ordinary work.

I can hear the machine guns rattling from the ground as they desperately try to rake us from the air as we swoop down and pour deadly streams of lead into masses of troops. A single bullet in the motor, a pierced gas tank and a burst of flame, a broken wire or a broken feed line and the game is over—lost.

I can hear the archies as they burst uncomfortably close. I can feel the plane as a bursting shell upsets it and starts it spinning, but a quick movement of the controls rights it and on I fly. A burst of black smoke on my right, flying splinters, crumpled wings. The archies have scored another victory—another dear friend gone west.

Over and over I live a terrible moment. Glancing quickly behind I see the sinister silhouette of two Hun planes diving directly at me from above. I am alone and escape seems impossible. One is now almost on top of me and as I make a quick turn he fires at close range. I see again the streaks of fire. Phosphorus fumes of the incendiary bullets fill the cockpit full of that sickening odor and with a damaged motor I fight the fight over again for my life.

I fly again with great formations of bombers in their daylight raids and take my place above with the other scout planes as we sweep the sky for the enemy. The enemy appears and puts up a stubborn fight. One, two, perhaps more, flaming planes crash to the ground, friend and foe, and the bombers return, their mission accomplished.

"One of our planes did not return," says the official report of the day and we each wonder but dare not ask aloud, "Who will be next?"

Oh, fateful vision that now appears of three comrades, three friends that shared the same billet in the home of a French family near the flying field where we worked and played together. I am one of the three. The other two are dead.

How can I ever forget that evening as we sat before the open fireplace. I was writing a letter with a single candle as light. Roth, you were reading aloud from a book of poems, and your sudden burst of enthusiasm would make the flames leap. Kinney, you were making and remaking the fire, playing with the embers with the fire tongs and returning the jumping sparks to their bed.

How little we knew what the morrow would bring. The next evening, Kinney, you and I sat by the fire alone. And a few evenings later, I alone sat by the fire and wondered. The story is always the same: a combat with the enemy and one of our planes did not return.

I walk again over a battle field fresh with its dead and ruin; shattered villages standing as monuments of destruction. Tangled and torn wire litter the barren fields and slopes, barren of life but littered with the waste of war—broken guns, bits of clothing, shells, and the sad remains of life.

There was a war, a great war, and now it is over. Men fought to kill, to maim, to destroy. Some return home, others remain behind forever on the fields of their greatest sacrifice. The rewards of the dead are the lasting honors of martyrs for humanity; the reward of the living is the peaceful conscience of one who plays the game of life and plays it square.

Love,

Lt. Lewis C. Plush

~⌒~

American Red Cross Nurse Maude B. Fisher Writes to the Mother of a Young Soldier About Her Son's Tragic Fate After the War

Over 25,000 American women volunteered to support U.S. troops abroad during the war, the majority of whom served in the Red Cross and the U.S. Army and Navy Nurse Corps. Some were killed and wounded in air raids and from artillery fire, and hundreds died from a particularly virulent strain of influenza they caught primarily from infected soldiers. Nurses not only tended to wounds and helped patients with their rehabilitation, they offered emotional comfort to men who were often homesick and still shaken by the horrors they had experienced. One of the most valuable services they performed was writing letters for men who were too injured or too ill to do so themselves. Maude Fisher, an American Red Cross nurse, cared for a young soldier named Richard Hogan hospitalized with influenza just days after the armistice was declared. Within two weeks of being admitted, Hogan, who had survived the war unscathed, was dead. Recognizing that his mother would receive only a terse notification from the government about her son's death, Fisher decided to send Mrs. Hogan a more personal letter of sympathy about the boy she had come to know.

November 29th, 1918.

My dear Mrs. Hogan:

If I could talk to you I could tell you so much better about your son's last sickness, and all the little things that mean so much to a mother far away from her boy.

Your son was brought to this hospital on the 13th of November very sick with what they called Influenza. This soon developed into Pneumonia. He was brave and cheerful though, and made a good fight with the disease. Several days he seemed much better, and seemed to enjoy some fruit that I brought him. He did not want you to worry about his being sick, but I told him I thought we ought to let you know, and he said all right.

He became very weak towards the last of his sickness and slept all the time. One day while I was visiting some of the other patients he woke up and seeing me with my hat on asked the orderly if I was his sister come to see him. He was always good and patient and the nurses loved him. Everything was done to make him comfortable and I think he suffered very little, if any pain.

He laughed and talked to the people around him as long as he was able. They wanted to move him to another bed after he became real sick and moved the new bed up close to his, but he shook his head, that he didn't want to move. The orderly, a fine fellow, urged him. "Come on, Hogan," he said, "Move to this new bed. It's lots better than the one you're in." But Hogan shook his head still.

"No", he said, "No, I'll stay where I am. If that bed was better than mine, you'd 'a' had it long ago."

The last time I saw him I carried him a cup of hot soup, but he was too weak to do anything but taste it, and went back to sleep.

The Chaplain saw him several times and had just left him when he breathed his last on November 25th, at 2:30 in the afternoon.

He was laid to rest in the little cemetery of Commercy, and sleeps under a simple white wooden cross among his comrades who, like him, have died for their country. His grave number is 22, plot 1. His aluminum identification tag is on the cross, and a similar one is around his neck, both bearing his serial number, 2793346.

The plot of the grave in the cemetery where your son is buried was given to the Army for our boys and the people of Commercy will always tend it with loving hands and keep it fresh and clean. I enclose here a few leaves from the grass that grows near in a pretty meadow.

A big hill overshadows the place and the sun was setting behind it just as the Chaplain said the last prayer over your boy.

He prayed that the people at home might have great strength now for the battle that is before them, and we do ask that for you now.

The country will always honor your boy, because he gave his life for it, and it will also love and honor you for the gift of your boy, but be assured, that the sacrifice is not in vain, and the world is better today for it.

From the whole hospital force, accept deepest sympathy and from myself, tenderest love in your hour of sorrow.

Sincerely,
Maude B. Fisher

Unbeknownst to Maude Fisher, less than a month before Richard's death, Mrs. Hogan lost two of her other children—one son and one daughter—to the influenza epidemic back home in Woburn, Massachusetts.

≈

Col. Robert T. Oliver Shares a Poignant Story with Veteran Frank Cashin About a Memorable Encounter with an Elderly Frenchman in Château-Thierry

Exactly five years to the day after nineteen-year-old Gavrilo Princip assassinated Archduke Franz Ferdinand, the official peace treaty was signed in the Hall of Mirrors at the Versailles Palace. President Woodrow Wilson received a savior's welcome when he strode through the French capital after the war, greeted by adoring Parisians who chanted "Vive l'Amerique!" and showered him with fresh flowers. (Wilson found a less enthusiastic response, however, back in the United States; his proposed League of Nations—an international body that would, among other goals, arbitrate disputes between nations to prevent future wars—was spurned by the U.S. Senate. On October 2, 1919, six weeks before the Senate's first rejection of the League, President Wilson collapsed from a massive stroke, leaving him an invalid for the rest of his presidency.) While traveling through France in the summer of 1919, Robert Oliver, a colonel with the Dental Corps in Washington, D.C., discovered that the French people remained enormously grateful to the young Americans who left their homes and families to fight in a foreign land. After returning to the States, Oliver wrote to a veteran of the Battle of Château-Thierry to pass along a small relic Oliver had been given in France.

January 15, 1920.
Mr. Frank J. Cashin,
Brooklyn, New York.

Dear Sir:

Your letter of the 9th instant informing me that you are the man referred to in my letter of the 7th instant, who served as Corporal, Company "H", 308th Infantry, has been received.

Referring to the incident mentioned in my last letter: I visited the Battle Field of Chateau Thierry (and Belleau Wood) on August 8, 1919, taking lunch there at a small cafe recently opened by an American, about in the center of the town on the south side of the river. After a good luncheon, our party of four officers made an additional round of some of the side streets and buildings of the town to observe the effect on the buildings of shell fire and machine-gun bullets. Naturally, we had quite a following of idle persons and children in our wake, all eager to advance various kinds of information.

Finally, we were approached by a very old man, grizzled and bent with years, supporting himself by a long staff, who stopped in front of me, saluted, then took off his hat, and with tears in his eyes, began his peroration. His speech was not typically French, being a Patois that rendered it hard to follow, but with numerous questioning I elicited the information that he was filled with great gratitude and love toward the American Army for coming to the assistance of his beloved France; that his heart was full of sorrow for the fine fellows who fell and their families at home; that he was an old man and would, therefore, have no chance to let the American people know how much he personally loved them and how deeply he felt for them in their sorrow; but as a mark of his gratitude and deep sentiment, he was bringing to me now, whom he recognized as a Superior Officer, a little token as proof of his deep emotion, which he hoped I would be instrumental in having returned to the family of the brave man who died in battle at Chateau Thierry, where it was lost off of his body.

With that, he dug up the ordinary aluminum tag, bent and soiled by earth, which contained the name F. J. Cashin—Corporal, Company "H", 308th Infantry, and the number 1709293. From his statement, we naturally assumed that the Corporal Cashin, to whom this originally belonged, was killed in the Battle of Chateau Thierry or, perhaps, Belleau Wood; that this tag—the lower one—had become detached in some way and lost either during the battle or incident with the disposition of the wounded or dead man. I accepted the identification tag from the hands of the old man, stating I would surely use every endeavor to send the tag to the family of the man to whom it belonged, with statement of the occurrence, in order that it would be retained as a souvenir of the beloved one who lost his life in the World's War.

Owing to stress of business after my return to this country, I failed to follow up the incident, but finding it in my locker a few weeks ago, I made inquiries from the Record Division of the Adjutant General's Office and ascertained that Corporal Cashin had not been killed in France but was discharged under date of May 9, 1919, and your address was Brooklyn, New York.

It is needless to say that I am pleased to be able to deliver this souvenir into your own hands and not to those of your relatives, as was originally expected, and in doing so, I desire to congratulate you heartily upon your service during the great War, upon your apparent recovery from the wound obtained in the heat of the Veale Sector. I also want to congratulate your dear one, whoever she may be—mother, wife or sister—on being able to hear of this incident through your own words instead of having been obliged to receive knowledge of the dramatic little incident as a posthumous narrative.

With best wishes for your success and happiness in whatever endeavor you engage, I am

Yours very sincerely,
Robert T. Oliver
Colonel, Dental Corps, USA.

World War II

I like to sit up these warm bright nights and watch the white clouds and dark shadows move in the night. That's when I miss you the most darling. On the nights that I sit up alone I can feel you very close to me. Sometimes we sit and talk and sometimes I pretend we are just sitting there with our arms about each other. Best I don't dwell on the subject just now cause I miss you so much right now it seems as though my heart is going to burst.

—*Lt. Jack Emery to his fiancée, Audrey Taylor, July 6, 1944;*
Emery was shot down three days later over Burma.

I had always hoped and wanted to see this part of the world, but not like this. I would much rather be there, and long for the lush mountains of WVA in summer and the snow capped hills in winter where pop let me come along on his hunting trips—a different kind of hunting than this. I don't think that I will ever go hunting again.

—*Cpl. John Hairston, U.S. Marines, to his mother;*
April 1944

I don't know how long you'll be gone—and I don't even know if you'll want me when you come back. I think about you often Nat—and when I heard there was a letter from you I rushed home and devoured it! And after I read it, I said to myself, "I love you, Nat." I want more than anything right now to fall completely in love with you. I hope I'm not pinning you down to anything you don't want to say, Nat—and I hope that either way, everything will turn out for the best.

—*Evelyn Giniger to her sweetheart Nathan Hoffman,*
September 21, 1944

For the past six weeks we've had rumor and counter-rumor of going home. Tonight is New Year's Eve. For most of us, our celebration is in the fact that tomorrow we are scheduled to struggle up that gangplank. This is the last day of the last month of the year, and this should be the last letter that I shall write to you. So long, honey, and pucker up—'cause here I come.

—*Sgt. Nathan Hoffman to his fiancée,*
Evelyn Giniger, December 31, 1945;
they married less than two months later.

Alexander Goode, an American Jew, Writes a Prophetic Letter in 1933 to His Beloved, Theresa Flax, About Adolf Hitler
&
Rabbi Goode, a Month Before His Legendary Act of Heroism, Reminds His Wife, Theresa, How Much He Loves Her

Darting through enfilades of machine-gun fire to carry urgent messages to the front lines, the young dispatch runner frequently came within inches of being killed in the First World War. Twice he was struck by shrapnel, and once he barely survived a lethal gas attack. His name was Adolf Hitler and, after Germany's crushing defeat, he vowed revenge for the draconian sanctions imposed by the Allies at Versailles. (Stripped of over 10 percent of its prewar territory, Germany was required to pay tens of billions in reparations and prohibited from amassing an army of more than 100,000 troops.) Just months after the war Hitler became the chief propagandist for the National Socialist German Workers Party, which blamed all of the nation's woes—particularly soaring inflation and unemployment—on Jews and Marxists. Hitler became president of the organization, better known as the Nazi Party, in 1920. Imprisoned in 1924 for trying to overthrow Germany's new government, the Weimar Republic, Hitler wrote Mein Kampf *(My Struggle), a bestselling anti-Semitic screed that outlined his blueprint for world conquest. After his release he swiftly rose to national prominence by preying on Germans' postwar humiliation, and, on January 30, 1933, he was appointed chancellor of Germany. The United States was in the throes of the Great Depression and paid scant attention to Hitler, who, from across the Atlantic, seemed little more than a megalomaniacal buffoon easily caricatured for his shrill, almost convulsive oratorical style. American Jews, however, were considerably more wary. They knew that German Jews were being harassed and persecuted and that Hitler's rhetoric was becoming increasingly venomous. Alexander Goode, twenty-three years old and studying to be a rabbi, was especially mindful of the ominous developments unfolding thousands of miles away. In a letter to his sweetheart, Theresa Flax, Goode reflected on Hitler's anti-Semitism and its inevitable consequences, both to Jews and Germany itself. The letter, dated April 3, 1933, was written well over eight years before the U.S. went to war against Germany. (The long ellipses are in the original.)*

Cincinnati, Ohio

Darling. . . .

Theresa, dear, why don't you write me sometime more intimately about yourself, what your opinion on things is, what you think about, what your interests are, anything at all so that I can feel I am closer to you when I read your letters, something that will reveal you yourself, in all your charm and sweetness, just say anything at all as long as it concerns you and I will love it. . . . . . .

Recently I have cultivated a taste for poetry, a sure sign that I have become a mere shadow of my stern self and now am as sentimental and love-smitten as all the fellows I used to laugh at in former years. Keats and Shelley are my high-brow recreations now and fine fare they are too. If it were not for my infernal habit of reading so terrifically fast I could no doubt appreciate far more their charm and beauty. It is not at all mushy either. Perhaps when I become more familiar with them I'll try to impart some of the joy I get from reading their poetry to you. The Bible is not so bad for poetry either. Just read the Song of Songs sometime. It is not long, but its beauty is overpowering. They are the lovesongs of the ancient Hebrews and as love poetry they have never been surpassed.

Speaking of the Bible I might mention that by this time in my preparation for the career of a Rabbi I have read most of the Bible, and when I say read I really mean studied carefully, at least three times, so that I am more familiar with this great library of our people than I am with any other volume I have ever studied or read. In it is stored such a mine of information and beauty that I am tempted to think with our ancestors who absolutely believed that everything in the Bible was true and that all things that man can experience under the sun are contained therein. So much is treasured up that I could not begin to describe its contents. It really is heartrending that more people do not seek out its treasures. Perhaps if Hitler read some of its valuable sayings he would be a wiser ruler than he is destined to become.

His policy now means utter ruin, not only to the Jews, but to the whole of Germany itself. He can no more injure the Jews of Germany without seriously depriving the nation itself of all its wealth and position than he can cut off his nose without detriment to his Charlie Chaplinesque physiognomy. I see no hope for our kinsman abroad. Germany's loss, however, is our gain for expulsion of the Jews from Germany means that many of the greatest Jews alive today will emigrate to America and greatly promote the development of Jewish culture in this country. As long as their lives are not injured it will be a gain to American Jewry to have these Jews here. There should be no difficulty in the way of their entering America. This country will be glad to have them.

There I go veering off at a tangent. I am grateful to this letter indeed because it has caught my interest and made me lose sight of my own mood, blue as blue can be, of an hour ago. I think I feel better now. May my slumber be as peaceful as I hope yours will be tonight . . . so with a tender caress . . . . . goodnight.

Alex

What is extraordinary about Goode is not merely the prescience of his observations, but what he, himself, would go on to do in the war. Five years after beginning his rabbinical studies at Hebrew Union College in 1930, Goode and Theresa Flax married. Four years later they had a baby daughter, Rosalie Bea. Fiercely patriotic, Goode had trained as a national guardsman in high school, and, when war was declared in December 1941, he volunteered to serve as a U.S. Army Chaplain. After completing his orientation at Harvard University, Rabbi Goode, age thirty-one, headed overseas. Hours before embarking on the USAT Dorchester *in early January 1943, he dashed off the following message to Theresa, now settled in Washington, D.C., with Rosalie.*

Wednesday

Darling:

Just a hurried line as I rush my packing. I'll be on my way in an hour or two. I got back yesterday afternoon just before the warning. Hard as it was for us to say goodbye in N. Y. at least we could see each other before I left.

Don't worry—I'll be coming back much sooner than you think.

Take care of yourself and the baby—a kiss for each of you. I'll keep thinking of you.

Remember I love you very much.
Alex

It was the last time Theresa Goode ever heard from her husband. At 1 A.M. on February 3, 1943, 100 miles from the coast of Greenland, a German torpedo exploded in the Dorchester's *engine room. The ship immediately rolled to its starboard side and began to sink. Panic ensued. Goode, along with three other chaplains—George Fox (Methodist), John Washington (Catholic), and Clark Poling (Dutch Reformed)—calmed frantic and wounded men and helped them with their life jackets. But only minutes later they made a horrible discovery: there were not enough life preservers for everyone onboard. According to eyewitnesses, the chaplains removed their own preservers and, without hesitation, gave them to the first young soldiers they could find. The last anyone saw of the chaplains was the four of them standing on the* Dorchester'*s hull, arm in arm, praying together as the ship went down.*

~~⌒

Ned Black, Visiting England in 1939, Relates to His Family in the United States How Anxious Londoners Are Bracing for War

Throughout the 1930s, as much of the world suffered through a punishing economic crisis, Adolf Hitler brazenly defied the Treaty of Versailles and trampled on basic human rights in Germany. After becoming chancellor he dissolved all other political parties, purged his enemies, eliminated freedom of speech, and, in 1935, instituted the Nuremberg Racial Laws, which deprived German Jews of citizenship and forbade them from marrying gentiles. On March 7, 1936, Hitler again violated the Versailles treaty by sending troops into the Rhineland—a buffer zone between Germany and France. The French had a substantially larger army but did not retaliate. (Hitler later conceded that "if the French had marched into the Rhineland we would have had to withdraw with our tail between our legs.") The First World War was still fresh in the minds of millions of French men and women who had served or lost loved ones, and few were enthusiastic about the idea of another confrontation with Germany. When Hitler occupied his native land of Austria in March 1938 and invaded Czechoslovakia a year later, Europeans readied themselves for the worst. George Edwin "Ned" Black, a nineteen-year-old American, was traveling with a college friend throughout Britain in the summer of 1939. Black wrote home to his parents in Fargo, North Dakota, describing the preparations being made in London as tensions mounted. (The letter, reprinted in its entirety, is one in a series written over several days.)

On Board R.M.S. "Queen Mary"
August 30, 1939

Dear Family,

But a moment ago I began to write you when the trumpet sounded the muster at the life stations; so I was forced to give up my work and attend. That completed now and being thoroughly safe and saved, I may return to my original plot and write as intended—but starting anew, and I am hoping for it, better.

I have very grave concern for the nervous health of all of you—and particularly Mother. Dad's two cables have had a convincing nature— that worry is an uninvited visitor at our house. I am much afraid that crises have made the position of anyone, near or about London, that of a manifestly and thoroughly dead man—requiring only an early burial.

I need hardly tell you that the continent and Britain are on the threshold of another war. I need not say that all are prepared to fight again in the names of justice and peace, corrupted and perverted—you probably know more of all this than I do.

I knew little of the crisis until my first day in London. I was astonished and astounded that, during these weeks of apparent apathy, the crisis had taken on such grave nature again. Don told me of it my first night in London. The next day we were advised to evacuate! I will tell you more of this when I am returned.

Preparation for defense was being advanced in every quarter of the city. Sandbags (and their number is increasing rapidly) were being placed in important buildings to absorb shock. Blimps are stationed in Green Park, ready to arise at a moment's warning to drop cables to ward off enemy planes. Anti-aircraft guns are stationed at located points—notably Hyde Park. Troops are constantly being called up—and our second night there, several especially-commandeered buses were loaded with men directly in front of our hotel—or better said, our pension. In the streets aluminum paint is daubed upon curbings and pedestrian islands, as traffic precaution in a blackout. Street lights are being dimmed, changed, removed, or screened (even to the traffic lights). Tubes are being prepared to carry women and children to remoter quarters immediately upon the declaration of war. Museums are being closed, art treasures are fast disappearing into safe caverns or cellars.

Naturally, all citizens hold gas masks, have alloted shelters to give them sanctuary, if there is a sanctuary from a posse of shrapnel and bombs. Hundreds—nay thousands—have left the city for the south of Wales: yet there is no panic, no riot, no confusion. All moves on at its usual pace—and, but for a few wild-eyed Americans, calm and quiet confidence and strength is everywhere, in every face, on every lip, in every eye. They seem to feel that this will be a messy little business, but the policing must be done—and after it's all over, there's plenty of soap.

In Canterbury the stained glass was all being removed and the crypt was in a clamor with partitions, packed with sand, appearing as the workmen labored hurriedly. Students at Cambridge are crating old manuscripts. The thirteenth century West Gate at Canterbury has a small garrison of artillery in the north tower. Banks, stores, offices of the government have established rural centers for records and archives. Even the boat on which I travel will be under partial black-out when night comes (the lounge windows by which I sit are blinded) and smoking will not be permitted out of doors.

And in the churches the faithful gather in a silent prayer for peace. But peace is lost. As I stepped aboard the ship this morning from the pier, a man called to his friend from his bicycle, passing by, "I think we shall be over there again," and the friend replied, "Yes, I think we shall." And, lacking the intervention of something greater than we, they will.

They will die, these men. They will believe to the last that they know why they die. But I do not believe they do. I think no one does. . . .

My love to each
Ned

On September 1, 1939, just two days after Black wrote his letter home, Hitler's forces invaded Poland. Britain and France declared war on Germany four weeks later. Ned Black would, himself, be one of the war's casualties; in September 1944 he was shot dead by a sniper at the age of twenty-four while serving in France.

~~~

Lt. Cdr. Paul E. Spangler Gives His Old Friends Back Home an Eyewitness Account of the Bombing of Pearl Harbor on December 7, 1941

A war machine of overwhelming power and ruthlessness, the German Wehrmacht *had crushed one European nation after another—Denmark, Norway, Belgium, the Netherlands, Luxembourg, and France—by June 1940. British Prime Minister Winston Churchill implored President Franklin D. Roosevelt to join the Allied effort to conquer Hitler, but Roosevelt offered only limited funding, weapons, and supplies. The American people were adamantly opposed to going to war, and Roosevelt, months away from an election, assured parents: "I have said this before, but I shall say it again and again and again. Your boys are not going to be sent into any foreign wars." Everything changed on Sunday morning, December 7, 1941. As droves of low-flying planes approached the Pearl Harbor naval base in Hawaii and began spitting out live ammunition, a sailor aboard the battleship USS* Arizona *exclaimed, "This is the best goddam drill the Army Air Force has ever put on!" But it was no drill. Japan, a German ally, had launched a massive surprise attack against the United States. In less than two hours, approximately 350 Japanese warplanes wiped out 10 percent of the entire U.S. Pacific Fleet, including almost all of its battleships, and killed an estimated 2,400 Americans, many of whom were burned to death or drowned when the* Arizona *exploded and sank. (The bodies of over 900 sailors remain entombed there to this day.) Lt. Cdr. Paul E. Spangler, M.D., a surgeon stationed with his family at Pearl Harbor, provided the "Izee Reds," his hunting buddies back in Portland, Oregon, with a firsthand account of the historic event. (Although the letter, which has some minor misprints, was typed ten days after the attack, Spangler decided to wait a year before mailing it due to censorship.)*

December 17, 1941

Izee Reds:

Just a note to tell you hams that you ain't seen no shootin yet. We had a little disturbance out here a week ago Sunday and it was sumpin. I must hasten to tell you that we all survived it without a scratch but I expected to see my maker most any moment that Sunday morning. They are begining to evacuate those who want to go but the family will stay here untill ordered home.

I was resting peacefully in bed when I noticed rather more "practice fire" than I had heard before and then I realized that it was strange to be practicing on Sunday morning. About that time Clara and the kids came home from Church and their curiosity was aroused. Then I got the fatal word to report to the Hospital immediatley. I still was not certain what was going on untill I came off of the hill on my way to the Hospital. Then I saw the smoke from the several fires and saw the antiaircraft shells exploding. I opened her up then and with my Pearl Harbor plates on I had the right of way and I was out there in nothing flat. I arrived just in the lull between waves of attacks about 30 minutes after the first shooting.

There was one big Jap bomber in the sky flying over Hickam Field and Fort Kamahamaha but no one seemed to be doing anything about it. One Jap plane was down in flames at the Hospital and it had fired the Laboratory and one of the quarters which fortunatley had been vacated because they were starting a big new dry dock. I met the Exec. at the door and he told me to go up and take charge of the Surgery. I hurried up to the Surgery and all ready the casualties were pouring in. I did the first operation on a casual in this war if that is anything.

I spent the next 72 hours in four hour shifts at the operating table. During my first shift we were under almost constant bombing and the A-A fire kept up a constant din. They didn't actually hit the hospital but one explosion was so close it blew all the windows out of the work room which was right next to the room I was operating in. I thought my time had come for sure. It was hell for a while. These poor devils brought in all shot up and burned. Many of them hopeless. We gave them plenty of morphine and sent them out in the Wards to die. The others we patched up as best we could. Some we opened their bellies and sewed up perforations in their bowels. It was all a nice party but personally I dont want to see any more like it.

You have read the official accounts given by the Secretary of the Navy. I note relief in the mainland that it was not as bad as feared. If the truth were known I don think they would be so optimistic. Dont quote me, but this is the real dope. We have just three battleships that can fight now. The Arizona and West Virginia are shambles. The Oklahoma is belly up and I doubt she will ever be of further use, if so it will be a full year. The California is sitting on the bottom but is still upright and may be salvaged. The Nevada is aground just across from the Hospital and they hope to float her this week but it will be a year before she can be fighting again. The Utah is a total wreck but she was not used except for training anyway. I think they thought she was a carrier as she was tied up at the carriers berth and they certainly gave her plenty. Four cruisers are badly damaged. Three destroyers are gone. Aircraft lost are certaily over two hundred. The hangers at Hickam Field, the mess hall, post exchange are all shot to hell. Many Flying Fortresses and PBYs destroyed.

If you think these damn slant eyes didnt do a thorough job, guess again. They certainly knew where they could hurt us most and they droped their bombs and torpedos right there. They had all the information. They needed even to the exact locatin of the most vital targets and as to our ship movements and disposition. I cant understand why they soft pedal things back there. I think the people should know the truth. Then they would be roused to the necessary pitch to bring this thing to a successfull conclusion. It is not going to be an easy job in my opinion. I only hope the country will now take off their coats and go to work. We have the ability and skill but it is going to mean many sacrifices for all and a long hard pull. What we need is planes, carriers, and subs. Thousands of them.

Things are pretty calm here now. There are subs in the waters about and we dont know how many we have but it is quite a number. The Enterprise came in yesterday and I hear they think they have sunk about forty since the war started. They have touched none of our carriers. Many reinforcements have come over in the shape of Bombers that can fly over but but the fighters will have to be shipped over and they are short now. The morale here is very good. The jap situation is well handled and the FBI and Naval intelligence has been very active. No sabatage of any moment. We are under strict military law. Blackout every night. Food and gas rationed but adequate suppy of all for the present. I get home every other night now but that is just the last few days. Schools are closed so the kids are home with Clara all day long. No liquor or beer is sold but fortunatley I have an adequate supply for New Years if I live that long.

I must close now and get this on its way. Please do not broadcast the source of this information as I am in a bad spot I guess if I was caught sending this sort of dope. But I thought you all would like to know the real dope and I think you should.

We are all well and I think we have seen our last big engagement here unless Singapore and the Phillapine should fall, then I expect we would be in for some more fun. Just heard today our chief Surgeon is being transferred to Command the Mobile Hospital and I am told unofficially that I am to be made Chief Surgeon. If true I hope a promotion goes with it. I still am in the red and if they evacuate the family my financial trouble will be multiplied.

I hope this note gets through the route I have chosen. It certainly would not by the regular channels. We all send you our love and best wishes. We wish you all a Merry Christmas and A Happy New Year. And Remember Pearl Harbor.

Paul

"Yesterday, December 7, 1941, a date which will live in infamy," thundered President Roosevelt before the U.S. Congress, "the United States of America was suddenly and deliberately attacked by naval and air forces of the Empire of Japan." Roosevelt demanded a state of war be recognized, and the Congress—with only one dissenting voice (Rep. Jeannette Rankin of Montana)—readily agreed. Germany and Italy, Japan's Axis partners, declared war on the United States three days later. Roosevelt immediately dispatched a top-secret cable to Prime Minister Churchill: "The Senate passed the all-out declaration of war eighty-two to nothing, and the House passed it three hundred eighty-eight to one. Today all of us are in the same boat with you and the people of the Empire and it is a ship which will not and cannot be sunk. F. D. R."

~~~

World War I Veteran Dwight Fee Offers Some Fatherly Advice to His Son, William, "Off on the Great Adventure"

Over twenty years of American isolationism had evaporated in an instant. Recruitment centers throughout the country overflowed with young men hellbent on avenging the attack at Pearl Harbor. "I'm going all the way to Tokyo to kill that Jap emperor myself!" boasted one eager recruit to a reporter. William Fee, a high school student from Pittsburgh, Pennsylvania, went to the Selective Service office the day he turned eighteen, and, less than three months later, he was heading off to basic training. His father, Dwight, had served in World War I and fought in the brutal Meuse-Argonne offensive that finally defeated Germany in 1918. Throughout William's childhood, Dwight had instilled in him the values he held dear—duty, honor, and integrity. Flooded with memories of his own wartime departure, Dwight wrote the following letter to his teenage son.

Dear Will:

Well, I figure you're off on the Great Adventure. There will be many disagreeable experiences; soul-shaking experiences; tragic experiences; uplifting experiences. You will see examples of selfishness and selflessness that will stir you tremendously. I have no doubt that you will develop the same respect that I have for the Infantry, the Gol-Darned Infantry, and the same awesome regard for the Medics.

I have no fears for you; you will do well. You have the finest spirit of any one I know of. I wish I could go FOR you, or at least WITH you, but this is your war. Mother and I will pray that God will give you courage for any danger you will have to face; that you will be given steadfastness, and patience, and resolution. We believe that God lays on nobody more than he is able to bear; that through all trials God will provide the qualities needed to meet them. I believe David: The Lord upholdeth all that fall; The cast-down raiseth up again.

Just be your own self: and there are not many people to whom I could say that.

You are serving in a great cause. Because of you and those like you millions of fathers and mothers and children again will be able to think and speak freely without fear; to live their lives without oppression. And we here at home will be spared what most certainly would have been the fate of those people if all of you had not gone out to prevent the domination of the world by Japan and Germany (and Italy)—and don't think for a minute that they wouldn't have dominated it. And they'll try again in another generation if they can. Goodnight, son. Have at em!

As always, Pop.   Keep busy.

Keep bucking.

William Fee would eventually be sent into the European Theater where he saw combat, as a private first class with the Eleventh Armored Division, in the Battle of the Bulge. Fee was seriously wounded in the Rhineland, but recuperated fully and returned home after the war to proud and very relieved parents.

—◡◞—

President Roosevelt Receives an Extraordinary Appeal from a Half-German Immigrant Who Wants to Join the War Effort

His first attempt to register for military service was denied. The twenty-nine-year-old enlistee was disqualified on the grounds that his uncle had served as a corporal in the German Army during World War I. His uncle, in fact, was Adolf Hitler. William Patrick Hitler, who arrived in the United States in March 1939, was born in England in 1911 but moved to Germany in the early 1930s where Uncle Adolf (who also happened to be Chancellor of the Reich) reportedly helped him gain employment in Berlin. Although prone to exaggeration, Hitler claimed his uncle had issued an ultimatum: acquire German citizenship or leave the country. Hitler left, ending up in the United States, where he exploited his famous last name on a paid speaking tour—a "daring exposé," as one advertisement trumpeted it—revealing "the sensational truth about the leaders of Nazi Germany." Over six feet tall with dark, slicked-back hair and a thin mustache (he bore a passing resemblance to Clark Gable), Hitler was a popular draw and was profiled frequently in the media and the New York society pages. After war was declared, Hitler, having already been rejected by the draft board, appealed to President Roosevelt directly in early 1942.

> March 3rd. 1942.
> His Excellency Franklin D. Roosevelt.,
> President of the United States of America.
> The White House.,
> Washington. D.C.

Dear Mr. President:

May I take the liberty of encroaching on your valuable time and that of your staff at the White House? Mindful of the critical days the nation is now passing through, I do so only because the prerogative of your high office alone can decide my difficult and singular situation.

Permit me to outline as briefly as possible the circumstances of my position, the solution of which I feel could so easily be achieved should you feel moved to give your kind intercession and decision.

I am the nephew and only descendant of the ill-famed Chancellor and Leader of Germany who today so despotically seeks to enslave the free and Christian peoples of the globe.

Under your masterful leadership men of all creeds and nationalities are waging desperate war to determine, in the last analysis, whether they shall finally serve and live an ethical society under God or become enslaved by a devilish and pagan regime.

Everybody in the world today must answer to himself which cause they will serve. To free people of deep religious feeling there can be but one answer and one choice, that will sustain them always and to the bitter end.

I am one of many, but I can render service to this great cause and I have a life to give that it may, with the help of all, triumph in the end.

All my relatives and friends soon will be marching for freedom and decency under the Stars and Stripes. For this reason, Mr. President, I am respectfully submitting this petition to you to enquire as to whether I may be allowed to join them in their struggle against tyranny and oppression?

At present this is denied me because when I fled the Reich in 1939 I was a British subject. I came to America with my Irish mother principally to rejoin my relatives here. At the same time I was offered a contract to write and lecture in the United States, the pressure of which did not allow me the time to apply for admission under the quota. I had therefore, to come as a visitor.

My mother, having been rendered stateless by the Austrian authorities, left me with no British kith or kin and all my relatives are Americans.

I have attempted to join the British forces, but my success as a lecturer made me probably one of the best attended political speakers, with police frequently having to control the crowds clamouring for admission in Boston, Chicago and other cities. This elicited from British officials the rather negative invitation to carry on.

The British are an insular people and while they are kind and courteous, it is my impression, rightly or wrongly, that they could not in the long run feel overly cordial or sympathetic towards an individual bearing the name I do. The great expense the English legal procedure demands in changing my name, is only a possible solution not within my financial means at present. At the same time I have not been successful in determining whether the Canadian Army would facilitate my entrance into the armed forces or whether I am acceptable to them. As things are at the present and lacking any official guidance, I find that to attempt to enlist as a nephew of Hitler is something that requires a strange sort of courage that I am unable to muster, bereft as I am of any classification or official support from any quarter.

As to my integrity, Mr. President, I can only say that it is a matter of record and it compares somewhat to the foresighted spirit with which you, by every ingenuity known to statecraft, wrested from the American Congress those weapons which are today the Nation's great defense in this crisis. I can also reflect that in a time of great complacency and ignorance I tried to do those things which as a Christian I knew to be right. As a fugitive from the Gestapo I warned France through the press that Hitler would invade her that year. The people of England I warned by the same means that the so-called "solution" of Munich was a myth that would bring terrible consequences. On my arrival in America I at once informed the press that Hitler would loose his Frankenstein on civilization that year. Although nobody paid any attention to what I said, I continued to lecture and write in America. Now the time for writing and talking has passed and I am mindful only of the great debt my mother and I owe to the United States. More than anything else I would like to see active combat as soon as possible and thereby be accepted by my friends and comrades as one of them in this great struggle for liberty.

Your favorable decision on my appeal alone would ensure that continued benevolent spirit on the part of the American people, which today I feel so much a part of. I most respectfully assure you, Mr. President, that as in the past I would do my utmost in the future to be worthy of the great honour I am seeking through your kind aid, in the sure knowledge that my endeavors on behalf of the great principles of Democracy will at least bear favourable comparison to the activities of many individuals who for so long have been unworthy of the fine privilege of calling themselves Americans. May I therefore venture to hope, Mr. President, that in the turmoil of this vast conflict you will not be moved to reject my appeal for reasons which I am in no way responsible?

For me today there could be no greater honour, Mr. President, to have lived and to have been allowed to serve you, the deliverer of the American people from want, and no greater privelege then to have striven and had a small part in establishing the title you once will bear in posterity as the greatest Emancipator of suffering mankind in political history.

I would be most happy to give any additional information that might be required and I take the liberty of enclosing a circular containing details about myself.

Permit me, Mr. President, to express my heartfelt good wishes for your future health and happiness, coupled with the hope that you may soon lead all men who believe in decency everywhere onward and upward to a glorious victory.

> I am,
> Very respectfully yours,
> Patrick Hitler

The letter was forwarded to FBI director J. Edgar Hoover, who investigated Hitler's past and any involvement in subversive activities. The FBI concluded that his request was sincere, and Adolf Hitler's nephew—with cameras flashing—was inducted into the U.S. Navy in March 1944. Although he was never in combat, Hitler served for two years as a seaman first class. After being honorably discharged in 1946, Hitler faded into obscurity.

Sgt. J. M. Smith, Before Being Forced on the "Bataan Death March," Tells His Wife to Have Faith He Will Return Home Alive
&
Capt. James Sadler, Smith's Brother-in-Law, Adds a Brief Note at the Bottom of the Letter, Sending His Love as Well
&
Lt. Tommie Kennedy, Captured at Corregidor and Imprisoned on a Japanese "Hell Ship," Scribbles Two Short, Last Letters to His Parents

Only hours after the surprise attack on Pearl Harbor, the Japanese struck U.S. forces stationed in the Philippines commanded by Gen. Douglas MacArthur. Few soldiers would find themselves in a more brutal nightmare than the 80,000 mostly American and Filipino troops cornered on the Bataan Peninsula. For four months they battled not only a superior number of Japanese troops, but debilitating diseases like malaria and dysentery, hunger, thirst, sweltering jungle heat, and repulsive sanitary conditions. When defeat seemed imminent in late February 1942, MacArthur (alone) was ordered by President Roosevelt to abandon the peninsula. Vowing defiantly, "I shall return," MacArthur left for Australia. Fighting continued until the Americans and Filipinos were forced to surrender on April 9. By this time the men were so famished, dehydrated, and ill, they were scarcely alive. The worst, however, was yet to come. Despite having access to trucks and transport vehicles, the Japanese ordered the emaciated prisoners to walk sixty-five miles to a railway junction without food, water, or medicine. Many collapsed along the side of the road and were left to die. Japanese soldiers arbitrarily whipped, beheaded, bayoneted, and tortured men as they marched. An estimated 10,000 men, including British and Australian soldiers, perished along the way, and those who survived spent the next three years as prisoners of war. Three brothers—Sgt. J. M. Smith, Capt. Burney Smith, and Sgt. Clark Smith, as well as their brother-in-law Capt. James Sadler—fought at Bataan and were captured. Six weeks before the April 9 surrender, J. M., a father of two little girls (Patricia, who had been born while he was away, and Judy, who was not yet two), wrote to his wife Martha in Clovis, New Mexico, to downplay the severity of their situation and to assure her they would all return home.

Somewhere in Bataan
Feb. 22, 1942

My Sweet,

Well darling life has been good to us and God has surely been with us—in many ways and if we carry on as we have in the past. He will stay in our hearts and by our side as long as there is need of him—So I open my letter asking his blessings for you all—

I can't exactly say it has been easy for us yet it hasn't been too awful bad as yet—I can't realize yet how people can be <u>such fools</u> to cause so much trouble and suffering and heart aches not only for the ones actively engaged, but, also to those left behind—I know you have suffered and have grieved many times since I have left but chin up and look the world in the face for you have 2 of the sweetest things in the world to brighten your life—God bless them. I miss you all so much—but with God's will I will return some day and that in its self is all we could ask of anyone—

The boys here are in high spirit, and there could never be any equal to these fellows, all of them, I mean soldiers here in Bataan—you would never know what it could be like unless you were here—

Jim is my Btry Commander now so I see him every day. Clark is feeling very well, Burney is O.K.—but they said they would sure like to see the Squirts—

Did Judy have a big Xmas? I wanted to be there so much and I wanted her to have a big Xmas and if I ever get home I will sure throw a big party for you all—

Well my sweet you know I miss you very much and I would give anything under the sun to be with you, but, I am not so just have faith in me and in God and I will be home some day—

I could write a lot of nonsense and a lot of foolishness but I know you will read between the lines and see more in spirit than in what I write—

> God Bless you all, and I pray
> that he keeps you well and happy—
> I love you all,
> JM

J. M.'s brother-in-law, James "Buddy" Sadler, was also his commanding officer and therefore responsible for inspecting his mail. Sadler saw J. M.'s letter and penciled a special note to Martha.

Dearest Sis,

I have to censor this so I will add a few lines to send you my deepest love to you and to ask the blessings of our Dear Father in Heaven and the blessings of our Lord Jesus on yourself and the babies. Jake is doing ok. I have his Battery now and so am in constant touch with him and each night I ask God's protection and that it be His will that we both be spared to return to our beloved wives and our other loved ones at home.

It hasn't been too bad so far, and with God's blessing and His help, we will come sailing back someday to you.

I haven't heard from home since the war but my prayers are ever of loved ones at home. I would give a lot to see my newest neice—if she is as cute as Judy she's some baby. Keep in touch with Carmen for news and so good bye dear sister and may the Good Lord above keep and bless you and may he will that this reach you soon

Your own loving Buddy

Martha Smith never heard from her husband or brother again. Burney Smith was also killed. Only Clark Smith, who, with several thousand other men, had escaped to the island of Corregidor (just south of Bataan), survived the war. Living in tunnels on the fortified island, the troops endured an almost month-long bombardment before finally surrendering to the Japanese on May 6, 1942. Twenty-one-year-old Lt. Tommie Kennedy was one of the thousands taken prisoner at Corregidor, and he spent nearly three years as a POW. Fatally malnourished and incarcerated on a Japanese hell ship, Kennedy sensed, by early January 1945, that the end was near. On the back of two family photographs he had saved throughout the war, Kennedy handwrote in tiny letters a farewell message to his parents. He began with a note to whoever found his body.

Notify: C. R. Kennedy, Box 842 Maricopa, California. Death of Son. Lt. Thomas R. Kennedy 0–890346.

Momie & Dad: It is pretty hard to check out this way with out a fighting chance but we can't live forever. I'm not afraid to die, I just hate the thought of not seeing you again. Buy Turkey Ranch with my money and just think of me often while your there. Make liberal donations to both sisters. See that Gary has a new car his first year hi-school.

I am sending Walts medals to his mother. He gave them to me Sept 42 last time I saw him & Bud. They went to Japan. I guess you can tell Patty that fate just didn't want us to be together. Hold a nice service for me in Bksfield & put head stone in new cematary. Take care of my nieces & nephews don't let them ever want anything as I want even warmth or water now.

Loving & waiting for you in the world beon.
Your son,
Lt. Tommie Kennedy

Kennedy lived for a few more days, and, after finding a larger scrap of paper, wrote the following:

Enroute Japan. Jan. 18, 1945

Dearest Momie & Dad,

I am writing this so that you will know exactly what happened and won't be like so many parents. I guess I really made a mistake in not listening to you & coming over here. If I could only have been killed in action, its so useless to die here from Disentry with no medicin. Walt & Bud went to Manchuria Sept '42. We have been since Dec 13 from Manila. Bombed twice from 2 ships, on the 3rd now. Use my money to buy Turkey Ranch so you will always have some place to always go. Also give both sisters liberal amounts & see Gary has Sport model auto his 1st year hi school. Also nieces are always best dressed. Write: Mary Robertson at Houtzdale, Penn. Her son Melville died of disentry on the 17th of Jan. with his head on my shoulder. We were like brothers. He was buried at sea somewhere off the China coast. Tell Patty I'm sorry, guess we just weren't meant to be happy together. I weigh about 90 lbs now so you can see how we are. I will sign off now darlings and please don't greave to much. These are my bars & collar ensigns. The medals are Walts, please see his mom gets them. I'm not afraid to go, and will be waiting for you.

All my Love,
Tommie Kennedy

Kennedy's final letters and medals were smuggled from one POW to another. Each made certain that, before dying, the items were passed to someone else. When the survivors were liberated at war's end, Kennedy's belongings were mailed to his parents in late 1945—well over four years after their teenage son had left for the Pacific.

~

Pvt. Morton D. Elevitch, in Basic Training, Informs His Mother He Is Learning How to Shoot, Beat, Stomp, and Bayonet Another Human Being

At the beginning of World War II, the U.S. Army ranked eighteenth in the world— behind that of such nations as Italy, Portugal, Sweden, and Romania. Millions of young Americans had to be rushed into basic training, where they were drilled, taught, disciplined, tested, and marched to the point of exhaustion. Morton D. Elevitch, a red-headed eighteen-year-old from Duluth, Minnesota, chronicled his wartime life—beginning with his enlistment—in hundreds of letters to his parents. Occasionally bawdy, frequently lighthearted, and always candid, Elevitch related anecdotes about his fellow trainees and the relentless instruction they endured on an almost daily basis. Writing from Fort Benning, Georgia, Pvt. Elevitch sent the fol-

lowing letter to his mother. (His mother's name was Evelyn, not Louisa; he often playfully addressed her with made-up names and salutations such as "Moomu," "Dearmadre," and "'Allo mama," and occasionally signed his letters with aliases or a simple "Yo honey chile.")

Dear Louisa:

For the Nth time, thanks for your package. Please don't send me any more underwear, socks, or candy. The Milk of Magnesia was absolutely unnecessary. I'M HAVING NO MORE BOWEL TROUBLE AND DON'T ANTICIPATE ANY.

This week they are teaching us to kill. Now you probably looked away and shuttered. Well, mom, I don't like the idea, either, but we all know it's for our own good. The most strenuous work we do takes place as we stand in one place—bayonet drill. We lunge about in definite movements and are required to growl, grimace, and look at each other with hate. Five hundred of us dance about, screaming, shouting and snarling.

A rifle seems to weigh a ton more with a bayonet on. Our arms feel as if they're going to drop off as the Lt. holds us in one position and talks! Our bayonets have sheaths on them so that no one has his head cut off. They teach us how to withdraw our bayonets in a certain manner, too, because steel sticks to warm human flesh. (This sounds awful bloodthirsty, but everyone keeps serious minded about it.)

We are learning jiu jitsu holds — and to put it bluntly — plain dirty fighting. This will be invaluable in case anyone ever tries to pick on me. Maybe I shouldn't put this in — in fact I know I shouldn't — but it is going on so — Our instructors emphasize that we should be quick or be dead — always try to kill a man — break his arm first — then clip him under the nose — throat, neck or kidneys to kill him.

I'm afraid I'll never be an expert at this, because I just can't bring myself to go at this in earnest. Surprise is a very important element — I know how to break any hold, grip and throw a man flat on his face — They even teach us how to scientifically stomp on a man. I've left out many gory details.

By the way everything is done in double time this week. We move in place and from place to place on the double — puff puff.

Confidentially, I'm tired.
S'long
Mort

Shipped to Europe, Elevitch and his division joined Gen. George S. Patton's Third Army. On January 27, 1945, during the Battle of Sinz in Germany, Ele-

vitch was struck in the chest by mortar fragments. He survived, but was hospitalized for six months. Elevitch returned to the States by Christmas of 1945.

~~

Pfc. Edgar Shepard Promises the Parents of Pfc. Russell Whittlesey, Who Saved His Life at Guadalcanal, That He Will "Avenge" Russell's Death

Mauled at Pearl Harbor and the Philippines, U.S. troops were out for blood, desperate to retaliate against the Japanese. In April 1942 Col. James Doolittle spearheaded the first air attack on Japan, striking Tokyo itself and other major cities. (Although the bombings were, militarily, a mere pinprick, they burst Japan's aura of invincibility and did wonders for American morale.) Less than three months later, a Japanese armada bore down on Midway Island, a small atoll held by American troops. But due to the work of a brilliant team of cryptanalysts who had broken the Japanese code and deciphered their intentions, U.S. warships were already there—waiting. Initially overpowered by superior strength, the Americans orchestrated one of the most dramatic and ultimately pivotal reversals in the Pacific war, destroying four aircraft carriers and hundreds of planes. Now on the offensive, the U.S. began pounding the Japanese-held island of Guadalcanal for six months from the air, sea, and land beginning in August 1942. Japan suffered its first ground defeat of the war at Guadalcanal with an estimated 24,000 dead. Over 1,700 Americans, mostly marines, were killed in the fighting. One of the casualties was a young marine named Russell Whittlesey. Russell's parents learned the details of their son's death from a close friend of his, Pfc. Edgar Shepard, who was not only there when Russell died, but had Russell to thank for his own survival. Shepard's account, written in September 1943, recalled Russell Whittlesey's extraordinary sacrifice.

Dear Friends:

Through change in address, your letter mailed in February, did not reach me until a few days go. Knowing how you feel, I will give you all the details of Russ's death. Russ and I were attached to each other like no other people could ever be. We lived together several months before seeing action and shared everything from small bits of food to each others personal affairs and feelings. Being scouts, we were alone together a great deal and learned to depend upon each other. I knew his past life like a book, the food he liked best and even his favorite music and songs. We went through several battles together, never leaving each others side.

It all happened one year ago tonight. We had just returned from the raid of Toranboca and set up positions on a barred ridge (later called "Bloody Ridge"). At dusk we were ordered to advance several hundred yards into the jungle and dig in at the edge of a lagoon which the japs were expected to cross to reach Henderson field. All was quiet until about 9:00 o'clock except for the movement of small animals in the lagoon and surrounding jungle, a half moon hung on the c and then we could hear the japs cautiously advancing. They reached the far edge of the lagoon. The word was passed to hold our fire until they started crossing. Then all hell broke loose, the jungle was lit up like a stage, battle cries broke out from both sides above the screams of dying and wounded men. We were outnumbered five to one and were soon hand to hand. After about thirty minutes, I was hit and dropped to the ground. Russ stood over me and fought like a madman. I asked him to leave me and he only said, "go to hell Shep!!"

Things began to quiet down and reorganization began. Russ worked over me about an hour trying to stop the blood flow, tearing his shirt into strips for bandages. His rifle had been shot from his hands and mine had fell into the lagoon and all we had were knives. With Russ's assistance I could walk a bit. My right lung being punctured made it difficult to breathe, the bullet had penetrated both my arms which made them useless. We found ourselves behind the jap lines and we had to go through to get to our own outfit. Moving along a narrow trail, we ran on into a jap patrol, and Russ instead of getting away, chose to die fighting to save my life. He dropped me to the ground and stood with a knife in hand and the three japs charged him with bayonets. With the cool art of a true Marine he used certain tricks (we had often practised together) to kill the first two and the third one stabbed him in the back with a bayonet. He fell and the jap ran. He put a finishing touch on the two japs and lay down beside me. He was hit in the stomach several times of which I was not aware. He said "Well Shep I guess this is where we came in" & smiled, & began to try to hum his favorite tune "I'm getting Tired so I can Sleep." Then he just went to sleep. I put my hand on his heart and started crawling toward the jap lines. By some miracle of God, I reached the hill and a corpsman gave me a shot and I went to sleep.

I'm in training again and in perfect condition. I swear by God to avenge the death of the best pal I ever had before I'm another year older.

Sincerely,
"Shep"

~

Capt. Ed Land, an American Pilot Flying with the Royal Air Force, Expresses to His Brother Frank the Exhilaration—and Risks— of His Job
&
1st Lt. Charles S. "Bubba" Young Chronicles for His Family a Dramatic Bombing Raid on Ploesti, Romania

Well over a year before the United States entered the war, Adolf Hitler was plotting Operation Sea Lion, an invasion of England that, if successful, would mean German domination of virtually all of Western and Central Europe. First, however, Hitler's Luftwaffe would have to destroy the Royal Air Force (RAF) and gain control of the skies over the English Channel. In the summer of 1940 the Battle of Britain was on, and German air power unleashed a furious blitz on both military and civilian targets in England, killing thousands of innocent men, women, and children. Outnumbered by the German warplanes three to one, the RAF nevertheless outmaneuvered and outlasted their enemies through sheer skill and determination. Landing only long enough between missions to resupply fuel and ammunition, the relatively small band of airmen slept little and relied on adrenaline to keep themselves going. The Luftwaffe was unable to neutralize the RAF, and Hitler ordered Operation Sea Lion postponed. "Never in the field of human conflict was so much owed by so many to so few" extolled Prime Minister Winston Churchill of the RAF. Captivated by the gallantry and heroism of the British pilots, many young American men volunteered for the RAF before the U.S. declared war on Germany. Ed Land left his hometown of Houston, Mississippi, for Canada to train with the Royal Canadian Air Force and then headed off to England in November 1941 (a month before Pearl Harbor). Land began flying with the RAF soon after his arrival, and on April 22, 1942, he wrote to his brother about his experiences.

Frank,

I'll have to hurry with this letter for I'm flying again tonight. In 45 minutes I'll be eating and filling myself full of hot tea to last me through the night. Shortly after, I'll be roaring down the runway and climbing slowly into the gathering darkness, those little red lights there on the ground flicking away behind me until they are all at last from sight.

Behind me, and with me, my crew will be going about their duties, all enveloped in the black curtain of the night that is around us, and holding us there in its bosom. All is quiet except for the sweet steady drone of my engines, and the whisper of the radio waves coming through my earphones. Before me—my instruments—my controls—my love—my life.

Behind me—my men—their lives, their all depending on me, the captain of the ship. Ahead of us all what? Only God could say. I know I don't have much longer to live. Don't ask me how I know or can say that. I'm just being fatalistic. I can see it and feel it around and about me. I know down deep within myself that one of these nights I shall go out and not return. My pals, one of these mornings will all be sitting down to breakfast without me. A few empty chairs—someone raising his eyebrows in silent query—someone else nodding in silent confirmation. A moment's reverent silence and quiet; then all will continue as before. "Tough luck, Eddie, see you later." Yes, I know! Because all the time this goes on about me, one day I have a pal—the next day I don't. Through the months they've come and gone. Here today, gone tomorrow. It used to shake me when I lost a friend—but now—well, I suppose one gets hardened to it all and it's just to be expected.

I do know though, that I'm happy with my job. I would not trade it for a war job on the ground at all. I'm fighting in this war the way I want to (in the air). Never shall I the least bit regret the work, the hell, I've gone through to get where I am today. I am today what I've always wanted to be (a pilot). Many thousands of dollars have been spent on me, getting me ready and capable of striking a lick for freedom, and life of a united people. I'm striking that lick, again and again, and all about me my comrades likewise—until the day comes when there's nothing left to blast—nothing left to blow up in smoke and flame; and all is quiet where once was hate and death.

I must be getting along now. Wish I had some plain old Mississippi cornbread to eat instead of what I know I'll get. Haven't seen a piece since I've been in the foreign service. Englishmen have never heard of it.

So, until later,
Your bud,
Ed

Five months later, in late August, Captain Land shot down his first German fighter. In a letter to his family dated September 12, 1942, he reported how close he came to being killed himself:

> *I had one cannon shell burst two feet beneath my seat, it having come through the aircraft and between my navigator's legs before it exploded beneath me. . . . My mid-upper gunner had a thermos of coffee beside him and one slug tore through it. Another cannon shell just missed his head. The entire aircraft was riddled from end to end. . . . We crash landed back here in Eng-*

*land and walked away from the wreck without a scratch on a single one of us.
Miracles do happen.*

*It was Land's last letter; while returning from an attack on Germany a week later
his plane sent out an urgent SOS before plummeting into the ocean just off the coast
of Denmark. Similar to Ed Land, Charles Stenius ("Bubba") Young, from Day-
ton, Texas, enlisted in the Royal Canadian Air Force in the fall of 1941 and went
on to serve with distinction in the ranks of the RAF. (The Army Air Corps initially
rejected Young for being too short.) Having proven himself in combat, Young was
eventually commissioned as a flight officer with the Army Air Corps in March 1943.
On August 1 of that same year the Allies launched a massive but perilous raid on the
heavily defended oil refineries in Ploesti, Romania, the source of half of Germany's
petroleum. The Allies suffered tremendous casualties, losing almost 25 percent of their
men. Lieutenant Young, who was on one of the 178 B-24 bombers that bombarded
Ploesti, wrote to his family about the mission from North Africa.*

Just Outside Bengazi in Libya.

Dear Mom & Dad & All:

This I hope is an uncensored letter which I am sending by Lt. Hap
Kendall. He is going to send you some pictures and this letter if he can
get it through.

Well I will try to tell you everything that I possibly can remember at
this time for he is leaving tomorrow morning.

Went on the raid in the heart of Romania. Just northwest of Bucharest
at the city of Plocsti. We had our squadron Commanding Officer on Board
as command Pilot and Technical observer. Jake Epting Capt. my first pilot
was flying and I was Co-pilot. Before we came to our turning point into
the target which was the Vega-Romano Refinery our left waist gunner was
killed by machine gun fire. I asked Major Dessert to take over as co-pilot
and I went back and took the waist gun. We were down to 50 or 60 feet
above ground and were just coming over a village before Ploesti. The people in their very pretty native costumes (the day being Sunday) were waving and standing in the streets.

Just after we passed over that village I saw an 88mm flak battery consisting of 4 guns. They were pointed at us. Four Germans or Romanians
were handling shells over the revetments and I opened fire on them.
Killed all four of them and blew up something in the battery. Those 4
guns did not fire anymore.

We then were coming into the edge of Ploesti and I saw a 6 gun battery
of 37mm. and 100 yards on a 20mm. battery composed of 8 guns. I shot

approximately 150 rounds into each battery and completely wiped both out. But not before they got one of our wing men. I must have killed 30 or 40 men in the 2 batteries. There was a woman standing by the 20mm. battery and I killed her with a shot in the back. I felt sorry but she should have never been there.

Then into town I go and on every house top and building there were guns. I fired constantly and killing and wrecking as we go. On my left I see a B-24 Liberator go down in flames and I see the battery and I get it. I hear our bombardier say there is the target at 12 O'clock. Then another one of our planes go down. That was Nick Stompolis of Kalamazoo, Michigan. His co-pilot is Ivan Canfield of San Antonio, my very best friend in the 409th. From their bomb bay doors on back he's in flames. He is trying to hold the ship in the air till he gets over the town but can't make it. So seeing that he can't he turns for the biggest building in town and goes head on to make it quick. Which in my estimation was the most heroic move on the raid.

I look up ahead and see black smoke and then back to the left I see our Commanding Officer Lt. Col Baker pull up and straight down he goes. Then there is the target with oil storage tanks blowing up all around us. I machine gun the distillation columns and the boiler house and storage tanks. And we are still being fired on.

I chance a look up there's a bunch of fighters coming in on us besides the fire from the ground we have to contend with them. I looked down and there's a marshalling yard so I open up on an engine and a full train and when my incendiaries hit the tank cars up they go and steam pouring out of the engine and men running everywhere.

We are getting close to the edge of Ploesti and I think now only fighters to bother with but lo and behold. Farm houses and haystacks and trees drop their sides and start firing at us, and I see a Liberator with its wheels down it's Ben W. Willie. The pilot is Hubert H. Womble from Caldwell, Texas. Another swell guy and he lands in a field and the last thing I saw was 6 guys running like mad to escape capture and try to get to Turkey and internement or to Yugoslavia and join the Guerilla Bands or Chetnicks. Dad if you get the chance go to Caldwell and see Mr. H. H. Womble and tell him that his son is pretty positively alive and either a prisoner of war or a guerilla warrior now in Yugoslavia.

Well so much for all that. We turned for home and made it back okay. The mission was 13 hours long and a little over 2400 miles. And the 409th is only a shadow of its former self. We've lost Lt. Pryor and crew from Texarkana, Texas. Lt McPeters and crew. Lt Womble and ship. Lt. Stompolis and crew. And Lt. Wilkinson interned in Turkey. And after yesterday's raid in Germany Lt. Gerons and crew interned in Switzerland.

It's really rough losing all those boys. I did 22 missions with the RAF and they don't count here. I'm going to work hard and when I finish my missions am going to try to get into Headquarters or Operations and advance myself and get higher rank and learn something.

My estimation is that the Ploesti Raid was the roughest mission of the war and should be given more credit than Tokio, Rome, Berlin and all the raids put together. And the Liberators haven't been getting the credit they deserve cause some people in the states think the only 4 engine bomber is a Fortress. The Libs can outfly, carry more bombs faster and over a greater distance than the Forts. And also if the Fortress boys got all the enemy fighters they claim why is it when they go back to the same place they meet the same number the next day.

We cruise 35 miles an hour faster than the Forts and our bomb load is 8,000 pounds and theirs 3,500 pounds. We can carry 4,000 lbs for 2,500 miles while they can carry 3,800 for 1,200. So there.

All first pilots probably will be awarded the silver star for the raid and all the rest of the crews the Distinguished Flying Cross probably.

If I ever have to go on another mission like that I think I will balk.

Tell everyone including my two sisters I send my very best of love to all. And to you Mom and Dad if I don't come back from this war you can say I was a fighting fool. But I'm coming back.

Well, that's a little story of my life away from home. I broke off all marriage ideas so you don't have to worry about that.

> I'll close now.
> Love to you all.
> Bub

Less than a year later, Young was killed in England during a routine training flight.

⁓

Maxine Meyers, Working as a Welder, Describes to Her Husband, Nove, a Historic Explosion Near Their Home in California

By the time she was fifteen, Maxine "Max" Richards had lost both of her parents and was raising her three younger siblings by herself. Six years later Max met the love of her life, a handsome twenty-five-year-old named Nove Meyers. The two courted for six months and then married the day before he was inducted into the army. During the three years Nove was off fighting in the Pacific, the couple exchanged thou-

sands of letters. Meyers updated her husband on news from the homefront and frequently described the various characters she met on the graveyard shift as a welder at the Henry J. Kaiser Shipyard. Millions of women like Meyers had, almost overnight, become an integral part of the war effort, churning out a seemingly infinite supply of tanks, ships, guns, planes, grenades, and other weapons. No nation in the history of the world overhauled its manufacturing as dramatically as the United States did in the early 1940s, and much of the credit was due to the women—white and black—who labored backbreaking hours in hot, dirty, and sometimes hazardous factory jobs. With millions of men off to war and millions of women now in the workforce, social dynamics shifted dramatically in the U.S. "The yard has been drained of its younger men," Meyers observed in one letter to her husband,

> *No one is left except the middle-aged, the 4-F's, and the very old. I have failed to see any men who, in my opinion, could be classified as "attractive". But the women, so it seems, have gone "nuts" and "gush" over anything that can be identified as a man. Not all the women have gone nuts, but the majority of them have, at least around these parts. Consequently, the men have become egotistical and bold. As for yours truly, all men are just fellow workers or shipyard wolves that I want no part of, and my attitude towards them reflects the way that I feel.*

In another letter to her husband, Meyers recorded one of the worst war-related accidents on American soil—the explosion at Port Chicago, California, just north of San Francisco. On July 17, 1944, well over 300 men, the great majority of them African American, were quite literally blown to pieces when ammunition they were loading onto a ship suddenly detonated. Meyers, who had actually helped build one of the ships destroyed, felt the blast. (Ringling was her baby brother; Bonnie was her sister.)

July 19, 1944

My Darling!

Ten twenty is the time it happened. Unusual for me, to be ready for work so early, I was all dressed and sitting on the couch reading, "Return of The Beloved", by Thomas Mann and Ringling had just gone to bed and was dozing off to sleep. He was on the back couch and I was sitting on the front couch. Bonnie had just left after asking me if she could go stay awhile with a girl friend whose mother had gone to a party.

You would expect me to be frightened, wouldn't you? But I wasn't, honestly I wasn't. My reaction was one of excitement and thrills. I know that I shouldn't feel like that, but it is just the way I felt. As I began reading, "My love for Ottili makes it easy for me to acknowledge that her original character . . . ." my book took a rankish turn and almost dropped from my hands. At the same instance, I was aware of the motion of the trailer. The night was quiet, most of the people were in bed and not even the usual wind was having it's fling. As though a giant stood on the right side of the trailer and with a mighty hand playfully rocked the trailer from side to side.

I tried to rise from the couch, but only one well schooled at sea could have walked the short distance from couch to door over the floor beneath that rolled as the waves. As the trailer rocked, I heard a loud rumbling noise like thunder. Of course it only lasted a few seconds maybe just one or two, the time rumbling and rocking continued, but to me it seemed hours. Ringling had locked the door, so that detained me that much longer as I was so eager to get out and see what had caused such an unusual thing.

Of course my first thought, as most people, was that the Japs were bombing us and that is why I can't understand not being frightened. Ring called to me: "Is it buzz bombs"? he had been reading about the buzz bombs, just before he went to sleep, so he thought that was what it was. Just as I opened my door, lights came on all over and people came running out from everywhere. I called Mrs. Blackstone, the lady who lives behind me, and her husband came out just then and people started gathering in knots and expressing their opinion. It was generally conceded that we had just gone through an earthquake, but Mr. Blackstone said that it felt like a mighty explosion and I said that the noise seemed to come from the east, (I was right), and one woman across the way, laughed at our predictions and said it was thunder. "I know," she said, "for I saw the lightning in the sky just as I went out the door". (She saw lightning all right, but not the kind made by storms).

Always your loving baby,
Max

The Port Chicago explosion became a racial flashpoint when fifty African-American crew members, claiming the job was too dangerous, refused to continue loading ammunition. Shaken by the carnage—"there weren't any bodies," recalled Freddie Meeks, one of the seamen at the base, "just pieces of flesh they shoveled up"—the men asked for a temporary leave "to get [their] nerves together." The request was denied. Still unwilling to handle the explosives, the men were charged with mutiny and sentenced to fifteen years in prison. (Like most of the men, Meeks was released after a year and a half in a federal penitentiary. On December 23, 1999, Meeks, one of the only survivors of the fifty who had been convicted, was granted a symbolic pardon by President Bill Clinton.) Max Meyers was reunited with her husband in November 1945, and, in the years after the war, they raised six children together.

~

Journalist Ernie Pyle Sends an Explicit, Profanity-Laced Letter from North Africa to His Lifelong Friend Paige Cavanaugh

"They are the mud-rain-frost-and-wind boys," the venerated war correspondent Ernie Pyle said of American infantrymen, "and in the end they are the guys that wars can't be won without." Wire thin, 5' 8", and in his early forties, Ernie Pyle lived, slept, ate, smoked, bunked, drank, and marched with the young GIs he so admired in order to depict the daily hardships they endured. By 1943 he had won the Pulitzer Prize, and his syndicated columns were appearing in hundreds of newspapers back in the U.S. While his letters to his wife Jerry in Albuquerque, New Mexico, were guarded in what they revealed about the underbelly of army life, Pyle was more candid in letters to old friends about such matters as sex, booze, and the latest dirty jokes. Pyle's raunchy humor and raw stories, however, concealed a deep sadness; three months after he left the States in 1941 his mother died from cancer and his wife, who suffered from depression, had tried to commit suicide. She divorced him in April 1942, but they remarried again a year later. Writing to his lifelong friend Paige Cavanaugh in June 1943, Pyle began by needling him about a voluptuous music teacher Cavanaugh had previously mentioned. Pyle then updated him on his life in the sands of North Africa covering Operation Torch, the first major joint Allied offensive of the war. (Please note: Pyle's letter uses graphic language inappropriate for young readers.)

Dear Egbert—

Congratulations, my friend. Must say you were in excellent literary form in your May 13 epistle which reached my tent flap some four or five days ago. Must be the influence of your new music teacher. Give them protuberances you spoke so highly of an extra stroke or two for me, will you? Who cares if she can play the piano when there are other and better things to play with? I'll bet you actually don't get within ten feet of her, and then jack off as soon as she leaves.

I'm in a tent-camp on the Mediterranean shore, starting my first day of a solid week of rest. Since coming back from the front I've been working like a bastard trying to get all caught up, and now I haven't got a thing left except to write a couple of dozen letters. You'd like it here. We're on a sand dune with scrub pine growing out of the sand, and the beach of the blue Mediterranean is about 100 yards away. I have my own tent, and have it fixed up like home, with grass mats on the ground, a light over my cot, a table to write on, and a low wicker settin' chair just outside the tent. The nights are cool and the days are not too hot. It's just damn near ideal, and

I'll sure hate to leave here and go back to war. We're a little self-contained camp, with our own mess, and as there are only two or three other people out here, it's as quiet as the grave. I don't go into town but once a week, for my cigaret rations, and then it damn near kills me to go in.

I understand the secret is out at last. They tell me Time Magazine has arrived over here with a full-page piece about me, in which it estimates my annual income at 25,000. Ha ha, you indigent cocksucker. And don't start that old shit about you being happier than me on account you don't make much money, because I'm as happy as a fuckin' jaybird. So yah! How much do you make, incidentally? Think you ought to tell me now. Although of course I aint coming right out and saying that Time is right. Might be more than that for all I know har har.

Your letters are so good I read them aloud to a small circle of select friends, but nobody thinks they're funny except Chris Cunningham, and he thinks they're wonderful. Chris is a wonderful little guy. He's good-natured as hell, gets tight on wine very easily, and soon reaches a stage where he can neither walk nor talk. From then on he just staggers around making vague blubberings which if you listen closely turn out to be the constantly repeated phrase "pig-fucker, pig-fucker!" You'd like him.

Yes, I've become quite familiar with soil conditions in Africa. I can quote you the shovel-resistance content of every type of earth from solid rock to playbox sand. Sand is the nicest in our type of work, except it caves in on you. Your suggestion of taking up a little piece of land over here and starting life anew is not a bad one; in fact I've given it considerable thought myself. Might as well do it somewhere, I suppose. I have very little faith in the future. But I still want to try the South Sea Islands first.

Nicotine still has me in its grasp, but my mind has been cleared of women for a year now, and of alcohol for some seven months. And I must grudgingly admit that I feel a hell of a lot better being rid of both of them. In more than six months I've had exactly two bottles of whiskey. I've always hated wine, and in the first month here I swore completely off of wine and haven't had a drink of it for more than six months. However, last week I did run onto two bottles of whiskey at $10 per bottle. I was so out of practice that two drinks before supper almost laid me away, and I had a hell of a hangover next day. So I gave most of it away. I did however have a couple of before-supper drinks every day for about four days, and I'll be damned if all the old symptoms didn't come back—eyes out of focus, faintly upset stomach, that tense pain in the back of the head. I never knew all those years they are from the venomous worm, but they must have been. It wouldn't surpise me at all if I'm not carrying a white banner the next time you see me. The years were dealing heavily with me. No wine, no women, no song, no play—soon nothing will be left to me but my shovel and a slight case of athlete's foot.

If Tom Treanor doesn't start home pretty soon (at least by fall) I'll be catching up with him. That piece you enclosed was kinda thin. Damn near as thin as mine are getting. I'd come home and give it all up except what would I give up to?

So Mrs. Cavanaugh thinks I look like a billy-goat does she? Well, all I can say is, in the language of my esteemed compatriots, the military—fuck Mrs. Cavanaugh. Why don't you try it yourself sometime; you certainly owe her something for putting up so cheerfully with your mooning all these years.

A funny thing happened at the front just before the finish. A new correspondent arrived from America, and he was a balmy character if I ever saw one. Absolutely psycopathic. Completely devoid of any quality of fear, loudly braggart, always picking quarrels with everybody he met, completely uninhibited as for example, upon being introduced to a very dignified British colonel, his first words were of what wonderful "blow jobs" the British girls can perform.

Well one evening when we got back to camp from Bizerte the boys got about ten gallons of wine in celebration, and everybody got good and tight except me—and I would if I wasn't off wine. Everybody in camp took a turn of trying to out-insult and out-shout this guy. The arguments went on all evening and could be heard for miles. Finally they went into their own tent; five of them were in a big tent, and Chris and I in a small tent nearby. Being sober, I could hear all that was said in the next tent.

Finally this guy got tired of arguing over which was the best division and who took what hill, and decided to brag about his beautiful wife back home. He got out a picture of her and was saying "Now my wife . . ." when I heard a voice from the same tent say to him in disgust and with dead seriousness "Fuck your wife." He let that one pass and then started telling about his eight-year-old daughter. He said "She's got an I.Q. of 145 . . ." and the voice said "Fuck your eight-year-old daughter!" That's the end of that story.

I am not sure what goes on in Albuquerque. Letters from friends there, and from several Washington visitors who were out there in April, report Jerry working hard at her new job, thinner and more beautiful that at any time in years, extremely proud of the house and keeping it neat as a pin, taking Spanish lessons on the side, quite abstemious, and apparently getting over her introversions and aversions to people.

Yet I have not heard from her in almost two months, and a cable to Lee a week ago asking for a cabled message from her has gone unanswered. I can't make it out. The few letters I did get in the spring were grand, and she said she was writing twice a week. I find it hard to believe that other people's letters all get through, while all of hers are lost. I try not to think about it too much.

Finally got around to reading Beau Geste last week. Quite a book. I've also read James Hilton's "We Are Not Alone", Thornton Wilder's play "Our Town," and any number of short stories by Maugham, Conrad, and so on. Wish I had some of the new books at home to read. I get an old New Yorker once in a while and see what books are out. Did I tell you they're reprinting the African columns in book form? Due out in August, I think. Better buy one. Don't suppose I'll ever get home to give you one.

Had a nice letter from Gene Uebelhardt. Said he might get released from the Army. Any news of the Hardies? Katie Miller has gone to London with OWI. Dick Hollander is over here with same. Hear Palmer got fired again from some other job, but reinstated. How is Joe doing with those tires? Suppose Earl Mount is overseas somewhere by now (Lt. S. G.) in Naval SeaBees, but haven't heard where. I get mail from a lot of people, but am gradually sinking into my oldtime funk (from which I've been free for several months) about Jerry. I've a premonition things have gone bad again. God if they have, I don't know what to do. Don't think about the war brother, I'll wake you up when it's over.

—Mohammed.

In an earlier letter to Cavanaugh, Pyle named several colleagues lost in combat and remarked, almost off-handedly, that the war had "been tough on newspapermen." In fact, of the estimated 100 American war correspondents killed in combat during the twentieth century, almost half died in World War II. On April 18, 1945, Pyle himself became one of the fifty. Following a convoy of trucks on the tiny island of Ie Shima (near Okinawa), Pyle and four other men were driving in a jeep that was suddenly raked with machine-gun fire. No one was hit, and they all dove into a roadside ditch for protection. After a few seconds passed, Pyle poked his head up, smiled, and called out to one of the men, "Are you all right?" In that instant a Japanese sniper shot Pyle right through the head.

1st Lt. Paul Skogsberg Flirts with a Beautiful War Nurse Named Vera "Sheaf" Sheaffer Through a Series of Letters
&
Seaman Sylvan "Sol" Summers Receives an Unexpected, Crushing Letter from His Fiancée
&
1st Lt. John David Hench Expresses His Disappointment to His Wife, Barbara, Over Her "Nocturnal Adventures"
&
Hench, Writing Three Days Later, Assures His Wife She Is Forgiven

Smitten the moment he saw her, 1st Lt. Paul Skogsberg approached an American nurse named Vera "Sheaf" Sheaffer at a Red Cross dance in Oran on May 19, 1943. He was part of a reconnaissance unit with the First Infantry Division, she was with the Ninety-third Evacuation Hospital, and they were both temporarily stationed in Algeria. The next night they listened to swing music on the BBC with a group of friends, and a few days later they drove to the beach, made a picnic of tinned ham and eggs from their K rations, and went swimming in the Mediterranean. For a month they spent almost every night under the North African stars and moon talking, laughing, and (innocently) keeping one another company. On June 20, the day before Skogsberg was to leave for Algiers, he feared he would never see Sheaf again and expressed how much he had enjoyed his time with her:

My Dear Sheaf,

Well, sister, I am afraid you have seen the last of me, for a while at least. I'm off on a mission. Without me to darken your doorstep you should be able to stay out of trouble. All joking aside, Sheaf, I want you to know that this past month has been grand for me and I want you to know that I think you are super. You cannot imagine what it has meant to me to meet a girl such as you and to be able to enjoy her company for those many evenings, after being away from civilization for so long. But this is the Army, "here today, and gone tomorrow."

So long, good luck, thanks a million for all the memories, and I hope we meet again soon.

As ever,
Paul

Fate conspired in their favor; Sheaf, too, was sent to Algiers with the Ninety-third, and they were able to spend another week together. All the while, however, Skogsberg had been keeping a secret from Sheaf, and he knew the time had come to reveal the truth. "In the last month I have done a lot of thinking—a lot of soul-searching. There is something I should have told you a long time ago," Skogsberg wrote on July 26. "Sheaf, I am a married man." Skogsberg's predicament was one that innumerable married couples, severed by the war, struggled with during their long-distance separation. Letters helped, and billions of correspondence flowed between those in the military and their loved ones back home. But to many young men and women overseas or in the States, a letter was no substitute for the intimacy they craved after months and even years apart. "I am sure you will never want to see me again," Skogsberg concluded in his letter to Sheaf, "and you have every right to feel that way, but I want you to know that you are still very dear to me. So long and good luck." Much to his surprise, the very next evening he was handed a message from Sheaf, assuring him she was not angry and still wanted to correspond with him. (Regrettably, all of Sheaf's wartime letters have been lost.) In August 1943, when Skogsberg's unit and the Ninety-third went their separate ways, the two continued writing to one another. Skogsberg, however, was becoming increasingly anxious about the relationship, and on January 1, 1944, he sent Sheaf the following:

Dear Sheaf,

Here's that man again. How goes the battle in Italy?

This being New Year's day I suppose resolutions are in order. I don't usually make New Year's resolutions and when you hear this one I'm pretty sure you will think, "What a crazy mixed-up kid this is!" And you will be right, I really am crazy and mixed up. My conscience has been gnawing away at me for some time and has finally gotten the best of me. To put it in a nut-shell, it is, "No more hanky-panky!" This means no more dating and no more letter writing. In truth, I hate making this resolution as your letters have meant so much to me. But I keep thinking, "What if something happened to me and one of your letters was sent to my home." Maybe my wife would understand, for there has never been anything in any of our letters that either of us need to be ashamed of. But then again, maybe she wouldn't. And what about my parents, would they be ashamed of me?

Well, I don't want to hurt any of them, but I don't want to hurt you either. Maybe I am flattering myself to think you would care. At least, I know you will understand. Anyway, it was great while it lasted. Wish it could continue.

Well Sheaf, I hope that '44 will be a good year for you and I wish you the best of everything. And I hope that if you ever run into a guy like me you will recognize him immediately for what he is.

Thanks for everything.

As ever,
Paul

Skogsberg immediately regretted mailing the letter. But it was too late. Three months passed and he didn't hear from Sheaf, not even to say she agreed, or was hurt by his comments, or hoped to change his mind. On April 2 he read that bombs had fallen on hospitals at the Anzio beachhead in Italy, killing two nurses. Certain that the Ninety-third was there, Skogsberg wrote to Sheaf. Almost two months later, just as he was about to give up hope, a letter arrived from Sheaf apologizing for the delay and explaining that she had been in the hospital to have her appendix removed. (She had indeed been at Anzio during the shelling—a silver-dollar-sized piece of shrapnel had even zipped through her tent—but she was unhurt.) Once again they were correspon-ding regularly, and Skogsberg could not have been more elated. "You have no idea what you do for me," he gushed in August 1944. "Half an hour ago I was ready to burst and then I am handed your letter of 30–31 July and what do I do? I melt." What he wanted most of all was to see her again. After winning a three-day authorization pass in a card game, he planned to surprise Sheaf in Paris, where he had learned she would be visiting. It had been eighteen months since they had seen each other, and Skogsberg could hardly contain himself. The night before they met, Skogsberg—after a few drinks—revealed his feelings for her. (Lorraine was Sheaf's middle name.)

23 Feb '45

Dear Lorraine,

Good evening, Honey. Tonight I am celebrating and as you can guess I have had a few too many. You see, there is plenty of bourbon and gin at this club and tonight I have had more than my share. First I went to a movie and then it was booze time. But there are others that have fared worse than I. There are several "out cold" in the halls here.

Honey, have I ever told you that I love you. No? Well Sweetheart, I am telling you now, and not just because I am tipsy. To confirm it I will tell you again in the morning when I am cold sober. I've kept this inside me as long as I could. So, until then, Sweetheart—I love you, and I'll be dreaming of you until then. Goodnight kiddo.

Love and Kisses,
Paul

Here I am again, Honey. It is morning, not bright yet, but it is early and I am cold sober. Yes, I do love you and have been bursting at the seams for a long time wanting to say that to you. See you soon.

All my love and kisses
Paul

Sheaf never responded directly to the letter and their correspondences remained those of close friends or pen-pals. Skogsberg was torn. Sheaf was the woman he loved, but

if they married he would have to go through an agonizing divorce back home. But,
he also reasoned, it was a separation that might happen anyway; he and his wife had
married hastily when war was declared, did not have children, and had not spent
more than a few months together before he was shipped overseas. Skogsberg also
rationalized that, if he didn't survive the war, there would be no need to choose. And
this was not unthinkable. Skogsberg was seriously wounded in action in February
1943, and he had had a close call in April 1945 when a bullet struck him in the
head. (Luckily, he was wearing his helmet.) When the war ended that May, he and
Sheaf were very much alive, and Skogsberg was still in turmoil.

June 2

Dear Sheaf,

I don't suppose you are sitting in tonight thinking of me, but I will write to you anyway. I must admit that I am a bit on the lonely side tonight and I am feeling blue. I don't know what's wrong with me, do you? I guess you do. Couldn't be that I miss you, could it?

You know Sheaf, my mind has not been at ease for a long time. I've got troubles and need someone to talk to. Should I tell my troubles to you? No, maybe that's not such a good idea. It might complicate things more. We never were ones for saying much, were we? I believe we have both been doing a lot of thinking. I have found myself deep, deep in thought lately and saying over and over "I wish, I wish, I wish." And what do I wish? I wish I could tell you. Maybe someday I will. It is hard to say and it is even harder not to say. Yes, maybe I will tell you. I am not much of a letter writer and probably a lot of them sound silly, but at least these letters let you know I am thinking of you. And this is probably the dopiest one of all.

I suppose you are having a good time on your leave. At least the guys who manage to date you will be happy. I don't suppose you are having a moment to or by yourself. I am green with envy. I might as well admit it. I know I have no right to feel that way, but there are some things you just cannot control. I suppose I should say, I hope you meet some nice guy who will treat you right, but I wouldn't be telling the truth if I said that.

I guess I had better sign off before I crack wide open! Nite, see you in dreamland, and as the song goes, "You Can't Stop Me From Dreaming."

Love,
Paul

Two weeks later, Skogsberg made up his mind and proposed to Sheaf. She did not say
yes—right away. First, he had to promise to explain everything to his wife. (He did,
and they divorced three months after he returned.) Second, she said, "You'd better not
get into any more messes." He gave his word he wouldn't. (He did not, and they mar-

ried in 1947 and have been together ever since.) Not all such affairs, of course, occurred abroad. The strain for spouses and sweethearts on the homefront proved excruciating for many of them as well. The wait was too long, the uncertainty too great, and the temptations too overpowering. Serving aboard the USS Ajax, an auxiliary repair ship in the Pacific, twenty-five-year-old Seaman Sylvan "Sol" Summers had the wind knocked out of him by a succinct, handwritten letter from the States. Dated March 25, 1945, it was from his fiancée, back home in the Bronx.

Dear Sol,

I know its been quite some time since you last heard from me and no doubt you've been wondering why the long absence. This is by far the most difficult thing I've had to do and you must realize how much it pains me to do this.

I've always been honest with you Sol & I believe you deserve only the truth from me, for you yourself are so fine & wonderful a person. So I'll be perfectly honest with you, I've met someone I care for very much.

I realize too well how you must feel right now, but do you think it fair to give only part of my devotion to you? You deserve more than that, for you are too fine a person to receive anything half way about it. And it would never be fair to either of us.

Don't think for a moment that it was your fault Sol. I don't believe it was either of our faults. Neither of us wished to have things happen as they did. It just happened & we can't do anything about it. Guess they call it fate.

You've been wonderful to me all along & I think you are one of the grandest, sincerest people I've had the honor of meeting. I'm certain you'll meet someone in the very near future who will be able to give you what I can no longer give. For someone as fine and understanding a person as you Sol deserves only the best in life.

I'm returning your gifts & the ring to your mother, which I believe is the only fair thing to do. Thank her & your Dad for being so wonderful to me. If I could but spare you & them all this, believe me Sol, I would, but I see no way.

Please try to find some forgiveness in your heart, for I honestly didn't want it this way, but I guess it just had to be.

I'd like very much to remain friends but that of course is entirely up to you.

Here's wishing you the very best in life, for all who know you, know full well, that you certainly deserve it. Good luck to you always & here's wishing you a happy voyage home & soon.

Annette.

Although his crewmates made a ritual of gathering together their "Dear John" letters into a small pile, lighting them on fire, and ceremoniously dumping the ashes into the sea, Summers never threw Annette's letter away. (As heartbreaking as the rejection was, it turned out for the best: after the war Summers met and proposed to the love of his life, Rose Lee Nowack. She said yes, and they remain happily married to this day.) Some couples endured rocky times even before the men headed overseas. 1st Lt. John David Hench, in training in Corpus Christi, Texas, received a letter from his wife, Barbara, confessing that she had been unfaithful to him. Overwhelmed with remorse, she emphasized she still loved her husband and did not want to end their marriage. Hench, understandably upset but remarkably forgiving about the matter, explained why her actions pained him.

March 8, 1943

Dear Bobs:

There is nothing for me to say as far as I can decide concerning your nocturnal adventures. I am deeply hurt, more so than I ever dreamed I could be, but I think I know why, and I'll try later to explain my reasons. Regardless of your strength of character and will, I love you and consequently, the whole matter is finished with the completion of this sentence!

The reason behind my hurt, however, cannot be disregarded. I find it comes from being or at least trying to be an officer in the United States Marine Corps. I am no longer an individual. My ego, which has always been large, is now part of the Espirit de Corps that make the corps the fightenest bunch of men in the world. A Marine is more honest, more truthful, more military in his bearing than any other type of man. He is forced to be all Marine by those under him and unless those under him respect and admire his judgement, ability and character, those above him will soon lose faith. To be a good Marine is to be more than a man, and to be, as I want to be, the best Marine is to draw more outside of myself and make me more than I am now. I am fighting every weak impulse, every soft tendency in my body to gain for myself the respect and approval of other Marines. This is hard. I work long hours, fly long hours, and study long hours to be all that I dream you, staying behind me, hope I am. The forgoing gives you some background as to why I was so dreadfully hurt by what you told me. Now, a failure of will or character to me, regardless of reason, is so much graver an offense than ever before, primarily because if I ever failed in one of those respects, I'd have to quit.

I hope you understand now something of the life I am trying to carve out for us. I am proud of my uniform and my title of officer; surely, I can't be requested to be less proud of those I love even more dearly, and of whom am even more proud.

I am sorry not to have written sooner, but I just didn't have anything to say.

New: I AM FINISHED PRIMARY!!

My new address is: BOQ Aux. Cabiniss Field, Corpus Christi. I am house hunting after I finish this letter. So I should be able to let you know the 15th!

I start in Basic tomorrow and my new ground school starts Monday! So I'll be rushed for a while.

Must close now.

Love,
J.D.

P.S. I hope you all are feeling a hell of a lot better!

Several days later Hench wrote again to his wife, who was still consumed with guilt about the incident. ("The boys," mentioned at the end of the letter, are their two young sons, Michael and Christopher.)

March 11, 1943

Dearest:

Spent another hour or so on the phone today with no luck whatsoever. We may have to take one of these little 3 room shacks for the time being, but even that would be better than this ghastly separation.

All your letters which I got today are so sad and mournful of your midnight adventure. Forget it—it's not going to change anything. Our life together has never had sex as its main and unfailing point of contact. We have evolved some relationship between ourselves which far transcends the mere physical contacts of sex. Sex, as we both agree, is a wonderful emotional background for marriage, but it is by no means the cornerstone of the foundation. That is "Sense of Humor" or at least as far as I am concerned, sense of humor is much more important than Sex. This, of course, doesn't mean that I shall condone or even put up with any more nonsense like that, for the act of yours was, as far as I'm concerned, about the lowest anyone can pull. Because it was just giving in to promiscuity. If you thought or believed yourself dreadfully in love or something like that, I might understand it. But just leaping into bed with strangers is the business of some women, the pleasure of others, but my wife fits neither of these categories. Enough said!

Keep right in with your plans for moving. I'll find something. If necessary you could always get a room or two in a tourist court until we can find a home.

I started formation today. How I hate it. It keeps you keyed up fit to kill. Got two 4.0's in my first two tests in ground school. Looks like I'm doing all right. Keep the letters coming. I love you dear. Kiss the boys for their Dad.

Less than a year later Capt. John David Hench was in the Pacific, where he earned the Distinguished Flying Cross for his skills as a marine Corsair pilot. His relationship with his wife was stronger than ever. "I love you darling," he reminded her in a letter dated March 6, 1944, "and each day apart from you is only a half a day lived." Soon after writing this, Capt. Hench was returning from a mission in the Solomon Islands when the throttle went out in his plane. He successfully ditched in the ocean, swam to his inflatable life raft, and, once in, waved to his comrades circling above. It was the last anyone saw of him. Devastated by her husband's death, Barbara Hench never remarried.

Extended Correspondence

**Fifteen-Year-Old Pvt. Bill Lynn Implores His Mother
to Send His Birth Certificate and "Get [Him] Out" of Boot Camp,
but Then Later Tells Her Not to Worry About Him
&
Mrs. Lynn Mails a Series of Short Letters to Bill Asking Where
He Is and Updating Him on His Brother Bob, Also in Combat**

In a fit of youthful bravado, fifteen-year-old Bill Lynn from St. Louis, Missouri, joined the marines in the summer of 1941 after lying about his age. (Many teenagers did the same.) Almost immediately after he got to boot camp in San Diego, California, he discovered he had made an awful mistake. Lynn desperately wanted to quit but, being tall for his age, could not convince the marines he was really only fifteen. In a letter to his mother dated August 29, 1941, Lynn begged her to help him come home. (Lynn's education was limited, and he dictated some letters to older privates, who penned them on his behalf. The following letters, which Lynn wrote himself, have an occasional grammatical or spelling error.)

Dear Mom,

This is the lousy place in the world. Our clothes they gave us are to big for some of us. I got my shots today & they really do hurt me. The sargents crabby. Just because a boy forgot something when we were moving the man kicked him & made him run all the way over to the other camp & get it. We go to bed at 9:00 & get up at 5:00. Mom tell them the truth about my age and get me out of here. I am getting so lonely I think I will die. We had to get all of our hair cut off but about half an inch. Hurry as soon as possible if you can. Try to get me out by Sunday at least. We had to polish & wash windows last night until 9:00 o clock. I have enclosed the bill. Sorry I did not write sooner. Oh, mom if you only knew how I feel you would not wait to get me out. Send me some clothes when you come get me out. Write me some because I have put some stamps in for air mail. You have to walk on you tiptoes so it will not make to much noise. The sarg. made that up. Tell everybody I said helo. How's Sandy.

> Your son
> Bill
> Write to me.

It is not known for certain if Mrs. Lynn withheld her son's birth certificate on purpose, forgot to mail it, or simply couldn't find it, but she did not send it after receiving her son's letter. On top of the rigors of training, which he continued to find onerous, Lynn was also being introduced to the brutality of war, as evidenced in the following letter dated January 13, 1942. (Betty is his sister; Bob is his older brother; and Toot, mentioned in later letters, is the nickname for his other sister, Alline.)

Dear Mom,

Please tell Betty that I got her package and I thank her very much. I got a box of candy and I guess you sent it & thanks a lot. Tell Bob that I will send him a Xmas present when I get paid. How did you like the pillow case I sent you.

Mom, I am standing guard by one of these English ships that came in last week. They took off 600 dead & wounded from it. You could not even go down in the hole it stunk so bad. As soon as it landed I went on board and went up forward and there sat a guy with half of his head blown away. There sure were soom of the bloodist sight on that ship that I every saw.

I have a new address now Mom, you will find it on the back of the envelope. I'm just 30 miles north of San Franscico. I am trying to write this letter and listen to Bob Hope at the same time. Mom, if Bob has to go to the Army tell them my right age and tell them I have to get out and help you make a living. If you see Emmett around enywhere tell I said hello.

Don't get worryed if you don't here from me very often because when I go on guard for 24 hours I haven't any time to write. When I get off I have to get caught up with my sleep. If every thing turns out right I will get my first stripe in about 1 month from now. Well mom I guess that about all there is to write now so I will close this letter now. Write soon.

You Son
Bill

Sixteen years old now, Lynn, despite the promise of a budding relationship with a local girl, reminded his mother he was still determined to leave the marines.

March 9, 1942

Dear Mom,

I am sorry I did not write you sooner but I have been to busy out here in California to do anything but guard duty. I am writing this letter from the guard house where we stay before going on guard. It is 8:00 now, at 11:30 I go on guard until 2:30 in the morning, then I come back & sleep until 10:00.

Mom, I am going to have a big picture taken of myself the 20th & I am going to send one to you & one to Eleanor. This is a Navy yard where I stand guard at and is it noisy out here. Tell Toot it was very nice of her to send me those Valentine cards. Mom, <u>Please,</u> make Betty go to school all the time because I know what it is like to not have the education since I got in the Marines.

Is it very cold in St. Louis now mom? We have been having fine weather out here in Calif. for about a week now. In the mornings when we go on guard we're in shirt sleeves until about 5:00 in the evening. Mom, when I want to go on liberty I go to San Francisco about 30 miles from here. Sometimes I go to Oakland, just 26 miles away.

Mom, it sure is bad to see these service men that have been fighting over in Pearl Harbor coming back with one leg or one arm. Some of the have got big cast over their chest where it was broken.

Mom, I use to go to Frisco and just walk around the streets and then go to a show by myself & it was so lonely that it nearly drove me crazy. So last week a guy took me out & I met a girl that is so nice. Everytime I get a chance I hitch-hike 40 miles to see her. I go up to her house & if she is not at home her mother will not let me leave until I have had a glasss of wine or something to eat. Her family is so nice to me. She ask me to come up Thursday night & she would teach me how to dance. Mom, everybody thinks I am 18 out here, for one reason I am 5ft. 9inches tall and weight 157 pounds. Was I that big when I left for the Marines?

Mom, will you write to Jefferson City & get my Birth Certificate for me? There was a boy up here just a week ago got his mother to get his for him. When he got it he went down & seen the Captain & told them he wanted out. About a day later he had $155. to go home on & a honorable discharge from the Marine Corp. So will you write up there & get mine & sent it to me so I can come home. There should be plenty jobs open buy now with all the boys going in the service. Mom, I am so lonely I don't know what to do. I sure would like to see St. Louis again.

Well Mom it took me 1:45 to write this letter but I got it wrote after all. Well that is all I can think of for the time being so I will close this letter.
Bye.

Your Son
Bill Lynn

P. S. Get my Birth Certificate as soon as you can. <u>Please</u>.

At long last, she found it. But, having now spent almost a full year in military service, Lynn realized he was actually developing a fondness for the marines and becoming more mature as a person. A little too mature, in fact. "If you can spare it," Lynn wrote to his mom, "please send me some smokes. (Camels)." And, in a later letter: "We had some Rum over here two weeks ago. Boy, it sure tasted good. It was given to us by the officers." Lynn even learned to build a small, makeshift distillery: "In case I haven't told you," he reported with pride, "the 'still' is doing OK. Made two nice rums & expect them to get better." On July 2, 1942, he sent his birth certificate home along with the following letter:

Dear Mom,

I got your letter & was very glad to hear from you. There is not much to say. I got out of the Mess-Hall the other day after serving another month. Mom don't get worried about me because nothing is going to happen. I doubt if I will see Bob when he comes to Calif. because I will be gone.

Mom don't let Bob get drafted & be a Dog face. Make him join the Marines. I will not be hear another 2 weeks, so do not get worried if I do not write to you for a long while. I met a girl out here in Calif. & went head over heels for her. If Bob would join the Marines I would not be with him because I will be gone by the time he got out of Boot Camp.

I am sending you a trunk with some old clothes that I had. Do not think that I am dead because you get some clothes. Mom just take care of them in case I don't come back. I will have a year in the service in another month. It does not seem right does it. You will find my birth certificate in a book in the trunk. It won't be long till I am 17 will it. You will find my new address on the front of the envelope. That's about all for now so I will close for now.

Your Son
Bill

P.S. Don't get worried if you don't hear from me for a while.

A year later Bill Lynn was in the Pacific. His mother hadn't received word from him for several weeks and did, in fact, begin to worry. "Sorry I haven't written," he apologized in a November 5, 1943, letter, "but I just haven't been able to. We are kept pretty busy here." The word "busy" meant combat, but Lynn spared his mom the grim details and referred to the fighting only vaguely.

Jan. 27, 1944

Dear Mom, & Betty,

Well here is your baby boy again, writing a letter to you from the front lines. I don't know if I told you before, but I am now in action again. It was pretty tough for the first three day, but now things are pretty quiet.

I met a boy from St. Louis the other day. He came from the same neighborhood as I did.

How is Betty getting along in school? Fine I hope. Tell her to keep going & be sure to finish because she is going to have to teach me when I get back.

After I get out the Marines, which is next year I am going to live in Wash. State. A man has got me a job up there with Pan-American Air Ways.

I have not heard from Bob in about 2 months. Write & tell him to write, because I lost his address.

Well that's about all for now so I'll have to close. I hope to be home for Xmas in 44.

Your Son
Bill

Letters came in only sporadically from Lynn, which made his mother all the more anxious. On August 21, she sent the following:

Dear Billie. I will drop you a few lines as I havent heard from you in 2 weeks. And I get so worried when I dont get letters from you boys. I hope you are well and O.K. I sure hope you are getting my letters, for I do write you often. Gee I sure am lonsome since Toot went back home. The baby didnt want to leave me. She cryed after she was on the train. I sure am glad you hear from them. And I am glad you got the pictures that Toot sent you, and I do hope you have gotten the picture of Bob by now. Honey I sure wish you could have some made and send me one, as I am so lonsome to see you. I know you are a big boy now. Billie you had a letter this morning tell you that your Service life Insurence has elapsed. since april 5, 1944, so write and tell me if you know about it. I guess I will close so write me soon. With Love Mom

When he had not received any replies from his brother Bob, fighting in Europe, Bill was now the one sounding like the concerned parent. "Have you heard from him lately[?]," Lynn asked his mom in August. "He has not written to me in almost a month now." Three weeks later, Mrs. Lynn informed Bill of his brother's whereabouts.

Sept 5, 1944

My dear little Son Billie sure glad to hear from you and to hear you are well and O.K. and honey I sure hope it wont be to long before you get a 30 day furlough. I sure want to see you. and honey I have kept away from you about Bobbie. but I will tell you as I hope and think he is OK now. he was taken a prisoner of Romania in June 23 but I hope he is back safe agine. for there was 11 hundred relesed last week. I have allmost gone crazy. but I am trusting in God that this war ends soon. and that you boys will get to come home. honey I am living in hopes of having some better news for you soon. I hope I hear that he is save and well. Everything is OK here at home. I hear from the girls often. ans soon

with love Mom

Several weeks later Mrs. Lynn was able to report that Bob was safe. But she had not heard from Bill for some time.

Sept. 21, 1944

Dear Billie will drop you a few lines as I havent heard from you. and I have good news, from the last letter I sent you. Bob will be back in the States at the last of this month. I sure was happy when I read the telagram from the government last night. I hope you are well and O.K. I have a pretty bad cold but I guess it will leave. I had letters from the girls they are getting along fine. honey you ask me why I didnt go out to Calif to see Bettie. well I have been working since she left. but I may decide to go now since I have heard that Bobbie is O.K. well honey I dident know what to send you for xmas but you can be looking for a box. and I hope you will like it. so write me soon.

Bob made it back to the States in October, and sent a short note to his younger brother. "How are you doing? I haven't heard from you in a long time. When are you coming home? Wish you were here now. Well answer soon, would like to hear from you very much." The letters and Christmas package Bill's mother and brother sent him in the fall of 1944 were returned unopened; although the exact circumstances are not known, Pfc. Bill Lynn was killed in the Pacific three days after he turned nineteen years old.

Shizuko Horiuchi, an American Citizen Detained for Being Japanese, Depicts for Her Friend Henriette Von Blon Life in an Internment Camp
&
Pfc. Ernest Uno, with the Famed 442nd Regimental Combat Team, Writes to His Sister Mae in an Internment Camp About Why He is Fighting

"I AM AN AMERICAN" exclaimed a sign on a grocer's storefront in California. But it was to no avail; the owner, an American of Japanese descent, was evicted from his home, forced to close his business, and sent to an internment camp for the next two years. In the spring of 1942 approximately 120,000 Japanese-American men, women, and children were rounded up and imprisoned for no other reason than their ethnicity. Euphemistically called "relocation" or "resettlement" centers, they were in fact penitentiaries surrounded by armed guards with orders to shoot anyone who tried to escape. (Shootings, although rare, did occur.) Two-thirds of those detained were American citizens, and even distinguished veterans who had fought for the United States in World War I were taken into custody. Incarcerated with her family at the Pomona Assembly Center, a young Japanese-American mother named Shizuko Horiuchi maintained a correspondence with her friend and former neighbor Henriette Von Blon. In the following letter, Horiuchi articulates the feelings of many Japanese Americans dismayed and disheartened by their plight.

Dear Mrs. Von Blon,

It does seem as if it's getting to be a habit of mine to be neglectful in writing, but truly, I'm so busy, I haven't found much time.

It's been a one round of washing, ironing with all the dust, soot from the mess hall kitchen, that it isn't an easy life for us. Especially, with three children, it's double work.

This is a very belated thank you, but I sincerely mean it. Thank you ever so much for your kindness and thoughtfulness. Your visits to our home made us very happy. I guess it would be hard to convey our dire feelings in these times and to be brightened by our dear American friends is really more than words can express.

The life here cannot be expressed. Sometimes we are resigned to it but when we see the barbed wire fences and the sentry tower with floodlights, it gives us a feeling of being prisoners in a concentration camp. We try to be happy and yet, oftentimes, a gloominess does creep in. When I see the "I'm an American" editorial and write-ups, the "equality of race etc."—it seems to be mocking us in our faces. I just wonder if all the sacrifices and hard labor on part of our parents has gone up to leave nothing to show for it? Well, I hope after this is all over they'll find some compensation waiting for them.

While Hitonie is sleeping, I'd better have my work done, so I'll be closing now. Please extend our best regards to Mr. Von Blon, Marie Adele and Philip. We do think of all of you often.

Very sincerely yours,
Shizuko

The "compensation," which was not offered until forty-three years after the war (half of the survivors had already passed away), was an official apology from the U.S. Government and a check for $20,000. Ironically, one of the most highly decorated units in American history remains the combined 100th Infantry Battalion and the 442nd Regimental Combat Team—all of whom were young, Japanese-American men eager to fight for the United States. The 442nd achieved particular acclaim when, in late October 1944, it rescued the 141st Regiment's First Battalion, which had been cut off and surrounded by enemy forces for eight days in France. The 442nd suffered over 800 casualties to save the 211 men of the "Lost Battalion." At the age of eighteen, Ernest Uno volunteered for the army while detained at the Amache, Colorado, War Relocation Camp and eventually became a member of the 442nd. (Uno's two older brothers were already in the U.S. Army working as translators and interpreters in the Pacific. Many Japanese Americans worked in the military, utilizing their knowledge of the Japanese language to break Japanese codes and inter-

rogate Japanese prisoners.) Three months before the "Lost Battalion" rescue, Pfc. Uno wrote from Italy to his sister—still imprisoned in the Amache camp—with observations and reflections about the war.

July 29, 1944

Dearest Mae,

I promised you I'd write every chance I had so here I am again. In the lull, between firing, I've found that scribbling off a few lines of a letter was the best way to ease the tension of fighting. Any little thing we do to divert our mind and keep us busy when the fighting comes to a temporary halt, relaxes the nerves and rests our bodies. That's why receiving mail from home is so important. I've got a bunch of letters in my pocket that are dirty and falling apart. They are the letters I have received from you, and the rest of the family. I almost know each one, word for word, 'cause I've read and re-read them so often. They are the ones that have kept me going until new ones come.

Of all the people who are good enough to sacrifice a few moments to drop me a line, you have become my favorite. Yours come regularly, and I've gotten to expect at least one a week from you. I couldn't begin to tell you how much each letter from home means to me. Maybe I haven't been so faithful in answering them all on time, but there have been reasons for the delay. I know you understand.

There isn't much I could tell you, except that I am well. Things I can't write about are in the newspapers, and over the radio anyway.

One thing I do like to talk about, is the people here. Their welfare, and their conduct with the presence of Allied Troops in their towns instead of the dreaded Germans. Being part of front line troops we are usually the first to march thru the towns which have cost so much blood and sweat to liberate. But the people are not ungrateful. They know that when we come, we mean to stay. That means that the war is over for them, and an end has come to their long oppression. As soon as we enter we are showered with all they have to spare. Wine, water, and fruits. And many times, they wait along the roadside to offer us warm, fresh milk. What they have to give is simple and little but when you're tired from lack of sleep, worn out from fighting without rest, dirty and unshaven, you accept their gifts with a lump in your throat. The poor peasants never asked for this hell, and they want to make good our sufferings.

There was one time while we were fighting, that one sniper killed one of our men. A woman saw him die, and she sat by his body and wept. Maybe she had a son once, who knows? But she refused to leave the body, and between tears, she tried to tell us how horrible it was to see an American soldier die for their sake. It was very pathetic.

This is a grim war, Mae. Our enemy is no longer the great superman he was once thought to be. Instead, he is a tired discouraged, dispirited young boy, fresh out of grade school! It's a pity. I've seen these boys, and thanked God that our younger brothers will not have to suffer the same fate.

I know now, for certain, what we are fighting for! Our mission is to free all the nations of oppression. Give the children of this, and the coming generations a chance to grow decently, and learn the true meaning of the "Four Freedoms".

Please give my regards to the Morimotos, your new neighbors and Amy Kamayatsu. Good luck, and lots of love.

Ernest

Ernest Uno survived the war and returned to the United States, where he finished his schooling. (Uno was a high school junior in Los Angeles before his family was detained in Amache.) After a thirty-year career with the YMCA, Uno studied for the diaconate in the Episcopal Church and became a deacon.

～

Lt. Walter Schuette Sends His Newborn Daughter, Anna Mary, a Letter to Be Read to Her in the Event He Does Not Come Home Alive
&
After Learning That His First Child Has Just Been Born, Capt. George Rarey Exclaims to His Wife, June: "I'm a Father— I Have a Son! Thank You, Junie!"

"Dear Harriet: Daddy thanks you for all those swell letters you have written," Sgt. Sol P. Shakofsky wrote to his two-year-old daughter back in St. Louis. "Some day you will understand why I could not answer them as often as I wanted to. You understand that daddy is not away from home because he wants to be. . . . As soon as I can I will hurry home to you and mother and will never, never have to leave again. . . . Good night little sweetheart." Sgt. Shakofsky, who did make it home alive, voiced the sentiments of countless servicemen with wives and children back in the U.S. The separation was painful for all parents, but especially so for those who were overseas when their children were born. Thirty-five-year-old Lt. Walter Schuette, a school principal from Bethalto, Illinois, was in England when he learned that his baby daughter, Anna Mary, had come into the world on December 15, 1943. Recognizing that there was the possibility he might not return, Schuette

*wanted Anna Mary to remember that, no matter what happened to him, he loved
her dearly.*

Dec 21 1943

My Dear Daughter, Anna Mary,

Some day I shall be able to tell you the conditions under which I write
this letter to you.

You arrived in this world while I was several thousand miles from
your mother's side. There were many anxious moments then and since.

This message comes to you from somewhere in England. I pray God
it will be given to you on or about your tenth birthday. I hope also to be
present when that is done. It shall be held in trust by your mother or
someone equally concerned until that time.

Also I pray that the efforts of your daddy and his buddies will not have
been in vain. That you will always be permitted to enjoy the great freedoms for which this war is being fought. It is not pleasant, but knowing
that our efforts are to be for the good of our children makes it worth the
hardships.

With this letter you will find a war bond of $2500 maturity value, and
a list of names. A list of names to you, honey, buddies to me. Men of my
company, who adopted you as their sweetheart when you came into the
world. It is these men who bought you the bond as a remembrance of
when they were soldiers with your daddy. The money values are in the
current English denominations.

I shall ask your mother to obtain the bond with the money sent her
and keep it with this letter, envelope, and list of names until such time as
she sees fit to give it to you, Anna Mary.

You will never know the joy I knew when I received word that you had
arrived. Suddenly the sun shone through the fog. The mud paths seemed
paved with gold. The boys thought I had gone stir crazy or maybe slap
happy. I guess I was a little daft.

I want you to know that God gave to you for a mother the finest
woman of his creation. I pray that you will grow to be as fine a person as
she. I ask that you follow her guidance and her teachings. I know how
much you mean to her at the time I write this letter. Such a love can never
be forgotten.

It is time that I close this short message to you. Should God decree
that you never know your father I want you to have this sample of my
handwriting. I want you to know and understand that with the help of
God, He will spend his life trying to make you and your precious mother
happy, and to provide for your needs and wants.

Sketch by Capt. George Rarey, on the birth of his son, Damon.

I place you now in the hands of God. May He care for you and love you. May He see fit that we shall see one another very soon and keep us together into eternity, ever as He gave us His son to seal our salvation.

Your loving dad
Walter Schuette

Lt. Walter Schuette did make it home alive and was able to read his letter to Anna Mary on her tenth birthday. Capt. George Rarey, also stationed in England, was informed of the birth of his first child just moments after coming back from a mission on March 22, 1944. Overwhelmed with joy, Rarey sent the following letter to his wife, Betty Lou (nicknamed June), in Washington, D.C. A talented artist, Rarey drew a sketch to commemorate the event.

Darling, Darling, Junie!

Junie, this happiness is nigh unbearable — Got back from a mission at 4:00 this afternoon & came up to the hut for a quick shave before chow and what did I see the deacon waving at me as I walked up the road to the shack? A small yellow envelope — I thought it was a little early but I quit breathing completely until the wonderful news was unfolded — A son! Darling, Junie! How did you do it? — I'm so proud of you I'm beside myself — Oh you darling.

All of the boys in the squadron went wild. Oh its wonderful! I had saved my tobacco ration for the last two weeks & had obtained a box of good American cigars — Old Doc Finn trotted out two quarts of Black and White from his medicine chest and we all toasted the fine new son and his beautiful Mother. Old Bill is proud and almost as excited as I am — He told me that he has known all along that Old Damon would show up ahead of schedule but he didn't say a word until after the fine news — Junie, you rascal, why didn't you let me know?

I think that I've had just about the easiest time of it that any father has had — I was just getting down to the really serious part of the floor pacing — When, Wham! I find that Old Junie has done the whole thing without the unecessary moaning and hollering from the Old Man — And they say that the Woman is the weaker of the sex — Fooie — You're terrific!

Gaily I'm anxious to know all of the details — I figure Damon was born on the 19th — I wonder what he weighs and all about him. Tell him that he has the proudest, happiest and luckiest Pop in the whole world.

Junie if this letter makes no sense forget it — I'm sort of delirious — Today everything is special — This iron hut looks like a castle — The low hanging overcast outside is the most beautiful kind of blue I've ever seen — I'm a father — I have a son! My darling Wife has had a fine boy and I'm a king — Junie, Darling, I hope it wasn't too bad — Oh I'm so glad its over — Thank you, Junie — Thank you — Thank you. This is really living! I shall dash into town in the morning and get a wire off to you — You send them from the post office & their hours are rather odd — I'll have to check on it — Junie, thank Emily for sending the news so quickly — She's wonderful!

Oh, Junie, I wish I could be there — Now I think maybe I could be of some help — There are so many things to be done — What a ridiculous and worthless thing a war is in the light of such a wonderful event. That there will be no war for Damon! — Junie, isn't there anything I can do to help out —

This letter is pretty jumbled — I haven't been alone yet — My thoughts are jumbled and the happiness and joy just sort of overwhelm me. I want to take a walk by myself tonight & just sort of order my thoughts a little — I might even pray a little — But Junie, when I think of you and Damon that's in the nature of a prayer — I worship you both and believe in you as in nothing else —

Oh my beautiful darling, I love you more and more and more — Gosh, I'm happy! — Sweet dreams my sweet mother, Love — Rarey.

Less than three months after writing this letter, twenty-six-year-old Capt. George Rarey was flying over France when German antiaircraft guns shot his plane out of the sky. He did not survive.

~

Army Nurse Vera Lee Writes to Her Family
About a Deadly German Attack on Her Ship in the Gulf of Salerno
&
Pvt. Paul Curtis, Fighting at Anzio, Responds to a Letter
from His Younger Brother, Mitchell, Asking What Combat Is Like

"It wasn't just my brother's country, or my husband's country," said Beatrice Hood Stroup of the Women's Army Corps, "it was my country as well. And so this war wasn't just their war, it was my war, and I needed to serve in it." During World War II literally hundreds of thousands of American women volunteered for military service in the Women's Army Corps (WACs), the Marines, the Women's Air Force Service Pilots (WASPs), the Navy's Women Accepted for Voluntary Service (WAVES), and the Coast Guard's SPARS, derived from its motto Semper Paratus—*"Always Ready." Employed as radio operators, mechanics, cryptographers, truck drivers, gunnery instructors, electricians, intelligence analysts, air-raid wardens, control-tower personnel, and pilots, their responsibilties extended far beyond the cler-*

ical work that some, uncomfortable with the idea of women in uniform, had argued they were best suited for in wartime. Over 72,000 women also served as war nurses, many of them working in or very near to combat zones. Hundreds of American women died as a result of their service in the war, and in the middle of September 1943 army nurse Vera Lee came close to being one of them. Beginning on September 9, Allied forces began a ferocious six-day invasion of Salerno, Italy, that nearly failed. Lee, with the Ninety-fifth Evacuation Hospital, was aboard the HMS Newfoundland *in the Gulf of Salerno. Despite its colored lights identifying it as a hospital ship, the Germans targeted the* Newfoundland *on September 13, killing several nurses. Two and a half months later, Lee wrote to her family in Lewellen, Nebraska, to describe the bombing.*

Wed - Nov 24 - '43

Dearest all:

Just yesterday I wrote you a letter but your air mail of Oct 30th & V-mail of Nov 7th came this morning so will answer them today. Jan and I got up for breakfast this morning and made a dashing trip with our mail man to another town to have my picture taken for my Identification or a.g.o. card. I've been without a bit of Identification since the bombing — no dog tags, no pay datta card — I'm almost not in this army. It has sort of worried me to — because something could have happened & no one know who I belong to. I still have my chain around my neck but the dog tags were torn off — Guess that something fell on my chest that morning & took them off.

I still don't know if this will pass this the censor but will try & tell you what happened the 13th of Sept. We tried to land in Italy all day Sunday the 12th but they were too busy fighting to worry about a hundred nurses on a hospital ship. Several bombs just missed us several times but we didn't really realize what it was all about. Evening came & we had to go out of the harbor because our ship was all lit up. We taxied around in the sea off shore about 30 miles all nite — our ship & 4 other Hospital ships — at 5 a.m. we were awakened by a bomb falling very close to us — Some of the girls dressed then but most of us went back to sleep. (We all slept in the nood because all our clothes were packed & ready to get off the ship the next morning.)

At 5:10 we heard a plane & then that bad awful whistle a bomb makes & bang!—You'll never know of the thousand things that flashed thro my mind those few seconds. I thought sure I was dying — could feel hot water falling on my face & body — Had heavy boards on my chest that had fallen from the ceiling — I shut my eyes & thought it was the end — Then the next second I thought "What the hell, I'm not dead — get out of this place" — then I could see poor Wheeler & Waldin without a stitch of clothes on trying to find anything to put on. I couldn't see for the terrific smoke in our room — but was a mass of motion trying to find my coveralls which I had hung on the post hole the nite before. I found them on the floor — all soaked with water & black with dirt — put them on & found my shoes — grabbed my helmet & water canteen & grabbed on to someone's arm & followed the light that Claudine was holding. She couldn't hardly find where the door was because the wall had all been blown out.

When we got on the deck we all had to get on one side because the bomb had torn away the other side of the ship. I'll never forget seeing this one British nurse trying to get thro the porthole but was too large to make it. She was screaming terribly because her room was all in flames. One British fellow saw that she could never get out so he knocked her in the head with his fist and shoved her back in his room — She died but it was much easier than if she had burned to death.

We loaded in a life boat — 70 of us in one boat that had a capacity of 30. Were taken on another hospital ship & given tea & hot coffee. I felt a darn good cry coming on so some British fellow took the 4 of we girls to his room & we drank a bottle of Scotch. I got "stinko" drunk — cried & when I snapped out of it, I felt fine. All the bruises I got out of it was a scratch on my knee, a cut on my left foot and marks & scratches on my chest where debree fell from the roof.

— Someday I'll tell you more about it. . . .

Love,
Vera

By the time of the Salerno invasion, neighboring Sicily had already been overtaken by Gen. George S. Patton Jr.'s Seventh Army and Field Marshal Bernard Montgomery's Eighth Army. (It was in Sicily on August 10, 1943, that Patton sparked an uproar by striking a quivering, shell-shocked soldier for, in Patton's view, being a "goddamned coward.") Italian forces surrendered to the Allies on September 8 and, a month later, declared war on Germany. Benito Mussolini, the fascist dictator and Hitler ally blamed by Italians for dragging their country into war, was arrested. (Months later Mussolini would be executed, and his bullet-ridden corpse hanged upside down by its heels in Milan.) Furious at the betrayal, Hitler ordered 640,000 Italians taken prisoner, the majority of whom were shipped to slave labor camps where many of them died. German troops still held Italy in a stranglehold, and on January 22, 1944, Allied divisions hit the beaches of Anzio, over thirty miles south of Rome. Despite a successful landing, precious time was squandered and German forces were able to mobilize a punishing counterattack. Paul Curtis, a twenty-three-year-old army private from Oak Ridge, Tennessee, was one of thousands of soldiers pinned down at Anzio. Curtis had received a letter from his younger brother asking for his thoughts on combat, and, after participating in the hellish fighting that eventually broke through the German lines, Curtis was able to tell his brother exactly how he felt.

May 28, 1944
Anzio, Italy

Dear Mitchell:

I just finished writing you a V-Mail, but it seems I had something else to say, so I attempt this air mail. I haven't had a chance to write you for the past four or five days.

As I told you in the V-Mail, I have seen some action—a few hard, hard, days in which I saw more than I imagined I ever would. I don't think any man can exactly explain combat. It's beyond words. Take a combination of fear, anger, hunger, thirst, exhaustion, disgust, loneliness, homesickness, and wrap that all up in one reaction and you might approach the feelings a fellow has. It makes you feel mighty small, helpless and alone. It's a comfort to know there's one who is present at all times and anywhere ready to help you through. My faith in God has been steadily growing stronger all along. Without faith, I don't see how anyone could stand this. It all seems so useless, but I realize Germany must be stopped; but they will rise again for peace will be settled by men who have never known combat and naturally they will hold no bitterness nor dread of another war, for they don't know. This war could have been avoided.

I thought I had been tired before in my life, but nothing like this; but still you can and do go on. Every time you stop you dig a hole which has saved many lives. The ground is so hard and dry that digging is very hard. You don't get so very hungry, but thirst drives you crazy. I have drunk water with everything in it and liked it. You have no energy but still you go on.

The battle seems like something in a faraway land, and everything seems sad, lonely, and dark. The roar is even as bad as the movies have it. The cries of the wounded are pitiful. They seem so helpless. The dead seem forsaken, but they are out of it all as in the Masonic textbook—"The gentle breeze fans their verdant covering, they heed it not, sunshine and storm pass over them, they are neither delighted nor disturbed"—so it is in this battle, the things rage on all around them, but they are still and quiet.

You wanted to know how I felt after I saw action and I have told you all I can that will pass the censors; I imagine all new men feel about the same and I know old men feel differently and so will I, but that's for now.

Love,
Paul

This was Paul Curtis's last letter home; he was killed three days later, only fifteen miles from Rome. (Two of Curtis's other brothers—John, eighteen, and Lee, twenty-six—also died in the war.) On June 4, U.S. and British soldiers marched triumphantly into Rome, the first European capital wrested from the control of the German Wehrmacht. Allied forces a thousand miles away would storm the beaches of Normandy less than forty-eight hours later.

~⁀⌒

Pfc. Dom Bart Provides His Wife, Mildred, with a Moment-by-Moment Account of Going Ashore at Normandy on the Morning of June 6, 1944
&
S. Sgt. Eugene Lawton Shares with His Parents What Was Going Through His Mind Before, During, and After the D-Day Invasion

Pacing in his headquarters in England as torrential rains and wind rattled the windows, Supreme Allied Commander Dwight D. Eisenhower carefully weighed his options. An estimated 175,000 Allied troops were awaiting his command to begin the largest, most logistically complicated amphibious invasion in history—Operation Overlord. Launched from England's southern coast, an armada of 6,000 warships and 12,000 planes were to cross the English Channel into German-occupied France to begin the liberation of Europe. The problem was the weather. Reports were conflicting, some indicating continued thunderstorms, others clearing skies. A cross-Channel assault of such magnitude would be impossible in raging seas and overcast conditions, but postponement only increased the odds Overlord would be exposed. And surprise was essential. Eisenhower turned to the fourteen principal subordinates he had gathered in his headquarters and asked for their advice. They split right down the middle. Eisenhower paused, and then said simply: "OK, let's go." On June 6, 1944, British and Canadian troops hit the beaches on the Normandy coast designated "Gold," "Juno," and "Sword," as the Americans descended on "Utah" and "Omaha." German forces barraged incoming troops on all five beaches, but Omaha suffered the most; a steel blizzard rained down on the men from cliff-top bunkers, wiping out almost entire companies in minutes. Weighed down by their backpacks, many drowned as they struggled ashore. But the Americans, through individual acts of heroism, prevailed and the beachhead was secured by nightfall. "What memories dear," Pfc. Dom Bart, who was with the Twenty-ninth Infantry Division and part of the first wave that took Omaha, recalled to his wife, Mildred, back in Brooklyn.

It was 6:30 in the morning and just about to land between Point-du-Hoc and Vierville-sur-Mer on the beaches of Normandie, Omaha Beach, the Allies called it.

In the far away distance I could hear the rumble of the artillery and the brrrp-brrrp of machine gun fire.

The elements were at their worst and our landing craft was half filled with water. We used our helmuts to throw it overboard and I never thought we would make it. Some of the boats never reached shore. It was a horrible sight.

Finally the word came—Let's go—and there we were in combat, something new in my life. But oh, what an experience.

We didn't have a chance to fight back, as we were dropped in water over our heads. No one's fault as the entire beach was strewn with mines. With a stream of lead coming towards us, we were at the mercy of the Germans and we had all to do to reach shore and recuperate. I floated around in water for about one hour and was more dead than alive. Tried to land at several places, but always had to withdraw. It was impossible to get ashore.

I lost all hopes and said my last prayer to the Good Lord. The prayer was a passage to safety, but I sure was in a bad way. Got to the beach half frozen and almost unable to move and then I passed out. How long I remained there, I don't recall, but when I came to, the fighting was at a climax. Pulled myself together and sought a rifle and around I went trying to locate my outfit. It didn't take long to spot them and was I glad. But gracious Lord, what was left of them, just a handful, about 25 out of 160. The battalion was almost wiped out, 800 casualties out of 1000 men.

Our position was desperate, but with sheer will, fear and luck we overcame all obstacles and pushed inland to capture Vierville-sur-Mer, our first town. The price was high but covered ourselves with glory and for that we received the Presidential Citation. Later on we received another at Vire, France.

Yes darling, our outfit can be proud for the part it has played in helping to win this war. Whenever there was a tough nut to crack, the 1st BN., 116th Infantry, 29th Division was called on and always came through with flying colors. I'm very proud of it.

Let's forget about the past for awhile and talk about today.

Today was declared a holiday by Eisenhower and church services were held for all, in memoriam of the boys who paid the supreme sacrifice on D-Day and hereafter. It was a simple requiem but with plenty of meaning behind it.

> Bye sweet, until tomorrow.
> Love and kisses,
> Dom

Twenty-eight-year-old S. Sgt. Eugene Lawton, with the Second Infantry Division, also went ashore at Normandy and wrote home about it less than two months after the invasion. In the following letter to his parents in Tarentum, Pennsylvania, Lawton not only related the drama of the landing, but articulated what he was thinking during this historic moment.

August, 31, 1944

Hello Mom and Dad,

Have had plenty of time to review the past two months of my life. In the following paragraphs shall try and explain or perhaps should say put into words a few of my experiences. Of course a few of the events must wait until after this war, as censorship closes the door on many military problems.

One's thoughts go deep into the past when moving across water on a troop ship. And can say the move to France left me with the feeling of "seeing the past and trying to look through the fog into the future."

Long before we landed on enemy soil, saw that here was what my years in Army had come to. Again I wondered if I remembered all my training that was going to be called on in next few hours. For you see a maneuver may answer a few of the questions, but no man can put his mind at ease as to what he will do under fire, till he's actually under the fire. Didn't have long to wait.

We hit water from an assault boat and waded ashore. Didn't try running in water as this only uses up one's energy that will be needed later on. (Here for the first time my training was being put to use against the enemy) Never run in water as you can be carried along by waves much easier. Touched solid ground and we all were on the move at a run. There was quite a bit of noise around of big guns being fired from ship to shore. So didn't realize was being shot at until saw slugs leaving their calling cards on the sand. No time to stop and think right now, must get some protection. So covered ground at full speed, ending up under cover of rising in the ground. Again my training was put to use. (Never hit the ground in the open when under fire) Here for the first time believe me all my training in the states saved my life.

Now under cover of this high ground we were safe for the time being. But somewhere in front of us was an enemy who knew how to soldier.

I guess I did like the rest of the boys. Looking around saw that ones who had gone on before us, left the silent of every battle behind. Here I was with two other soldiers behind this ground not knowing just what to do. This in my opinion is the worst time in any soldier's life. I knew the other two fellows were waiting on me as was the only Sgt. among the three. Saw a Lieutenant off to my right with a few men. Never was so glad to see any one man in my life as right now. Lay there listening to firing up front. Was quite away up there so didn't have a great deal to worry about at the present time.

Again looked across at the Lieutenant, he was still in the same place. In fact he hadn't moved a bit. In next few minutes saw him looking around and getting a picture of what was before us. Saw him move and yell at the same time to move up on the hill. I yelled to men on my left and we moved on up towards the front.

So this was my first time under enemy fire. Still wasn't up in the thick of the fight. Couldn't figure out where the enemy was that fired at us coming in on the beach. Later on in rear area found out was a sniper giving us trouble. He from all reports will give no one else any trouble.

My first night in France was one I will remember always. We dug fox holes and had guards placed along line the whole night through. Each and every one of us taking our turn. The ones who weren't on guard could sleep if possible but can say that not a man went to sleep that first night.

Just at dark heard planes overhead very high. Had no way of knowing if ours or was Jerry himself. Hadn't long to wait for within the next few minutes saw a sight that will always be very vivid in my mind. The planes droned out over our ships anchored along the coast. Up went more anti-aircraft fire than from all reports has ever been concentrated in one spot before. The amazing sight of these tracers going up into the sky left it a complete mass of red death to any plane within this protection circle of anti-aircraft fire. It was a beautiful sight from our point of view but to the Jerry it was something beyond his own imagination. If you have followed Ernie Pyle's column you may have read his opinion on this scene of coast of France. Yes, it was beautiful, but a kind of beauty only a soldier can understand.

You can readily see why no one slept that night. For right here was history in the making. Events taking place that kids will be reading about in future at school. Yes I for one was proud that I had the honor of helping in my small way in this present conflict.

I noticed many more things but have given you the ones that seemed to stand out above all the rest. Some things I can't write about so will skip that and drift on into the next events that have already made headlines in the states.

The green fields and hedge rows of Normandy was our next problem. We had already a working plan of just how to go about getting the Square heads out of these blasted hedges. Of course just how we were going to do it must wait until after the war.

The next morning we were all set for running the Germans clear into Berlin. We moved up to the jumping off place and was ready for Fritzy along the hedges of the the fields to our front. My first look-see along the banks between fields reminded me of hunting ground-hogs back home. The Super race (I hope Goebbels won't mind) was dug down and into the banks. But as said before we had a way of getting them out. After putting it into effect we had some coming up with the old term "Kamarad" and some didn't get up. The rest were on the move towards Berlin.

This much I can say it takes team work between Infantry, Tanks, Artillery and Air Force. Perhaps I can give you a better understanding of what I mean. Football is a great game but it takes eleven players working together. One fellow moves under the protection of his team. Apply that to fighting over here and you have an idea of what I mean.

Yes Mom and Dad, I have told you about a few things up to a certain time. Am afraid I can't go beyond what have already told you. You see events that happened the past few weeks am not allowed to write about. Can say I was hit but as to date, time, and place, well as censorship doesn't permit it, why try to write about it. Take up where I left off when time allows it.

Am doing fine here in England. Up and around now, even played a game of horse shoes to-day, so you all haven't a thing to worry about.

I have my own opinion of what the censor may think of this letter. Yes, there is an end and this is it.

Love always,
Son-ny.

This was one of Staff Sargeant Lawton's last letters home; he was killed months later in Belgium during the Battle of the Bulge.

～

Gen. George S. Patton Jr., Removed from the Main Action on D-Day, Offers Some Fatherly Advice to His Son George

"It is Hell to be on the side lines and see all the glory eluding me," wrote Gen. George S. Patton Jr. on June 6, 1944. But as much as he hated it, Patton was an integral part of one of the most brilliantly orchestrated deceptions in military history: Operation Fortitude. As tens of thousands of Allied troops poured onto the beaches of Normandy, Adolf Hitler was certain it was a feint. The real invasion force, he insisted, would leave from Dover (the English port closest to France), and strike at Pas-de-Calais. German reconnaissance had determined that an army of enormous size was mobilizing near Dover under the command of Patton, the Allied general

the Germans most feared. In fact, there was no army. Hollywood set designers had
helped the Allies construct dummy airfields, oil storage depots, and landing craft
near Dover. Full-size inflatable rubber tanks were lined up in massive rows. Fake
messsages were transmitted to simulate radio traffic, and double agents fed the Ger-
mans misleading information. Field Marshal Erwin Rommel pleaded with Hitler
to release armored divisions from the Calais region after the Normandy landings,
but Hitler refused, convinced the main assault was still to come. (By the time Hitler
recognized his folly, the Allies were firmly established in France.) On D-Day, itself,
the commander of the phantom army had virtually nothing to do. Crushed he was
missing "the opening kick-off," a restless Patton whittled away the hours writing in
his diary and sending off letters, including the following to his son George, enrolled
at West Point. (Excerpts of this letter have been published before, but they were
edited for length and clarity. The entire letter is transcribed below as it was originally
typed.)

Dear George:

At 0700 this morning the BBC announced that the German Radio
had just come out with an announcement of the landing of Allied Para-
troops and of large numbers of assault craft near shore.So that is it.

This group of unconquerable heros whom I command are not in yet
but we will be soon-I wish I was there now as it is a lovley sunny day for
a battle and I am fed up with just sitting.

I have no immediate idea of being killed but one can never tell and
none of us can live for ever so if I should go dont worry but set your self
to do better than I have.

All men are timid on entering any fight whether it is the first fight or the
last fight all of us are timid.Cowards are those who let their timidity get the
better of their manhood.You will never do that because of your blood lines
on both sides.I think I have told you the story of Marshall Touraine who
fought under Louis XIV.On the morning of one of his last battles-he had
been fighting for forty years-he was mounting his horse when a young
ADC who had jsut come from the court and had never missed a meal or
heard a hostile shot said: "M. de Touraine it amazes me that a man of your
supposed courage should permit his knees to tremble as he walks out to
mount." Touraine replied " My lord duke I admit that my knees do tremble but should they know where I shall this day take them they would
shake even more." That is it. Your knees may shake but they will always
take you towards the enemy.Well so much for that.

There are apparently two types of successful soldiers.Those who get
on by being unobtrusive and those who get on by being obtrusive I am
of the latter type and seem to be rare and unpopular: but it is my method.

One has to choose a system and stick to it people who are not them selves are nobody.

To be a successful soldier you must know history.Read it objectively—dates and even the minute details of tactics are useless.What you must know is how man reacts.Weapons change but man who uses then changes not at all.To win battles you do not beat weapons you beat the soul of man of the enemy man.To do that you have to destroy his weapons but that is only incidental.You must read biography and especially autobiography.If you will do it you will find that war is simple.Decide what will hurt the enemy most within the limits of your capabilities to harm him and then do it.TAKE CALCULATED RISKS.That is quite different from being rash.My personal belief is that if you have a 50% chance take it because the superior fighting qualities of American soldiers lead by me will surely give you the extra 1% necessary.

In Sicaly I decided as a result of my information,observations and a sixth sense that I have that the enemy did not have another large scale attack in his system.I bet my shirt on that and I was right.You cannot make war safely but no dead general has ever been criticised so you have that way out always.

I am sure that if every leader who goes into battle will promise him self that he will come out either a conquerer or a corpse he is sure to win.There is no doubt of that.Defeat is not due to losses but to the destruction of the soul of the leaders.The "Live to fight another day"doctrine.

The most vital quality a soldier can possess is SELF CONFIDENCE utter complete and bumptious. You can have doubts about your good looks,about your intelligence, about your self control but to win in war you must have NO doubts about your ability as a soldier.

What success I have had results from the fact that I have always been certain that my military reactions were correct.Many people do not agree with me;they are wrong.The unerring jury of history written long after both of us are dead will prove me correct.

Note that I speak of "Military reactions"no one is borne with them any more than any one is borne with muscles.You can be borne with the soul capable of correct military reactions or the body capable of having big muscles but both qualities must be developed by hard work.

The intensity of your desire to acquire any special ability depends on character ,on ambition.I think that your decision to study this summer instead of enjoying your self shows that you have character and ambition-they are wonderful possessions.

Soldiers ,all men in fact, are natural hero worshipers.Officers with a flare for command realise thisand emphasize in their conduct,dress and deportment the qualities they seek to produce in their men. When I was a second lieutenant I had a captain who was very sloppy and usually late yet he got after the men for just those faults;he was a failure.

The troops I have commanded have always been well dressed,been smart saluters,been prompt and bold in action because I have personally set the example in these qualities.The influence one man can have on thousands is a neverending source of wonder to me.You are always on parade.Officers who through lazyness or a foolish desire to be popular fail to inforce discipline and the proper wearing of uniforms and equipment not in the presence of the enemy will also fail in battle and if they fail in battle they are potential murderers.There is no such thing as : "A good field soldier"you are either a good soldier or a bad soldier.

Well this has been quite a sermon but dont get the idea that it is my swan song because it is not I have not finished my job yet.

Your affectionate father

Seven weeks later, on August 1, Patton's Third Army officially became operational. "The waiting was pretty bad and lasted well after Bastile day, but now we are in the biggest battle I have ever fought and it is going fine except at one town [St. Malo] we have failed to take," Patton wrote to his wife, Beatrice, just days after resuming command. "I am going there in a minute to kick some ones ass." The old general was back in action and could not have been happier.

~∿

Pfc. Charles McCallister, with the 101st Airborne, Describes to His Aunt Mima Her Son Jim's Heroic Last Moments Before Being Killed
&
Shaken by the "Terror" of Battle, Capt. George Montgomery with the Eighty-second Airborne Tells His Fiancée, Arline, He Loves Her More Than Ever
&
2nd Lt. Jack Lundberg Assures His Parents That, If He Should Die in Combat, Sacrificing His Life for the United States Is More Than Worth It

Just after midnight on June 6, 1944, 23,000 paratroopers, comprised mostly of the American Eighty-second and 101st Airborne Divisions, were dropped throughout the French countryside. Fooled as they may have been by the amphibious landings at Normandy, the Germans were thoroughly prepared inland. Fields were flooded so that paratroopers would be drowned upon landing. (Many were.) Strategically placed machine-gunners shot men to pieces as they helplessly floated to earth. Widely scattered and separated from their units, which made them easier to kill or capture, the surviving U.S. troops rallied as best they could and seized key bridges and cross-roads against tremendous odds. Pfc. James W. Dashner, with the 101st Airborne, staved off approaching German soldiers with a machine gun before a shell blew him apart. His cousin Pfc. Charles McCallister, also with the 101st, "liberated" a German bicycle and rode around trying to find Dashner, not realizing he was already dead. After learning what happened from an eyewitness, McCallister wrote to Dashner's mother with the terrible news.

My dearest Aunt:

I suppose this is the first time I have ever written to you Aunt Mima. I have always been able to maintain the closest contact through Mom and it never seemed necessary. I am sorry that this first letter must be written under such a sad circumstance but I hope we may come to know each other better through future correspondence and that we may be able to comfort each other in some way.

At a time like this, it's hard for any one, especially one who isn't good at words such as I, to say anything that might be of comfort to someone who has suffered a great loss like you have, but since I can at least tell you how James met his death, I feel that it might be of some comfort to you.

When Jim came to see me a few weeks before the invasion, I knew instinctively when I first saw him that I would like him. First of all his wonderful physique and handsome features command respect and once you talked with him his honest ways and great personality made you like him very much. We were friends from the start. We had a pleasant afternoon of talking of home and loved ones and then I walked out on the road with him where he flagged a truck going toward his camp. We shook hands and wished each other luck and I thought as I watched him running to catch his truck—"What a great guy!"

That was the last time I saw him. I knew he jumped in France because he is in the same division as I am and I hoped to meet him there. His regiment was close by all the time but there was no time to try to get together until the 10th day when I located his company and went over to see about him. I found his platoon and it only took a glance around to prove to me Jim wasn't there. I hoped for the best but dreaded to ask about him. By chance I approached a former very close friend of his who was with him at the time, and when he told me what had happened it was quite a blow. By this time I had lost many friends and thought I had become hardened to it, but this was different. Jim was part of the family, the same blood as mine and that was different. But the battle field is no place to grieve so I made an effort to control my feelings and asked the fellow to tell me the details. This is what he told me:

"Jim's Section Leader had been killed and Jim was in charge so he took over the machine gun himself. His platoon was sent out on a flank and ran into plenty trouble. The enemy had them surrounded on three sides and had them pinned down with fire. Jim took the machine gun and crawled forward to a good position and set up the gun and began firing. He was in a spot and was doing plenty of good, so the heinies started concentrating all their efforts on him. They were trying to get him with a mortar. His platoon leader saw they were getting close and yelled to Jim that he'd better get out of there. The boys in the platoon said it was possible Jim didn't hear as they had never known him to refuse to obey an order but his friends seem to think he was just mad and was doing so much good at the time he didn't want to move. So he stayed right there and fired until his gun was red hot. Then they got zeroed in on him and landed a mortar shell right on top of him. He died instantly but his hand was still clutching the trigger. As a result of his continued fire, the platoon was able to advance on their objective."

On the way back to my outfit I let myself go and cried like a baby but I wasn't ashamed of it.

When his son gets old enough, tell him how his father died and his son's son, for our family must never forget him. Let's try to replace grief with pride in the way he died and the things he died for, as that is the way Jim would want it.

Yes, his outfit has lost a great soldier, his buddies have lost a great friend, but you have lost a son. God has not left us with out consolation. We know that all is done in fulfillment of God's will and that not even a sparrow falls that He does not know, and though we are inclined to ask the reason why—who are we to question His will. He has promised that we shall one day all be together again and there find happiness that shall never end, where there is no sorrow, tears nor grief. Jim is there tonight under God's loving care. He will never again have to experience the horrors of battle. I can hear him saying—"don't grieve for me, I'm happy here, and when we meet again, we will never be separated." I talked to Jim, Aunt Mima. He was ready to go—I know.

No one knows how heavy your heart is tonight, but if I could in some small way help to take his place, I would like to be your son. I know that I could never fill his place in your heart just as no one could take the place of my mother if God should see fit to take her away, but we can be a comfort to each other.

I want you to let Jim's wife and baby know that if there is any way in which I might ever help them, for them not to hesitate to call on me. There is nothing I wouldn't do for them for Jim's sake.

Give my love and sympathy to them and Martha and his brothers.

With all my love,
Charles.

McCallister later learned that, although everything about his cousin's actions under fire were true, the shell that killed Dashner was fired not by the Germans, but from an American warship off the coast of Normandy. In the fury of battle, a miscalculation caused the round to fall short. It was this very randomness—the bullet that missed by only a few inches or the enemy grenade that dropped at one's feet but inexplicably failed to explode—that so unnerved soldiers and other servicemen. Capt. George Montgomery, with the Eighty-second Airborne, also parachuted into France on D-Day and came within inches of being killed numerous times. Shaken by three weeks in combat, Montgomery wrote to his fiancée, Arline, who was serving as an army nurse in New Guinea, to let her know he was still alive—so far— and that his love for her had only grown.

Arline, my dearest—

Today is our 20th day in action, yet it seems like years. What has happened to me and my Battalion would be scoffed at, even in a 10¢ novel, as being impossible. Why the few of us left alive—are alive—is something to figure out in church. I've seen as many of my very best friends killed beside me. I just can't believe it is all really happening. I never in my wildest dreams knew such terror could grip your very soul. The business of landing deep in enemy territory & trying to hold a position assaulted and shelled from 4 sides until friendly troops break through is something I hope they never ask me to do again.

The night we jumped, D-Day—6 hrs, was the pay off night. The Jerries knew our plans down to the last detail and were waiting for us with everything they had. My chute was on fire from tracer bullets when I landed—right in front of a machine gun emplacement. I cut out of my harness & crawled for a couple of hours with bullets whistling past my ears coming from seemingly every direction. I can't tell you what else went on—but the story gets good from there. I hope it won't be too long before I can tell you personally all that has happened. Anyway—God alone brought me safely through this far—of that I'm sure.

We have had mail brought to us twice and have been permitted to write twice. Both mail calls brought me letters from you Arline—& I could have wept with joy & relief to hear from you & that you were still of a mind to be Mrs. G. Montgomery one of these days. I'm being as careful as I can be so as to get back to you—but there are times when it's just up to the good Lord whether you get it or you don't.

My darling, I love you more than life itself—I've realized that many times these last 3 weeks when I thought I was going to be killed & always the regret of missing seeing & marrying you was topmost in my mind at the time. I think I can say my love for you has been pretty well tested.

Goodbye for awhile,

—George

Capt. George Montgomery returned home to Iowa after the war and married Arline in 1946. But, as Montgomery hinted in his letter, he was well aware of how precarious life was in battle and that every day could be the last. This realization plagued those who fought, and many made certain they wrote an "in the event I don't make it back. . . ." letter just in case. Some gave the letter to a friend with instructions to forward it should the worst happen. And some, like twenty-five-year-old 2nd Lt. Jack Lundberg, mailed it home themselves before they went into combat. Lundberg wrote his "final" letter a few weeks before D-Day to assure his loved ones in Woods Cross, Utah, he was more than ready to die and only regretted the pain it would cause them, and his new wife, Mary.

19 May 1944

Dear Mom, Pop and family,

Now that I am actually here I see that the chances of my returning to all of you are quite slim, therefore I want to write this letter now while I am yet able.

I want you to know how much I love each of you. You mean every-thing to me and it is the realization of your love that gives me the courage to continue. Mom and Pop—we have caused you innumerable hard-ships and sacrifices—sacrifices which you both made readily and gladly that we might get more from life.

I have always determined to show my appreciation to you by enabling you both to have more of the pleasures of life—but this war has pre-vented my so doing for the past three years.

If you receive this letter I shall be unable to fulfill my desires, for I have requested that this letter be forwarded only in the event I do not return.

You have had many times more than your share of illness and deaths in the family—still you have continued to exemplify what true parents should. I am sorry to add to your grief—but at all times realize that my thoughts are of you constantly and that I feel that in some small way I am helping to bring this wasteful war to a conclusion.

We of the United States have something to fight for—never more fully have I realized that. There just is no other country with comparable wealth, advancement, or standard of living. The U.S.A. is worth a sacrifice!

Remember always that I love you each most fervently and I am proud of you. Consider Mary, my wife, as having taken my place in the family circle and watch over each other.

Love to my family,
Jack

Almost prophetically 2nd Lt. Jack Lundberg had, indeed, written his last letter home. Two and a half weeks after D-Day, Lundberg was the lead navigator on a B-17 flying over Abbeville, France on a mission to bomb the town's railroad station. Struck by German antiaircraft fire, the plane burst into flames and crashed. His body was not recovered until nine months after his death. Although Lundberg's family had the option of having him returned to the United States, they chose to have him buried with his comrades at the American Cemetery in Normandy, France.

―――――― *Extended Correspondence* ――――――

**Combat Nurse June Wandrey Describes to Her Family
the Challenges of Working in a Field Hospital,
Receives a "Dear June" Letter from Her Beau in the U.S.,
Writes to Her Sister About a Memorable Visit to the Vatican, and
Grieves Over the Fate of a Young Patient**

Decades after the war, June Wandrey thought back fondly on one of her first assignments as a nurse at Fort Custer in Battle Creek, Michigan. "One ward was full of fellows suffering from pilonidal cysts, affectionately called Jeep Seats," Wandrey recalled. "It was the most cheerful ward. Each AM, when the Major and I walked in to change their dressings and check their surgery, I'd call out, 'Bottoms up, fellows.' Thirty plump pairs of smiling buns would turn skyward." Twenty-two-years-old when she enlisted in the Army Nurse Corps, Wandrey was 5' 2" tall with, in her own words, "finely honed muscles that were dynamite ready." (She signed one of her first letters away from home, "Your littlest tomboy.") In March 1943 Wandrey journeyed across the Atlantic where for the next two and a half years she would serve throughout Western Europe and North Africa as a combat nurse. The work was bloody, often exhilarating, sometimes tedious, and very dangerous. Almost a year after her arrival, Wandrey wrote to her family in Wisconsin to give them an idea of the conditions in which she and her colleagues lived and, quite literally, operated.

2–9–44 Somewhere in Italy

Dear Family,

It has been a hellish bit of night duty. Admitting critically wounded patients on the double, getting them cleaned up, starting I.V.s, changing dressings, getting them something to eat (if they could), and giving medications. You have to keep involved records of everything for the Army; that's as it should be.

To compound the misery, it started to pour and the tents leak. They are filled to over capacity and there is no place to put the poor soldiers to keep them dry. We're high up in the mountains and it gets bitter cold, noisy too. The big guns boom all night long and shake the ground. My fingers are so cold I have to warm them over my candle so that I can hold the pen to write.

The Germans bombed and strafed a hospital on the beachhead a few days ago. Latest reports listed 23 dead and 68 wounded. The dead included two nurses, six patients, 14 of the hospital personnel, and a Red Cross worker. The dead patients were in the receiving ward with wounds suffered at the front and were waiting to be operated on. The hospital was more than half a mile from the nearest military target. Fragmentation bombs were dropped on the operating and administrative areas and the ward tents. Two litter bearers were hit while carrying a "chest case" to the operating ward. The men tried to hold up the litter but they had to let it drop. The report said the patient has a chance of pulling through.

Incidentally, we, too, were scheduled to go in on the beachhead but our orders were cancelled at the very last minute. Mother, I feel your prayers for me are getting top priority. We were also scheduled for the Salerno landings, and they also were cancelled at the last minute.

I wish you could see me tonight. For a change, I swore that I was going to be WARM. Over the first layer, (my long woolen underwear, a wool sweater, a wool olive drab shirt), I wear a pair of men's fatigues. My GI shoes, which are two sizes too big for me, are also men's. They are covered with mud to the tops.

Wearily,
June

Less than two and half months later, in late March 1944, Wandrey was stunned to receive the following letter from her beau, an officer residing in the States. (Names have been changed to protect the privacy of certain individuals.)

June Darling,

Had intended writing to you on Saturday evening and at the same time take care of a lot of old correspondence which I've accumulated over a period of months. Was OD that night and, after making early rounds, I stopped at the Club for supposedly a few minutes but got stuck in a bridge game, which lasted out the evening. Had a few good cards and also a lot of bad. Haven't played much bridge since Mary left.

Yesterday was another beautiful day, just about as nice as any spring day could be. Went for a long walk in the afternoon and then last night went to the show in Bay Shore with Pat the WAC officer. The picture we saw was "Up in Arms", very good but somewhat misleading as to the grand and glorious life of the Army Nurse Corps.

Received two letters from you this morning, darling, both quite old, and another on Friday written March 14th. Am very happy to hear that you have had the opportunity to go to the Rest Camp for a little vacation. It was long past due, and I know has been pleasant. I still so much wish, however, that you might have been returned to the States instead and still hope that that day will not have to be too far in the future.

Darling, there is something I have wanted to write about for the past several weeks and is something I feel should be discussed. Regardless of the final outcome, I feel that it is no more than fair to all concerned that I tell you now, otherwise I'm afraid that some day I might feel the perfect heel and be ashamed even to face myself. If you've not already guessed, I am referring to the love tangle I've become involved in.

On one or two previous occasions, I've mentioned Mary in my letters. Whether you had ever thought or wondered if I was becoming too interested in someone else, I don't know, but it almost seems that at time you must have.

Our friendship started very casually with an occasional date, never dreaming of or having any desire to go steady with anyone. In a short while, however, it became quite apparent that ours was to be more than just a casual acquaintance, at which time I laid the cards on the table and told Mary all about you because I did not want to find a one-sided love affair developing, and then some day for her to be badly hurt. After that I felt much better, had a clear conscience and things went along fine. Months went by and friendship turned to love, I know we both realized it but were afraid to face it. Was even afraid to admit it to myself, not knowing just how to cope with the situation. She felt much the same, not wanting to hurt you nor wanting to be hurt herself. I never once thought it would be possible to fall in love with someone else nor that I could be so much in love with two different persons. I found that I was wrong.

Mary was transferred and has been gone five weeks, which has given me the opportunity to think this through more clearly and on an unbiased basis but still has not enabled me to arrive at any satisfactory decision. Darling I've had many sleepless and worried nights but can't see through the fog I'm engulfed in. This, June, is just one more and important reason why I want you to return to the States now, because I don't want this to drag out indefinitely. It has been more than difficult to write this letter, darling, but at least I now feel as though a heavy weight has been lifted from my heart and mind.

My love, Del

Wandrey sent the letter to her family, along with the attached note:

Mother, Daddy and Ruthie, it is cruel "To lift the weight from a man's heart and mind," who is living stateside in great comfort and luxury in his custom-tailored uniforms and dump it on another's heart and mind, who is living in a tent in the mud, being rocked by artillery fire in the mountains, and harassed by low-flying German fighters. I can understand civilians not knowing how war is fought, but I cannot understand how officers can be so naive. He says, "Return to the States now." Am I supposed to go to General Mark Clark, letter in hand, and get permission to leave the battle zone? Lying creatively, in a short letter, I gently let him off the hook. In spirit, I joined the legion of soldiers in ETO who received a Dear John letter. "Love postponed on account of war" became my battle cry.

Just,
June

Despite the heartache, Wandrey maintained her sense of humor. Throughout her hundreds of wartime letters to friends and family, Wandrey was constantly making puns, relating humorous anecdotes, and sending mildly risqué poems. In June 1944 she had the opportunity to see the Vatican, and the visit, as described in the follow-ing letter to her older sister, turned out to be rather eventful.

6–15–44 Italy

Dear Betty,

Today was my turn to go to the Vatican; I wore my dress uniform with a skirt. I went with our Catholic chaplain. Two Catholic nurses from another hospital joined us as we were crossing the Piazza S. Pietro. The Swiss Guards wear the most colorful garb, big black tam-o-shanters, blue and black leg-o-mutton blouses, and knee breeches. They carry staffs. The men who guard the Pope have helmets with plumes, spears, and multi-colored garments on the same order as the Swiss guards. They are the Papal colors of the early Roman Empire. There were thousands of GIs at the audience with the Pope.

We stood in the front row. The Pope stopped right in front of me. He's as small as I am. I gave him a big smile and he extended his ring to me to kiss. Methodists just don't go around kissing old men's rings as you well know, so I didn't. If one thinks of the sanitary aspects of that antiquated custom, it's repulsive. Instead I extended my hand to him, gave him a happy, hearty handshake. We chatted briefly. I told him I came from Wisconsin. Also about the great fishing there and put in a good word for Father Nurnberg. Are he and Mom still discussing religions? The Pope blessed a rosary and gave it to me. I'm going to give it to Mrs. B. when I get back. It isn't safe to send things home.

Perhaps I rattled his Papal cage, but I meant no disrespect. His position I salute. The Catholic nurses on either side of me wanted to hit me over the head after it was over. They were burned up because he didn't speak to them and wasted his attention on me. They broke out a package of cigarettes and started to smoke in the Vatican. To me that was a sacrilege. The Vatican is a wonderful, incredibly beautiful building made so by the paintings and sculptures. The Judgement Day is magnificent. There must be a thousand rooms in the compound. I think even an atheist would be moved by the Holy nature of this place.

I have an infected finger from a jab with a dirty needle in the OR. The sulfadiazine I'm taking has made me absolutely sluggish and it doesn't become me.

Love,
June

"Dearest family," Wandrey reported from Germany on April 6, 1945, "It's mid-night and the church bell in the village is toiling; it sounds so mournful. At the

moment, I'm sitting here alone with Sammy our only patient." Wandrey became *especially fond of Sammy, whom she described as a "young, handsome, black-haired, married, Italian-American enlisted infantryman [with] an angelic singing voice." Fragments from a German grenade had ripped through his chest, legs, skull, and right arm, and there was no chance he would survive. The next day, an anguished Wandrey wrote home after Sammy succumbed to his injuries.*

4–7–45 Germany

Dearest family,

Despite Sammy's desperate battle to live, he slipped away just as morning broke. It broke my heart. Desperately tired, hungry, and sick of the misery and futility of war, I wept uncontrollaby, my tears falling on poor Sammy's bandaged remains. Later this morning, our long overdue ambulance came to retrieve us. I couldn't bear to leave Sammy; I sat on the ambulance floor next to his litter and held his corpse as we bounced over the pockmarked roads on his last trip to Graves Registration. When he died, part of me died too. His magnificent singing voice was stilled forever, but 'til the end of my days, I will still hear him say, "Nurse, you have a smile like a whooooole field of sunflowers."

So sadly, June.

Exactly six months and ten days later June Wandrey was heading back to the States. In her last overseas letter to her family, she wrote: "I have no idea how long it will take us to cross the Atlantic this time. It's incredible that I should be coming home in one piece. Love, June." Wandrey would receive a total of eight battle stars for campaigns in Tunisia, Sicily, Naples-Foggia, Anzio, Rome-Arno, Southern France, Rhineland, and Central Europe.

Lt. jg. George Bush Updates His Parents on His Recovery After Being Shot Down and Nearly Killed During a Bombing Mission in the South Pacific

Burning to enlist after the Japanese attack on Pearl Harbor, George Bush was barely out of high school when he volunteered for the Navy's flight training program on his eighteenth birthday—June 12, 1942. "[T]hough I know I can never become a killer," he wrote to his mother on Thanksgiving Day 1942 from the Wold-Chamberlain Naval Air Station in Minneapolis, "I will never feel right until I have actually fought. Being physically able and young enough I belong out at the front and the sooner there, the better." Bush received his wings in June 1943, becoming one of the Navy's youngest pilots. Less than a year later he was aboard the USS San Jacinto flying combat missions, and it was proving to be a sobering introduction to warfare. "Oh mum," he wrote on June 26, 1944, "I hope John and Buck [his brothers] and my own children never have to fight a war. Friends disappearing, lives being extinguished. It's just not right." Five weeks later Bush almost became a casualty himself; on September 2, 1944, he was piloting an Avenger torpedo bomber when it was attacked just off the island of Chichi Jima. As the cockpit filled with smoke, Bush called to his crewmates John Delany and Ted White to bail out. Bush jumped from the plane, striking his forehead on the tail, and parachuted into the ocean. Injured but conscious, he was picked up hours later by the submarine USS Finback. (White and Delaney, much to Bush's great distress, were never found.) During the thirty days he was with the Finback, Bush regularly typed letters to his parents. The following was written on September 16, two weeks after he had been rescued. (Bar is his fiancée, Barbara Pierce; Nance is his sister, and Pres is his oldest brother.)

Dear Mum and Dad,

Several days have slipped by since I last sat down before this machine-days not without excitement, but unfortunately the details will have to remain unrelated for the present.

Gradually I am becomingmore used to this life. At first I missed my daily bath but now I am used to my weekly one.I will say that I certainly do look forward to the day when my bath is due.Today was the big day.Water is precious , but soap is plentiful,so I soap and soap and finally rinse.It is amazing how much better I feel after this weekly pleasure.With my bath comes a clean set of clothes.I hate to have to borrow other peoples things,but unfortunately I came equipped only with pants,drawers and flying jacket.They have a laundryman aboard which helps some.

I have been on the mid watch for the last few days.That puts me on watch from 12–2 at nite and from 12–3 during the day.This way I get a little sun once in awhile.If we are submerged I don't stand a watchfor obvious reasons.

There is a fellow aboard here named Jerry Redmon.He graduated from Harvard in '42.They live right next door practically to the Lovetts on Long Island-Glen Cove I believe.

The food continues to be excellent.I have not beeen sleeping as well lately,and I am sure it is because I never get any exercise.I could take calisthenics I suppose.I better start soon because I really do feel sluggish and rotten without at least a trot down the old flight deck.

I am certainly eager to get back to the squadron now.It seems like ages since I have been back.I can just picture the letters on my desk and I long to be able to tear into them. I haven't heard from Bar in almost a month now.Did I tell you about my gotee.It started off beautifully,but gradually developed into a joke-sort of like Gruff's moustache,so today off it came. If worse came to worse ,however, I am now convinced that I could grow a fairly presentable gotee,given plenty of time. Most of the enlisted men aboard here have big full faced beards. It is indeeed quite a sight.

I have been doing quite a bit of reading lately. Retreat From Rostov;and Dos Passo's "Number One" plus "Captain from Connecticut" and now "The Robe".The latter appeals to me a great deal.So far I have only read a hundred pages or so but it has been deeply absorbing.

I wonder if you have seen Bar since you have been back from Maine.I imagine so if she didn't go back to college. By now Nance is undoubtedly back at college and Buck and John almost rady for school now.Wheere is Buck going to go?In one of your letters you said that Pres was coming North for a week or so to see about his eyes.I wonder if he made it.I feel so darn out of touch with you and I hat that feeling.This great distance seems so much closer when I have your letters to fall back on.

My eye has completely heeled now-there is no scar and the only visible sign of the accident is a big bare spot where eye brow should be growing.They were all kidding me because I have no scar or evidence of my wound now by which I can claim the PURPLE Heart.

I still think about the accident a good deal.So many thing that I could have done come to my mind and bother me. It was a terrible thing alright.

Getting on to another subject.Did you ever see that Oakes girl with the funny nick-name,I can't remember it for the life of me.She was my downfall. I hope your last letters have included bits of news about Ed,Vinny,Red Dog,etc.Perhaps some day I will run inot them out here.I hope,however,that it will not be out here,but at the Field Club or some such spot.

Well,I have rambled on long enough,and shall secure for now.The steaks are on the table.Much much love to all the afmily and to yourselves,

Pop

Foregoing a rotation home, Bush rejoined the USS San Jacinto *in November. (After the war, Bush learned that the Japanese commander in charge of Chichi Jima was tried and executed for eating the livers of captured American pilots. "I like to tease Barbara," he later recalled, "that I almost ended up becoming an hors d'oeuvre.") Bush returned to the States on Christmas Eve 1944, one week before marrying Barbara Pierce. He later received orders to head back to the South Pacific for the invasion of Japan, but, when the Japanese surrendered in August 1945, Bush was able to stay home with his new wife, begin college, and start a family. (George Walker Bush, their first child, was born July 6, 1946.) Awarded the Distinguished Flying Cross, George Bush flew fifty-eight combat missions in the war. He went on to serve as a representative in the U.S. Congress, ambassador to the United Nations, liaison officer to China, director of the Central Intelligence Agency, vice president of the United States, and president.*

~~⌇~~

1st Lt. George S. McGovern Shares with His Friend Bob Pennington a Few (Surprising) Comments on the 1944 Presidential Race

"We've lived in a funny era and sort of a mixed up one, but I'm still glad I'm living in this age," twenty-one-year-old George McGovern wrote to his friend (and future brother-in-law) Bob Pennington on December 28, 1943. "If we can just get this war completely over with and make damn sure we've won it we may be able to spend the rest of our lives doing things we've been dreaming about for so long." McGovern, who had confided to his young wife, Eleanor, that flying "scared [him] silly," was in Kansas training to be a combat pilot. What he dreamed about was returning to South Dakota and becoming a teacher, and he left for Europe months later armed with a stack of history and philosophy books. Whatever fears he had confessed to Eleanor were not apparent to the crew of his B-24, nicknamed the "Dakota Queen"; McGovern quickly earned a reputation for being a steel-nerved pilot in the most life-threatening situations. (McGovern would be awarded both the Air Medal and the Distinguished Flying Cross for his bravery and heroism under fire.) Days before the election back in the States between President Roosevelt and the Republican candidate, New York Governor Thomas Dewey, McGovern wrote to Lt. Pennington in Rome with observations about life in combat, Eleanor, and the presidential campaign.

Nov. 4, 1944

Dear Bob,

Well I'm writing this from a 15th Air Force Base in Italy, Bob. We haven't been here so very long, but are beginning to get into the swing of combat flying. It's a great deal like I expected it to be. Perhaps a little rougher in some respects and not so rough in other respects. At any rate I'm glad to get started on that string of missions we've been preparing for the last year and a half. I'll confess we're going to need and are already using the major part of what we learned back in the States. It seems that while training gets tiresome back home it seems scantly enough when you have to put it into practice to save your neck. We really haven't done much of anything yet over here, but we're beginning to see that there's a damn big job ahead of us before we'll ever see home again.

Eleanor tells me that she's beginning to look the part of an expectant mother. I noticed it a little before I left, so she must be "showing" considerably by now. The baby's E.T.A. is supposed to be around the first week in March so it isn't so very far off. I guess I'll miss his entrance, though, but if we aren't held up too much I should be able to see him around next summer. (Notice that I use "him" and "he," etc.) I hope it is a boy, but a doctor friend of mine is betting me that it will be a girl due to the fact that in his observations he has found that the children of airmen flying at high altitude are in the great majority of cases girls. I hope he's wrong in our case, though, even though I'd be almost equally happy to have a girl.

I suppose you have been following the political battles of Dewey and F.D.R. with your usual interest, Bob. I've sort of lost track of them lately, but the Stars and Stripes have sort of revived my interest. I'm going to be more than disgusted if Dewey doesn't win. I really think we need a man like Dewey in there now! I like the vigor, and efficiency that he has shown in the past and even in the way he is conducting his campaign. I think he'll do a lot toward clearing up all the dozen and one messes that the government is in now. For one thing he has a fairly definite attitude toward everything really vital and that's something the New Deal certainly hasn't had. I believe Dewey will give business a confidence in the government that they haven't had for quite awhile now. I like his plan for a simpler and definite tax policy. He also seems to be concerned with regaining the confidence of the people and of Congress in the president. I believe he can do it if he continues to stick to his guns and follow out a definite and straightforward platform. Have you read his recent eight point platform? It seems very good to me.

I hope this letter finds you O.K., Bob, and in good spirits.
Your friend,
Mac

McGovern's first child was a girl—Ann. And Franklin D. Roosevelt trounced Thomas Dewey to win an unprecedented fourth term in office. (The twenty-second amendment to the Constitution, preventing a president from serving more than two terms, was not ratified until 1951.) McGovern returned home from the war and pursued his goal of becoming a professor. But he eventually went into politics and was elected to the House of Representatives in 1956 and the Senate in 1962. Ten years later he became the Democratic nominee for president, but lost to Richard Nixon in one of the worst electoral defeats in American history. McGovern, a vocal opponent

to the war in Vietnam, was pilloried for being a "left-wing, liberal peacenik."
McGovern rarely mentioned his wartime experiences—or decorations—during the
presidential campaign.

~~~

CPhM Fritz Houser Describes to His Parents the Critically
Wounded Patients He Treated During the Invasion
of the Philippines
&
Lt. Cdr. Douglas Fairbanks Jr. and John Steinbeck Offer Words
of Condolence to the Widow of Their Friend, John Kremer,
Killed in a Kamikaze Attack

Gathering like a storm in the Pacific, an armada of U.S. warships and hundreds of
thousands of American troops under the command of Gen. Douglas MacArthur
began preparations in October 1944 to recapture the Philippines. MacArthur, who
had famously pledged that he would return, landed with his men at Leyte and waded
ashore through the knee-high waves on October 20. (Expecting the invasion to begin
on Luzon, to the North, the Japanese had left only a small ground force at Leyte.)
Three days later the Japanese Imperial Navy tried to divide and conquer the U.S.
Third and Seventh Fleets at Leyte Gulf, but, after the largest naval battle in world
history, the Americans were victorious. On October 25, the last day of the mammoth
sea battle, the Japanese introduced a terrifying new tactic—the kamikaze strike.
Japanese for "divine wind," kamikaze pilots intentionally flew their planes, loaded
with explosives, straight into American warships. The ground battle for Leyte
dragged on into December after the Japanese rushed in reinforcements, and the
kamikaze suicide missions were beginning to inflict enormous casualties on the
Americans. Twenty-year-old Chief Pharmacist's Mate Fritz Houser watched as one
bloodied young sailor after another was brought into the medical station aboard their
destroyer as a result of the attacks and on December 9, he wrote the following letter
to his parents while aboard the USS Mount McKinley. (Prevented from sending
the letter due to censorship, Houser brought it home with him after the war. Portions
of this letter include graphic descriptions of injuries that may not be suitable for
younger readers.)

USS Mount McKinley (AGC-7)

Dear Folks,

This letter cannot be sent now but eventually I hope that you get to
see it. The reason I am writing this is more or less to let you know what
Hell this war can be.

About 1200 on the 6 of December I came up to sick bay from chow and

Doctor Hopkins told me to get a few things ready to go on independent duty for a few days aboard another ship. I packed my things and a Lt. from a destroyer took me up to Captain Graham to get permission for me to leave. The Captain got quite angry because they were trying to take somebody from his ship to replace a PhM who had been taken ill. The Captain refused and said that he would not transfer me until he received written orders from the Chief of Staff. I went back to sick bay a little relieved because this Lt. said to forget about the whole deal but by the time I began to relax he was back and said I was going. We left the ship on the Crash boat and pulled along side the Destroyer and boarded her.

The Lt. introduced me to the Doctor and then I found out where we were going. This destroyer was to go with a convoy to take troops for a landing at Ormoc Bay on the opposite side of Leyte Gulf. This is the part of the island where the Japs had been bringing reenforcements in to help the Japs already on the island. There were no supplies sterilized on the destroyer so Ed Kissick, Hal C and myself got to work and started to make vasoline gauze, wrap instruments, gloves, and all the other hospital supplies needed to take care of casualties. We worked on that and sterilizing until 12 o'clock that night.

The supplies of a destroyer are pitifully small. In all we had about 30 units of blood plasma, 24 packages of 4x4 dressings, some battle dressings, 9 cans of vasoline gauze, roller bandages, sulfa powder, and an inexperienced doctor and a willing Hospital Apprentice and myself. I won't say what I think of myself—that doesn't count. What other people think of you is the important thing.

I tried to sleep but couldn't do anything but roll around because I wasn't used to the new surroundings. At 2 in the morning of 7 December we had GQ. My battle station was forward, topside. I had to cover the two forward five inch guns, three 20 mm guns, fire rooms 1 & 2, the bridge, radar shack, and the gunnery directors. We went to our battle stations and just sat around and watched the stars, moon, and water. The only thing we encountered on the way were some flares, probably dropped by Jap planes.

At 6 in the morning the destroyers opened up with a bombardment. Each destroyer fired about 200 rounds at the beach without any return fire from the beach. Six LCI's went in close to the shore and opened up with rockets. When that was over the first wave of Higgins boats started to move in. We couldn't quite see what opposition they were meeting but it sounded like a lot of machine gun fire. About this time six unidentified planes came in at a fast speed. They looked like they were going to dive bomb so the whole convoy opened up with anti-aircraft fire. One of the planes was hit and made a forced landing on the beach. We then realized that they were American P-47's and ceased firing.

The landing continued and we found out that they were meeting no opposition from the beach. At 11:30 the ship's began to form into a convoy ready to make the return trip back to Leyte Gulf. Just about this time about three or four Jap planes appeared overhead and the guns let loose. One of the planes came down but the other ships began to bomb the Destroyer Mahan. I don't know if they hit her with the bombs or not but they followed up with a suicide dive and hit the bridge. We saw a big flash and then smoke rose high into the sky. Another destroyer pulled up along side to help but evidently she was too badly damaged because half an hour later one of our destroyers opened up and sank her (Mahan). The first few shots didn't hit the right spot but the fourth or fifth one did. We saw a huge flash and that was the end of the ship.

The convoy was moving out by this time and things seemed to be a little quiet so I decided to sack out on the deck for a little while. I must have slept about an hour when our guns opened up. I couldn't quite collect my senses for a few seconds because the firing had scared the living hell out of me. I tried to put on my helmet, put cotton in my ears, put my first aid kit on and get the hell out of the way without much success in any direction. I finally accomplished all of these things and watched what was going on. Our ship shot down one of the planes that was overhead. They were not after us on this particular occasion because they went over to the DD Lampson and three planes, one after the other went into a dive and crashed on the Lampson. We saw smoke rise from her and we hauled ass to give her assistance. Just as we were getting close to her a number of Jap planes started for us. We shot one down and some P-38's took care of the rest. We went back to the scene of the crippled Lampson and found a lot of men floating in the water. I went to the Officer's ward room to get ready for casualties. This was the battle dressing station on the ship. They started moving patients into the ward room and the first few we got weren't too badly hurt. I thought this was going to mean a few hours work and that was all but how wrong I was on that thought.

We started to work on one fellow who was burned on the face, arms, hands, shoulders, and legs. We took care of him with comparative ease. Then the bad cases started to come in. One kid about 19 years old had his leg shattered about four or five inches from the hip. The leg was held on by a few shreds and could not be saved so with a few snips the leg was off. The doctor tied off some of the veins and we bandaged the stump. The kid was in a hell of a lot of pain so morphine was administered. Another young fellow by the name of Tony Santos was laying on the table and looked as though he were taking his last breaths. The doctor started working on him while I mixed some blood plasma. I took the plasma over to the patient and started that. I looked him over to see what his wounds were and found out that he had four gaping wounds in his left arm, shrapnel wounds of both legs, and a shrapnel wound in the left eye. He was unconscious at this time and looked to be in very bad shape.

By this time the ward room was full of horribly wounded men, groaning, dying and pitifully helpless. We couldn't work on them all at once so we did our best and went from one to the other. I have no idea in what order we worked on the patients but I'll just describe them as I can remember them.

One fellow by the name of John B. Johns had flash burns that covered about 60% of his body. Most of the skin on his face was hanging down in shreds. His hands and legs were in the same shape. He was conscious but not in his right mind and I remember his eyes in particular. They had a terrified look and you could almost feel the pain yourself that he was going through. As soon as we tried to touch him he started to fight and we had to have someone hold him down while we bandaged his burns. He also had a shattered lower leg that looked pretty bad. Later on in the night he became unconscious and went into convulsions about every fifteen minutes. We had to have a constant watch on him but every once in a while we'd all be doing something and he'd go into one of these fits. Once he fell off the couch on to two other casualties.

Working on these few casualties took about two hours and it was beyond me how some of the other cases waited so patiently for us to get to them. One fellow sat on a chair and watched what we did, didn't make a noise and when I went over to find out what was wrong with him I found a hole about 2 1/2 inches in diameter in his back through which was protruding part of his lung. I applied sulfanilamide powder to the wound and put on a compress dressing.

We had a CPhM who had numerous shrapnel wounds in his legs and abdomenal cavity. I noticed he was in a lot of pain but didn't know at the time how badly wounded he was. The doctor had me working with other patients, making plasma, and doing a thousand and one other things that I had no chance to investigate the case. It turned out that the shrapnel had punctured the peritonium, broken the spleen, and penetrated some of his vital organs. We gave him penicillin, sulfa drugs, and bandaged his wounds. He later died on a hospital ship. I also found out that when he was picked up out of the water he was holding a fellow up by wrapping his legs around him. It just so happened that the man he was holding was dead but he had no idea what condition the man was in. It seems strange what a man will try to do to save another man's life when his has almost been expended.

By this time we had most of the casualties taken care of with the exception of an officer who was badly burned and had a broken leg. Like many of the other cases his skin in a lot of places had been all but peeled off. As I looked at him I saw that he was a handsome fellow, young, and good natured. We applied vasoline gauze, cotton compresses, and roller gauze to his burns. I talked to him just before we transferred the patients to a hospital ship and he really was a swell fellow. He wanted to know if his face was going to be scarred, how the other fellows were doing, and where I was from. He thanked me several times for what we had done as though we were doing him a great favor. That is one of the strangest things about casualties. We are trained for one purpose—to take care of the sick and wounded—we know it's our job and then they want to thank us. We should thank them for what they have given. We may work on them for 60 hours without sleep or a chance to even sit down but that is a damn small price to pay when they are going to bear the signs of battle for the rest of their life. When we thought we were almost caught up with ourselves and may get a minutes rest they told us we were taking more casualties from another ship and were going to leave the convoy and come back at full speed to Leyte Bay.

While all this was going on we were constantly under attack by the Jap planes. I hate to say this but I didn't think much of the doctor we had. Whenever we were attacked and our ship opened fire the doctor stopped whatever he was doing, even if it was giving plasma or anything, grabbed his helmet and went under the table. The rest of us paid no attention and went right on with our work. I don't know how the others felt but as for myself I figured that the patients couldn't go for any added protection, so why should I. If a bomb was going to hit us I didn't think that a table would help me much. I later found out that the ship shot down a number of Jap planes and also that they dropped eight bombs at us, two of them landing a hundred feet off our port and starboard bow.

About this time the other casualties were brought aboard and we started all over again. The ship got underway, darkness came and I thanked God we were getting out or at least starting to go towards safety. I know that when I prayed I was selfish and was thinking of my own skin a little more than I was thinking of what great help the hospital ship was going to be to the casualties.

The new casualties were practically the same as the other ones. One man had wounds of the head, a punctured lung, shrapnel wounds of his legs and was in shock. He had a horrible moan all the time and this bothered me more than anything that I saw. I can stand to see practically any kind of wound but when they start moaning it gets me because I can't do much to help them.

Another of the new cases had a broken lower left leg but wasn't in too bad shape. Another had a compound fracture of the femur plus a large flesh wound but he had been taken care of fairly well on the other ship so we left him for other cases until later.

Another fellow had a punctured lung and a shattered left arm. He was having a tough time breathing but never complained once. It's patients like that who make you think that what you're doing is really worthwhile. Many times he saw how busy we were and just waited until he saw we had a breathing spell and then would politely ask you for some water or some other small favor. I know that if I were in his place I'd probably be bitching to high heaven trying to get people to wait on me.

Some of the other minor cases we had were—a man with burns of the arms, chest and shoulders—a man with a broken ankle but no flesh wounds, another man with a three-inch open wound of the lower leg, and about eight or ten men with numerous small shrapnel wounds in many parts of their body.

After all the immediate first aid was taken care of we had to continue with the million and one jobs that are necessary to make a patient a little comfortable. We mixed plasma, gave albumin, dextrose, morphine, drinks of water so many times that it seemed I was always carrying water, explained to some what actually was wrong with them, turned them over from side to side to make them a little comfortable, gave them urinals and last but not least occasionally prayed for them.

By this time most of the men who were helping us had gone to get a little sleep and the doctor had retired to his state room likewise. Ed Kissick, myself and a radioman were the only ones left. We decided to have a little water and a cigarette ourselves and we took out about five minutes for a rest. While hunting for cigarettes we found a few bottles of brandy and we proceeded to drink that. It was a good bracer and morale builder.

We pulled up along side the hospital ship at 0400 in the morning and immediately started to transfer the patients. Almost every one that was conscious thanked us several times, wished us good luck—yes, wished us good luck when some of them will probably die soon.

When all the patients were finally on the hospital ship we sat down to look the situation over. The ward room was a mess of blood, skin and flesh. My clothes were soaking wet from sweat and blood, my eyes were blood shot, and I was damned tired but deep down in my heart I was happy that I had the chance to help such a swell bunch of fellows.

I have only one regret about the whole affair but there isn't much that I can do about it. I regret that the sons-of-bitches back in the States who go on strike, think the war is over, think that it is somebody elses war, moan about the sacrifices they are making by working overtime, getting very little gas, butter and meat, and the inconveniences they must go through—can't come out into a battle area and get a little or see a little of the HELL for themselves.

Love,
Fritz

Thousands of American servicemen were injured or killed as a result of the Japanese kamikaze attacks, and one of them was a forty-five-year-old father of three from Philadelphia named John Kremer. An extremely popular commander, Kremer was befriended by the movie star Douglas Fairbanks Jr., who served in the U.S. Navy, saw combat, rose to the rank of lieutenant commander, and earned, among other medals, the croix de guerre, the British Distinguished Service Cross, and the Silver Star. (Many celebrities fought in the war, including Clark Gable, Charlton Heston, Lee Marvin, Paul Newman, and Jimmy Stewart. And some, like the famed band leader Glenn Miller, were killed during their service.) On December 30, 1944, a kamikaze plane deflected off the water and crashed into the USS Orestes *killing Commander Kremer and approximately twenty other men. When Fairbanks learned of his friend's death, he immediately sent Mrs. Kremer the following handwritten letter:*

Jan 9th

Dear Mrs. Kremer—
    Word has just reached me about John.
    No words of mine will supply the comfort and the strength which these days require. However, I could not let the day pass without letting you know how very deeply I am feeling the effects of this crushing news.
    To say I was fond of John would merely be the echo of any and all who ever knew him. He was a man whose courage I admired, whose wisdom I respected and whose friendship I treasured. No one will miss him as much as you, but I know that I, for one, will remember him with affection and count myself fortunate for having known him,—for as long as I linger with "this mortal coil."
    Dick Barthelmess wrote me the news and said, in part, "I hope he is sitting on a nice comfortable cloud, conversing in Greek, with a quartet of harps playing soft chamber music to him. He'd like that." I feel sure that's right.
    This sort of letter should be brief but I've gone on because I did

want to say my say about a fine man, a courageous warrior and a great friend.

My wife joins me, dear Mrs. Kremer, in sending you and the children our most very sincere sympathy & friendship and the hope that the great sorrow you have will somehow be mitigated by the pride you must also feel.

> Yours
> Douglas Fairbanks Jr.
> Lt. Commander USNR

John Steinbeck, who had earned international acclaim for Of Mice and Men *in 1937 and* The Grapes of Wrath *in 1939, worked for the* New York Herald *during the war as a correspondent. Steinbeck and Kremer had also become close friends (Kremer was a featured character in several of Steinbeck's wartime articles), and on January 14, 1945, Steinbeck sent Mrs. Kremer the following brief but heartfelt note:*

Dear Mrs. Kremer:

There's nothing whatever to say except I wish, very profoundly, that I had been with him. I'm so sorry.

> John Steinbeck

~⌒⌒

Pfc. Richard Cowan, Just Before the Battle of the Bulge, Writes a Profound Letter to His Mother About Ethics and Morality
&
Pfc. DeWitt "Chick" Gephart Informs His Parents He Has Been Seriously Wounded in the Battle But, Nevertheless, Is in Very Good Spirits
&
Warrant Officer Frank J. Conwell, Having Survived the Battle of the Bulge, Sends His Family a Poetic Reflection on War and What He Has Seen

"Compared to war, all other forms of human endeavor shrink to insignificance," remarked Gen. George S. "Old Blood and Guts" Patton Jr. as he drove past the battle-scarred fields of France. "God, how I love it." By August 1944 Patton was commanding the Third Army as it barreled through France toward Berlin. Allied troops had punched through St.-Lô and Caen in July and liberated Paris in late August. Hammered by the Allies in the west and the Russians in the east, German forces were disintegrating and their high command was corroding from within. (On

aus

**Pacific
Biological
Laboratories**

Pacific Grove, California

January 14

Dear Mrs. Kramer:

There's nothing whatever to say except I wish, very profoundly, that I had been with him. I'm so sorry.

John Steinbeck

July 20 Hitler narrowly escaped an assassination attempt by his own officers, who had planted a bomb in his East Prussian headquarters. Hitler, partially paralyzed and deafened in the blast, had 5,000 suspected co-conspirators, including Erwin Rommel, executed.) So depleted was the German army, sixteen- and even fifteen-year-old boys were being thrown into combat. In October the Allies captured their first German city, Aachen, and total victory seemed imminent. No one was expecting a massive German counter-offensive. But in a last, desperate attempt to inflict catastrophic losses on the Allies, Hitler ordered 250,000 troops to strike the thin line of Allied forces stretching from Belgium to Luxembourg. It would prove to be the largest battle ever fought by the U.S. Army. Eleven days before the German blitz, Pfc. Richard Cowan, in Belgium with the Second Division, was celebrating his twenty-second birthday. Finding himself in a pensive mood, Cowan responded to a letter his mother, back in Wichita, Kansas, had recently sent him about the importance of adhering to certain values in life. ("Chas." is his brother Charles.)

December 5, 1944

Dear Mom,

I guess 22 years ago was a pretty important day for both of us. But after all, it was only the start — the days that have come since — all 8036 of them — have meant as much, I think — a whole lifetime in one sense — because you and I shared the same life and it's left me wanting no more.

It's an awfully solemn mood in which to write a letter, Mom, but then it's not that I've lost the willingness to look at the humerous side of it, so much as to agree with your slant of things as in your last letter.

It makes a guy think, all right, all of it. Like today — of all days — the rather determined and prolonged efforts of a sniper to erase me from the company roster. Artillery and machine guns can never be quite so personal as a persistent sniper. And it makes every fellow here play his real part — not that part that he'd like to play.

It's like you wrote, Mom, you talk your ethics and you live them; and then the day comes when you feel they ask too much — they ought to be modified — they're right but they're superhuman.

And believe it or not, Mom — it sounds like a very irrelevant reason, perhaps, but that's really the main reason I tried so long to get into the army. To join so much in the action that there would be no moral tie to the ten commandments, as it were — to base my actions on a rawer creed — or rather lack of creed — as Chas. would say, live honestly with myself.

But I think the beauty of it is that when the going shades off into the rough, then the old creed comes shining through. And it's easy to see that nothing's changed. Quite the contrary—that the old law was built from out of the same indecency; that it is quite the logical development from this realistic off-color life of ours. In fact I think it is proof that to know one extreme, its antithesis must first be realized.

And it means that everybody shares the same universals — hope, love, humor, faith. Being 22 is to have a chance to hit everything no holds barred. And it's damned comforting to have made the loop of most of the attitudes towards things, and come out near where you started.

Pretty convinced I'm grown up, ain't I, Mom? Well, I still count on your tucking me into bed when I get home.

Love,
Dick

The next message the Cowans received was from the War Department, stating that their son had been missing in action since December 18—two days after the Germans launched their sweeping assault. Mrs. Cowan contacted the Red Cross and was told not to worry; there was every possibility Dick was still alive. In February, an elated Mrs. Cowan wrote to Dick's older brother, Bob, and his wife, Dot, to say she had received a newspaper clipping announcing that Dick was a bona fide war hero. The January 23 Stars and Stripes *army newspaper reported that as a Tiger tank and 80 Germans closed in on Cowan, he machine gunned half of them and held off the rest, allowing his comrades to retreat to safety. Cowan himself only pulled out when his ammunition had been exhausted. Mrs. Cowan, in her letter to Bob and Dot, could not have been more proud:*

> *Gosh, I don't know how Dick had the intestinal fortitude to do such a thing, unless he had his old Irish up, and could have licked all Hitler's army, after what had happened to his pals. For my part, I think all the Germans would ever have seen of me would have been my heels. Well, it's pretty grand to have a son like that.*

But the Cowan family's worst fears were realized when another telegram came informing them that Dick was no longer considered missing; it was now confirmed that he had been killed the very day of his courageous action, for which he was posthumously awarded the Congressional Medal of Honor. "It is such a bitter dose to have to take," mourned Mrs. Cowan in another letter to Dick's brother, "and I am not a bit brave about it." The Cowan family was not alone in their grief. Tens of thousands of soldiers were killed, seriously wounded, or captured by the Germans, who had pushed the Allied line back—in a "bulge" shape—forty-five miles. Unprepared for the harsh winter conditions, American troops fell ill and, in some cases, froze to death. Even General Patton, who had arrived with his Third Army, was growing anxious, and on December 23 he appealed right to the top: "Sir, this is Patton talking," the general prayed aloud in a Luxembourg chapel. "The past fourteen days have been straight Hell—rain, snow, more rain, more snow—and I am beginning to wonder what's going on in Your headquarters. Whose side are You on anyway? . . .[I]n exchange for four days of fighting weather, I will deliver You enough Krauts to keep Your bookkeepers months behind in their work. Amen." The weather cleared the next day. Christmas Eve, no less. By the middle of January the Germans were in full retreat, having suffered an estimated 120,000 to 200,000 casualties. Pfc. DeWitt "Chick" Gephart, one of 40,000 Americans wounded in the month-long battle, described his injury in the following letter to his parents back in El Reno, Oklahoma. ("Vi," short for Violet, is his wife.)

Feb. 3, 1945
France

Dear Folks,

I'm really ashamed of myself for not writing but it is rather hard to write left handed, and then I thought Vi would tell you everything.

On Jan. 13, we started out to attack a town before dawn, it was daylight when we reached an open field on the approach to the town. When we got about 600 or 800 yrds. from there, they opened up with small arms fire on us. We dropped flat on the ground but couldn't dig in because the ground was frozen and covered with several inches of snow. Jerry then opened up with mortar and artillery and just started blasting us with everything they had. I was lifted off the ground twice by concussion but not hit. Then, about 0900 a mortar shell landed quite a ways from me, and I got a piece of shrapnel in my left side just above the hip. It wasn't but a few seconds and another piece got me a couple of inches above the wound. There was hardly any pain and I kept on firing my weapon.

About 0930, an 88 MM zoomed past me. I looked down and my rt. hand was gone. Well, it was about 1500 before I got back to a station to get morphene, and my stub bandaged. They gave me blood, fixed me up, and sent me back to an evacuation hospital. They operated about 2000 that nite, took the shrapnel out, trimmed my arm up, about one half inch above the waste. So from then on I decided I would be left handed.

I thought I would wait to tell you about it on my arrival in the states but then changed my mind. I didn't write Vi to tell her this because I knew she would be alone when she read the letter. You can let her read this or tell her about it whichever you think best. Hope I didn't break the news too abruptly but couldn't think of any way to do it except the way I did. Don't worry about me because I have the best of medical care, and my morale is very good.

After I get to the states, I will be given a pretty good furlough, and then will have to report to a hospital probably in Calif. for three to six mos. to learn how to use my left hand, and also my artificial rt. hand before getting my discharge.

The cookies arrived today, and they were surely good. Have a few left yet.

Keep smiling and I'll do the same.

Love to all,
"Chick"

Dad: You'll have to be patient with me until I learn to bowl left handed.

Frank J. Conwell, a thirty-four-year-old warrant officer, also survived the fighting and was fortunate to have come through unscathed. The snow-covered Ardennes Forest, where much of the Battle of the Bulge occurred, inspired Conwell to reminisce on his childhood, when wintry conditions meant frolicking outside in the snow. Struck by the surreal juxtaposition of the war-related horrors he had witnessed amidst the beauty of the Ardennes, Conwell wrote a lyrical, almost whimsical letter to his aunt and uncle that masked great sorrow over the buddies he had lost during the war.

February 6th 1945

Hello John, Ann and all the Little Ones:

Greetings and salutations.

I received your most welcomed letter of Jan. 11th today and it was good hearing from you. When I read your letter I re-read it again and again for I really couldn't believe so many changes have taken place since our last meeting. Just as you said John, it has been difficult for me to know where to start. So light up a Camel, be calm, cool and collected and I shall try to give you a bird's eye view of what yours truly has been doing these past 34 months, which I have spent overseas. Hold your hat here we go.

This will be the third invasion to my credit. I went through the No. African, Sicilian, and present invasions and without a single scratch, what a lucky guy and I sincerely hope my luck holds out. During these campaigns I have been all over Ireland, England, Scotland, Algeria, Tunisia, French Morocco, Sicily, France, Belgium, and Germany. Sounds like a Cook's travel tour—but definitely. I have seen plenty of the sights of the various countries and Paris is on the top of my list. I managed to spend a few days there and had the time of my life. I also visited the Cathedral of Notre Dame and paid my respects to where the boys of the last war use to hang out, need I say more—ahem. I also have seen plenty of action and have just about had my fill. It's pretty tough stuff to take to see some of your buddies getting knocked off; especially the ones who sweated it out together away back in our training days, but as the french say "C'est la guerre."

Thanks for wishing me the best for the New Year, I'll need it. While we are on the subject I'll give you a vague idea of the jolly New Year's Eve we had. Wined and dined on the Siegfried Line. Visited the Club Cologne on the Beautiful Rhine. Big "88" (heavy mortar guns) piece band and that famous singer "Screaming Mimi" (shells). All came — the mortar the merrier.

Well what can I talk about now. As a last resort we can always talk about the weather. The weather has been very cold over here with plenty of snow, snow, and more snow. As I look at the kids sledding, throwing snow balls, etc., it brings back many memories of the good times I had when I was a kid. All us lads from the Northern states remember it well. As kids we loved it. Took out our Flexible Flyers and went belly whopping down the hills. Made snow men with it. Packed it into hard, round, balls that caught other kids in the head and melted down the backs of their necks. When our hands got red and our feet got cold we would call it a day. We would go indoors to a hot fire and a good scolding for getting our feet wet. We would put on dry socks and shoes and eat hot chow to take off the chill. When we were kids snow sure was fun.

There's a lot of snow on the Western Front these days and the country looks like a Christmas card. The trees are like old queens stooping from under the weight of their ermine robes. The wires loop from pole to pole like tinsel on a Christmas tree, except where the weight of the ice and snow has pulled them down and the signal repairmen are patching them. Snow lies smooth on the hill sides—it's beautiful.

But the Flexible Flyers have turned into tanks. The snow men are Schutzstaffel. The snowballs are grenades. The wet stuff trickling down the back of necks is often blood. And when you're wet and numb with cold there's no place to go to. Nothing to look forward to. Nothing but snow, Cold, wet, beautiful snow.

The news certainly is good these days and I hope it continues. With so many Nazis dying for Der Fuehrer there is a possibility that Hades is beginning to look like Times Square on New Year's Eve. And with all the bombing and shelling of Germany today, Hitler has achieved what he always strived for A CRATER GERMANY.

Well folks this is all for now so I'll say so-long for awhile. Hoping this letter finds you all in the best of health, I remain

Sincerely,
Frank

P.S. Gosh darn I almost forgot. I am the Asst. Adjutant of my outfit and that means plenty of paper flak — but definitely.

His citizens starving to death and virtually homeless and his army all but vanquished, Adolf Hitler refused even to contemplate surrender. Any officer who ordered a retreat was to be shot for treason. Hitler celebrated President Franklin D. Roosevelt's death on April 12, 1945 as a harbinger of good fortune, a notion seconded by his propaganda minister Paul Joseph Goebbels. "It is written in the stars that the second half of April will be a turning point for us," a cheerful Goebbels told Hitler. Indeed it would. By the end of the month both men would be dead and the Nazis' "Thousand-Year" Reich would be soundly annihilated.

~

1st Lt. James Carroll Jordan, in a Letter to His Wife, Details the Atrocities Committed in the Buchenwald Concentration Camp
&
1st Lt. Fritz Schnaittacher, a German-Born Jew Serving in the U.S. Army, Writes to His Wife After the Liberation of the Dachau Concentration Camp
&
S. Sgt. Horace Evers, in Adolf Hitler's Munich Apartment, Uses Hitler's Personal Stationery to Describe to His Family the Horrors of Dachau

"Dear Betty Anne," James Carroll Jordan wrote from Buchenwald, Germany, to his wife, serving with the Signal Corps in Washington, D.C., "I saw something today that makes me realize why we're fighting this war." Jordan, a twenty-three-year-old P-51 pilot from Saint Paul, Minnesota, was with the 109th Tactical Reconnaissance Squadron (attached to the Ninth Army). He continued his letter, dated April 21, 1945, to Betty Anne:

We visited a German political internment camp. The camp had been liberated only two days and the condition of the camp has changed very little. The American Red Cross just arrived.

The inmates consisted of mostly Jews, some Russians, Poles and there were six American pilots that they shot almost immediately.

When we first walked in we saw all these creatures that were supposed to be men. They were dressed in black and white suits, heads shaved and starving to death. Malnutrition was with every one of them.

We met one of them that could speak English so he acted as a guide for us. First we saw a German monument that stated 51,600 died in this camp in three years. They were proud of it. Second we went in the living barracks. Six sq. ft. per six people. Hard wood slats six ft. high. Then we went down through rows of barbed wire to a building where they purposely infected these people with disease. Human guinea pigs for German medics.

In this medical building were exhibits of human heads in jars and tatooed human flesh or skin on the walls.

After that we went up to the torture dept. Here were beating devices that I won't explain. The clubs, by the way, are still lying there with blood on them. In another room in this building were 8 cremator furnaces. The doors were open and in one I noticed one body 1/2 done. A horrible sight. After I snapped a few pictures I walked out side and noticed a truck with 50 naked bodys piled up six deep. Turning my head away from that I looked over against the wall and here were about 30 more. Their eyes open, their mouths open, blue, and purple, cut and some with holes in them.

The guide told us he lived with some of these men for years. He said most of them died with-in the past 24 hrs. In fact a medical Red Cross man told us they are dying like flys. Nothing can be done for them. It's too late. They are much too far gone.

There is another place I never told you about. The latrine. I won't tell you about it, because you won't believe me. It's unbelievable.

It was about time to leave so we started out the big gate. As we were nearly out we saw one of the men that looked like a ghost, fall over. They put him on a coat and headed for the truck.

One of our pilots is Jewish and as you know the Jewish language is somewhat similar to the German language. He stopped one of the men in the striped suits. He was a young boy. The pilot asked him several questions such as, how long has he been here. Three years he said. How old was he. 16 years old. He asked all type of questions about the camp which was exceptionally interesting and no doubt true.

We gave him some cigarettes and candy. He forgot how to smile, but you could see the happiness in his sunken eyes.

We still had about an hour before leaving so we went back in. We wandered in to a barracks. What kept us from getting sick I'll never know. On some of these wooden slabs were half alive, half dead men, lying on some dirty rags and clothes. It was the sick barracks, you might call it. These men were cut deep in the flesh with knives, infected of course. Some of them were not off of these beds for days. They were lying in their own body waste. Yes, for days.

The Red Cross was there and were removing one of the men. They told him they were going to take him to a hospital and make him well again. He didn't want to go. He thought they were going to take him out and kill him. I doubt if he even knew who they were.

Naturally, the Krauts had to benefit by these people for bothering with them at all; so they had a factory in which the men had to work 12 to 15 hours a day. If they refused to work or couldn't work, Well — there was always more.

We were naturally interested in the six American pilots and crew men, so we inquired around. We couldn't find out very much; only that these bomber crews were shot down from a bomb run over the town. The inmates said they were put in a barraks by them selves. If they were tortured or not they didn't know, but they did know that they were dead in a few days. One man stated that their clothes were taken away from them so they couldn't escape.

We found a Russian that could speak a little English and he told us some incidences that took place.

He said that if the guards were feeling good they would get soup, very greasy soup. He said that he survived because he would warm the soup by putting his hands in it and melt the grease. If things weren't too good for the guards they wouldnt eat anything for 8 days. The men naturally wouldn't be able to walk so they put about 50 hungry dogs in the camp and let them gnaw on the dying men.

When the American tanks charged through the prison gates the guards naturally evacuated deeper into the father land, but the inmates caught one of them. I saw this SS guard among the dead bodys. When I saw him I thought he was odd, because he had long blond hair. His head was all bruised, his neck was slashed with a knife. The inmate watched him kill himself just 48 hours ago. They drove him mad.

Our time was up so we boarded our truck and rode home, just thinking.

Enclosed you will find some pictures that I took while going through the camp.

All my love darling
Carroll

One by one the Nazi concentration and extermination camps were liberated—and exposed to the world—by Allied forces coming from the West and Russian troops arriving from the East. Fritz Schnaittacher, a German-born Jew who fled to the United States in October 1933, was nearly imprisoned in the Dachau concentration camp as a young man. Schnaittacher had left Europe just in time; millions of Jews who tried to escape the full fury of the Nazis beginning in the mid-1930s discovered it was too late. Immigration quotas prohibited the majority of them from entering the U.S., and many consequently perished. In 1942 Schnaittacher joined the U.S.

Army and, being fluent in German, served as a military intelligence officer with the Seventh Army as it tore through Germany in 1945. In the middle of April, a German POW Schnaittacher was guarding begged to be released so he could return to his wife in the village of Forth, only a few miles away. "Who is your wife?" Schnaittacher demanded. "Gunta Has," the prisoner told him. "Oh yes, Gunta Has." Schnaittacher said, "She lives in house #35, and if you look across the street there is house #52, and the Protestant minister's house is on the left, and the firehouse is on the right." Flabbergasted, the prisoner exclaimed, "If American intelligence has all this information, how can we win the war?" The POW was unaware that Forth just happened to be Schnaittacher's hometown. Weeks later First Lieutenant Schnaittacher was at the gates of Dachau, and on May 1, 1945, he sent the following letter to his wife, Dorothy, in Brooklyn. (The "SS," alluded to in Schnaittacher's letter, is the abbreviation for the Schutzstaffeln, the Nazi security force infamous for its sadism.)

My dearest Dottylein,

Twelve years ago to day I came to Munich—yesterday we took it—to day we were in the heart of it—another coincidence. The past few days were some of the greatest and saddest in my life. Our regiment took Dachau or should I say liberated the human wreckage which was left there. This I consider one of the most glorious pages in the history of our regiment, not because the fighting was tough, it wasn't, but because it finally opened the gates of one of the world's most hellish places.

Twelve years ago I missed it by the skin of my teeth. This time I saw it — I shall never forget it, and nobody will, who has seen it. You know that I had never doubted the truth of all the atrocities, of which we have been reading—I know they could never be exaggerated, but at the same time I could never visualize this insane cruelty until I was confronted with it now, and now I cannot comprehend it, and it almost seems more unbelievable than before I had seen the victims of Nazi German culture.

You have heard the stories over the radio—I don't want to add much more—the most striking picture I saw was the "death train"—I say picture, no not picture, but carload and carload full of corpses, once upon a time people, who were alive, who were happy and people who had convictions or were jews—then slowly but methodically they were killed. Death has an ugly face on these people—they were starved to death—the positions they were lying in show that they succumbed slowly—they made one move, fell, were too weak to make another move, and there are hundreds of such lifeless skeletons covered by some skin. I tried to find out the origin of this train. Some of the stories corresponded—whether this train was to leave Dachau or had just arrived is not essential—essential is that they were locked into these cattle cars without sanitation and without food. The SS had to take off in a hurry—we came too fast—it was too late to cover up their atrocities.

Yet there were even worse scenes at Dachau than the one I tried to describe. And still Dachau was considered only a drop in the bucket in the eyes of an experienced observer, a high ranking SS officer. He had been in a hospital in camp as a convalescent. I was called in as an interpreter, and first when I met him I was unaware of his identity, but expected him to be a political prisoner who was anxious to help us in the elimination of those who were guilty for all these crimes. I greeted him accordingly. Then I found out he was an SS officer—my hand, which had shaken his, felt as if it wanted to shrivel up. I told him so too. Then he made the following statement, take it for what it's worth "Yes I am an SS officer, not because I wanted to, but because I had to—still I am proud to have been an SS officer, only as such I was able to see the true face of Hitler and his system, and only as such I was able to help the unfortunate ones a tiny bit." Then he told us about the Concentration Camp near Katowicz—Dachau is just child's play in comparison to Katowicz.

Dottylein I hate to close this letter so abruptly—this is all dark, but there are some light aspects in all of this nightmare too—they will follow shortly.

I love you my Dottylein with all my heart and soul.

Your Fritz

On the very day First Lieutenant Schnaittacher was writing home, a staff sergeant named Horace Evers, also with the Seventh Army (Forty-fifth Infantry Division), was walking through Dachau after Gen. Dwight Eisenhower ordered American troops in the vicinity to bear witness to what the Nazis had done. "The things I saw beggar description," Eisenhower wrote to Gen. George C. Marshall on April 15, 1945. "I made the visit deliberately in order to be in a position to give first-hand evidence of these things if ever, in the future, there develops a tendency to charge these allegations merely to 'propaganda.'" While setting up a command post in early May during the Allied invasion of Munich, Evers and his men found themselves in none other than Adolf Hitler's private apartment. (This was the same residence where Hitler's niece and lover, Geli Raubal, killed herself in 1931.) In an adjoining room Evers noticed a long wooden conference table, where sheets of Hitler's personal stationery—with the Nazi swastika embossed in gold over Hitler's name—lay scattered. Evers sat down in Hitler's chair and, still sickened by Dachau, wrote the following letter to his mother and stepfather back in Long Island. ("Weeds," mentioned in the beginning of the letter, was 1945 slang for cigarettes.)

2 May — 1945

Dearest Mom and Lou,

Just received your 19<u>th</u> April letter and was glad to hear you are all well and the tractor business is still intact.

So you went to N. Y. and had a big time. I'd give most everything I have to be able to see Lou with his pants rolled up and a baby cap on. — Gawdamighty! Did Mom get a jag on and smoke weeds? — Have you ever learned to smoke, Mom?

A year ago today I was sweating out shells on Anzio Beachhead — today I am sitting in Hitlers' luxuriously furnished apartment in Munich writing a few lines home. — What a contrast. — A still greater contrast is that between his quarters here and the living hell of DACHAU concentration camp only 10 miles from here. — I had the misfortune of seeing the camp yesterday and I still find it hard to believe what my eyes told me. —

A railroad runs alongside the camp and as we walked toward the box cars on the track I thought of some of the stories I previously had read about DACHAU and was glad of the chance to see for myself just to prove once and for all that what I had heard was propaganda. — But <u>no</u> it wasn't propaganda at all — if anything some of the truth had been held back. In two years of combat you can imagine I have seen a lot of death, furious deaths mostly. But nothing has ever stirred me as much as this. I can't shrug off the feeling of utter hate I now hold for these people. I've shot at Germans with intent to kill before but only because I had to or else it was me — now I hold no hesitancy whatsoever.

The first box car I came to had about 30 what were once humans in it. — All were just bone with a layer of skin over them. Most of the eyes were open and had an indescribable look about them. They had that beaten "what did I do to deserve this" look. Twenty to thirty other box cars were the same. Bodies on top of each other — no telling how many. No identification as far as I could see. — And then into the camp itself. — Filthy barracks suitable for about 200 persons held 1500. 160,000 persons were originally in the camp and 32,000 were alive (or almost alive) when we arrived. —

There is a gas chamber and furnace room in one barracks. — Two rooms were full of bodies waiting to be cremated. — In one room they were all nude — in the other they had prison clothes on — as filthy as dirt itself.

How can people do things like that? I never believed they could until now.

The only good thing I noticed about the whole camp were the scores

~~ADOLF HITLER~~ X
S/Sgt Evers

MÜNCHEN, DEN

2 May–1945

Dearest Mom and Lou,

Just received your 19ᵗʰ April letter and was glad to hear you are all well and the tractor business is still intact.

So you went to N.Y. and had a big time. I'd give most everything I have to be able to see Lou with his pants rolled up and a baby cap on. - Gardemighty! Did mom get a jag on and smoke weeds? - Have you ever learned to smoke, mom?

A year ago today I was sweating out shells on Anzio Beachhead - today I am sitting in Hitlers' luxuriously furnished apartment in Munich writing a few lines home. - What a contrast. - A still greater contrast is that between his quarters here and the living hell of DACHAU concentration camp only 10 miles from here. - I had the misfortune of seeing the camp yesterday and I still find it hard to believe what my eyes told me. -

A railroad runs alongside the camp and as we walked toward the box cars on the track I thought of some of the stories I previously had read about DACHAU and was glad of the chance to see of SS guards freshly killed. — Some of the prisoners newly freed could not control themselves and went from German to German and bashed their heads in with sticks and rocks — No one tried to stop them for we all realized how long they had suffered.

I guess the papers have told you about the 7th Army taking NURN-BERG and MUNICH by now. — Our Division took the greater part of each place and captured many thousands of prisoners. We also liberated Russian, Polish and British and American prisoners by the thousands — what a happy day for those people.

> Well enough for now —
> Miss you all very much
> Your Son
> Horace

An estimated 6 million Jews—nearly one-third of world Jewry—were murdered by the Nazis. Millions of Gypsies, homosexuals, Catholics, children and adults with mental illnesses, and others deemed "socially undesirable" were also targeted, but not as relentlessly as the Jews. In October 1946 ten of the highest-ranking Nazis were sentenced at Nuremberg to hang for "crimes against humanity." Adolf Hitler and Joseph Goebbels, the propaganda minister, were not among those tried and executed. At the end of the war Goebbels poisoned his six children and then instructed an SS guard to shoot him and his wife. On April 30, 1945, as Soviet tanks rumbled into Berlin, Hitler and Eva Braun, the woman he had married only the day before, ingested cyanide. Hitler simultaneously put a gun to his head and pulled the trigger. On his orders, their bodies were carried to the chancellory garden, doused in gasoline, and set on fire. Hitler wanted his corpse cremated before the Soviets got hold of it.

~

2nd Lt. Richard Wellbrock Chronicles His Remaining Days as a Prisoner of War in a Letter/Diary to His Wife, Mary

Plummeting to earth in a crippled B-24, 2nd Lt. Richard Wellbrock was pinned beneath a broken, 700-pound turret and barely conscious. After a violent explosion of antiaircraft fire, which killed five of his crewmates and dislodged the turret, Well-brock was able to stagger to an opening and parachute out of the spinning plane with only moments to spare. With one broken leg and another cut up on impact, he crawled for four hours away from the crash site before being apprehended by German soldiers on August 22, 1944. Wellbrock was marched (on two bad legs) from one POW camp to another, interrogated, tortured, and ultimately imprisoned in Moosburg, twenty miles northeast of Munich. On Red Cross paper Wellbrock secretly penciled a diary in the form of letters to his wife, Mary, and their two-year-

old son, Kent, back in Peoria, Illinois. For eight months he recorded his hellish existence battling chronic hunger, subzero temperatures, loneliness, and infections. "Things here are critical, with over half the men down with GI's flu. The fleas are in every bed," Wellbrock wrote in one message. "Have been lying in my bunk dreaming about us. It's my favorite pastime, although it hurts like the devil at times." Holidays and anniversaries were the hardest.

> *Mary, my darling: It is Christmas Eve and, darling, if I've ever needed you, I do now. I've such a lost feeling and bluer than I have ever been in my life. I've spent the evening with the other men, just staring into space. A strange sight, darling, and not a pretty one, of 17 men in old clothes, heavy hearts, and hungry, bitter forlorn faces, as they think of home, etc. "Peace on Earth, Good Will to Men" is hard for me to visualize. I only hope this bitterness will fade, but I've seen too many sights and too many men's souls to ever be quite the same. I still wake up in the middle of the night with nightmares. Some of the men who have been down two years wake up screaming, so the nights don't lack interest.*

In April 1945 Wellbrock's spirits soared as he heard the muted thunder of distant shelling; Allied troops were fast approaching. The following are Wellbrock's final entries in captivity:

Mary, darling: April 27, 1945. Still a POW but it is definitely looking up. It is rumored we will not be evacuated from here, but will be left to be liberated. If so, we should be free in a week. It can't be put into words how I feel at that prospect. After eight months, the thought of freedom is almost frightening. We are hearing demolition and artillery fire day and night now, and the bombers have passed on, so it can't be long. Darling, the thought of soon being with you again leaves me so impatient I can't sleep or even wait for the day. May it be very soon. Yours forever, Dick.

Mary, my darling: April 30, 1945. This in all probability is the last entry I'll make. Anything after this would be anticlimactic. Yesterday at 12:40 the American Flag was raised over Moosburg. The battle for the area started at 9:00 and continued until then. It was a tense three hours for us, but we had few casualties. It is impossible to describe my feelings. To be free once again and to describe it is far beyond my ability. It is a man's greatest possession and without it, he finds he is only half alive. I find my entire nature has changed already. The lines have moved on at least ten miles and we are told we will be moved soon. We are supposed to be flown to LeHavre and then from there home, which should be soon. Darling, it doesn't seem possible I'll be with you in a month. For eight months that has been my prayer and hope and now at last I can finally realize it. Mary, I love you with all my heart and always will, darling.

It was indeed a spectacle that I'll never be able to fully describe—to be one of 175,000 prisoners in this camp and see them all, English, Poles, Indians, Russians, Senegalese, French, and Americans, fall to their knees to pray as they watched the American Flag rise over this "hellhole." Many of these men have been here for five years, so I can consider myself fortunate.

We are to receive liver shots and a bland diet for about two weeks, then will be on our way toward home. Do you remember the last night in the States, when I told you I would make it O.K.? Well, darling, I've done it, and will be there soon. The thought of you and Kent had made it possible, believe me, and putting those thoughts in here has helped. I hope and pray that Kent will never have to keep a record such as this, and that man, in his little weak mind, at last has learned that wars can only cause suffering. My love forever, Mary.

Thirty-year-old 2nd Lt. Richard Wellbrock was able to deliver his letters to Mary personally; he returned to the States alive and well by Christmas 1945.

~

1st Lt. William Lee Preston Characterizes for His Brother, John, a Parade of German Soldiers—Once the "Terror of Europe"— Now Defeated and Powerless

Berlin fell to the Soviets' Red Army on May 2, 1945. At 2:41 A.M. on May 7, Germany capitulated. Representatives of what was left of Hitler's regime signed the surrender in a small schoolhouse serving as General Eisenhower's headquarters in Rheims, France. The Soviets demanded that the ceremony be repeated in Berlin the next day, and May 8 officially became V-E (Victory in Europe) Day. Cities throughout the world exploded with joy. People took to the streets, dancing, singing, yelling, and blowing whistles and horns. Cloaked in blackouts for years, Europe was now ablaze in lights. But underlying the revelry was a stark realization of all that had been destroyed in the past six years. Over 50 million people were dead, including 20 million civilians, and entire nations lay in ruins. Twenty-two-year-old William Lee Preston, a first lieutenant with the Sixty-fifth Infantry Division in Patton's Third Army, had witnessed firsthand the ferocity of combat in France, Belgium, and Germany. Forty-eight hours after V-E Day, Preston wrote to his older brother, John, back home in Monroe, Georgia.

May 10, 1945

Dear John,

The war is over. The war in Europe is over. I can hardly believe it, for it seems only yesterday we were seeing our first action in the Siegfried line.

Two nights ago, John, I sat by an open window on the second story of the building my platoon occupies, and listened and watched for over an hour as German prisoners, thousands, passed below me on their way to a prisoner of war enclosure. I listened to the tromp, tromp, of Nazi boots, no longer in cadence, no longer marching proudly, a beaten, tired mob of German soldiers—surrendered.

I recalled the many pictures and newsreels I had seen of the German Wehrmacht on parade, while thousands of cheering civilians watched the spectacle before Adolf Hitler. The super race they were—the world's best soldiers then. I looked at them now—hungry, shoulders stooped by the heavy equipment on their backs, uniforms dirty, and a haggard expression on their faces. Hitler's soldiers on parade before the Yanks, and the G.I.s watched intently. Then I recalled the scene I had witnessed of those same soldiers—they had left a string of dead and dying from Cherbourg to the Siegfried line—from the Rhine to Austria, in retreat. I had seen them lying in roads, streets, ditches, fields, wherever we went—sometimes with G.I.s near them. And still they came on the street below me, marching four abreast.

Two afternoons ago I saw another group, a column of Hitler's SS troops who had surrendered. I watched as M.P.'s took them to a prison camp. They still wore their insignia, the skull and cross bones, but they were no longer arrogant, their pride had gone with surrender. Hitler's crack troops with the insignia that had meant terror and torture to the people of Europe for years. And not only to Europeans, but terror and torture to American soldiers surrendered. And now I saw them stop for a rest, and was amazed to see them begging G.I.'s for a smoke, a cigarette butt. We felt like spitting on them. The terror of Europe—begging for a smoke. How things change. The M.P.'s moved them off again. They walked with shoulders stooped, heads bowed looking at the ground—beaten. I was glad to see them so. We didn't mock them as they passed, for our hatred was deeper than mocking.

Another column of German soldiers came by. I was amazed. Can you imagine Kent Lawrence, Jo, and men dad's age fighting the war for America? Most of them were 14, 15, 16, years of age, with an old man here and there in the column. The youngsters were the Hitler youth (Jugend), fanatical boys fighting for der Fuhrer. In America, kids the same age are reading Superman and going to junior high school, I hope. Yet these German boys were old soldiers, prisoners of war. A shame, I agree, but indicative of the desperate measures the Nazi leaders took in a last ditch fight against us.

Yes, the war in Europe is over. I don't know what the reaction was in the states on a whole. Over a patched up radio we heard that ticker tape and paper floated down from New York buildings. We heard that there were wild celebrations in the streets in London by civilians, English and American soldiers. But, John, the front line troops didn't celebrate. Most of the men merely read the story of victory from the division bulletin sent to the troops, said something like "I'm glad," and walked away. Perhaps it was a different story in their hearts, or perhaps they were too tired, or thinking of home too much, or thinking of their buddies who didn't live to see the victory, to do much celebrating or merry making. But I'm sure of one thing—the troops were glad they wouldn't have to fight any-more—I was.

What our future is we don't know, but everyone is sweating out the South Pacific troop movement.

> My love to Eleanor and Troy.
> Your brother,
> Bill

P.S. Some boys who left Camp Shelby with me didn't get to see V-E day. Others are in hospitals in the U.S., England and France who used to be in my company. I'm thankful John, to be sitting here writing to you, and I'm still a very lucky fellow. Yes, I'm thankful.

As Preston indicated, the worst was by no means over. Some of the bloodiest and most ruthless fighting of the war was raging in the Pacific with no end in sight.

～○

Seaman Robert Black, Aboard the USS *Swenson,* Berates His Father in a Blistering Letter for Embarrassing Him in Front of His Crewmates

Losing a child in the war was unbearable for any parent, but the loss was especially devastating when it came after peace had been declared. Henry Black, a business-man in Manhattan, had not heard for some time from his son Bob, a seaman aboard the USS Swenson, *and he feared Bob was critically ill or dead. Mr. Black went to extraordinary lengths to send a shore-to-ship message (which was usually reserved for emergencies) simply to "check in" on his boy. Bob, very much alive and now very much humiliated, explained to his father in no uncertain terms why the call to the ship was a stupendously bad idea.*

R. Black S 1/C
USS LK Swenson
DD 729 C/O F. P. O.
San Francisco, Cal

Dear Dad,

Notice the above address. That's just in case you have forgotten that I can be reached at it. Maybe you also think I'm the big hero type who may be dying of a tropical disease but gayly writes home of the beautiful landscape and fine feathered birds. Well, you may have forgotten, but I'm just as blunt and tactless as I've always been. If I don't like something or someone everyone's quick to hear about it. If I have a gripe the above still holds true. Take it from me — If I were in bad health the Navy would be the first to hear about it. The fact is I'm disgustingly healthy, if I weren't, I'd be homeward bound with my discharge flying at the mast head.

I take it that the cause of your little communique was no mail. I wonder what you would have done if I had been out here during the war. I hope you realize that no. 1. I'm on a ship that is continually on the move, 2, I'm 10,000 miles away in a half civilized part of the world where it is extremely difficult to find quick and sure means of communication, and 3, the human element is not infallable. Any one of the above listed reasons might have slowed the mail.

To touch another facet of the situation — the Navy is the Navy, an organization of supposedly grown and well balanced men. The above mentioned organization is not to be confused with the 4H Clubs of America or the Boy Scouts of America. The men in the Naval Service have a reputation that is practically a tradition. Namely, as individuals they are the sweet, innocent, sons of ordinary American families. Once they get together in uniform, though, they are as tough and efficient a fighting machine as they are a suave, smooth functioning team when it comes to the women. If you need a personal example to confirm the above statement I've cracked and been cracked over the head with beer bottles in the toughest and most notorious dance halls and bars of the West Coast and Orient. Secondly, I've a girlfriend in every port you have marked on that map I sent home as well as in 'Frisco, Oakland, San Jose, and Mt. Vernon, but I'm still Mom's little Bobby.

All the above mentioned is just to clearify the fact that I can take care of myself physically and mentally.

Still another fase of the situation is that in your shall we say immature haste, you failed to realize that a message like that must go through the "Chain of Commands" and eventually ends up among my friend in radio on this ship. As a result I got a terrific ribbing as well as being placed back in the limelight and under the Captain's Blue Beardish Scrutiny. Being that I just got through with him or rather he just got through with me I'm none too happy about the situation.

After careful consideration of all I've said and a great deal more that I could add I hope you can see that your unnecessary attempted easing of your mind may have made you happy but has made a devil of a mess on this end of the line. If you had my interests at heart you can see how they have taken quite a beating. I hope you are satisfied because I had to use the money I had been saving for toothpaste and my brand of razor blades to answer the message.

I'm positive that Mom knew nothing about what you did because I think she would have laughed it off as a fantastic idea. Remember you used the route reserved for messages telling of mortal sickness or death in the family. Compared to those messages yours seems, let's just say, uncalled for.

How about knocking off this anxious father over infant son situation. I'll consider the incident closed if you will reimberse me for the return message and this letter.

As usual,
Bob

Extended Correspondence

**2nd Lt. Sidney Diamond Writes to His Fiancée, Estelle
Spero, to Remind Her How Much He Loves Her, Shares His Fears
About How Veterans Will Be Treated After the War, Reflects
on His Fellow Soldiers Who Have "Departed," and Describes
the Melancholy Among the Men on Christmas Day 1944
&
Estelle, During the Final Months of the War, Tells Her Fiancé
She Is Thinking of Him Always and Loves Him Dearly**

They met in August 1938 at the Mullaly playground in the Bronx. He was sixteen. She was fourteen. His name was Sidney Diamond, hers was Estelle Spero. Pals at first, they played Ping-Pong, handball, and badminton together, and went on long, meandering walks through the neighborhoods of New York. The following summer they went to Coney Island, where Sid kissed Estelle for the first time after a ride on the Caterpillar. After only the second time he walked her home, Sid recalled many years later, he said to himself, "I want to marry that girl." A precocious fifteen-year-old, Estelle was accepted at Hunter College, where she majored in speech and English literature. Sid enrolled at New York's City College and studied to be a chemical engineer. By 1940 the relationship was serious and the two began to discuss marriage. And then came Pearl Harbor. Over the vociferous protests of family and friends, Sid dropped out of school in April 1942 and volunteered for the U.S. Army. They had never argued until that time, but Estelle was upset with Sid for succumbing to what

she believed were romantic notions of warfare. After graduating from Officer Can-
didate School, Sid was sent to Fort Bliss, Texas, as a second lieutenant in the
Eighty-second Chemical Battalion, 4.2 mortar outfit. Attached to the infantry, it all
but guaranteed Sid would end up in combat. "I know you'll be in the middle of it,"
she chided him in a letter, "you have that luck. Trouble seeker that you are. You do
ask for it." Corresponding regularly, Estelle occasionally reminded Sid of her dis-
pleasure at his decision but affirmed she still loved him. Sid felt they had been
"engaged to be engaged" long enough and wanted to make their commitment official.
In a playful tone characteristic of so many of his letters, Sid feigned bewilderment—
not to mention a bad Brooklyn accent—concerning what they should do next.
(Ronald Colman and Charles Boyer, mentioned by Sid, were famous movie actors.)

May '43

Darling—

Me? I'm tough, see! — I sleeps on de ground. I eats rough "vittles." — nobody gets de better 'a me — no siree — Dere's only one ting whats got me perplex - er - perp - er a — screwy — and dat's a dame — see? Whatta babe — cute? — nothin' better! a looker? — tops! — Yeah — and even talks intell — intel — er — a — smart-like! ya get me? Yeah!! — Once she tells me I'm nuts — dat don't botter me none! — She tells me I'm an imbe - imibec - er - a dope! —

Foist she's sugar, honey and schmaltz — Den she gets to naggin and raisin de roof wid me! — she treats me rough and tough — whadda I do? — whadda I do??? — I takes it! — takes it wid all de screwy looks 'n ways of Charles Boyer — I suffers like who's dat guy — a — Ronal Coleman! — 'o course I ain't as pretty as dat guy — no, I aint got a line, but cripes I'm in love!

I tries to tell her of de sky, de trees, de boids, de scenery. — She tells me I'm childish? — Smart like a whip, my babe! Uses big woids — ain't "childish" a big woid?? —

Sweetheart — joking aside I love you, love you to the utmost. My dar-ling, listen — if this war takes ten years, yes even twenty years I'll finish college! For more reasons than one! — Did you know I was born under the sign of Aries, the goat — or something — according to my horo-scope, they tell me, I have all the persistency, revolting stupid stubbor-ness of the goat. A goat would bat his head against a wall until dead — maybe there's something in this horoscope deal huh??

Marry you?? — get us all the things we need?? — — — — I will!! —

Darling, let's both thank heavens we both have a healthy sense of humor. My little silk-stocking-selling-saleswoman. —

No, I haven't grown up — not at all — I still blush when people tease me about the "notorious Stelle!" — Get flustered like an adolescent school boy —

So I suffer from softening of the brain — that's really getting down to fundamentals! — basic!!

You "want to know where we stand in my estimation" —

I can only speak for myself. I know I love you. I know things have not changed as far as I'm concerned. — A little dubious, perhaps, about fitting in to the scheme of civilian living when this is over — but I imagine I'll get into the swing of things after a few weeks — a trifle worried about being teased about this deal for the rest of our blissful (and it <u>will</u> be happy) lives — Regardless of how you think — please respect my right to believe in certain stupidities —

Sure, I'm a dumb idealist. I'm a shameful cad for running out on you — okay — you're in a position of some buying and selling. Weigh the good qualities against the bad. Buy that which will give you the most of what you desire. Again getting down to the brutal facts which are, to say the least, disgusting —

I offer nothing but a pig-headed dreamer — when the conflict is ended there will be even less because I'll no longer be a dreamer! —

Here's the story and let's settle it once and for all time — and by heaven's let's not continue discussing this matter — I want to marry you — to spend the rest of my life with your telling me to stop biting my fingernails — when? — tomorrow, if it were possible — the day after the "duration plus six months" definitely! — Now we place the dilemma in your lap — you choose the most suitable time! —

The more I write the more confusing I get — even to myself! —

Today we went through a very dull R. S. O. P. — we've done this so often it isn't funny — R. S. O. P. — always called "arsop" — Reconnaissance, Selection, Occupation of Position — Dull to say the least —

I phoned mom tonight — I'll try to get you later this week — say, when is Mother's Day. —

Next time I mention what we did during the day tell me to keep my mouth shut — that's restricted information — "for those people concerned only."

Darling, the radio blares forth that "Romanian Rhapsody" Enesco — recall the Russian Kretchma, the violinist, the soul stirring crying, spirit rising, swift music. — Memories hide thyself!!! How unfair to come after me thus!!! I love you.

Your —
and I do mean your
Sid

Almost immediately after writing the letter, Sid received word he had been granted a temporary pass to go home. He promptly dashed off a quick note to Estelle: "Hyah — Ought to be home for extremely short leave beginning the 8th — I'll try to fly home — leave so very short it's cruel — 10 days — disgusting — about five days home. I repeat — Will you marry me ??? — Yes?? — no?? — Your, Sid." On May 14, 1943, Sid Diamond dropped to his knee in the middle of Central Park and placed the ring on her finger. Two days later Estelle and Sid's parents accompanied him to Penn Station, where Sid, decked out in his full uniform, boarded a train bound for Texas. Estelle graduated Phi Beta Kappa from Hunter College that June and started a job at Bell Laboratories as a technical assistant focusing on war-related projects. Some time after Sid had left, his parents, who sold dresses from an apartment on Nelson Avenue, told Estelle about a chance encounter with a girl from Sid's past. (In fact, Sid barely knew the young woman; they had met only briefly when he was working as a waiter at a children's summer camp.) Estelle couldn't resist teasing him about it, and Sid replied with mock horror.

Darling,

Dilemma! confusion! distraction!! — My past returns to haunt me — skeletons rattle their bones in my closet. Once more the Nelson Dress Shoppe is my undoing —

So a girl from Concy Island walks in to buy a dress. She spots my sorry puss hanging from the wall — She swoons and shrieks in terror — "Is that — is that-that Monster Sidney Diamond" — (It must have happened this way) — So my picture leers back at her and says, "What's it to ya bub?" —

"Sure," she says, "I knew him in Parksville — He used to call me fat & when I was sick with appendicitis he sent me a lollypop — " — "Evelyn something or other's" my name she states —

Nights of tossing and turning. Who the hell is Evelyn — I've called a lot've 'em fat — (Candid Sid) — The lollypops — oh — oh — oh — It hit me like a flash —

It was one of those Irv (Charlie) Jacobson, Phil, Diamond screwy escapades —

Some guy writes a book "Out of the Night" — Mine's — "Out of the Nelson" — Some say that if you stand on Brodway & 42nd St. you'll meet someone you know — the Nelson apparently has taken over some of the work — all of my "lurid" past parades before that photo on the wall — Ah yes — I shall drink me a bottle of the "Green Death" and retire to the ignominious hovel —

She says she took pictures of us — Yoiks, they hitched the five miles from town and grabbed us for the pictures before we knew what was going on — Women — are crazy — insane — and should be watched carefully —

A guy can't get engaged in peace —

I fully expect a bare breasted native girl in a sarong to walk into the Nelson — glance at the photo — and shout — "Uggle bub — sut phlub — Heel — me him see 'em — no good Joe — Double bubble — rubble!"

What a life!! — What a world!! — damn I could make a good strategist for this war — I read all the funnies — to quote a rotten gag in a rotten paper —

For you — alone — a very fond caress — a kiss — because — just because —

Your
Sid

Not all of their letters focused on their relationship. By July Sid was stationed in the South Pacific, and news from the homefront prompted reams of commentary from Sid. He and his comrades were especially steamed by reports that folks in the United States were complaining in late 1943 of "war fatigue"—the shortages, the blood donation drives, the endless pitches to buy war bonds, the rationing, the workers' strikes, and so on. Was the war no longer considered an honorable one, Sid and his men wondered? How would they be received when they eventually returned home? In a letter updating Estelle on an otherwise uneventful day, Sid articulated the group's thoughts and fears concerning their postwar lives.

South Pacific
Jan 2, 1944

Darling —

This morning I went into the jungle to inspect the impact area of yesterdays firing. My guns were on line but over by 50 yards. — I think its good. Particularly since it was impossible to see more than ten feet ahead and I ranged in by ear. — Me — the guy that couldn't tell a C from a C sharp trying to determine how far away a shell burst. — A new tune!!!

This afternoon Cotton, Hindman, and myself took two cases of empty beer bottles — our carbines and played coney island. We put the beer bottles up in trees, on the ground, on bushes. Then we just potshotted at the beer bottles. — It's like I said — this war business is an overgrown carnival — shooting gallery and all — Sunday was topped off by a "social" gathering of the remaining battalion officers. Everything from whores of Juarez to post war activities was discussed. Lt. Gutman raised this question — "What will the people back home say to us when we return? Will they call us suckers? They did those who fought in 1918!" — A strange hush fell over the officers, as if that was the question that all had thought about — all had worried about — We all realized how little people at home can conceive of the suffering, hardships, loneliness, violence of war. —

We talked of the new generation — the teen agers that would look at their war tired brothers and fathers and speak of us as we once spoke of the men of the last war. — It wasn't pleasant — We knew then why so few veterans speak of their experiences. — no, not because they weren't exciting, new, dangerous — but because the squirts, the snot-noses, the know-it-alls had driven their souls to the background.

"What will we do if they call us suckers?" —

What will I do?? — I often wonder — my equilibrium is a bit changed — Well — we'll see.

The young fathers wondered whether their kids would slam the door and run to mother shouting "There's a strange man outside!" — Captain Smith remarked "You single men will have the biggest worry — how'll you get wives? — All your gals will be taken and the new ones won't go for your old fashioned stuff." I said,

"It may be old fashioned but that stuff will go any time, any place, — There's nothing new in that field."

We had egg-noggs — peanuts, cake, toast, cheese — Somebody's Christmas packages just opened — I like these gatherings, particularly because they don't play charades!! — Ugh!! —

Of course you and the Copacabaña came up — damn 'em! —

Enough said — I love you — endlessly

Your Sid

Sid's mood turned somber again as he and his fellow troops thought of their comrades half a world away landing on the beaches of Normandy. "The news of the continental invasion is the primary source of conversation," Sid, recuperating from noncombat-related back surgery, wrote to Estelle on June 7, 1944. "I heard the report during a movie in the hospital — Picture was stopped — news announced — 'Stelle — there were no cheers — no shouts — we all sat still — we'd fought — we'd made beach heads — ours was a deep sympathy — a silent prayer — 'Good Luck brothers — good luck. . . ." Sid's loneliness and yearning for Estelle grew more pronounced as the humid summer months in the South Pacific plodded sluggishly along. Facetiously addressing his letter to Estelle's mailman, Sid pined for some goodies from his sweetheart which he had long been expecting:

Dear Postman,

You look like a very happy man. You probably come from a happy home. Yes, your wife probably loves you — I love you — this girl admires you — We all have an affection for you — so please allow this lady — no you dope, not the one on the left — the good looker in front of you — allow her to send me a pen & cigarette lighter — and a kiss — Hey!! — in the letter! — in the letter! — Tend to your own business and sell stamps!! . . .

A month later Sid, once again in a lively mood, dispatched an "official" memo to Estelle enumerating the tactical qualifications and classifications of their two-person squad.

17 August 1944

Subject: Miss Estelle Spero
To: The World

1. On several occasions there has been questions posed as to rank and authority in the Diamond combat team. Also some people have asked about who is most beautiful. — The following paragraphs supercede any previous bulletins on these matters.

2. Commander of the organization will be Miss Estelle, who upon assuming command will be responsible for the maintenance of discipline amongst her subordinates in particular Lt. Diamond. Miss Estelle will be charged with the morale and well being of this officer. Lt. Diamond will assist in all possible ways and continue to show the same respect and affection to his superiors.

3. Careful studies of photograph II MIAI — GARFIELD indicate that the C.O. is by far the best proportioned, most attractive of all models heretofore presented — The mark IAI reveals the following assets.

    a. irresistable lips
    b. Clear vision —
    c. black, long eyelashes
    d. Long flowing hair, slightly kinky
    e. Eyebrows (note: one must be careful of these, when they are raised duck for cover, when normal proceed as usual, when lowered and wrinkles form at brow kiss lips immediately — or else hear the burst of a severe tongue lashing)
    f. Nose — very adaptable for biting — also very pretty.
    g. Ears — Be careful of these. They are usually hidden and well camouflaged — If you get too close you will be caught by booby trap

M2 EARRING — they are excellent receptacles for hot air but receive best when the truth is told —

h. The neck is streamlined and especially designed to overcome wind resistance

i. The overall picture indicates an extremely efficient fighting machine combined with an obvious beauty which is dangerous for the unschooled — Although rugged in appearance it has a few delicate mechanisms which must not be fooled with by the novice —

j. The instrument on the whole has no liabilities that we can see

4. We recommend that this equipment be requisitioned for Lt. Diamond's organization and that they get married at the earliest possible moment — Despite Lt. Diamond's demonstrated lack of skill in handling this equipment we feel he is sufficiently interested to study and learn this instrument — its nomenclature, its functions, its use, its quirks and needs. He will be responsible for the care of this instrument.

5. This item is a critical one and numerous requisitions have been made for it. Lt. Diamond, however, has A-1 priority as soon as it becomes available.

General E. Motors

In October 1944 Gen. Douglas MacArthur was leading the climactic U.S. invasion of the Philippines, and Sid and his men were heading toward the main island of Luzon. Sid had already endured combat as a forward observer on Bougainville in the Solomon Islands from late January through April of 1944. (During this time, he was promoted to first lieutenant and received two commendations for bravery.) Sid could not give Estelle the particulars of his whereabouts or what he had experienced, but it involved (he would later tell her) seeing the aftermath of Japanese brutality against innocent civilians. And, for the first time, Sid was losing friends in battle. Sid tried to maintain his sense of humor, but the grim business of war was dampening his spirits. He sent the following to Estelle on November 1, 1944:

Darling,

Almost seventeen months overseas. It seems like such an endless interlude. Yet, somehow, the day of departure is so clear. — The way we walked from camp through sidestreets to the pier. There were no bands, no flourishes, few people. A few lonely citizens watched us go by with a dull expression of having seen the show before. Many other troops, on many other days had preceeded us — and there were many more days and troops to come. A woman cried. A young girl waved. The men were too hot and impressed by the occasion to whistle at her. Then the morning when the ship went around the harbor checking the instruments. We did a lot of thinking that morning.

There was a peculiar sensation that all this wasn't new — that our ancestors somewhere had experienced the same tightening around the stomach. Perhaps the feeling was inherited from our animal forebears. Were we not about to engage in the birthright of beasts? — Soon we were to live, eat, hate, fight like the beasts of yesteryear. Man hadn't changed much. Sure, we had tanks, carbines, mortars, planes — They were only aids to man's ativism.

Some of us felt cheated — We had gambled but believed our losses to be excessive. The man with the new born baby, the man who just got married, the younger boys who wanted only to live in dreams of youth — no, 'Stelle — There were no bands!

Then in retrospect came the second departure — A soldier always "departs" He never "arrives" — When we left New Caledonia — We'd gone speeding through the streets of the capital city —

More departures, more thoughts, more wondering about the "arrival" — Each island is only a place to depart from to go to another island — You never get where you're going. The morale services and motion picture heroes say we won't stop until we reach Tokyo — We know our departures, leave takings, will never end — Sometimes one wonders as he sees the white crosses neatly lined up in well formed ranks — Sometimes the cemetery brings the question to one's mind — — — Are these the men who have finally "arrived"? The chaplain calls them the "departed" ones — but their journey is over — "Last Stop — All Out!"

This letter may well be titled "Random melancholias" and politely dumped into a trash basket.

The ghost of Johnny Martin parades before us now — a nice kid — about twenty — The army hadn't aged him much — He laughed a lot. Johnny never complained. I can remember, so vividly, so cruelly clear — our last few days before we left the States. We had a beer party. Johnny played the guitar and sang western and hill billy music — Sometimes, when I'm not watching myself I catch myself humming the "Truck Drivers Blues" his favorite — They didn't allow men to carry excess baggage so I carried his guitar with my equipment when we left. — Martin wasn't brilliant. What he lacked in education he made up for by his cheerfulness and eternal smile — He was just another guy — who got off at the "end of the line."

Don't mind this morbid nonsense. Sometimes the loneliness overwhelms me — the noises of the insects, birds, small creatures seem to crowd into my tent crushing against me. It is terrible to live with memories only. — The soldier doesn't think of the future, His "present" just exists and the Past is all he can think about

'Stelle I wouldn't write or speak this load to anyone but you because it sounds so childish and you're the only one to whom I can moan. Reminds me of a ditty make up fad we have here. Once I complained about some nonsense so now, every time I open my mouth I'm greeted with a

> "Moan and groan
> With Sidney Diamōn'"

Ted Bochstahler gets

> "Yell and holler
> With Ted Bochstahler"

and so on —

Anyway I'm moaning and groaning on your very nice, soft shoulders — I want to be with you — I love you

Your,
Sid

The weight of the war—the physical and emotional exhaustion, the isolation, the fear, the sheer enormity of death and destruction around him—was grinding Sid down. On what should have been a day of joy and celebration, Sid and his comrades found themselves at one of their lowest points. His love for Estelle was all that made it tolerable.

December 25, '44

Darling,

Christmas occasions thoughts of warmth, of friendship of giving — It says in all the papers!! — The spirit of the holiday, whether it be Chanukah, Christmas, or what have you is a noble and satisfying one. You and I agree that to give and love but once a year is close to the ridiculous — We, at least know the happiness of Christmas all year 'round. The pleasure of giving is ever present with us. It is not so much with the material creations that we reward each other but each day we give a little of ourselves to each other. —

It would sound inane for me to speak of how "different" our love is —
Somehow ours fills all the requirements. Poems, songs, stories of love
and eternal devotion were written about everlasting, enduring, powerful
affections such as the one which holds us together —

Don't mind the overdose of sentimentalism — Maybe it's the night —
the radio which moans "Little Town of Bethlehem" — Perhaps the carols
the men sing — or the quiet tropical night with the cool breeze and twin-
kling stars — or the remoteness of home — the loneliness of the moment
— Yes today we had a community of thought. All the men — together —
in a community of homesickness — Do not think harshly — or scoff at
our childishness — We have so little — so little else but dreams —

It is difficult at present to be the cold, the practical. — Even more is it
hard to be humorous or laugh — to joke — I cannot say where we are,
what we are doing, what we will do — There's been so much between us
unsaid and undone — So much of our lives missed —

'Stelle, for my part in this denial — I beg forgiveness — For my part in
being such a fool, such a child — will you understand? Sweetheart —
Would I were with you so that I could tell you of these things. That I have
contributed to your unhappiness — again — I humbly request you try
and be patient with me — I would like to fill the air with plans, dreams,
hopes — But — 'Stelle — — all there is, is a choking in the chest —
Every once in awhile a guy gets himself overcome by despair; despondency overwhelms him. — It is so-oo long — so very very long —

I love you darling. — whatever happens — be happy — that's my only
request — get everything we would have liked — fill your life — (er —
only keep my little niche open — so if I ever get home — I'll know there's
one place waiting for me — my corner of the world — Let it be a small
alcove in your heart — put a comfortable chair there and always keep a
warm fire glowing — Because if I come home in any recognizable form
I'll head directly for that chair — That's where I belong — that's my
home — with you —)

Stelle, it's not weakness, it's not softness — it's a fact — I need you !!
— I need you !! — I need you!! —

Enough of this — I love you — "extensively"

Your,
Sid

*The next letter Estelle received from Sid was written over a period of days while he
was aboard a ship heading for the Philippines, and he forewarned Estelle that it
would be difficult for him to send mail for some time. Indeed, almost a month passed
before his next letter, which was hastily written in the midst of battle.*

January 19–1945

Darling,

Somewhere in the Philippines — In combat again — a lot to say but — A. very tired — B. very very dirty. — C. Busy, Busy, as all hell — Been moving constantly — Excuse brevity — I love you — you make my foxhole warm and soft — sweetheart — your

Sid

At nearly the same time Sid had sent off his message, Estelle, now a graduate student at Northwestern University, was lamenting in a letter to him: "Dearest, the emptiness of everything without you is appalling. The simplest things depend on you . . . a walk, a conversation, a whim . . . everything needs you for completion and enjoyment." Weeks passed and still no word. Concerned, but not panicking, she wrote to Sid while listening to President Roosevelt discuss his meetings in Yalta with Soviet leader Joseph Stalin and Prime Minister Winston Churchill. Estelle concluded her letter with two poems by Emily Dickinson. ("SAD," mentioned at the end of the letter, was Estelle's sobriquet for Sid: "Such A Darling.")

March 1, 1945

Darling —

I'm listening to President Roosevelt as I write. I have been concentrating on him, but it wasn't worth it. He has said, fifty different ways, that Joe, Winnie, and he get along just fine. I don't know what else he can say, but I was hopin.'

I'm going mad over that platform test. I don't like the way I've written it, I haven't learned it yet, and I'm sure I'll make a darn fool of myself Saturday. Probably make a fool of Emily Dickinson, too.

I was in most of the day, had scenery class at 2:30, sat through it in the usual foggy state, and went over to Scott Hall with Jan, who's in my scenery class. Jan Hall, this is, not Frankel. We chatted away over Hostess cup cakes and coffee, then went on our separate ways, I, to the library, to look up editorial opinion on the way the Yalta conference settled Poland. By now I'm hopelessly confused on what happened in the Atlantic, Terehan, Bretton Oaks, Dumbarton Oaks, Crimea, here, there and everywhere. If anything did happen, which I doubt. I want to write a prospectus for a program which would read editorial opinion on a matter like Poland. I think it would be interesting, although very difficult to handle. I probably wouldn't listen to it, of course.

I wonder whether you get my mail. I wonder whether you will get this V-mail letter any faster than a regular one. I wonder where you are, what you're doing, how life is treating you.

Suspense is hostiler than Death,
Death, tho' soever broad,
Is just Death, and cannot increase - -
Suspense does not conclude,
But perishes to live anew,
But just anew to die,
Annihilation plated fresh
With Immortality.

You see, I cannot see your lifetime,
I must guess,
How many times it ache
For me to-day - - Confess

How many times for my far sake
The brave eyes film.
But I guess guessing hurts,
Mine get so dim!

Too vague the face
My own so patient covets,
Too far the strength
My timidity enfolds;
Haunting the heart
Like her transplanted faces,
Teasing the want
It only can suffice.
— Emily Dickinson

I love you, dearest SAD, sweetest —
E

It had been almost a month since Sid's last letter, and Estelle was now genuinely worried. Just after 11:00 P.M. on March 5, Estelle returned to the boarding house where she was living while at Northwestern and found an envelope addressed to her in unfamiliar handwriting. There was nothing to indicate where it came from, and there was no letter inside—only a small newspaper clipping. "First Lieut. Sidney Diamond, who was with the Eighty-second Chemical Battalion," the March 2 article reported, "was killed on Luzon." On January 29, 1945, Sid was shot through the stomach during an assault on Fort Stotsenburg, north of Manila. He was twenty-two years old when he died. The last time Estelle had seen him was May 16, 1943, two days after their engagement in Central Park.

───────── ⟋⟍ ─────────

Pfc. Bill Madden, Wounded Twice in Combat, Describes to His Father Coming in with the First Wave at Iwo Jima

A speck of land only eight square miles in size, Iwo Jima was of immense strategic value to the B-29 bombing campaign against Japan. The Japanese had established an early warning radar system on the island, located 800 miles southeast of mainland Japan, and they launched fighter planes from its airfields to intercept incoming B-29s. Tiny as it was, Iwo Jima was defended by 22,000 Japanese troops entrenched in a honeycomb of camouflaged caves, pillboxes, and tunnels—all carved out of volcanic rock and protected by innumerable boobytraps and minefields. As the first wave of U.S. Marines struggled ashore on the morning of February 19, 1945, the Japanese unleashed a withering onslaught of machine-gun fire and mortar shells. Rushing headfirst into this deluge was Pfc. William Madden with the Twenty-seventh Marines, Second Battalion, "Easy" Company. Madden watched as some of his closest friends were critically injured or literally blown to pieces. Madden, himself, was shot in the right wrist and arm on March 6. Recuperating from his wounds in a hospital in Hawaii, Madden wrote to his father in LaPaz, Indiana, about the battle for Iwo Jima. (Bob, mentioned in the letter, was Madden's older brother.)

April 22, 45

Dear Dad,

I read once that a Dad likes to get mail addressed to just him sometimes, so if you can stand lefthand writing this is for you. I'll tell you a few things about Iwo.

It all started in the Hawaiians months ago. On every problem, we practiced landing, pushing across an imaginary island, then making a right turn and knocking out pill-boxes for miles.

We were crammed aboard transports (5 high in bunks & 2,000 to a ship) and began a 40 day voyage stopping for fuel & supplies, only at the Marshall Islands & Saipan. During the entire trip, we were schooled on maps & fortifications of Iwo, especially the 6 days between Saipan & there. We had a large clay model to study too, although we weren't told the island's name till 0–3.

0–1 was my birthday and as the fellows sang greetings to me I wondered if I would see my 20th one.

At Saipan we transferred to (L.S.T's) ships that carry amphibious tractors inside. The initials stand for "landing ship tank", but we renamed it "large stationary target" because it's so slow.

We got up at 4 o'clock on D day & could see the flashes of gunfire from battle ships & cruisers in the distance as we ate our last warm chow for a long time.

At 6 o'clock we were packed in the amphibs. & the bow of the ship swung open. At 6:30, we left the ship & spent 2 1/2 hours on the ocean forming into waves. 9 o'clock was H-hour, & as we neared the beach, Jap shells were falling close. The amphib. on my right was blown up 2,000 yards from shore, & one of our planes was shot down near us.

I was in the 1st wave of troops to land, but a wave of armored tanks landed 2 minutes earlier. This would have been swell if there hadn't been a 15 ft. embankment of loose sand in my sector. The tanks didn't get off the beach, & you can imagine the trouble we had!

The Nips pattern-shelled the beach with mortars, cross fired it with pill-boxes, block houses, & individual nambu & heavy machine-guns. They had the beach mined too, & I saw plenty of Marines die before they got over the first bank.

Just before we hit, the Navy gave the beach a thorough going over & then raised their fire to give us a "Rolling Barrage" in front. While we were only 200 yards from the beach, the ships hit it with a rocket barrage that even shook us. Our planes took over from there & strafed enemy emplacements till we got there (also laying us an ineffective smoke screen.)

Yes, I know it sounds like nothing could be living there, and it looked that way too, but we found them still waiting in their emplacements & ready when we arrived. There were no buildings. The entire population lived underground in their defenses & there were no civilians to bother with, so you can see it was a natural fortress.

After the first bank of sand there were two more and just as well defended. I got my first Nip on the second bank. He raised up to throw another grenade & I shot him in the neck with an armor piercing shell. You can imagine what was left of him!

Do you remember me telling you about "Best" winning the "Silver Star" overseas before? This time I saw him charge a Jap pill-box alone while they threw grenades at him, keep on going when shrapnel from one hit him in the mouth and jaw, shoot one, & kill the other two by beating them over the head with his rifle butt when it failed to fire. He did it so fast they couldn't even use their bayonets on him. Best wouldn't go back till he was hit again when I was. He's going to the states now & is recommended for the Navy Cross. Chicago is his home & his Dad's a cop.

My out-fit (27th) drove across the island at the narrow part with the 28th on our left. We sure caught a lot of shell-fire from the volcano, too, especially when we reached the other beach & turned right, with our backs to it. It certainly felt good to see the "Stars & Stripes" raised there, believe me!

Dad, a friend here at the hospital is going to the states to-morrow & says he'll take this letter & mail it there. It'll miss the censors, so I can tell you about my "company". Out of 252 officers & men, only 12 men came through the campaign without being killed or wounded. None of these 12 were officers or sergeants. One corporal who was back at the C.P. was the only N.C.O. left. It was awful to watch steel crash into human flesh & rip it apart. I saw a lot of good men die & I never want to see it again.

It seemed that every Nip had a mortar. One fellow said every one he saw carried a mortar but one, & that one had a requisition slip to get one.

They were plenty accurate too! One fellow said, "If you held up a tobacco tin, a Nip would drop a mortar shell in it without touching either side," and that's about the truth too.

The Nips had a German made rocket that we called "Box-Car Bessie." It was a 2000 lb. shell that made a red streak across the sky. Our artillery couldn't knock it out because they pulled it back in a cave in a cliff by the use of rails.

In the northern part of the island we had to take one cliff after another, all full of caves. A lot of caves were hidden & facing backwards. We got their fire in our backs as we advanced. This gave us the feeling of being surrounded at all times. Our outfit was machine-gunned by our L.V.Ts, hit by our own mortars, bombed by our rockets, shelled by our naval gunboats, and was hit hard by our artillery as we began an attack. The barrage broke it up & the attack failed. Now I know how a Nip feels!

After a few days on Iwo a guy can dig a 4 ft. foxhole with his bare hands. I don't know who killed the most Marines; the Japs or the men behind us. As Bob tried to tell me before I enlisted, I'm in the wrong outfit! It's a great one though!!!

We were told we'd be bombed by hundreds of carrier & land based planes, but the reason we weren't is the action of "Task Force 58." They hit the planes before they took off, & intercepted & destroyed the ones that did. I'll always be grateful to that task force

I had plenty of close calls in those 16 days that I'll always remember.

When I was finally shot they shipped me to Guam & then Pearl Harbor. I'm just a little ways from Honolulu now.

You know our casualties were given at 4,000 dead & 16,000 wounded. Well 2,000 more died of wounds & several thousand men are crippled for life. Do you think that rock was worth those men's lives, Dad??

Well, I haven't said all I wanted to, but it's all I can think of now. My arm is doing o.k., so don't worry about it.

Oh yes—Happy Birthday Pop!

Love, Bill

The raising of the Stars and Stripes over Mount Suribachi, which Madden alluded to in his letter, was photographed by Joe Rosenthal on February 23 and has become one of the most famous and dramatic war pictures ever taken. (Total victory over Iwo Jima was not achieved until over a month later, and three of the six flag raisers were killed in the fighting.) With more than 6,800 Americans killed and nearly 20,000 wounded, the battle for Iwo Jima remains the bloodiest in Marine Corps history. Nearly all of the Japanese defenders were either killed or, like their commander Gen. Tadimichi Kuribayashi, committed suicide. Thousands of U.S. airmen used the island for emergency landings in the war's remaining months.

Pfc. Richard King Chronicles the Fighting on Saipan and Okinawa in a Graphic Letter to His Parents

Almost ten times larger than Iwo Jima with five times as many defenders, Okinawa represented the final major showdown of the war. American troops stormed the island's beaches early on April 1 (Easter Sunday) encountering—much to their astonishment—scant resistance, and they advanced for five days essentially unimpeded. It was a trap. On April 6 the Japanese, having drawn the Americans inland, launched a massive counterattack from all directions. Kamikaze planes rained down on U.S. warships off Okinawa's coast, and concealed machine guns and artillery opened up on U.S. ground forces. Ambushed by Japanese soldiers hiding in caves, the Americans began flushing them out with grenades and incinerating anyone inside with flamethrowers. For two and a half months the savage fighting, including hand-to-hand combat, continued but, by June 21, the island was finally secured. Pfc. Richard King was sent with the Twenty-seventh Infantry Division to Okinawa after earning a Silver Star for gallantry during the battle for Saipan. (In preparation for the assault on the Philippines, the United States invaded Saipan in the Marianas in June 1944. An estimated 3,400 Americans were killed and 13,000 wounded.) King, twenty years old and a native of Muscatine, Iowa, sent his parents the following narrative detailing the bloodshed he had seen during almost two years in the Pacific.

Okinawa Island
Sept 8, 1945

Dear Folks,

We left the States, Dec. 14, 1943, on the luxury liner, Lurline. Arrived in Honolulu the 20th. We were in a replacement depot about ten days, then went to the Ranger (Refresher) school for a month, and joined our respective companies. Started training for Saipan, right away. Amphibious operations, rough training, and long hikes.

I went to Honolulu a few times, not much to do, went to Waikiki Beach, and other famous places.

On May 31, we got on transports at Pearl Harbor. (The Battleship, Oklahoma, had just been raised from the ocean, and was getting a paint job.) One week later we arrived in Eniwetok in the Marshalls, stayed one day, and continued to Saipan. On June 16th we dropped anchor off the coast of Saipan. As we drew close we saw enemy landing barges burning, live and dead Japs floating in the water. The navy was throwing thousands of tons of shells onto Saipan. In the afternoon at 3:30 we were told to prepare for debarkation, at 5:30 we went over the side into landing barges. We were on the water from 5:30 to 10:30, then headed for shore. About 75 yards from shore the barges grounded, and we waded shoulder deep to land. Just as we set foot on the beach, the Japs opened up with rifles, machine guns, and mortars, and we laid in the water on the beach, the rest of the night, waves washing over us, continually. At 4:30 next morning we moved to front lines, to relieve the Marine sector. That started our 23 straight days on the lines. At 7:00 we shoved off in the attack. That night was the most horrible, I will ever remember. The Japs pulled a banzai attack, before we could dig in. We had taken a hill, and they forced us to withdraw to safer lines so we could bring up supplies. Before we took the hill, we had a gigantic machine gun duel, and believe it or not, I went to sleep in No Man's Land for 45 minutes.

When I woke up, the duel was over and 3 Jap guns knocked out. Our destroyers were throwing plenty of lead at a ridge, directly to our front. Then when we retreated from the hill, the Japs really cut loose, we were wading down the coast, and boys were being killed right and left. Mortar shells lit on their heads, and this really did something to all of us. Some boys were jumping into the sea, when their faces were blown away. Two of us, carried one boy back with us, and our aid man gave him plasma all night, but he died next morning. He had his jaw, tongue, and nose blown away. This is a horrible thing to write about, but people should understand what war means, then maybe they wouldn't start another, so soon. They should be able to live together in peace.

To continue, it was late and we were tired as hell, but the order came through, "Get ready to move out." We opened fire, and moved up the hill. The Japs moved back, and we started settling for the night. It was all coral, so that prohibited our digging in. We picked up coral rocks, to form fox-holes. Finally, we just fell on the ground and went to sleep. All that night our artillery and navy guns pounded the hill. The Japs started using their famous knee mortars next morning. One shell lit behind me, about eight feet, shrapnel went all around me, and hit several boys. That was when I knew God would be with me. We had to fall back when they pulled a ban-zai attack. We were out of water, food, ammo, and there was nothing else to do, but withdraw. There was only one way to get out, we got into the water, and back down the coast, until at a safe distance to reorganize.

All along the beach, men were dying of wounds. Maybe you will think this is cruel, but I want you to know what it was like. Mortar shells dropping in on heads, and ripping bodies. Faces blown apart by flying lead and coral. It wasn't a pretty sight, and I will never forget the death and hell along that beach. It rained all the night and mud was ankle deep. Our artillery fired all night, and we shoved off next morning. Our regiment (the 165th) took Aslito airfield from which B-29's bombed Japan. This night passed uneventfully. Third day we were to clear out Magicienne Bay, where the Nips cut us off from our supplies. There were plenty of Japs there, and many of my buddies were killed and wounded.

That was another day that is burned in my memory. We were unable to bring up water or food, the night before. It was 120 degrees and we stayed on the coral, all day in the hot sun, and were slowly going crazy. I couldn't open my mouth at all, my tongue was swollen 5 times its normal size, my throat burned to a crisp, and blood coming out of my nose and mouth. Below us about 15 feet was the sea and the water looked won-derful. About 5:00 we were pulled back for a rest, and met our supply jeep. There was plenty of water, and I drank a helmet full, and didn't even notice it. We were supposed to get 3 day rest, but next morning we shoved off on a 7 mile hike to Mt. Topatchena. We were to relieve the Marines there. This was the 5 or 6th day and we were fagged. A lot of things happened then. My second scout and I moved out in advance. We came upon a Jap ammo dump and were fired on by a machine gun. We took up some very good positions facing down aisles between the rows of ammo. Every time a Nip came to get ammo, we let him have it. At this ammo dump, the fellow that sponsored me at Baptism was killed. He was a grand guy.

A few days passed, and we were up North and had them in one last pocket. On June 7th, they threw their big banzai attack of 9000 Japs on 4 companies of the 105 Infantry. This regiment did one of the most out-standing jobs in the Pacific. When they counted next morning, about 8000 Japs were killed. Nearly all the Americans were killed and lots of them were my friends. When they ran out of ammo, they used axes and their fists. Both Americans and Japs had axes buried in their chests, and stomachs.

You asked how I got the Jap saber. On June 8th, we were cleaning out caves, I was first scout on patrol, and moving down a valley of vines and coral. My second scout yelled to duck, and I turned around as I ducked. A Jap officer had the saber just ready to chop my head off. I knocked it out of his hands, and bayoneted him. That's the story. Look at the nicks on the blade where my bayonet hit.

After the battle was over we went to Magicienne Bay for a rest. There was nothing restful about it, it was so hot, and Dengue fever broke out, everyone came down with it. Your body literally shakes to pieces, tem-peratures at 104. We lived like pigs, after it was over, we were forgotten entirely. We stayed in that place until we left Saipan.

Can you wonder why the Smalley twins said we were a tired, sick out-fit when we reached Espirita Santos? The New Hebrides was heaven after Saipan. Really a swell camp area, in long rows of palms. We rested 2 weeks, then I got on Malaria Control Board. I did absolutely nothing and soon gained back the health, and weight, I lost. I had a jeep to go places, and had plenty of fun. Went to the Beach club every day, for ice cream and cokes. Meantime the boys were training for Okinawa. I missed out on all that training, being on Malaria Control.

On March 19th we left New Hebrides, and were in the Carolines, April 1. Stayed one day, shoved off, and landed April 8, on Okinawa, and moved inland to get straightened out, loafed around for a week, then moved up to front lines. Was there ten days. Took over in front of the lit-tle Siegfried line, and after plenty of casualties we broke the Western flank of the line and were relieved by the Marines. The night we were relieved, the Japs attacked and drove a full strength company back 500 yards. Our company was down to a handful. I had 4 men in my squad at the finish. One man was badly wounded and is in a Spokane hospital for 9 months. His wife had there marriage annulled. He was splattered all over Okinawa. One of my best friends died in my arms. He was hit in the chest by a knee mortar shell. I cried when he died. We had spent most of our time together and it hit me hard. I can't describe the men that fought in this campaign. They are a great bunch, and wonderful friends.

I took over a squad that day. We got a few new men and they were scared plenty. They had seen this boy get killed, so I talked to them and they grew quiet. We had 16 men in the platoon after it was all over, that is 1/3 strength. The Marines relieved us, and that night, the Japs attacked and drove the Marines back over that hard won ground. We went back for garrison because we were so cut up. We rested a week, then started on the biggest mop-up, in the Pacific. Before the mop-up, my platoon went to Tori-Shima. The landing was unopposed and secured in a short time.

The artillery on Okinawa was terrific. Shells would hit, and bury you, or blow you out of your foxhole. The Catholic Chaplain was killed as he was blessing each foxhole. An artillery shell cut him in half at the waist.

The Japs stacked lots of Americans in a big pile, poured gas on them, and touched a match. These atrocity stories are true, not propaganda.

We had a medic in my platoon, whose home is in Brooklyn. He is one of the finest boys, I know. Afraid of nothing, and always there when you needed him. All the medics were swell, and did a wonderful job.

In both operations I knew that God was with me. I prayed every time I had a chance. Silent prayers. Most of the time, I had only time to say, "God be with me," and then did my best. I had some close calls. Lost those chains on Saipan, and Okinawa. Both times I felt them break when bullets were singing pretty close.

That about tells you the story of the past 21 months. It has been a long time to be over here. Is it any wonder we were so excited when the news came over. I guess I cried and laughed at the same time. I want to get home to see all of you.

Your Loving Son,
Dick

With Okinawa captured, the United States was now in control of a formidable staging ground 350 miles south of Japan. Gen. Douglas MacArthur, leading all army forces, and Adm. Chester Nimitz, commanding all naval forces, prepared for Operation Downfall—the full-scale invasion of Japan. Dwarfing the D-Day landings at Normandy, Downfall would involve over 5 million troops. American casualties were estimated at 250,000 to one million with Japanese losses several times that. But as MacArthur and Nimitz huddled with their advisors to hammer out plans for a November invasion, a group of scientists in Los Alamos, New Mexico, were constructing a weapon so lethal it would change not only the course of the war, but human history.

A Survivor of the USS *Indianapolis* Disaster,
RT 2/C Herbert J. Miner II Assures His Parents He Is Alive
and Recuperating After Being Lost at Sea for Four Days

The first torpedo slammed into the hull of the USS Indianapolis *just past midnight on July 30, 1945. The second torpedo struck the ship's fuel tanks and powder magazines, setting off a chain of explosions. Of the approximately 1,200 men onboard the cruiser, which had been on its way from Tinian to Leyte, 300 were either killed instantly or went down with the ship. The other 900 leapt into the sea. In the final, frantic minutes before the* Indianapolis *sank, several distress signals were sent out, and the stranded men hoped they would be rescued in a day or so. They would not. As a result of both human error and security precautions that hindered an immediate search, the dwindling crew, spread out over twenty miles, floated in shark-infested waters hundreds of miles from land for four days with almost no food and water. Herbert Jay ("Jack") Miner II, a nineteen-year-old radio technician second class, wrote to his parents in Glencoe, Illinois, from a hospital on the Philippine island of Samar to tell them what happened beginning on July 30. Miner downplayed some of the more horrific details, and he was also fortunate not to have witnessed—for the most part—the shark attacks that claimed the lives of many of his crewmates. (A "CRE" is a Chief Radio Engineer, and an "RT" is a radio technician. Although it is implied in the letter that Miner salvaged supplies from the sunken ship, the incident was, in fact, a hallucination. The death of his friend Ray was not.)*

Dear Folks:

Still here and still don't know when we are to go. Can't tell you where I am but you might call up Mrs. Louis Richburg and ask where the Dr. is. Through a strange coincidence I ran into him yesterday and we had a friendly little chat. He is a Lt. Com. and a very busy one it seems. I was talking to one of the nurses the other night and when I mentioned being from Glencoe she thought a while and then asked if I knew Dr. R. That's how it started.

Are you curious as to what happened to me when the ship was sunk? I think it's legal to tell about it now.

To begin with, we got hit about 0005 on July 30. Some damn deck ape had stolen my mattress a few days before so I was sleeping on a cot, topside, just forward of our radio shack. There was an explosion and I woke up in time to see another one through the port. I just sat there wondering what they were practicing now. Then I heard guys milling around and figured it was time to arise and dress. Then I whipped into the shack and within about a minute all the rest of the radio techs were there. Most of us slept topside due to stolen bedding and because it was considerably cooler. About three minutes had passed since the explosion and the ship was already listing 10 to 15 degrees to the starboard. Most of the power had been killed so we were unable to communicate with any other part of the ship, particularly the main radio shack. Lots went on in the next five minutes, including the inflating of life-belts, transmitting a couple of messages, and plenty of scared and wild faces. By then the list was so severe that we could not work any longer. The CRE told us to get the HELL out, which we did with a most ready spirit. Until then, no one had been able to believe that we were down — not the USS Indianapolis — and of course we hadn't received any abandon-ship orders. Due to Fate, and not my own will, I was the last guy to get out of the shack. Almost broke a chief's leg in the mad scramble.

I came out the st'bd door and almost fell down the ladder. I managed to hoist myself down onto the hangar deck suffering nothing worse than two barked shins. It was preternaturally quiet and I was mumbling — gotta keep calm no matter what, try to be careful, don't hurt yourself getting off.

A voice was yelling "Go off the high side — off the high side." That was O.K. by me, but how to get there? The ship was at about a 45 degree angle and time was getting mighty short. After a couple of seconds I spotted a figure who had a grip on something and was working his way across the deck. "Mind if I hang on you long enough to get a hold of that too?" says I grabbing him firmly by the ankle. A short but powerful struggle ensued from which I gathered that he meant "no." I started to slide slowly across (or down) the deck and the water began to close in around me. I went under and came up with a thud against something hard. Again I was inwardly chanting "Don't get panicy — take it easy." I was only caught for a few seconds but it seemed considerably longer. Finally got my head out of water in time to see, hear and feel the after super-structure scrape past my fanny. I paddled away as fast as possible. I wasn't scared anymore, and for the first time in a mighty long ten minutes I relaxed to watch the show. You should have seen that baby go down! It had turned completely over. The stern was poised for a moment and then the whole works slid forward, down, and out of sight. There was a hazy moon so that the ship had been clearly silhouetted.

The first hour or so I was busy paddling around, shoving life jackets at guys who didn't have any, and looking for my buddies. Finally a life-net appeared out of nowhere with a few guys on it. Some more of us climbed into it, and we put up a yell for stragglers. Pretty soon another net showed up which we latched onto. The remainder of the night I was busy (1) pewking oil, (2) holding a sicker guy up, and (3) trying to convince everyone that a message had been sent so there was nothing to worry about.

By morning, three life-rafts had joined the party. They were ten-man rafts but were loaded with about twice that. Shortly things were arranged so that the sick, guys who pretended to be sick, loafers, and a pharmacist mate were permanently stationed on these rafts. It got to be a nasty situation later on. The sum total of our group must have been about 200, including a very few officers. The officers were afraid to assert themselves and do some organizing until it was almost too late. There were supplies, though for only ten men, on each raft. Towards evening of the first day I noticed some guys stuffing their faces with crackers and actually guzzling the few ounces of water. A few of us started to bitch and yell for justice. The whole trouble was that no one guy could do a thing. We were packed together so closely that any motion was next to impossible without exerting a week's store of energy. You had to arouse the spirit of the rabble to accomplish anything. Eventually the officers did get most of the supplies together on one raft and managed to keep the robbers away.

The first day a plane flew directly over us, and low. Everyone yelled and screamed, but it availed us naught. That was the first support kicked out from under our morale.

That afternoon someone started yelling and beating the water. Guess what? A nasty looking fin was cruising up and down only a few yards from us. That scared me about as badly as anything ever has. I'd read so many stories about huge schools of sharks gobbling men up and leaving nothing but the bloodied waters. I immediately began working my way (as surreptitiously as possible) into the very center of the mob. I figured that even by morning they could not have eaten more than halfway into the circle. Much to my surprise, no one was consumed that night.

The second day, one man was bitten. The shark took a hunk out of his rear-end, which was hanging over the edge of the raft. By the way, I managed to put in two hours on a raft that day by trading with a guy. That was a blessed relief, believe me.

We were all completely covered with oil, and some had gotten in my right eye. Due to the sun and salt and oil, it filled up with goo and closed completely. That made me a little nervous so I took great care of the one that was left. I didn't relish being blind amongst a bunch of guys that would gladly kill for a sip of water, a shirt, or a life-jacket. Rations, consisting of half a cracker and one malted milk tablet, were handed out this day and each of the following days. Naturally some of those bas_ _ _ _s took three or four and some got none. I almost went crazy 'cause those guys were out of reach. I had my knife and I was gonna kill 'em or worse.

Planes passed over us about every eight hours or so. We shot flares at night and waved a cloth during the day. We also flashed mirrors, but nothing seemed to work. That was also hard on a man's sanity.

Three other RTs were with me, but one of them was a gonner from the start. He <u>knew</u> we'd never be found. He must have gone down the third night. That was about the time our number began to decrease noticeably. Most of the men just floated away. About midnight someone came paddling up and said he was a Dr. from a large ship standing off a few miles away. He had just come over to see how badly we were hurt and how many there were. Everyone believed it at first and we were happy as could be. In a few minutes it was apparent however that it was just one of us, completely off his nut. Lots of men were crazy by morning. The third day someone snatched my sun shield so I cut another huge chunk out of my precious shirt. I lent my knife to someone and the louse refused to return it. His face was just like all the rest — bearded, haggard and begrimed with oil so I couldn't even decide who had it.

I'd had no water at all, but for some reason I wasn't horribly tortured by thirst. When you remain nine-tenths submerged and don't sweat, bodily absorption must be considerable. However I could readily picture myself sitting out on the back porch drinking great quantities of ice-cold beer, and I vowed that I would live to realize my ambitions, earthly as they were. My mind was troubled by very few noble thoughts. I prayed to God to pull me through because I knew what it meant to you two and because it meant nearly as much to me personally. There was no other man in that bedraggled crew who wanted to live any more than I.

The fourth night my mind began to lose control of itself. I could no longer distinguish between dream and reality. The ship lay directly below us and only a few feet down. I made a trip down to my locker and to the radio shack with Rudy and Griff (both dead). The morning of the fourth day I wanted to go back down to the shack and some of the oranges we had cached there, but I wasn't sure how to get down. Several had gone down to get various things but they went for good. I kept asking why the ship's evaporators weren't turned on to furnish a little water, and I got varied answers. Most of the guys didn't know just why they weren't turned on either. Some crude guys told me I was nuts. I ignored the stupid fools.

We were spotted that morning and the planes were really buzzing around by mid-afternoon. For some reason it did not impress me much. I would just have been hurt if they hadn't. I just floated there like a jelly-fish, watching the boats, rafts, and supplies being dropped to us. I was too tired to move — but not to notice the way things were being bungled. The guys in boats wouldn't help those in the water or pass out drinking water, etc., etc.

Evening came and we were still there. The one remaining RT and myself were telling each other that our troubles were over. Only hang on for a few more hours and we'd be picked up. Finally he cracked. He came up behind me and threw his arms around my neck and would not let go. He said they'd taken his lifejacket and were trying to kill him. I got a lifejacket around him and then the nightmare started. We were picked up and I buried my face in a sparkling silver scuttlebutt and the clear, bubbling water turned out to be salt. I woke up and Ray was beside me crying and again without a jacket. I shoved another one into his arms and cursed him wildly. He unsettled me completely. Whether dream or reality I don't know but this was the worst of all — he was unconscious and I was trying to hold his head out of water but he kept slipping down, down, down. I yelled at everyone near me to help for a moment, but no one even looked up. He finally slipped loose and I could feel him bump my feet on the way down.

We were picked up about four the next morning. The few hours between when I lost Ray and when the APD found us were a horrible mixture of dream and truth. Each fantasy was worse than the preceding one. The second I felt that deck under me I just gave up all my efforts. They poured a thin stream of cold water into my face and nothing has ever felt so good. The crew treated us magnificently. They gave up sleep for a couple of nights and devoted all their time to us. They all had huge beards. It must have looked mighty strange to see those great bearded guys gently squeezing an orange into my mouth or holding my head up for a glass of water. They gave me two pints of plasma, but some of the guys were able to walk and eat.

At Samar they greeted me with an IV. In a couple more days I stood up a while and was soon able to eat and walk. I was one big mess of pimples, boils, ulcers, sunburns, and oil.

Anyhow, I'm O.K. now and I'll relate the rest of the story next letter. Hope this will go on two stamps,

> All my love,
> Jack
> Herbert Jay Miner RT 2/C

Of the original 1,200 crew members, Miner was one of only 317 who survived. The ship's captain, Charles Butler McVay III, also lived through the disaster but became the only U.S. naval commander court-martialed for the sinking of a ship. (Although survivors would later defend McVay, family members of sailors who perished were less forgiving. "Merry Christmas!," read one letter to McVay, "Our family's holiday would be a lot merrier if you hadn't killed my son." Racked with guilt, McVay committed suicide.) The USS Indianapolis *would be remembered not only for the fate of its captain and crew, but for the top-secret mission it had successfully completed in late July 1945; unbeknownst to even those onboard, the* Indianapolis *had delivered to Tinian the atomic bomb that would obliterate Hiroshima less than two weeks later.*

~~᠔

Fireman Keith Lynch Describes to His Parents the "Dead City" of Nagasaki, Japan

"Sixteen hours ago an American airplane dropped one bomb on Hiroshima," announced President Harry S Truman in a radio address to the American people on August 6, 1945. "If [the Japanese] do not now accept our terms, they may expect a rain of ruin from the air the like of which has never been seen on this earth." At 8:16 A.M. the uranium bomb, nicknamed "Little Boy," had detonated over Hiroshima. No one knows exactly how many people were killed in the blast—many were vaporized instantly and left no trace—but most estimates range from 70,000 to 100,000. After Japan's military leaders refused Truman's demand for "unconditional surrender" (which included the removal of their emperor), a second bomb—"Fat Man"— decimated Nagasaki on August 9, killing approximately 60,000 people. Even after receiving reports of the almost apocalyptic destruction to Hiroshima and Nagasaki, Japanese military commanders still advocated "fighting to the death." But Emperor Hirohito proclaimed that they must surrender, and on August 15 the Japanese people heard the voice of their emperor for the first time in a message broadcast throughout the country stating it was time for "a grand peace." Keith Lynch, a nineteen-year-old fireman first-class on the USS Rutilicus, *wrote home to his parents in Crab Tree, Nebraska, after visiting Nagasaki only six weeks after the city had been reduced to rubble. He could hardly believe what he had seen.*

Sunday, September 23, 1945

Dear Folks,

Here it is Sunday, Holiday Routine again. Boy, does the time fly. It seems as if it were only yesterday that I sat out here topside of the veranda and wrote the last time. We've gotten mail twice this week and I've my share, eight of them. The last one I got was mailed the 10th of September, the same day we left Okinawa. A letter in twelve days. That's not so bad.

There has been quite a bit happening since last week, especially the last two days, to us anyway. During the week it was just about the same. Things are pretty quiet around here, or were, at any rate. It's been raining quite a bit. Wednesday night I had to go up to the top of the mast to put in a bulb in the truck lights. As it was raining I had to take a bag to put over me and the light to keep from blowing out the fuses and stuff. I also had a climber's belt to hook on with besides the tools and bulb, etc. All in all I was a bit top heavy and I don't mind telling you I was glad to get down, as it was also a trifle windy.

Well, to come to one of the two main topics I am to discuss (like they say in the movies): yesterday I went on my first, and most likely, only liberty in Nagasaki. The crew was divided into six sections and one went every hour. Each tour lasted two hours. We went to the beach and were put in trucks and given a tour of the city of Nagasaki. First we visited the main part of the city. It wasn't hurt so much by the atomic bomb. The only activity you see is people walking, going nowhere, it seems. Just walking. The only people doing anything were some men working on telephone lines. Everyone, even a quarter of the women, have on uniforms. Army, Navy, what appear to be WACs, Army and Navy cadets (about 8 to18 years old), etc. A lot of the younger boys carry what look to me like junior Sumari swords. A couple of us came close to relieving one of them of his sword. Or maybe bargain him out of it. But the chief persuaded us to forget it. Then we left that part of town and went to the other, the one that was hit by the bomb.

Now I know what they mean when they say a dead city. You remember when I first described the place to you? About the city being in two valleys going at right angles to each other from the harbor, with a string of mountains between them? The smaller of the two, about the same size and five or six times the population of Tecumseh, was the first we visited. It was damaged of course by the concussion of the atomic blast and also by two previous bombings. But the main part of the place, in the other valley, about the size of Lincoln I would say, and five or six times the population, was completely inundated. The sight I saw from the top of the hill, over which it was approximated the center of the blast, was a sight I hope my children, if I am so fortunate, will never have to see, hear of, or ever think of. It was horrible and when you got to thinking, unbelievable.

To think that a thirty-pound bomb the size of a basketball, exploding a thousand feet in the air, could cause such a holocaust was simply unbelievable. I shudder to think what these people underwent when the blast occurred. A blast that literally dissolved their homes, family, friends and any other material thing in the vicinity. A blast that pushed over huge steel structures a mile and a half away as if they were made of blocks. Now I can see what they mean when they say Dead City. A city with no buildings, no trees, no facilities, and no people. All you see from the top of the hill is a ground covered with bricks, burned wood, twisted and pushed over steel frames of buildings for several miles in each direction. There is nothing for the people of this Dead City to do but walk around and think, "What manner of people would do such a thing to us, who are a peaceful, courteous, and civilized people?" I wondered what they thought when they looked at us as we were driving along. "Are these the barbarians who did such a thing to us? What can we expect now that we are at their mercy?" I only wish they could be made to suffer a tenth of the atrocities that they performed on our men whom they held prisoner. People can say these people are simple, ignorant of the facts, or under a spell, but a nation cannot wage war as they have without the backing of the majority of their people.

Such a thing as I saw yesterday cannot be described in words. You have to see it and I hope no one ever has to see such a thing again.

Well, today the occupation forces came into Nagasaki. The Sixth Marines, I think they are. If anyone ever says to someone from the Wichita Hospital Ship House or the USS Rutilicus that they were the first to land on Nagasaki, that person will be viewing the world through what is known as a mouse, or breathing through what is known as a busted nose.

Well, I found out that my enlistment expires next March. If I get out then it'll just about be right. Here's hoping.

Well, folks, I've got a couple other letters to write before the movie. I'll see if I can't get another letter off before next Sunday.

Til then,
Love,
Son

The relentless B-24 and B-17 raids over Dresden, Germany, in February 1945 as well as the fire bombings of Japan, which consumed much of Tokyo and other Japanese cities in oceans of fire, killed more people than the two atomic bombs dropped on Hiroshima and Nagasaki. But that is what so horrified the world—there were only two bombs, and yet each was nearly powerful enough to wipe an entire city off the face of the earth. "I realize the tragic significance of the atomic bomb," President Truman stated in August 1945, "but [we have] used it in order to shorten the agony of war, in order to save the lives of hundreds of thousands of young Americans." After the war Truman's decision to use atomic weapons was increasingly assailed as inhumane and unnecessary. Truman was unapologetic. When Irv Kupcinet of the Chicago Sun Times wrote a column in 1963 arguing that, even in hindsight, Truman's actions were justified, the former president was grateful for the support. "I knew what I was doing when I stopped the war that would have killed a half million youngsters on both sides if those bombs had not been dropped," Truman wrote, "I have no regrets and, under the same circumstances, I would do it again."

~⌒

Cpl. Robert S. Easterbrook Writes to His Parents
from the Hospital Bedside of Ex-Premier of Japan, Hideki Tojo,
After Tojo's Failed Suicide Attempt

At approximately 4:17 P.M. on September 11, 1945, the ex-premier of Japan, Hideki Tojo, intending to spare himself the dishonor of arrest and certain punishment by the Allies, picked up a .32 Colt automatic and fired a single bullet into his chest. Police guards, correspondents, and several U.S. military officers who had been outside Tojo's modest Tokyo home rushed in as soon as they heard the gunshot. Although no one expected him to survive, Tojo was taken to the Ninety-eighth Evacuation Hospital in Yokohama—the closest hospital still standing after Allied bombings months earlier. Doctors discovered that the bullet had just missed Tojo's heart, and they were able to stabilize him. Cpl. Robert S. Easterbrook, a graduate of the Northern Illinois College of Optometry, was an assistant to the army physician instructed to monitor Tojo and keep him alive. Writing to his parents in Davenport, Iowa, Easterbrook reported what it was like tending to one of the instigators behind the war that killed millions of men, women, and children throughout the world.

(12:00 Noon) 12 Sept. 45

Dear Mom & Dad: —

I don't imagine you could ever guess where I am as a write this letter. At present, I'm sitting in a chair about 3 ft. from the bedside of the ex Premier of Japan — Hideki Tojo.

We were in duty last night, in surgery — when he arrived at approximately 9:40 P.M. — & I've never seen so much "brass", correspondents, & photographers in my life. From Lieut. Gen. Eichelberger (C.O. of 8th Army), on down to a smattering of Lieut. Colonels. And when Capt. Speelberger (attending physician) shoved the stethoscope in my hand & said to check him every 5 minutes, I didn't know whether to "shi- or wind my watch." Ha!

As there was no whole blood available at the moment, we gave him 600 c.c of blood plasma after which he perked up enough to make a statement. He told Gen. Eichelberger (thru the interpreter) that he was sorry to cause so much trouble. He had planned on shooting himself in the head, but had been afraid it would muss up his face to much — so had decided on the heart. He used a 38 Cal. automatic, & the bullet entered just below & medial to the left breast & emerged from the back about two inches higher. I'm damned if I know how it missed his heart.

It's almost 1 o'clock & time to check him. Back in a few minutes.

1:15 P. M.

Two nurses just arrived from the 42nd Gen. Hosp. (which hasn't set up yet). Everyone (including the C. O.) is pretty well griped at this — as after 18 months over here, taking care of about every type of case imaginable without nurses — they sent some in expressly for the purpose of taking care of Tojo! Oh well — such is the Army.

The Col. just came in & asked me to get things ready for a whole blood transfusion at 2 o'clock. One of the boys in the outfit has the same blood type & is donating a pint. Must go for now. Back later.

2:25 P. M.

Blood transfusion started. It will take about an hour. So far he has shown very little improvement over last night & they hope this fresh blood will help. The photographers have just left. They were allowed in for a few minutes just after the transfusion began.

3:40 P. M.

The transfusion has ended & everyone except the two nurses, the guard & myself has cleared out. Tojo is resting quietly & the color is coming back a little. In a way I hope that he recovers, so that he can stand trial & be executed the proper way. I believe if he died now, the Japs would have him up as a national hero — but if we finish him off, I don't think they'll have much to say. He has admitted that he was the cause of the war — something's wrong

4:25 P.M.

Phew, that was nice! He developed a severe chill & pain in the heart & wound from the blood given him. It was a little questionable there for awhile, but he came out of it O.K. (damit). You know it's funny to be taking care of some one, & not knowing whether you want him to live or not.

Well folks, it's almost time for my relief; so I'll close off for now, take another check on him & call it a day.

Love,
Bob

P. S. In my next letter I'll send a piece of his shirt. It has blood on it—but don't wash it. Just put it away in my room.

The American doctors were successful and Tojo recovered fully. But, as Tojo feared, he was tried before the International Military Tribunal for the Far East and sentenced to death for crimes against humanity. He was hanged on December 23, 1948.

Gen. Benjamin O. Davis Sr. Reports to His Wife, Sadie, His Efforts to Promote Racial Equality and Understanding in a Postwar Era

While traveling through the South in the spring of 1944, a young corporal named Rupert Trimmingham was refused service in diner after diner for one reason only— he was black. The proprieter of a railroad depot in Louisiana agreed to sell Trimmingham coffee and a sandwich, but only if he went around to the back and ate in the kitchen. Trimmingham then watched as a group of whites entered the station lunchroom and were promptly seated and served. The final insult came when he realized that all of the men, with the exception of two armed guards, were German prisoners of war being transported to an internment camp. Trimmingham's ordeal was symbolic of a larger irony; as an estimated one million African-American servicemen (and women) fought for President Roosevelt's "Four Freedoms" (freedom of speech and worship, and freedom from want and fear) abroad, they were denied basic equality in both their own country and the armed forces. "Double V!" became their rallying cry—victory in the war overseas, and victory against racism and oppression at home. And in both places they proved themselves time and time again. Facing enormous manpower shortages in the winter of 1944–45, U.S. military leaders (temporarily) desegregated the army and placed black platoons with white units during the Battle of the Bulge, where the black soldiers performed valiantly. In the air, the all-black 332nd Fighter Group—also known as the "Tuskegee Airmen"—earned 150 Distinguished Flying Crosses and hundreds of other medals for their heroism. Benjamin O. Davis Sr. (father of the 332nd's commander, Benjamin O. Davis Jr.) was named America's first black general in 1940, and during the war he was sent to Europe to head a special investigation into the treatment of African-American soldiers. Davis often shared anecdotes and observations about race relations with his wife, Sadie, and on September 22, 1945, the sixty-eight-year-old general expounded on the issues he thought needed to be addressed now that U.S. troops were preparing to return to the United States. General Davis suggested that Americans might even have something to learn from their wartime ally, the Soviet Union.

Headquarters Communications Zone
EUROPEAN THEATER OF OPERATIONS
United States Army

Dear Sadie:

This is another quiet day. So far no mail. The morning paper prints a dispatch from Pasadena, California, Sept. 21—Lt. Gen. John Clifford Hodges Lee and Mrs. Eve Brookie Ellis were married there on Wednesday. We are wondering if he is returning to us. Other than that news is as of yesterday and many days before.

I can hardly believe that today is Saturday. I have done nothing much during the week, except get ready to make the trip to England which begins on Monday. This should be very interesting as I am looking into the Information and Educational Program not only in its application to colored troops but its whole plan. I am particularly interested in the Orientation Programs. These have to do with citizenship. Here are examples: 1st Question: Do you believe there should be such a thing as "second class" citizenship? 2nd Question: Why is second class citizenship, which results from an un-American discrimination, harmful to our future stability after the war?

In these discussions questions are framed so as not to mention races or origins. Quotations are made from Abraham Lincoln's statements made in 1855—"As a nation we began by declaring all men are created equal. We now read it 'All men are created equal except Negroes.' When the Know Nothings get control it will read 'All men are created equal except Negroes, foreigners and Catholics.'" Discrimination makes all of us Poorer.

We cannot have a prosperous democracy with minority groups so poor that they cannot afford to buy the goods America produces.

This is a sample of how we are trying to make the soldier going back to civilian life think. I have tried to get them to eliminate the term Negro as far as possible. I have tried to impress them of the necessity of improving and lifting up the man farthest down. The man who is too poor to be self-supporting be he Negro, white man or any other kind of a man does not help our country. That the ideal democracy is one where all men mutually respect the rights of others and secure to them by training and privileges to labor, support themselves and enjoy the fruits of their labors.

I think we are making progress. We can discuss the question from the standpoint of groups rather than just Negroes or Cullud Folk. I am impressed with the earnestness and apparent sincerity of these men. Most of them are younger men who can be expected to carry on a number of years. The Reader's Digest for Sept. 45 has an articles on the Soviet Union by William Hard. Under pages 7 & 8 there are some very positive statements. The two most effective characteristics of the Soviet Union in dealing with Asiatic peoples: The absolute renunciation of all racial discrimination. Its earnest efforts to improve the economic conditions of Asiatic life. America and Britain thus far have been unable to do just that. We talk a lot and say nice things. It ends there.

Well let us hope that we can at least get these men who have been snatched away from their homes and seen much suffering, to thinking with the idea of trying to get along with their fellows. Perhaps we shall develop a better world.

I've filled you with a lot of "Shop." It will give you something to read. It will give you an idea of the lines along which I am trying to make folks think. In the midst of it all I'm loving you, thinking of you and longing to be with you.

Lovingly,
Ollie

Indeed, many of the "younger men" General Davis hoped would carry on efforts to improve race relations back home would do just that; after the war thousands of veterans—black and white—helped set the foundation for the civil rights movement that flourished in the 1950s and 1960s. In 1948 President Harry S Truman issued Executive Order 9981, officially ending segregation in the military and mandating equal treatment and opportunity "to all persons in the Armed Services without regard to race." Gen. Benjamin O. Davis Sr. retired that same year, and his son, after serving in the Korean War, became the first African-American air force general in history.

~

Stationed in Japan, Sgt. Richard Leonard Explains to His Friend Arlene Bahr Why, Despite All That Has Happened, He Does Not Hate the Japanese

Throughout the war, both the Japanese and the Americans vilified one another in vicious, dehumanizing propaganda campaigns. U.S. prisoners of war suffered some of the worst, most sadistic treatment imaginable in the hands of Japanese troops, and the hostility countless servicemen felt for the Japanese surpassed even their revulsion of the Nazis. But for many soldiers who were sent to Japan as part of the U.S. Army of Occupation, it was difficult to continue hating "the enemy" once they met with them face to face in times of peace. Four years of animosity would not fade quickly, but for men like Sgt. Richard Leonard, a twenty-four-year-old native of Ridgewood, New Jersey, the possibility of reconciliation was not inconceivable. Leonard even found himself becoming sympathetic toward the civilians he encountered, who, in his mind, were bullied into the war by imperialistic Japanese generals and warmongers. Leonard shared his postwar feelings in a letter to his friend Arlene Bahr after walking through what remained of the city of Kure, only miles from Hiroshima.

3 November 45

Dear Arlene,

Greetings from downtown Kure. Only it really isn't "downtown" because there just isn't a town. According to advance propaganda, the

Army of Occupation was supposed to get "the best living quarters available." The only hitch turned out to be that there are <u>no</u> living quarters at all. All that is left of Nagoya, Koyoto, Wakoyama, Kobe, Osaka, and Kure is a pile of ashes and burned steel. The bombing far exceeds anything I saw in London and that is saying a lot. I omitted Hiroshima from the above list of cities because you can't even find the ashes there.

Take Nagoya, for example. It once had a 3,000,000 population — now there are 10 buildings left standing and acres of desolation. The casualties were tremendous, and for all practical purposes you can say Japan is at least 50% destroyed. The cities are about 90% destroyed.

We made an "assault landing" at Wakayama. (Our outfit is famous for making assault landings in peaceful countries.) We made our customary climb down the side of the transport into the assault boats armed to the teeth. We hit the beach fast and there were hundreds of Japs to meet us — selling souvenirs. From Wakayama we went to Nagoya and spent a week rebuilding some Jap barracks into liveable quarters. We finished rebuilding just in time to get moved to Kure. Here we have quarters on the second floor of what used to be an airplane factory. It's pretty nice except there isn't any roof on it and the nights are cold. The days are cold, too, and we still have our tropical clothing from the Philippines — so I'm pretty much in a state of shiver.

The food isn't bad — if you can get any. Our outfit has actually been unable to draw any food since we've been here. The only way we've been able to eat is by splitting the outfit into groups of 20 and sending them out to beg meals from other outfits. But things are going to be better, they say. The army has promised to build a roof over us, and if we're real good they're going to give us some food and clothes! Lucky us!

Meanwhile we're fraternizing to beat hell. The Japs are being as polite as they can be and are treating us like kings. They bow, salute, and felicitate us into extreme egotism and you just can't hate them for hate's sake. The average Jap doesn't give a damn about "ruling the world" anymore than you or I do. He's just an ordinary joker who went to war because he was told to, and he did the job the way he was told.

War is all phoney in the first place — I know that now. It's just the vested economic, political, and military leaders of the world fighting for personal prestige and fortunes at the expense of their citizens. I believe that common people the world over share the same dreams of peace and security. I mixed quite thoroughly with German POW's, and now the Japs. I've been to their homes for dinner and crowded into streetcars with them — and I find them as human as any people I've seen.

I don't think I've been taken in too easily. I'm pretty skeptical by nature, but who am I supposed to hate? Can I hate the boy who ran along side my train window for 50 yards to pay me for a pack of cigarettes that I had sold him just before the train left the station? Can I hate the old man who took us to his home for dinner and made us accept his family heirlooms for souvenirs? Can I hate the kids that run up and throw their arms around me in the street? Or a Jap truck driver who went miles out of his way to drive me home one night? Or the little girl (about 4) who ran up to me and gave me her one and only doll for a present? My answer is that I can't. This may all be a big show of phoney hospitality, but if it is the players are all expertly rehearsed. Personally I don't believe they could fake the basic emotions with such perfection. I could be awfully wrong, but I have tremendous confidence in the common man of any country and the Jap is no exception.

It would have been easy for me to hate blindly. I hated their guts when they killed my brother a year ago, but hate leads only to more hate and it's only if we can get together — work and live together — and develop confidence in each other that there is any hope of a better tomorrow. Sure, we've go to occupy their country — watch them — but at the same time we've got to help them and do everything possible to reconstruct them as a peace loving nation. It can and must be done through the common man, by elimination of imperialistic industrialists. They are the ones I hate, not the Jap who is farming or working for his family security — not even the ones who sank my brother's submarine. They were just the pawns in the big game, it is the big men at the top in industry, trade, politics, and the military that we must hate and punish — and eliminate. Our building for a better world must begin at the bottom with you, me, and ordinary people all over the world. Capitalism is fine if the people have sufficient checks on the bosses — it can and does work well in our country, but we must work from here on to see that the interests of capital and humanity are the same, not merely manifestations of the financial lust of a greedy minority.

Whoa, babe, it's taps time. Sorry this letter has been so long, but I've been thinking a lot lately and had to share my conclusions with someone.

Thanks for the picture.

> Be good, and write some more,
> Dick

THE KOREAN WAR
& THE COLD WAR

Well Mother I am in a fox hole writing this letter   I am still hear on the front line   I praye ever night. How is the family getting along   fine I hope so. Well I will sent my birthday on the front line. It look like it. I am on a machine gun. I haven't no sleep for 6 days. Well Mother will close hoping to hear from you. Your loving son Bill

— Pvt. William Geary, writing from the Pusan Perimeter
to his mother on September 6, 1950, his twenty-second birthday;
Geary was killed nine days later.

Shot During One of the U.S. Army's First Major Defeats in Korea, Pfc. Donald Luedtke Tells His Mother His Fate Could Have Been Much Worse

"If the best minds in the world had set out to find us the worst possible location to fight a war," lamented Secretary of State Dean Acheson, "the unanimous choice would have to be Korea." War came to Korea—a thumb of land jutting out directly below China's Manchuria—on June 25, 1950, when 90,000 Soviet-backed North Korean troops stormed across the Thirty-eighth Parallel, which marked the border between the two countries, in a predawn invasion of U.S.-supported South Korea. "By God," President Harry Truman remarked when informed of the surprise offensive, "I'm going to let them have it." Truman saw a larger, more insidious Communist threat at work. In June 1948 the Soviets began an eleven-month blockade of Berlin, prompting the United States and Britain to airlift food and supplies to the city. In September 1949 the Soviets tested their first atomic bomb, ending America's four-year nuclear monopoly. And in October 1949 the world's most populated country, China, became a Communist nation. "We've got to stop the sons of bitches no matter what," Truman said to Acheson. With the sanction of the fledgling United Nations, U.S. air and naval forces were rushed to South Korea to prevent further advances by the North Koreans. In early July, Maj. Gen. William Dean's Twenty-fourth Infantry Division arrived at Pusan, a strategically vital city located at the southeastern tip of the peninsula. Outgunned and outnumbered, the Americans suffered defeats outside of Pusan and in neighboring Taejon. General Dean, himself, was captured and spent the remainder of the war as a POW. By July 21 an estimated 1,100 Americans were killed, seriously injured, or missing. Twenty-year-old Pfc. Donald Luedtke, a radio operator with the Thirty-fourth Infantry Regimental Headquarters Company, was one of the wounded. On August 20, 1950, Luedtke wrote a long but dramatic letter to his mother in Arcadia, Nebraska, explaining how fortunate he was to have survived the battle of Taejon. (Unlike in World War II, GIs' letters home from Korea were uncensored and, on the whole, more graphic.)

Dear Mom:

    Well, I suppose you wonder where I am, and where I have been.

    I will start at the beginning. We left for Korea the 1st of July. We were the first regiment to hit there and fight. The North Koreans had about ten divisions to our one regiment. About all we could do was hit them and back up and they would get us surrounded all the time. And now we will get to Taejon — one place I will never forget. Good size town. We were there for about four days. Last two days we were there we caught hell. Morning of the 19th, July, I woke up, enemy planes came over and strafed a little and they shot down one of our own jet fighter planes, nothing left of him when he came down.

Nothing too much happened 'til the morning of the 20th, July. That is when all hell broke loose. The enemy got the airfield to the north of town and they sent tanks in on us. They would go by our Reg't Headquarters and shoot up everything. They had men in them going to the other end of town to surround us. We would get their tanks knocked out but after they got to the other end of town, and by 4:30 that afternoon we all got on trucks and jeeps and started out, all shooting into the buildings as we went down the sreet. The enemy was all over in them. We were sitting ducks for them. Then we had to go through about five blocks of fire. All that end of town was on fire. Some places the streets were nothing but fire. There were tanks, trucks and everything else burning in there. We made it. A lot of them didn't. I just about cooked. Then after we got through, they shot our driver through the head and we hit a telephone pole and that stopped us. I got out of our truck — it was a radio truck — one that I worked in all the time. I got my carbine and started shooting at the dirty blanks. They had us from both sides with machine gun fire and about everything else they could throw at us — hitting guys left and right. We were just on the edge of town now — we were laying along the side of the road pinned down. We would try and make a break for it. We would get in the trucks and jeeps and we'd not move and I saw we would never make it out of there. I tried to help some of the wounded but that was hopeless. It was every man for himself.

I made up my mind to get out of there, so I and four other guys took off over a little hill to the left of the road into the enemy and I guess they saw me. Bullets started hitting all around me. I was in the back of the other guys. I was laying down — one missed my face about four inches — knocking dirt in my eyes and mouth — it gave me a bloody mouth and I could not see too good. I started to get up and go when a bullet hit me in thru the back end and down through my leg — did not go clear through. I just took off and got in a little washout. I about dropped dead when I got there and raised up and saw an enemy machine gun about twenty yards to our one side on a side hill and there were about three North Koreans that we could see. We could have killed them but I don't think I would be here today. I don't see how they could help but see us. That was one place I said my prayers.

We lay there until it got dark — about ten. There was a town about mile to our front that was all on fire and everything was about like day light. But we had to take the chance. I was not thinking about my leg — we started out of that place — got just about to the top and some "gook" took a shot at me, good thing I was about four yards from his hole for I would have walked right in on him. Guess he did not sight his gun — all I saw was the flash and I hit around to one side. Guess that gook was as afraid as I was because he never came up any more and I took off — didn't go too far and we ran into one of our G.I.s — that guy that was hit in the head. I was surprised that he was still going. He was in bad shape. He was hit in the upper part of the cheekbone and it went through his face just under his eyes. He had blood coming out of both sides of his head, nose and mouth. Both his eyes were shut and he couldn't see. We had to lead him and that made six of us — three of us were hurt. We hit for the mountains. It was hard going, for the enemy was all around us and we had to stay low a lot of times. We got up in the mountains and stopped at a stream to get a drink of water — I was about dying for a drink. My mouth was still full of dirt. Darn if we didn't get lost from that G.I. — that left me with that guy that could not see and another guy that was not hit. We kinda came down out of the mountains and hit machine gun fire again. That guy that was not hit said he was going no more, said he was going to stay there and die.

I stayed there for about fifteen minutes — told him he was crazy if he did, and I got mad and took that other guy and left him there. We went back up into the mountains. I could not go too good myself and I had to lead that guy that was shot in the head. We kept going all night stopping only when my legs would go no further and that was not very far. We had gone a long ways that night and we took a chance on coming out of the mountains the next day. There was a road at the bottom. We thought if we could get there we could go fairly fast, but we hit gunfire, so we went back up in the mountains. Do not know if they were firing at us or not, and I wasn't going to find out.

That afternoon we came out again and we were safe. We got down on that road and the South Koreans tried to help us as much as they could. We came to one place and ran into other guys and we all kept going. We got to a small town and there was some South Korean soldiers there — we stayed for about two hours. Everybody was leaving that place and I was too tired and could not go any further, so a South Korean soldier helped me down and asked me if he could take my watch and gun. I said O.K. — he said he would be back in fifteen minutes. He did come back and he said he was going out again but would be back. About that time two guys came in and told me everybody had left — they were not hit so they helped me. I was so darn weak — when I would get on my back I could not get up. There were four of us together. One guy could not go too fast — he was shot through the leg and side and that slowed us all up but we kept going 'til it was dark and I ran onto one of the guys from the radio section. Sure was glad to see him — then we left the guys that were wounded at a Korean place. They wanted me to stay there and they would get help. I said, "Nothing doing." I went the worst part and I was not going to stop. I got a ride for a ways in an old cart pulled by a cow — it was better than nothing.

We kept going — til about 2:30 that night, then we stopped at a Korean place and he fixed us up and we slept for the night. My leg was swelled up in the knee. The next day we made a Korean take me in a cart — this time pulled by a little horse. He took me a long ways into a good size town where we met a Captain. He said we had to go east to get back to our lines. He said it was about 25 miles to Yonkdong — that was where the 1st Cavalry Division was. They had just come from Japan and had not met the enemy yet, and so we took the road east. I got a ride for a little ways and ran out of road so had to walk — and ran onto a Korean that would help me. He gave me support.

Then about sundown we came upon a M.P. Patrol that was picking up guys up that road. We had just made it because they could just go so far on this road and it ran out. We had to walk along the side of a mountain with a river down below. It was just a trail until we hit the road again, where a jeep could go. I was never so glad in all my life to see those guys. We told them about the wounded guys we had left behind. They said they wouldn't take a chance to get them out so I guess it was a good thing I kept coming. Three full days to get out of that place back to our lines. I had not eaten in four days, after I got out they tried to feed me and I could not eat. All I wanted was water. They took us to the aid station and gave me some first aid. The bullet in my leg was just under the skin. We stayed there until morning, when we got on a train for Pusan. We got into Pusan that night and they cut my bullet out — next day they put us on a ship for Tokyo and was I glad. I still feel for the guys that were left in Tae-jon. There were a lot of them. They would holler, "Don't leave me." Fellows that were shot and couldn't move, but there wasn't anything we could do for them. Gen. Dean was left in there and never came out. He was at the head of the Company. When we started out of Taejon he was our Division Commander.

Well, I'm here in the Tokyo Gen. Hospital — still kicking, but not too good. My leg is still weak and I'm sick to my stomach. I think I drank too much of that dirty water from those rice paddies. I don't think you would know me now. I lost so much weight, nothing but bones. I hardly know myself and I still can't eat too good. I keep telling these people and they will not give me anything. I get so darn mad, they can send me back to Korea anytime. I don't give a damn if they send me to Siberia. I wish they would get all these big wheels from all these countries and make them fight their own wars. It may sound a little bad — there should be better days ahead. Guess maybe I shouldn't write home such things as this. I don't think it will hurt to let you know the inside picture of things.

Never worry about me, they can't get the best of a man from Nebraska. You just don't find men from that state. Most all of them are from New York and Pennsylvania, along the east coast states some place.

I do not know when I will get home now. Could have told more, but I'm getting tired. Write soon.

Lots of Love,
Donald

By early August 1950, the North Koreans controlled all of Korea except for a 5,000-mile area of land known as the Pusan Perimeter in the southeast. The American-led UN troops holding the perimeter were pounded relentlessly but never surrendered. On September 15 Gen. Douglas MacArthur, commander of all American and UN forces, orchestrated a daring amphibious invasion far behind enemy lines into the northwestern port of Inchon. After successfully capturing the city, U.S. Marines went on to recover the South Korean capital of Seoul. In an extraordinary reversal, the bloodied North Korean army was scrambling back to the Thirty-eighth Parallel by the end of September. Despite the catastrophic beginning in July, the liberation of South Korea had taken less than three months.

～

In a Letter Home, Sgt. John Wheeler Harshly Condemns the Communists Fighting in Korea and Their Sympathizers in the States
&
Wounded Twice in Action, Sergeant Wheeler Assures His Father He Will Not Be Sent Back into Combat
&
Sgt. Gordon Madson Provides Sergeant Wheeler's Father with a Firsthand Account of His Son's Fate

The United Nations mission in Korea "to repel armed invasion and restore peace and stability to the area" had been achieved. But public opinion polls in the United

States indicated that pushing the North Koreans back to the Thirty-eighth Parallel was not enough; Americans decided they now wanted (as did many in the UN) all of Communist Korea defeated. Gen. Douglas MacArthur adamantly agreed, promising President Truman a complete victory and dismissing the possibility that the Chinese would intervene, despite their warnings to the contrary. Truman gave the go-ahead, and on October 9, 1950, the Eighth Army crossed the Thirty-eighth Parallel and moved rapidly up the peninsula. Two weeks later South Korean forces reached the Yalu River, which marked the border with China, and Communist North Korea seemed on the verge of collapse. And then Trumans' worst fears were realized—the Chinese attacked. After secretly mobilizing in the hills of North Korea, they swiftly descended on and thrashed South Korean forces and isolated U.S. troops in early November. Truman, furious, considered halting the American drive, but was persuaded by MacArthur that the Chinese forces were paltry and would be beaten. Sgt. John Wheeler, with the Second Infantry Division, was dismayed to learn of growing ambivalence in the States about the expanded UN mission after the Chinese assault. Wheeler wrote to his father in Borger, Texas, to emphasize his unwavering commitment to their presence in Korea and the larger cause of eradicating Communism. Like many in the armed services, Wheeler believed that President Truman had gutted the military too severely after World War II. (The "WCTU" Wheeler alludes to is the Woman's Christian Temperance Union, an organization founded in the nineteenth century to protest the "dangers of alcohol.")

5 November, 1950.

Dear Dad:

Sorry I haven't written sooner. Have been working 7 days per week, day and night, sometimes as late as 11 oclock.

Glad to hear from you on my birthday. I must admit there are a lot of other places I'd rather be, but for the present I'm a hell of a sight better off than a few of my good friends who I'll never see again.

Can't say as I blame you, Dad, for your opinions of Mr. Truman and his administration. However, you must remember that his opinions as well as his actions represent the vast majority of the "Soft-bellied Americans" who, for the life of them, couldn't see giving up a few of the needless luxuries of life to support a military machine big enough to protect the peace and liberty that they take for granted. Only those who have visited foreign countries can realize what they mean. It would be a good lesson to the Americans if they had to fight a war on their own soil, and had to lie for a short time under the sadistic rule of this band of perverted sadists who call themselves communists. They claim that they want to help the "worker"—all they want to do is to help themselves. Mass murder, rape torture, and starvation is the rule and not the exception with them. They have proved it here as well as everywhere else. I could see nothing more fitting for a young man to do then to devote his entire life to killing everyone of them.

I intend to get out of the Army myself as soon as I can, but hate to miss the chance of carrying out the aforementioned in the event there's another war. The local Oriental population so bitterly detest them that collaborators during their short reign of power in this area are torn to pieces, or beaten to death by mob violence before they can even hope to be saved by a sentence to confinement for their acts. Americans had best prepare themselves for a bitter struggle in the years to come between two ideals, i.e., freedom and communism, both of which could never exist, and I think one of which will be totally destroyed.

I don't like to sound like a pessimist (hope that is spelled correctly), or a ham actor, but above is the opinion of everybody over here. Their treatment of American prisoners of war is typical; at a place not too far from here bodies were found, some had been shot, some bayoneted and some wounded soldiers who were too sick to move were burned to death. I suppose you'll read about this, or are the papers afraid to print such material, for fear it will shock some of the members of the WCTU. This organization should be put on the subversive list by Mr. Truman. It is too bad they can't utilize some of their energy donating blood to the men who need it so badly, instead of displaying their morbidness by attempting to shut off our free beer ration.

Well, Dad, that's about all I can say for now, except that the people in the US ought to do the same thing to their Communists that those people do over here. Since part of my work is in war-crimes, it might well be the reason for my violent conclusions.

Hope to be home next birthday.

Lots of Love,
John N. Wheeler

As suddenly and as stealthily as they had appeared in October, the Chinese troops seemed to vanish in mid-November 1950, pulling back into the northernmost mountains of North Korea. Their "warning" had been issued, and the world took heed; several nations proposed ending the fighting and relinquishing the northern provinces of Korea as a buffer zone to appease the Chinese. MacArthur would have none of it. "To give up any portion of North Korea," he argued, "would be the greatest defeat of the free world in recent times." MacArthur then launched a massive offensive on November 24 to overrun the North entirely. Once again confident of victory, MacArthur declared that American troops would be "home by Christmas." And once again the Chinese mounted a savage counterrattack, pouring hundreds of thousands of troops into North Korea. Three months after he had written to his father vilifying the Chinese, Sgt. John Wheeler was face-to-face with the enemy and, wounded twice, came literally within millimeters of losing his life. Evacuated to a hospital in Japan, Wheeler was allowed only a brief recuperation. In a May 8 letter to his father, he related what had happened to him and expressed how stunned he was, considering the severity of his injuries, to be back in Korea.

Dear Dad:

I know the change in address is a surprise to you. It was to me too. Please excuse the long period between letters. I didn't know where they were going to send me when I was discharged from the hospital about two weeks ago.

I was slated to go to the States for plastic surgery on my right ear, but the Chinamen started their big offensive and here I am. Still haven't regained much hearing in the punctured right ear drum, and have been informed that I will never get all of it back. However, the aforementioned operation is forthcoming.

Me being back here is a typical example of some of the stupid and self-centered birdbrains who have never heard artillery or witnessed death, and who manage to stay in the rear echelon. I so heartily detest them for their stupid blunders and their soft lilly-white hands that I'd let the Chinaman take another crack at me before I'd go back and be amongst them.

At the present this regiment is in the rest area, and will be for about two more weeks. I'm serving as assistant platoon sergeant for the time being. Will probably be reassigned in the rear as soon as the regiment goes back in the combat zone; so I don't think you'll have to worry about me being on the line again. I have enough points to go home in a couple of months.

Was surprised how happy all of the boys were to see me when I got back. Some of them thought I had died and that they were seeing a ghost.

I found out that I got hit twice that day. The first was a bullet that went through part of my right temple, through the right ear and out the back of my head never going all the way into my head, but grazing it leaving quite a scar and a hole in the ear. Good thing it didn't go all of the way in, or I would have come home sooner than anticipated, in a pine box. The second time was with mortar fragments while I was on my way to the aid station.

Found out we lost almost half the men in the company that day and the next. However, I was very pleased to find out through my buddies here that the gook who got me in the first place is now with his honorable ancestors.

Will probably be assigned to division rear as soon as the regiment moves back up. Could make Master Sergeant if I stayed here. However with this bum ear, I'd be six feet under before the orders were out; so I guess I'll bid good-by to combat, at least for the rest of this war.

Well that is about all the news for the present. Will write as soon as I get reassigned. By the way, I've found out that George Swetich is not only alive but in his usual good state of health. Wrote him a ten page letter. Information was based on a Q. M. Graves Registration Report of the death of some one with a similar name. Never was dead sure about it in the first place.

> Will write again soon,
> Your loving son,
> John

Incredibly, Sergeant Wheeler found himself in battle only a week later, and on May 18, 1951, he was taken prisoner by the Chinese. For over two and a half years Wheeler's father heard nothing from his son. And then, in late September 1953, Mr. Wheeler received a typed letter from one of John's friends, Gordon Madson, from Gowrie, Iowa, who was with John when he was captured.

My dear Mr. Wheeler,

I'm taking this oppurtunity to write you the complete details concerning your son whom was my very close friend and companion thru some of lifes darkest experiences.

John and I were captured on the same date, but not in the same position on the battle line. I was charged with the responsibility of defending my battalions rear during a withdrawal and protecting the evacuation of the wounded men. In my performances of these duties elements of my platoon including myself were overrun and cut off from main body. Although surrounded with just our rifles and what limited ammo. we carried we held out for over an hour and a half replusing three banzi charges and inflicting great losses on our enemy and enabling the rest of the battalion to withdraw successfully. Being the assistant platoon Sgt. (platoon guide) I had upon me maps of our supply dumps of ammo. and rations I also had a complete roster of the men and weapons of my platoon. I could not afford to have the enemy obtain this valuable information so I withheld my identity as a Sgt. until I would have a chance to destroy this information. I succeded in destroying it a few days later and decided that I would carry out my mascarade as a Pfc. to the end.

The day after our capture we were taken to a collecting point for POW's and it was there that I first met your son Sgt. John N. Wheeler. We were kept at this collecting point for two days and then began the long trek back and forth along the front line in the enemies rear. In my opinion they were using us for propaganda to instill courage in their own fighters by marching back an forth to show there men that after all americans are just flesh and blood and can be killed and captured. The food was terrible a handful of bug dust (Finely ground rice millet sorgum and wheat) or a small bowl of rice or one of sorgum. We got this twice a day and water was available only when we were marched across a mountain stream or by rice paddies. Disease and filth were the rule rather than the exception and we were not allowed the facilities of cleanliness. We were covered with body lice and various other parasites it was not long until men began to drop out and not be heard from again.

Your son was made squad leader of the first squad by the chinese (every eleventh man was a squad leader) and I was made squad leader of the ninth squad. On June 13th we arrived at a rest stop where we were to spend a few days. It was here that your son and myself were seperated from the main body of POW's. The chinese knew that I had a few years of college and also that your son spoke very good english I believe that for this reason they took us away. We were taken to a place way back in the mountains with only a few Korean mud houses so far back in the mountains that there were not even any road or cart trails only a narrow foot path. They kept us there and used us to practice there English on. All the Chinese in the vicinity from the various Battalions Regt's. Division's at one time or another came to this Hdq. and talked to us interrigated us and asked thousands of questions concerning our families, our homes, about america and about our lives in the US Army. John and I were all alone with about two hundred Chinks. We ate with the common Chinese soldier and our duty was to make all the supply runs (approx. 15 miles one way) to bring rice sorgum ect. for everyone to eat.

While we were there and doing all this walking and marching our combat boots soon wore out and fell to pieces from the rough rocks and stones of which Korea is composed John wore a size 12 combat boot and when the Chinese gave us these rubber tennis shoes they had none large enough to fit him. Myself I wore a size eight combat shoe and they did have tennis shoes I could wear. Then along in July we were hauling logs on our backs and digging bunkers with Chinese guards on us. We were both very weak, I weighed less than a hundred pounds and I would say John probably didn't weigh more than 115, but never the less they made us work. They said no work no eat and after all they had the weapons. Well during these heavy labors John contacted a skin disease, the backs of his hands, his nose, the backs of his ears became a real dark brown, yellow matter would form under the skin and break through and drain. He was given a small tube of our captured sufa salve and it seemed to dry it up and begin to heal, but we soon used it all up and then there was no more medical attention. They would give us none of there own. They made us eat alone then because they were afraid they would catch John's disease.

On August 6th 1951. The Chinese told us that they were going to take John to a place where they were many american soldiers and that there were good Chinese doctors and medicene. John and I were very close friends after being through so much together we had often talked of our families and friends and I felt that I knew you and John's sister real well. I am writing you this frankly and as in as complete a detail as is possible. I know that you and your wonderful family would want it this way and I do know that John would want me to. You have my most complete and heartfelt sympathy, John was the finest friend and buddie a fellow could ever have.

So on August 6th John left me along with three guards who accompanied him. The guards returned in about three days saying that John arrived safely at this camp and was taken immediately to the hospital. Just as John left me he presented me his most treasured belonging. I had no Bible with me at the time of my capture so John gave me his because he felt that I would need it being alone with the Chinese with no one to talke to noone to remember all the things we so dearly loved about our wonderful United States. I was deeply moved and as John walked away with his guards there were tears in my eyes and after he had disapeared over the mountain and I let my feelings go and had a little cry for no one ever had a truer friend or ever knew a better man. It was like losing a life long companion.

Well I stayed on alone with the Chinese there until Nov. 11, 1951 when I was also taken to the same place John had been sent to. We called it the mining camp for we did not know the name of it but it did have a big mine there. The Pow's had already been sent to the rear and there were only a few of us there. A new group of prisoners arrived and we all went back to the far rear together on trucks. I arrived in Changsong camp #1. on Nov. 18, 1951. Most of the men there were at the mining camp at the time of John's arrival on or about Aug. 8th. Needless to say that I enquired of many of them if they had ever known John, or had ever seen him. They told me that the so called hospital there was nothing more than the death house and that about one out of a hundred ever came back from there. They seemed to remember a Wheeler coming in there about that time and going straight to the hospital, and that he died shortly after that.

Now this is not conclusive evidence, but myself I can not help but feel that that is what must have happened. For there are hundreds of good american soldiers buried there at the mining camp that if they would have had just a little food and a little medicene would still be alive and able to return to there families. Life to the oriental is so very cheap they care not if you live or die had they given us enough food, clothing and medical care thousands more of americas finest youth would be alive to day. I have a deep hatred for the chinese and koreans for they are outright murderers and hope that some day they may be made to bear the full responsibility for there crimes against the human rights of man.

I still have with me John's Bible and I would like to send it to you as a dear rememberance. I have read it through many times and it was a constant source of inspiration and strength to me, but as his next of kin and immediate family it should be yours so If you will please drop me a line I will forward it on to you. I have kept it in excelent condition always keeping it wrapped to protect it from the elements.

I am very sorry Mr. Wheeler that I cannot send you encourageing news, but I know that you would want to know exactly how it was and I have endevored to tell you. Once again I would like to express my condolences to you and your daughter your loss has been a very great one. I pray that the lord will grant you strength and guidance in this your hour of great sorrow.

most sincerely
Your friend always
Sfc. Gordon L. Madson

~~⌒

Writing from the Osaka Army Hospital, Pvt. Bob Hammond Describes to His Father the Brutal Fighting at the Chosin Reservoir

"Well, by now you all have probably got a telegram saying I've been wounded in action," Pvt. Bob Hammond, a survivor of the Battle of the Chosin Reservoir, wrote to his distraught parents in Henderson, Nevada, on December 7, 1950. "Don't worry . . . I got shot up a little and I got frozen hands and feet, but I thank God I was so lucky. I had to run three miles with a bullet thru my knee. I'll tell you about it when I can write better." General MacArthur's Home-by-Christmas Offensive (as it was christened by the media) was torn to pieces by the Chinese in late November and early December 1950. One of the most horrific clashes of all occurred at the Chosin Reservoir deep within the frozen, wind-swept mountains of North Korea. "Don't let a bunch of Chinese laundrymen stop you," barked Tenth Corps commander Gen. Edward M. Almond to a group of shivering men, "we're going all the way to the Yalu." But as temperatures plunged to thirty degrees below zero, 15,000

members of the First Marine Division and 3,200 soldiers with the U.S. Seventh Infantry Division found themselves surrounded by 120,000 Chinese troops. It was a bloodbath. Having recovered the use of his frostbitten hands two weeks after his first note home, seventeen-year-old Pvt. Bob Hammond was able to describe to his father their desperate attempt to escape.

Dear Dad,

I received your letter, Joyce's, George Guthrie's, and Grandma's and the family's Xmas cards. I thought the card from "The House of Hammond" was pretty cute. I liked the poem you wrote too.

Dad, you asked me to tell you what I went thru. Well, you know I am a gunner on a 105 Howitzer in the artillery. The 57th, which is part of the 7th Div. We are usually a few miles behind the front lines. We have had mortars drop in on us, knocked out 5 tanks, killed hundreds of Commies we have never seen. But I have never seen anything like what I just went thru. The "Vets" of World War II agree also, that this is the worst they have seen.

On Nov. 27, we went into a new position. That night everything was quiet until about two o'clock the next morning. Then Hell broke loose. They charged the Infantry, went thru their lines and came right down into the Artillery position. "A" Battery had over half their men wounded and four were killed. Just before daybreak, hundreds came charging 30 of us. The rest had retreated to "B" Battery about 1/2 mile back.

We ran for it. My feet were numb from the extreme cold and I fell down. Three bullets hit a yard from me. I jumped to my feet, fired once and killed one and then ran back to "B" Battery. Five hours later we came back and took our position back.

Three days and nights of bitter fighting went on with heavy losses on both sides. We were outnumbered 10 to 1. We were also trapped and surrounded. We had over 200 wounded guys. I watched a good buddy of mine die of wounds and lack of medicine. I cried, I felt so utterly helpless. On Dec. 1, 1950, we were ordered to fight our way back to the Marine Div. which was 8 miles back. We had about 30 trucks which were carrying the wounded. We went about 2 miles and suddenly a slug ripped thru my knee and chipped the bone. I got into an ambulance which had 16 men in it.

We moved slowly and passed a few roadblocks and before I knew it, it was dark. They were on all sides of us and we were masecured. Our driver got killed and the ambulance crashed into a ditch. Machine gun slugs tore thru the ambulance killing a G.I. and a Capt. sitting across from me. He slumped on me and I shoved him back in order to get the rear door open. It was jammed, but I jarred it open in a few minutes and fell out.

Pain shot thru my leg, but I crawled into a ditch and then got up and ran. I ran about 3/4 mile and then slowed down to a fast walk. There were 18 other G.I.'s with me. We went along a railroad track for quite a way, then up into the mountains where we stayed till just before daybreak. We then went over a few more mountains and saw the 1st Marine Division. I felt tears come into my eyes, and I realized we were safe now. My pants leg was ripped wide open and I saw my leg was a mass of dried blood. I could hardly walk by then, and a couple of Marines came out and carried me in. The wounded were taken to a plane and flown back to a hospital in Japan. I stayed there two days and then took a train ride to Osaka Army Hospital, the one I'm in now. For the first week I was on my back, but in a while I could walk on crutches. Now they put me back to bed and put a traction on my leg to straighten it out.

But, I'm okay now and I feel great. Don't worry about me. I am sending a picture I had taken here. I am also sending a picture of a 105 Howitzer. My job is doing what the fellow at the extreme left is doing. The fellow on the other side of the gun with his arm crooked has just fired it. The two guys falling down were standing on the trails to help dig them in as the gun fired. The fellow in between them loaded the gun.

By the way, how much money do I have in the bank. Should be about $150.00, shouldn't it? I'm going to boost my allotment to $65.00 as soon as I have a chance. Well, take care of yourself. <u>Happy</u> <u>New</u> <u>Year</u>.

Love,
Your Son,
Bob.

P. S. Out of 1,400 men we had, just 400 got back. A Battery had 180 men. We now have 42. —32 are wounded.

The First Marine Division that Hammond praised had fought back tenaciously despite the insurmountable odds against them. The division's commander, Maj. Gen. Oliver Smith, uttered one of the most famous lines of the war after being asked by correspondents on the scene why the marines were retreating; "Gentleman, we are not retreating. We are merely attacking in another direction." The Chinese suffered approximately 40,000 casualties by the time the marines had withdrawn to the port of Hungnam for evacuation. By the middle of December 1950, UN forces were pulling out of North Korea. Not only had they lost everything gained in the North, they watched as Communist troops began to march south, once again on the offensive.

In a Letter to Carlos P. Romulo, Gen. Douglas MacArthur Defends Himself Against the "Radical Fringe" Maligning His Leadership

"If Washington will not hobble me," boasted Gen. Douglas MacArthur after North Korea invaded the South in June 1950, "I can handle it with one arm tied behind my back." At seventy years of age, the five-star general had lost none of his famed bravado. And his extraordinary September 15 landing at Inchon bolstered his reputation as an audacious military leader. By Christmas 1950, however, MacArthur's luster was dimming. After erroneously assuring President Truman that China would not intervene in the war, he drastically miscalculated both the enormity and potency of their army. MacArthur faulted "Washington" (i.e., President Truman) for prolonging the war by forbidding him from striking China itself—possibly even with nuclear weapons—and denounced the restriction as "an enormous handicap, without precedent in military history." Truman, who was trying to prevent World War III, was incensed by MacArthur's temerity. Although dissatisfaction with MacArthur's judgment was growing in political and diplomatic circles as well, the general still had his supporters. A former press aide of MacArthur's, the Filipino Secretary of Foreign Affairs Carlos P. Romulo, sent a message of encouragement to his old friend, and MacArthur replied with the following:

26 December 1950

Dear Carlos:

I am most grateful for your fine note of the 14th and the heartening loyalty it reflects.

The commitment of the military resource of China to war against the United Nations Command was of course a risk inherent in our decision to give military support to the Republic of Korea. That risk from the start hung over our heads like the sword of Damocles, and I realized that our only hope of avoiding it lay in speedily bringing the campaign to a close. In retrospect, it is now clear that the decision of the Chinese authorities was taken even before launching of the North Korean aggression on June 25th, and that nothing we did or could have done could exert the slightest influence upon that decision.

The campaign of vituperation initiated against me as a result of Red China's entry into the war was not unexpected. I had warnings from various sources, all reliable, long before Inchon that such a campaign was being planned by the radical fringe. Success at Inchon caused the plan to fail to materialize, but the new situation created by the Chinese offensive was apparently seized upon as the most favorable opportunity for its revival and effectuation. Calm judgment on the issue in the long run will prevail and the understanding will govern that the cards were stacked against us from the start, and campaign strategy alone gave us timely warning of political decisions and military preparations, both aimed at the build-up of an offensive so powerful as to destroy the Command, if caught off guard, with one mighty blow. The Chinese failed to achieve this decisive result but their eleventh hour intervention did block our efforts to complete the prescribed mission.

The efforts through a shocking perversion of truth to shape public thinking along the line that the entry of Communist China into the war was responsive to incidents of the campaign has been scandalous. The dominant group spearheading the drive has of course been the Communists and their friends, but they have received powerful assistance from those who are so infatuated with the safeguard of Europe that they would sacrifice Asia rather than see any support diverted from Europe. My views, of course, are well known. I don't believe either Europe or Asia should be abandoned if American resources can effectively assist toward their security, but the problem is a global one and must be considered on a global basis if it is considered at all. This group of Europhiles just will not recognize that it is Asia which has been selected for the test of Communist power and that if all Asia falls, Europe would not have a chance—either with our without American assistance. In their blind and stupid effort to undermine public confidence in me as something of a symbol of the need for balanced thinking and action, they do Europe the gravest disservice and sow the seeds to its possible ultimate destruction. Asia no less than Europe must be free if global peace is to be secured.

I see by the press that you are soon to return to Manila. Yours is a continuing and vast opportunity for public service, and I know that the free world may continue to look to you during these troubled times for wise and fearless counsel.

> With warm regards,
> Most faithfully,
> Douglas MacArthur

On January 1, 1951—just six days after MacArthur wrote to Romulo—Chinese and North Korean soldiers charged across the Thirty-eighth Parallel and forced the already demoralized UN troops into a hasty retreat. The Americans had lost Gen. Walton Walker, commander of all ground forces, just over a week earlier when his jeep crashed into another UN vehicle on an icy road. General Walker's replacement, Lt. Gen. Matthew Ridgway, mounted a formidable counterattack, and by March 1951 the revitalized UN troops had fought their way back to the Thirty-eighth Parallel. With a fragile equilibrium established, President Truman made preparations to negotiate a truce. Despite strict warnings to clear all foreign policy declarations with

Washington, MacArthur issued an ultimatum on March 24 ordering the Chinese to surrender or risk "imminent" destruction. MacArthur had—intentionally or not in Truman's view—ruined any chance of an early settlement. After MacArthur made several more incendiary statements, President Truman's patience was exhausted. "I deeply regret that it becomes my duty as President and Commander in Chief of the United States military forces to replace you as Supreme Commander," he began a terse message to MacArthur on April 10, 1951. "My reasons for your replacement will be made public concurrently with the delivery to you of the foregoing order." The accompanying release stated:

In view of the specific responsibilities imposed upon me by the Constitution of the United States and the added responsibility which has been entrusted to me by the United Nations, I have decided that I must make a change of command in the Far East. I have, therefore, relieved General MacArthur of his commands and designated Lt. Gen. Matthew B. Ridgway as his successor.

Full and vigorous debate on matters of national policy is a vital element in the constitutional system of our free democracy. It is fundamental, however, that military commanders must be governed by the policies and directives issued to them in the manner provided by our laws and Constitution. . . .

MacArthur, believing that Americans might receive him with indifference or possibly even hostility, instructed his aides to schedule his return to California at night; "We'll just slip into San Francisco after dark," MacArthur said, "while everybody's at dinner or the movies." Over 500,000 cheering admirers were waiting for him. Millions more turned out for ticker-tape parades throughout the country. And on April 19, 1951, he had the honor of addressing the full Congress, where he concluded with a line from the old ballad, "Old soldiers never die, they just fade away." (Truman, now loathed by the general public and many politicians for firing MacArthur, was overheard calling the speech "nothing but a bunch of damn bull_ _ _ _." After Senate hearings investigated MacArthur's dismissal, Truman seemed more justified in his actions.) The war in Korea raged on.

~~

A Young Officer, Feeling Ignored, Implores His Wife to Send More Letters—and to Stay True to Him Back Home
&
A Nineteen-Year-Old Soldier Replies to His Sweetheart After She Rejects Him for Another Man

"More mail came in to-day, but I still didn't get a letter, and I really feel blue & disappointed," wrote a twenty-four-year-old officer to his wife on January 20, 1951.

"Everybody kids me now because I never get any mail from the states. I can take a little kidding, but it's getting to hurt a little now. It's bad enough not eating & sleeping and freezing night and day, but to feel cut off completely is too much." By January 1951 many Americans fighting in Korea had been away from the States for six months, and all the usual wartime anxieties about sweethearts back home remaining faithful were creeping into their thoughts. Although the forlorn officer did begin to receive mail from his wife, his fears that she was neglecting him—or worse—had not abated. (The names of the couple have been omitted to protect their privacy.)

My Darling:

Just a couple of lines to tell you I love you. I got a letter from you that you wrote Jan. 8. It sure was good to hear from you. That's the first letter I've had since I left the U.S.

I can't see to write very much! I'm writing by the lite from under the hut, and it's almost out! Please don't worry about me, I'm all right.

I hope you are doing things right by me back there. If not, I want you to tell me so <u>now</u>. Because if I come home and hear one word the wrong way, you have had it. A lot of the fellas have had trouble from their wives back home, and not hearing from you has got me to wondering! So you had better let me know what is going on. Maybe I won't get back; right now it looks pretty bad, but if I do, lady, you had better be right on the level with me, and if there is anything to tell me, start talking now. You said in your 1 page letter you couldn't think of anything to say, well, you better start thinking, or quit writing. I'm the only dam fool around here who never seems to get any mail.

30,000 estimated enemy troops have gotten behind us. That's bad. I'm going up on "forward observation," probably tomorrow. (That's to spot enemy and direct fire on them.) So now I will really be right on the spot. So if you aren't living right, you better hope I don't make it these next few weeks. I love you more than you realize. I always will. I won't be able to write for a while after tonight. Please love me and pray. It isn't worth it to be wrong, I know. Bye Bye my Darling.

I love you.

The officer survived the war and eventually returned to his wife, and the two remained happily married. A nineteen-year-old artillery gunner named Leon was not so fortunate. (His full name must also be withheld in the interests of privacy.) Serving with the Thirty-fourth Field Artillery Battalion, Twenty-fifth Infantry Division, Leon received a "Dear John" letter from his fiancée on June 14, 1952. Heartbroken, he responded the next day.

Dear Babe,

I just received your last letter in this morning's mail. I held it in my hand for a minute while a little voice in the back of my head whispered, "This is it. This is the one." Oh yeah, I knew it was coming. I could tell from the tone of your last few letters. Have you forgotten how well we know each other?

You tried to "let me down easy." Well, if it's any consolation to you, you did it about as well as a thing like that can be done. But, then, we wouldn't have wanted it to have been too easy, would we?

You ask me if I understand. I do. I never said I was the greatest guy on earth; you did. I just agreed with you: but, to be fair, we didn't mention any other places. You didn't mention what planet you were going to live on, either; this, or his. Anyway, he's there. I'm here.

"Be careful," you tell me. "Take care." I almost laughed out loud. We wouldn't want to see me hurt, would we? There's no need to worry about me. I'll be all right. I swear it. You have other things to think about now. Hopes to hope. Wishes to wish. Dreams to dream. A life to live; and, I wish you the best of all there is.

Now? Now I will do what I have no choice but to do. But how? Do I say something brilliant like "may all your troubles be little ones"? Or do I treat this like a tennis match? "I did my best; it just wasn't good enough, and the best man won." How's that?

How about "If you ever need a friend"?

That presumes a future. There are 500,000 N. Koreans and Chinese on the other side of that hill bound and determined to make sure I don't have a future. Over here where your past is your last breath, your present is this breath, and your future is your next breath, you don't make too many promises. Which leaves me <u>what?</u>

Goodbye,
Leon

Two days later Leon single-handedly charged a Chinese machine gun nest on his own initiative. He was killed instantly in a hail of bullets.

—————— *Extended Correspondence* ——————

**World War II Veteran S. Sgt. Joe Sammarco Bids His Wife, Bobbie,
Farewell as He Embarks for Korea, Tells Her He Has Survived
the Battle of Chipyong-ni and Other Close Calls, and,
After Witnessing the Accidental Killing of Two Korean Children,
Pleads with Bobbie to Take Extra Care of Their Little Girls**

*A highly decorated veteran of World War II, Joe Sammarco was twenty-four years
old and attending airline management school in Kansas City, Missouri, when the
fighting in Korea erupted. Sammarco, who had experienced combat with the
Eleventh Airborne Division during the ferocious invasion of the Philippines, had no
intention of serving in another war. But when a Kansas City newspaper published
a photograph of kneeling, blindfolded American GIs being executed with a pistol shot
to the head by Chinese soldiers, Sammarco was so enraged he enlisted immediately.
After a brief retraining at Fort Hood, Texas, in the fall of 1950, Sammarco left
behind his wife, Bobbie, and two young daughters, Gracie (age three) and Toni (age
one), in Midland City, Alabama. On November 20, the day before he was to pass
once again underneath San Francisco's Golden Gate Bridge on a ship bound for
Asia, Sammarco wrote the following to his wife.*

My Darling Bobbie,

Well, tomorrow at noon I will be on my way. Bobbie darling, it is going to get so very lonesome for me now. Going farther away from you is going to hurt so much. But it won't be for long sweetheart. And then there will be no more of this running around all over this world. Just promise me honey, that you will continue to take such wonderful care of our babies! And above all honey, don't let them forget me.

Don't worry about me sweetheart, I have no ideas about becoming a dead hero! At the same time, I don't think there is a chinaman in Korea that can give me too much trouble. I've got some good equipment this time, and I think I know how to use it pretty well. Just don't you worry too much, and be sure and write often as soon as I give you an address to write to. And Bobbie, be sure and say your prayers every nite, and see that Gracie says hers also, and say some for Toni too.

I love you my darling, forever, with all my heart. Just keep loving me, won't you honey? That's all I want sweetheart.

Well, I've got to go and get some copies of my orders and finish packing. Good nite my darling.

I'll write again from California, Mon. or Tue.

I love you, so very much Bobbie, and I will always love you my darling.

Joey

"I was going to write last nite, but my ink was frozen in the pen," Staff Sergeant Sammarco wrote to Bobbie two days before Christmas 1950 from an abandoned schoolhouse 100 miles southeast of Inchon. Thrust into battle with the Second Infantry Division soon after his arrival, Sammarco was quickly discovering how intolerable winter in Korea could be. "Honey, this is really rough. I have been so cold & hungry for so long I think I am getting used to it. Haven't heard from you since I left the states, but we are not getting but a very few letters here. Bobbie, don't let anybody kid you, we are really losing men, by the thousands." Attached to a French battalion as a forward observer and liaison sergeant from the Thirty-seventh Field Artillery Battalion, Sammarco encountered the full savagery of the war less than two months later in Chipyong-ni. Four divisions of Chinese and North Korean troops unleashed a five-day blizzard of mortar, machine-gun, and shell fire on the town beginning on February 12, 1951. Although airdrops replenished food and supply shortages, ammunition constantly ran low, and at one point the UN soldiers resorted to bayonet charges and hand-to-hand combat. But despite the lack of firepower and a casualty count that numbered in the thousands, the surrounded UN troops repelled the Communist forces. In a letter to his wife dated February 22, Sammarco offered a firsthand account of what he had endured.

Bobbie Darling,

Sorry I haven't written, but I have not been able to! If you heard the news, maybe you heard about the French & Americans that were trapped in the town of "Chipyong." Well, I was one of them. It was a nitemare that lasted for 5 days & nites. We were completely cut off and surrounded with no food and very little ammunition. There were 4 divisions of Chinese around us, and the last two nites they broke through our lines and we were fighting hand to hand in the streets & houses, (what was left of the houses.)

Bobbie, you will never know how lucky I am to be alive. I was on my switchboard when they broke into the house, and at first I was too scared to move. Then they killed my Buddy (Johnny) and I got over being scared. I don't know what happened after that except that as the sun started to come up there were several hundred dead & wounded Chinese all over the place and they retreated (what was left of them) back to the hills. We had about 200 Americans killed, twice that many wounded, and I don't know about the French. My Battery Commander, my 1st Sgt., 3 wire Sgts, and several of my buddies were killed & wounded. Several times I thought it was all over for me, but I was lucky. Right now I am still with the French down in the Wonju area. I hope it will be over soon. I love you so much, and I must get home to see you again. I am all right now honey, and I think it will be quiet here for a little while, anyway. Please keep writing, and remember how very much I love you & miss you,

Kiss the babies for me,
I love you,
Joey

For his "magnificent example of courage" demonstrated during the battle at Chipyong-ni Staff Sergeant Sammarco became one of few Americans ever awarded France's croix de guerre with the Silver Star. As part of the UN drive pushing north toward the Thirty-eighth Parallel in early 1951, Sammarco was caught in one skirmish after another. "Honey, I've had a couple of close calls, too close, but I've been very lucky," he wrote on February 29. "I've seen my best friends blown all to pieces, I've been less than 1 foot from fellas that have never moved again, and it's right at those times when I think of you, and wonder if you are thinking of me." Sammarco frequently expressed how worried he was about Bobbie and his little girls, and on March 1 he asked Bobbie to assure him all was well back home. (Like many of his comrades, Sammarco often referred mockingly to the war in his letters as a "police action"—the term used by the Truman Administration and the UN to describe the fighting in Korea. Despite the Constitutional imperative, President Truman never requested a formal declaration of war from Congress.)

My Darling Bobbie,

I got a letter and a birthday card from you to-day. And it sure was wonderful hearing from you. But you also told me that Toni had a sore mouth & Gracie was sick also. That worries me very much, but I know that you will take good care of our babes. Please tell me if you are getting enough money! And if you are getting the things you need.

We have been moving right on up without too much trouble, but the Chinese seem to be massing for a big, and final attack. It doesn't look good, but I just know it is coming. After the next big ATTACK, (which is predicted to be the biggest of the "Police Action", (ha! ha!) I think the Chinese will be about washed up, if they don't get the best of us. I guess it will really be a bloody mess.

Incidently, in that article with this letter, I happen to know what happened to that chink field officer, and I've got the proof right here in my pocket. I also snapped a picture of him. I went with the French just before we got trapped at Chipyong, and am still with them.

I sure hope that it will all be over soon, I am sick of this whole mess over here, and if I stay too long, I'm just liable to get hurt, but I'm not worried about that.

Are the babies any better now? I just pray so much that you all are all right. Does Gracie even mention me anymore? I hope so. I know that Toni doesn't even know who or what I am, but when I get home we will make out all right. Please tell me more about the babes, and honey, please tell me all about <u>you</u> and what you are doing and how you are feeling. I love you so much honey, and if I don't seem to tell you often enough it is only because I don't have the time, paper & pencil all at the right time. But you must know how very much I love you, I just worry sometimes that you may grow tired & weary of waiting & waiting. I hope that someday I can make it all up to you, —maybe I won't get the chance, but if I do I will always love just you sweetheart. Well, I've got to get my rifle cleaned & my knife sharpened up. Where we are now it doesn't pay to have your weapon apart many minutes. These nites sure are getting on my nerves. Well, it's getting dark, so I must get going,

Good nite Sweetheart,
I love you with all my heart,
<u>forever,</u>
Joey

On March 7 UN forces launched Operation Ripper, a massive initiative to regain the Thirty-eighth Parallel. As Sammarco feared, he was right in the middle of it.

Mar. 16, '51.

My Darling Bobbie,

Well honey, I guess the lord is working overtime for me lately. Yesterday afternoon I got the purple heart. But I am all right, so don't you worry about me. I was about 10 yds. behind the red panel that shows the end of friendly territory. I was relaying fire missions on my radio. All of a sudden a Chink mortar came in. It hit my Captain & killed my radio operator. My Capt. started walking towards me holding his chest, and I was lying on my stomach looking up at him. Just before he got to me another mortar hit just about a yard to my left on the road. It lifted me about a foot off the road and I got a piece in my leg & another piece in my arm. But please believe me, I'm O.K., just a little nervous.

What kept me from being killed Bobbie, I will never know. Maybe I was too close to the explosion and the stuff flew over my head, I don't know, but anyway, after it went off I couldn't find my Capt. so I went back down the road, fast, about 100 yds, and just sat there in a ditch waiting, for nothing. Then I saw the blood coming through my sleeve & my pants, but I knew it couldn't be too much or I wouldn't still be sitting up. So, I stopped a medic and he sent me back & now I am all right & don't you worry. And if you happen to get a wire saying I am wounded, disregard it, cause honey, ah is all rite! ! !

Honey, I got another letter from you this morning, and it sure came at the right time. But honey, you must stop worrying, I'll be all right. It just isn't my time to go, and I just know that I will get back all right. And Bobbie, this stuff is getting old, and if I'm not worried, sure you can stop worrying. I'll be all right. But you will be sick if you don't stop worrying. I love you honey, and nothing will keep me from you, ever. Bye for now, and promise me you will stop worrying.

I Love You —Joey

After receiving only basic first aid to treat shrapnel wounds to the leg and arm, Sammarco was back in combat. By the beginning of April 1951 the UN forces were on the offensive and crossing over the Thirty-eighth Parallel into the North. (President Truman hoped to seize the opportunity and begin peace negotiations—until General MacArthur undermined them with his belligerent ultimatums to the Chinese and was dismissed by Truman on April 10.) Weeks passed before Bobbie heard from her husband again. "Sorry I haven't written for so long," Sammarco explained in a short note dated April 14, "but I haven't had a chance, and I have been so far up in the mountains that I could not have mailed a letter anyway." A week later Sammarco was able to send another letter during a lull in the fighting.

Apr 21, 51

Bobbie Darling,

Just a few lines to say hello & to tell you I love you. I have been back here at the Bn. for 2 days now getting a little rest, and thought I would have a couple more days, but, to-nite around midnite I will be on my way back up to the front, about 12 miles. It sure feels good to get back this far once in a while where you can sleep all nite long and close both your eyes. But then I am not doing any good when I am way back here.

One of my buddies got killed this morning. They just brought him in a few minutes ago. Last week he told me if anything ever happened to him for me to write his wife and send some of his pictures on home. Well, I just don't feel like it and I think it would be better if I didn't write. He has a boy, 3, and a little girl, 1, and when I think about it I get so nervous I don't know what to do. Anyway, I can't write.

This afternoon I took a walk down to the river and that is where I found the violet I enclosed. It was so peaceful & quiet down there and its just like spring anywhere in the world. That clipping was in Readers Digest, and it reminded me so much of Gracie that I thought you might like to read it also.

I may not be able to write for a few days now, but don't worry, I will be all right.

I don't know when I will be able to come home, but it should be in the next 3–4 months at the latest. Unless, of course, the "Police Action" (HA! HA!) takes a turn for the worst, which it might easily do.

Well, I'll have to sign off for now, and besides, I have a bad headache.

Bye for now,
I Love You,
Joey

P.S. Please kiss Gracie and Toni for me, I love you, Joey

The very next day the Chinese army hurled itself at the encroaching UN forces, which withdrew almost entirely into South Korea in less than a week's time. The war had become a human tide of troop movements ebbing and flowing across the Thirty-eighth Parallel with no end to the fighting in sight. In the middle of May the Communists—who outnumbered the Americans and their allies three to two—hit again, hard. Throughout the war the Chinese frequently struck at night and began their raids by banging drums, shrieking at the top of their voices, and blowing bugles and whistles. Originally it was believed they did this only to scare the wits out of the enemy (which it did), but, lacking in radio communication, the Chinese were also signaling fellow units. Sammarco alluded to the unnerving tactic in a letter dated

*May 12: "The Chinks are coming in again and we can hear them. I will not sleep
I guess. But then I have such nightmares when I do sleep I guess it does not make
much difference if I sleep or not. Every nite the darkness gets a little worse for me."
Daytime proved even more frightening for soldiers who traveled in the UN convoys
that snaked their way through the narrow valley roads of Korea. Hidden Chinese
snipers shot the drivers in the first vehicles, and then, as the UN soldiers fled from
their trapped jeeps and trucks, Chinese machine-gunners and artillerymen opened up
on them from all sides. In a letter dated May 28, Sammarco mentioned an ambush
he barely escaped:*

Well, I am still pretty lucky. We were cut off and trapped again the other day,
and had to try and run through a Chinese roadblock. It was at the town of
"CHAUN-NI." . . . My 3/4 ton truck got machine-gunned before I went 1/2
mi. down the road. It wounded my Captain, & killed my other two men. I fell
off the truck & was hit & crawled down into the creek. The Chinks had all the
high ground along the road and I watched them come down from the hills like
flies & kill our men & take a lot of my buddies prisoner. And I just about gave
up too, but I couldn't do it. I worked my way down the stream a ways and then
up into the hills. I kept crawling until I didn't think I could go any further, then
I would think about you & the babies, and go on some more. I guess I am pretty
lucky to have you praying for me so much. . . . [W]hen we got back to
Chaun-ni it was the worst thing I've ever seen. All the vehicles were shot up
& burned & the place had hundreds of dead all over. Dead G. I.'s all over. After
we got out of Chaun-ni the Air Corps & our big guns just about blew that place
off the map. There were pieces of "meat" hanging from the tree-tops.

*Despite initial defeats, the UN forces rallied and set in motion a major counterat-
tack. On May 30 Sammarco wrote: "Well, we are pushing ahead, after our latest
'strategic' withdrawal!! We are killing many many Chinese,—but of course we are
losing men also." Sammarco survived the sweeping UN assault, which inflicted
catastrophic losses on the Communists in late May and early June 1951. In July
both sides called for peace negotiations, which was especially welcome news to
Korea's civilian population, ravaged by almost a year of war. (The first round of
peace talks would unravel a month later.) Sammarco was devastated by the suffering he saw among Korean families and children, and he often wrote to his wife
about their plight. In a letter concerning mostly routine financial matters, Sammarco added the following:*

It all seems so futile sometimes, this waiting & crawling around like an animal nite & day. But it must end soon, because I have just got to see you & be
with you again before long. After this mess over here I don't know how I can

ever get over it. Everybody is so unhappy everywhere I look. And it seems that there is absolutely no future for all these sick & weary people. Even if the war did end, there is no place for anybody to go. No homes, no food, and for thousands of kids, there are no parents. I wish I could bring one of them home with me. If there was a way, would you want me to bring one with me? I found one yesterday in a house, sitting on the floor crying her little heart out. Everybody else was dead. . . . [W]hen you see it nite & day, week after week & months on end it just gets to you. You cannot even conceive of the situation as it actually is. But I am glad you don't have to see it.

Although they would both later realize the many complications involved with trying to adopt a Korean child, Bobbie was not opposed to the idea. Sammarco was confronted with an even more terrifying incident involving Korean children on June 11, 1951, which he described in graphic detail that night.

My Darling Bobbie,

Here I am again to say hello and to thank you very much for the sweet Fathers Day card which I received today. It is so nice honey, and I was happy to get it.

Well, in a couple of days I am supposed to receive a medal and citation from the French Government. I don't know just what it is, but I was told that it is in connection with Chip-Yong-Ni, but at any rate I will let you know more about it in a few days. Also I was told today that I am to receive the American Bronze Star medal for action at Chaun-ni a couple of weeks ago. One more thing, I am now back in the rear area of the division for a while. I was sent back a couple of days ago. It seems that they think that I need a little rest, which suits me fine.

As I told you before I have not been sleeping too good lately, and the other nite I came close to shooting one of the Korean guards for a Chink. It's just that my nerves are a little worn, and I know that a few days back here will do a lot of good. Now don't you go and worry about me, because I am perfectly all right, believe me. It is not unusual for a man to be sent back here for a few days to rest, in fact there are a couple of other boys here from the outfit with me. We can sleep all we want back here, eat good, and see a few movies and drink a few beers, and that should certainly get me in good shape, but quick. And it also gives me more time to think about you and the babies.

I am glad that you feel as you do about my bringing home one of these little Koreans if it is possible to do so. Even if I can not do it, I appreciate your feelings concerning these people. It is such a very sad picture, and the more that I see of it, the more I feel that any little thing that I might do to alleviate the situation is completely worth the time, trouble, and money it might take to do so. I have not had the time to look into it very thoroughly yet, but I hope that I will have the time before I leave here.

Bobbie, please keep a close eye on the babies all the time for me, and I mean just as much as you can. I saw two little kids get run over and killed today, in less than two hours. It makes me sweat just to think about it, it was the most horrible thing I have seen yet. In the first one it was a little girl that was run over, by a jeep. The jeep was coming towards me, the little girl ran right in front of it. It knocked her down, ran over her, caught her under the jeep, dragged her a ways, and when he tried to stop he just ran right over her little head. I have seen some pretty dirty things over here, but those two incidents today were the worst. I stopped my truck, and for a few minutes I just couldn't believe that it had happened. I kept thinking about it and as I started to leave Wonju to head back here the little boy got hit. And it was even worse, but I won't go into that one too, it's not very nice.

What I am driving at is that I immediately thought about our babies, and Honey, I worry so much about them. I know you take wonderful care of them, but I just can't stand to think about even the smallest little thing happening to either of our babies. Please sweetheart, be so very, very careful with them, and with yourself too darling. I love you all so much sweetheart, and just have to stay well all the time. So please Bobbie, promise me now that you will be especially careful all the time, and watch the babes real close, especially during this hot weather, and watch out for snakes and bugs and anything else that might hurt you all in any way.

Well, I guess that that is all for this time honey, but I will write again real soon, and thanks again sweetheart for that very sweet card. I have your pictures out right here next to me now, and honey I miss you all so much. I would give so much to be able to be with you right now, to hold you and love you so much the way I want to. But honey, don't you worry, I will make it all up to you just as soon as I can get my arms around you again.

> Good Nite my Darling,
> I Love You So Very Much,
> I Love You Sweetheart,
> With All My Heart & Soul,
> Joey

Wounded three months earlier in the right arm (which still had shrapnel in it) and left leg, Sammarco had an aggravated limp which was becoming increasingly painful. In mid-June his superiors ordered him to the army hospital in Osaka, Japan. After a successful operation on his leg, Sammarco was sent home to his wife and children in January 1952. But his stay was short-lived. Months later, after pursuing a job with the State Department, Sammarco headed to Taiwan to work for an import/export company named Western Enterprises, Inc. In fact, the company was, according to Sammarco, a CIA front; Sammarco's real assignment was on the island of Tachen, only a few miles off the coast of mainland China, where he trained former prisoners of war captured in Korea to subvert China's Communist dictatorship. (When Mao Zedong's revolutionaries overran the U.S.-backed regime of Chiang Kai-Shek in 1949, Chiang and what remained of his Nationalist government fled to Taiwan.) The POWs Sammarco was training in Tachen were the very same young Chinese men he had been trying to kill, and who had been trying to kill him, in Korea. After a year in the region and approximately three months in Saipan, Joe Sammarco was on his way home for good. Still a young man (he was only twenty-eight) he settled into a long—and refreshingly calm and quiet—career in the automobile and truck business.

Sgt. Don Gore Informs His Girlfriend That, If Ordered to Korea, "[He] Ain't Goin'"

By July 1951 support in the United States was waning for the now one-year-old "police action," which virtually everyone recognized was a full-scale war. When the hostilities began, telegrams and letters poured into the White House lauding the decision to send troops to Korea by an overwhelming margin. But after tens of thousands of American casualties, UN forces had failed to defeat the Communists, and Truman's popularity, which had always been tenuous, began to plummet. When a music critic named Paul Hume panned a performance by the president's daughter, Margaret, Truman shot off a venomous letter, warning that if they ever met, Hume would need "a new nose, a lot of beefsteak for black eyes, and perhaps a supporter below." Americans were not only shocked by the president's outburst, they questioned his priorities. A couple whose son was killed in Korea mailed Truman the following letter, accompanied by the Purple Heart medal their son had been awarded posthumously:

> Mr. Truman:
> As you have been directly responsible for the loss of our son's life in Korea, you might just as well keep this emblem on display in your trophy room, as a memory of one of your historic deeds.
> Our major regret at this time is that your daughter was not there to receive the same treatment as our son received in Korea.

In April 1951 Truman's dismissal of General MacArthur ignited another firestorm of protest, and the collapse of the July 1951 peace talks prompted fears that Ameri-

can soldiers would be mired in Korea indefinitely. (His public approval at its nadir, Truman would ultimately decide not to run for reelection in 1952. Dwight D. Eisenhower became the Republican nominee and pledged he would personally go to Korea to see firsthand how peace could be achieved. Eisenhower would win by a landslide—and, after the election, would fulfill his promise and travel to Korea.) Desertion rates, although still low, were rising in 1951, and even servicemen in the States were becoming increasingly cynical about the unfolding debacle overseas. In a letter to his girlfriend, who was living in Detroit, Michigan, twenty-one-year-old Sgt. Don Gore articulated the growing disillusionment of many young American men. (J.D., mentioned in the letter, was a childhood friend who had been serving with Gore at Fort Bragg, North Carolina.)

Dear ——,

Thought I would answer your letter dated September 25, 1951. Enclosed is a copy of it in case you forgot what you asked. I sure enjoyed spending time with you, too. And it wasn't because of your pin curlers that I didn't wake you up to say goodbye. You looked so peaceful and happy laying there sleeping so I just kissed you on the forehead and left because I had to get back to Ft. Bragg and help J.D. pack up his personal belongings and put his guitar in the trunk of my car and take it to his mother's house. J.D. has to leave for Korea this week, but I ain't about to go.

General McCarthur told them that this Korean war was a stupid war and unconstitutional because they wouldn't let us win the war and wouldn't let us lose it. All they want to do is to send us over there with gigantic war machines and grind up barefooted peasants and let the American soldiers get captured by the enemy and live the rest of their lives in a communist slave labor camp. General McCarthur told them that this is a bunch of BS and they fired him for insubordination.

I am with General McCarthur. We need leaders who will lead us not stick us and bleed us, and since General McCarthur got fired I've become one dysfunctional Sergeant. And they have left me full of rage and contempt for everybody in Washington, and without General McCarthur to lead us I ain't going.

I had my cousin write a letter to my Company Commander telling him that she was only 17 years old and that I got her in trouble and that she wanted me to come home and help support her and the baby. It didn't work, but they did bring me up on moral charges, which let me accomplish my mission. If I can postpone my hearing and manipulate the court for three months then I won't be eligible to go to Korea. If my plan falls through you may have to write my Parole Officer and tell him that I am a high moral man and this whole thing is a big mistake.

If J.D. and I get out of the Army with a sound mind and all of our body parts in good shape we are going to California and start a Hillbilly band, so if you don't hear from me too often don't get worried and think that I don't love you no more because I do. I am standing on a bridge that just won't burn. When I get enough money to buy a new car and a house I'll come back and we'll get married. You wouldn't like California though because they have cockroaches out here bigger than my car. We'll move to Florida, there we can teach our kids how to water ski and fish and boat ride and after we get settled we can talk your mom and dad to move close by so that the kids will have their Grandpa and Grandma and we'll have a babysitter.

Love,
Don

Although Sergeant Gore remained in the military, he was not sent to Korea.

~

Cpt. H. Richard Hornberger, M.D., Shares with His Parents the Antics of His Fellow MASH (Mobile Army Surgical Hospital) Doctors

"The surgeons in the MASH hospitals," Cpt. Hiester Richard Hornberger recalled of his days in Korea, "were exposed to extremes of hard work, leisure, tension, boredom, heat, cold, satisfaction and frustration that most of them had never faced before. . . . A few flipped their lids, but most just raised hell." A chest surgeon from Maine, Dr. Hornberger served for a year and a half in Korea in the 8055th MASH unit. Sparing his parents the gory details of body counts and casualties in his letters home, Hornberger chronicled instead baseball games in ankle-deep mud, late-night poker marathons, and other diversions the doctors turned to when things were slow. From time to time Hornberger also offered wry commentary on the war. "Off and on we get some interesting work to do," he wrote in January 1952, "some of it caused by the Chinamen, much of it caused by our own soldiers being hit by our own mortars, or trying to cross our own minefields. If we stay here long enough, the American Army may annihilate itself." After recovering from a bout of chicken pox, Hornberger sent the following on February 17, 1952. (A. D. Hall, mentioned in the letter, was his lifelong friend Arthur Dudley "Dud" Hall, who was serving in the Merchant Marines; "Horny" was Hornberger's college nickname.)

Dear Mother and Dad,

Well, except for my complexion & skin, I'm a well man. Tomorrow I'm going to shave for the first time in 10 days & go over to the 22nd Evac for a couple days before returning north.

Jenner, having saved the Captain's nose, was the guest of honor and occupied the seat of honor, in which he immediately passed out as a result of before dinner refreshment. The meal proceeded uneventfully and was followed by conversation and alcohol, probably in ever increasing quantities. Finally one of the more alert noticed that Jenner P. Coil was no longer with them. A search was forthwith instituted and sometime later Jenner was found down in the hold, draped over a pipe, sobbing, and mumbling over & over again "I am lost in the bowels of the ship."

Without knowing Jenner, you cannot fully appreciate the humor of this, altho I must admit there's a little pathos mixed in with it.

I have to laugh at the whole thing. And invariably makes a good first impression, particularly if he can impress a bunch like that by taking them aboard his ship. Just wait till he comes to Pusan and brings his whole crew up to have their appendices out; the boys may feel a little different about him then.

Well, that's the tall tale for today.

So long
Dick

Having nothing else to write about I will tell you more that I have learned about the adventures of A.D. Hall in the Orient. He apparently made a big hit at the 22nd Evac Hospital. The most disturbing thing is that everyone who's visited me says that the consensus of opinion is that "He sounded just like Horny"—to which I have taken violent exception at every opportunity. This was due, mostly, to one or two down east profanities we have in common.

His first night there he helped my friends Jeet & John Glynn drink up a bottle of John's scotch. At his time he met my old roommate, Jenner P. Coil (the 46 yr old Oklahoman lush of whom I once told you). Finding that Jenner was classified by the army as a CNT man, and being an excellent judge of character, Dudley decided that Jenner was just the man to take care of the nasal polyps which were afflicting the captain of his ship. So the next P.M. up came Captain & First Mate. The Captain submitted to the tender ministrations of Jenner P. Coil (a braver man than I) while the first mate proceeded to get around a bottle generously provided by my friends.

Well, the Captain survived, and that night Jenner, Jeeter, Big John Glynn, & Cy Schwolben, my other old roommate, were guests at dinner aboard ship. Jenner, having saved the Captain's nose, was the guest of honor and occupied the seat of honor, in which he immediately passed out as a result of before dinner refreshment. The meal proceeded uneventfully and was followed by conversation and alcohol, probably in ever increasing quantities. Finally one of the more alert noticed that Jenner P. Coil was no longer with them. A search was forthwith instituted and sometime later Jenner was found down in the hold, draped over a pipe, sobbing, and mumbling over & over again "I am lost in the bowels of the ship."

Without knowing Jenner, you cannot fully appreciate the humor of this, altho I must admit there's a little pathos mixed in with it.

I have to laugh at the whole thing. Dud invariably makes a good first impression, particularly if he can impress a bunch like that by taking them aboard his ship. Just wait till he comes to Pusan and brings his whole crew up to have their appendices out; the boys may feel a little different about him then.

Well, that's the tall tale for today.

So long
Dick

After leaving Korea, Captain Hornberger, using the alias "Richard Hooker," wrote a fictionalized account of his wartime experiences in a book titled M★A★S★H, *which became a movie and then an enormously popular television show that ran for eleven years.*

≈

Capt. Molton A. Shuler Jr. Describes to His Wife, Helen, the Makeshift Church He and His Friends Have Created in the Midst of Battle

With the exception of a relentless air campaign that pounded Chinese and North Korean troops and military targets, the UN did not launch another major offensive in the war after the late fall of 1951. Two more years of savage fighting would continue on the ground, however, as the Communists tried several times to punch through the line of UN forces just north of the Thirty-eighth Parallel. Diplomatic talks sputtered on and off, and were frequently suspended after petty squabbling. But in 1952, as truce negotiations languished and headlines about the fighting in Korea dwindled in the United States, reflecting a larger apathy toward the war, thousands of American soldiers and marines were still being killed and wounded in smaller though no less terrifying battles. Confronted by fears of insignificance, many struggled to retain a sense of greater purpose and meaning amidst all the bloodshed. Cpt. Molton A. Shuler Jr., thirty years old and the father of a four-year-old son and a one-and-a-half-year-old daughter, was fighting in Chorwon, just north of the Thirty-eighth Parallel with the Forty-fifth Infantry Division. Shuler related to his wife Helen in Kingstree, South Carolina, a moment that illustrated how essential it was for him and his comrades to maintain their faith.

Helen my Darling -

You are perfection — the paragon of womankind — and you're my wife — and I adore you! And what's more, you're first 6 letters came today! With them came my very life — for my heart was slowly breaking for words of love and tenderness from you, my beloved wife. It's impossible to describe what your letters meant to me. More than you can possibly imagine I appreciate your love. I know full well you love me — but I can't see quite why. But I'm not going to quibble. I'm only going to love you more for loving me as you do.

Then there is another reason for my good spirits tonite — as if your letters were not enough. I went to church tonite. Let me paint you a word picture of the "church". Picture a grassy hillside surrounded by mountains. And a rugged looking — crew hair cut and all — chaplain dressed in fatigues standing by a Government Issue folding podium with a red velvet cover and brass candelabra minus candles, all placed on a couple of ammo boxes.

Then just left of the "pulpit" as you face it you find a battered, 30-odd key, olive drab organ, a GI pianist seated on a 5 gallon gasoline can. And in the background you find blasted Chinese bunkers and old gun emplacements. Then if you look way to your left you'll see a battery of 6 105 howitzers, their ugly muzzles pointed menacingly toward the North. To the right and on up the valley are bunkers of our company, a couple of tents from which winds a road (one way) behind our "church".

But what about pews and who occupys them? Well, they are roughly terraced rows with a handful of soldiers, mostly a little dirty and bedraggled, trying to keep from becoming more soiled by sitting on their helmets. You find a rifle loaded with a full clip, or a carbine with a jam-packed magazine beside each man. Over there is a blond and baby faced young man, and beside him is a tough looking hombre with a dark beard and dirty fingernails. And down in the front row are three Korean boys who just sang a couple of hymns in their native tongue, self-conscious to be sure, but, even so, attesting to God's presence in the hearts of a people torn by war.

And God is in this "chapel" — so near you can almost reach out and touch Him. And the chaplain says, "And men, in the days to come, you must remember the words of Christ when asked where He lived; 'come and see'".

Only a couple of times in my life before this evening, have I felt God's presence in such a way. Perhaps it was the place and the time — I don't know. Be that as it may, I liked the way I felt.

'Scuse me for trying to be literary. I didn't mean to — as my efforts no doubt reveal.

Goodnite, Dear, and love our children for me — and miss me, please.

Your man always —
Molt

Over three weeks later Mrs. Shuler received another letter that began: "By now you have no doubt been notified that I was scratched up a bit on the morning of the 16th 'in the vicinity of Chorwon, Korea.' I only wish I could have beat the wire with a letter—this letter—for I know you were shocked." The UN soldiers at Chorwon found themselves overwhelmed three to one by the Chinese, and Captain Shuler was hit by shrapnel in the neck, the back, and on his right leg. Evacuated to a MASH unit, he was treated and then sent to a hospital in Tokyo. Although the wounds were not fatal, Captain Shuler received infected blood plasma during his treatment and died of hepatitis on August 24, 1952.

Ardith Morrisseau Gently Chastises Her Former Boyfriend, Lt. jg. Carroll Briggs, for "Getting Himself in Such Messes" with Other Women

&

Briggs Confesses to Morrisseau That He Has Fallen in Love with Her

&

Hardly Able to Contain Himself, Briggs Declares He Has Come to a Decision He Is "Just Dying to Tell [Her]"

Patrolling the coast of China in the summer of 1953 on the USS Gurke *DD-783, Lt. jg. Carroll Briggs, age twenty-five, was consumed by thoughts of a young woman named Ardith Morrisseau back in California. Briggs had been engaged to another girl a year earlier, but his fiancée ended the relationship in May 1952. Briggs was crushed. "I tied your letters / In a neat bundle," he would later write in a poem recalling his heartache, "With my 1928 silver dollar / And dropped them / Off the fantail / Into the sea . . ." In the fall of 1952, when the* Gurke *returned to its home port of San Diego for a seven-month rotation, Briggs and Morrisseau began dating. But Briggs had still not recovered from his break-up, and when he could not commit to a more long-term relationship with Morrisseau, she curtly informed him, "Never darken my door again." Back to sea in March 1953, Briggs wrote to Morrisseau and was resoundingly ignored. But after a few more persistent letters, Morrisseau began to warm to him. She was not, however, going to make things easy, and, after Briggs waxed nostalgic about moments they had shared before his departure, she responded on May 19 with a mild rebuff:*

> *Reminiscing is fun — but make sure you don't connect the wrong feelings with the memories. Don't put things there that weren't. For instance, as I recall — both the nite we stopped at Santa Cruz and the time you stepped on my shoe (which, incidentally, is now fixed) we were both trying to create something that wasn't. Remember also the fun and companionship we really did have, though. What I'm trying to say is don't remember something into a situation that wasn't there, and don't leave out what was there. Don't get any ideas from things that have happened. Let's accept what we have — which certainly is something — and go on from there. Don't worry — if there is or could be more — it will take care of itself —*

Much to Briggs's elation, there was more, and by the summer of 1953 their affection was slowly catching fire again. They had both been dating other people, and they both ended these relationships. This proved more problematic for Briggs, however, who had been receiving torrid love letters from a girl he had met while at San Diego's Naval

Training Center the previous summer. Briggs lamented to Morrisseau how difficult the situation was, but promised her it was over and sent her a few small gifts as well. (It cannot, alas, be determined what the gifts were.) Morrisseau addressed Briggs's ordeal in a letter dated June 2, 1953.

Carroll Gray Briggs,

What am I going to do with you?

They're very beautiful, of course — but why me? I just don't understand. Besides, I thought you were saving your money. This sounds as though I don't appreciate them — I really do — but — oh to heck with it — thank you very much, they're lovely. I don't understand men in general, and you in particular — and let's leave it at that.

My last letter must have left you in suspense. I forgot to send the cartoon I referred to. Let's hope I remember to send it this time.

I don't mind your reminiscing — in fact, I like to do it myself — I just don't want it to lead you astray — if that's the right phrase.

It's a good ~~think thingk~~ (ye gads I can't think straight) thing (<u>there</u>) you're not here — I think I could talk for hours — afraid you wouldn't even have a chance to get one word in edgewise. Well, maybe one.

Well, to start with, I don't mind your "blowing off steam" to me. (I'm used to it.) I do wish you'd stop getting yourself in such messes, though. Yes, it's your own fault. You should be able to handle it differently. I don't know how you acted before you left, but at any rate — you were all right up to that point. Your trouble was in not setting her straight when she began writing that you didn't want her to write. For heaven's sake — no girl likes to be squelched, as the saying goes, but it's a darned sight nicer to be stopped before you've made a fool of yourself. It's not as though you didn't like her. (Although, that sometimes makes it tougher.) Most girls like to know where they stand, and appreciate straightforwardness in a fellow. (There are exceptions!) You have to make up your mind what you want out of the relationship, and let her know. Then it's her perrogative to accept or not on your terms. This cuts many beautiful friendships down, but who wants someone that doesn't want them? Maybe none of this is applicable — but — anyway — take it for what it's worth.

"I remember, I remember, the day" . . . or should I say night after the party at Stetson's. Maybe it was the excitement, maybe the atmosphere, maybe the moon (was there one?) or maybe two kids who had managed to make something tangible out of something intangible — if only for one evening — who knows. At any rate, if that "magic" remains illusive, at least we caught it once. It's sort of nice to remember things like that, isn't it?

I didn't think the boat ride was such a flop — I enjoyed it! So there, too! Your almost right on the phonetics. Maybe I'll explain further, at a later date — when I'm at a loss for something to write — or say — or —

Ardi

By the middle of June, Briggs realized he was passionately in love with Morrisseau, and he wanted her to know that, although separated by 10,000 miles, he had never felt closer to her. ("Kilowana," which Briggs refers to in the letter, was the camp in the Silverado region of California where Morrisseau was a counselor.)

19th of June
2300

Ardith Morrisseau —

You ought to be ashamed of yourself, keeping me up like this — I should be getting a little sleep before going on watch but no — I lie down and WHOOSH, you come tromping thru my head and I lie and start thinking — well you know that's quite a process. Young lady do you know what I think about — for instance the thing that really shook me out of bed to write — to write words which should be spoken — Was the terrifying thought that come October you might be some place else — Suppose, — suppose you went back east to that silly school or something like that — Do you know what I would have to do? — And don't think I wouldn't —

You know darn good and well what I'm thinking about and you are probably laughing (and I hope you are —) But this is a serious matter and I am warning you, I have done my very best to try not to make any leading statements — I just don't need them — and that is that. My mind is made up — .

Now — see what you have done — in 40 minutes the messenger will be down here calling me — There isn't any point in trying to go back to sleep — [go back to sleep heck, I never got to sleep] — so prepare your self for a harangue — If this is all you can take, then stop here otherwise, read on —

Come into my parlor — little fly!

So — you are gonna persist — (you had darn well better) Now that I am here, I don't just exactly know what to say — Of course I could go ranting on as before — however maybe I had better save some of that for later. Just one little word of warning —Woman, you be available.

Now to pick up some kind of a thread of conversation (you will probably continue to read between the lines any way, — I might as well just spend the next (let me check, —) 30 minutes (my time passes quickly with you — would you mind spending the next four hours up on the bridge I'll really bend your ears!) [to continue —] writing something like, "The quick brown men to come to the aid of the lazy dogs country" But in case . . . . Where in the Paren am I any way??

— Good, a new clean white piece of paper and I can start fresh anew. Ah the rippling streams of Kilowana in the hills of Silverado — What? No streams? — Well you can't fool me about Silverado every thing in Calistoga Countree is called Silverado. Hey, teacher, teach me how to swim, I can't swim a stroke! —

Guess I ran out of words, look at the doodling on the bottom of the page — yep, — I'm all run down — Nothing but real serious thoughts running thru my mind —Thoughts like the ones I was thinking one day as I drove from Monterey to Salinas — and from Monterey to Berkeley. Thoughts which I would like to speak — and very much like to write but am afraid to — for fear they will lose their magic

For they are magic thoughts Ardi —

If only I could speak them to you

Love —
Carroll

By August 1953 Briggs had made up his mind; Ardith Morrisseau was absolutely without question the woman with whom he wanted to spend the rest of his life. He had said as much "in code" in one letter, but he recognized he had to do more than just hint. (Briggs and Morrisseau often tried to outwit one another by putting the first letter of each word of a sentence on the back of their envelopes. This could be as simple as "I. L. Y."—for "I love you"—to "M. W. B. M. I. S. T. D. W. D. Y. T.?"— which even Briggs, who wrote it, couldn't decipher when Morriseau later challenged him on it.) On August 30, Briggs came one step closer to formally asking Morrisseau to marry him.

Sunday Nite 30 Aug.

Hi Sweet Heart —

Shall we go for a ride? — No telling what might come out on here to nite — so watch out — I am in a kind of philosophical mood —

Lets talk about 'Lil Ardith Morrisseau — You know her? She's a pretty special girl. I have learned a lot about her in the last few years and every-thing seems to indicate that — Gosh, what do I say here? The idea that should be conveyed is that she has very high ideals and lives up to them — I guess that says it as well as anything — Did you know that she is very artistic? —(No, I am not speaking as one who desires to be artistic himself — I am speaking as a "student of human nature" — We all are you know!)

But look at the way she works with design — She has an excellent sense of design — and very much of an individual style. In the confused world of today an individual style in design is a rather hard attainment yet it is quite natural with her.

I remember, one nite I drove up to see her — Don't remember just when — That's not important anyway — but I drove down Clay Street — and there she was down at the end — out in the street — in an old leather jacket and Levis playing some sort of game with the kids. I stopped and watched for almost a half hour — then drove on — she was enjoying herself so much that I didn't even bother her —

Do you know what she told me in a letter once? — She said — She said — "Regardless of what else I have written — and dependent on talks after you get back I think I can honestly write that I do want you, Carroll — Love Ardi" — Isn't that wonderful — That was the 30th of July — Since then, a lot has been said — and gone on — I can't say that I have grown more sure of my — self — intentions — since then, — Because I have already reached the most sure point — I think if you read back a few months, you can find where it was — Most sure.

This Ardith Morrisseau — sometimes Ardi — and sometimes (real privately —) Ardito — (Remember the purse seiner — you always said it was named for you). She is pretty wonderful — No, most wonderful — and I love her very much —.

Gosh Ardi — here we are almost to San Simeon — guess we'd better turn around and go back. — You are always complaining about me keeping you up too late — know how to solve that problem — ! — Do you know what the trouble with this letter is? — Well, there is something I am just dying to tell you — But I am not gonna untill I find out for sure — I put it on the back of a letter once in initials — (several weeks back) — Since then it looks even more likely — ! Now don't get too big ideas — This is just a small thing but — I've already talked too much —

Ken Masters and I ate dinner down at the club tonite — had a buffet dinner pretty good. After dinner, we went down town and bought some photo chemicals — I will have some time Wednesday nite — and will see if I can make some more prints for you — maybe I will get some films developed on the Base tomorrow.

Well Ardi — I guess I have about talked myself out tonite — Some of it got on paper — I have been writing this since 9:30 now it's almost 11:30 — so you can see, there was some blank time where just thoughts were going by — sometimes they get written down — Sometimes no — (Sometimes — I must admit, — I throw the paper away and start over —

even tho I know that most of the time you seem to know exactly what I
mean —) —

    Really what I mean is so very simple — I love you Ardi —

I want you for my own always —

Love Carroll —

*Soon after writing this, Briggs and several of his closest friends were in the Officers
Club in Naha, Okinawa, discussing their sweethearts back home. Briggs was the
only one who did not have a wife, and hearing his friends expound on their marriages
and how profoundly happy they were, inspired him to make his own engagement
official. Briggs grabbed the nearest piece of paper he could find—a coaster—went back
to the ship and scribbled his proposal to Morrisseau. Later realizing this might not
be the most romantic parchment for such a moment, Briggs wrote out a longer letter
which he sent (along with the coaster, as a keepsake) to Morrisseau. For six long
weeks there was no reply. Briggs' letter and Morrisseau's response, it turned out, were
delayed by a typhoon. (Letters usually came every six days when a tanker would sidle
up to the* Gurke *and unload food, mail, and fuel.) Morrisseau's answer was yes, and
on Sunday November 22, 1953, Carroll Briggs and Ardith Morrisseau were
married in Carmel, California. They became the parents of three boys and two girls
and remain happily married to this day.*

～↝

Demoralized by His Experiences in Korea, Pfc. Jack Train Jr. Instructs His Friend, Kathie, to Tell Her Younger Brother the Realities of War Before He Enlists

*"I'm almost looking forward to going to Korea," Jack Train wrote to his parents in
December 1952 from boot camp. "With the grace of God, I'll be able to come through
it okay, and I'll at least have the knowledge that I did my share." Train, a nineteen-
year-old private from Somerville, Massachusetts, was sent to Korea with the First
Marine Division in February 1953. For the past year and a half, Chinese and
North Korean soldiers had tried repeatedly to smash through the formidable line of
UN troops just north of the Thirty-eighth Parallel, but were unsuccessful. Fierce, iso-
lated battles exploded on hillsides known as Bloody Ridge, Pork Chop Hill, Bunker
Hill, and Heartbreak Ridge, but the UN line proved virtually insurmountable. By
March 1953 negotiations were once again in progress and a truce seemed imminent,
but this made combat all the more harrowing; no one wanted to be a casualty when
peace was so close at hand. Even Pfc. Train, once so enthusiastic about fighting in
Korea, was thoroughly dispirited within a month's time. In a letter to Kathie
Thompson, a close family friend back home whose teenage son (nicknamed*

"Brother") wanted to be a soldier, Train encouraged her to pass on what he had seen firsthand after two months of war. (Charlie is Thompson's husband; Robert, Maureen, and Carol are her other children; and Joseph Byrne is her brother. There was speculation that Train had a slight crush on Maureen.)

May 29, 1953

Dear Kathie,

Hello again, I trust all is well with you; the situation here is not greatly changed, we're still taking that foolish training, which will do us no earthly good, since, if we don't know how to keep alive by now, we never will. The replacements who have joined us since we were relieved aren't even getting anything out of it, as they were taught the exact same things back at the States, and they pick up all the extra little tricks after about ten minutes in combat. But I suppose the big wheels think it's benefiting us, and you can't fight City Hall, as the saying goes.

This ought to be a little lesson to Brother—he should be learning by now that the military takes a lot out of a man and gives very little in return; it is not, despite anything people say, glamorous, exciting or enjoyable. You live constantly in dirt, hunger, anger (at the sometimes brutal treatment of the lower classes/enlisted men, especially low-ranking ones like me, of which there are many, by the higher ups); and even though the first two conditions are found mostly in combat areas, the last one is prevalent all over. No matter what he thinks (and I know, because I thought that way, too) he's not likely to be an officer, I'm sorry to say, and if he's not, he'll have to start from the bottom & work up, and he will be stepped on all the way.

The service has no regard for the individual, and the personal feelings & priveleges of the lower-ranking personell mean & rate a big fat nothing. It's a hard & merciless taskmaster, and he's a fool to even consider it—never mind about the glory of a uniform, or the supposed "honor" of serving your country. There are too many dead & maimed glorious & honor-bound boys, poor young fellows who never hurt a soul, and were blinded by such baloney. God knows I was blinded too, and Heaven forbid, but I might yet be one of them.

Ask him to read this letter, & perhaps he'll wise up before it's too late; consider, Brother, if you will, all your buddies in school. If you make the same mistake I did, you may someday be carrying what's left of them back on a stretcher, or burying them—don't think it doesn't happen to the Navy, because they have corpsmen and fliers over here, and they take their share of casualties.

If you <u>have</u> to get it out of your system, join the Reserves; you'll see why I hate the service, even the Stateside service, and you'll be a lot better off. No matter what you read, or are told, it's no fun dodging bullets and artillery shells, never knowing from day to day whether you'll ever see your home, family or parents again—no, it's a Hell on earth, and you'd be a lot wiser to spare yourself from it.

Forgive me for going overboard, Kathie, but I can't stand thinking of more poor kids being dragged into this mess. Sorry to sound so melodramatic; my love to Maureen (hah!), Carol (ha-ha!), hello to Robert & Charlie, my best to Jos. Byrne, & company. So long for now, must close as my time is up.

Love
Jack

To the outrage of almost everyone involved, South Korea's leader Syngman Rhee— clinging to the dream of a unified Korea, which he, of course, hoped to rule—temporarily sabotaged the peace negotiations by threatening to launch a new offensive against the Communists. It was meaningless bluster (his soldiers were no match for the Chinese) but Rhee was able to delay the talks. Train, echoing the views of many exasperated troops, wrote to his parents on June 22:

> *The truce talks drag endlessly on, seeming always nearer to peace, and yet not settling a thing—I don't know, it's a senseless war at best, and it's not really accomplishing a lot, except to kill off some more of our boys; these people don't seem to want it; I know (and you do too, from the news) the South Koreans don't want it over—and we're letting them make suckers out of us.*

After Rhee undermined the diplomatic talks, clashes between the UN and the Communists flared up in June and early July. Train was back in battle, and on July 8—his twentieth birthday—Chinese forces bombarded Train's outpost with heavy mortar and artillery fire. Pfc. Jack Train was killed in the attack. Two days later the peace negotiations resumed, and on July 27, 1953, an armistice was declared. After three years and one month of fighting, the border between North and South Korea was reinstated at the Thirty-eighth Parallel—almost exactly where it had been before the June 25, 1950, invasion. Hundreds of thousands of Chinese and millions of Koreans had been killed in the war, and 37,000 Americans had died. Approximately 8,000 are still listed as missing in action

∾

Julia Child Admonishes Aloise B. Heath for Questioning
the Patriotism of Smith College Professors
with Alleged Communist Connections

"I am avidly following all the international goings on," Julia McWilliams reported to her beau Paul Child on March 2, 1946. "I am particularly interested in the Russian game of imperialism. . . . To me the Russian business is the historical and crucial happening—in that, on its outcome depends the future of Europe, Asia, and us." McWilliams's comments were not those of an idle observer casually interested in geopolitical dynamics; during World War II she served, with high security clearance, in the Office of Strategic Services, precursor to the Central Intelligence Agency. Over six feet tall, she was rejected by the WAVES, the women's branch of the navy, but was accepted by the OSS in December 1942 to do clerical work in Washington, D.C. A year and a half later McWilliams was assigned to Ceylon (now Sri Lanka), where she collected and processed highly classified information. After the war she returned to the United States but maintained a strong interest in world affairs. On March 5, 1946, former British Prime Minister Winston Churchill warned that the Soviet Union, once allied with the United States and England during World War II, was lowering an "iron curtain" over Eastern Europe to suppress democracy and dominate the region. Joseph Stalin angrily denounced Churchill and insisted the Soviet Union had every right to "ensure its security" by encouraging pro-Soviet governments in neighboring countries. Writing to Paul Child on March 19, McWilliams was not, at least initially, entirely dismissive of this view.

Two very interesting letters from you—which I can at least answer in my leisure and beatific mood. I have recently and successfully made a most satisfactory, light, delectable bernaise sauce (awfully easy when the tricks are known), and have laboriously practiced on my piano. . . .

I felt Stalin had quite a few points on his side in his speech. (I wonder how accurate or how "shaded" the translation was—is the meaning of "lie" retranslated into the original Russian that Stalin used, as rude a word in Russian as it is in English—etc., etc.) For one thing, I am inclined to forget that Russia was almost beaten to the knees by the German advances into Stalingrad, and that they lost an in-numerable amount of people—far more than we did. Why, also, is it not quite rational for them to want pro-Russian governments in their adjoining territories? His point seems well taken, indeed about our toleration and support of former fascists in government posts rather than Communists. Our position seems to have been so often "<u>anything</u> but the Communists"— which is such a negative and disastrous position = viz: Spain from 1933 on.

I notice so much of your "obfuscation" in people's thinking—or rather their un-thinking mind-patterns which have been conditioned and chan-

nelled by bewilderment, fear, and the loud-blabbing propaganda pressure groups. RUSSIA, as a word, is a symbol for FEAR. Ain't it? . . .

McWilliams *later condemned the Soviets after the brutality of Stalin's regime was exposed, but she remained troubled by anti-Communist hysteria in the United States in the years after World War II. The "loud-blabbing propaganda" she alluded to in 1946 found, in her belief, its mouthpiece in a little-known senator from Wisconsin named Joseph McCarthy. "I have here in my hand a list of 205 [names]," McCarthy declared on February 9, 1950, "a list of names that were made known to the secretary of state as being members of the Communist party and who nevertheless are still working and shaping policy in the State Department." Challenged to substantiate the charges, McCarthy refused. He later said he had only eighty-one names. Or possibly fifty-seven; he wasn't certain. Living with her now-husband Paul in France, where she was studying cooking, Julia Child followed McCarthy's rise to power from international newspapers and through letters from friends and family in the United States. In March 1954 Child learned that an ad hoc committee established by Smith College alumnae had succumbed to McCarthyism as well. Child, who graduated from Smith in 1934, was livid. On March 12 she fired off the following:*

> Mrs. Aloise B. Heath, Secretary
> Committee for Discrimination in Giving

My dear Mrs. Heath:

Another fellow alumna of Smith College has forwarded to me a copy of an undated form letter containing your printed signature as secretary of a committee whose members are unidentified. This letter names five members of the Smith College faculty as having been or as now being associated with organizations cited as Communist dominated or as Communist fronts, etc. I have also a memorandum, dated February 26, 1954, signed by the President of Smith College and the Chairman of the Board of Trustees of Smith College, stating that your committee never presented its letter either to the President or to the Board of Trustees for comment or investigation.

I know you feel you are doing your patriotic duty towards Smith College and towards the United States, or you would not have allowed your name to be used at the end of your committee's letter. But I respectfully suggest that you are doing both your college and your country a dis-service.

We, as alumnae, have voted, in the correct parliamentary fashion, for each member of the Board of Trustees to act in our behalf. Our trustees, who are answerable to us, have duly selected President Wright to administer the college. It is an extremely serious matter to accuse by implication five faculty members of being traitors to the United States; and further-more to accuse the college of knowingly harboring these "traitors". According to proper democratic methods, charges of this grave nature should first be brought to the attention of the President and the Trustees. You have assumed a responsibility for which you were not appointed. It is clear that you do not trust your own elected officers, and that you do not have confidence in democratic procedures.

David Lawrence, the newspaper columnist, has an article in today's Herald Tribune in which he states again a principle he has stated before in regard to fighting Communism: "The followers of Senator McCarthy believe in fighting fire with fire, and they are not too concerned with the methods, etc." This is the theory of the "end justifying the means." This is the method of the totalitarian governments. It makes no difference how you do it: lie, steal, murder, bear false witness, but use any method fair or foul as long as you reach your goal. I am sure Lawrence has not thought through his thesis to this length, but carried to its logical conclusion, it is the nullification of all that the United States stands for. In Russia today, as a method for getting rid of opposition, an unsubstantiated implication of treason, such as yours, is often used. But it should never be used in the United States.

In the blood-heat of pursuing the enemy, many people are forgetting what we are fighting for. We are fighting for our hard-won liberty and our freedom; for our Constitution and the due processes of our laws; and for the right to differ in ideas, religion and politics. I am convinced that in your zeal to fight against our enemies, you, too, have forgotten what you are fighting for. Certainly democratic procedures are often slow. But their very slowness gives full opportunity for free debate, free investiga-tion, the right of the accuser to present his case, and the right of the defen-dant to hear the charges and be faced with the evidence. None of these rights are available in the totalitarian countries; nor have you made them available to the persons you have accused.

One of the purposes of Smith College, and the main reason why its alumnae support it, is that it is a free, democratic institution, privately endowed, and subject to no political pressures from any government or any party. It can operate freely as long as its Trustees and its President have the courage to act as they see fit, with the support of the alumnae. In this very dangerous period of our history where, through fear and confusion, we are assailed continually by conflicting opinions and strong appeals to the emotions, it is imperative that our young people learn to sift truth from half-truth; demagoguery from democracy; totalitarianism in any form, from liberty. The duty of Smith College is, as I see it, to give her daughters the kind of education which will ensure that they will use their minds clearly and wisely, so that they will be able to conduct themselves as courageous and informed citizens of the United States.

I am sending to Smith College in this same mail, along with a copy of this letter, a check to duplicate my annual contribution to the Alumnae Fund. I am confident that our Trustees and our President know what they are doing. They are only too well aware of the dangers of totalitarianism, as it is always the great institutions of learning that are attacked first in any police state. For the colleges harbor the "dangerous" people, the people who know how to think, whose minds are free.

Very sincerely yours,

Julia McWilliams Child

That same March the esteemed CBS newsman Edward R. Murrow broadcast a withering profile on McCarthy, and senators from McCarthy's own party began to criticize him publicly. The backlash had begun. When McCarthy assailed the U.S. Army for harboring spies and Communists, the military refused to be bullied. "Have you no sense of decency, sir?" the army's chief counsel Joseph Welch reproached McCarthy on June 9, 1954, before a televised audience of millions. On December 2 the Senate voted by a three-to-one margin to condemn McCarthy for his behavior. He died two and a half years later of acute alcoholism.

In a Letter to Reverend G. A. Zema, Helen Keller Denies That She Is a Communist Sympathizer

Despite Senator Joseph McCarthy's personal demise, the spark of recrimination, fear, and mistrust he ignited continued to blaze throughout the 1950s. Civil liberties were trampled on, teachers were forced to sign loyalty oaths to the United States, and many books and other publications deemed "leftist" were banned and, in some cases, even burned. The famed social advocate Helen Keller, herself, was tarnished by allegations that she had associated with the avowed Communist leader Elizabeth Gurley Flynn, who was serving a twenty-eight-month prison term for "conspiracy to teach and advocate the overthrow of the government." Stricken as a young child with an illness that left her blind and deaf, Keller matured into a brilliant, articulate advocate for human rights, suffrage, and international peace. Keller was the spokesperson for the American Foundation for the Blind when the Flynn controversy erupted, and she worried it would adversely affect the Foundation. Although Keller had, in fact, greeted the Russian Revolution with great enthusiasm— "March on, O comrades, strong and free!" she exclaimed in 1920—she distanced herself from the Communists in the following letter to Reverend G. A. Zema, one of many supporters who had written to Keller demanding an explanation for her relationship with Flynn.

September 15, 1955

Dear Father Zema,

I want to thank you for writing me about the message I sent to Elizabeth Gurley Flynn. This encounter with the Communists has taught me, as I should have known before, how exceedingly alert and careful we must be at all times. I will tell you how it happened.

I met Mrs. Flynn some forty years ago among a group who advocated the formation of unions for miners and other workers who were struggling for fair living conditions. I was trying to understand labor problems, strikes, and the tangled history that surrounds them. She was among those with whom I discussed these tormenting questions.

Since then I have had no contact with her and no correspondence except when I sent her a message of condolence several years ago after the death of her son. Since I joined the American Foundation for the Blind in 1924 I have been so absorbed in work for the exiles of the dark that I have had little time to devote to other activities.

In June of this year Mrs. Flynn's sister with whom I had never had any connection wrote me that Mrs. Flynn was ill and in prison. Shortly afterwards a friend of Mrs. Flynn's with whom also I had never had any connection asked me to send Mrs. Flynn a message for her 65th birthday. I felt that I could not be a Pharisee in spirit and refuse a friendly word to one whom I had seen long ago standing up for the rights of those who were wounded and crushed in the battle of economic life. I was thinking of her services at that time and not of what she has since done for the Communist Party.

I want you to know that if Mrs. Flynn was a member of or connected with the Communist Party at the time of our meetings forty years ago, I was totally unaware of the fact. I want also to assure you that no plan, purpose or conspiracy for the violent overthrow of the United States Government could awaken any response in my soul. I am not a Communist now and never have been a Communist. In responding to the plea for a message to Mrs. Flynn I let my heart rule my head and I am deeply troubled by the distress that it has caused among my friends and the friends of the blind.

Sincerely yours,
Helen Keller

Lt. Jack Sweeney Sends a Letter to His Future Wife, Beebe Matthewson, After a Disastrous "Trans-Oceanic" Phone Call
&
Cdr. Sweeney Assures Beebe That Even if He Should Die on One of His Missions, He Considers Himself "One of the Luckiest People" to Have Lived

Throughout the 1950s, '60s, and '70s, thousands of U.S. airmen flew covert missions to probe weaknesses in Russian radar and electronic defenses and to photograph military bases, missile silos, and similar installations in the Soviet Union and other potentially hostile nations. In 1956 Naval Cdr. Jack Sweeney, a veteran of both World War II and the Korean War, patrolled for Soviet submarines in the Atlantic along America's East Coast. Ten years earlier he had been stationed in Saipan and China as part of a military presence working to stabilize the region after World War II. "I'm certainly glad I figured out I was in love with you," Lt. Sweeney wrote to his future wife, Marie "Beebe" Mathewson, back in Coronado, California. "It explains a lot of queer things that have been puzzling—for instance, why I think of you most of the day and dream about you most of the night and why I'm so eager to return to the States." Mathewson and Sweeney first met in late December 1945 and spent a mere ten days together before he was off to the Pacific, and for the next seven months they courted by letter. "It seems incredible I could miss anyone so much that I've only known for a couple of weeks," Sweeney wrote. "But I do." One month before he returned to the United States, Sweeney was desperate to hear Mathewson's voice, and he contacted her by telephone. He discovered, however, that international phone calls were not all they were cracked up to be.

Monday, June 3.

Dearest Beebe,

Just got back from that confoosin but very amoosin' trans-oceanic coast-to-coast Sweeney-to-Mathewson telephone conversation. I don't know what we said, but I got a big bang out of whatever it was. My shorthand expert was along and took it all down for the newspapers and here's what came off, according to ~~her~~ him:

Operator: Go ahead
Jack: Hello — Beebe?
Beebe: What?
Jack: Hello — is that you, Beebe?
Beebe: Okay.
Operator: You have one minute left.
Jack: What happened to the first four minutes?
Beebe: What?

Monday, June 3.

Dearest Beebe,

Just got back from that confoosin but very amoosin' trans-oceanic coast-to-coast Sweeney-to-Mathewson telephone conversation. I don't ~~know~~ what we said, but I got a big bang out of whatever it was. My shorthand expert was along and took it all down for the newspapers and here's what came off, according to ~~the~~ him:

Operator: Go ahead
Jack: Hello - Beebe?
Beebe: What?
Jack: Hello - is that you, Beebe?
Beebe: Okay.
Operator: You have one minute left.
Jack: What happened to the first four minutes?
Beebe: What?
Jack: I think you're the most wonderful girl I've ever known, and I adore you, honey.
Beebe: Huh?
Jack: I said howmuch weight have you gained?
Operator: What?
Beebe: Why, you — gribble smock diffuser gamble sweater.
Jack: What did you say about the sweate

Jack: I think you're the most wonderful girl I've ever known, and I
    adore you, honey.

Beebe: Huh?

Jack: I said how much weight have you gained?

Operator: What?

Beebe: Why, you— gribble smock diffuser gamble sweater.

Jack: What did you say about the sweater?

Beeb: Huh?

Jack: Are you mad at me?

Beebe: Naturally.

Operator: Yer five minutes is up. Tell 'er goodbye.

Jack: Huh?

Operator: Goodbye, Beebe. (Hangs up.) That'll be $734.26, Mr.
    Sweeney.

(end of conversation)

Well, that's the last time I'll spend $734.26 on a trans-oceanic phone call,
even to you. Unless something big comes up. I could hear you fairly well,
but you weren't receiving me. I'd say something clever as the dickens, and
you'd ask for a repeat, and by the third time I'd said it, I'd decide it
wasn't funny after all, and off I'd go on another tack. But all in all, I enjoyed
it a lot and it was swell hearing you again. That was the shortest five minutes I ever saw. Next time I'll ask for ten.

I wish that mail would start coming again. I feel as if I haven't heard
from you in several months.

All my love,
Jack

*In July 1946, Sweeney and Matthewson were married in Coronado. Sweeney
attended the Air Force Command and Staff School at Maxwell Air Force Base in
Montgomery, Alabama, and eventually joined Patrol Squadron Forty-nine. By
1956 Sweeney, Beebe, and their four young sons—John (age seven), Bill (five), Al
(three), and Dan (one)—were all living at the Hamilton Air Force Base in
Bermuda. Although Cdr. Sweeney's reconnaissance patrols were not considered terribly dangerous, they were not without risk. Sweeney wanted Beebe to know that,
should the unthinkable happen, his life could not have been more joyful or fulfilling
because of her and their children. (Undated, the letter is believed to have been written in early November 1956.)*

To the best wife a man ever had:

Honey, I am writing this letter to you to say a few things that I might
leave unsaid if I should depart this world unexpected-like. In this flying

business you never can tell when you might all of a sudden get mighty unlucky and wake up dead some morning.

I suppose this shows me up for the old sentimental fool I have always been, but I thought if I could make sure you know how I feel about such things it might be a little comfort to you.

First of all, let's face one fact—everybody ends up dead. Think of all the infants and children and people who had the misfortune to die before they got very much of anything out of life, and then think of all I got out of it.

Even if I should die the day after writing this, I still claim I am one of the luckiest people who ever lived, and you know it. I've got a lot to live for, as I write this, but when I count up all the blessings I've had, I can see that I have already lived a lot. When you come right down to it, I've done just about everything I've wanted to do and seen about everything I've wanted to see. Sure, I'd like to stick around while the boys are growing up, and to have fun with you again when we have time after they grow up. But you and I agree so closely on how to raise a family, the boys are going to be all right; I'm sure of that. And I've had enough fun with you to last anybody a lifetime.

Don't let the memories of me keep you from marrying again, if you run across somebody fit to be your husband, which would be hard to find, I know. But you're much too wonderful a wife and mother to waste yourself as a widow. Life is for the living. (That's not original, I'm sure.)

So get that smile back on your face, put on some lipstick and a new dress, and show me what you can do toward building a new life. Just remember me once in a while—not too often, or it'll cramp your style, you know—and as long as I'm remembered, I'm not really dead. I'll still be living in John, and Bill, and Al, and Dan, bless their hearts. That's what they mean by eternity, I think.

My love as always,
Jack

Astonishingly, this was Cdr. Jack Sweeney's last letter; he and his crew were killed on November 9 when their plane went down in the Atlantic for reasons that are still unknown. Beebe Sweeney was pregnant with their fifth child when Jack was killed. A beautiful girl, Emma, was born in March 1957.

～

Convicted Spy Alger Hiss, Writing from Prison, Advises His Young Son Tony on What Is Required for an Individual to Be Truly Happy

&

In a Letter to the Writer James Rorty, Whittaker Chambers Reflects on the Explosive "Hiss-Chambers Case" Twelve Years After It Was First Reported

Ordered before the House Un-American Activities Committee (HUAC) on August 3, 1948, Time *magazine editor Whittaker Chambers admitted that from 1931 to 1938 he had allied himself with the Communist party. But Chambers's most shocking revelation was that Alger Hiss—president of the Carnegie Endowment for Peace, a senior State Department official under presidents Roosevelt and Truman, and a former clerk to the legendary Supreme Court Justice Oliver Wendell Holmes—had been a friend of his and accomplice in an underground Communist spy ring in Washington, D.C. Outraged, Hiss emphatically denied the charges under oath and claimed he had never even met Chambers. (When it later became clear that he had, Hiss explained that Chambers introduced himself fifteen years earlier using the alias George Crosley and that they had not seen one another since.) Handsome, charming, and articulate, Hiss cut an impressive figure and initially was given the benefit of the doubt. HUAC even considered dismissing the accusations. But a thirty-five-year-old congressman named Richard Nixon insisted on further investigations, leading to a dramatic confrontation between Hiss and Chambers. The climax came in early December 1948 when Chambers presented classified State Department documents on microfilm, purportedly given to him by Hiss, which Chambers had been hiding in a hollowed-out pumpkin on his farm. The evidence convinced a jury to convict Hiss for perjury, and he began a three-year, eight-month prison term on March 22, 1951. Permitted to write home only three times a week, Hiss addressed his letters to the family as a whole, but occasionally wrote directly to his son Tony, who was nine when Hiss left for prison. The following was sent on March 10, 1953. (Hiss was allowed only one piece of paper to write a letter, so he indicated shifts in thought and new paragraphs with "x"s to save space. Hiss also affectionately used "thee" and "thy" when writing to his family.)*

Dearest Tony, About time for a letter all of your own. I wish that we were permitted to write often enough so that I could send full-length letters to thee regularly—little bits in my regular letters home are not adequate to talk about all the things thee + I need to share with each other. x-x-x This letter is going to be mostly about a very big subject that we will often discuss, thee + I. The subject is: What makes people really happy inside themselves?—the kind of happiness that keeps on shining day after day, not just now + then; and the kind of happiness that lasts in spite of discouraging disappointments + sad events. I don't mean that sorrow isn't real; I do mean that it doesn't continuously darken the skies of a truly happy person. x The answer isn't simple + various ways exist for stating it. I'm forever changing, at least slightly, my way of saying it. Thee will in time decide on thy preferred formulation of it. The important part, which is itself quite simple + has been understood for a long, long time by wise people, is that happiness is a natural result of a full + healthy growing. In that respect men + women + children are like flowers; when they are healthy they grow continually—+ they blossom. The blossom is our happiness. Or it can be compared to a bird's song — the natural result of living fully. So, if there is continuing sorrow or anxiousness or crossness or even boredom, this is a sign that something is wrong. The Romans knew this long ago. The wise Emperor Marcus Aurelius said: "A man's happiness,—to do the things proper to man." The ancient Chinese knew it. One of the followers of Lao Tze said to keep the mind easy (not worried) + the body healthy "since both mind + body have no inherent defect or trouble." x-x But the really important words in all these statements are "proper," "full," "healthy." This is where so many people, even kind + intelligent ones, get confused + this is where the question gets more complicated, where the more the world learns the surer the answer. This is the part of happiness that for a long, long time only the most wonderful + remarkable men understood, men like Buddha + then, later, Jesus. They learned that no one person can live fully or healthily or properly (or happily) by himself or for himself. Now more + more people have come to understand this. We are lucky that we live at a time when this is no longer hard to grasp. x Perhaps you remember a kind + quiet older woman, Dr. Richards, who visited us at Peacham with Aunt Anna for just an hour or so in the summer of 1950. Dr. Richards is a psychiatrist + she says her pleasure in life comes from "pumping air into other people's tires." No one can live well with out both giving to + getting from other people that kind of help. x-x These are not normal times in our country. Many people are confused or frightened so that they are not naturally — + hap-pily—helping each other. And — a strange thing — it is so natural + necessary for all to love + help that one who stops gets twisted. The energy for helping is still there, but when it doesn't get a chance to be used naturally, it sours + turns to hate or miserableness. When President Roosevelt was alive he encouraged most people to bring out their natural kindness; he "pumped" lots of "air" — good fresh air — into people's spirits. And Adlai Stevenson had some of this quality as thee + many others realized. Thee knew then how happy-making it is to wish others well. Just because there came, after Roosevelt's death, so much confusion + twisting of love into hate, there is much to be done by all of us who know what people need to be happy. As long as some are hungry + cold + sick + rejected no one can feel as good about life as he should, because we are all like members of one big family. But those of us who are fortunate in having enough to eat + to wear (+ MUCH MORE than merely enough), who are well + strong + loved, we can find great happiness in pumping friendliness + cheerfuness into the lives of others — including each other, of course! x-x-x That is why I thought thee would now enjoy the book about Boston during the years when Justice Holmes was just the age thee is now. His friends, young + old, were the people who did most to end slavery in our country. And they didn't lose heart though there was even more confusion + fear + hate than there is today. Much happy love to dear Tony,

Daddy.

P. S. Today the "Astronomers Club" had wonderful views of Venus by day. I hope that N.Y.'s smog let thee + Mommy see it, too. It is especially bright as I am writing for the sun has now set + the sky is not so dazzling.

Alger Hiss, who maintained his innocence until his death in November 1996, rarely mentioned Whittaker Chambers in his prison letters. He did, however, refer to the 1952 publication of Chambers's bestselling autobiography Witness *as "the product of a seriously disturbed psyche." The foreword to* Witness *was a letter from Chambers to his children John and Ellen about the Hiss-Chambers case. "The Communist vision is the vision of Man without God," he wrote to the two teenagers. "At heart, the Great Case was this critical conflict of faiths; that is why it was a great case. On a scale personal enough to be felt by all, but big enough to be symbolic, the two irreconcilable faiths of our time—Communism and Freedom—came to grips in the persons of two conscious and resolute men." Almost a decade later, and a year before his death, Chambers expounded on his momentous clash with Hiss and how misunderstood it was by past and present generations in a typed letter to the journalist James Rorty, who had written a play about the two men. (Tukhachevsky, Bukharin, Muralov, Smirnov, Rakovsky, and Ovseenko, alluded to in the letter, were all Russians falsely accused of treason and executed during Stalin's purges of the late 1930s. The last page of the letter has been lost.)*

July 1960

To James Rorty—

What a generous letter! Especially after my bare-handed treatment of the tissues and ligaments. I purposely left out of my letter (during surgery) an appreciation of your kind treatment of me in your play. It is so unusual that I was a little incredulous at first, but grateful.

There is a built-in handicap in dramatizing the Hiss Case. It was (perhaps I should say: it is, for it will never end) an epitomizing drama—on at least two levels. On one level, it was a drama of historical epochs—the signal that an epoch was ended. This is one of the things that so misled many liberals, who imagined that Alger was the rallying figure of an age coming to flower, whose tender shoots must at all costs (and some of them were pretty extravagant) be protected from the little foxes.

In fact, The Hiss Case was a disclosure that the historic bases of several kinds which more or less give shape and direction to eras were changing at extreme speed; had, to a large degree, changed for an unguessable time. Since the mass of men seldom understand the history they live through and act in, nothing falls more quickly into oblivion than any given historical period. Even the facts of the fathers are unknown to the sons, who find the past generation almost entirely baffling. "Papa, who was Mussolini?" my daughter asked me mid way of her career at Smith, Then I knew. I said that she probably did not know, either, who Georges Sorel was, though Reflections On Violence was on our bookshelves—a book that Mussolini read and reflected on, so that, by reading it, one might grope better toward what Mussolini was than by reading stacks of the grotesque accounts in the press, or even Balibanova. The campus generation that I am so curiously embedded also does not know who Mussolini was—except as a name.

Last semester, I would often hear, coming from somewhere on the campus, a strong unself-conscious whistling: Mack The Knife. Those whistlers would have been astonished (and, I think, in some curious way, angered) if any one had told them that Mack The Knife was written by a Communist, who was a friend of several friends of the old man in their midst. Of course, the old man would never tell them, though he never ceased to be bemused by those innocent whistlers. Nothing marks so clearly the absolute cleavage between concurrent generations, or the complete ending of the historical epoch, than the revival of this theme song of the 1930's without the slightest knowledge of what it is.

How long has Brecht been dead—three years? Yet almost certainly none of those whistling Mack The Knife even knows his name. Yet he wrote in their own life time and toward the end of his great assertion of basic faith: "In the bloodiest times, there are kind people.—In den blutig- sten Zeiten, gibst gütige Menschen." He also wrote:

> The sons of the tiger
> Are the horse's brothers;
> The child of the snake
> Brings milk to the mothers.

What are the completely new dialectic minds of the campusmates to make of this riddle?

Now, Alger and I are dialectic. What ever differences of mind and character set us apart, we are held in this one consistent bond—the habit of our minds is essentially dialectic. So, once events had disclosed that Alger was still a Stalinist, I always felt that I knew what, in the main, he would do. For example, the notion was popular for a time in certain quarters that Alger would kill himself. I never believed this for a moment. Not that it could happen—There are limits to human endurance, but as we know it in hind sight, his are high enough to make him an extraordinary figure. My view was based on something else—a dialectical reading of the circumstances as a whole, how Alger read them and his role in them. Suicide was simply not what it was all about. I might commit suicide (for reasons implicit in the same reading). It was unlikely to the point of unthinkableness, that he would. To do so, would be to negate his reading of history, of reality, his own meaning in the total process. And to such men as we were (as the breed was that grew us), our meaning was the most precious thing to us in life. It was precisely the recovery of meaning in a world which had lost meaning that made us Communists. But our meaning lay in our active purposeful life which we could sacrifice only if a threat to our essential meaning left no other means but self-slaughter to rescue and reassert that meaning—our reality, our truth.

It was I, not he, who was especially vulnerable on this side: since there were recurrent spins when it seemed that there was no means left but self-destruction to assert my truth and, therewith, everybody elses. Alger had, not only a grasp of what the whole struggle was about on the historic plane, and what he must do. I had, I should think, an almost identical view. The difference lay in interpretation. It was as if the history of our time had been reduced to an equation filled with x's, y's and z's. Alger read the value of X as human hope and Y as man's salvation etc. But I read the same X as human night and the same Y as man's damnation etc. But we both knew the same algebra and read the same equation in its terms. A paradox was that, while we were both algebrists, the mass of the onlookers had never got (in this direction) beyond simple arithmetic. Hence, the quite extraordinary public befuddlement about his motives and mine, the preposterous motivation assigned to us even to this day (and which, incidently, it was, and is, to his tactical interest to befuddle further). This is what Ralph de Toledano means when he says in his recent Lament To a Generation, that neither the American nor the public ever knew what the Hiss Case was about. Nor would it have done more than compound the confusion if any had known that, in certain frightful turns that were beyond my strength, I would try to recoup some force by saying to myself: "This effort for Tukhachevsky and his little girl (she hanged herself, age 6, a few days after he was shot). Or, again, this effort for Muralov, for Smirnov, for Rakovsky, for Antonov Ovseenko." The problem was not vengeance (though who would reject an adrenolin of vengeance in those terms if it would strengthen us at such times?) The problem was to defeat what had defeated those men before it should defeat all men.

Do you remember Bukharin's last words to the Purge court: "For when you ask yourself: 'If I must die, what are you dying for?'—an absolutely black vacuity suddenly rises before you with startling vividness. And when you ask yourself: 'Very well, suppose you do not die; suppose by some miracle you remain alive, again what for? Isolated from everybody, an enemy of the people, in an inhuman position, completely isolated from everything that constitutes the essence of live.' And at once the same reply arises. And, at such moments, Citizen Judges, every thing personal, all the incrustation, all rancour, pride, and number of other things, fall away, disappear' ".

Through The Hiss Case, I said to Bukharin's memory that I had heard his words that all the world has forgotten; that there is not an absolutely black vacuity; that there is still the possibility of struggle while men live who dare to struggle. I knew this then and Alger knew it too. We both knew what, under all appearances (many of them perfectly valid in themselves) the struggle was all about at root. In a way, it simply continued in open form the substance of our last conversation. Little can be so improbable in history (so full of improbabilities) than that, in the land the most remote from the epicenter of the age's central conflict, and most ignorant of it, two such men as Hiss and I should continue the struggle in public. Not because either of us wished to. Each of us, I imagine, down to his last drop of all plasm, wished not to. But forces, moving in an infinitely complex web of history, brought it to pass. "He and I are caught in a tragedy of history," I said while he listened in public hearing. Though there is a sense in which this is the kind of thing, one does not say: one hears one's self saying it—if the distinction is allowed—since the words well up, unpremeditated, from—where?

> When winds were in the oaken straws,
> And all the cauldrons tolled.

And never more than in an instant, we were both anachronisms—I of the revolutionary epoch that was ended; he of the long Thermidor whose true nature I find it difficult to believe he has yet assessed, but to which he has brought an individual fortitude—the ? of what gave force to the original revolutionary formations.

As you can see, at this point I am no longer writing a letter; I am bleeding at the pores. I will let it go because I have a sense that you will return (in writing) to these matters. By that date, I may not be around. My comments on these things may be of some small interest or help. I said, way back toward the beginning, that the Hiss Case was an epitomizing drama. It epitomized a basic conflict. And Alger and I are archetypes. This is, of course what made The Hiss Case. Though almost no one grasped what was afoot, this is what gave the peculiar intensity to the struggle. If he and I had not been gladiators of the revolution (though of different vintages and schools), if we had not fought, knowing what was at stake, to the end, The Hiss Case would have been just another Boris Moross case. It is all this, and much more of the same, that makes it all but impossible, or so it seems to me, to make a play of the Hiss Case. . . .

~

Writing from Moscow, Francis Gary Powers Sends His First Letter to His Parents After Being Shot Down Over the Soviet Union

Hours before his May 1, 1960, mission over the Soviet Union in a U-2 spy plane, Francis Gary Powers dropped a silver dollar in the pocket of his flight suit. It was not for luck; pilots were offered the coins, each containing a pin loaded with lethal toxins, and "exhorted but not ordered" to kill themselves if they were captured and in peril of being tortured. Privately, though, the CIA did not believe there was even a "scintilla" of a chance any pilot would survive if the notoriously flimsy plane were hit with antiaircraft fire. The planes flew at seventy thousand feet, well out of range of Soviet defenses, and in the four years they had been photographing strategically vital civilian and military sites, not a single U-2 had been lost or shot down—until May 1, 1960. Approximately thirteen hundred miles inside the Soviet Union, a surface-to-air missile exploded behind Powers's plane, sending it into a tailspin. Powers parachuted safely onto a field in Sverdlovsk, where he was taken into custody. The timing could not have been worse. In two weeks, President Dwight D. Eisenhower and Soviet Premier Nikita Khrushchev were to meet in Paris for a highly anticipated summit. Relations between the two nations, which had been warming, immediately soured. (The meeting went forward, but Khrushchev stormed out of the negotiations when Eisenhower refused to apologize for the U-2 affair.) Over three weeks after his arrest and imprisonment, Powers was permitted to send his first letter to his parents in Kentucky. (Barbara is his wife.)

Moscow USSR
26 May 1960

Dear Mom & Dad,

I was told that I could write a letter to you and Barbara. I have finished the letter to Barbara and am now writing to you.

I sincerely hope that you both are well. I was very worried about how the news would affect you. Mom please take care of yourself and you can believe me when I say I am being treated much better than I expected to be. I get more than I can eat and plenty of sleep. I have been furnished books to read and I get to walk in the fresh air every day that it doesn't rain. So you see that there is no need for worry.

Dad, you see that mom takes care of herself. Don't let her worry too much, for all the worrying in the world cannot accomplish anything.

I know that you know that I am in a bad situation. I don't know what is going to happen. I do know that the investigation and interrogation are still going on and after they are over there will be a trial. I am being tried for espionage and according to Article 2 of the Criminal Code, which has been read to me, I can be punished by from 7 to 15 years imprisonment or death in some cases. Where I fit in I don't know. That will be for the court to decide.

I maybe should not tell you what the punishment may be but I think you should know the truth.

I am very sorry about all this. I am sorry for all the pain and anxiety I have caused you and am still causing you.

When I first arrived here in Moscow I had no appetite at all. All I could do was think about you and Barbara and all the worry and anxiety I was causing you. Believe me, I am sincerely sorry for all this.

When I had to bail out of my plane I got a few scratches on my right shin and a black eye. Other than that I was in good health. A lady doctor has treated both and now everything is fine.

On May 2nd I was taken on a tour of Moscow. I enjoyed it very much. It is a beautiful city and the people here seem very proud of it.

I have been told that there has been a lot about me and the situation I am in written in the papers. I was also told that an article appeared in one of the papers where you, dad, ask for permission to come to see me. I was told that if the U.S. government gave you such permission that you would be allowed to see me if you came here. I would prefer that you wait until the trial or after when I would be able to tell you the results. I will leave the decision of when to come up to you. I hate for you to go to all the expense to come here even though I would like to see you. I have also written Barbara about this.

Tell all the sisters and their families hello for me and tell them that I am as fine as can be expected.

I know that you worry about me but I don't want you to. I assure you that I am being treated good, and as I said before, much better than I expected.

I guess you have the impression that I had before, that I would be treated badly, but it is not so.

It is dark outside now and I should go to bed. I am anxiously awaiting a letter from you. I do get fairly lonely here even though I spend most of my spare time reading. It is not a loneliness for people but for people I know.

Please take care of yourselves and try not to worry too much. Remember that I love all of you very much and miss you more than I can say.

May God bless all of you and keep you well.

Your Son,
Francis

P.S. My return address is:
Mr. Francis G. Powers
USSR Moscow
Dzerzhinsky Street 2

Powers was sentenced, at the age of thirty-one, to ten years in prison. In February 1962 he was returned to the United States in exchange for the Soviet spy Rudolf Abel.

～⌒

Former President Dwight Eisenhower Tells His Friend Jock Whitney That All Americans Must Be "Unified" Behind President Kennedy After the Bay of Pigs Disaster

"Let every nation know," President John F. Kennedy declared on a frigid January afternoon during his inaugural speech, "that we shall pay any price, bear any burden, meet any hardship, support any friend, oppose any foe to assure the survival and the success of liberty." It was not an idle pledge. Less than three weeks after his election in November 1960, Kennedy began plotting with his advisors how to destroy Fidel Castro's Communist regime in Cuba. (Castro had come into power in early 1959 at the age of thirty-one after overthrowing Fulgencio Batista's government, which even Kennedy perceived as a "brutal, bloody, and despotic dictatorship.") On the morning of April 17, 1961, Brigade 2506—comprised of an estimated fifteen hundred CIA–trained Cuban exiles—went ashore at the Bay of Pigs, hoping to inspire a popular uprising. They hardly made it off the beach. Without the air and

naval support they had been promised by the U.S., virtually all of the invaders were easily overwhelmed by Castro's forces. Many were killed. "I am taking to the swamps," radioed one survivor to his American contact. "I can't wait for you. And you, sir, are a son of a bitch." The assault was a public relations catastrophe for the young American president, and he called on his predecessor, Dwight D. Eisenhower, for advice. The two men met for lunch at Camp David on April 22, and a few days later Eisenhower wrote a personal letter to his old friend John Hay "Jock" Whitney to express his views on the debacle.

April 24, 1961

PERSONAL AND CONFIDENTIAL

Dear Jock:

After talking to you on the phone, I began to fear that I might have expressed myself unclearly or inadequately, and this decided me to write you.

My feeling is that particularly in any period of crisis—and the present is one of strain—the attitude of all Americans must be of a unified front before the world—and this can be achieved only by support of our Constitutional leader. This does not mean blind approval of every diplomatic or operational tactic, but it does place upon each of us such a burden of personal responsibility that any criticism, if voiced, must be clearly on the constructive and helpful, and if possible, on the confidential side.

The foregoing deals, as I said, with basic considerations applying to the citizen's duty. While all of us support the purpose of excluding Communism from our hemisphere, the details of techniques, timing and other deciding factors in the Cuban operation may never be known to all of us until history will make them available. We of course could neither approve nor disapprove of these unless such knowledge should be in our hands.

Since the Administration has already said that a military man is to be called in from the outside to examine into all these things and point up lessons from the experience, I assume that the added intention is to make these findings public, although even on this point I have no assurance. But if the assumption is correct, I see no reason for failing to express an opinion at that time as to the wisdom or unwisdom of any such detail and to editorialize concerning the matter if in your judgement this seems desirable.

You will recall that in the U-2 incident—which in magnitude and in real significance to our nation was not to be compared with what we now know about the action in Cuba—newspaper and political criticism was frequently bitter and persistent. It may be because of the newness of the present Administration that both editors and political leaders are making excuses for lack of experience and therefore exercising some moderation in these respects. <u>Whatever the reason I approve of the moderation</u>.

We cannot now be speaking to the world with many voices. There will be plenty of time when the facts all become known to the public to express personal and institutional convictions on the matter. None of this means that we surrender our wills and our souls to any one individual or to any one idea, but I believe that our own enlightened self-interest compels us to take an attitude that gives the fact and the appearance of strength in unity, not of futility in division. Timing, in such criticisms, could easily become just as important as was the matter of timing in the action under discussion.

When Batista was dictator of Cuba, he was of course a thorn in our sides. While he appeared to be friendly enough to the United States, it had been for many years our policy to try to develop Latin American governments that were responsive to the will of their people rather than agencies of repression. So when Castro started fighting in the hills, we were very much in favor of his success except that we suspected one of two things might happen. The first was that he might take his government, when established, into the Communist camp, and the other—which would have followed the traditional Latin American pattern—to establish himself as just another dictator in that region.

We of course watched developments very carefully and as quickly as Castro succeeded in driving Batista out of the country, we found that he was turning into a vindictive and almost irrational type of man that we would have to watch very closely indeed. Within a short time his selection of assistants who were known Communists and his establishment of close and friendly ties with the Soviets convinced us that we had a real problem on our hands.

It was not long after this that refugees began coming out of Cuba, many of them landing in Florida, others in different countries of the hemisphere. Those remaining in Cuba were helpless under the strong arm methods of Castro and, of course, successful revolution can come from only one source—the people of the country affected. But the refugee bands grew rapidly in numbers and these included many of the natural leaders of the country. It was only natural that they began to plan the overthrow of Castro and their return to their homeland. For a time the different bands and leaders seemed to be pulling in different directions, and it was likely that each leading figure wanted to become the "Big Boss." In the meantime, however, all of them wanted to get the equipment and the training by which they could hope, when the time came, to overthrow the new dictator.

In March, 1960, our government decided to move forward in several ways, the most important of which were propaganda, and training and equipping of volunteer refugees. Locations were selected where the training could go forward. But much time consuming work had to be done by the refugees themselves.

Up to the time that I left the White House, no definite plans had been made, or could have been made, for a future invasion, to say nothing of such details as timing, location, strength and the commander of the invasion forces.

Two other factors helped slow up the development and for this I think the two principal reasons were the lack of early action on the part of the refugees themselves to choose a man who would, in effect, head a government-in-exile, and so energize the whole movement, and the other was the need for keeping the matter as nearly secret as possible. It was clear, of course, that finally all these matters would become known, but under the circumstances that then existed, specific planning was impossible.

All of the above is meant for your eyes only; it may be or may not be helpful. It is one of those things that cannot be completely black or completely white, and we have to deal with it with this truth always in our minds.

Give my love to Betsey and, of course, the best to yourself.

As ever,

D. E.

The repercussions of the Bay of Pigs invasion extended far beyond mere national humiliation. In August 1961 Soviet Premier Nikita Khrushchev brazenly defied the West by constructing a twenty-eight-mile wall around East Berlin to keep its citizens from fleeing to the West. Fourteen months later the Kennedy administration discovered that Soviet nuclear weapons were being installed in Cuba. (Castro had aligned himself with the Soviet Union after the Bay of Pigs and allowed the Soviets to use Cuba as a military base.) Just ninety miles from the U.S., the missiles could kill an estimated eighty million Americans within minutes of being launched. Kennedy ordered a naval blockade of the island and demanded that Khrushchev have the remaining missiles dismantled. After the world held its breath for nearly two excruciating weeks, the Soviets relented. (Khrushchev was appeased by Kennedy's pledge that the United States would not attempt another invasion of Cuba and that it would remove its missiles from Turkey.) In the decade to come, the world's attention would turn to the Southeast Asian country of Vietnam, where the United States would become embroiled in its longest and most divisive war of the twentieth century.

THE VIETNAM WAR,
THE PERSIAN GULF WAR,
SOMALIA, & BOSNIA

Please disregard any small note of flippancy that might reveal itself in this letter. I try to avoid it, but when one is having such a good time it is hard not to be cheerful. I've thrown off the shackles of silly society. I've cast out my razor, divorced my soap, buried my manners, signed my socks to a two-year contract, and proved that you don't have to come in out of the rain. I scale the mountains, swim the rivers, soar through the skies in magic carpet helicopters. My advent is attended by Death and I've got chewing gum stuck in my mustache. I beat the draft.

    —*Lnc. Cpl. Thomas P. Noonan Jr., in Vietnam,*
      to his sister and brother-in-law, October 17, 1968;
      Noonan was killed on February 5, 1969, and posthumously awarded
      the Congressional Medal of Honor

We have seen many tragic cases and marvel at the spirit of these fine young men. They are so grateful for hot food, showers, and a bed to sleep in. Once a week we send our Air-Evac patients home and those fully recovered back to duty. There's always a lump in your throat when they leave, especially for those who must return to duty. Our prayers go with them.

—*Lt. Claire M. Cronin (Nurse Corps, U.S. Navy)*
aboard the hospital ship USS Sanctuary
to her family, December 1967

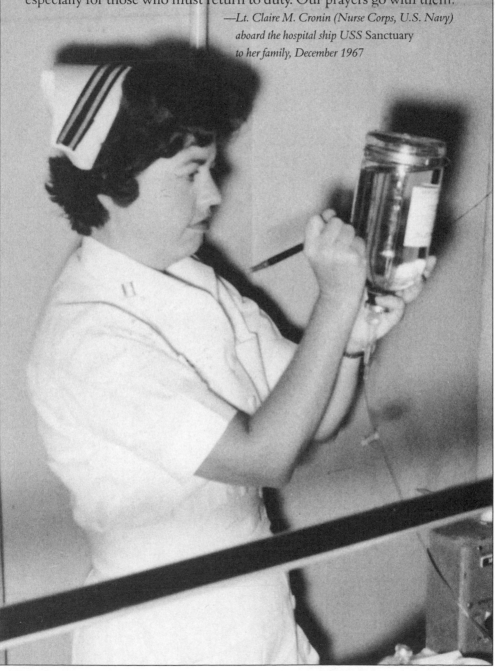

The Sister of an Army Specialist Killed in Vietnam
Asks President John F. Kennedy "If a War Is Worth Fighting—
Isn't It Worth Fighting to <u>Win</u>?"
&
President Kennedy Responds

In early 1919 a twenty-eight-year-old Vietnamese anticolonialist named Nguyen Tat Thanh, dressed in a rented black business suit and bowler hat, walked the corridors of the Palace of Versailles during the World War I peace negotiations and petitioned Allied leaders to end French control over Vietnam. Thanh had been inspired by President Woodrow Wilson's "Fourteen Points," which called for national self-determination, and hoped the American president would be sympathetic to his concerns. But Wilson, like the rest of the Allied leaders, brushed him aside. Thirty years later, the United States found it impossible to ignore Thanh, who had adopted the name Ho Chi Minh (One Who Enlightens) and was leading a nationalist movement against the French in Vietnam. After China and the Soviet Union officially recognized Ho Chi Minh's revolutionaries in 1950, President Truman directed modest military support to French troops in Vietnam. In 1954 the French lost a decisive battle at Dien Bien Phu and conceded to dividing the country almost in half at the Seventeenth Parallel, creating a Communist north and a non-Communist south. President Eisenhower's administration, worried that Ho Chi Minh's forces would overwhelm the entire country, dispatched financial aid and hundreds of military advisers to the south to train the Army of the Republic of Vietnam (ARVN). Like his predecessors, President John F. Kennedy feared a Communist "domino" effect in Southeast Asia and, by the beginning of 1963, he had sent to Vietnam an estimated ten thousand American military personnel to serve only as advisers. Although U.S. fatalities were rare, they did occur, and in January 1963 army specialist James McAndrew became one of the war's earliest casualties. Devastated by her brother's death, Bobbie Lou Pendergrass wrote to President Kennedy to question why Americans were in Vietnam at all.

February 18, 1963

Dear President Kennedy,
My brother, Specialist James Delmas McAndrew, was one of the seven crew members killed on January 11 in a Viet Nam helicopter crash.

The Army reports at first said that communist gunfire was suspected. Later, it said that the helicopter tragedy was due to malfunction of aircraft controls. I've wondered if the "malfunction of aircraft controls" wasn't due to "communist gunfire". However, that's neither important now, nor do I even care to know.

My two older brothers entered the Navy and the Marine Corps in 1941 immediately after the war started. They served all during the war and in some very important battles. Then Jim went into the Marines as soon as he was old enough and was overseas for a long time. During those war years and even all during the Korean conflict we worried about all of them — but that was all very different. They were wars that our <u>country</u> were fighting, and everyone here <u>knew</u> that our sons and brothers were giving their lives for their country.

I can't help but feel that giving one's life for one's country is one thing, but being sent to a country where half <u>our</u> country never even <u>heard</u> of and being shot at without even a chance to shoot back is another thing altogether!

Please, I'm only a housewife who doesn't even claim to know all about the international situation — but we have felt so bitter over this — can the small number of our boys over in Viet Nam possibly be doing enough good to justify the <u>awful</u> number of casualties? It seems to me that if we are going to have our boys over there, that we should send enough to have a <u>chance</u> — or else stay home. Those fellows are just sitting <u>ducks</u> in those darn helicopters. If a war is worth fighting — isn't it worth fighting to <u>win</u>?

Please answer this and help me and my family to reconcile ourselves to our loss and to feel that even though Jim died in Viet Nam — and it isn't our war — it wasn't in vain.

I am a good Democrat — and I'm not criticizing. I think you are doing a wonderful job — and God Bless You —

Very sincerely,
Bobbie Lou Pendergrass

Less than three weeks later, the president replied.

MAR 6 1963

Dear Mrs. Pendergrass,

I would like to express to you my deep and sincere sympathy in the loss of your brother. I can, of course, well understand your bereavement and the feelings which prompted you to write.

The questions which you posed in your letter can, I believe, best be answered by realizing why your brother — and other American men —

went to Viet Nam in the first place. When this is understood, I am sure that the other related questions will be answered.

Americans are in Viet Nam because we have determined that this country must not fall under Communist domination. Ever since Viet Nam was divided, the Viet Namese have fought valiantly to maintain their independence in the face of the continuing threat from the North. Shortly after the division eight years ago it became apparent that they could not be successful in their defense without extensive assistance from other nations of the Free World community.

In the late summer of 1955, with the approval of President Eisenhower, an Advisory Group was established in Viet Nam to provide them with adequate weapons and equipment and training in basic military skills which are essential to survival in the battlefield. Even with this help, the situation grew steadily worse under the pressure of the Viet Cong. By 1961 it became apparent that the troubles in Laos and the troubles in Viet Nam could easily expand. It is also apparent that the Communist attempt to take over Viet Nam, is only part of a larger plan for bringing the entire area of Southeast Asia under their domination. Though it is only a small part of the area geographically, Viet Nam is now the most crucial.

If Viet Nam should fall, it will indicate to the people of Southeast Asia that complete Communist domination of their part of the world is almost inevitable. Your brother was in Viet Nam because the threat to the Viet Namese people is, in the long run, a threat to the Free World community, and ultimately a threat to us also. For when freedom is destroyed in one country, it is threatened throughout the world.

I have written to you at length because I know that it is important to you to understand why we are in Viet Nam. James McAndrews must have foreseen that his service could take him into a war like this; a war in which he took part not as a combatant but as an advisor. I am sure that he understood the necessity of such a situation, and I know that as a soldier, he knew full scale war in Viet Nam is at the moment unthinkable.

I believe if you can see this as he must have seen it, you will believe as he must have believed, that he did not die in vain. Forty-five American soldiers, including your brother, have given their lives in Viet Nam. In their sacrifice, they have earned the eternal gratitude of this Nation and other free men throughout the world.

Again, I would like to express to you and the members of your family my deepest personal sympathy.

Sincerely,
John F. Kennedy

In the first draft of his letter, which was sterner and more official in tone, Kennedy wrote: "Why did [your brother] have to prove his belief in a war which is not our own? That I can answer with certainty. We must continue to express our belief that every man has the God-given right to freedom, and we must continue to help those whom we can. We must not, however, spend our strength recklessly in danger of provoking a world conflict which could destroy our friends, our enemies, and ourselves." Five days after President Kennedy was assassinated on November 22, 1963, his successor, Lyndon B. Johnson, stood before the United States Congress and declared that "there can be no losers in peace and no victors in war." Within a year, Johnson increased America's military presence in Vietnam by almost fifty percent.

~~

Lt. Roy Boehm, "Father" of the U.S. Navy SEALs, Wishes His Mom a Happy Valentine's Day from Vietnam— the "Damndest Craziest War" Ever

"You can get yourselves another wife and have more kids," Lt. Roy Boehm repeatedly told his men, "but you can never get another Team." Unapologetically blunt, profane, and hotheaded, Boehm volunteered for the navy in April 1941 and, as one of his first assignments, dove into the waters of Pearl Harbor to recover munitions and corpses from the USS Arizona. He survived the sinking of the USS Duncan during the Battle of Cape Esperance in October 1942 and went on to serve in Korea and, covertly, in Cuba during the cold war. In 1961 Boehm was selected to develop, select, and train an elite, special operations commando group that could "go any place, any time, any where to do any thing." Within a year it evolved into the U.S. Navy SEALs (for SEa, Air, and Land), and under Boehm's leadership it would become one of the most effective and lethal fighting forces in the world. Boehm was sent to South Vietnam in November 1963 to advise troops battling the Communist Viet Cong, nicknamed "Charlie," trying to conquer the south from within. (Ho Chi Minh's troops in the north were referred to by servicemen as both the People's Army of Vietnam [PAVN] and the North Vietnamese Army [NVA].) Over three months later, the forty-year-old Boehm sent a handwritten letter to his mother explaining what he and his men were up against. (Polly was his wife; John was his stepfather; Roy, Katy, and Bob were his children; Weege was his aunt; and Tom was his cousin.)

14 Feb 1964

Dear Mom:

Hello Sweet heart, no Valentines card for Mothers Sons Daughters or Sweet hearts to be found. I did find one for Polly. This and also your beloved Dad's Birthday I know has made you go back over the years. Well Sweet heart I am busy losing the war in Vietnam My frogmen, although not to my satisfaction upon my arrival and some what lacking here, improved by leaps and bounds, and are completely loyal and devoted to me if not the cause. I have repeatedly been in action since my arrival and my status has improved from the $50 reward on my head by the Viet Cong to $450,000. I am now on the same level as the Junk Force — if given the equipment we need the price should half itself again.

The Viet Cong are either sniping at us or bombing us A Captain Copeland that lives here in Vung Tau was killed in the bombing of the theater in Saigon along with four or five others. 25 dependents including children pretty much maimed Honest this is the damndest craziyest war I ever fought A farmer lays down his tools picks up a gun shoots at you and when you chase him he stick his gun in a hole pick up his tools and claims imunity because he is only a poor farmer but I guess thats the name of the game.

To-night is the 18th as in the middle of your letter I had to leave, this is also my Christmas as Pollys package just arrived and my check which I sent off to Polly so we can pay you back and thank you ever so much I have three pictures of my son and one of my Polly in front of me the pictures make me long to be with them.

Well old gal hear your knees are going. I sure hope you and John have weathered the storm as for me I came limping in with that right knee that had Polly waiting on me hand and foot I kind of busted it up again jumping into a rice paddy of all places had to come in a little hard to miss some anti personell stakes the V. C. put in. and as I limped in my counterpart was loading he said Ah Mr Boehm the team is yours

I leave an operation and thats the way it has been so against all regulations I find myself in command of my loyal little group as we only have one Vietnamese officer and beloved friend Mr Ninh. Well Sweet heart I owe my God child a letter little Tom and Weege not to mention Roy Katy & Bob and of course Polly Baby so I'll sign off wishing you good health. and please don't fear for me as my frogmen are devoted to me as I to them and protect me as if I were something sacred although they continuously steal my ciggaretts and think that they are fair game. I wonder why I always wind up with rogues, Highwaymen, and rascals.

> Good health and I'll add peace of mind to you and John
> your loving son
> Roy

Boehm returned from Vietnam in October 1964 and retired from the navy, after thirty years of service, in 1971. He has not, however, lost his sense of adventure; Boehm regularly drives race cars, pilots a private plane, and has learned aerobatic flying. At the age of seventy-six he began ultralight parachuting—but, he admits, it was partly to spite his wife, Susan, who had taken away his motorcycle.

~

Cpl. Mike Jeffords Offers His Parents His First Impressions of Vietnam and Describes the Experience as "Something of a Vacation"

On August 2, 1964, North Vietnamese boats in the Tonkin Gulf purportedly fired without provocation on the destroyer USS Maddox, *and, soon after, on the USS* Turner. *(Later investigations would cast serious doubts on these reports.) With assurances from President Johnson that he had no intention of dramatically escalating U.S. involvement in Vietnam, Congress almost unanimously passed the Tonkin Gulf Resolution. It was a functional—but not formal—declaration of war, and it authorized President Johnson to "take all necessary measures" to assist South Vietnam. In March 1965 the marines landed at Da Nang, representing the first official U.S. combat presence on the ground in South Vietnam. (A mammoth air campaign, "Operation Rolling Thunder," had already begun.) Twenty-two-year-old Cpl. Mike Jeffords, who had enlisted in the marines three years earlier, came in with the initial wave on March 8. Jeffords wrote to his parents back in Milwaukee, Wisconsin, to let them know he had arrived safely.*

Dear Folks,

I'm writing this on top of a c-ration box so if it's difficult to read you'll know why. The Air Force is making a hell of a racket outside and me trying to write. They are not very considerate. Neither is the weatherman—it must be 90° outside. My shelter-halve is ten degrees hotter. You are either soaking wet from rain or broiling in the sun. I'm laying on my bullet-proof vest and wondering how to break the news to you. I wrote a note on the way down here that explains a lot of the way I feel but it comes out morbid when I read it. Anyway, if you haven't thought of it seeing the newspapers and television my battalion was moved some. I'm at Da Nang Airfield in South Vietnam. Ha! It makes me laugh. Everything I told you wouldn't happen—has happened. It makes me look like a liar.

Funny, I used to watch movies, see television and read books about combat in war zones and get excited. The funny part is I'm not excited but calm—even bored from the heat! It isn't anything like I thought it would be. The excitement just isn't there.

One thing I've found is that all the days, months, and years that went before the last two days seem like a dream—unreal. Here, my senses of sound, sight, and touch have sharpened. And my awareness of reality. Every second—every minute I breathe I'm very aware of it. I'm enjoying life like I had never lived before. Maybe it is the purpose—feeling that you're doing something besides marking time. Doing what you've trained for. I wouldn't want to be anywhere else.

I just read over what I wrote and I'm afraid you'll get the impression that we're engaged in combat. We're only guarding the airfield against a Viet Cong attack. There haven't been any I've seen or anybody else yet. We expect it and we're ready but there isn't any trouble from them.

I'm telling you the facts so you don't get all excited over everything you read in the papers.

We aren't doing much here. Just watching and waiting.

We took off in such a hurry when Johnson ordered us in that I didn't have time to pick up my pay record at disbursing. I was going to Vietnamese language school when the mount out order came in. I was about twenty-five miles from my home base. I only had a certain time to make it back or they would have left without me. So, I left and didn't have time (actually I forgot to in the excitement) and it will be a while before I'm paid. Until the record catches up. So, until it catches up with me here in Vietnam the allotment will be late. I only hope you aren't counting on it too much.

Hey, how about telling Pat to change frequencies when she goes to church. Somebody's got their wires crossed. For eight months she's been praying I didn't go to Vietnam. Wha' Hoppen??? It must have been me praying I did.

I can't tell you how much peace of mind I've had since I've been here. The games are over. We know just what's expected of us.

I've been rambling on and on. Listen, this operation isn't any worse than Lebanon in 1958 or Cuba in 1962. If you remember nothing happened in either of those places. Don't you think if there was any <u>real</u> immediate danger I would never sound as good and high-spirited as I do. I'd be scared to death and crying to go home. Right? So don't worry. I'm having something of a vacation. Don't sweat it.

Let me know how the family is. Remember, I'm as happy as a lark. Keep me informed about Tim. I like to hear how he's doing.

I have to get this done. They only pick up mail once a day. At night we can't move around too much and I want to make <u>one</u> trip. There and back. I'm too <u>lazy</u> to make more than one, that's why.

See you soon—
Sincerely,
Mike

P. S. I never felt better. DON'T WORRY!!

A week later, Jeffords again described to his parents the relative tranquillity of his surroundings, especially in the evening: "At night it cools down to about 60° until midnight. Then a ground fog about knee-high moves over the deck. It's eerie as hell. Much like a graveyard or a spooky picture—it's that quiet. Not even a bird chirp." In the morning the only "invaders" Jeffords had to contend with were stealthy but not life-threatening:

> [W]hen you wake up you shake out your mosquito net, blanket poncho, and pack and watch the menagerie take off. First, a cloud about six feet high of mosquitos takes off, then the frogs hop out to get them, the lizards crawl away to find a cooler spot before the sun comes up, one or two mice vamoose, the snakes head for their holes, the chiggers come out of your skin when you fry them with a cigarette, and finally you knock a 1 inch spider off your rifle who has been indifferent enough to build a web between it and your tent pole. All this happens at different times. They don't all appear at once. The variety keeps you guessing. The mosquitos get high on the repellant we put on.

Jeffords ended the letter by assuring his family, once again, all was well: "I feel good and healthy and alive most of the time. Don't sweat it!" After two months of combat, Jeffords was less sanguine, but still committed to being in Vietnam. "We've been engaged in combat action (company size patrols) against the Viet Cong," he wrote in May 1965:

> [T]he squad, (8 men), I was leading was ambushed in the jungle from a distance of 15–20 feet away by two VC with carbines. One second we were stumbling along in the stifling heat; the next second a round came very, very close to me again. I know because I heard it and literally felt the "breeze." When I turned to fire I saw a kid I had trained go down in a heap. . . . What has been happening and will happen in the future is better left forgotten. What I've almost done, will have to do, or have already done is better forgotten, too. . . . I'm no war-lover—I don't enjoy this. But it has to be done.

Cpl. Mike Jeffords survived the war and was honorably discharged in March 1966.

~❧~

In a Private Letter to Lt. Col. Lewis L. Millet,
Gen. William C. Westmoreland Articulates the Difficulties
American Forces Are Up Against

"The situation is unbelievably complex and the challenge is beyond dimension," Gen. William C. Westmoreland wrote to a colleague on July 23, 1964, one month

after Westmoreland was named by President Lyndon Johnson to command all American forces in Vietnam. "This is not an easy task and will involve blood, sweat, tears, and many years," the general concluded. A highly decorated veteran of World War II and Korea, Westmoreland believed Vietnam would be a "war of attrition"—a conflict that would not be won by seizing territory and holding clear boundaries, but by slowly and systematically rooting out and killing enemy forces. Faced, however, with a seemingly invisible and ubiquitous foe, Westmoreland acknowledged that his objective was a daunting one in a letter to his friend Lt. Col. Lewis L. Millett, commander of the U.S. Army Security Agency Training Regiment.

July 15, 1965

Dear Lewis:

It is a pleasure to forward the enclosed autographed picture for use in connection with your training program.

As you can appreciate, our Army is faced with a tremendous challenge here in Vietnam. Initially our soldiers were committed strictly in an advisory role, and as such the number required was relatively small. But now it has become necessary to commit more and more US troops to actual combat. It is necessary therefore that our training programs in the United States be oriented toward the type of fighting we are involved in today in this country.

Here we have an enemy who operates covertly. The battlefield is everywhere — no front to it nor rear. The enemy is here today and gone tomorrow. He moves at night, concentrates, attacks, and then he disappears into the wilderness of a jungle or into the landscape when reaction forces are brought to bear.

The basic squad tactics we have taught our soldiers over the years are still applicable here in Vietnam. But in addition, we must stress the importance of knowing how to search and destroy in difficult terrain and how to counter ambushes and other tactics used by guerilla insurgents.

The importance of training programs such as yours cannot be overemphasized. I am confident that your work will add significantly to the Army's effort in Vietnam as your trainees begin to join their comrades over here. I look forward to their joining us in the fight against this cunning and persistent enemy.

Best wishes.
Sincerely,
W. C. Westmoreland
General, United States Army
Commanding

That same month President Johnson sent an additional 50,000 troops to Vietnam. By the end of the year, the number had surged to 185,000. The vast majority of Americans supported Johnson's policies in Vietnam, but impassioned voices of dissent were becoming more audible. On November 30, 1965, thirty-two-year-old Norman Morrison, a father of three children, doused himself with gasoline in front of the Pentagon and set himself on fire. Over a week later another young man, Roger Allen LaPorte, immolated himself outside of the United Nations. Morrison and LaPorte were the first, but not the last, protesters to die over the war in Vietnam.

~~

Airman 3/C Robert Zwerlein Sends a High-Spirited Letter to a Friend Back in the States Only Days Before the Fatal USS *Forrestal* Fire

Just after 11:00 A.M. on July 29, 1967, a sudden electrical charge launched a six-foot Zuni missile from a stationary fighter jet on the deck of the USS Forrestal. The missile struck the fuel tank of a nearby plane and exploded (the plane's thirty-one-year-old pilot, John McCain, miraculously survived the blast), setting off a chain reaction across the flight deck. Bombs weighing a thousand pounds detonated. Chunks of flying metal ripped enormous holes in the carrier's sides as burning fuel consumed men frantically trying to extinguish the spreading flames. Four days before the fire, twenty-one-year-old Airman 3/C Robert Zwerlein—who happened to be John McCain's plane captain—wrote to an old friend from Port Washington, New York, to say that, despite whatever grumblings she might be hearing on the homefront, morale was still high. (The last page of the letter is missing.)

July 25

Hi Sue,

This letter comes to you <u>LIVE</u> from Yankee Station, Gulf of Tonkin. Today we finally started flying missions against North Viet Nam and in about an hour we'll stop flying for 12 hours. So far we've lost no aircraft or even had one damaged. But, this is just the first day. Two pilots from my squadron were the first to drop bombs on N.V.N. from this carrier and they blew up a bridge. Beginners luck I guess! My "bird" didn't fly at all today though, as they were installing a camera in it. I hope it goes up tomorrow. If you want I'll dedicate a bomb to you and Terri. You should see some of the things the guys write on the bombs. Its really funny. Here's a few that I can think of. FROM THE V.C. FOR LUNCH BUNCH; NO DEPOSIT NO RETURN; IF YOU CAN READ ENGLISH CHARLIE HAHA!!; ITS WHATS UP FRONT THAT COUNTS;

MAKE WAR, NOT LOVE; CHARLIE KILLER; MERRY CHRISTMAS HO; TO HO WITH LOVE; DO NOT DROP ON THE FLIGHT DECK; then there are always a few with, THIS ONE'S FOR MOM or FROM SIS; of course there are a few I can't print.

I got all my mail in the Philippines but I can't answer your letters because I can't find them. I've got so much mail my lockers getting crowded. Right now I'm working on 12 hour shifts so I'll be able to write more than I thought I would. Guess what, I came within a few miles of Bill MacCarthy's ship yesterday. I also saw Viet Nam yesterday and could see two shell bursts along the shore. Wasn't anywhere near us though but that suits me fine. Just think, the next time I touch land it will be almost September and our schedual says we start for home January fifth '68. That's not too long. I finally wrote to Hank last nite. It wasn't long but at least it was something.

Ya know Sue, the night before we pulled out of the Philippines to leave for Yankee Station some guys and I went to the club for a couple (80 or 90) drinks. Well, as you probably know there are guys from all over the USA and as it always happens the band would play DIXIE and all the guys from the south would start singing and yelling and cursing the Yankees from the north and the same thing would happen when the band would play Yankee Doodle only we got up. But as soon as that band started to play God Bless America, everyone, no matter where they were from, just stood up and started to sing. It was really great. It made me feel real good. I wish the people back home could have seen it.

I imagine a lot of them would just say it was a bunch of drunken sailors that didn't even know what they were singing. But it wasn't that at all. It was a bunch of guys that are proud of their country and will fight and die if necessary for it. That's a lot more than I can say for some people in our country. Now, it may seem like I copied this out of books or something but I didn't and its just as it really happened and that's how I feel. That's probably how your brother feels too.

Did you know that your little brother has been writing to me, keeping me up to date on the Rangers. He's sent me about five little letters, one was even typed. Have you been home lately? Would you believe my little, six foot three inch, brother is starting to drive! He'll be almost old enough for me to get him loaded when I get back. Have you ever

One hundred and thirty-four young men were killed in the Forrestal *fire, including Robert Zwerlein. After being engulfed in the blaze, Zwerlein was transferred to the hospital ship* Repose *with burns on over 80 percent of his body. He died on August 1, 1967.*

～〇

Pvt. Brice E. Gross Offers His Younger Brother, Jerry, Words of Advice and Encouragement After the Death of Their Father
&
In a Letter to His Wife, Joyce, 1st Lt. Dean Allen Reflects on the Physical and Emotional Challenges of Leading a Platoon

By the end of 1967 the number of American troops in Vietnam was nearing the five hundred thousand mark, a 5,000 percent increase since late 1962. Approximately 3 million sons, husbands, brothers, and fathers would ultimately pack up and head out for Southeast Asia throughout the course of the war. (An estimated 10,000 women served in Vietnam as well, primarily as army, navy, and air force nurses.) For twenty-year-old Brice E. Gross, a private with the U.S. Army, saying goodbye was especially difficult because his father had died from a heart attack months before he was shipped overseas, leaving his thirteen-year-old brother Jerry to be—in Gross's words—"the man of the house." Just over halfway through his tour of duty, Gross (who would return home alive) wrote to his brother back in Fresno, California.

Hello Jerry, how is my "big" little brother? I trust you're doing good and keeping yourself out of trouble. I figured I'd write you a special letter because if I was home, we would have had some serious brother-to-brother talks, but I guess a letter will have to do.

Well, to get down to business, I've been doing a lot of thinking and wondering about how things are going back at home. You well know by now that you're taking Dad's and my place in the family now that I can't be there and for such a young man you've got quite a load to bear. I may just be repeating what other folks have told you, but I believe you'll understand it as my duty. You're going to have to sacrifice a little to keep things going smoothly around the house now. All the things that our Dad or me or all of us did before, are now your responsibility. It's quite a task to undertake, but I'm confident you can do it. Now that you're out of school for the summer and ready to be off, you'll have to curb your wandering spirit a little for the sake of your Mother. Before you do something, consider carefully the consequences of your actions. I know it's a lot to ask, but you're going to have to spend an equal amount of time at home with Mom as you do out on your own. Remember, you're filling Dad's shoes, and he was the best husband any woman ever had. Mom and Dad have devoted the last 25 years of their lives to raising us kids, and now our time has come to repay them for at least some of their love and care.

You know well now that you are by no means a "kid" any longer even though you are still young. Try your best to keep yourself straight and be especially kind to Mom, because for a while you're going to be her only son. Treat her to a movie now & then, buy her a flower or some candy, use your imagination and think of your own special ways to make her day a little brighter. <u>Remember</u>—she's the only Mother we've got, so take good care of her.

You can see that I worry a bit about you & mom, but I have a lot of trust in you Jerry. Not many people are lucky enough to have a brother like you. And once in a while, take time out for yourself and maybe ride out somewhere alone on your bike & think things over & consider that even though we've lost a lot, we still have a great deal to be thankful and happy for.

Before I left for Vietnam, Dad said something to me and these were the last words I ever heard from him. He said, "Be a Man." You and I both know what that means, and I want to repeat the same admonition to you. If ever you are in doubt, think of your Dad and those words and you can't go wrong.

> Bye Jerry & be good.
> Your Brother
> Brice

Young couples separated by the war also turned to letters to share words of support, love, and reassurance during their time apart. Dean Allen, who had been married for only two years, was ordered to Vietnam after attending officers' training school. Although externally he seemed like an imposing, no-nonsense leader, First Lieutenant Allen was, in fact, a compassionate, thoughtful twenty-seven-year-old who had a genuine concern for the men in his platoon. In the following letter to his wife, Joyce, in Pompano Beach, Florida, he confided in her the feelings and insecurities he could not express to anyone else.

July 10

Dearest Wife,

There are many times while I am out in the field that I really feel the need to talk to you. Not so much about us but what I have on my mind. I can tell you that I love you and how much I miss you in a letter & I know you will receive it and know what I mean, because you have the same feelings.

But many times like tonight — I am out on ambush with eleven men & a medic — after everything is set up and in position I have nothing to do but lay there and think — why I am here as well as all the men in my platoon — age makes no difference — there are very few kids over here

— a few yes but they grow up fast or get killed. Why I have to watch a man die or get wounded — why I have to be the one to tell some one to do something that may get him blown away — have I done everything I can do to make sure we can't get hit by surprise — are we really covered from all directions — how many men should I let sleep at a time, 1/4, 50% or what. I know I want at least 50% awake and yet those are the same men who have to hump through the jungle the next day carrying fifty to seventy five pounds on their back and still be alert and quick if they run into Charles the next day. If I have four or five man positions, and only have one man awake per position they like me because they get some sleep. If I have them in two man positions and have one man awake they bitch and moan & aren't worth a damn the next day. If I don't we may all get our shit blown away — excuse the language but that's what they call it over here.

Babes, I don't know what the answer is. Being a good platoon leader is a lonely job. I don't want to really get to know anybody over here because it would be bad enough to lose a man — I damn sure don't want to lose a friend. I haven't even had one of my men wounded yet let alone killed but that is to much to even hope for to go like that. But as hard as I try not to get involved with my men I still can't help liking them and getting close to a few. I get to know their wives name or their girls and kids if they have any. They come up and say "hey 26 (they call me 26 because that is my call sign on the radio) do you want to see picture of my wife/girl" or "look at what my wife or girl wrote." Like I said it gets lonely trying to stay seperate.

Some letter, huh! I don't know if I have one sentence in the whole thing. I just started writing.

July 11

It got so dark I had to stop last night it got to dark and rained for twelve hours straight. Writing like that doesn't really do that much good because you aren't here to answer me or discuss something. I guess it helps a little though because you are the only one I would say these things to. Maybe sometime I'll even try to tell you how scared I have been or am now. There is nothing I can do about it but wait for another day to start & finish. If I had prayed before or was religious enough to feel like I should — or had the right to pray now I probably would say one every night that I will see the sun again the next morning & will get back home to you. Sometimes I really wonder how I will make it. My luck is running way to good right now. I just hope it lasts.

I have already written things I had never planned to write because I don't want you to worry about me anyway. Don't worry about what I

Don't worry about what I have said these are just things I think about sometimes. I am so healthy I can't get a day out of the field and you know I'm to damn mean to die. Hon I better close for now & try to catch a few z's. It will be another long night

Sorry I haven't written more but the weather is against me. You can't write out here when it rains hour after hour. I love you with all my heart

All my love always
Dean

have said these are just things I think about sometimes. I am so healthy I can't get a day out of the field and you know I'm to damn mean to die. Hon, I better close for now & try to catch a few z's. It will be another long night.

Sorry I haven't written more but the weather is against me. You can't write out here when it rains hour after hour. I love you with all my heart.

All my love always
Dean

Soon after receiving Dean's letter, a telegram arrived from the war department. Joyce Allen could barely get past the first sentence.

The Secretary of the Army has asked me to express his deep regret that your son, Lieutenant Dean D. Allen was wounded in action . . . He received multiple wounds to the brain, the left eye, the face, the chest, the abdomen, both arms and both legs. He has lost his left eye and is in a deep coma. He has been placed on the very seriously ill list and in the judgement of the attending physician his condition is of such severity that there is cause for concern. . . .

Clearly, Joyce thought, there had been a mistake. Dean was her husband, not her son, and his middle initial was "B," not "D." But despite the errors in the message, it was, in fact, her Dean who had been fatally wounded. Four days after writing to Joyce, Dean stepped on a land mine while on a search-and-destroy mission. As he was being evacuated, a second mine exploded. 1st Lt. Dean Allen, a recipient of the Bronze Star, Air Medal, and Purple Heart, died three days later.

~⌒

**Chaplain Ray W. Stubbe Writes to His Parents
from the Marine Base at Khe Sanh on the First Day of What Was
to Become a Lengthy and Terrifying Siege
&
Lt. Col. Gerald W. Massy III Offers His Daughter Lynn a Firsthand
Report of the Tet Offensive as It Unfolds All Around Him**

By late fall of 1967 hundreds of flag-draped coffins containing the bodies of dead Americans were returning to the United States each month for burial. An estimated fifteen thousand soldiers had been killed since the beginning of the war. Violent clashes were erupting between antiwar and prowar demonstrators on college campuses, city streets, and even the grounds of the Pentagon. Led by students and civil rights activists, the peace movement was gaining momentum. President Johnson and his military advisors were adamant that America was winning the war in South Vietnam

and bringing stability and security to the region. But that assessment would be shat-
tered abruptly after the new year. On January 21, 1968, Communist forces—which,
according to President Johnson, were on the verge of collapse—blitzed the heavily for-
tified marine base at Khe Sanh and, nine days later, launched massive, coordinated
attacks throughout the South. Twenty-nine-year-old Lt. Ray W. Stubbe, a chaplain
with the navy reserves, was one of six thousand troops pinned down by the North
Vietnamese at Khe Sanh. Stubbe knew his parents in Milwaukee, Wisconsin, would
soon learn of the assault, and on January 21 he sent the following:

Dear Folks:

First, I'm OK, not even a scratch. The casualties have been comparatively small. So don't worry.

I wrote my last entry in my log beginning Dec. 1st. Since our post office
was hit this morning, I gave it to one of the pilots of one of the planes to
mail via registered mail. I don't know if it will ever get home, but there's
a lot in it; it's very important to me. So I hope it gets home. Please write me
if it does. It's a green record book diary, covering the period 1 Dec. to today,
plus a lot of personal papers.

We are, as you probably hear on the news, under attack. It's the scariest
thing I've ever had to face. I awoke at 5 o'clock to the sound of incoming
rockets and mortars exploding just outside my hooch! They hit our
ammunition dump, and rounds of ammunition were flying all day long.
Practically half the base is in ruins, but the casualties were very few
because everyone got in bunkers. The only casualties were from the lines
on the perimeter of the base from Hill 861. I am writing this as the sun is
setting today. I don't know if you will ever receive this, but I must write it
anyway.

The base is quite safe. The airstrip wasn't harmed, and planes keep coming and going. We still have our artillery for counter-mortar attacks. My
hooch's well-built, sturdy. We have a lot supporting us. So don't worry.

I feel I'm needed here. I give my every waking moment for these
men. They are basically good men, but not particularly religious as such,
although I'm quite sure many prayed today! Yet I love them all, and give
my daily life for them, and I do it not for personal satisfaction or companionship or a sense of personal accomplishment, but because I feel this
is God's will.

You of course know my love for you both and grandad and all — Peg
and Jeane, Jackie, Henry — everyone, but especially you and grandma. I
have not always been a good son and I know I've caused you grief at times,
unsureness and anxiety at other times. But I've always loved all of you very
deeply.

Well, there's really not too much more to say in this situation — I've recorded all the details of everything in my log.

Love,
Ray

Unbeknownst to Stubbe, the 21st marked the beginning of an eleven-week seige that would leave hundreds of Americans dead and 1,500 to 2,500 wounded. Haunted by the specter of the French defeat at Dien Bien Phu in 1954, President Johnson ordered that Khe Sanh be held at all costs. Tens of thousands of American and South Vietnamese troops were rushed to the marine outpost, and the North Vietnamese were repelled in early April. (Ironically, the base was closed only months later.) After being safely transferred from the base in March, Stubbe described the experience in a letter to his parents:

So many things happened at Khe Sanh — it's good I didn't write earlier — practically anything I might write would either sicken or scare you. But that's all past now. I must say the good Lord was very merciful and gracious. I didn't even receive a cut or bruise. But there for a while I was having very close calls every day. One noon, while eating brunch in my hooch, an incoming round went into my wall — through four feet of dirt, 3 feet of sandbags, and bent my steel walls held up by u-shaped engineering stakes — it was a dud!

One evening at midnight, a rocket round — 100 pounds — exploded just 2 feet from my hooch entrance. One day I was walking through an excavated trench about 10 feet deep, a mortar round exploded on the top edge, just above. . . .

Things were very ghastly. I stayed one night at a hooch on the perimeter. It was a bunker for the men manning a 106 gun. One afternoon they took two incoming rounds — only one lived; all the rest were killed. One man's head was never found — pieces of finger, hand, flesh, blood, all over. One man came into our medical area. He'll lose both legs, his right arm, and be blind. Our medical area took quite a few hits, but fortunately no one there was hurt.

The slogans the men have on their helmets and flak jackets changed from "KILL, KILL, KILL" and "In many a strife we've lost our life and never lost our nerve," etc. to "mom and dad forever," and "you and me, God," and "Please, Mr. Cong, I don't want to die," and crosses.

Many times our water supply would get shot up and we'd go several days without water.

There was always fear of incoming — it might come in anywhere; it might land anywhere. No place, no bunker, was absolutely safe. . . .

The initial attack on Khe Sanh was only a preamble to the most sweeping Communist offensive of the war. On the eve of Tet, the Vietnamese lunar new year observed at the end of January, Viet Cong and North Vietnamese soldiers swarmed out of the jungles and struck airfields, military installations, and over a hundred towns and provincial capitals throughout the South. American and South Vietnamese troops—many of whom were on furlough to celebrate the holiday—were caught entirely off guard. In a move more symbolic than tactically significant, Viet Cong commandos infiltrated the courtyard of the American Embassy in Saigon and blasted a hole through an embassy wall. Hue, the ancient imperial capital, was entirely overrun. The liberation of the city would take weeks and was one of the bloodiest battles of the war. Fifty-two-year-old Lt. Col. Gerald W. Massy III, a reconnaissance pilot with the "Antique Airlines" (the name a group of older U.S. airmen flying in Vietnam had affectionately chosen for themselves), wrote frequently to his eighteen-year-old daughter Lynn about his service. During the Tet Offensive, Massy provided Lynn with an eyewitness account of the firestorm raging outside his base.

2 Feb 68

Dear Lynn,

I have just sent a message to Mama through MARS, the only fairly rapid means available to me now, that I am okay and I assume she'll phone you. I know that you are all worried and I'm sorry that you must suffer such anxiety, but you understand, of course, that I am only one of a half million American troops, plus many State, AID and other American personnel, who are caught here in this all-out attack by the Viet Cong and the North Vietnamese—all supported by Russian and Red Chinese arms, of course. We all have anxious families and are all in the same boat—we cannot get word home yet. But MARS told me that the message, which is a standard message and I cannot personalize it, will reach Mama in one to thirty-six hours. It's the best I can do, though I have written to Mama since the attack began. Heaven knows when she will get the letters. No mail has entered or departed here since the attack and that's understandable, since conditions are such that other, more urgent cargo must now be handled by the greatly reduced airlift capacity now available to us.

I am now on Tan Son Nhut, living in an unfinished barracks, with no screens, windows, doors, sills, or lights, except emergency lighting in the halls. And there is no operational latrine. I am sleeping on a mattress without bedding, on the floor and there is no furniture. I have devised a table from a door (not yet installed) laid across two high saw horses and am seated on a small step ladder and that is where I am typing now. We were evacuated from our off-base BOQ late yesterday, after 36 hours of small arms fire near by, often within a block. We had no phones and no weapons at first, but managed to get some M-16 rifles and pistols late Wednesday, so that Wednesday night we could mount an additional guard to supplement the Chinese Nung guards who are hired by the Air Force to guard our quarters.

Last night, after we arrived on base, the enemy attacked the base again from all directions and there was much gunfire. I spent much of the night at my open window, pistol drawn, expecting an attack on these and nearby barracks, for gunfire within a block of us erupted frequently and our Army and Air Force security guards, in flak vests, helmets and full battle gear, were moving about in darkened vehicles, or on foot, crouching and darting from cover to cover, looking for the enemy. Flares filled the sky and helicopter gun ships roared around at rooftop level. Now and then a furious gun battle would erupt, then subside, with only occasional, sporadic light arms fire to punctuate the silent darkness.

The enemy has apparently launched a massive, all-or-nothing assault on all our major installations throughout South Vietnam, timed to coincide with the Vietnamese New Year, called TET. He has achieved some initial successes, but is now being driven back with huge losses and I think the critical danger has passed. There is still danger, though, and we have seen a remarkable demonstration of what the enemy can do. Hue Phu Bai, where I was recently stationed for a couple of weeks, may have been overwhelmed. I am not sure at this moment, but I do know that all the troops of my outfit there were successfully evacuated to Danang and subsequently to Nha Trang.

I am finding it a bit difficult to type, for I burned myself with hot grease quite severely on the head, right hand, right arm, and right leg just hours before this attack began. If I must use my pistol, it will have to be in my left hand and I have been practicing holding and aiming it that way, steadied by my bandaged right hand. The burns are bad and painful, but not crucial and I'll be back flying in two or three weeks.

Your letter expressing concern about the latest development in Korea reached me a couple of days before the attack and I understand your feelings, while at the same time I am glad to hear you express faith in your country. You ask for my opinion for guidance and I am glad to give it. I want first to point out that American history is filled with dark moments when the odds were great and we have never failed to meet each challenge. The present situation is no more urgent, or filled with danger, than was the attack on Pearl Harbor, nor is this moment in history any blacker for us than it was at Valley Forge, or Gettysburg, or Bataan, or the Alamo.

There is one big difference now, and this is the area of our greatest concern: In those days Americans were not so adept at wringing their hands despairingly as seems to be the case with many of our countrymen now, young and old. If fears were felt in years gone by—and you can bet they were—people had less trouble concealing them because it was the unpopular thing to show fear, or conversely, not to appear brave and resolute. Today, in some circles, it appears to be the thing to do to reject our previous ideas about the virtue of personal courage. In my judgement, these people are more dangerous as enemies of our country and our liberty than the Nazis or Communists ever were.

Our national anthem has a line which is appropriate to quote here: "The land of the free and the home of the brave." The two go hand in glove. If we are not brave, we soon will not be free. No nation, or person, ever achieved greatness, or even success, without courage.

I would hate to think what would happen to America if all those of us who are now in Vietnam, in the face of this attack (which is more real and personal to us than all the academic discussions on all the campuses of America) were to turn tail and run. Can you imagine such a thing? Neither can I—so why should comfortable civilians back home quit in despair?

Maybe some do not appreciate America. Let them visit many other lands, as I have, and they will thank God for the blessing of being an American. Maybe some fear the nuclear weapons of the day. You die just as dead from a bow and arrow. And in numbers just as great from pogroms by Ghengis Khans, or Hitlers, or Stalins, or Maos.

You are growing up, Sweetie, and more and more you will come to know that life rewards the strong and punishes the weak. So does history. The greater the heights of achievement, the greater the strength and resolution demanded. America is now the greatest human achievement in history, in spite of some of the weak among us (can you suppose that they contributed to our greatness?), and the length of the shadow which we cast into the future depends on how tall we stand now, just as it always has.

Don't worry about our country and don't worry about me. I'm not afraid, so don't you be either. And you might recommend this kind of attitude to any of your friends who could profit from it.

Your loving,
Daddy

The Tet Offensive reverberated like a thunderclap throughout Vietnam—and the United States. Militarily, it was a disaster for the Communists, who failed to maintain a foothold in a single town or city and lost up to half of their troops engaged in the assault. But politically it was catastrophic for President Johnson. Accused of misleading the public that the U.S. military was decisively winning the war, Johnson watched his approval ratings plunge. He was burned in effigy in rallies throughout the country as protesters chanted "Hey! Hey! LBJ! How many kids did you kill today?" Challenged by antiwar candidates Robert Kennedy and Eugene McCarthy, Johnson announced at the end of March a partial halt to bombing raids on North Vietnam, as well as an offer to begin peace talks, and, most dramatically, that he would not run for reelection. General Westmoreland's request for an additional 200,000 troops (there were over 500,000 in Vietnam at the time) was rejected, and although denying it was related to recent events, Johnson relieved Westmoreland of command and appointed him army chief of staff. Richard M. Nixon, the Republican candidate for president, hinted he had a secret plan to end the war and would bring "peace with honor." Nixon was elected president in 1968. American troops continued fighting in Vietnam for four and a half more years.

～

In a Letter to His Parents, L. Cpl. Stephen Daniel Laments the Death of a Close Friend "in a Damn Country Not Worth Fighting for" & SP4 Richard Baltzegar Shares with His Friend Mike Engel His Disgust for the U.S. Army "and the Country It Represents"

Outrage and disillusionment about the war was not confined to the United States. Countless GIs and marines vented in their letters home about being entangled in a conflict that appeared increasingly hopeless. With no clear objectives or perceptible gains, the very strategy they had to follow—"victory by attrition"—was psychologically debilitating. Risking their lives to fight an intractable enemy with a seemingly inexhaustible number of guerrilla soldiers at its disposal was, to many, an exercise in futility. L. Cpl. Stephen Daniel volunteered for the marines in October 1967 and left for Vietnam full of pride and confidence. Only three months after arriving, Daniel began to articulate the sentiments of many demoralized young men in his letters to his parents back in Waco, Texas. The following letter was written on August 9, 1968, after a friend of his had been killed. ("Ralph," mentioned in the letter, was how Daniel referred to God and fate.)

Mom and Dad:

Well its Friday morning. Last night one more Marine died. No one will ever here or care about it except his parents and us. A good Marine has died and there is no nation to mourn for him or fly our flag at half mast. Yet in one night this Marine did more for his country than any President or Senator ever did. His name was Corporal Lee Clark. He was the guy who took my picture standing in front of the bridge. I hope you have received that picture and if you have it has a name on the back. He was a good marine and a better person. He didn't deserve dieing in a damn country not worth fighting for. He didn't deserve diein' for people who won't even fight for themselves. But he is dead and those back home who's freedom he was defending will never know his name. He is just another number. But we will here about it and we will remember. Cpl. Lee Clark is dead but those who knew him and fought with him will never forget him. He had about 38 days left in the Marine Corps and in Viet Nam. 38 days left and he is dead. 38 days to start living again, to see the world, and home, but he will never see it. But besides his parents and those who new him, who will care. After all Marines are expendible so who cares when they get it. It makes you wonder when you see a good man die. When you know that those people in the world will never here about it and could care less. It makes you wonder. 38 days left. All he wanted was 38 days. Ralph cut him no slack. But Ralph had a purpose.

#2 Son

Eight months later, on April 5 (Easter Sunday), 1969, nineteen-year-old L. Cpl. Stephen Daniel was killed by a sniper. Other servicemen lashed out with even more hostility in their letters home. Twenty-year-old Army SP4 Richard Baltzegar frequently railed against the war in letters to his friend Pfc. Michael Engel, who was serving as an army clerk in Augsburg, Germany. Baltzegar held particular contempt for the United States, which, he argued, had betrayed its founding principles and was therefore worse than the Soviet Union (CCCP).

September 6, 1968

Dear Mike,

I guess it has been quite a while since I last wrote: a lot has happened, but I can't think of a thing about which to write.

KP has been discontinued, but I was lucky enough to have it the day before it was discontinued. We always had civilians (Vietnamese) who did most of the KPing; we, the KP's, just had to help them—I guess they (the mess SGT's) finally decided they didn't need us after all. I'm glad; I was getting my share.

My brother has decided to put in a 1049 (2496) asking to be assigned to something other than RVN. I finally got through to him—he's gonna get out of it. (At least he said we would.) Remember how I used to get a letter from him everyday? Now I'm lucky to get a letter once a week. Something else is bothering me now: He apparently likes what he's doing. He likes being a drill SGT; I can tell. He tells me of how his "men" come to him with their troubles. He tells me of how he is the only SGT who has control of the men. He is the only one the "men" listen to. He stops fights; he gives out passes; he delegates details. He told me of how the "men" cheered him when he walked up after being absent for 4 days. He reprimands them for not calling "at ease." Is this my brother? I'm rather disappointed in his attitude toward the Army. He no longer criticizes the Army—only talks about his job.

He is a part time company clerk: they (CO and cadre) asked him to be one, since he will be a holdover until he gets his new orders. Damn, his new outlook bothers me. Well, if he is enjoying himself, I should say that's good. I wish I could be that way. All I see is the corruption of this representative organization of the great US. I see people everyday that I have to salute—people I have no respect for; people who lack the intelligence to be anything other than an Army Major. I see a country equally agressive as (aggressive?) CCCP—more disgusting than CCCP because we (America) is backhanded about the whole deal—using words like "freedom," "preservation of Freedom," "heritage of founding forefathers," People tell me that there is no better country. That may be true, but I plan to find out for myself. I'm going to Sweden, Norway, West Germany, England, Luxomburg, even CCCP, and see if I can't find something a little better. If the US is the best, then the rest of the world must be in some hell of a shape.

I was disgusted with the outcome of the Democratic convention. Americans are such fools. (I wonder if public opinion had anything to do with the way the delegates voted. I thought McCarthy was very popular.) I was for McCarthy 100%. Need I describe the rage within me? I guess I'll campaign for Aretha Franklin for President. I was very proud of Aretha Franklin: she sang the National Anthem at the beginning of the convention, and she forgot the words. Words can't describe the joy I felt. I hate that song—and all it stands for. Oh yes, I'm gonna see what Israel is like, too.

I now have a little war story to tell. On bunker guard two weeks ago my bunker received ten minutes of sniper fire. You should have seen little old me peering over the sandbags trying to see who was shooting at me. No one was shot, though. And the NCOIC wouldn't let us fire back—thank goodness. (I don't blame whoever it was who was shooting at me.) (If there were invaders in my country, I would shoot at them, too. What in the hell am I doing here?)

That same night the Bien Hoa Air Base was mortared. All of a sudden a large red ball of fire soared into the sky. The ball expanded, and almost instantaneously emerged into a huge red mushroom cloud. (You can imagine how scared we in the bunker were—we thought the ammo dump had been hit.) From the red mushroom vibrated pink shockwaves, and we could see them (the shockwaves) heading toward us. We gripped the walls of the bunker, but the blast almost tore us loose. We later found out that a rocket fired by a VC hit an RVN bomb storage area on Bien Hoa Air Base. The concussion broke out the windows here at the headquarters. Boy! That was some night to be on the bunker guard.

Every second I was expecting to die; I really was: I regretted everything I had done for the AUS and the USA. I still do. God, I hate the Army and the country it represents. Look at the infamous job I am forced to do. Everyday I am sickened by the gripes of others. "I hate Vietnam." Hell, no one had to come over here if they didn't want to (if he didn't want to). Americans are ruthless and violent: I hate 'em.

I looked up Furlow's address in the in-country alpha. I wrote to him, and He wrote back. (My typing is getting worse, because I'm running out of time.) He is with G4 of the 25th Inf Div at Cu Chi RVN. He is a SP4. He has KP and other details, too. He asked me to send him DiDio's address, so I looked it up. Mike, I fear Fearless Didio may be dead. He is not listed, and unless he was called back to CONUS for some reason, he has been killed. I know he arrived in-country, because I saw him when I first got here.

The past week has been one continuous HIGH for me. Everynight I "lose" myself. Like you said, the first few times, I felt nothing. I fear I am becoming a connoisseur. And that's not all: I went to Saigon two weeks ago and smoked opium. The setting was great. A dark room with an old man lying on a table (his head resting on a wooden block), a lamp with a small red flame, and a Vietnamese woman softly singing some weird song. The withered man cooked the opium over the flame into a long wooden pipe. I rested my head on a wooded block, lay opposite him and quickly inhaled and exhaled the smoke that came from the pipe that he held over the flame. Then a little pot—God, I don't know how I made it back here to Bien Hoa. The greatest feeling. The guy I was with said that I looked as if I were in a trance. I could have taken it mainlinerly, but I was afraid—my partner wasn't.

> Write to me soon.
> Rick

According to the Department of Defense approximately 70 percent of all American servicemen in Vietnam used drugs. Marijuana was the most popular, but amphetamines, opium, and heroin were also common. Government studies also indicated that a majority of all first-time users stopped taking drugs after the war. But many, like Richard Baltzegar, became hooked for life. Although he returned to the United States alive and uninjured after his tour of duty, Baltzegar came home an addict. He died in 1992 at the age of forty-four as a result of substance and alcohol abuse.

—————————— *Extended Correspondence* ——————————

Pfc. Timothy Robinson Chronicles His Combat Experiences in Vietnam in a Series of Short, Descriptive Letters to Anxious Family Members Back in the States

"I sure would like to sit down and write you all seperet letter's but my time is small," twenty-one-year-old Pvt. Timothy Robinson wrote in October 1967 to his family from Fort Campbell, Kentucky. Robinson struggled with dyslexia and found writing difficult, but he regularly updated his parents, his sister Ruth, and his fifteen-year-old brother Patrick back in Hoyt Lakes, Minnesota, on how he was progressing in basic training. (Robinson's twenty-two-year-old sister Peg was in college, and his eldest sister Nancy was married and living with her husband in Minneapolis.) Although notorious in his family for being extremely self-disciplined and something of a neatnik, Robinson was also a free-spirited soul who chafed under strict conformity. "What ever you do," he remarked a few days later,

> I hope you can keep Pat out of this type of mad world of uniformity and do what you are told and not to think for yourself because this is all what this army is. We had four men go A.W.O.L. in the last week and three were back

within the next day but one is still gone. One nite when I was on fire watch two of them went A.W.O.L. an I was supposda turn them in but if they won't to go thats their bussiness I wasn't going to turn them in.

In March 1968 Robinson was shipped to Vietnam. After landing in Bien Hoa, he sent the following:

22 March 68

Dear Mom, Dad, Ruth, Pat,
    I got to my unit now and have a address
                Pfc Tim Robinson US 56502427
                Co. C. 2nd Bn 2nd Brg
                101st ABN Div
                APO 96383 S. F. Cal.
We are located some were around Phu Bai and Hue North. It sure is a durty hole here You were the same cloths untill they fall of you and then they give you a new pair. This country is not worth fighting for but the good we do for the Viet Nams is good. Theis people are so far back in the world that it sad. You just cant explain it in word's. But I got pitchers to be devloped and maybe they can tell you better then I can.
    Did you get my picther that I had taken when I was home? I whish I could see it. Writ soon now so I can see what is going on in the world Over here we don't know even how the war is coming along. Haven't seen rain over here yet It's dry and hot but at night it cools off. They say that some were in Viet Nam it is raining every day.
    Boy would give ever thing in the world to be home. That the place were ever one belong's. You should see my nice tan I have already. I think some of it is durt.

                    "Love" your son
                    Tim

Only days days later Robinson was in combat. He related his first impressions on March 28.

Dear Mom, Dad, Ruth, Pat
    Im in the field now in the hills. From the hill Im on now you can see Hue, so we are far north. We have a battalen of NVA traped down in the valley and have been hitting them with mortur and boms for the last 3 or 4 days. The first day they sent me out here to meet up with my platoon We moved out from the top of one hill to the next and on the way we ran in to snipers and had four men killed and four wonded.

The good Lord was with me coming down the hill because I wasn't hit but some of the men in front of me and along side of me were hit. Death is sad over here to these young men. To see them rolled up in a poncho. I had to go out and get one guy that had got hit and then got on fire, he was still burning when we got to him. It was a sad mess. I've never been so scared in my life as I was that day and Iv been praying ever since that day.

Im the mechine gunner in my squad. If you think this letter is grubby that because we live that way. On top of the hills for weeks with out shaving, washing, or brushing your teeth. You cloth get so dirty they fall of then you get a new pair. At night you have to sleep with a few gernads in your pocket because you never know when you'll get hit by something.

Get them letters rolling and say a prary for me every night and I'll do my best.

Much love.
Your son & brother
Tim

"Humping" (GI slang for marching) through the jungles, villages, mountains, and rice paddies of Vietnam, soldiers were well aware that every step could be their last. They had to be on constant alert for ambushes, as well as for land mines and booby traps, which caused over 10 percent of all U.S. casualties in the war. (Some of the most crippling were punji pits—shallow, concealed ditches embedded with knife-sharp spikes that, when stepped on, pierced right through the foot. Fecal matter often was smeared on the tips of the stakes to cause infections.) On April 7, Robinson referred to several of the potentially lethal threats they contended with daily, including one nobody had expected.

Dear Mom, Dad, Ruth & Pat,

Still at it going strong. We are down and out of the mountens now and sitting on the bech of Utah up North

We are guarding part of the perimeter and go out on patrolles and ambushes. So far all we have run into was one man step into a pungy pit and one man triped a bobee trap gernaded. Both are out of action. Yesterday A Co ran into a ambush in a village that we had swep through the day befor and the last I heard they had 10 killed and 11 wonded.

A few days ago we were standing in the chow line and bullets started flying at us. Everones was hitting the ground and crualing for cover. Half of us had are weapanes with us and started to move in the diraction of the shots

When we got up to it we found a couple of Merines that were taking target practzes at something with a 60 cal. mechine gun and a M-14. They said they didn't know the bondres of the perimeter. They sure had me scared with bullets flying about one and two feet along side of me.

Im still waiting for my first letter from some one back home. It would be nice to get a package from home about once a week if you could because your son is starving over here. Some of the things you can send are: cans of fuirt, cokies, hard candy, caned meat, anything in cans our jars, hony or some strawbarry jam, joke book, comics book, hot rod books, paper's, baked food's and "kool-aid" The water over here teast like "H" apple sauce. About once a month send some stationary like Im writtin on now. Im going to try and write grandma, Nancy, and Joyce to because they always have good coked foods around but it is hard to get the time and the equip. over here.

I heat to write and ask for food like a pig, but I losing whiegt fast. Dad I would love to have that big hunting kinef with me over here Do you think you could send it to me. Dont get any cold beer or Coke any more. Maybe one or two cans a week

Haven't seen a base camp in a mounth That's why we can't get any of that good stuff. Im still wearing the same cloth as when I got over here but they gave me new socks last week. We get a chance to swim in the ocean hcrc but the water is to salt to get clean. We have a mud piled in front of our bunker to wash up and shave in. Got to go now

Love and miss ya all lots
Your loven son and brother Tim

P. S. I don't know what good Im doing over here but I'll keep fighting in hopes that my brother may never have to see this dam land.

One week later, Robinson wrote a nostalgic letter to his family about a certain holiday tradition his mom continued even after her grown children had left the house.

April 14, 1968

Dear Mom, Dad, Ruth & Pat,

I finally got your first letters you sent and it sure was good to here from ya. Thanks Pat for your letter I enjoy getting them from you. I would write you a seperrate letter but I just dont have the time. Hope you dont minde. Right now Im sitting in front of my bunker pulling guard and it's 2:00 in the morning which would make it 12:00 afternoon April 13 at home. It is light out tonight so that I can see to write. I may miss the lines a few times but that's my excues.

Here is the money you asked for Pat. We use to differont typs. The 50 P's is what the V.C. use for money They call them peasstas Im not to sure on the spelling The other money is what the American troops use They have some coins but I dont have any. I'll try and send some more thing's home when and if I ever get to base camp. I have some things now I would like to send. Iv got $200 dollars of last month pay that Im trying to send back to the bank. But no money orders and it's almost pay day for this month. Just know place to spend money over here where I am. I'll be sending about that much back every month. I should be getting Spc/4 pay next month becauce Iv been put in for the next rank.

I hope the Ester Bunny doesn't for get me this year because the last 21 years it been real good to me and will always be so dear to my heart, "Right Mom"

Remember when we were kids on Ester The grils would be all dress up in new hats, pretty dresses and new gloves and us boys with new shoes and shirts and off to church we would go and after come home to look for our Ester baskets. What good times. I hope God will bring me back home so, that I may marry the girl I love, "Wich will be in March if things go OK." Then I can watch my kids all dress up and head for church and live them day over again.

Today we went out on patrole today and it wasn't to good for a Ester Sunday. One man triped off a boo bee traped 105 Round and killed himself and wonded one other. Holidays are know different then any other day. Every day is Monday in Viet Nam. Just about ever day we walk between 3 to 12 miles through rice paddy up to our knees in mud. Up and down hills. Through jungles What a drag.

Must go now, "God Be With You All"
Your fighting son & Brother
Tim

The special care packages the family had put together for Robinson were returned several weeks later. On April 19, 1968, Robinson caught his foot on the trip wire to a booby-trapped mine and, quite literally, was blown to pieces. Two days before his death, Robinson sent the last letter he ever wrote to his "second family"—his cousins, aunt, and uncle, who owned a small farm where Robinson worked during the summer. (His Aunt, Joyce, suffered from arthritis, which Robinson alludes to in the letter.)

Dear Herman, Joyce, & Kids,
    Thanks much for the letter
    It's always good to here from you good people. (I sure hope the doc's are

taking good care of you Joyce so that you can get better.) I know you all would like to know what Im doing and wear I am over here. Im a mechine gunner in my squad. I hump that and about a 65 pound pack over mountens across the flate lands through the rice paddies and fight my way through the jungles. We move every were between 1 mile to about 12 a day. We dont have a base camp to work out of so they move us all over Viet Nam, Long Ben, Bien Hoa, Phan Rang, Hue, Phu Bia, Utah Beach.

Ive been shot at and had gernades flip at me, helped put dead in ponchos and seen wonded bleed. And can tell you for a fact that this war is hell and that more praying goes on over here in one day than it does in a week back in the world.

Joyce I sure could go for some of your good home made cookies if it's not to much trouble for you. You always did make real good cookies. Thanks for the picture of the family It's a good one. Got to go now

Write again soon and may the good Lord take care of you all as good as He been taking care of me. "Love" your old son and brother

Tim

**SP4 Bob Leahy Explains to His Family Why One
of the Worst U.S. Atrocities of the War Was No Surprise
&
Another Army Specialist Four Describes to His Parents
the Extent to Which Accidents, Friendly Fire, and Fragging
Are Killing U.S. Troops**

The official press release detailing the March 16, 1968, incident could not have been more perfunctory: "[I]nfantrymen from Task Force Barker raided a Viet Cong stronghold known as 'Pinkville' six miles northeast of Quang Ngai, killing 128 enemy in a running battle." The "stronghold" was, in fact, the small hamlet of My Lai and the "battle" was a massacre of hundreds of defenseless Vietnamese villagers, many of them children. The true nature of the killings was exposed over a year later by a Vietnam veteran named Ron Ridenhour, who appealed to members of Congress to begin an investigation. (After a congressional inquiry, only platoon leader Lt. William Calley was convicted of murder. Calley was sentenced to life imprisonment but was released after serving just over three years.) Antiwar activists claimed My Lai symbolized everything that was wrong with the war and vilified U.S. soldiers as "baby killers" intoxicated by wanton destruction. Twenty-year-old SP4 Bob Leahy, like many young men sent to Vietnam, took offense at this characterization. What happened at My Lai, Leahy contended in a letter to his family in Yorba

Linda, California, was terrible, but the truth was more complicated than what some in the media were reporting.

February 2, 1970

Dear Mom, Dad, and Grandma,

Enclosed are some pictures you may enjoy. Included is a picture from <u>Life</u> of a CA (combat assault). It is the best I have ever seen. It is from Life's article on the My Lai massacre. This is the first time I saw Life's article, and I was impressed. Could you send me the earlier Life article on My Lai? The one I read was January 17, and had a picture of an antelope on the cover. Several comments published, especially those by Vietnam veterans, were thought provoking. Others missed the point completely. One Captain said some trash about lack of discipline being the problem. Rubbish. It would take a Marine Corps lifer to think of a stupid thing like that. Frustration and impotent rage cause things like My Lai. One student said, quite rightly, that "I don't think that people put in a situation that requires them to kill can be punished for killing the wrong people."

In an operation of this size, there is a lot of confusion. Intelligence reports said the hill was heavily fortified and that only NVA, VC and their families live there. A report of that kind makes you trigger happy. There is a saying here, "better safe than dead." Everyone is nervous when moving in. All it takes is one person firing in the air, and everyone assumes that there is contact and they are under fire. Any civilians nearby become expendable on the theory that you can not take a chance on their having concealed weapons or chicoms (grenades). Then, with everyone firing in all directions, people get carried away, like a mob. Everyone is doing it, but no one is leading it. All non-GI's become suspected enemy. By the time you find out if someone has a weapon or is a simple farmer, he could empty 30 rounds from an AK-47 in you.

Sure, as Life Magazine points out, no enemy fire was encountered and there were no wounded in action, but no one probably was sure of that until the next morning. By then it was too late. People who assume that the fire you hear is only friendly fire are the ones who make up our 40,000 dead in Nam. You must always act under the assumption that the fire you hear is enemy fire. When you find out to the contrary, it is often too late. Here on the center (B Battery Fire Base), when we get incoming mortars, sometimes they are not sure until the next morning whether it was our own mortar or not. And here there are only 4 mortar tubes to check. Out in the field, how are you supposed to find out if it is incoming rounds or a GI firing into the air? You cannot sit in the open for 10 minutes and check your platoons to find out. You act under the assumption that it is enemy.

I am not condoning My Lai. There is no doubt that a massacre took place. If you enrage and tease a lion, and then an innocent person comes along and pets the lion, the innocent person will be mauled. People who think that troops should always restrain themselves are simply asking too much of human nature. They sit in their carpeted homes and say, "Control yourselves, don't give in to your emotions." They've never had a friend hit a booby trap and shipped the pieces home in a rubber sack. Let them tell me what to write to a man's wife or parents. Control yourselves, your husband/son is dead. Or to his buddies. Control yourself, your friend who you slept with, ate with, and patrolled with, is dead; but don't feel any hatred. They say, "But you can't blame innocent people for the actions of a few." They are the ones who condemn the Negro race because some riot or because some are shiftless.

Or when a man comes back from R&R and everyone is looking at the pictures he took and joking with him. He looks around and says, "Where is Monte?" The joking stops and there is silence. Finally someone says, "Monte died two weeks ago, a 105 booby trap." Then everyone just sort of drifts away to let the returning man grieve alone. Tell <u>him</u> not to hate Vietnamese people in general. I cannot. This is not a soap opera. This happened in my platoon. People do not live happily ever after and come back to life for tomorrow's episode. This is war and I'll give a news flash to everyone back in the states — they're playing for keeps over here.

You cannot ask a man to risk his own life and chance of going home in one piece for a Vietnamese civilian who might not have a weapon. Especially when, as in My Lai, they were told only enemy troops and their families lived in the village. It is asking too much.

You cannot demand that an individual refuse to obey orders he feels are wrong and then turn around and allow laws that will send him to prison when he does. If someone had refused to obey orders, and My Lai had not become a national incident, that person would now be serving 5–10 in Leavenworth and nobody stateside would have said anything in his defense. Cowardice in the face of the enemy or some trash like that.

We have crisp weather here. It is warm during the day, but cools off rapidly at night. We see the stars almost every night. When there is no industry and almost no vehicles, you have no smog. Fog is very heavy every day. You can watch it flowing from valley to valley. I'm going to take some pictures of it.

Love,
Bob

From the chaos of Vietnam emerged another horror: An astonishing number of American soldiers were being killed by their own men. Unintentional deaths from "friendly fire" were deemed a regrettable but inevitable consequence of combat in any war. What concerned the military about Vietnam, however, was that hundreds of deaths were believed to have been from "fragging," the intentional killing of sadistic or dangerously incompetent officers by their subordinates. (Although fragmentation grenades were the weapon most associated with the practice, the term fragging assumed a more general definition as officers were murdered by other means.) During the later years of the war, as unit cohesion and discipline unraveled, combined with increasing drug abuse and racial tensions, reports of fragging rose to their highest levels. In April 1970, an infantryman in Cu Chi and Tay Ninh alluded to both friendly fire and fragging in a letter to his parents back in Fort Atkinson, Wisconsin. (The soldier's full name has been withheld for reasons of privacy.)

Dear Mom & Dad:

Got your letter today containing the stamps. Was really glad to get them. Sent three more rolls off to be developed and am sending a packet of slides with this letter.

Sounds like Theresa can really sing. Wouldn't it be great if she really made it big like T.V., records and live performances. Hollywood here I come! No, really it sounds like she's got talent though.

Seems Scott has the same problem with clothes I had. I'll give him a hint next time look on the floor. He'll find enough to dress himself 3 or 4 times I'll bet.

Well, I'm playing chicken for a few days now.

I volunteered for K.P., trash run and other nasty details, like burning _____ in a barrel while my Co. went out on this four day mission.

It sounded as though they'd see some certain action. Our company linked up with two other battalions to sweep a 4 mile area, trying to flush a regiment of expected V.C. Then last night the artillery had an hour fire mission giving them rear support so they must have made contact last night. At 10:00 we had 6 incoming rounds expected from a V.C. 82 mortar. We manned bunkers and were expecting a follow up ground attack but nothing happened.

Then this morning while we were dumping trash in the dump, someone had set fire in the dump and off went what we thought a grenade. Threw shrapnel all over. I only caught a couple small pieces in the right pectoral muscle and luckily the trailer and truck were between me and the explosion which was only 10 feet away. One other guy got his face messed up pretty bad and had to dust him off to a hospital.

It's so stupid and ridiculous of how so many of our boys are killed by accidents due to some careless mistakes.

Like the guy I saw die, the helicopter crash killing 13 people, and for another example, 2 nights ago, B co. blew an ambush on their own people due to a simple communication mistake and these two squads started blasting away at each other. Two men were killed instantly by Claymore mines, another lost his legs and 5 more injured. All due to GI mistakes. They say as high as 50 % of deaths and casualties are caused by our own men and so many parents never know how their son was killed because all the Army tells them is that they are combat casualties.

That's why I was afraid of this mission. Because our commanding officer is insane. Gungho lifer looking for nothing but a body count of enemy so he can make a stupid promotion.

Like on this last 9 day mission, one night he made us fire mortars from our night position ambush saying we needed practice. All the V.C. had to do was zero in on the noise with their mortars and we'd be hurting. The Lieutenants tried to explain the hazards of doing this but he pulled rank on them and that's all that could be said.

I know for one fact with the hatred his men have for him, that if we ever got in a fire fight someone will knock him off. It happens quite a bit and I'm for certain It'll happen here. I've never seen such hatred.

With all the war atrosities, people act like animals. That's why they happen. It seems these lifers go nuts. Army means battle, death and victory to them.

Enough about him.

I've been wondering if you ever received a $20 money order I sent about a month and a half ago. Please afirm this if you should remember next time. Not that I'm worried, but I like to keep track of the money I send and I could forget and never even miss a $200 check. . . .

Finally got a hair cut. Glad to be rid of that stuff over here. Hot, dirty and hell to keep up.

Well, I have to go now so say hi to Grandma & Grandpa for me. Thanks again for the stamps.

Love
Steve

In another letter home the writer related in graphic detail the accidental death of a comrade who was trapped in a fire ignited by American mines. "We were so damn helpless. We couldn't get in to help. We were watching our friend get burned mother," he wrote. "For once I'm afraid of dying and wish I could find that helping hand like a little child being shielded by his parents. . . . Damn this war and every-thing that's put us here. If I'm to die here, I only wish it were for something I believed in." Steve survived the war and was honorably discharged in February 1971.

~

The Parents of Sandy Scheuer Receive a Series of Letters, Including One from President Richard Nixon, After Their Daughter Is Shot Dead at Kent State

At 12:24 P.M. on May 4, 1970, over two dozen Ohio National Guardsmen aimed their M-1 rifles at a crowd of Kent State University students and began fir-ing. In thirteen seconds of shooting, the guardsmen killed four students—Sandra Scheuer, Allison Krause, Jeffrey Miller, and Bill Schroeder—and wounded nine more. Although most of the students were protesting President Richard Nixon's announcement that U.S. troops would invade and attack Communist staging grounds and sanctuaries in Cambodia, many, including Bill Schroeder, were only watching the demonstration out of curiosity. Sandy Scheuer, an attractive, studious, and outgoing twenty-year-old, was heading to her 1:00 P.M. class when she was shot through the throat, causing her to go into convulsions before she died. A poll conducted after the shootings found that a majority of Americans—almost 60 percent—blamed the students, while only about 10 percent condemned the guardsmen. (Their defend-ers claimed the students had been taunting them and hurling rocks in their direction.) Incredibly, the parents of the slain students received letters accusing them of being responsible for their loss. Sandy Scheuer's parents had been celebrating their twenty-seventh wedding anniversary when they learned their daughter had been killed. After they publicly expressed grief over Sandy's death, the following handwritten letter arrived in their mail.

Dear Mrs. Scheuer —

Our hearts are sad also in the death of your daughter. Why — why don't you mothers take more interest in the activities of your children? Why do you allow them to participate in these terrible demonstrations? You know, and we all know — there is no such thing as an <u>innocent</u> by-stander. If she was in the crowd, <u>she was</u> a <u>part of it</u>. If she was <u>against</u> this militant rad-ical <u>Communist</u> inspired upset — she would have stayed <u>away</u> from it.

You & you alone are to blame — you say "<u>they</u> just let it go on & on, rioting here — rioting there, it's just not right, <u>it's unexplainable</u>." No, it is <u>not unexplainable</u> — <u>you parents</u> are the ones, especially the <u>Jewish par-ents</u> — for so many many of these leaders of student uprising are Jewish children. Did you think this kind of thing can go on forever? Do you <u>not care about our Country,</u> don't you care about what happens to it, can't you concern yourself at all, how do you justify all the burning and looting, breaking windows, tearing up classrooms? —

It is a good country & if it is not, it is the laxity of parents like yourself, that sit back & close your eyes to all the destruction. There were rocks & bullets, & construction pipe, re-inforcing sharp-rods and they were used on the national guard — yes — they were justified in shooting, it is long, long overdue. If we are to have any protection from these radical mobs, our National Guard is our only source of safety. Did you think this was a Sat. nite picnic, your daughter was going to? Don't you watch t.v., you and thousands of other parents? I would feel safer in Vietnam than on many of our college campuses today. Again, I ask you, why are so many of your Jewish sons & daughters allowed to participate and take such active parts in this attempt to overthrow, so violently, and no where, do I ever see or read objection from these parents. These children should be in school & busy learning —

You say — "No one listens to them" — this is the statement of the year & you a parent. Let them learn first, let them learn the right thing to say — then, when the right time comes, and their turn comes, and they have something to say — do so the American way. This thing has gone as far as it can go. People will not let it go on any longer for most of us do not believe in mob rule — "stoning" — is long past. J. Edgar Hoover has told us who is overthrowing or attempting to disrupt & overthrow the gov't of our country — through our youth & their lax, uninformed, or possibly too-well informed parents.

I've no doubt every parent of every child, & there are thousands upon thousands, in these mobs at various colleges, would say the same as you, that their son or daughter had no part in it all. This, we know, is untrue. "They should be free to express their thoughts & their feelings" — yes, at school, not in mob violence — not at the expense of our freedom — or anyone elses freedom. It must be stopped, it will be stopped. You, the parents, become more concerned, become aware that freedom, here, is for all — not just a mob of loud, radical, demanding students. Don't blame our Country. Don't blame our President — put blame where it should be — on all parents' shoulders. We are weary to death of rock throwing mobs, & we are weary of crowds of dissenters. Whether you think so or not, the National Guard would not shoot if they had not been driven & forced to. Don't blame your governor, blame yourselves.

In this "write-up" in the paper I note about 25 why's — why this & why-not that — The answer to all these why's & why-nots is — it is a free country — the free-est one in the world and it must not be ruined — you ans'd your own questions when you said — "When I compare my youth to theirs, I came from Germany, and <u>there</u> we did not <u>have a chance</u> to develop like the children here." Yes, this country is <u>great</u>, our laws are just & fair and <u>must be obeyed</u>. It grieves me to hear you say — you don't think much of this Country <u>now,</u> or you won't vote for our president again. It is our President Nixon that will end our war — It was started with the democrats. <u>You,</u> no doubt, will be one of the first to say, send men & arms to Israel — but that is the same thing — again — Vietnam.

Believe me, when the war is over — the student revolt will latch on to another cause to riot & be led (by communists) down to ruin. Then there will be <u>more National Guard</u> & <u>more guns</u> — for it will <u>have to be</u> so, we cannot allow our Country to be taken over by <u>uneducated, undis-ciplined, uncouth, un-American, unpatriotic</u> youngsters — whose parents couldn't care less. All 4 parents have said — "My child was an <u>innocent by-stander</u>" — Maybe so, but they were in the thick of it or <u>they were taking part.</u>

May God comfort you, in your grief. May you now be God's instrument in helping stamp out this rioting. The place for students is in school, learning, and learn it well, <u>student</u> & <u>parent</u>.

Remember this — the National Guard are also young people, <u>young</u> & <u>patriotic</u> and also loved by parents, such as you.

Anticipating the aforementioned, another mother, who was genuinely sympathetic, wrote to the Scheuers:

> *One thing has been on my mind in particular. One understands that people who experience tragedy are often the recipients of hate-filled letters, or worse, from ghouls, often in large numbers. No doubt you have received some of this kind of stuff. Please don't let it touch you. Statistically there have to be some sick people like that. You cannot let what they say represent any kind of reality to you, except that they are vicious and sick. Reality for you is the millions of young, middle-aged, and old who wept and still weep for you.*

Students throughout the country were particularly upset by the Kent State killings. "It is so hard to know what to say at a time like this," a sophomore at Middlebury College wrote to the Scheuers,

> *Words are not the best means of expression, yet hopefully a real feeling will be conveyed to you through my words.*
>
> *Everyone here is still shocked at the news and the pictures in the newspapers. School has been called off for 5 days so that we'll not only have time to think about what has happened but most important do something about it.*

Last night the college held a memorial service for your daughter and the other three Kent St. students. It was a beautiful service and I have never heard such fullness of singing before in our chapel, as it was completely filled. I realized that the students that we were mourning could have been Middlebury students and that their parents could have been our parents. . . .

I wanted you to know personally that this community is behind you in try-ing to understand and accept the present tragedy and with you in spirit to give you strength to continue to go on.

Ironically, a letter of support even came from President Nixon, who had publicly assumed a less sympathetic posture: "When dissent turns to violence," he remarked coolly after the shootings, "it invites tragedy." Nixon's brief, handwritten note was dated May 6.

THE WHITE HOUSE
WASHINGTON

Dear Mr and Mrs Scheuer

I realize that there is little that I, or anyone, could say at this point that would lessen your personal sense of grief. But I want you to know that I share, as does the entire nation, your sorrow at the tragic death of your daughter Sandy.

As parents of two daughters, Mrs Nixon and I feel especially keen the loss of one so young, so happy, so much a source of joy to her friends, and so full of promise of life ahead. You, and she, will be in our thoughts and our prayers —

Richard Nixon

After an extensive investigation, the U.S. Justice Department concluded that the shoot-ings were ". . . unnecessary, unwarranted, and inexcusable." No one, however, was ever convicted or punished. Less than two weeks after the Kent State shootings, police killed two African-American student protesters—James Earl Green and Phillip Lafayette Gibbs—and wounded twelve at Jackson State College in Mississippi.

~

2nd Lt. Scott Alwin Shares, in a Letter to His Father, a Secret He Has Been Keeping from Him for Some Time

Hovering above dense carpets of jungle as camouflaged Viet Cong sprayed them with gunfire, helicopter crews endured some of the most harrowing moments of the war. In Vietnam—considered the first "helicopter war"—they performed tens of millions of sorties, transporting ground troops, scouting for enemy forces, delivering supplies, escorting unarmed aircraft into hostile areas, and rescuing trapped and wounded comrades. "I don't tell mom and dad much about what I do so don't you mention it either," 2nd Lt. Scott Alwin instructed his younger brother Lance. A pilot with the Sixty-eighth Combat Assault Helicopter Co., Alwin had his share of close calls but rarely reported them to his entire family. There was, however, one subject matter he was even more reluctant to tell his parents, especially his father (whom he feared would be less understanding), even though he suspected he had already surmised the truth. After a brief visit home, where he evaded the subject altogether, Alwin mustered the courage to write to his father soon after he returned to Vietnam.

Bien Hoa R.V.N.

Dear Dad,

Felicitations from your all to often unfilial eldest son.

I'm sure you're wondering what elicites such an early letter. I guess its business which I should have attended to quite some time ago but put off until I can't stand my procrastination any longer.

I'm sure that this letter will become rather disjointed and rambling but I think you will get quite a bit of the information that I want to pass on.

The subject of this whole thing is a young Vietnamese girl you may or may not already have heard something about from some of the other kids.

You can probably glean some good and bad stories and opinions from my brothers and sisters who speak through curtains of love and fear.

I did everyone a disservice when I was home and let a couple of letters she sent get opened by the others and then I didn't comment on it. Her letters are a poor reflection of the girl because I'm afraid they really only reflect the fact that she only had one year of formal english and was a young girl dealing with her first venture into the somewhat bewildering field of romantic love. I'm sure that it would be difficult to give in a few sentences a comprehensive insight into the difficulties surrounding any type of a relationship between a middle class Vietnamese girl, and a G.I.

I guess I will quit writing this because I will never be able to say anything worthwhile in a letter.

Why do I suddenly love some girl in a far away place? That is a difficult question. Maybe you only see so much death and destruction and do so much killing and that part of you that is kind and gentle cries out for some object to direct itself toward. I've thought of all the possible reasons and problems etc and finally let the whole thing lie at the point that there are some things that you do with your heart as well as your mind.

A couple of times while I was home I started to work toward talking with you about this but I never managed it. Now it'll have to keep until the end of March.

All of this is just for your use in possibly better understanding any of the things I do. Don't let this new facet loom to large when you analyze my motivations for whatever things I may do.

I'll write again soon. Until then may that grace and peace that was Christs be yours and mine.

Love
Scott

Far from being angry about or uncomfortable with the relationship, both of Scott Alwin's parents welcomed the news—and the young woman—with open arms. Alwin, twenty-four, had met seventeen-year-old Du Thi Duong at the Bien Hoa Officers Club, where she was working part-time. After dating for approximately two years, they were married in 1970 and went on to raise two children.

~

Tom McCabe, Writing to His Parents from the Hospital, Reflects on Being Back in the States After Fighting in Vietnam
&
Shaken After an Attack at Fire Base Mary Ann, an Anguished Young Sergeant Tells His Mom He Wants to "Get the Hell Out of Here"

"The idea that I might not return haunts me," Pvt. Tom McCabe wrote to his parents in February 1969 while in advanced training.

> *One thing is very evident since having more contact with returning troops & that is that no one really feels like he is a great patriot or that he has fought for any apparent justifiable reason. Going to Nam, for the soldier, is simply an unavoidable obligation that one has to fight to stay alive to finish. It rather makes the whole affair more frustrating.*

McCabe's discouragement was understandable; he was plunging into the war at precisely the time overall U.S. forces were being reduced. (From a high of approximately 540,000 in 1968, troop levels dipped to 330,000 in 1970 and steadily declined in the years to follow.) Only months later McCabe was an infantryman in combat, prompting even more intense opinions on the war:

> *I saw a friend brought out on a home-made litter with his head hanging loosely over the end with his blonde hair hanging in loose curls. Now I know why war*

is so meaningless & wasteful—my heart is heavy. Not one square inch of Vietnam was worth that young soldier's life—not to mention the 35,000 other boys that have so far died over here. It seems that firefights are the only time we get really good food in the field. It is undoubtedly to keep up the morale of the company, but it is a heck of a way to earn a hot meal. . . . It will never cease to amaze me how unorthodox this war seems compared to how I imagined it. There are no set lines of battle & it is usually over as fast as it starts.

The war was over for McCabe soon after writing this letter when he received a "million-dollar wound," a nonfatal injury that was severe enough to guarantee a trip home. Recuperating at Fort Knox in Kentucky, McCabe expressed to his parents how elated he was simply to be alive. It was a joy marred, however, by thoughts of buddies still in Vietnam.

Howdy—

What a marvelous feeling to be back in this glorious country of ours. I am still awed every morning when I wake up and I can look out over the plush country side with its green grass, rolling forested hills and blue skies over head. It seems like I've been thru some sort of nightmare, but dawn has come and the bad dream has vanished with the coming of a new day. It is hard to believe that I was ever in the Nam, altho an occasional sharp pain in my shoulder brings back the reality of that experience. My wound is much better, altho it is still open, but the infection is no longer present. The doctor said that as soon as the bone is covered with muscle he can let me have a convalesence leave since I could take care of the wound my self. I suspect that it won't be for another two weeks before I'm ready to come home. It would only be for 14 days, but that is better than nothing. I would like to be home for my birthday and Dick's and Big Steve's wedding on Aug 2nd.

I have a slight guilty feeling leaving my good friends back in Nam, but I guess it wasn't done intentionally so I didn't exactly abandon them. I hope that they will all survive their miserable year overseas and return to resume natural and productive lives without a bitterness towards America. Even the short time that I was over in Nam I developed a bad taste for what our gov't. was doing and the way the people allowed it to continue. For those who are subjected to more killing and destruction that bad taste may turn into a permenant dislike and distrust of our American system, and then this country will really suffer. I was very happy when you said that you wanted to send my friends a care package; I know they will enjoy it and the thought behind it. It is a shame that we can only do so little for these men over there fighting a futile war.—Well, so much for my thoughts about the war.

As it is now I have no idea what the army has in store for me. I doubt very strongly that they will send me back to Nam, but there is a slim chance that I can get sent to Korea. God forbid. Well there is nothing to do but sit and wait until I heal then try for a good stateside post; altho I wouldn't mind being stationed in Japan—that is a beautiful country.

I hope all is well at home & I will write again soon!

Your ever-so-happy-to-be-back son

As an ever dwindling number of American troops slogged on in Vietnam, the desire to forever abandon "this goddam useless piece of shit country," as one GI bluntly put it in a letter home, burned at fever pitch. After surviving a ferocious assault by NVA sappers—enemy soldiers specially trained to penetrate and sabotage American bases—a twenty-year-old sergeant from Illinois wrote home to assure everyone he was unharmed. His sense of rage and desperation, however, could not be contained. (The sergeant's name has been withheld for reasons of privacy.)

30 Mar. 71

Dear Mom and all,

We made it back to LZ Mary Ann. C Company was there 2 days till the attack started Sunday morn. at 230 AM. Mom we got our ass kicked badly. The dinks fired approx. 200 rds. of mortar and RPG's, small arms, m-79, and heavy machine gun fire.

You wouldn't believe it if you saw it. GI bodies laying all over, and buried. The NVA sappers numbered 100 and each had an Ak-47, grenades, and sapper charges.

I had to write to tell you I'm OK but my buddies are all dead. Out of our Infantry Company 21 killed, 29 wounded, and 27 of us are left to talk about the 5 hrs. of hell we went through.

We were extracted to Chu Lai for regrouping and resupply till we get enough men to replace the ones we lost. I'm OK and they didn't see me. Thank God I was on the river side the only side they didn't come up.

The total for the battle was 33 dead, 74 wounded, plus missing in action 12 (means blown to bits and can't identify.) We killed 12 NVA.

Don't worry I didn't get another purple heart. As close as the lifers can figure the S. Vietnamese soldiers helped the NVA murder us. It was not even a fight. It was a massacre. The dinks ran from one ammo dump to another blowing it up with grenades or satchel charges.

All the men in the hospital are alive mostly because when the dinks stole their watches and wallets they went limp and played dead. This I saw 6 times. One buddy Mike who was shot in his chest and legs groaned when a dink kicked him to see if he was alive. John saw the dink beat his head with a rock till he died.

John layed 5 feet away and took 5 rds. from an AK-47 they thought he was dead. I patched a few guys up and played dead too. Ronald had both legs blown off and I saw him die from shock. I hate this war. Please don't worry I'm AOK but scared to death to go out again.

Doubt if we'll go to the bush again. The guys that are left can't hear plus we are getting 40 or so new guys and we'll have to train them before they go to battle.

Mom don't worry OK., we are in Chu Lai. The dinks shoot rockets at Chu Lai but they always aim for HQ or airport or fuel dump. That's 3 miles away. Usually they send helicoptors armed with rockets to shoot back.

I can't sleep too good anywheres now. I'm drinking lots of Pepsi to try to forget the horror of Sunday morning. They found half of our Captain. He was a damn good guy and always took care of his men.

They had newspapermen and ABC cameramen here at the rear area talking to us and we told him the dying truth how the South Viets helped let the NVA in our wire. He then twisted the truth so the people who made the mistakes that costed 33 lives and 74 wounded. These men are a Colonel and the General. We had no recon elements searching the area, no M-60 machine gun ammo, no mortars to shoot up illumination so we could see who to shoot.

It's too late to bitch, the truth will not be told to the U.S. because the war over here is ended. Bull Shit. They kill a lot of men and tell you only half the number. Mom I'm sick of this shit. Take care and don't call the Red Cross because I'm OK. All the guys are getting told to call home but I won't—OK? I am shaken up but really want to get the hell out of here. It's not worth the cause. I have seen the real war and the jarred paper figures, lies and body counts.

Take care every one and I love you all so don't worry I'll come home in one piece. It's late but I'm safe. I have to go drink some Pepsi. I haven't got drunk in over a year.

Love

After two years of secret meetings in Paris, Secretary of State Henry Kissinger and the North Vietnamese signed the "Agreement Ending the War and Restoring Peace in Vietnam" on January 27, 1973. Among other stipulations, the treaty called for an immediate cease-fire between all parties and the withdrawal of American troops from Vietnam within sixty days. "As we have ended the war through negotiation," President Nixon said in a message directed to the North Vietnamese, "let us now build a peace of reconciliation." It was not to be. Although the U.S. finally had extracted its military forces from the conflict (leaving behind, in accordance with the peace talks, only a small diplomatic presence and truce observers), fighting between the Communists and the South Vietnamese continued for more than two years.

~

Ambassador Graham A. Martin
Dispatches Three Urgent Telegrams from the American Embassy
in Saigon Pleading for More Helicopters

Early on the hot, humid morning of April 29, 1975, Bing Crosby's wistful voice crooned "I'm dreaming of a white Christmas" over the U.S. military radio network in Saigon. The song was a prearranged signal to all Americans that the final evacuation of the city had begun. It was precisely the outcome South Vietnam's president Nguyen Van Thieu had most feared. President Richard Nixon had promised Thieu that he would retaliate with "full force" if the North Vietnamese violated the peace settlement and tried to conquer the South. But as the Viet Cong gutted Thieu's country from within and the North Vietnamese invaded from above, Nixon was powerless; he had resigned the presidency in disgrace in August 1974 after the Watergate scandal. His successor, President Gerald Ford, implored Congress to direct emergency assistance to Thieu, but Congress refused. As the North Vietnamese troops surrounded Saigon in late April 1975, mass pandemonium ensued. South Vietnamese citizens frantically tried to scramble aboard aircraft ferrying Americans out of the city. When the airport was closed, thousands of South Vietnamese, many of whom were U.S. allies promised safe passage out of Saigon, swarmed the American embassy where helicopters were airlifting evacuees to offshore warships. At 10:00 P.M. on the twenty-ninth, Ambassador Graham Martin rushed a cable to Brent Scowcroft, one of Ford's national security advisors, requesting more helicopters. Predicting resistance, he appealed to Scowcroft from a public relations perspective. (Edited versions of these cables have been previously published; they are transcribed below uncut and exactly as they were originally typed.)

TO THE WHITE HOUSE
SECRET 291400Z APR 75 VIA SRF CHANNELS
CITE SAIGON
TO: FLASH WHITE HOUSE..
FOR: BRENT SCOWCROFT
    PERHHPAS YOU CAN TELL ME HOW TO MAKE SOME OF THESE

AMERICANS ABANDON THEIR HALF VIETNAMESE CHILDREN, OR HOW THE PRESIDENT WOULD LOOOK IF HE ORDERED THIS.

FOR MORE THAN TTHAN 50 MINUTES THERE HAVE BEEN NO CH-53'S HERE, AND ONLY ONE CH46.

COMMANDER SEVENTH FLEET MESSAGED ME ABOUT HOUR AND HALF AGO. SAYING HE WOULD LIKE TO STAND DOWN ABOUT 2300 HOURS AND RESUME 0800 TOMORROW MORNING.

I REPLIED THAT I DAMN WELL DIDNT WANT TO SPEND ANOTHER NIGHT HERE.

FOURE HOURS AGO I TOLD NOEL THE NUMBER OF SORTIES WE NEED. NOW THE NUMBER IS 30 CH53 SORTIES. I DONT REALLY MIND GIVING DAO COMPLETE PRIORITY -- THEY WERE MORE EXPOSED THAN WE WERE HERE. I NEED 30 CH53'S SORTIES DAMN QUICK AND I HAVE RECEIVED NOTHING BUT SILENCE SINCE I ASKED FOR THEM.

I AM WELL AWARE OF THE DANGER HERE TOMMORROW AND I WANT TO GET OUT TONIGHT. BUT I DAMN WELL NEED AT LEAST 30 CH53'S OR THE EQUIVALENT TO DO THAT. DO YOU THINK YOU CAN? GET PRESIDENT TO ORDER CINCPAC TO FINISH JOB QUICKLY.

I REPEAT, I NEED 30 CH53'S AND I NEED THEM NOW!
WARM REGARDS.

Scowcroft replied: "DEFENSE PROMISES 30 CH-53S ON THE WAY." A colossal helicopter, the CH-53 normally carried forty people but, during the evacuation, was often packed with more than sixty. (The smaller CH-46s, which held twenty-two persons, were being crammed with up to thirty-six.) It still was not enough. At 11:45 P.M. Martin wired:

SECRET 291545Z APR 75# VIA SPECIAAL CHANNELS
CITE SAIGON
TO: FLASH WHITE HOUSE.
FOR: GENERAL SCOWCROFT
SINCE MY LAST MESSAGE 19 REPEAT 19 CH46'S HAVE COME AND GONE. THEY CARRY ABOUT 2/5THS OF C-53 CAPACITY.

I NEEDED 20 C53' SORTIES CAPACITY. I STILL DO. CAN'T YOU GET SOMEONE TO TELL US WHAT IS GOING ON?
WARM REGARDS

The embassy compound was growing more chaotic, and Martin sensed that time was running out. The small group of U.S. pilots shuttling back and forth between the embassy and the aircraft carriers were all dangerously fatigued. Weather conditions were abominable and there was no moonlight, increasing the possibility of midair collisions in the pitch-black night. Two pilots were killed when they flew into the sea. Martin was assured that another nineteen CH-46s were on their way, but they were nowhere to be seen. Just after midnight on April 30, he wired:

SECRET SPECAT EXCLUSIVE
FOR ADMIRAL GAYLOR.
INFO GENERAL BROWN CJCS
BRENT SCOWCROFT, WHITE HOUSE.

THANKS FOR YOUR MESSAGE

19 CH46 SORTIES ARE MOST WELCOME. THER IS NOW ANOTHER LULL. NOTHING IN LAST 20 MIN. WE NEEDED THE CAPACITY REPEAT CAPACITY OF 30 C-53 SORTIES TO GET US OUT OF HERE. AS I RECALL, A CH46 HAS ABOUT 2/5THS THE CAPACITY OF A CH53.

WE STILL NEED THE CAPACITY RPT CAPACITY OF THE 30 CH53 SORTIES REQUESTED IN MY PREVIOUS MESSAGE.

IT NOW SEEMS I WILL SPEND PART OF APRIL 30 HERE — A VERY SMALL PART I HOPE.

BUT I SURE DONT WONT TO SPEND MAYDAY HERE.

WARM REGARDS

Patience was exhausted on both sides. The president and his advisers wanted all Americans out of Saigon immediately, and they were convinced that Martin was delaying his own departure so that he could continue demanding helicopters for the South Vietnamese. "On the basis of the reported total of 726 evacuees," stated a terse message to Martin from the White House, "CINCPAC [Commander in Chief, Pacific Command] is authorized to send 19 helicopters and no more. The President expects Ambassador Martin to be on the last helicopter." Less than two hours later Martin was whisked away. North Vietnamese tanks rolled into the city later that morning. South Vietnam had fallen to the Communists. Saigon was now Ho Chi Minh City.

Maj. Michael O'Donnell Sends His Friend Marcus Sullivan a Poem That, Decades Later, Would Be Read and Cherished by Thousands of Vietnam Veterans and Their Families
&
Gold Star Mother Theresa O. Davis Writes to Her Son Richard, Killed in Vietnam, Thirty Years After His Death
&
Richard Luttrell Leaves a Heartfelt Letter of Reconciliation and at the Vietnam Veterans Memorial in Washington, D.C.

Unlike their fathers and grandfathers who served in the First and Second World Wars, the generation of soldiers who returned from Southeast Asia were greeted by an apathetic, and in some cases, even hostile nation. There were no ticker-tape parades, no mass celebrations. Only an embittered sense of how much the war had traumatized the United States. But as time passed, the mood of the country changed. Amid a renewed sense of national optimism, Vietnam veterans were increasingly shown the respect and honor accorded to veterans of other wars. In November 1982, the country formally recognized their sacrifices with the dedication of the Vietnam Veterans Memorial. Etched in the immense black granite walls of the monument are the names of the 58,216 men and eight military women killed in the war. Each year tens of thousands of visitors to "The Wall" leave photographs, flowers, personal belongings, and letters in memory of those who died. One of the poems left most frequently at the Wall was written by Michael Davis O'Donnell, a young helicopter pilot from Springfield, Illinois. The untitled poem was actually part of a handwritten letter O'Donnell sent to his best friend, Marcus Sullivan, who had served as a combat engineer in the war from 1967 to 1968 and had returned to the United States. O'Donnell's poem has been published before, but the full letter, below, has not. It was also the last letter Sullivan ever received from his friend; Maj. Michael O'Donnell's helicopter was shot out of the sky on March 24, 1970, during a rescue mission. His body was never recovered.

9:00 PM
2 Jan 70

Dear Marcus,

I guess we are not very good correspondents. I have raced thru the month of December and found I was not entirely unhappy to see it leave. I am, right now, in the middle of being positive I was never anywhere except Pleiku, Vietnam this whole lifetime and am sorry to report that I've already played the same good times over and over and they are beginning to fade out. I think you must know what I mean. It's hard to make the old dreams last—especially when you have no one to make the new ones with.

At any rate I should not complain, it could be much worse, I could be a combat engineer or something.

I enjoyed the poems you sent me, I really did. I have typed them up and added them to A Leaf of Life.

I have written a few new things. I will send them later. I do want to give you this one I wrote last night:

> If you are able
> save a place for them
> inside of you . . .
> and save one backward glance
> when you are leaving
> for the places they can
> no longer go . . .
> Be not ashamed to say
> you loved them,
> though you may
> or may not have always . . .
> Take what they have left
> and what they have taught you
> with their dying
> and keep it with your own . . .
> And in that time
> when men decide and feel safe
> to call this war insane,
> take one moment to embrace
> those gentle heroes
> you left behind . . .
>   1 Jan 70 MDO

I am convinced this will be worst or the best year I have had. Ask me this time next year. Let me wish you a good year and when you have the time write me and take care of yourself.

Until that time,
Michael

Visits to the Wall are understandably painful but often cathartic for family members of those who died in Vietnam. On June 6, 1968, Theresa O. Davis, from Quincy,

Massachusetts, learned that her nineteen-year-old son, Richard, a Green Beret with the Fifth Special Forces, was killed near the Cambodian border. Mrs. Davis had lost her husband, also a serviceman, ten years earlier, and the death of her eldest son was overwhelming. The heartache never subsided but, after going to the Wall to find his name, Davis wrote a letter to Richard expressing how much she loved him and how deeply he was missed. ("Gold Star Mothers," alluded to by Davis in her letter, date back to World War I, when the mothers and wives of men killed in battle began wearing a black band with a gold star in memory of their loved ones.)

Dear Dick,

You were my first born. With your laughing eyes and mischievous grin, you stole my heart. I remember you as a little boy—the forts you built, the adventures you took, the "rescued" critters you brought home—and the friends that surrounded you. I'll never forget, when you were twelve years old, you stood so proudly beside me as they played taps for your Dad, and gave us his flag.

My darling son, you were the brave one—you tried so hard to be a father to your younger brothers and sisters.

But you grew up so fast. As soon as you were out of high school, you signed up for the Special Forces—and you were so happy when they accepted you. How proud you looked when you came home on leave wearing your Green Beret. Captured forever in my mind, is the image of your final hug, as you raced for the plane that would take you to Vietnam. You didn't say too much in your letters—but I knew you were in danger, because you always used to tell me "what you don't know, won't hurt you." I found out later—on June 6, 1968, you were on a team with some South Vietnamese soldiers, and your group was pinned down under fire. You were hit several times before you died. You were only 19 years old.

There are no words to describe how I felt. I was so empty—but I had to put up a front for your brothers and sisters. Little Kevin was only seven. He kept saying it wasn't fair—he'd already given up his Daddy. I pretended to be brave. But inside, the empty space just grew larger.

It's been a long time my son. I still miss you. I will always miss you. Sometimes I look at your friends that you went to school with, and I wonder what you would be like now; what my grandchildren would have been like. But you will never come back. You're gone forever.

They gave you a Silver Star. Now they call me a Gold Star mother. I spend a lot of time with the other Gold Star mothers. Every Monday night, a group of us go to the homeless shelter for Vietnam Vets. I know if it was you in that position, I would want someone to do the same for you. I guess that's what moms do. A lot of the guys have family problems. When they came home from Vietnam, they just couldn't talk about it; and they alienated themselves from their parents.

We try to give them support—talk to them like a mother would talk to a son. One of them even came over and asked me if I could sew some buttons on for him. I did, but I also asked him, "Have you called your Mom, have you called your Dad?" They think their family doesn't want to hear from them. But when they do call, and go visit, the healing can begin.

We also go to the Vietnam Memorial whenever we can. We can tell when one of the vets is having a hard time. Even now, so many of them feel guilty because they came home, and our sons didn't. We give them a hug, and tell them it's not their fault; we're glad they're home. Dick, I'm sure wherever you are up there, you approve of what I'm doing. You were such a people person; always trying to help someone.

Besides, when I go to the Wall, it's almost like you're there with me. Each time I run my fingers over your name on that cold, granite wall, I can feel the warmth of your laughter as if you are saying, "It's okay, Mom. I'm here." I know I will never hold you in my arms again. But I will forever hold you close to my heart because you will always be my firstborn—my shining star.

Love, Mom

All letters and artifacts left at the Wall are collected, catalogued, and preserved by the National Park Service, National Capital Region. Duery Felton Jr., a park service curator (and a Vietnam veteran himself), was organizing a container of memorabilia gathered at the Wall when a small photograph and letter left by another Vietnam veteran caught his attention:

Nov 18, 1989

Dear Sir,

For twenty two years I have carried your picture in my wallet. I was only eighteen years old that day that we faced one another on that trail in Chu Lai, Vietnam. Why you did not take my life I'll never know. You stared at me for so long armed with your AK-47 and yet you did not fire. Forgive me for taking your life, I was reacting just the way I was trained, to kill V. C. or gooks, hell you weren't even considered human, just gook/target, one in the same.

Since that day in 1967 I have grown a great deal and have a great deal of respect for life and other peoples of the world.

So many times over the years I have stared at your picture and your daughter, I suspect. Each time my heart and guts would burn with the pain of guilt. I have two daughters myself now. One is twenty. The other one is twenty two, and has blessed me with two granddaughters, ages one and four.

Today I visit the Vietnam Veterans Memorial in D.C. I have wanted to come here for several years now to say goodbye to many of my former comrades.

Somehow I hope and believe they will know I'm here, I truly loved many of them as I am sure you loved many of your former comrades.

As of today we are no longer enemies. I perceive you as a brave soldier defending his homeland. Above all else, I can now respect the importance that life held for you. I suppose that is why I am able to be here today.

As I leave here today I leave your picture and this letter. It is time for me to continue the life process and release my pain and guilt. Forgive me Sir, I shall try to live my life to the fullest, an opportunity that you and many others were denied.

I'll sign off now Sir, so until we chance to meet again in another time and place, rest in peace.

Respectfully,

101st Airborne Div.   Richard A. Luttrell.

Felton instantly knew he had to include the photograph, as well as several lines from the letter, in an upcoming publication the National Park Service was assembling called Offerings at the Wall. *In 1996 a good friend of Luttrell's saw the book and shared it with Luttrell, who had not seen the photograph and the letter since he had left them at the Wall seven years earlier. Suddenly confronted with them again, he broke down and cried. The pain of the memory was so great that Luttrell realized it might never go away unless he tried to return the photograph to the daughter of the slain Vietnamese soldier. Although he realized that, without an address or even a name, the odds of finding someone in a country of 80 million were astronomical, he was determined to try. Luttrell contacted Felton, who flew to Illinois and personally returned the items. And then, with assistance from the Vietnamese Embassy in Washington, Luttrell was able to convince newspapers in Hanoi to publish the photograph with an accompanying article. Miraculously, a copy of the paper made its way to a tiny farming village where the family of the soldier recognized it. Several days later Luttrell received a short, translated letter, forwarded from Vietnam by fax, written by a woman identified only as Lan. The message read:*

> *Dear Mr. Richard, the child that you have taken care of, or through the picture, for over 30 years, she becomes adult now, and she has spent so much sufferance in her childhood by the missing of her father. I hope you will bring the joy and happiness to my family.*

Luttrell immediately responded and asked Lan if he could visit her in Vietnam. She said yes, and in March 2000 Richard Luttrell traveled to Vietnam—the first time he had been back in thirty-two years—and found himself face-to-face with Lan in her village. The moment she saw him, Lan burst into tears and embraced Luttrell. "I'm so sorry," he said to her, also crying. Lan forgave Luttrell, and the photograph of her and her father now rests on a small altar in Lan's home.

~

Bill Hunt Shares with Fellow Vietnam Veteran David H. Hackworth His Concerns About an Impending U.S. War with Iraq

The shadow of the Vietnam War loomed ominously over the United States armed forces in the late summer of 1990. Although victorious in relatively minor invasions in Grenada (October 1983) and Panama (December 1989), the military was now confronted with an infinitely more threatening situation. On August 2 the Iraqi army, the fourth-largest standing army in the world, devoured its tiny neighbor Kuwait in less than a day. Iraq's dictator, Saddam Hussein (a U.S. ally in the 1980s), controlled one-fifth of the world's oil and was poised to invade Saudi Arabia. President George Bush imposed economic sanctions on Iraq and ordered two hundred thousand troops to Saudi Arabia in a defensive operation named Desert Shield. Undaunted, Hussein held Americans and Europeans who had been residing in Kuwait as hostages and even placed them in and around vital Iraqi installations as "human shields." President Bush doubled the number of forces in the Gulf to four hundred thousand and activated Reserve and National Guard combat units. As the U.S. seemed to be mobilizing for an offensive strike, many questioned whether a small, feudal monarchy in the Middle East was worth a single American life. Vietnam veteran Bill Hunt, a part-time writer and columnist, believed President Bush and Secretary of State James Baker had been successful in restraining Hussein's troops, but had failed to articulate a convincing justification for initiating a full-scale war. After a mutual friend forwarded Hunt an editorial by David "Hack" Hackworth, a highly decorated Vietnam veteran who became one of the Vietnam War's most vocal critics, Hunt sent the following:

November 28, 1990

Hack:

Mike Kelley asked me to respond to your column "Before Storming Iraq, Remember Vietnam."

We've met, briefly, Hack. I was at the luncheon in Stockton, and we spoke at Doug Durham's house. I'm the vet who gave you the field map showing Muc Hoa and my old advisory post, Long Knot.

Congratulations, by the way, on your latest appearance on the Larry King show. It was two against one, but I thought you took 'em both out.

I do a little opinion writing myself. I won't bore you with all my columns, but I've enclosed a couple you might find interesting.

Your column was right on, of course. I could nit-pic over some of your points, but your final recommendation to Bush was exactly correct. We <u>have</u> won. We should declare victory and get out.

I hope you have time to wade through this. For the sake of speed, I'm just going to ramble on a bit and share my scattered thoughts on the subject at hand. Like Bush, I've flipped and flopped over this thing.

Initially I liked the rapid response Bush took at organizing the naval blockade and world opinion. But realizing that a guy like Hussein only understands force, as opposed to saber rattling, my attitude was hawkish. I would have backed an immediate air strike as soon as we had at least two carriers in the region. It would have made sense to take out Hussein's air force, while the dust was still settling. It would have been a fair price for Kuwait, and it would have secured our fleet. Our goal at the time was clear: guard Saudi Arabia. I think air power would have achieved that goal, especially if we had used it early to let Hussein know we were serious. Of course, to do any of that we would have needed a treaty with Kuwait.

But when a congressman or two started saying "we've got to get a few troops on the ground to let Iraq know we're serious," my attitude started to turn cynical. That's a type of phoney gunboat policy that usually gets us into trouble. It stems from an arrogant attitude that thinks if we arrive in force the bad guys will pee in their pants and just give up. I had this image of "a few troops" being nothing more than a target, a la Beirut. Flippity flop.

And so, when we actually sent in several divisions, I started to feel a little better. Flip, flop again. Our objective was still clear in the early stages, the protection of Saudi Arabia, and when it comes to a defensive force, the more the merrier.

And then our goals changed. Somehow we went from a clear defensive posture to "it's about jobs." Flop.

Well, Mr. Baker is right. It is about jobs, but it is not about a global recession. It's about Mr. Baker's job. We got in deep because President Bush needed a diversion from election troubles on the S&L front, the "read my lips" front, and the budget debacle front. The military-industrial-complex, MIC, has always wanted a base in Saudi Arabia. And Hussein, bless his murdering heart, provided the opportunity to shift the cold war to the Middle East. It was the perfect opportunity for opportunists. Yes, it is about jobs. It seems there's a tyrant under every rock just when MIC needs a boost.

And now let the race begin, because the objectives of Bush and MIC are at odds. To save his presidency, Bush needs to win "big". He needs to push Iraq out of Kuwait, with maximum destruction and minimum loss. If Hussein should suddenly give up the hostages, pull back to the sea lanes and northern oil fields of Kuwait, and worse, allow the Kuwait population to move back in, what then? The Arab world would rejoice, Hussein would win his original objectives, and Bush would lose "big". MIC, on the other hand, would silently join the celebration. Having a "Hitler" fully armed in Iraq is good news to personnel staffing, promotions and arms sales.

Cynical? Yeah, I can hardly believe what I'm saying, but I've been able to draw no other conclusion from the information I've been provided.

Maybe I'm missing something. Maybe that's because I'm looking way too hard for a small glimmer of "honor" in the midst of this mess. Honor is not something we can define, so we seldom even talk about it. But any soldier who has had to make a sudden personal decision, regardless of "orders" or "duty", some deadly commitment to some grim action on the battle field can testify that honor is not something anyone can fail to ignore. Honor, in spite of our more primative inclinations toward self preservation, stands in total defiance to common sense, sometimes, and reminds our most unwilling self that some things are worth dying for. At the top of everyone's list is simply family and friends. Truth and dignity play in there somewhere, but that can get pretty obscure when the shooting starts.

And in the end all wars are about dying. When the dying is about honor it is somehow OK, even to, and maybe especially to, the dead. Only the folks back home have the luxury of viewing war as about living.

As a war vet, I can't ask a young soldier to go into combat unless the mission is something I personally feel equals the value of my own life.

So, where's the honor? Well, if the President asked me to walk point all the way to Baghdad in order to secure the release of a single hostage, I'd say yes. But I've been told that the taking of hostages "shall not be allowed to effect our policy." From the way we talk they don't officially exist. Hummmmm.

If the President convinced me that Iraq was about to attack Israel and I needed to be the sacrificial lamb, I'd say maybe. But I would want to know a lot more. Israel has been a real problem lately. My personal blood would require one heck of an explanation. But in this deal, Israel doesn't exist either.

Oil? No, Mr. President. This ultimate value of crude on the world market will never go higher than about $60 a barrel. That's because alternative fuels can be produced more cheaply than that, and we the people, if not the President, are starting to understand that. We really need a national energy policy that <u>requires</u> energy independence. We've needed it for years. I'm not going to die for oil.

To liberate Kuwait? Well, frankly, Mr. President, is Kuwait some flowering democracy? Can you get the Emir to go on TV and talk about the new constitution that provides rights for <u>all</u> citizens? Perhaps the Emir will call for an election after I liberate the place? If I die in Kuwait, will they stop calling me an infidel? And do you really expect me to go in with Syria on my flank?

Then, shall we just protect Saudi Arabia? Well, yes, Mr. President, with serious reservations. I think I could be friends with the people of Saudi Arabia, in time. But our presence may very well bring on a smoldering unrest, and even civil war. If that happens, Mr. President, you've got to promise me one thing. Promise me we'll get the hell out. The one thing I learned in Vietnam is that you don't mess around in someone else's civil war. Not unless you're nuts.

As an American citizen I feel pretty helpless in the face of foreign policy that I know is short sighted or patently wrong. Nothing I've said here will change what happens in the Middle East one iota. It's all happening too fast.

But I wish, as a citizen, I had more influence. I would like to ratify a treaty or two, every election day. I think every American needs that kind of personal commitment. I'd like to be able to turn to my constitution for basic wisdom on the principles of foreign conduct. Is not a blockade an act of war? I should expect my constitution to define conditions of war, police actions, and state clearly when certain actions need to be automatic, if ever.

As it stands we know that the President can't declare war, but we know he will take us to war nevertheless. And we know from history that congress <u>won't</u> declare war until it's too late, if then. Consider this crazy thought: maybe foreign policy today is too important for politicians.

Let me stop banging on these keys now and get this in the mail.

Keep the faith, Hack
Bill Hunt

The very next day, November 29, 1990, the United Nations Security Council approved Resolution 678, authorizing the use "of all necessary means" against Iraq if Saddam Hussein did not withdraw his army from Kuwait by January 15, 1991. Even President Bush's political opponents acknowledged that Bush had orchestrated a diplomatic masterpiece in creating a broad, international coalition—including most Arab nations—committed to liberating Kuwait. On January 12, 1991, after many impassioned appeals to give economic sanctions more time, the U.S.

House of Representatives and Senate also voted to permit the use of force. (A differ-ence of three votes in the Senate would have defeated the measure.) At this time—only six months after the Iraqi invasion—there were almost as many U.S. troops in the Persian Gulf as there had been in Southeast Asia at the height of the Vietnam War.

~

Sgt. Tom Shaffer Jokes with His Friend Kathleen Williams About the Precautions They Have Been Given in the Event of a Chemical Weapons Attack

Of paramount concern to the Americans and their allies was the possibility that Sad-dam Hussein might utilize chemical weapons, which he had used during Iraq's eight-year war with Iran and against Iraqi Kurds in 1988. Servicemen and women in the Gulf loathed the chemical protection gear they had been issued; in a desert envi-ronment where temperatures could soar to 120 degrees, the full-body suit became insufferably hot in seconds. Some were skeptical of the pills and shots administered to protect their immune systems from chemical agents. (In the years after the war, an estimated one hundred thousand Gulf War veterans, many of them only in their twenties and thirties, would complain of an array of chronic ailments now referred to as "Gulf War Syndrome." Although a host of studies and tests have proved incon-clusive, the antibodies distributed before and during the war have been blamed for the illnesses, which include intestinal problems and even brain damage.) Tom Shaffer, a twenty-three-year-old sergeant from Richmond, Virginia, served with the 43rd Engineering Company, 3rd Armored Cavalry Regiment, and he frequently updated his friend Kathleen Williams on his life in an army tent city in Saudi Arabia. In a brief, lighthearted letter to Williams, Shaffer alludes to suspicions about the inocu-lations the military was dispensing.

10 JAN 91

Kathy,

Hey, it's me again! Aren't you just privileged to get so much mail from me?! Anyway, today is Thursday, and they aren't taking out boxes until tomorrow, so I might as well write to you some more. I also found the shirt in the bottom of one of my bags, and I thought you might want it to wear around the house or something, so I sent it to you instead of throw-ing it away.

Really nothing new has happened since I wrote last. We finished the ramp project today. My old squad leader from third platoon had a heart attack today. They took him to the hospital around dinner time. I hope he is okay, because he was a really good squad leader. We are still preparing to move. I have to wash my clothes tomorrow, and finish packing my bags, and then I'll be ready. We never got our anthrax shots. They changed their minds I guess. I just heard on the radio that the troops are still getting vaccinated. Well let me tell you that we aren't. They said that our mask will protect us against biological weapons, but there is no way to tell if we are in a biological contaminated area unless someone gets sick. By that time, everyone would probably already have contaminate in them, so what good is our mask going to do?!

We are also supposed to start taking some pills that are supposed to slow down a nerve agent once it's in our system. I really don't trust taking them, and I'm really thinking about throwing them away. Many people think we are being used as guinea pigs over here. The side effects for these pills are actual nerve agent poisoning! That's one thing I could do without at this point of my life. I don't want to end up going sterile, and not being able to have any kids! They had the talks last night and nothing came out of it, so that's not good news.

I hope everything with you is fine. I sure hope I hear from you soon before I go crazy over here! I think this place has finally gotten to me! Well I'll let you go, so I can seal this box and get to bed. Take care.

Love,

Tom

Shaffer, who never ingested the pills or received the shots, did not raise the issue with Williams again, and his attention was turned to the imminent assault on Iraq. "The night before last a guy in first platoon shot himself in the leg, because he said 'God doesn't want us to kill each other over here, and I'm not going to shoot anyone.' Now that he has shot himself, he has to pay for all his medical treatment and will be sent to prison for 6 months–1 year. We will probably be home by the time he gets out. He blew the whole calf off his leg, so he'll probably have trouble with it for the rest of his life." Shaffer, himself, would return from the war alive and well, free of any symptoms of "Gulf War Syndrome."

～

S. Sgt. Frank Evans Describes to His Mother and Stepfather the Anxious First Hours of the Air Campaign Against Iraq

"Just two hours ago, Allied air forces began an attack on military targets in Iraq and Kuwait," President George Bush announced from the Oval Office on January 16 (January 17 in the Persian Gulf). "Our goal is not the conquest of Iraq. It is the liberation of Kuwait." Broadcasting live from Baghdad, network and cable news reports beamed the first, dramatic images of the war as air raid sirens blared and anti-

aircraft fire streaked wildly across the dark, predawn sky. Carrier-launched cruise missiles and stealth aircraft pounded Iraqi communications centers, radar sites, air force bases, chemical and nuclear warfare facilities, and other heavily defended targets. Desert Shield was now Desert Storm. Twenty-seven-year-old S. Sgt. Frank Evans served with a weapons ground crew on an airbase in the United Arab Emirates. On January 24, Evans wrote to his mom and stepfather in West Virginia about the evening the war began. (Toni is his wife, seven months pregnant with their first child, a son they planned to name Gage.)

4 Jan

Dear Mom & Jim

Just want to let you know I'm doing fine. I think I've told you before that any chance of Iraq's weapons reaching us here is extremely low. But of course, we're ready for the unexpected. I'm lucky to be this far from the trouble, since many A.F. people are very close. Things around here aren't much different than they were before the war. We practiced for this day after day, so everything has been going well. We have been doing our jobs just like we have any other day.

After the 15th of JAN deadline passed, we halfway expected things to start happening soon. The 16th came and went just like any other day, except that all of the phones had been disconnected.

I went to work on the 17th of JAN at midnight. One hour later our commander told us it was time. I don't think reality had set into us at that point. Hard to believe this was really happening. Pilots were strapping into their cockpits, our final checks being made, and then the engines started. I felt bad for the pilots. I could sense that they were nervous, but as they taxied their jets to the runways, the salutes exchanged between pilots and ground crews were noticeably sharper than usual.

Jet after jet screamed off into a pitch black night loaded to the hilt with bombs bound for Iraq. The ground trembled for nearly half an hour until the last jet lifted off. And then it was quiet. Almost six months wondering which would prevail. Peace or war. Now I knew. It had been a long wait, much too long. I stood there and felt sorry it had come to this, but I felt what we were doing was right. If not, God forgive us.

It was another 6 hours until the jets were due back. A tense time, just hoping for all of them to return safely.

Sometime during that morning, we all gathered around a radio and were able to hear President Bush's speech of his decision to go to war. He announced that the "Liberation of Kuwait had begun." No one clapped or cheered but the pride and determination showed. I'm sure I will never forget those words.

It was daytime when the jets began to come back, and we counted them as they appeared off in the distance and landed. They all made it. We loaded new weapons, fresh pilots were brought in, and the jets were off again.

I can't see how Iraq can take this pounding 24 hrs a day for much longer. I hope it ends soon. I've been working from 3 am to 3 pm. Didn't get much sleep the first couple of days. Must be why I've got this stupid cold. Since then I've been sleeping, eating, and feeling fine. I'm being as safe as I can possibly be and my spirits are good. I'll even be better when I'll be able to call Toni again to see how she's getting along. I'm sure I won't be with her when the baby comes, but like I told Grandma & Pop, if me not being there helps to make this a more peaceful world for Gage to grow up in, then my sacrifice will have been worth it. Now I just hope she'll be OK and our baby will be healthy. That's my biggest concern. It sure will be a special day when I see and hold our baby for the first time. Not to mention hugging Toni again too. I'm looking forward to seeing you both and I hope you're doing OK. Hope business is going good too, and I hope to see you soon.

Love,
Frank

P. S. Mom, I just got the box you sent with the candy. Thanks!

Gage Evans was born on March 4, 1991—the very day his father returned home safely from the Persian Gulf.

～

Writing to His Wife and Sons, Maj. Bob Munson Downplays a Scud Attack and Relates Some Lighter Moments on the Base

A fat, cloddish giant of a weapon, "Scuds" were long-range Iraqi missiles that, although inaccurate, inflicted enormous damage on impact. They were also mobile, making them easy to conceal and almost impossible to hunt down. Ravaged by the Allied air campaign, Iraq began indiscriminately firing Scuds into Israel, hoping to draw the Israelis into the war. President Bush warned Israel not to retaliate, arguing that if they did, Arab nations might withdraw from the international coalition and rally behind Iraq. Israel demonstrated remarkable restraint, and the coalition remained unified. The Iraqis also lobbed Scuds at Allied bases in Saudi Arabia, intending to kill or at least intimidate Allied troops. "It's an eerie feeling to hear across the airwaves to 'don full chemical protective gear: this is NO DRILL!,'" one young soldier (whose name has been withheld for reasons of privacy) wrote to a friend back in the United States. He continued:

In the bunker, there was a moment of total silence, and then bags, coverings, plastic and foil, exploded into the air like an instant blizzard. Shouts, prayers, curses, and the sound of weeping filled the space. Me? I was too busy trying to get into everything to talk. Just as we got it all on, we got the "all clear" signal. Another period of dead air. Then there was one voice cutting across the silence, who said, "Mommy, I want to go home." Instant laughter, and the spell was broken.

Over the next few nights, we went zinging through the dark for bunkers, more than once. At the time, it's the scariest feeling in the world. When the world returns to normal, you review things that went on that are startlingly funny. The 3rd raid caught some people in the latrine. Watching them bail out of it at a dead run, trying to don masks, hold weapons, and pull up pants is an arresting sight. You're praying for them to speed up and make it, but at the same time, you're dying from laughter. In the dark, why is it you run into things that you NEVER hit in the daylight? In the rush of the moment, you hear running feet, mumbled prayers and loud yells, and then, SLAM!!! Somebody hit a truck, fell in a ditch, or slammed into an airplane. I have learned words I never knew existed before.

Maj. Bob Munson, an aeromedical evacuation flight surgeon at the King Khalid Military City, endured his share of Scud alerts as well, but he did not want his wife and young sons, Michael and Daniel, to worry about him. In a letter home, Munson made light of the Scud attacks—which, he would later concede, were terrifying—and portrayed them almost as bit players in a war that, from his perspective, seemed to be becoming more and more of a sideshow.

22 Feb 91

Dear Pam & Boys,

Well, you may have heard that our area was targetted for Scuds. As I understand it, it was reported at the daily Saudi military briefing. Just like Riyadh it was pretty unimpressive. Two came in at broad daylight without warning and were intercepted by our Patriot missiles. Some small pieces fell at the other end of the runway but otherwise no big excitement. I didn't see anything as I was in the back of a Suburban at the time. The third scud came in at night & we had warning and so we were deep in our bunkers. That too was intercepted and the pieces fell far away from us.

Earlier that day Liz Kornegay (flt surgeon from Altus) & I were getting checked out on the ambulance so we could take alert rotations for airfield accident/emergency coverage. Just as our instruction ended news of a crippled F-16 came to us so we went out in the ambulance to watch the action (there was none). On our way back who should we bump into but none other than Sam Donaldson. Liz & I jumped out of the truck & unabashedly insisted that each of us have our picture taken with Sam. He was nice, but still rates an 8 on the Jane Fonda scale. Anyway, when the first scud attack occurred, Sam was seen driving off-base with a gas mask on.

The radio says that President Bush has given Iraq a deadline, so things may get busy for us in 48hr. We may be in pretty good shape here. Besides Londe & I we have 4 USAFE flight surgeons rotating through on flights to/from Europe. We've also recruited 2 local flight surgeons who are interested and may be available. Then there is a pool of physicians from CEEB (OMAN) which is a hospital manned by Scott AFB as well as an Army hospital. These guys may come forward and assist in whatever way they can. Ziggy Orzechowski is one of them. Londe is at Ramstein now but should get back tomorrow.

John Baxter & I borrowed a truck today to look for pieces of scud (we found none). While we were leaving the compound a Toyota landcruiser approached, chasing a sheep. The Saudi got out chasing the animal. I sensed a photo opportunity so I stopped and started taking pictures, then tried to help run down the animal. The Saudi ended up running over the sheep which slowed him down enough to catch. Once caught he slapped the sheep on the head and yelled at the animal. (Bad sheep! I guess)

I spent most of today buffing up our bunker. Barry Gardner and I shored up the wood roof & layed out sandbags while some of the flight nurses filled & tied sandbags. We'll use some of them to wall off our yard before putting in our gravel lawn. Then I built one of the nurses a vanity table out of scrap lumber & plywood. What's amazing is how everyone has adapted so well to living in tents—contrast us to the Army group across the street living in villas w/private shower & baths & even washing machines. All they do is complain how bad the Army is, while we borrow their washing machine.

Right now we're using 30mm shells as barter items. But these are so plentiful that they're losing their marketability. It's a form of inflation, I guess. That's why we were out looking for scud parts. Liz traded her flight knife (the one like I used to have in my flight suit leg pocket) to a guy from the French Air Force who promised her regular Perrier & bread. These guys have their own baker.

Time to go, tomorrow may be a long day. Don't worry about me, we're safe here. Give Michael & Daniel a big hug & kiss for me. I love you.

Bob

Three days after Munson wrote this letter, a Scud warhead slammed into the U.S. Marine barracks near Dharhan and exploded. An estimated one hundred Marines were wounded and twenty-eight were killed, representing one-fifth of all U.S.

deaths in the war. Powerless against the air campaign, Hussein was desperate to pro-
voke a ground war and fight the Allies to a bloody stalemate as he had done against
Iran. He was certain the Americans, who represented the overwhelming majority of
the Allied forces, were so tormented by Vietnam that they would retreat as soon as
their casualties started to escalate. Hussein had tried to spark a land battle in late Jan-
uary by sending tanks over the Saudi Arabian border and into the coastal town of
Khafji. They were soundly destroyed. In a move more spiteful than strategic, Hus-
sein ordered the torching of hundreds of Kuwaiti oilwells. Geysers of flaming oil
spewed out of the desert and into the sky, enshrouding the region in a bleak, smoky
haze. It would take seven months to extinguish the fires.

~

Capt. Samuel G. Putnam III Chronicles for His Wife and Family His Participation in the Ground War & S. Sgt. Dan Welch Reflects in a Letter Home How Strange the War Seemed and Expresses His Regrets the Allies "Didn't Go Far Enough"

After being pounded from the air for almost six weeks, Saddam Hussein's forces were
badly crippled but not defeated. Gen. H. Norman Schwarzkopf and his commanders
were anxious to end the war but agonized over how and when to begin the ground
campaign. They estimated that Hussein had four hundred thousand troops, includ-
ing his highly trained Republican Guard, entrenched throughout the mine-strewn
deserts of Iraq and Kuwait. They also feared that, if cornered, Hussein might use
chemical weapons. It was possible that up to ten thousand Americans, maybe twice
that number, would die in the offensive. But President Bush believed the time had
come, and the order was given: The ground assault would begin on Sunday, February
24. On her last mission ever, the USS Missouri—upon whose decks the Japanese
officially surrendered in 1945—bombarded Kuwait's beaches on the evening of Feb-
ruary 23, suggesting that an amphibious attack would follow. In fact, it was a feint.
The real invasion came hours later as the U.S. Marines charged straight into
Kuwait from Saudi Arabia. Hundreds of miles to the west, Allied airborne troops
headed north and then swooped east toward Kuwait in a flanking maneuver. The
army Seventh Corps, with its heavy armor, would follow a similar hook pattern in
the west to cut off Iraqi troops from all directions and ultimately crush the elite Repub-
lican Guard. President Bush was attending church services and had no idea how the
operation was unfolding. Secretary of Defense Richard Cheney received the first reports
from the field and passed a handwritten note up the aisle that read simply:

Norm says it's going very well!

Dick

In fact, Schwarzkopf and his generals were stunned by what they were hearing: Saddam's troops were surrendering in droves. Some did resist, and scattered firefights erupted. But after only one hundred hours, the ground campaign was over and the Allies were victorious. Thirty-one-year-old Capt. Samuel Grady Putnam III, a flight surgeon from Pennsylvania with the 1/1 Cavalry Squadron, 1st Armored Division, Seventh Corps, wrote to his wife back home the day the fighting stopped.

2/28/91

Dear Sharon,

It's great to be here, even if this place is windy, dusty & ugly — it's just great to be able to write a letter after the past 4 days.

We're now in Southeastern Iraq, about 12 miles west of the Kuwait border. It was a truly incredible trip to this spot, which I'll tell you about from the beginning.

On the 24th, at about 8 AM, we started moving north from our last holding area in Saudi Arabia. We've known for about 4 weeks what our mission was — to go into Iraq and outflank their forces, focusing in on the Republican Guards. So we headed north, thinking we'd stop just short of the border and spend the night. There was one unit ahead of us — the 2nd Armed Cavalry Regiment. Things were going so well for them, that we got the word we would go straight into Iraq that day. We stopped a couple miles south of the border, put on our chemical suits, took our PB tabs (anti-nerve agent tabs), and had a quick orders brief. . . .

Periodically I tuned into the BBC news on shortwave — the press still didn't seem to know that we were moving north. We thought this would be our first big battle day. We thought we'd be getting shot at as we moved north that day, but instead we ran into a bunch of surrendering Iraqi soldiers. The spot reports started slow, maybe 3 EPW's (Enemy Prisoners of War), then 7, then 15, then 60, then 120 Iraqis surrendering. There were a bunch at a bunker complex that was targeted for artillary, so we had to get them out before our artillary could blast it. It stopped us for a couple hours, so I stood up on the aid station and watched the entire 1st Armored Division pull up behind us — it was incredible. Thousands of vehicles rolling across the desert. It visually showed me what a feat it was getting all this stuff here — and that just one Division out of the 8 that the army has here. A herd of camels got caught up in the movement and were totally perplexed — didn't know which way to go.

Back to the EPW's — they knew exactly how to surrender, thanks to the leaflets that our air force dropped on them. They had no desire to die for Saddam. I saw lines of them, hands over their heads, waving anything white that they could find. One guy was dancing with a white sheet over his head. One group had a dog surrendering with them. They looked pretty hurting — torn up uniforms, thin, many without shoes. They just left their weapons sitting on the ground. We picked up so many of them that we stopped stopping for them and just pointed them south — let someone else in the Division pick them up.

Our troops made a bit of contact with Iraqi troops not willing to give up — but they blew up the vehicles & took care of that. None of our guys were injured. The day ended about 70 miles into Iraq. It was raining and very dark and we were the furthest unit into Iraq — half of our soldiers were on guard that night. I slept in one of our ambulances and got a great 8 hours of sleep.

We knew the war was going well. We were moving faster than expected and had very few casualties, so for us it was going real well. We also heard the reports of how other fronts were doing and they were all good. The Republican Guards were moving southeast, just like we wanted them to. Our move was a flank/encircle maneuver to isolate them. I was happy to just follow along & hear what was happening, as long as we weren't getting shot at and our squadron wasn't getting casualties.

The next day we moved out at first light. The terrain changed dramatically — it was hilly with lots of small scraggly bushes and more camels. We went through a large bedouin camp. I wonder what they were thinking as this division rolled through the camp. Our air troops found a bunch of enemy tanks to our south, so we stopped for a couple hours while we worked with air force to take them out. I was still just following along, looking at my map once in a while, and hoping that the battle would continue to go as well.

By nightfall we were at our objective that was supposed to take 4 1/2 days to reach. Things were going so well that we kept going. We were still the furthest unit into Iraq, and moving northeast towards Kuwait, we started to pass more enemy positions with blown up tanks & unexploded bombs & mines that we had to avoid. Everyone did avoid them.

Furthur on that night we started to hear and see a lot of boom - booms to our south. That was the Republican Guards fighting our 3rd Armored Division. Our guns wiped them out that night. That's also when our artillary started firing from behind us right over our heads. I was a bit nervous about a round falling short — but it didn't happen. At about 11:30 PM we stopped to let our artillary prep the battlefield in front of us. Our troops were sending mortar on a road to our north, artillary was going off to my west, there was a major battle to our south. I saw a vehicle blow up and fly about 100 feet into the air — and to our east were the Republican Guards that we were going after — the Medina division. Every direction I turned there were explosions. Our vehicles were lined up in columns, mine being the last vehicle of our column. I was standing outside, when I saw something fire into a hill not 200 feet from me. I dove behind my humvee along with 2 other guys — we were sure we were getting shot at. We had our weapons out, ready to shoot at anything that moved. I thought the worst, but it turned out one of our own bradleys had fired that shot at a bunker near us. Scared by our own troops.

We moved a little furthur after the artillary barrage, then stopped for another one. I can't describe to you the power that you feel when artillary goes off anywhere nearby. The earth shakes, your body vibrates, the sound is deafening. I watched as these rockets were being fired directly behind me — coming right at me and over my head, hitting about 10 miles to our front. They were beautiful to watch, but it must be hell on earth to be anywhere near where they land.

Most of our guys were sleeping at this stop, but I stayed awake and kept my eyes open to our rear. I wasn't going to take any chances. I saw about 10 people coming over a hill with their hands over their heads — figured they were Iraqis surrendering. I rounded up a few guys with M-16 rifles & drove over to them. It turned out they were 11 soldiers from the Tawakalna Division of the Republican Guard — supposedly the most elite forces, surrendering to me. My guys seized their weapons & searched them. They were thin, disheveled, cold & dirty. I asked if any of them spoke english and I got a resounding "no" from most of them. I laughed at that and most of them responded with a nervous chuckle. I'm sure they were worried that we might just shoot them. We put all their weapons in my humvee and pointed them west — towards the rest of the Division following us. They were a little hesitant to walk away — I think they thought we would shoot them. Eventually they walked. I was left with 7 AK-47's, Soviet made assault rifles. I got a picture of me holding them all, then Mascellino and I buried them. Now I can boast about how I single-handedly captured 11 enemy soldiers — could you imagine if that happened to Wags? Think how inflated that story would become.

We stopped again about 3 AM. Everyone was tired but ecstatic that things were going so well. It seemed too good to be true — and it was. We heard a loud "crack", — much closer & different sounding than the ones we'd been hearing the last 2 days. Mascellino & I jumped out of our humvee and beelined for the nearest armored vehicle — an ambulance 2 up from me. As I ran up I twisted my ankle & limped towards the ambulance. I saw multiple explosions very close — right in front of me. I heard guys screaming and saw people running as I dove into the ambulance.

It stopped soon after I got in. We had been attacked by someone, somehow, somewhere — no one knew where it came from. I hobbled out and heard we had a lot of casualties at the TOC (tactical operations center) where about 100 soldiers live. I drove over there & saw guys laying out all over the place. I went to each one & checked them out — we had 21 casualties, but no one had a life threatening injury. It was a miracle. The artillary that hit us exploded over our head, where it shoots out a bunch of little bomblets that then explode when they hit the ground. They send shrapnel in all directions. We dressed all the wounds, sorted the patients & put guys on ambulances who couldn't walk. By then it was 5:30 AM, we tried to get some sleep for an hour, but I don't think anyone slept. The explosions that we'd been hearing the last 2 days and had adjusted to now made everyone very nervous. When the sun came up we re-checked all wounds & I decided who needed to be evacuated & who could stop with us. We ended up sending eight guys back to hospitals — wherever they are now.

We were incredibly lucky. With all that shrapnel flying around, no one had any vital organs or eyes pierced. Someone was definitely watching over us then. You know I'm not too religious, but I just can't attribute our good fortune to luck alone. I think I may have seen the power of your prayers that night.

That scene totally changed the attitude of the squadron. Immediately, we all realized what war really meant, and everyone hated it. I have never been as scared as when that stuff exploded. Since then, everyone wore their frag vest (body armor) & most slept in armored vehicles. We all jump a bit more when we hear explosions.

We still don't know where that came from — but it was most likely from our own guys. Friendly fire that wasn't.

We moved up a few more miles yesterday morning, then stopped and let the Division pass us by. They battled all day yesterday with tanks, apache helicopters, artillary and jets going after the retreating Iraqis. By last night I was delirious — I hadn't slept in 38 hours. I crashed in the ambulance & slept a solid 10 hours, woken up intermittently by the explosions around us, hoping that they were outgoing and not incoming.

This morning I woke up and heard the <u>second</u> best news in my life — Pres. Bush announcing a cease fire. I was working on patients later this morning when I then heard the <u>best</u> news in my life — that Iraq had accepted the cease fire terms. Hopefully that's it, but I won't believe it for sure until I'm out of here.

The sun's now setting & to the east I can see the red glow of an oil field burning under dark clouds, with a full moon rising above the clouds. It's beautiful.

Dear Ya'll

I'm now back in Saudi Arabia. I'm in a maintenance collection point about 20 miles from King Faud Military City (K.F.M.C). The rest of my unit is still in N. Kuwait. My tank developed an oil leak part way through the fighting, and finally quit 2 days ago.

I don't know if KFMC is on the map, but if it is you know where I am. I sure don't. I wrote some place names I saw on the way here on the back of my hand, but I did my laundry today and......

We passed Kuwait City on the coast road in the middle of the night. I can't describe it. I mean the scene on the highway. We all just looked at it in the moonlight as we drove Throught the now silent carnage, going, "God damn, God damn....."

I talked to a lieutenant today who saw it during the day while it was still fresh, and he gave an interesting description of the dead that still littered the highway, vehicles, etc. He picked up a beret out of the front seat of a car, with a dead Iraqi in the back seat, eyes wide open, frozen in a silent scream.

Please save this letter — it's as much a journal as a letter. I don't think I'll write anybody else in this detail, so feel free to share this with anybody — ie. our parents.

I think about you & my sons all the time — you've kept me going through this ordeal, I can't wait to get home.

I love you,
Putt

S. Sgt. Dan Welch, a tank commander with the 1st Infantry Division, Seventh Corps, was also elated by Iraq's surrender. But in a letter written to his mother and extended family back in Maine a week later, Welch began to express more ambivalence about the brief, almost surreal war he had just experienced. Welch was also unsettled by the Allies' decision not to assist the Iraqi rebels struggling to topple Hussein. (Marianne is his wife and Chris is his three-year-old son. Although Welch states that he is writing from the "King Faud Military City," he later realized he was, in fact, at the King Khalid Military City.)

8 March 91

Dear Y'all

I'm now back in Saudi Arabia. I'm in a maintenance collection point about 20 miles from King Faud Military City (K.F.M.C). The rest of my unit is still in N. Kuwait. My tank developed an oil leak part way through the fighting, and finally quit 2 days ago.

I don't know if KFMC is on the map, but if it is you know where I am. I sure don't. I wrote some place names I saw on the way here on the back of my hand, but I did my laundry today and . . . . . .

We passed Kuwait City on the coast road in the middle of the night. I can't describe it. I mean the scene on the highway. We all just looked at it in the moonlight as we drove through the now silent carnage, going "God damn, God damn. . . . . ."

I talked to a lieutenant today who saw it during the day while it was still fresh, and he gave an interesting description of the dead that still littered the highway, vehicles, etc. He picked up a beret out of the front seat of a car, with a dead Iraqi in the back seat, eyes wide open, frozen in a silent scream.

I still think of the guy I shot the day before we attacked. If I hadn't done it, he could have been in an EPW camp right now, waiting to go home, just like me. He probably would have surrendered along with most of the others, just one day later.

We should be able to get to the phones in the next day or two. You'll already know if I did when you get this.

They're talking we'll be here like probably three weeks or so, then move into the KFMC itself for 3 weeks or so, and then move from there toward the aircraft. We heard the first guys got home today. 100 from 24th Mech at Ft. Stewart.

I guess I haven't said anything much about what I'd done during the ground war. I started writing to Marianne about it, but it didn't come out right. We didn't do much shooting, though we (my tank) expended more ammo than any of the others in my platoon. We never shot another tank or vehicle, except one suspect tank, that, after the dust from the artillery settled, ended up an already dead heavy truck. We shot up some trenches and bunkers, mostly empty. But you never really know. We ran over some AP mines and unexploded DPICM and cluster bombs here and there, received some incoming artillery off to our flank once, etc. Mine missed an anti-tank mine by about 2 feet on the right side once coming around a dune, and at our speed would have probably gone off under my gunner and I.

It never seemed like a war. More like a field problem. Even when stuff was burning all around you and firing going off all over the place, artillery firing from behind you and landing to your front. It was very real, but more a curiosity than anything else. I just can't describe it.

Like one time 21 was right next to me, and we were on the move. He was on my right, and ran over an AP mine or submunition with his left track. It exploded and sent shit flying past me. I was up out of my hatch, and the first thing that came to mind was can I get to my camera before the smoke clears? I didn't even think to duck. And the L.T. (21) just throws his hands up and smiles, like "Oh well".

The first time I ran over one I thought that 23, to my left had fired his main gun. I didn't realize 'till one of the others ran over one what had happened. Sometimes the stuff blows a hole through the track, etc. Sometimes it doesn't scratch it.

When we were breaching the main Iraqi defense line in the neutral zone, an idiot popped up with an AK from a trench and started firing. Mine was the first to return fire, and he didn't pop back up. Although the muzzle fask was pointing at us, you just don't think of it as someone shooting at you. Just a target and you engage it, like on a range.

Right after I released the mineroller and was linking back up with the platoon, some incoming artillery rounds landed maybe 300–400 yards from us to the left and my only consideration was that it wasn't a very good shot. And the second volley never came, so I just figured that our counter-battery must have had better aim.

Can you understand what I'm saying? I think I would have had to have gotten hit for it to seem different. I guess I've played it so much for the last ten years that it just didn't seem much different than the training. I've had field problems that were tougher. This only lasted for four days. It wasn't even long enough to seem like a war. The waiting and worrying before we did it were worse than doing it.

The only time I was ever really afraid was a couple of weeks before we did it. Then I got over that. After that, the only time I thought much about it was when I would picture that split second as the impact would rip my cupola from the turret and half my body would collapse onto my gunner's back, and the resulting tears back home. But not even that from the time the prep bombardment ended and we rolled forward through the cease fire.

The thing that was hardest for me was knowing how Marianne and you, Ma, were probably taking this back home. The image I've had of you two sitting in front of the T.V. afraid that I'm already dead, can and has choked me up and brought tears to my eyes. Even now as I write this I'm hoping that Marianne isn't still waiting for the "We're sorry" Team to come knock at the door. I wish I could get to a phone to relieve the pain.

You don't know what it's like to hold an M-16 up to a man's back and make him clear out of a trench, and pick up a few pieces of rock hard bread, blue and green with mold, and break pieces off and eat them.

Or realizing you came a few feet from crushing live men that you thought were dead, and only saw at the last moment because they were too afraid to stand up.

It's only been the last couple of days that I've come to realize the horror that has taken place here. It's not a personal feeling of horror, but more an overall picture of horror. And I think it's taken so long because with only the small number of exceptions on our part, it was almost entirely theirs.

I can only imagine what it was like for those who were part of the carnage of which we witnessed the silent aftermath on that highway. It is just so very strange.

I'm just now realizing the significance of all these things I've been through and seen, that were at the time merely curiosities. It's just different now. I don't know if I'm really explaining it or leaving you wondering what the hell I'm trying to get across.

I wish that that night that we were mopping up the remains of that republican guards division that there had been another one behind it, so that there would be less of them left. We have now left the rebels in Iraq with a much harder problem to solve in their struggle. And when we pulled up to Basra, we had to halt for about an hour while a battalion of

Rep. Gds. T-72's pulled out of the positions that we sat in for 3 days before we withdrew. They left one behind that they couldn't get started, and I smashed out all the optics and visions blocks with a tanker's bar with delight, knowing how much work and money they'd spent fixing it. We should have torched it after we stripped it, but by that time it was a no-no.

The news said that rebels had come to our lines asking us to join them, and also said they were running short on ammo. Of course we couldn't join them, but I and others would have led them to the vast stock piles in our vicinity if they had come to us.

I think we've made a mistake and not finished this the way it should have been ended. There is now a weakness in my heart for the people of Iraq. I'm still trying to explain what has gone on here. The next time you go to the drive-thru at McDonalds, remember that you haven't been living off rice, onions, and radiator water in your hole in the ground for the last month and a half, hoping you won't be exterminated by a pilot you don't hate, because someone told you if you didn't they would kill you and your family.

The next time you see someone throwing garbage at the White House, know that a helicopter is not going to spray them with nerve gas.

Don't hate the guy that has been busy burning Kuwait hotels and dragging people off, because it's been happening in his hometown for quite a while now, and by now he probably doesn't even realize what he's doing.

It may appear to most of us over here and to you back home that we've done our jobs, but we've screwed up and didn't finish it. He's still alive, and unless somehow the rebels finish what we've started, we may be back.

I guess I'm finally starting to feel I've fought in a war.

This is what I expected it to be like in the first place before I came over here. It just took a while for it to sink in that it really was. I think the easy victory just clouded the undertones until I reflected on it for a while here tonight.

But I still think we did the right thing, although we didn't go far enough. I still like what I do, this hasn't changed that. And I'm not psycologically scarred or maimed for life. If anything, this has just reinforced all I've believed in before I came over here. And I'll be home soon.

Love,
Dan

P.S. I hope you're saving all my letters. Someday I'd like to go through them with Chris.

"The specter of Vietnam has been buried forever in the desert sands of the Arabian peninsula," President Bush declared after the war. With a staggering 90 percent approval rating in 1991, Bush's reelection seemed guaranteed. But after the U.S. economy slipped into a recession, Bush was defeated by Governor Bill Clinton of Arkansas in 1992. Upon hearing the news, a jubilant Saddam Hussein stepped onto the terrace of his presidential office and celebrated by firing a pistol into the air. Hussein would outlast President Clinton as well.

~⌒

Gen. H. Norman Schwarzkopf and Gen. Colin Powell Console the Families of Two Men Killed in the Persian Gulf
&
General Powell Responds to a Withering Onslaught of Questions— from a Class of First Graders

Rumbling through the jungles of South Vietnam on February 14, 1966, in a personnel carrier, thirty-two-year-old H. Norman Schwarzkopf came within inches of being shot dead by a Viet Cong machine gunner. Twenty-five years later Schwarzkopf, nicknamed "Stormin' Norman" for his indomitable will power and volatile temper, was in command of all U.S. and non-Arab coalition forces in the Gulf War. Gen. Colin Powell, appointed by President Bush as chairman of the Joint Chiefs of Staff, also served two tours in Vietnam as a military advisor, and also survived his share of close calls. Both men were profoundly affected by the carnage they witnessed in Vietnam and were determined not to repeat the mistakes of their predecessors. Allied forces in the Gulf War would, they vowed, go in with clear objectives and overwhelming firepower. Although Americans suffered relatively few casualties— approximately 150 battle fatalities in all (over 20 percent of which were caused by "friendly fire")—Schwarzkopf and Powell were well aware that each death was profoundly traumatizing for the families who lost a loved one. After learning that an army nurse in the Persian Gulf named Karen Bnosky had lost her twenty-five-year-old husband (who was also serving in the Gulf) in a jeep accident, General Schwarzkopf sent the following:

15 April 1991

Dear Karen,

I received a beautiful letter from your parents today. They spoke to me of your grief and asked if I would write to you. I am indeed proud to do so.

I join you in your grief for the tragic loss of your husband, Jeff. Since both you and I are members of the military service, we knew that some day we might be called to serve our country in time of war, and we also fully understood that this service could result in our death. Nonetheless, because we believe in a cause higher than self, we chose to serve our country and take that risk. Few who have never served their country will ever understand a soldier's heart. Just as Kipling once said, "In time of war the public adores soldiers and in time of peace they are slighted." Even so, because we choose to serve our country we become part of a very special and honorable group of Americans and we can take pride in ourselves and our accomplishments. I am sure that Jeff felt this way about his military service.

Even though we understand that we might give up our lives for our country in times of war, none of us are prepared for that reality, and particularly when that reality is a tragic accident rather than a fierce battle. For this reason I will constantly badger my commanders about taking care of their troops. I badger them even more about the prevention of careless accidents that might result in a senseless loss of life. Your story and similar stories of over 150 family members who have lost loved ones as a result of accidents renew my conviction to continue to insist that our leadership remains vigilant to the prevention of such tragic accidents. I will never cease in my efforts until the day I remove my uniform and probably not even then.

I am very proud of you that despite your tragic loss you have chosen to continue with your life in the Army. Simply stated, that is the epitome of selfless service to your country. Your country should be proud of you also. I am also proud of your efforts to see to it that our country does not forget that when we send our service men and women abroad that they face many dangers in addition to the enemy. Those who lost their lives in Desert Shield deserve to be recognized by their countrymen just as much as those who lost their lives during Desert Storm. It is because of people like you that their sacrifices will not be forgotten.

I pray that your grief will soon pass and I know that your memory of Jeff will never fail. I hope that eventually you will draw strength from the fact that your husband thought enough of his country to give his life for it and that this strength will cause you and all who you meet to rededicate themselves to the values and ideas for which our great country stands. God bless you.

Sincerely,
H. NORMAN SCHWARZKOPF
General, U.S. Army

General Powell, whose correspondences tended to be more formal in nature, received a letter from the mother of a thirty-four-year-old marine captain, Jonathan Ross Edwards, killed in the Gulf on February 2. Captain Edwards, who had a wife and children back in Grand Rapids, Michigan, was piloting a medical evacuation mission when his helicopter crashed. Ms. Edwards wrote directly to General Powell to request information about her son's two-year service in the U.S. Army, beginning when he was seventeen. Powell replied with the following:

Dear Ms. Edwards,

Thank you for your letter concerning your son, Jack. Please accept my heartfelt sympathy at his loss during Operation DESERT STORM. Your letter has conveyed the pride you have for Jack's distinguished service to our Nation. I share your pride in him, and I share your sorrow over the terrible sacrifice he, and you, had to make.

It took us some time to trace Jack's Army service record. I enclose the awards you requested as well as a copy of his Record of Separation from Active Duty and a copy of a letter of Commendation he received during his service in Korea. In staffing your letter, we learned from the Marine Corps that an additional service award, recently approved, also should be sent to you soon.

Finally, I must tell you that I firmly believe that the cause for which Jack fought and died was a noble and necessary one. And while I also believe that the decisions we made during the Persian Gulf crisis were the right ones, I deeply regret the cost so many good Americans like you had to pay. The very gracious words at the end of your letter meant a great deal to me personally and will continue to have a special place in my thoughts long into the future.

Once again you have my sincere sympathy and best wishes.

Sincerely,
COLIN L. POWELL
Chairman of the
Joint Chiefs of Staff

During the war General Powell earned high praise for his public relations skills, answering a barrage of questions from the media with charm and, in as much as wartime secrecy would allow, candor. After the war, Powell received a veritable grilling from an unexpected source: a class of first graders from Ypsilanti, Michigan. The chairman of the Joint Chiefs of Staff—the most senior military advisor to the president—dutifully replied to the inquisitive tykes with the following:

May 24, 1991

Dear Ms. Dusbiber and First Graders,

Thanks for all the wonderful pictures. They did, indeed, make my day. In fact, of all the correspondence I have received as a result of

DESERT STORM, I have found none more enjoyable than your collection of drawings.

In response to most of your questions, I can drive a tank, have been scared, like to read, travel frequently, eat snacks, have a family, smile often, sometimes get angry, love pizza, have attended many schools, watch lots of television, like sports, enjoy exercising, cannot fly a plane, have eaten at the White House, and have very little spare time. There are female generals; my boss is the Secretary of Defense, and my wish is for a peaceful earth where every individual is free.

My best wishes to all of you. Thanks again for thinking of me.

Sincerely,
COLIN L. POWELL
Chairman
Joint Chiefs of Staff

In January 2001, Colin Powell became the first African-American secretary of state in U.S. history.

~~

Photojournalist Dan Eldon Sends a Short Note to His Girlfriend from Mogadishu About the Plight of Somalia

"I am in Somalia now," photographer Dan Eldon wrote to his girlfriend on September 10, 1992.

> *The rains are coming, it's a full moon and tensions are very high. A boy guard was shot dead at the airport and our guards at the house want revenge for the killing. . . . The UN are sending 300 troops into Somalia and we're discussing with the General the details. This could mean hope for the people or more fighting and suffering.*

A seahorse-shaped country on the coast of East Africa, Somalia was ravaged by famine and civil war in 1992 as despotic warlords and gangs of armed and intoxicated teenagers terrorized the capital of Mogadishu. Millions of Somalis—many of them children—were perilously malnourished, and a humanitarian crisis of staggering proportions was developing rapidly. In the spring and summer of 1992 the United Nations coordinated relief efforts in the region, and in August President George Bush announced that the United States would airlift food to Somalia. Eldon, a world traveler raised in Kenya and later the United States, went to Somalia as a Reuters photographer to put a human face on the tragedy. A handsome, gregarious young man, Eldon befriended many Somalis and was nicknamed the "Mayor of Mogadishu" by the locals. But as the days passed, he became more and more exasperated by the violence and misery around him. Eldon wrote few letters while in Africa (he kept in touch with his sister Amy and his mom back in the United States mostly by telephone), but on September 14, 1992, he sent the following to his girlfriend in Nairobi, Kenya:

Hello, it's me—two days later, still in Somalia, still scary. I went to the Red Cross hospital yesterday. So sad—I saw a 13-year-old girl covered in bandages—a grenade had exploded in her face. I also saw a really beautiful Somalia girl named Hos. Her hair was just like yours, and she had washed it. She made me think of you so much. She looks like she could be one of your sisters. I wanted to tell her about you but she spoke zero English. Today was the usual collection of psychopaths trying to threaten to kill me. It must be so tiring being a Somali and having to argue about absolutely everything. Honestly these people are really too much. I was talking to some last night who said they wanted to invade Kenya after their war was over. They are crazy. The nights are so boring here. It's 9:00 and I'm already in bed—alone—thinking about you—

I hope there is a letter waiting for me when I get back to Nairobi.

Upon learning that much of the aid airlifted into Somalia was being stolen by the warlords and sold on the black market, the United Nations sent a U.S.-led task force to Mogadishu in December 1992 to oversee the orderly distribution of the food. Operation Restore Hope, as the effort was called, was successful and prevented mass starvation. The following spring the United Nations broadened its mission by attempting to break the warlords' stranglehold on the country and help Somalis build a democratic society. On July 12, 1993, a failed UN raid on the headquarters of Mohamed Farah Aidid, one of the region's most powerful clan leaders, resulted in numerous civilian deaths. A crowd of enraged Somalis, wielding guns and machetes, saw several journalists—including Dan Eldon—photographing the bloody aftermath of the attack and quickly surrounded them. After butchering three of his colleagues (Hansi Kraus, Anthony Macharia, and Hos Maina), the mob descended on Eldon. He was twenty-two years old when he died.

~

Black Hawk Pilot Michael Durant Writes from Captivity in Somalia to Assure His Wife and One-Year-Old Son That, Although Injured, He Is Still Alive

On October 3, 1993, a Black Hawk helicopter flown by thirty-two-year-old CWO Michael Durant was shot out of the sky by a rocket-propelled grenade. The attack on Durant and his crew came during a U.S. attempt in Somalia to apprehend two "lieutenants" of clan leader Mohamed Farah Aidid. Knocked temporarily unconscious by the crash, Durant opened his eyes and realized he was stranded in the middle of Mogadishu with a broken back and a leg that had snapped apart on impact. Immobilized by his injuries, Durant was unable to escape, and he knew it was only a matter of time before hordes of Somalis would find and most certainly kill him and his crew, all of whom were severely wounded. A rescue convoy searching for another downed Black Hawk was being chewed up by gunfire as it crawled through Mogadishu's labyrinth of narrow streets and alleyways. Any hope of being saved was fading. Durant's worst fears became reality as a crowd of armed Somalis approached from all sides. They had just killed the last of his crew as well as two Delta Force commandos who had courageously volunteered to be dropped into the crash site to stave off any attackers. As dozens of screaming Somalis swarmed over him, Durant folded his arms on his chest, looked skyward, and prayed the end would at least come quickly. After beating him savagely, several Somalis decided the American pilot might be worth more alive than dead. Durant ended up in a small apartment where he was guarded by Aidid's propaganda minister. Several days later Durant was allowed to write a single, brief letter to his wife and one-year-old son in Clarksville, Tennessee. Although there remained a very good chance he would not return home alive, Durant tried to sound upbeat.

Dear Lorrie & Joey,

I know you must be worried about how I am doing. They are treating me well. The Somali doctor comes every day and cleans my injuries. The people taking care of me also are treating me well. They get whatever kind of food I ask for but there is no pizza available unfortunately.

I want nothing more in the world than to be with you and Joey again. I see his face and I pray that this will all turn out OK. Please tell everyone else in the family that I hear their prayers and things will work out OK.

Nothing else matters more to me than to see my family again. I think I will, I really do. You stay positive and be strong and give Joey more hugs and kisses for his Dad that misses him so.

I broke my leg (compound fracture right femur) and injured my back in the crash. I think my nose is broken but it does not hurt. I have a superficial gunshot wound in my left arm. The leg & back are the only real problems but as I said the medical care has been very good.

I hope to see you soon and I pray for the others who are missing, Ray, Bill, Tommy, and anyone else.

I love you.

Unbeknownst to Durant, a total of eighteen Americans had been killed and more than seventy had been wounded in the seventeen-hour battle in Mogadishu. It was the largest number of U.S. deaths from a firefight since Vietnam. (An estimated one thousand Somalis were casualties as well.) The dead body of Bill Cleveland, Durant's crew chief, was dragged through the city's streets by cheering Somalis as television cameras beamed the images worldwide. After the United States negotiated a peace with Aidid's militia, Durant, having spent ten days in captivity, was released. American forces withdrew from Somalia six months later.

~

1st Lt. Erin Shuler Writes an E-mail from Bosnia to Her Family Back in the States Detailing Serbian Atrocities
&
Maj. Thomas O'Sullivan Sends His Son, Conor, a Special Gift from Bosnia for His Seventh Birthday

Not since 1945 had Western Europe witnessed such slaughter; from 1991 to 1995 almost three hundred thousand men, women, and children were killed in the Balkans as a civil war raged in the former Yugoslavia. A cluster of republics cobbled together at the end of World War I, Yugoslavia began to unravel in 1980 when its Communist dictator Josip Broz Tito died after a thirty-five-year reign. In June 1991 Yugoslav republics Slovenia and Croatia officially declared their independence, followed by Bosnia-Herzegovina in early 1992. But one-third of all Bosnians were Serbs, and they vehemently objected to seceding from Yugoslavia. Political debate within the country exploded into bloodshed and the Bosnian Serbs, aided by neighboring Serbia, systematically began killing and raping Muslims and Croats in Bosnia to gain total control of the country. In July 1995 the Serbs besieged the Bosnian town of Srebrenica—which had been designated a "safe haven" by the UN—and massacred an estimated seventy-five hundred Bosnian Muslim men and boys. When economic sanctions failed to stop or even slow the ethnic cleansing, NATO air strikes led by the United States in 1995 pounded the Serbs into submission. Leaders from the former Yugoslavia came to the United States in November and, after protracted negotiations, signed a peace agreement that established new boundaries in Bosnia and the surrounding territories. Twenty-four-year-old 1st Lt. Erin Shuler was one of twenty thousand American troops sent to the area as part of an implementation force (later renamed SFOR for "stabilization force") to monitor the fragile peace plan. Serving as a military press officer at Eagle Base in Tuzla, Shuler dashed off an e-mail to her family back in Dallas, Texas, to relate stories she had heard of Serbian atrocities.

Hi all,

I hope that everybody had a nice weekend! I just wanted to thank everybody for their messages of concern. It makes me feel really good to know that everybody is out there thinking about me and the welfare of all of the troops stationed in this area. I know all this Kosovo stuff sounds pretty bad on the news but, just know I am very safe.

I am more than ready to be home. I really miss everybody and just having a normal life in general. As I think most of you know I spent almost a whole week in Germany last week during my leave. It was wonderful to wear jeans, eat with silverwear instead of plastic and to drink water from the tap!! It's amazing the things that you miss. I didn't even realize I had missed alot of these things until I was able to use them again.

I took many pictures during my R&R but before I show those I wanted to send some more of my pictures from Bosnia. They are more interesting to me than the Eifle Tower anyway.

batteryfactory—This photo is of an old bombed out building which used to manufacture batteries. It was a Serb stronghold during the war. If you look very closely on the top floor to the far right of the building you can see a defensive position with a bunch of sandbags. They would herd the muslim men into the parking lot and then just spray them with gun fire. Many massacres took place here. Some of the men were able to escape into the mountains very near but walking the mountains was very greuling and physically demanding so many of them did not make it. It is actually not at all unlike the situation in Kosovo right now. The similarities are striking really.

church—This church is in the town of Srebrenicia. Prior to the war, Srebrenicia was 95% muslim. Now, it is 99% Serb. American troops stationed at our base camp Camp Dobol, conduct regular presence patrols into the city to help build relationships and trust among the Serbian people. We accompanied the group during one of these patrols and it was truly fascinating to watch how the soldiers interacted with the people of the town. Many of the people, in particular the older ones, made no secret of the fact that we were not welcome there. But, the majority of the people were relatively nice . . . at least they tolerated us. It was amazing to see how the patrol commander, who is very well known in the town interacted with the locals. It is obvious that they genuinely trust him. He is their friend. That, I think is the best way to establish a lasting peace. Show all these different people from all sides that we are all human. We all have families, lives, ambitions and fears just like them. We are all humans and we can all live together. But, we have to be able to understand and appreciate our differences as much as our similarities . . . sorry about the preaching . . . . moving right along!

Dam—the dam is on the way to Srebrenicia. Just on the other side of the reiver is Serbia. I certainly wouldn't want to be there right now. The story behind this river and this dam is interesting but kind of disturbing. Apparently, during one particularly greusome battle of the war, this dam became clogged and had to be shut down because of all the bodies in the river. The water was completely red with blood. I don't know if that story is true but I certainly could believe it.

Grave—This was the the site of a mass grave that has been excavated. You can see how deep it is by looking at the ground were the digging occured. The graves were very shallow. SFOR is actually very involved with helping with mass grave excavation. They had to stop for the winter but excavations will more than likely be starting again soon.

Helo—This is just another picture of me. This was in the helicopter that we took down to Brcko, north of Tuzla. It's always cool to go on a helicopter.

Well . . . I guess that is all for this round. But, as always, there is more to come. Again, I think everybody for their thoughts. I will continue to keep you all posted on activities here but please don't worry. We are all safe so there is nothing to worry about. :)

I love and miss you all and can't wait to be home!!

Love,
Erin

Thirty-six-year-old Maj. Tom O'Sullivan was also in Bosnia, serving as the officer in charge of the First Armored Division Assault Command Post and, later, as the operations officer of the Fourth Battalion, Sixty-seventh Armor at Camp Colt. O'Sullivan frequently wrote home to his wife, Pam, and their two children, Tara and Conor, and on September 16, 1996—the day Conor turned seven—O'Sullivan sent a birthday gift he hoped would have special meaning to his son.

Dear Conor,

I am very sorry that I could not be home for your seventh birthday, but I will soon be finished with my time here in Bosnia and will return to be with you again. You know how much I love you, and that's what counts the most. I think that all I will think about on your birthday is how proud I am to be your dad and what a great kid you are.

I remember the day you were born and how happy I was. It was the happiest I have ever been in my life and I will never forget that day. You were very little and had white hair. I didn't let anyone else hold you much because I wanted to hold you all the time. That day was so special to me that I think it is right to have a celebration each year to remember it.

There aren't any stores here in Bosnia, so I couldn't buy you any toys or souvenirs for your birthday. What I am sending you is something very special, though. It is a flag. This flag represents America and makes me proud each time I see it. When the people here in Bosnia see it on our uniforms, on our vehicles, or flying above our camps, they know that it represents freedom, and, for them, peace after many years of war. Sometimes, this flag is even more important to them than it is to people who live in America because some Americans don't know much about the sacrifices it represents or the peace it has brought to places like Bosnia.

This flag was flown on the flagpole over the headquarters of Task Force 4–67 Armor, Camp Colt, in the Posavina Corridor of northern Bosnia-Herzegovina, on 16 September 1996. It was flown in honor of you on your seventh birthday. Keep it and honor it always.

Love,
Dad

AFTERWORD

There was never any intention of doing a book. Launched in November 1998, the Legacy Project was created solely to preserve American war correspondence so that future generations would better understand warfare and the sacrifices made by those who have served this nation. When I asked veterans and their families to share photocopies of letters that were particularly meaningful to them, I expected to receive a few hundred at best—not fifty thousand, as was ultimately the case.

With permission of those who contributed these never-before-seen correspondence (and with a promise that all earnings would be donated to veterans' organizations), I featured two hundred of them in *War Letters*. Our efforts to preserve this irreplaceable material did not end, however, with the publication of the hardcover book in May 2001. Indeed, since that time the Legacy Project has received an additional ten thousand war letters. With the release of this paperback edition, it seemed the ideal opportunity to add new correspondence—again, all previously unpublished—to emphasize that our mission continues.

Instead of weaving these new letters chronologically into the body of the book, I wanted to include them here, with commentary, to explain why they are unique. (Although I was adamant about not cutting letters in the first edition, those presented here have been slightly edited due to space constraints.) Over the past year I have been asked if we are looking for specific types of letters or why certain subject matters were not addressed in the hardcover edition. These letters represent answers to many of those queries.

A question I am asked frequently is whether or not the Legacy Project seeks out letters by veterans from other nations. The answer is yes. Although our focus is on American wars, our understanding of those conflicts are illuminated, I believe, by the insights and observations of those who fought both with and against this country.

One of the most astonishing letters I discovered concerned a heartbreaking story from World War II, involving the only fatalities on the continental U.S. caused by enemy weapons. In May 1945, Reverend Archie Mitchell was picnicking with his pregnant wife and five children on Gearhart Mountain, near Bly, Oregon. Rev. Mitchell watched with horror as one of the children picked up an unexploded "balloon bomb"—an incendiary weapon built by the Japanese that was floated over the Pacific Ocean and toward the United States, where it was intended to ignite on impact. The bomb blew up in the child's hand, killing him, the four other children, and Rev. Mitchell's wife. Only Rev. Mitchell survived.

Recently I received a remarkable series of letters written in 1987 by seven Japanese women who, decades after the deaths in Oregon, learned for the first time of the suffering these bombs had inflicted. In 1945 these seven women, although only high school students at the time, had all helped make the balloon bombs that killed Mrs. Mitchell and the five children. These women felt enormous guilt for what they had done, and with the help of a professsor in the United States named Yuzuru Takeshita, they sent letters of condolence to the surviving members of the Mitchell family. They also enclosed a thousand paper cranes they had folded, symbolizing the earnestness of their sorrow. Below is one of the letters, written by a woman named Ritsuko Kawano and translated by Professor Takeshita.

We learned concretely as to what happened with the balloon bombs only recently. The more we learned, the more we came face to face with the terrible past that involved the regretful loss of innocent lives. If the six persons who are resting in the hills of Oregon were alive today, they should be close to our age. They would be fine husbands and beautiful wives, with children and being a source of strength to their country. How regretful and painful to think of what might have been had they lived! I vow that I shall join those who, with courage, fight for peace, by talking to as many persons as possible about the futility of war and by insisting more than ever on the sanctity of human lives. I pray wholeheartedly that the souls of the six victims rest eternally in peace.

I also recently received letters written by Russian, Italian, and German soldiers who fought in World War II. What is striking is not how different their letters are from those by U.S. combatants, but how similar. The following letter, mailed on December 12, 1943, by a Russian soldier, echoes many of the sentiments expressed by American servicemen who felt their sweethearts back home had forgotten them. (The "Komsomol" he alludes to was a youth communist league.)

Hello Zinaida!

If you want to write to me as if I were an old friend to whom you had no real feel-ings, but just a childish attraction, I'll be happy to answer. But what for??? I'll be dead, and you'll be living a happy life. So go ahead and forget about a poor wretch, abandon him on the road, don't lift his feelings from the mud. I often remember happy days and nights with you, especially the latter. I was very happy, because I thought you had loved me, and that made me so happy, but now I understand that I was a fool. I wish you well. Be happy. I joined the Komsomol in September. I'm not going to meddle in your life, I'm not the kind of man to make problems for a person I honor and love.

Best regards from Sergey

Sergey's words immediately reminded me of a letter written more than twenty-five years later by a young African-American soldier fighting in Vietnam. On May 3, 1969, he wrote to his girlfriend after she told him she had met someone else:

Little Butterfly:

I received your letter & at the time I didn't know whether to laugh or cry. Every-thing was confused & clouded you see, I had just had my second narrow escape in a row & I was attempting to erase my nerves with the first half of this quart of rum when a comrade handed me your letter.

All that I can say in reply is that you've let people take advantage of you again. You think the same way I think, you believe the same way I believe, the only real difference is that we come around to needing & wanting each other at different times. We're both so subject to ideals & therefore to disillusion. I love you but there is no way in the world that I can help you until you are ready to acccept the fact that life is not a dream & you can't make it what you want it. I had planned on a long elabo-rate "Critique" but I'm too high & too much in love with you to go on. I can't get rid of the thought that I want to marry you but that's foolish, you love someone else & I only have $1,000 in the bank so far with a good chance of an early demise tomorrow or in the next four or five days.

Yes, I'm going out again but this time I have the best team in the 4th Div. The three of us during the next five days will either kill or be killed. I have no compul-sion over killing or being killed for that matter; you have me so confused that I just don't care anymore. The only things that I worry about is that my equipment is packed, my knives are sharpened until I can shave with all three of them & placed correctly on my belt, that my rifle is clean & I write a letter to you. All else that mat-ters is your kiss & that's so far away that I may as well not even think about it. Well, I gotta get some sleep.

I love you & I will forever.

This young soldier—whose name has been omitted to protect his privacy—survived the war. (The fate of the Russian, Sergey, is not known.) Of the tens of thousands of letters sent into the Legacy Project, only about a dozen are by African Americans. Considering their distinguished service fighting in every war in this nation's history, it remains one of the Legacy Project's highest priorities to seek out and find previously unpublished correspondence by black soldiers, marines, airmen, and sailors. Several months ago a man named Philip Tibbs generously sent us a series of letters by his father, Howard A. Tibbs, who served with the famed Tuskegee Airmen. Writing on March 17, 1945, to his mother in Salem, Ohio, the twenty-six-year-old Corporal Tibbs confided how he and his comrades were feeling about racial injustice.

Dear Mother:

Sat. morning and very dull. Had a furious rain & electric storm last night so it's overcast and rather chilly today.

This is certainly a lovely base where we are stationed now. I haven't gone anywhere at all since coming here. Been broke because I missed the pay-day having been in the hospital when the men were paid. They've been having dances twice a week out here on Mon. & Fri. Mon. the girls from Indianapolis and Franklin came out and Fri. from Louisville. We are midway between the two towns so that makes it rather nice that way. The nearest town, Seymour, is very prejudiced toward negroes, and it was reported that there was danger of racial friction, but nothing occurred.

It is a pity, though, that we are supposed to be defending the welfare of the country and yet it really amounts to upholding just the injustices which contradict all that we are supposedly here to destroy in this war effort. At times it is certainly ironic and makes one feel utterly disgusted. There are some really fine chaps in here who are so mixed up, angered, and hurt by demonstrations of all these things that are a constant thorn in the side.

Being philosophical about it doesn't help one bit, because it doesn't solve the problem. I for one will definitely devote much of my time after this is over for a more clear and better understanding. Sometimes it seems almost cruel to know that people are still having children who are going to be faced with the same thing.

Maybe I seem a bit morose, I'm really sorry for I'm not. It's just that not facing this thing and overlooking it is just the reason it still exists. I certainly hope the people at home living in civil life will lay more ground work and try to reach a clear understanding. You Mother, nor I, nor my children, if I am fortunate to have any, shall not see co-operation, but I'm firm in my belief that one generation will see it when another generation decides that race will no longer be cause and cause alone for all this pure stupidity. My next letter shall be much brighter than this seemingly depressed one has been, and for troubling you I apologize.

I've always admired your strength, and philosophy, the good clean, and unselfish thoughts and actions that are part of you. It's these things that give me faith, as your loving Son.

Although stories of tensions between servicemen of different ethnicities and faiths were common, there were also inspiring examples of unity. Lt. jg. Syd Brisker, a twenty-eight-year-old sailor from Bethlehem, Pennsylvania, wrote to his parents in April 1943 to describe an extraordinary Seder he organized aboard the gunship USS *Beaumont*. It is a remarkable example of how essential faith was to these young men and women and the great lengths they went to maintain religious traditions and rituals.

Dear Mother and Dad,

The ghosts of thousands of years of Jews were with me tonight—from the first refugees of the Bible's fascist Pharaoh through two destructions of the Temple and through ages of wandering and persecution—they were with me tonight at the strangest Seder I've ever had.

In the jungle heat of Guadacanal and the torridness of the African desert, in the biting cold of Iceland and Alaska, and the foggy dampness of England, modern Maccabeans in the uniforms of their beloved countries gathered tonight to celebrate the deliverance of the Jews from the persecution of an ancient fascism. The modern parallel is quite startling at first. It can be said, without fear of contradiction, there are no Jews in the ranks of the enemy.

When I look back on all the Seders I've sat at, in my own home with my beloved family, and in strange cities with friends, I wonder if I could ever have dreamed that I might be spending Passover on a U.S. Warship, bound on a mission of war. Or perhaps, I should say, a mission of peace, because we are fighting for the peace for which each Passover we lift our voices in prayer.

One enlisted man (ship's cook, third class) and myself are the only Jews aboard the Beaumont, but we decided to spend the Passover with a Seder. At our last port of call we obtained two boxes of matzoh, and a hagadah from the Chaplain. Alcoholic beverages are prohibited aboard U.S. men-of-war, and grape juice was unobtainable, so we substituted prune juice for wine. The Captain said he would cooperate in every way possible to help us hold our Seder. We got two chickens from the chief commissary steward. (I am the commissary officer, a recent appointment, so it was easily arranged!) For bitter herb we used stalks of Chinese cabbage; and for parsley we used the celery tops. The officer's steward baked a sponge cake. Everything else was quite orthodox—to the salt water and hard-boiled egg. But lacking matzoh-meal, there were no knadels. That would have been something to see—the matzoh balls rolling around with the motion of the ship.

A bay in the Chief Petty Officer's quarters was partitioned off by hanging two blankets, and the Seder was set at a table large enough for eight. We had several guests, the Pharmacist's mate 1/C, a Protestant, another ship's cook, who is Catholic, as well as the officer's steward. And to this gathering I related the story of Passover in English to the Four Questions as asked by Goldstein.

The modern parallel was more startling. When I read "And it is this same promise which has been the support of our ancestors and of us too: for at every time enemies rise against us, to annihilate us; but the most Holy, blessed be He, hath delivered us out of their hands" I could substitute Hitler for the Assyrian Laban who intended to kill every Jew—root out the whole race. And I read a prayer, which has been repeated for centuries, and today more loudly than ever "May He who maketh peace in His heavens grant peace on us all Israel, and say ye, Amen."

But if I was startled by the modern parallelism, it was the myriad of ghosts of long dead Jews, visiting me tonight, who make me feel this prayer for peace need not be repeated year in and year out. We have the answer in our power now. The United Nations can make this Victory one of everlasting Peace, and build a world in which Jew and Gentile, white and colored, can live in peace, harmony and security—just like we of different faiths and races sat down at Seder tonight.

Good night, dear parents—God Bless You.

All my love, Syd

Syd survived the war and is alive and well to this day.

Frequently I am asked if the Legacy Project receives, along with the countless "why we fight" letters, correspondences written by pacificists and conscientious objectors. To date there have only been a handful, and not surprisingly, they are mostly from the Vietnam War era. One that struck me as particularly memorable was by a twenty-five-year-old Peace Corps volunteer in Liberia named D. Michael Van De Veer who wrote to his brother, John. The brothers were from Montgomery, Alabama, and John was in the army training for "graves identification registry," which entailed collecting the body parts of men killed in action and then shipping the remains back to the States. John found the work emotionally unbearable and deserted the army. Michael, who was recovering from both a serious illness and a car accident, offered moral support to his younger brother.

My Dearest Brother John,

I am not sure if you will ever read this letter but I needed to write you. If I could see you, and hold you in my arms, I would tell you how proud I am of what you have done. You know that is one of the reasons I joined the Peace Corps. I, too, am a "deserter" from that cruel, unjust war. On that day when all the soldiers show the same valor that you have, on all sides, and walk away, there will be no more war.

The suffering is not just limited to South East Asia and Vietnam. The money that is used to make one bomb, can build two schools.

You wouldn't recognize me. I am in the middle of a rubber plantation, with tubes running out of my left arm, and I weigh about 116 lbs. We are in the midst of a cholera epidemic and already 42 out of 165 have died. As you would expect, I did my best, but especially the old, and the young died too fast to bury. Some few days ago I developed diarrhea, vomiting and fever, like nothing I have ever known. I thought it would pass but it wouldn't let up. As no one else could drive, I tried to drive myself and remember leaving the road and smashing into the bush. When I woke up yesterday, much to my surprise, I was/am alive! I feel too dehydrated to cry and don't know how it will be to return to the village, but with all the troubles I have with the Peace Corps, I have found some kind of "true peace" there, even amongst all this poverty and death. I guess I will recover and at some point we will be reunited. Until then, and Forever, I Love and Respect You,

Your Big Brother, Michael
PS take care of yourself and remember you still owe me $40.

Not all of the letters sent to the Legacy Project are profound or philosophical. Funny things happen in wartime, and servicemen and women have penned their share of whimsical missives. These letters serve a valuable historic purpose as well, for they remind us that it is not statistics that head off to war, but individual combatants with their whole lives ahead of them. Humorous letters, no less so than battle accounts or messages of love, humanize these young men and women. The following was written during World War II by two mail-deprived ensigns named Nye Moses and Bill Wilhoit. The letter is self-explanatory.

Dear Elizabeth Jane,

This is a fan letter! You see, you wrote a letter to C.W. Faust on L.C.I. 540. My Executive Officer and I saw your beautiful and neat handwriting, smelled the sweet perfume on the letter and said, "Anyone who sends letters such as this must be more wonderful than Paulette Goddard, Lana Turner, Betty Hutton, and Ingrid Bergman all put together!" We then said, "Why not write her a letter?" So I (we) did, I mean we are now. This is it! How does it feel to have a "public"?

Before I begin, let me explain that we are two very lonely lads and our morale is very low. We have hearts of gold but girls never seem to bother finding it out after once looking at our comical faces. My Executive Officer's name is Bill. He graduated from Georgia Tech in February. He's a "rebel" from way back. As for looks— well, he doesn't really have any. Your first impression of him is Gargantua has arrived in England. But if you look closely, you will discover that he has yellow hair, it is not exactly hair, it is more like fuzz being only $1/4$ inch long at the present time.

For ears, he has sort of curley protrubances that look not unlike cauliflowers. He claims he was born with them that way, but I don't believe it. God couldn't make a man with ears like that. I don't think he has any eyes, at least I've never been able to find them. He says he can see so that settles it—he has eyes. His nose looks like a large, very red apple. It is his best feature. At least you know he has a nose. His mouth is really a good looking one except that he has no lips. We are at a loss to explain why, he just has no lips.

I should stop here, but I won't. His physique? Well, he has 26 shoulders and a 36 waist. His arms and legs are nice. They are only about the size of a baseball bat but are all muscle. He claims he had a girl once, but I doubt it. Anyway, every day he wishes he would get a letter from a girl, but he never does. Couldn't you surprize him with one?—just for the morale of the boys in the service?

Girls don't like me either, but I really am a swell guy. I am not good looking, but I think I have sort of an inner beauty radiating from my heart within. I can not explain why others don't discover it. To begin with I have beautiful red eyes (at least you can see mine), I have a long, finely formed nose. I have the best looking ears. They are real big and they sort of stick out, but attractively. I think my lips are a lit- tle thick, but you wouldn't notice them much if I didn't lisp. (At least I don't stutter like Bill.) My best feature, though, is my dark bushy hair. I am short and very round—just healthy looking. My name is Nye, and I never had a girl in my life.

Won't you write us a letter so we can see your handwriting and smell your beau- tiful envelope again? If you only knew how low our morale is, you'd rush right down and send a telegram only we'd rather have a letter so please, please write and send us a snap shot of yourself?

In ending, let us say it has been fun knowing you already and you haven't even answered us. Just think how much fun we'll have after you have answered us and we are old friends. We know you won't let us down. Now don't forget: First, fall in love with us. Second, write us a letter. Third, enclose a snap shot. So until we hear from you, good by and we eagerly await your answer.

Bubbling over with unwanted love,

Nye (Pinochio) Moses

Bill (Atlas) Wilhoit

President and Vice President E.J.K.F.C.O.E. (Elizabeth Jane Kivell Fan Club of England Post No. 1 membership closed)

Although Elizabeth Jane Kivell did respond to them, she was in love with—and would go on to marry—a pilot named Dale Leslie French. (Bill Wilhoit ultimately survived the war and married in 1949, but Nye Moses, tragically, was killed at D-Day.) Not all of the humorous letters sent to the Legacy Project were meant to be funny. Some are uninten- tionally amusing, such as this Civil War letter written by a Union soldier to President Lincoln, who almost certainly did not see it. I have not included his full name for reasons that will be obvious.

March 27, 1863
Dear Mr Lincoln
  When this Civil War broke out I went right in I did and fought and bled for the Cause and left my wife and family, and when I came home on furlough last month I found she had been diddling other men and I would like to have a discharge to take care of my children for I won't live with her, and I don't want any of my children to live with her for she diddles all the time, and has got the clap which I have got too and I want a discharge for me to take care of my children, when I get well.
  John N——

Another humorous letter (this one intentionally so) was written by Robert Guttman, who was serving as second mate with the U.S. Merchant Marine aboard the SS *Rover,* an ammunition ship delivering explosives to the coalition forces in Saudi Arabia during Operation Desert Shield. On October 11, 1990 Guttman wrote to his older brother Jon to describe the one bit of "entertainment" he and his crewmates were enjoying while at sea.

Dear Brudder,
  Can't say where I am exactly, loose lips and all that, but the postmark should give you some idea. Suffice it to say that it's the place to be this season. Clear skies, bags of sun, temperature in the low 110s. What more could anyone want?
  Everybody whose anybody is here as well, all you have to do is listen to the VHF Radio-Telephone.
  "THEES EES HESPANEESH WARSHEEP. IDENTIFY YOURSELF POR FAVOR. CAMBIO."
  "MENCHANT VAYSEL ON ME STAHB'D BAHW! THIS IS ASS-STAYLIAN WAHRSHIP, CAHM IN PLEASE, AHVER!"
  "GOOD DAY. THIS IS CANADIAN WARSHIP CALLING THE VESSEL ABOUT 3 MILES AWAY FROM ME. HOW'S IT GOING, EH?"
  "THIS IS BRITISH WARSHIP CALLING THE VESSEL 4 MILES OFF MY STARBOARD BEAM. DO BE SO GOOD AS TO RESPOND ON CHANNEL 16 OR I SHALL RELUCTANTLY BE COMPELLED TO BLOW YOU OUT OF THE WATER. OVER."
  "ZEES EES FRENCH WAR-SHEEP CALLING ZEE SHEEP ON MAH PORT QUARTAIR. IDENTIFY YOUR SELF, OVAIR."

"FRENCH WARSHIP BE DAMNED! BURN ME FOR A HAND-SPIKE, I FLY MY SOVEREIGN'S COLOURS AND I'LL NOT HEAVE-TO FOR ANY SNAIL-CHEWING, GARLIC-BREATHED SWAB OF A FROG, AND YE MAY LAY TO THAT! OVER."

And then, of course, there are the Americans. The Americans are immediately distinguishable from the foreigners in that the foreigners all speak better english than the Americans. The Americans don't actually speak english at all, they speak Navy, to wit:

"MERCHANT VESSEL ON COURSE THREE FIVE TWO SPEED ONE SEVEN THIS IS CHARLIE OSCAR U.S. NAVY WAR-SHIP THREE FIVE ZERO ZERO YARDS BEARING TWO FIVE FIVE RELATIVE WHAT ARE YOUR INTENTIONS REGARDING MY UNIT, OVER?"

This to an Indian Tanker where there may only be one person on board who even speaks english at all, and badly at that.

In any case you see that we don't lack for free entertainment. It's better than Bob Hope any day.

I don't know how long I'm going to be here, but I hope it won't be long because everybody expects the balloon to go up shortly. By the way, it may interest you to know that we have a couple of W.W.II veterans on board, both merchant marine vets. One is 76 years old. They both volunteered for this trip. After dodging U-Boats and Kamikazes, they both find this a bit of a yawner, except for the heat.

Give my best to everybody. Hope to see you soon.

Robert

Due to the relatively brief duration of Desert Storm and the availability of phones for the troops, there were fewer letters being written, relative to other wars. I am partial to Gulf War letters not only because they are more difficult to find but because they, for reasons that are still unclear to me, disproportionately capture the surreal nature of warfare. One example is the following letter by army specialist Don Odom, who found himself in a Saudi Arabian village that may have suffered an Iraqi anthrax attack. (Kim is Odom's girlfriend.)

24 December 90

Dearest Kim,

Well, it's Christmas eve and all is quiet on the western front. I know it's been a couple of weeks since I wrote last, so I'll try to fill you in on what's going on. My platoon was attached to an air cav unit with the 101st Airborne. These are the guys who get to fly all of the fancy helicopters, Apache's, Cobra's, Black-hawks. We travelled north for a couple of weeks to conduct training exercises, so that's why I haven't written. At one point, we were only a few miles from the Iraqi border.

After travelling through the desert for 2 weeks, there is only one thing I can say for certain about this country, There's an awful lot of sand. I'm making a promise, I swear I'm never going to the beach again.

We did get to travel through several Saudi villages. It's pretty amazing how different our cultures are, yet how similar the children at play. I saw a group of young children playing a king-of-the-hill type game on a pile of rubble. Of course the game broke up rather quickly when our convoy stopped for lunch. All the children quickly ran towards us begging for candy. We were mobbed by these dirty little hands reaching up in the air at us. Needless to say, no one got to eat the dessert in their M.R.E.'s for that meal. The kids horded the chocolate brownies and oatmeal cookie bars and ran off to taste their sampling of American food.

We came across another village that was really weird. As we approached the outskirts of the village, the desert was covered with the dead corpses of camels and goats and sheep. They were all just lying there rotting in the sun. We didn't actually go into the village, we just stopped in a grove of trees, almost like an oasis, on the outskirts of the town. We stayed there for the night. As I was laying in my cot, I looked up and saw a goat's leg in the trees above me. How it got there I'll never know. We were supposed to stay in that village for several days, but the next morning we had to pack up and move somewhere else. Lt. Bolluytt told us the village had been wiped out by anthrax, that's why all the animals were dead. I don't remember if anthrax is contagious or not, but if it is, I'll probably be dead by the time you read this letter. . . .ha ha ha. In all seriousness though, there were thousands of flies everywhere, buzzing from one carcass to another and then landing on our food. Pretty unsanitary conditions if you ask me. Some of the guys in the squad are wondering if this village was the result of one of Saddam's bio weapons. My thinking is that if that was the case, we would have heard about it all over the news. I don't know, then again maybe not.

By the time you get this, Christmas will be over and you'll probably be celebrating New Year's. I hope you had a great Christmas, and I'll try to beat the lines at the phone center tomorrow to call and hear your voice.

All my love,
Don

Neither Odom nor any of his comrades became ill after the visit, and to this day Odom does not know what killed the animals they saw.

One of the most remarkable Gulf War letters I found was notable not only for what it said but for who wrote it. Serving on a Coast Guard patrol boat in the Port of Dammam, Persian Gulf, PS1 Sandy Mitten manned (for lack of a better word) a 50 caliber machine gun. She also happened to be a grandmother. Mitten had joined the Navy in 1959 and then, in 1974, entered the Coast Guard Reserves. In 1990, Mitten's port security unit represented the first Coast Guard reserves called in for active duty, and she left for the Middle East one week before her oldest son was married. While overseas she wrote regularly to her family, and on January 22, 1991, she sent the following letter to her mother describing what it was like to be at war.

Dear Mom,

Well, we are 5 days into war. Amazing isn't it? It's been some trying times in the past 5 days and I'm sure there will be many more before I leave here.

We were awakened on the morning of the 17th at about 2:40 to "SKUD ALERT, MOP LEVEL 4. COME ONE, COME ON, OUT IN THE HALLWAY AS SOON AS YOU CAN!!"

Since this began the women have moved in with the men, at night. Otherwise our barracks is out at the end of our compound. These are our buddies, our compatriots. We felt stranded. Besides we're all scared—men & women and we need each other for support. We sit in the hall and hold hands and just wonder what will happen next. Some sleep, some cry, some just look straight ahead, but all are scared.

I'm fine and I plan on staying that way. We've had some pretty close calls. Two nights ago, the Patriots went off right from our Port which is about 1 mile from our compound. I though that the missiles landed right in our courtyard. A terrible BOOM when it took off and a second BOOM when it broke the sound barrier. There was debris all over.

If I ever had any doubts about whether

Next P.M.

Back again. In the middle of the sentence, we had a SKUD attack. You should have seen it. One of my people called me outside to tell them what was coming toward our tower. I ran outside and when I looked I saw these flashes in the sky. They looked like tracer shells off of a weapon being fired.

People are really doing strange things now and emotions are high. Tempers short. Iraq ended up putting a missile or two into Israel again. That country isn't going to hold back much longer. I can't blame them. That bastard Hussein is trying to kill civilians. He doesn't care. Rumor has it that his people are also uprising against him. He needs to be killed. That's how this whole thing will be eased.

Before this all came about, I wondered if I would really be able to use my weapon against someone else. I have no question now. You know, like so many others, I prayed for a peaceful end before this. But, now that it isn't peaceful & it won't be, I just want to do whatever has to be done to get this whole damn mess over with. It's now become a situation where you shoot if someone shoots first and they say shoot to wound. Bull, if I shoot and I end up killing someone, if they were trying to do me in, that's too bad. I really thought I wouldn't ever say that. It really does put a different light on things when you're right here, not knowing what to expect next.

Well, Mom, take care & God Bless You. Keep praying. Every little bit helps.
Love,
Your daughter, Sandy

Gulf War servicemen and women did not write many e-mails. A crude form of e-mail existed, but when military personnel wrote home, it was mostly by letter. Although e-mails tend to be more stream-of-consciousness, weaving together the profound with the trival, the Legacy Project has received many well-written and insightful e-mails. We are looking for more—especially by the men and women serving in Operation Enduring Freedom.

I personally prefer handwritten letters because their physical condition accentuates the conditions under which the letters were composed. Through the rips and tears, the splotches of mud and grease, and the hastily crossed-out words, one better understands that these letters were often written under punishing circumstances. What is paramount for those serving in the armed forces, however, is that their loved ones know that they are alive and well—regardless of how the message comes to them. Wartime e-mails may not have the physical texture and beauty of handwritten letters, but for speed and convenience they are unrivaled.

Many e-mails written after the September 11 attacks have been forwarded to the Legacy Project, and we save every one. The great majority have been heavily circulated over the internet, but one of the more unique (and, up to now, previously unknown) e-mail exchanges we have is between Rye Barcott, a twenty-two-year-old second lieutenant in the U.S. Marine Corps and Salim Mohamed, a twenty-five-year-old Muslim friend of his living in Kenya. Barcott and Mohamed are coleaders of a nonprofit organization called Carolina for Kibera (CFK) Inc., which created and now maintains a youth sports association, a medical clinic, and a nursery school in the Kibera slum of Nairobi, Kenya. (Barcott started the program after a summer visit to Kibera while doing research on his thesis at the University of North Carolina at Chapel Hill.) As soon as Mohamed heard about the attacks on the World Trade Center and the Pentagon, he rushed off a message to Barcott. (Barcott and Mohamed often wrote to each other in Shen'g, a ghetto youth dialect made up of Swahili, African tribal languages, and American slang. The English translations appear in brackets. "Semaj" is another friend of theirs involved with CFK.)

Rye beshte [friend],
We keep watching planes crashing into buildings in New York and Washington.
Uko wapi saa hii? [Where are you now?] Are you OK? What about Semaj?

Salim,
Thanks for your email. I don't have much time because our communications are limited. I'm sitting in a room with a dozen lieutenants wondering what the hell is going on. We are OK, but I have not heard from Semaj. He works in South Bronx though, so I would presume he is far from the World Trade Center. I hope that these events don't cause the Muslim community in Kibera to turn on CFK, or the US to react with violence before we know who perpetrated this and why.
Tucheckiane [Later], Rye

Barcott sent another e-mail which prompted a candid, but cordial, exhange on issues of faith and loyalty.

Salim kaka Vipi? [Salim Brother, How are you?],
You know, it's odd. We have been busy doing CFK business and never talked about US/Muslim relations. What are your thoughts? How is the Muslim community in Nairobi and Kibera reacting? I've been reading the Koran and came across a few puzzling excerpts. I'm wondering what you think of them.Surah V: Verse 51:
"O ye who believe! Take not the Jews and Christians for friends. They are friends one to another. He among you who taketh them for friends is one of them. Lo! Allah guideth not wrongdoing folk.
"Surah IV: 91
"Ye will find others who desire that they should have security from you, and security from their own folk. So often as they are returned to hostility they are plunged therein. If they keep not aloof from you nor offer you peace nor hold their hands, then take them and kill them wherever ye find them. Against such We have given you clear warrant."
Pamoja [Together], Rye

Rye,
There have been some riots by some Muslims in Nairobi. But those people are in the minority. It's too bad the press focuses on that. In the central Mosque downtown last week we prayed at mid-day for all the victims in your country. I think Bin Laden is really hurting the religion. I hope he is caught. In Kibera there is some anti-American talk. But it is not much. I get worried though that the US will just bomb and kill a lot of innocent people. There is a passage in the Koran that comes before Surah IV Verse 51. It condemns murder like your Commandment "Thou shall not kill." Verse 32: "For that cause We decreed for the Children of Israel that

whosoever killeth a human being for other than man slaughter or corruption in the earth, it shall be as if he had killed all mankind, and whoso saveth the life of one, it shall be as if he had saved the life of all mankind . . ."I think this verse is for everyone. But at the same time people need to defend themselves. So this is how I see verse 91 in Surrah IV. This is also how I can say the US is right in its war.

How are the Marines? Why did you join anyway?

Salaam [Peace], Salim

Salim,

Asante kwa email yako [Thanks for your email]. I joined the Marines back in high school because I was attracted to the image, wanted a challenge (and respect), respected my father's friends who were Marines, and wanted the autonomy and pride to put myself through school. The last two still apply, though I am most moved now by the astounding opportunity to take on a great deal of responsibility at a young age that the Corps offers. However, the decisions we made and make with CFK on a day-to-day basis will probably always weigh more heavily on my conscience because they have an effect, directly, on so many lives of people we know and admire. As a junior officer, even in the most intense combat imaginable, I will not face decisions of that magnitude (in part because I am now part of an enormous institution, instead of leading a smaller one).

So your turn, why Islam?

Rye

Rye, soldja wa ghetto [soldier of the ghetto],

I wasn't born Muslim. But when my mom died I lived on the streets. And one day a Lady named Mama Fatuma picked me up and took me to her home for chokora [street kids]. Mama Fatuma was a Muslim. She didn't force Islam on us, but I got interested in it because she saved me.

Islam is really important to me. I like the comfort it provides and discipline. In that way it is kind of like the Marines maybe. I found after I became Muslim that I had a community that cared about me. On the streets there was no one. The Marines helped you get educated. Muslims like Mama Fatuma helped me get educated too. So I feel a commitment and duty to Allah, praise be His name. I think we are all here for a purpose. I believe that purpose is guided by Allah. There is a lot of bad in this world. Allah I can count on to show us goodness and peace and so I hope this war will end and the terrorists will be stopped so that we can go back to goodness. Kibich damu [Kibera blood], Salim

The power of war letters (and now e-mails) is their ability to bring to life the individual voices and stories that might otherwise be lost in the blur of history. Ironically, of everyone whose correspondences and images were part of the first edition of *War Letters,* the only individual whose name I did not know was also the most prominent—the soldier featured on the book's cover. Found in an archive, the photograph gave no clues as to his identity, background, or fate. I often looked at this photo and wondered what happened to this young man. I wondered if he made it back alive and started a family. I thought of the children he might have raised and what, if anything, he told them of his war experiences. And, of course, I wondered what happened to the letter he was writing.

Twenty-four hours before my deadline to finish this afterword I received a call from a woman named Suzanne Kerr, who said she knew the young man in the photo—it is her uncle, Russell Helie. (We have since authenticated this.) Originally from Middlesex, Massachusetts, Helie was a private first class serving with the 7th Infantry Regiment, 3rd Infantry Division in Korea. All of his letters, except one, were lost when the family moved from Massachusetts to Tennessee several years ago. Helie's one remaining letter is dated November 22, 1950. It reads:

Dear Mom,

How are things at home? Everything is fine here. I got your letter written last month and was glad to hear from you. I am now in Korea and it isn't so bad. I am in a fighting zone but I am not doing any fighting. We are acting as a guard for some engineers who are about twelve miles up the road. We are not doing much except cleaning up and loafing around, getting ready for tomorrow which is Thanksgiving, and we are expecting some big brass to come down so we have to be all sharped up. I received the birthday greetings. I want to thank everyone for them and thank Gladys for the two dollars. It sure came in handy. I was broke. Mom I won't be able to send any Christmas presents so I dont expect any, as I am so broke it is pitiful. I have no place to spend any anyway. Well mom I guess I will close for now, as I have said about all the news for now. Your loving son, Russ

Three months later, on February 16, 1951, an artillery shell exploded near Pfc. Russell Helie. Slashed by flying shrapnel, Helie bled to death. He was only nineteen years old when he died.

For all those like Russell Helie who never came home, for those who survived but still live with the physical and emotional wounds of war, and for all those who lost loved ones in combat, the Legacy Project will continue to seek out, save, and share their words so that what they experienced and what they sacrificed is not forgotten. This is our mission, and it grows more urgent with every passing day.

EDITOR'S NOTE

AND ACKNOWLEDGMENTS

As best as we can determine, the approximately two hundred letters in this book are being published here, in their entirety, for the first time. The overwhelming number of these letters were contributed by individuals who have never before shown their wartime correspondence to anyone outside of their family. Some contributors have photocopied and bound their letters in self-published collections, but these were done on a strictly limited basis—usually no more than a few hundred copies—and distributed primarily to their friends and loved ones. Others have placed their family's letters on the Web, as have several archives. I think this is an ideal way to give these letters exposure, and the Legacy Project plans to feature many letters not included in this book, due to space limitations, on our own site.

A handful of the letters by the more prominent servicemen and women featured in this book have been quoted in other publications but were cut for length and edited to fix errors in spelling or punctuation. For this book, they are transcribed in their entirety and without revisions. These "mistakes," I believe, offer glimpses into the personality of the letter writers and the conditions under which they may have been writing. The excerpts of letters featured in this book as chapter epigraphs are also from previously unpublished correspondences. Some writers self-censored their letters, using dashes or underlines to indicate swear words. There are, however, surprisingly few words missing or censored from the letters here, and, unless otherwise noted, the ellipses in the letters are in the originals and were added by the correspondents for stylistic reasons.

The letters are arranged chronologically, except in the occasional case where, for narrative purposes, a letter was placed out of sequence. It was not always possible to discern a letter's exact date or find out the specific rank or division of the correspondent. The "Extended Correspondence" sections do not necessarily feature letters that are more historic or better written than others; they are merely a series of letters with additional biographical information and a photograph of the correspondent. The purpose of the "Extended Correspondence" is to offer a more detailed portrayal of who these young servicemen and women were.

It was not possible to verify for certain if some of these letters, especially those written during the Civil War, have not appeared in local newspapers a century ago or in a limited-circulation, out-of-print publication. Again, the vast majority of the letters listed in the table of contents can be confirmed never to have been published before, and all the rest are believed to be previously unpublished. All of them were selected for their literary and historical merits, and the decision to use previously unpublished material is to demonstrate, overall, how many exceptional wartime letters are still filed and boxed away in private homes and archives throughout this nation.

Although the letters span almost a hundred and forty years of warfare, there are several omissions—the Indian Wars (as they were called, and which spanned the latter half of the nineteenth century), the Spanish-American War, and the War in the Philippines. They are not featured in this book for one simple reason: The Legacy Project received virtually no letters from these wars. In fact, we received more letters written by Americans recently stationed in Bosnia than letters written during the aforementioned three wars combined. Ideally, I would have preferred to include every war in our nation's history, beginning with the War of Independence. But here, too, we received very few letters from the American Revolution, the War of 1812, and the Mexican War.

There is, however, a common thread that binds the wars ultimately featured in this collection, and it is the personal and emotional connection Americans feel toward them. It was not surprising to me that most of the letters in this book were sent in by the immediate family members of the 16 million American men and women who served in World War II. I did not expect, however, that many of the World War I letters in this book would come from the the children and even the wives of World War I soldiers, or that two of the Civil War letters would be submitted by the *grandchildren* of Civil War soldiers—one Union and one Confederate. It is a stunning reminder of how young our country is.

I cannot emphasize enough how grateful I am to the tens of thousands of people who have sent wartime letters to the Legacy Project, regardless of whether or not I was able to publish their letters in this book. I have gotten to know many of these families, and I am honored to call them friends. I offer my sincerest apologies to those whose letters were not included, and I assure them it was only a matter of space limitations.

Speaking of such limitations, it is not possible to list again the individuals who allowed me to use letters for this book, as they are mentioned in the permissions section. I would like to take this opportunity to thank all of the other individuals who made this book possible:

First and foremost, there would be no book and no Legacy Project if it were not for Jeanne Philips and Abigail Van Buren, who announced the Legacy Project in "Dear Abby" on November 11, 1998. This single column generated our initial avalanche of mail and set this project in motion. Abigail Van Buren, Jeanne, and Olivia "Newt" Vis have been more generous and supportive than I can express, and I will be forever in their debt.

I am also indebted to my agent, Miriam Altshuler, who is, quite simply, the greatest agent an author could hope to have. Miriam's integrity, sense of humor, thoughtfulness, and encouragement buoyed me every step of the way. Miriam is truly the gold standard of professionalism and friendship, and without her this book never would have been possible.

I am especially grateful to Miriam for finding Scribner and the most phenomenal group of individuals with whom an author could hope to work. Susan Moldow and Nan Graham understood the spirit of this book from its very conception. They recognized that this project represented a personal mission for a great many people, and I will never forget how much they have done to nurture that spirit. I adore them, I respect them, and I truly cannot thank them enough for letting me work with them on this book.

And then there is my personal editor, Gillian Blake. Who doesn't like me to begin sentences with conjunctions or use sentence fragments for emphasis or repeat phrases for dramatic effect. And who excoriated me vituperatively for my rampant verbosity. In all seriousness, Gillian Blake is one of the most brilliant, beautiful, and creative persons I have ever known. She endured my nervewracking delays with the patience of a saint and brought both heart and intellect to the editing process. Gillian will never know how grateful I am to her for all that she has done for this book and for putting up with me for the past year. Gillian's wonderful assistant, Rachel Sussman, was also more helpful and more patient with me than I deserved (especially considering my daily barrage of phone calls), and I am seriously beginning to suspect that Rachel is singlehandedly keeping the Simon & Schuster empire together. I am also enormously grateful to Pat Eisemann and Giulia Melucci for all they have done, are doing, and are about to do to help us spread the word about this book. They are truly incredible, and I look forward to working with them on this project and many more.

Along with the opportunity to read all of these exceptional letters, one of the greatest thrills of this project has been meeting, working with, and even becoming friends with people I have seen and admired from afar. Doug Brinkley is not only one of our nation's greatest historians, he is also one of the most gracious, generous, and thoughtful people I have ever known. Doug directed me to several letters in this book (including the letter by a young Lt. George McGovern), and spent his entire Christmas and New Year's writing the introduction. Doug would frequently call to just to check in and make sure I was alive, and I hope he knows how much these and a thousand other acts of kindness meant to me. Doug also introduced me to one of my other great heroes, Stephen Ambrose. Doug and Steve have inspired in millions of Americans a love for history, and I certainly count myself as one of those influenced by their passion. I also want to thank the folks at the Eisenhower Center (which Doug directs)—assistant director Kevin R. Willey, Erica L. Whittington, Michael J. Edwards, Matthew M. Ellefson, and Andrew Devreaux. They are a talented and all-around remarkable group of individuals.

When the first strangling sense of fear took hold of me as my deadline for this book loomed, a dear friend and former teacher of mine, John Elko, recommended having one of his students, Jake Jeppson, assist me. Well, if it were not for Jake, this book could not have been completed. Jake transcribed letters, hunted down information for the headnotes, traveled hundreds of miles to gather letters we needed, offered invaluable commentary, and even found, on his own initiative, several of the letters featured in this book. Jake's intelligence, integrity, discipline, sense of humor, and attention to detail make him not only an ideal assistant, but an exemplary young man. Jake is just graduating from high school, and I know he is going to go far in this world. If Jake is representative of his generation (and I believe he is), I have no fears for the future of this country.

I am also indebted to Deborah Baker, who fostered my passion for letters and helped me with the initial idea for the Legacy Project. Deb was there when it all started, and she has been an extraordinary friend over these past many years.

Several of the best letters in this book came from the U.S. Army Military History Institute at the Carlisle Barracks, and David Keough, Dennis Vetock, and especially Dr. Richard Sommers, were incredibly helpful and hospitable to me when I visited them. The Institute has many of this nation's greatest wartime letters, and I look forward to continue working with these incredible scholars and archivists.

Most importantly, I am eternally grateful to my mom, dad, brother, and sister-in-law, who could not have been more encouraging and loving, and who were more than understanding about my absence at certain family events and functions as I worked on this book. I am also grateful to my friends, who similarly put up with my overall crankiness, odd working hours, and occasional "disappearances" as I hunkered down to meet one deadline after another. Drinks are on me, fellas.

I am also indebted to the following individuals for all that they have done to make this book and the Legacy Project possible (several of them reviewed the chapters for historical accuracy; since, however, I added letters and headnotes after they reviewed the book, I take full responsibility for the final product): Ted Alexander, the park historian at Antietam National Battlefield, who reviewed the Civil War chapter and has been enormously helpful (I am also grateful to Brian Baracz and Mike Weinstein at Antietam); Meredith Ashley and Thomas "Lud" Ashley for their support and for helping me get a copy of the letter President George Bush wrote as a young lieutenant; Ted Barker at the Korean War Project, who reviewed the Korean War section of the book; Scott Baron, who is the author of a terrific book, *They Also Served: Military Biographies of Uncommon Americans* (Spartanburg: MIE Publishing, 1998), and who helped me find the Patrick Hitler letter; Peter Bartis, with the Veterans' Oral History Project at the Library of Congress's American Folklife Center; Jean Becker, who also helped me with President Bush's letter and could not have been more gracious; Judy Bellafaire at the Women in Military Service for America Memorial Foundation; Peter Bergman, who saved the day by meticulously typing in the last batch of letters as our deadline loomed; Jean V. Berlin, who is the editor of *A Confederate Nurse: The Diary of Ada W. Bacot 1860–1863* (Columbia: University of South Carolina Press) and coeditor, with Brooks D. Simpson, of *Sherman's Civil War: Selected Correspondence of William T. Sherman, 1860–1865* (Chapel Hill: University of North Carolina Press, 1999) and who generously found for me a previously unpublished letter by W. T. Sherman; Joseph E. Bles, Inspector General of the Young Marines; Erwin Blonder, whose World War II letter (which I used in a previous book) was influential in creating the Legacy Project; Roy and Susan Boehm for all their help with Roy's letters; Doug Bradshaw, who helped me respond to the first onslaught of letters the Legacy Project received; Preston Brown for sharing two of his best Sherman letters with me; Mary Lynn McCree Bryan for setting me in the right direction to find the letter by Jane Addams; Margaret Buchholz, who contributed Civil War and World War I letters to the Legacy Project; Christopher Buckley, quite simply one of the greatest people I know, for his support and encouragement; Ronald Bulatoff and Carol Leadenham at the Hoover Institution; Jim Burgess at the Manassas National Battlefield Park; Sylvia Helene Burley, for helping me find letters by African-American servicemen and -women; Chris Calkins at the

Petersburg National Battlefield; Richard A. Cameron at the National Historical Publications and Records Commission; Alan Canfora, who is the director of the Kent May 4 Center (www.May4.org), and who sent me the Kent State letters; Doran Cart and Lynn Ward at the Liberty Memorial Museum of World War I; Julia Child and everyone who helped me find her letters: her extremely gracious sister Dorothy Cousins, her biographer Noël Riley Fitch, author of the sensational *Appetite for Life: The Biography of Julia Child* (New York: Doubleday, 1997), Linda Morrison (who went through Julia Child's letters for me in Boston), and Elizabeth P. McIntosh, who wrote *Sisterhood of Spies: The Women of the OSS* (New York: Dell, 1998); Wendy Chmielewski at the Swarthmore College Peace Collection; Jonathan Y. Cole at the Center for the Book at the Library of Congress; Henry S. F. Cooper, who sent me the Edgar Shepard letter; the saintly "Brother" Bruce Cummings and the wonderful "Sister" Sandy Dennison for all their support; Robert J. Corrette, who alerted me to the sensational collection of Civil War letters at the Military History Institute; Richard Danzig, whose kind notes throughout this process were very meaningful to me; Kitty B. Deernose and John Doerner at the Little Bighorn Battlefield National Monument; Denali DeGraf, a brilliant young student who laboriously typed in many of the letters in this book; Megan Desnoyers at the John Fitzgerald Kennedy Library, who found the John F. Kennedy and Bobbie Lou Pendergrass letters; David Dunckel, who helped me search for Gulf War letters; Bernard Edelman, who found the letter by Bill Hunt in the Persian Gulf War section and who is the editor, himself, of what remains one of the greatest collections of war letters ever assembled, *Dear America: Letters Home from Vietnam* (New York: Pocket Books, 1985); John S. D. Eisenhower, for granting me permission to include his father's letter; Susan Eisenhower for all of her help and for putting me in touch with Daun van Ee at Johns Hopkins University and with James W. Leyerzapf, who ultimately found the letter by Dwight D. Eisenhower I included; Amy and Kathy Eldon, who shared two of the letters written by Dan Eldon, and who have inspired me more than they will ever know. Kathy also edited The *Journey Is the Destination: The Journals of Dan Eldon* (San Francisco: Chronicle Books, 1997); Robert G. Evans, who lead me to the William Harris Hardy letter; Horace Evers, who has become a dear friend; Duery Felton Jr., who helped me find Richard Luttrell and the letter he left at the Vietnam Veterans Memorial; Leslie Fields at the Morgan Library, who went out of her way to help me find Civil War–era letters; Liz Filler, who shared with me the extraordinary story of her great-uncle; Susan Finta at the Clara Barton National Historic Site; Jeffrey Flannery, at the Manuscripts Division of the Library of

Congress and one of our nation's greatest archivists (not to mention a man to whom I am eternally indebted for all his help); David Fox, a living saint who runs The Immortal Chaplains Foundation (www.immortalchaplains.org) and who helped me get in touch with Theresa Goode Kaplan (another person dear to my heart); Mary Folsom, who helped me find the remarkable Frank Conwell letter; Karen Fortner at Levenger for supporting the Legacy Project from its very beginning; John Gable, director of the Theodore Roosevelt Association, who graciously sent me the historic letter by Theodore Roosevelt; Jimmy Gaines, who delivers the mail at my building and always looks out for me; Brad Gernand at the Library of Congress; Jeff Giamborn at the Vicksburg Old Court House Museum; Patricia W. Gianneschi and her son Matthew for the William Byron letters; Hill Goodspeed at the National Museum of Naval Aviation; Philip Gourevitch, who wrote about the Immortal Chaplains in the New Yorker and put me in touch with David Fox; Bernice M. Grudzinski, Debra Beyerlein, and Gregory Grudzinski for the historic Tojo letter; Peggy Haile, city historian of Norfolk, Virginia; Shane T. Hamilton and Kathleen Wach at Miller & Chevalier, who very generously provided the Legacy Project with pro bono legal advice when we were just starting; Margot Hartmann, my wonderful aunt, who sends me letters and newspaper clippings on all sorts of issues of importance to me (and who understands how much I, too, miss Frank Hartmann—a true war hero); historian Rick Hatcher, who led me to the Marcus Morton letter; Philip Himberg at Sundance; Olivia Hines in Miriam Altshuler's office; Tony Hiss, who sent me the complete copy of the letter his father, Alger, wrote from prison; Nathan and Evelyn Hoffman, whom I love and admire, and who have essentially become my adopted grandparents; Bob Huddleston, who singlehandedly found the historic letter by Samuel Cabble and graciously provided me with additional information about Cabble; Terry A. Johnston Jr., who is the editor of the sensational book *Him on One Side and Me on the Other: The Civil War Letters of Alexander Campbell and James Campbell* (Columbia: University of South Carolina Press, 1999) and who went out of his way to help me find previously unpublished Civil War letters; Mary-Virginia Jones at the Virginia Historical Society; David Kennedy at Dan Curtis Productions, who has been supportive of this project from day one and has been a rock of friendship throughout; Robert Kenner, Paul Taylor, and Melissa Adelson, who are putting together the documentary for American Experience (to air November 2001) based on the Legacy Project and who helped me select many letters in this book; Carolyn Kingston, granddaughter of Major Edward Ball Cole, and Mary Sayward Cole, the daughter-in-law of Major Cole, whose thoughtful conservation of his letters was the source of the letter dated April 22, 1918; Thomas Knoles at the American Antiquarian Society; John Kremer, who contributed the letter by John Steinbeck; Robert E. L. Krick at the Richmond National Battlefield Park; Betsy Kuhn, who is the author of *Angels of Mercy: The Army Nurses of World War II* (New York: Athaneum Books, 1999), and who helped me find that gripping letter by Vera Rieck; Bob Leahy, who contributed an incredible letter and reviewed the Vietnam War section for me; Donna Lehmann at the Gerald R. Ford Library, who found the Graham Martin cables; Vickie Lewis, who edited the wonderful book *Side-by-Side: A Photographic History of American Women at War* (New York: Stewart, Tabori & Chang, 1999); Judy Barrett Litoff, who has done more to find and preserve war letters written by women than anyone else; Brian Lipson at Endeavor, who understood the spirit of this book and project from the beginning and who connected the Legacy Project with PBS's American Experience; Christina Lowery at the History Channel, who has done two sensational documentaries based on wartime letters and has been incredibly helpful in more ways than she will ever know; Ellin Martens, who singlehandedly helped us bring in hundreds of extraordinary letters; Helen Matthews at the Atlanta History Center; Jessica Mathewson at the American Foundation for the Blind; Yvette Mayo and everyone else at the post office where we have our PO box number; Toshiko McCallum at the Japanese American National Museum; Adrienne McGrath, who sent me a letter by her husband which is one of the most dramatic I have ever seen; James M. McPherson, one of the greatest Civil War historians alive, for offering me ideas on where to look for letters; Kirke Mechem (musician/composer extraordinaire) for putting me in touch with Larry Lawrence, chairman of the John Brown Society, who told me about the Aaron Dwight Stevens letters at the Morgan Library; Harry Miller, who shared with me several of the best Vietnam War letters at the State Historical Society of Wisconsin; Patricia Morse, who helped me with Maxine Meyers' letters; Barbara and Opal Nestingen; Lisa Newman and Eric Rosenthal for all their support and encouragement, and especially Lisa, who has helped the Legacy Project spread the word about its mission; Frank Niader, who sent in some exceptional letters to the Legacy Project and put me in touch with the Gold Star Mothers; Michael and Elizabeth Norman, author of an incredible book, *We Band of Angels: The Untold Story of American Nurses Trapped on Bataan by the Japanese* (New York: Random House, 1999); Julia Oehmig for transcribing Joshua Chamberlain's almost indecipherable handwriting; Betsy Paradis at the University of Maine's Fogler Library; Ben and Robert Patton; Jeanne Penfold, at the

American Gold Star Mothers, who introduced me to Theresa Davis; David O. Percy at the South Carolina Historical Society; Donald C. Pfanz at the Fredericksburg & Spotsylvania National Military Park; Cristy and Ray Pfeiffer, who run Historic Tours and who put me in touch with Gary Powers Jr.; Carolyn Ponte, for sending me the letter by Charles McCallister; Nancy Pope at the Smithsonian's National Postal Museum; Colin Powell and everyone who helped me find his letters: Peggy Cifrino and Bill Smullen in the general's office, Susan Lemke at the National Defense University, and his son, Michael; Francis Gary Powers Jr., who not only let me publish his father's letter from Moscow, but helped me look for other extraordinary Cold War–era letters. Gary started the nonprofit Cold War Museum (www.coldwar.org), which is actively seeking out items from this historical period, and he also operates "spy" tours in Washington, D.C.; Alfred Puntesecca, the man most responsible for the extraordinary letter by "Leon" in the Korean War chapter; Pam Putney and Ellen Wingard for their love and support, which has meant more to me than I can express; Steve Robinson, producer extraordinaire, who did a first-rate radio documentary based on war letters he acquired in Nebraska (two of which appear in this book) and also very generously put me in touch with Studs Terkel, to whom I am also enormously grateful; Joe "Buck" Rogers, my friend and neighbor (and World War II veteran) who read through several chapters for me; Chris Scheer at the Veterans Administration, who offered us his encouragement, guidance, and wisdom when the Legacy Project was just starting; H. Norman Schwarzkopf and his very helpful (and very kind) assistant Lynn Williams; Hunter Scott and his family for their assistance with the USS *Indianapolis* story; Jan Steinman for the Elijah Beeman quote; James O. Stinson, who sent me the wonderful Bob Brown letter mentioned in the introduction; Emma Sweeney, who generously shared her fathers' letters and has become a dear friend; Sam Tanenhaus, who is the author of *Whittaker Chambers: A Biography* (New York: Random House, 1997) and who went out of his way to help me find the letter by Whittaker Chambers; Donald E. Thies, who alerted me to the collection of Vietnam War letters at the State Historical Society of Wisconsin; Anne Tramer, a dear friend and the person who, in so many ways, was instrumental in starting the Legacy Project; Aileen Tu at the Japanese American National Museum; Dan Welch, not only for letting me use his phenomenal Desert Storm letter, but for reviewing the section on the Persian Gulf War; John Weisman, who put me in touch with Roy Boehm, the "father" of the U.S. Navy SEALS; William C. Westmoreland and everyone who helped me find his letter: Mrs. Westmoreland, their son, Rip, and Herbert J. Hartsook at the

University of South Carolina's South Caroliniana Library; Joe Williams at the Appomattox Court House; Kathleen Williams, who is the web site producer at A&E's History Channel and included us on their site (www.historychannel.com/dearhome), and who also helped me find Tom Shaffer's letters (and Tom, himself); Rob Wilson, who is the director of the exemplary Veterans Education Project in Amherst, Massachusetts, and who sent me the Fritz Schnaittacher letter; Eugene Winick and Matt McGowan at MacIntosh & Otis, for their assistance with the John Steinbeck letter; David F. Winkler at the Naval Historical Foundation; Terrence J. Winschel at the Vicksburg National Military Park; Albert H. Wunsch III, who has contributed numerous exceptional Civil War correspondence to the Legacy Project and is a true man of letters, himself; Mitchell Yockelson, reference archivist at the National Archives; James W. Zobel at the MacArthur Memorial Archives; and a special thanks to Margie Myrick for the William Harris Hardy letter.

For the afterword, I would like to thank Syd Brisker, Sandy Mitten, Don Odom, Bill Wilhoit, and D. Michael Van De Veer for their letters and Rye Barcott and Salim Mohamed for their e-mails. I would also like to thank: Terry Baxter, who put me in touch with Professor Yuzuru J. Takeshita, who provided the Ritsuko Kawano letter; John P. Coyne, editor of www.peacecorpswriters.org, who found the D. Michael Van De Veer letter; Katherine DaCosta, who sent me the "Dear Butterfly" letter; Dale Leslie French, who sent me the Nye Moses and Bill Wilhoit letter; Jon and Paul Guttman, who provided me with the Robert Guttman letter; Suzanne Kerr Wright and Gladys B. Larrabee, who found the Russell Helie letter; James Sackett, who provided the "Dear Mr. Lincoln" letter; Philip and Betty C. Tibbs for providing the Howard A. Tibbs letter; Jill Tubbs for putting me in touch with Don Odom; Gregory R. Wessel, who found the "Sergey" letter; and Dr. Richard Zeitlin at the Wisconsin Veterans Museum, who put me in touch with Sandy Mitten.

PERMISSIONS

The editor is extremely grateful to the veterans, families, archives, libraries, and estates who have contributed and/or granted the editor permission to publish the following letters: Jane Addams letter to Woodrow Wilson from The Jane Addams Papers, 1860–1935 (Bell & Howell Information & Learning, 1985; Ann Arbor, MI), Reel 9, Swarthmore College Peace Collection, Records of the Women's International League for Peace and Freedom, U.S. Section. Dean Allen letter © Joyce Hallenbeck. Reprinted by permission of Joyce Hallenbeck; Scott Alwin letter © Du Thi Duong. Reprinted by permission of Du Thi Duong; Richard Baltzegar letter © Joan Baltzegar. Reprinted by permission of Joan Baltzegar; Dom Bart letter © Mildred Bart. Reprinted by permission of Mildred Bart; Clara Barton letter from the Clara Barton Papers at the Library of Congress; Charles E. Bingham letter © Eunice Bingham Putney. Reprinted by permission of Eunice Bingham Putney; George Edwin "Ned" Black letter © Anna Jane Schlossman. Reprinted by permission of Anna Jane Schlossman; Patience and James Black letters © Cavitt Caufield. Reprinted by permission of Cavitt Caufield; Robert Black letter © Paul Steven Miller. Reprinted by permission of Paul Steven Miller; Roy Boehm letter © Roy Boehm. Reprinted by permission of Roy Boehm; John Bott letter © Wayne Bott. Reprinted by permission of Wayne Bott; Carroll Briggs and Ardith Morrisseau letters © Carroll and Ardith Briggs. Reprinted by permission of Carroll and Ardith Briggs; Walter Bromwich letter © Dorothy McGibbeny. Reprinted by permission of Dorothy McGibbeny; P. Burns letter courtesy of Laura Ulrich Brickey; John H. Burrill letter from the Robert Brake Collection, Manuscripts, US Army Military History Institute, Carlisle Barracks, PA; George Bush letter © President George Bush. Reprinted by permission of President George Bush; William Byron letters © Patricia W. Gianneschi. Reprinted by permission of Patricia W. Gianneschi; Samuel Cabble letter from the National Archives, Compiled Military Service Records of Volunteer Soldiers Who Served with the United States Colored Troops: 55th Massachusetts Infantry (Colored), Records of the Adjutant General's Office, 1780s-1917; Joshua Lawrence Chamberlain letter from the Chamberlain Family Papers, Special Collections, Fogler Library, University of Maine. Reprinted by permission of the Fogler Library, University of Maine; Whittaker Chambers letter © John Chambers and Elleb Chambers Into. Reprinted by permission of John Chambers and Ellen Chambers Into. Whittaker Chambers letter from the Duncan Norton-

499

Collections Library; Brice Gross letter © Brice Gross. Reprinted by permission of Brice Gross; John J. Hairston letter © Sylvia Helene Burley. Reprinted by permission of Sylvia Helene Burley; Bob Hammond letter © Joel Hammond. Reprinted by permission of Joel Hammond; John David Hench letters © Michael Hench. Reprinted by permission of Michael Hench; Lester Michael Hensler letter © Carole Hensler Varela. Reprinted by permission of Carole Hensler Varela; letter from Alger Hiss to Tony Hiss dated March 10, 1953 from the Alger Hiss Family Papers, Harvard Law School Library, reprinted by permission of the President and Fellows of Harvard College; William Patrick Hitler letter courtesy of Timothy W. Ryback, Director, Salzburg Seminar; Nathan Hoffman letter © Nathan Hoffman. Reprinted by permission of Nathan Hoffman; Shizuko Horiuchi letter from the Henriette B. Von Blon Collection, Hoover Institution Archives; Richard Hornberger letter © William Hornbeger. Reprinted by permission of William Hornberger; William T. House letters courtesy of Steve Domjanovich. Reprinted by permission of Steve Domjanovich; Fritz Houser letter © Betty Ganse. Reprinted by permission of Betty Ganse; Columbus Huddle letter © Robert W. Battin. Reprinted by permission of Robert W. Battin; Bill Hunt letter © Bill Hunt. Reprinted by permission of Bill Hunt; letter by Mike Jeffords from the Wisconsin Vietnam Veterans Collection at the State Historical Society of Wisconsin. Reprinted by permission of the State Historical Society of Wisconsin; James Carroll Jordan letter © James Carroll Jordan. Reprinted by permission of James Carroll Jordan; Helen Keller letter courtesy of the American Foundation for the Blind. Reprinted by permission of the American Foundation for the Blind; John F. Kennedy letter to Bobbie Lou Pendergrass dated March 6, 1963 from the "ND 9-2-2 M Executive" folder, White House Central Subject file, box 604, John Fitzgerald Kennedy Library; Tommie Kennedy letters © Jacque McNeely. Reprinted by permission of Jacque McNeely; David Ker letter © David K. Schermerhorn. Reprinted by permission of David K. Schermerhorn; Richard King letter © Marsha King Sepp. Reprinted by permission of Marsha King Sepp; "Dear Old Bunkie" letter © Susan Koelble. Reprinted by permission of Susan Koelble; Edward Land letter © Martha Button Ward. Reprinted by permission of Martha Button Ward; Eugene Lawton letter © Eileene Bohn. Reprinted by permision of Eileene Bohn; Bob Leahy letter © Bob Leahy. Reprinted by permission of Bob Leahy; Mary Custis Lee letter courtesy of and reprinted by permission of the Appomattox Court House National Historic Park; "Leon" letter dated June 15, 1952 © Alfred Puntasecca. Reprinted by permission of Alfred Puntasecca; Richard Leonard letter © Richard Leonard. Reprinted by permission of Richard Leonard; Hugh Alexander Leslie letter © Kenneth L. and Carolyn T. Cochrum. Reprinted by permission of Kenneth L. and Carolyn T. Cochrum; Donald Luedtke letter © Donald Luedtke. Reprinted by permission of Donald Luedtke; Edward Lukert letters © Ed Lukert Jr. Reprinted by permission of Ed Lukert Jr.; Jack Lundberg letter © Ann Lundberg Kronmiller. Reprinted by permission of Ann Lundberg Kronmiller; Richard Luttrell letter © Richard Luttrell. Reprinted by permission of Richard Luttrell; Keith Lynch letter © Lorraine Lynch. Reprinted by permission of Lorraine Lynch; Bill Lynn and Mrs. Robert Lynn letters © Rob Boyte. Reprinted by permission of Rob Boyte; Douglas MacArthur letter courtesy of the MacArthur Memorial Archives, Norfolk, Virginia; William Madden letter © William Madden. Reprinted by permission of William Madden; Gordon Madson letter © Gordon Madson. Reprinted by permission of Gordon Madson; Goldie/Edward Marcellus letter © Richard E. Leggee. Reprinted by permission of Richard E. Leggee; Graham Martin cables, Gerald R. Ford Library, National Security Adviser: Backchannel Messages (1974-77) Collection, Box Number 3; Gerald William Massy III letter © Lynn Massy Amos. Reprinted by permission of Lynn Massy Amos; William Mayberry letter © E. Dawson Fisher. Reprinted by permission of E. Dawson Fisher; letter by Tom McCabe from the Wisconsin Vietnam Veterans Collection at the State Historical Society of Wisconsin. Reprinted by permission of the State Historical Society of Wisconsin; George McGovern letter © George McGovern. Reprinted by permision of George McGovern; Maxine Meyers letters © Maxine Meyers. Reprinted by permission of Maxine Meyers; Herbert J. Miner II letter © Herbert J. Miner II. Reprinted by permission of Herbert J. Miner II; Robert Mitchell letter © Mary Ann Powers. Reprinted by permission of Mary Ann Powers; George Montgomery letter © Arline Montgomery. Reprinted by permission of Arline Montgomery; Marcus Morton letter from the Robert Anderson Papers at the Library of Congress; Robert Munson letter © Robert Munson. Reprinted by permission of Robert Munson; Richard M. Nixon letter and letters to the parents of Sandy Scheuer courtesy of Alan Canfora, director of the Kent May 4 Center; Thomas P. Noonan letter © Jeanne Leonard. Reprinted by permission of Jeanne Leonard; Michael O'Donnell letter courtesy of and reprinted by permission of Marcus Sullivan; Thomas O'Sullivan letter © Thomas O'Sullivan. Reprinted by permission of Thomas O'Sullivan; Robert Oliver letter © Mary E. Saitta. Reprinted by permission of Mary E. Saitta; George Smith Patton letters from the George S. Patton Papers at the Library of Congress; James Paxton letter courtesy of Frances Maxwell; William Pegram letter courtesy of the Virginia Historical Society; Bobbie Lou Pendergrass letter to John F. Kennedy dated February 18, 1963 from the "ND 9-2-2 M Executive" folder, White House Central Subject file, box 604, John Fitzgerald Kennedy Library; John Pershing letters from the Papers of John Joseph Pershing at the Library of Congress; April 19 Vietnam letter from the Wisconsin Vietnam Veterans Collection at the State Historical Society of Wisconsin. Reprinted by permission of the State Historical Society of Wisconsin; Lewis Plush letter © Gary Lee. Reprinted by permission of Gary Lee; Colin L. Powell letter © Colin L. Powell. Reprinted by permission of Colin L. Powell; Francis Gary Powers letter © Gary Powers Jr. Reprinted by permission of Gary Powers Jr.; William Lee Preston letter © Marie Elizabeth Preston. Reprinted by permission of Marie Elizabeth Preston; Samuel G. Putnam III letter © Samuel G. Putnam III. Reprinted by permission of Samuel G. Putnam III; Francisco Rice letter © Fillmore Cannon. Reprinted by permission of Fillmore Cannon; Vera Lee letter © Vera Rieck. Reprinted by permission of Vera Rieck; Tim Robinson letters

INDEX

ABOUT THE LEGACY PROJECT

The Legacy Project is a national, nonprofit initiative that works to honor and remember those who have served this nation in wartime by seeking out and preserving their letters. We are looking for letters from all of our nation's wars and on any subject matter, including descriptions of combat, expressions of love, encounters with prominent military leaders, humorous anecdotes, eyewitness accounts of historic events, advice to younger family members back home, letters from the homefront, words of condolence, letters written to or in memory of fallen comrades, and, above all, any well-written letter that describes an incredible story or offers insight into the nature of war and its effect on those involved. We are especially interested in preserving letters by veterans of color and women, whose correspondences, we have discovered, are harder to find. Although we appreciate the generosity of those who have offered, we do not accept monetary donations. (Nor do we solicit or accept grants, government funds, or any other form of financial assistance.) This project is able to support itself thanks to the assistance of an unpaid staff, who donate both their time and the necessary financial resources to cover expenses.

If you would like to contribute a war letter (or letters) to the Legacy Project, please send a legible photocopy or typed transcript of the material to:

> The Legacy Project
> Attn: Andrew Carroll
> PO Box 53250
> Washington, D.C. 20009

We prefer that you do not send originals, unless you are planning to dispose of the material otherwise and/or do not want the originals returned. We are a very small, all-volunteer organization, and due to the overwhelming volume of mail we receive, it can take us several months and possibly longer to respond. We would be grateful if you would include your address and phone number so we can reach you.

For additional information on the Legacy Project, as well as free information on how to preserve old letters (regardless of the subject matter), links to additional organizations and institutions preserving letters and similar material, and many other war-, veteran-, and military-related resources, please visit our web site: www.warletters.com